With more than 1.3 million readers worldwide, *Mothering* magazine is the premier publication for parents who choose a simpler, more organic lifestyle for themselves and their families. In-touch, outspoken, and always cutting-edge, *Mothering* magazine has advocated new and alternative ways to care for children for more than a decade.

Natural Family Living

embraces *Mothering* magazine's philosophy on every page. This unique sourcebook of all-new material addresses everyday child-care issues from a natural perspective, and helps parents to support their children at all levels of growth: physical, emotional, spiritual, and intellectual. No other parenting guide contrasts mainstream theories with holistic approaches—or gives parents a place to turn when intuition tells them the standard advice is not right for them. This guide features:

- all-natural approaches to pregnancy and delivery
- the latest medical and psychological perspectives on drug-free childbirth
- current research on eating and sleeping habits, circumcision, vaccinations, weaning, diapering, crying, night waking, and attachment parenting
- warm, intimate accounts, interviews, and advice from those who have been there
- creative and innovative ways to handle divorce, loss, and change
- tips for integrating technology—from computers to high-tech toys—into the natural family lifestyle
- a compassionate message of self-care and the importance of "time out" for parents

Natural Family Living

**The *Mothering* Magazine
Guide to Parenting**

Peggy O'Mara

with Jane McConnell

PRODUCED BY
THE PHILIP LIEF GROUP, INC.

POCKET BOOKS
New York   London   Toronto   Sydney   Singapore

PHOTO CREDITS:

Nancy Medwell ii, 3, 46, 51, 94, 108, 114, 145, 146, 186, 192, 202, 204, 243, 307, 320, 324
Michael Weisbrot 4, 31, 57, 58, 86, 90, 99, 132, 141, 158, 163, 174, 226, 230, 232, 263, 269, 292, 296, 317
David Kelly Crow 12, 17, 68, 121, 125, 143, 161, 181, 182, 185, 207, 214, 219, 220, 246, 252, 256, 260, 264, 273, 282, 298, 308, 311
Therese Frare 26, 45, 64, 72, 122
Jennifer Moller 71, 96, 111, 234, 242, 301
Greg Davis Photo 104, 216
Robin Kessler 118
Dave Rusk 130
Emily Bestler 155
© Marilyn Nolt 195, 244, 266, 291

The author of this book is not a physician and the ideas, procedures, and suggestions in this book are not intended as a substitute for the medical advice of a trained health professional. All matters regarding your health require medical supervision. Consult your physician before adopting the suggestions in this book, as well as about any condition that may require diagnosis or medical attention. The author and publisher disclaim any liability arising directly or indirectly from the use of the book.

An *Original* Publication of POCKET BOOKS

POCKET BOOKS, a division of Simon & Schuster Inc.
1230 Avenue of the Americas, New York, NY 10020

ISBN: 0-671-02744-1

First Pocket Books trade paperback printing March 2000

10 9 8 7 6 5 4 3 2 1

POCKET and colophon are registered trademarks of Simon & Schuster Inc.

Cover design by Elizabeth Van Itallie

Cover photo by Michele-Salmieri/FPG International

Design by Lindgren/Fuller Design

Printed in the U.S.A

Peggy O'Mara

I first want to thank Jane McConnell. Our collaborative process has been a joy. It has refreshed and revitalized me and made me feel renewed pride in the magazine. I want to thank her family for sharing her and mine for putting up with the madness.

The thanks really go to the readers of *Mothering,* the many natural living pioneers who supported us through our grass roots beginnings and grew up with us. Thanks to the contributors for being the fountainhead of inspiration. Thanks to the staff of *Mothering,* past and present, for perseverance and dedication.

Thanks to Ashisha for gathering the resources for this book, as well as for years of faith in the magazine and in me. To Ann Church for true partnership, co-leadership, and friendship and for bringing financial stability to our mothership. To Beth Stephens, Vickie Nelson, Todd McCoy, and Donna Patnode for managing and growing that stability. To Carly Newfeld for staying in touch with the readers. And, to Melissa Chianta and Ann Mason for continuing our tradition of editorial excellence.

I have enjoyed working with and owe much of our past excellence to Ellen Kleiner. And, I remember with fondness the unique contributions of Mary Steigerwald, Meria Loeks, Susanne Miller, Ellie Becker, Vicki Stamler, Pacia Salomi, Kay Cook, Joan Logghe, and Sara Corbett.

I will always remember the years of devotion to *Mothering* of Jennifer Miller, the quintessential *Mothering* reader, who died of breast cancer while we were writing this book.

And I especially thank my first partner, John McMahon. We learned how to be parents and publishers together.

Special thanks to Linda White, Joy Johnson of The Centering Corporation, Victoria Moran, Thomas Armstrong, Patrick Farenga, Kim Solga, Mary Ehrmin, Joan Armon, Paul Fleiss, Frederick Hodges, Janice Cox, Miranda Castro, Vimala McClure, Sandy Jones, Adele Faber, Elaine Mazlish, Eda LeShan, Tine Thevenin, Linda Caplan, Lynn Ponton, Nancy Wallace, Marion Cohen, Elizabeth Hormann, Gail Grenier Sweet, Peter Neumeyer, Kathleen Auerbach, Diana Korte, Nancy Griffin, Elizabeth Baldwin, Jackie Hunt Christensen, Sally Rockwell, and the many others who have enriched our pages over the years, as well as Philip Incao, Richard Moskowitz, Ranny Levy, Robert Van Howe, Sabrina Cuddy, Louis Slesin, and Jan Hunt for their professional insights.

And deep gratitude to Catherine Peck and Philip Lief for their great idea; to Kip Hakala for his friendly efficiency; and especially to Emily Bestler for her kindness and broad editorial vision.

The real thanks go to my children. My life began with them. I have learned how to love with them and they have given me a bigger, richer sense of myself. Thank you, Lally, Finnie, Bram, and Nora, for the wonder you bring to my life every day.

Jane McConnell

It always seemed appropriate to me that this book had a nine-month deadline. Throughout the gestation period of the book, I felt as proud and excited as a new mother all over again. I believe that we have given birth to a book that will change people's lives, by allowing them to parent in the most natural and instinctive way.

It has been an honor to work with Peggy O'Mara throughout this process. Her style of mothering has always been so far ahead of its time, and her words of wisdom have touched so many lives. As I put into practice with my own children the ideas presented in this book, Peggy was my sounding board for mothering advice. In long, loving conversations, she counseled me through so many of the issues that mothers face. I only hope her gentle wisdom comes through on these pages.

I want to thank my husband, TJ, for supporting me during this process and always; for keeping an open mind to parenting ideas that might have once seemed crazy to him; for patiently sitting up with me while I worked at night so I could be with the children during the day; and for being such a wonderful father that the children barely missed me in the busiest periods.

Thanks to Sheila Plunkett and Lisa Vernon for taking such good care of my children while I worked. Without them, I never could have gotten the book done on time. Thanks to my dear friends Erin Harding and Robin Luff for reading the manuscript and testing the ideas out on their own children.

Especially, thanks to my mother for showing me what it means to really love a child, and to my children—Lucy, Henry, and Jack—for teaching me so much about mothering and joy.

CONTENTS

As the father of eight, I have had the opportunity to observe how the parenting decisions of my wife, Martha, and me have affected our children as they have grown up. And as a pediatrician for almost thirty years, I have often been called upon to advise new parents. Always I have drawn upon my conviction that the decisions we make as parents can have long-lasting effects on our children.

I believe that parents who choose the kind of parenting described in *Natural Family Living* have a great chance of raising confident, sensitive individuals who will value intimacy with others and know how to stay connected to them

The kind of parenting described in *Natural Family Living* is just that—natural. It's the kind of parenting that people have used for thousands of years and it's what comes naturally when we trust our own intuitions. So many of the things advocated in this book—bonding, breastfeeding, co-sleeping, and attachment parenting—are things that I have seen work well at home as well as with the families in my pediatric practice.

But it's not important that these things are now popular. It's important that they work. As parents, we all want to find a balance between our own needs and those of our children. Yet our babies have needs that can overwhelm us when we don't have a trust in their inherent cues and our own inherent wisdom.

In *Natural Family Living* you can finally find all of the ideas of natural parenting in one place. I've found that this type of parenting—whether you call it attachment parenting or natural family living—results in more independent and self-confident children. Children who are accustomed to having their cues trusted by their parents grow up to trust themselves.

Parents who incorporate the ideas found in *Natural Family Living* into their own family lives will enjoy parenting more. The strong bond that comes from being sensitive to our babies helps us to form a relationship of mutual trust with our children, which serves us well throughout our entire lives as parents. Rather than overpowering our children in the name of discipline, we learn to be responsive and compassionate and to base our authority as parents on love rather than fear.

In *Natural Family Living*, you will find all of the fine ideas of *Mothering* magazine in one place. Their experience over the last twenty-four years is reflected in the comprehensive nature of this book. Where else can you find contemporary yet timeless wisdom on healthy pregnancy, drug-free childbirth, breastfeeding, circumcision, vaccinations, crying, night-waking, attachment parenting, good eating, natural health care, alternative medicine, discipline, a fresh look at teens, wholesome family entertainment, homeschooling, and new ideas in education all in one place? Nowhere!

I am so happy to be able to recommend this comprehensive book to the parents in my practice and delighted that these old ideas are really becoming new again.

William Sears, M.D.
Coauthor of *The Baby Book*

Natural Family Living

I've been a parent for over twenty-five years. My oldest child just recently celebrated her twenty-fifth birthday; it was my birthday too. I still remember vividly her early days and the early days of all of my four children. I remember these days as the beginning of my life. Being a mother has been a wonderful experience for me. And, sometimes it's been terrifying. Having the responsibility for a new life is a humbling experience. It is with this in mind that we offer up this book to new as well as seasoned parents who want to do everything right, but are imperfect like all of us.

I have had the privilege of being the editor, publisher, and owner of *Mothering* magazine for twenty years and as such have heard the stories of hundreds of parents who have been an enormous support group for me as I have parented in a new way. What's new about this way is that it is based on trust rather than on fear: trust in my children, trust in myself.

I called Jane, my co-author, the day after we had finished the last chapter of this book to go over a few final revisions. In the background I heard her four-year-old son, Henry, saying emphatically, "You're done! You said you were finished with the book!" I decided from then on, I had better get Henry's permission to talk to Jane.

Jane and I have written this book the way we do everything else as parents—in fits and starts, working it around our commitment to our children. Writing this book has allowed me to reflect on and revisit issues that I have faced with my children and that we have covered in *Mothering* magazine throughout the years, while Jane has been living the philosophy of the book day to day. She has three children under six. Twenty years ago, so did I.

Jane's children are Lucy (5), Henry (4), and Jack (2). Mine are Lally (25), Finnie (23), Bram (21), and Nora (17). Together, we bring you the experience of mothering seven children, as well as the wisdom of the many contributors, letter writers, and readers of the last twenty-three years of *Mothering* magazine.

I had the good fortune of sending an article, then a poem, to the fledgling *Mothering* magazine in 1978. They were both accepted, and the editor and founder, Adeline Evanson, called and asked me to become an editor. I lived in southern New Mexico at the time and was pregnant with my third child. As it turned out, our family was moving to Albuquerque, where the magazine was based, and I accepted the offer. I worked with Addie and her old friend, Kate Cook, in a ramshackle house in Corrales, New Mexico, as our children played about, and we reinvented magazine publishing.

In 1980 I became the owner of the magazine and have been publisher and editor ever since. I have seen the magazine grow from 3,000 readers to millions. I have seen the natural family living movement grow from twenty years ago—when breastfeeding was at an all-time low and herbs and acupuncture were considered fringe, at best to today, when the American Academy of Pediatrics recommends breastfeeding for at least a year and the United States government has created an Office of Alternative Medicine.

While it is good to see the things we like become popular, natural family living is more than the latest fad. It is about old-fashioned values, classic ideas, and relying on your instincts. The ideas about parenthood presented to you in this book have stood the test of time and are practiced widely in many cultures around the world. If some of these ideas are new to you, take what you like and leave the rest behind. If many of the ideas appeal to you, then read some of the books listed in the reference section, get support from other like-minded parents, and above all, trust yourself to know what is best for your child. That trust is what is at the heart of natural family living.

Hopefully, reading this book will help you to develop a personal ethic of parenting. It is natural to ask questions as a parent and to come up with personal, creative solutions to problems. Developing an ethic of parenting helps us to be proactive rather than reactive in our parenting and to answer the moral questions that arise once we have a baby. They are moral questions because the way we answer them influences all of the choices we make and underlies our relationship with our child.

An ethic of parenting must be based on the true nature of your child. It must not be based solely on the prevailing beliefs of the culture, because such beliefs are too arbitrary, transitory, and tenuous to sustain an ethic that will determine, to a large extent, the life history of an individual.

Parenthood is worthy of our best efforts, and raising the heirs of our civilization well is the prerequisite for a healthy society. That is why the magazine *Mothering* was started in 1976: to celebrate motherhood. At that time, motherhood was disparaged and considered by some to be no more than glorified servitude. Mothering set out to remind women that motherhood has immense importance in developing the full human potential of parents as well as children.

Today, women are again free to choose motherhood without apology. Being "just" a mother is once more good enough, a career choice worthy of respect. Popular magazines report that a natural lifestyle and motherhood are "in." The stature of parenting has improved in the United States, and although we have far to go in supporting families in this country, we have already come a long way.

For me, the experience of being a mother has been my greatest joy and deepest transformation. No one could have prepared me for the totality of my absorption in motherhood, or for how alive I feel as a mother. It is intoxicating to be as close to the miraculous as are the parents of a new baby.

PART 1 Preconception, Pregnancy, Natural Childbirth, and Midwifery

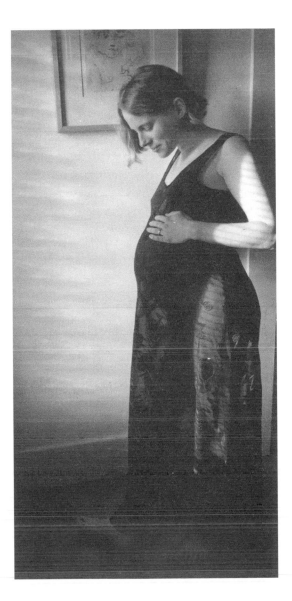

CHAPTER 1

Preconception

Becoming a parent can radically transform you. But long before you are even pregnant, you can begin thinking about how having a family may change the way you approach your life.

Naturally, you want to give your child as healthy a start as possible. Because you may be pregnant for several weeks before you are fully aware that you have conceived, preconception is the time to start examining the kinds of things your baby will be exposed to during pregnancy. At the same time, you can begin thinking about what having a family means to you—so you can start cultivating the qualities in yourself that will help you become the kind of parent you hope to be. Knowing that you want to create a certain kind of family life will allow you to consider what changes you need to make to bring your baby into a sensitive, responsive, and loving environment.

Out of the Mouths of Babes

Contrary to Freud's notion that every baby is a kind of *tabula rasa* or blank slate, recent research shows that infants have awareness and consciousness while in the womb. Studies have shown that babies respond to music in the womb and react to loud noises and bright light. They have even been observed to smile and to cry in utero. In one experiment by Italian researcher Allesandra Piontelli in 1992, a pair of twins, observed with ultrasound throughout their gestation, played affectionately with each other, touching each other cheek to cheek on either side of the membrane that separated them. Later, as toddlers, their favorite game was sitting, separated by a curtain, and rubbing their cheeks together.

If our memory begins in the womb, then it stands to reason that each of us might remember our own birth on an unconscious level. Indeed, children under three have been able to give detailed accounts of their experiences in utero and during their birth—complete with facts they could not have otherwise known. Under hypnosis, even adults have produced vivid recollections of their birth experiences.

Elaine and Thomas

On a long car trip, Eric, then three years old, suddenly asked us from the back seat, "Do you remember the day I was born?"

"Yes, do you?" we asked.

Eric responded, "Yes. It was dark and I was up real high, and I couldn't get through the door. I was scared, so finally I jumped and got through the door and then I was OK. Were you happy then?"

"Yes, we were very happy," we both responded, in shocked disbelief.

The interesting thing is, he remained high in my pelvis throughout twenty hours of labor, until very suddenly his position changed and he was born.

Linda Mathison, "Birth Memories: Does Your Child Remember?" *Mothering*, Fall 1981.

The Womb: Baby's First Room

The womb, then, is the baby's first environment, one in which he appears to have consciousness and feelings. As Leni Schwartz writes in *Bonding Before Birth*, "The moment of conception, the process of growing in our mother's womb, reacting to her hormones, digestion, smells, tastes, the air she breathes, her movements and emotions for nine formative months, and experiencing birth, are all part of our unconscious, affective memories." [1]

Just as you want to bring your child into a safe, healthy, supportive home, you want to make sure your child's first environment is a nurturing place. Thomas Verny asserts in *The Secret Life of the Unborn Child* that the womb sets the stage for the child's future development: "If it is a warm, loving environment, the child is likely to expect the outside world to be the same.... If that environment has been hostile, the child will anticipate that his new world will be equally uninviting." [2]

Such research suggests that we carry memories of the womb with us—memories that can influence the way in which we develop. It also suggests that you can create a nurturing place in the womb through your positive feelings about your baby. Your emotions of love and protectiveness towards your infant will be communicated to the baby in utero. Conversely, feelings of fear, anxiety, and ambiguity can affect the baby. Loving, nurturing thoughts can go a long way towards counteracting the effect on the baby of stresses that the mother can't control. Even if you are under extreme external stress, have financial problems or illness in the family, or feel ambivalent about the baby, you can protect your baby by keeping your feelings about him positive and loving. You can't control the external factors that are affecting you, but you can control whether or not they affect your baby.

Equally important are your partner's feelings. One study indicates that women involved in stormy relationships run a 237 percent greater risk of bearing a psychologically or physically damaged child. [3] A pregnant woman needs emotional support, and the baby's father is often the most important source of that support.

Food: Fuel for a New Life

Most of us readily recognize that a healthy diet is critically important during pregnancy. But it is also an excellent idea to start eliminating toxins from your diet and begin developing good eating habits while you are trying to conceive. Eat a wide variety of foods found in as natural a state as possible. Whenever they are available, choose unprocessed, pesticide-free, organic foods. Try to eat food that is locally grown and in season—check out your local farmers' market. Avoid additives and preservatives.

Vegetarian, vegan, and macrobiotic diets are all safe to follow during preconception and pregnancy as long as you are careful about following a balanced diet. You can get ample protein, for instance, from concentrated protein sources like tofu, tempeh, seitan, and nuts. Your calcium requirement can come from fresh greens sprinkled with sesame seeds and from sea vegetables, which are high in iron as well as calcium. Vegetarian diets have the added bonus of including lots of folic acid, which is necessary in the early development of the fetus. And, don't forget about Essential Fatty Acids (EFAs) which make up the membrane of every cell in the body as well as providing raw material for energy production. Make sure to get enough unrefined oils and fats. Good sources include sesame oil, safflower oil, sunflower oil, soy oil, flaxseed oil, organic butter, coconut oil, and various nut butters.

Although many women take prenatal vitamins as a precaution when they are pregnant or trying to conceive, current guidelines from the Institute of Medicine in Washington, D.C., note that they are not absolutely necessary. A well-balanced diet is the best way to get vitamins and minerals, as the body absorbs and assimilates them better through food sources, with little risk of overdose. In fact, vitamin supplementation can have adverse effects. For example, too much iron can inhibit the absorption of zinc, and high doses of vitamin A may interfere with fetal development. If you do decide to take a supplement, be sure you do not take more than the recommended dosage and be especially sure that you do not think of the supplements as a cure-all. No amount of supplementation can make up for a poor diet.

Besides making sure to include healthy foods in your diet, you should definitely give up tobacco and alcohol, and limit or avoid caffeine during pregnancy and preconception. After all, you may be pregnant before you realize it—and the first trimester is a critical time in the baby's development. Smoking greatly increases the risk of spontaneous abortion and fetal death as well as complications during labor. Babies whose mothers smoked during pregnancy may be born at a lower birthweight and have continuing health problems into childhood. Fetal alcohol syndrome is the name given to a host of ills in children, including mental retardation and growth deficiencies, that are a direct result of their mothers' alcohol consumption during pregnancy. Caffeine has been shown to increase the incidence of birth defects among laboratory rats.

If a cup of coffee in the morning or a glass of wine with dinner is part of your daily routine, eliminating these things may be hard for you. Try some healthy substitutes: a mug of herbal tea (preferably red raspberry and nettles—see "Herbs That Help," page 8) in the morning; sparkling mineral water with lime at night. Instead of putting your feet up with a cigarette after dinner, try taking a walk around the neighborhood. Exercise has the added advantage of producing natural endorphins, the same pleasure transmitters that are factors in addiction to cigarettes and caffeine.

Catherine

A few months ago my thirteen-year-old daughter asked if I had ever smoked. I admitted that I did until I got pregnant, at which point I gave it up for good. She looked at me admiringly and said, "You did that for me?" There is a beauty in knowing you're doing the best for your child, and in effect saying, "I respect you and love you, and I want to take care of you from the day you're conceived."

Start getting in the habit of drinking lots of water now—you'll need it when you're pregnant and nursing. Spring water and well water are best. If your tap water comes from municipal water system, you can have the water checked for things like lead, nitrates, and trihalomethanes, which have been linked with a higher miscarriage rate. If these are present, you can always use a water filter or buy bottled water instead.

HEALTHY EATING FOR TWO

Following are some suggestions for a balanced preconception and pregnancy diet for different food lifestyles. Key advice is to eat when you are hungry and stop when you are full, making sure you include a variety of foods from the groups listed below:

Calcium. Found in dairy products, tofu processed with calcium, soy milk, soybeans, sea vegetables, sesame seeds (tahini), almonds, dark leafy greens, salmon, mackerel, sardines, beans, lentils, blackstrap molasses, and dried fruit.

Protein. Chicken, fish, red meat, dairy products, eggs, tofu, tempeh, seitan, beans, legumes, nuts, and nut butters.

Grain products (supply carbohydrates for energy as well as a good source of B-complex vitamins, vitamins E and K, and zinc). Whole grain breads, cereals, pastas, cracked wheat, wheat germ, rice, millet, bulgur, quinoa, kasha, and amaranth.

Iron (iron requirements double in pregnancy, and may be difficult to get from diet alone). Red meat, liver, tofu, brewer's yeast, blackstrap molasses, dried fruits, whole grains, beans, legumes, dark leafy greens, seeds, nuts, and eggs.

Folic acid (critical in early development of the fetus). Liver, whole grains, legumes, sunflower seeds, beans, dark leafy greens, oranges, broccoli, and brewer's yeast.

Vitamin B6 (supplementation may aid in reducing morning sickness). Brewer's yeast, sunflower seeds, wheat germ, legumes, walnuts, whole grains, fruits, dark leafy greens, meat, fish, and chicken.

Vitamin C. Oranges, grapefruit, cantaloupe, papayas, guava, strawberries, lemons, limes, green or red peppers, broccoli, Brussels sprouts, cauliflower, cabbage, parsley, cucumbers, tomatoes, potatoes, turnips, watercress, and rose hips.

Vitamin A, E, and K. Dark leafy greens, orange fruits and vegetables (such as squash, sweet potatoes, carrots, peaches, and cantaloupe), and whole grains.

Zinc. Fresh oysters, pumpkin seeds, ginger root, nuts, whole grains, and lima beans.

Fats. Unrefined vegetable oils (olive, sesame, sunflower, soy, safflower, etc.), organic butter, mayonnaise, avocado, nuts, and nut butters.

HERBS THAT HELP
There are several herbs that are rich in vitamins and minerals and have properties that are beneficial during conception, pregnancy, and childbirth. (For more on using herbs, see Chapter 12.) The following herbs can be eaten as vegetables or steeped—alone or in combination—as a nourishing tea:

Red raspberry. Rich in calcium, magnesium, iron, phosphorus, potassium, and vitamins B, C, and E. Increases fertility, tones the uterus, eases morning sickness, and aids in milk production.

Nettles. Rich in iron, calcium, and protein. Increases fertility, reduces leg cramps and childbirth pain, helps prevent hemorrhage after birth, reduces hemorrhoids, and aids in milk production.

Alfalfa. Loaded with vitamins A, D, E, and K, digestive enzymes, and trace minerals. Reduces risk of postpartum hemorrhage.

Dandelion. Provides vitamin A and C, iron, calcium, potassium, and many trace elements. Acts as a diuretic to reduce water retention during pregnancy.

A Hazard-Free Environment

At the same time that you are nourishing your body to prepare for your baby, you will want to make sure that your external environment is also safe for a new life. There are many potential environmental contaminants, and while you do not want to be afraid of every little thing, neither should you hesitate to ask questions. If something concerns you, look into it through the resources in your community. Ask pregnant friends. Ask birth practitioners. The main thing is to be aware of what can harm the baby you are planning to conceive and to do all you can to reduce potential hazards.

- Electromagnetic fields (EMFs), emanating from power lines and electrical appliances, have been linked with reproductive problems as well as cancer. Although the research is inconclusive, it is probably best to limit your exposure to these potential hazards.
- Almost all major brands of computers now come equipped with low-emission terminals. To check yours, ask the manufacturer if it is TCO or MPR2 compliant. Of greater concern are EMFs emanating from office equipment such as copiers or printers. Sit at least four feet away from the back or sides of these machines, where the EMFs are strongest (even if a wall separates you from the machine). Microwave ovens are also a concern—not because of the microwaves themselves, but again, for the EMFs emanating from the machines' backs and sides. Stand back or leave the room when a microwave is in use. Electric blankets, because of their proximity to your body, should be avoided. Try using a hot water bottle instead of a heating pad. If you are concerned about a power line located near your house, you can ask your utility company to measure the magnetic field for you.
- X rays are another cause of concern. Robert Brent, MD, a distinguished professor of pediatrics, radiology, and pathology at Jefferson Medical College in Philadelphia, recommends that both a mother-to-be and her partner wait

three months after being exposed to radiation before trying to conceive. If you are counseled to get an X ray while you are pregnant or trying to get pregnant, always ask, "How much will it help? Is it indispensable? And how much exposure will there be?"

- The fumes from paints, some cleaning supplies, glues, and other noxious products can harm a baby in utero. As with substances you ingest—because you may be pregnant without knowing it—avoid exposure to such potentially toxic substances when you are trying to conceive.

- There is not much information on how safe food additives are during conception and pregnancy, because very few of them have ever been tested. Therefore, when you are trying to conceive, try to avoid foods that are heavily fortified with additives such as artificial sweeteners and replacements for oil and butter.

- Never take over-the-counter medications without first asking your doctor when you are pregnant or trying to conceive. Even if he or she gives you the go-ahead, it is wise to do all you can to solve minor complaints without the use of medication. Again, not much is known about some over-the-counter medications. Doris Haire, president of the American Foundation for Maternal and Child Health, cautions: "If you have a headache, try a cold cloth first; try anything other than a chemical product."

Use common sense. When you are in doubt about any choices you may make about food, medications, or potential environmental hazards while you are trying to conceive or when you are pregnant, always err on the side of caution.

How to Establish a Baby-Friendly Lifestyle

As hard as we may work at it, none of us can ever say that we have created around us the environment we consider perfectly safe, stress free, and supportive of the lifestyle we seek. Many factors are out of our control. But many are not. When you are thinking about having a baby is a good time to take stock of your surroundings, your support network, and your lifestyle, and to change the things you can to ensure that you will provide the best environment you can for your new family. Following are some concepts that can help you toward this end.

REDUCE STRESS IN YOUR LIFE

An extremely high-stress lifestyle is not conducive to conceiving or carrying a baby to term, or to getting a baby off to a good start. A study of forty-four women who were at risk of premature labor showed that they all had either a high level of stress in their lives, a high level of fear or anxiety about the birth, or many unrealistic demands placed on them with little support. Under hypnosis, many of the women revealed an unconscious perception that having a baby prematurely would make their lives easier because it would mean the hospital nurses would care for the baby. Through the use of further hypnosis, they were able to form intimate bonds with their babies, and in most cases, the premature contractions stopped without drug therapy.[4]

We all have a lot of stresses in our lives. Who can avoid it? But if having a baby is your main priority, start thinking now about rearranging your other priorities around this one. Consider reducing your workload—if this is an option for you—or cutting back on the obligations that may have accumulated outside your work. Start taking time out of your day to take care of yourself. This self-care will become even more important when you are pregnant and after your baby is born.

INCREASE YOUR SOCIAL SUPPORT NETWORK

Research shows that women birth best when they feel safe and cared for. Now, before you need to make all the decisions involved in having a child, you can begin to look at your support network and think about ways to augment it. Start to educate yourself about the resources that are available in your community for pregnancy, birth, and child-rearing. Is it important to you to live near relatives once you start a family? Or do you have close friends nearby who are like family? Maybe you

Susanna

As a partner in an investment fund, my career was intense and exciting, with frequent trips to Asia and big sums of money at stake. When my husband and I decided to start a family, I assumed it would be easy to get pregnant, since I thought of myself as healthy.

However, our long-awaited pregnancy ended abruptly in a miscarriage while I was on a business trip to New York. Over the next nine months, as I tried unsuccessfully to conceive again, I gradually realized that I was going to have to make some changes if I really wanted to have a baby.

I decided to stop working completely. It was a long process dissolving my partnership, but the very week that everything was finalized, I went along on a business trip with my husband to a place where I could just relax and walk on the beach. That's the week that I got pregnant, and nine months later, Elliot was born. I really had to create a space for the next phase in my life before it could happen.

want to make sure you are in a community where alternative medical practitioners are readily available. Or perhaps you want to be near a university hospital, big city, church group or spiritual community once you have children. In preparation for having a family, you might want to consider moving to a more family-supportive environment, but many new families find that there are abundant resources nearby, once they begin really looking for them.

If you do not have much flexibility in your choices, you can still create your own support network, by accessing resources over the phone or the Internet. The main thing is to begin to look at your options now, while you have time to think about your choices, and make any changes that are important to you.

EXPLORE YOUR EXPECTATIONS OF PARENTING WITH YOUR PARTNER

It would be a shock to discover after your baby is born that you and your partner have radically different ideas about how to raise a child. However, it is not uncommon for couples to make just that discovery. After all, if we go into parenting unconsciously—without much thought—we tend to do things the way our parents did them. If you and your partner had parents who raised you with very different sets of values and different styles of discipline, for example, it stands to reason that you will most likely find yourselves at odds when you try to parent your own child.

If we make conscious choices, we can choose the best of our parents' practices and try not to repeat their mistakes. Partners can do a great deal to help each other acknowledge what forces are at work in determining how they want to parent. As you prepare to conceive, now is the time to find out where you share common ground and to begin trying to build a consensus where you differ. To start, each of you should take a careful look at and talk about the role models you have had for intimacy, caretaking, and conflict resolution. Your goal is to build common values, but also to respect each other's differences of opinion.

BEGIN THINKING ABOUT BIRTH

Again, this is an area to discuss with your partner: You may have very different ideas about how and where you want the birth to take place. You will also want to examine your own attitudes and beliefs regarding birth. If you find that you are harboring fears and anxieties about birth, go through some exercises, such as writing down the fears you have been afraid to think about, and talking with supportive friends and relatives as well as with your partner. Often the simple expression of a fear helps you to let go of it. Most importantly, start to become comfortable with the notion that birth is normal. It is not a medical event, and it can be safe in almost any setting, as long as you have had good prenatal care and your birth attendant is experienced and has access to emergency equipment. Wherever you feel safe and cared for is the best place for you to give birth. (See Chapter 2.)

TAKE CARE OF YOUR SOUL

Now is the time to start thinking about babying yourself a little. It is a well-known psychological principle that men and women who have felt nurtured in their lives make the most nurturing parents. Conversely, those who do not experience nurture have difficulty nurturing others. You will be a better parent if you are loving and gentle toward yourself. Begin to notice the things that make you feel good—taking a bath, going for a long walk, or talking with a friend—and start to develop simple self-care routines. Laugh, dance, and sing. Most of all, recognize that you are a very important person, and learn to be easy on yourself.

CHAPTER 2 A Healthy, Wide-Awake Pregnancy

Pregnancy is a time to celebrate your femininity and to revel in the awesome changes that your body is going through. Powerful hormones are flooding through your body, helping you to feel motherly, making your skin and nails grow, and giving your complexion that pregnant "glow." You will become aware of your body and its capabilities in a whole new way. Pregnancy is a time to pamper yourself: to help yourself relax through techniques such as yoga or bodywork, to surrender to letting others care for you, and to treat yourself especially well. It is a time to enjoy your appetite and to eat better than ever.

Many women report feeling at their best during pregnancy. Your energy may be at an all-time peak, especially during the second trimester. This added energy makes pregnancy a wonderful time to take on a special project as a way to stretch your physical limits and to develop trust in your body. One woman began digging a well when she found out she was pregnant; others may start a garden. You would not want to undertake more than you are used to, but if you already farm, you can dig a well; if you already bike or hike, try a new or challenging trail. You will feel empowered if you focus on your strength rather than viewing pregnancy as a limiting condition.

Pregnancy is also a wonderful time for introspection. Towards the end of your pregnancy, you may feel your body giving you cues to slow down and reserve your strength for the hard work of labor. As you give in to this need for rest and contemplation, you can begin to focus inwardly and connect with your unborn child.

Marypat and Alan

That summer, as we paddled a canoe nearly 1,000 miles without seeing a human being, the 'pregnancy pace' came to be our motto. The knowledge of our extra cargo, our stowaway, never left our consciousness. It was as if, during moments of danger or exhilaration or fatigue, we could sense this third being participating as tangibly as if we'd had another paddler along. Our days were full of the cadence of wave and current, thunderstorms, the calls of loons and sandhill cranes. On some primitive sensory level the baby had to be taking in the experience, picking up on the environment, reading the joy coursing through Marypat.

Alan S. Kesselheim, "Am Pregnant, Will Paddle," *Mothering,* Summer 1997.

Prenatal Care: Giving Your Baby the Best Start

The statistics are dismaying: When a woman receives inadequate prenatal care, there is a 50 percent chance that her baby will be born with a low birthweight (less than five and a half pounds), and a low birthweight increases by forty times—

the risk that a baby will die during the first month of life. Yet one-quarter of the women in the United States receive little or no prenatal care. Put another way, there are twenty-one countries with lower infant mortality rates than the United States—and all of them provide universal prenatal care. It is impossible to overestimate the importance of good prenatal care. If detected early, most problems can be treated successfully.

PREGNANCY IS NOT AN ILLNESS

Prenatal care does not necessarily mean medical care. Pregnancy is a normal and healthy condition, not an illness. Good prenatal care simply means getting your vital signs checked regularly, eating an excellent diet, and perhaps most importantly, feeling well cared for.

Pregnancy and childbirth have always been considered natural biological processes. Only in the twentieth century did it become normal for medical doctors to assist in childbirth and for women to have their babies in hospitals. The change has altered the cultural attitude toward childbirth, making it seem more a medical procedure than a natural process. This approach to childbirth has not been universally positive for mothers and babies. In fact, since technology was introduced into birth, the impact on fetal and maternal outcomes has been mixed.

ARE PRENATAL TESTS ALWAYS NECESSARY?

One area in which the intrusion of the medical profession is most readily apparent is the realm of prenatal tests. It is a rare pregnant woman today who is not exposed to ultrasound, in the form of a sonogram (a scanning device used to get an image of the fetus) or a Doppler device to listen to the fetal heart rate, or an electronic fetal monitor to track the fetal heart rate during labor.

Ultrasound has proven useful as a follow-up test when multiple-birth pregnancies or birth defects are suspected. However, the American College of Obstetricians and Gynecologists, the American College of Radiology, and the United States Preventive Services Task Force all recommend against ultrasound screening during low-risk pregnancies. In spite of these recommendations, ultrasound is used routinely now to estimate gestational

---

Mothering Perinatal Health Care Index

- The twenty-one countries with lower infant mortality rates than the United States: Japan, Singapore, Sweden, Finland, Hong Kong, Norway, Switzerland, Denmark, Germany, Ireland, Netherlands, Australia, Austria, France, Canada, United Kingdom, Italy, New Zealand, Spain, Portugal, and Belgium
- Percentage of countries with lower infant mortality rates than the United States that provide universal prenatal care: 100
- Percentage of women in the United States who have no private health insurance: 25
- Percentage of women in the United States who receive little or no prenatal care: 25
- Chances that a woman with little or no prenatal care will give birth to a low birth-weight (less than 5.5 pounds) or premature (less than 37 weeks of gestation) baby: 1 in 2
- The factor most closely associated with infant death: low birthweight.
- Percentage of infant deaths linked to low birthweight: 60
- Chances that a low birthweight infant will die during the first month of life: 1 in 40
- Average cost of long-term health care (through age 35) for a low birthweight baby: $50,558
- Average cost of long-term health care (through age 35) for a baby of average weight: $20,033
- Cost of newborn intensive care for 1 infant: $20,000–$100,000
- Cost of prenatal care for 30 women: $20,000–$100,000
- Healthcare cost savings obtainable by providing universal prenatal care to all women in the United States: $7–$10 billion a year.

Mothering, Summer 1993.

---

age and size, although a woman's recollection of the date of her last menstrual period and an experienced practitioner's palpations of the uterus have proven to be just as accurate. Ultrasound is so standard today that photos and videos taken from sonograms are promoted as a way to "meet" and bond with your baby in utero.

New research has raised doubts over the safety of ultrasound scans used to view fetuses in the womb. A study by scientists at University College Dublin found that scans create changes in the cells. Patrick Brennan, lead researcher, said, "It has been assumed for a long time that ultrasound has no effect on cells. We now have grounds to question that assumption." It would certainly seem prudent to avoid all routine, but absolutely unnecessary, ultrasound scans for fetal observation. [1]

Electronic fetal monitoring has become standard practice as well. Most women who deliver in hospitals are hooked up to a monitor for part or all of their labor, which inhibits their ability to move around and makes labor more difficult in general. In addition, not one well-constructed scientific study has proven the use of an electronic fetal monitor to be any more effective than the use of a simple stethoscope.

Ruth

As soon as I got hooked up to the fetal monitor, all everyone did was stare at it. No one even looked at me anymore. Then I started staring at it, too, and pretty soon I got the feeling that it was having the baby, not me.

Amniocentesis—the withdrawal of a small amount of amniotic fluid to diagnose genetic conditions such as Down's Syndrome—is another prenatal test that has become a rite of passage for pregnant women thirty-five and over. However, the rate of miscarriage as a direct result of the procedure can be as high as one in 100. If her practitioner is not skilled in performing the procedure, a woman may be at greater risk of losing a healthy baby from the amniocentesis itself than of delivering a baby with a genetic problem.

The issues raised by across-the-board use of medical technology in pregnancy are many. Much of the technology has not been proven safe. There has never been a sizable, controlled trial, for example, to assess the safety of ultrasound, and there most likely never will be, because of the ethical dilemma of denying women access to a diagnostic tool that most people have been conditioned to believe is safe. A few smaller studies have indicated a link between children exposed to ultrasonography and symptoms of possible neurological problems in children. (The jury on ultrasound's safety may still be out, in a sense. It is interesting to note that fifty years after X rays had been routinely used during pregnancy and assumed to be safe, the procedure was found to be associated with childhood cancer.) Whether or not ultrasound is found to be dangerous, it is a fact that ultrasound testing is unnecessary in most pregnancies. Yet ultrasound testing has become so accepted that most doctors at the least recommend it strongly, and some even require it as a condition of care.

Medical technology poses other, more subtle, ethical and moral issues. Scientific tests like ultrasound and amniocentesis can give pregnant women a false sense of security about their babies, when, in truth, no test can guarantee a healthy baby. At the same time, these tests may undermine a woman's own intuition about her body and her baby, her own sense that the pregnancy is or is not going well. There are also moral concerns raised when an abnormality is found using technology. Women are usually offered the option of aborting a fetus believed to be carrying a birth defect. Because technology is imperfect, especially in the hands of an unskilled practitioner, women who have been warned that their children will have birth defects and have decided against abortion have given birth to healthy babies. How many healthy fetuses are aborted as a result of an erroneous reading?

If you are concerned about the medical, emotional, and ethical ramifications of prenatal testing, know that there are alternatives to obstetrical tests and technology. Depending on where you choose to have your baby, and with what type of birth attendant, you will have more or less control over which tests and procedures you will have. Some doctors insist on using the latest technology because, in our litigious society, they fear being charged with malpractice if something goes wrong. Their concern is legitimate, of course. Witness the number of malpractice suits brought against obstetricians in the last twenty years and the high cost of malpractice insurance. Yet midwives and other personnel at birthing centers can offer you alternatives to a technologically-centered pregnancy and childbirth by using tests, such as counting and recording fetal movements, that have been shown to be as reliable a method of determining the baby's well-being as any medical procedure.

The best way to avoid unnecessary and costly prenatal tests is to select a birthing practitioner who will not only provide prenatal care and birthing assistance, but who will also give you choices when it comes to which tests you will undergo. You need to become informed about prenatal tests, both from the information within this chapter and from discussions with your birth practitioner, so that if prenatal tests are recommended you will know their purposes, benefits, and potential risks. Then you can make your own choices.

Choosing a Birth Attendant

Prenatal care is essential to increasing the odds that you will have a healthy baby and that you will remain healthy during and after your pregnancy. However, prenatal care need not be approached as a medical procedure. Once you understand that there are choices open to you as to the kind of prenatal care you receive, you are ready to make the first important decision about whom you want to deliver that care. The three categories of birth attendants you can choose from are obstetricians, family physicians, and midwives.

OBSTETRICANS

These medical doctors have four years of residency in the field of obstetrics and gynecology following medical school. Their orientation toward prenatal care—whether they advocate complete choice for families regarding prenatal testing and natural childbirth—will depend a great deal on where they took their training. Some medical schools are more progressive than others. When interviewing an obstetrician as your potential birth attendant, you can ask where she received her training and what approach the institution took toward childbirth.

Choose a Person, Not a Category

Not all obstetricians and family physicians are technologically oriented when it comes to prenatal care and childbirth. Many embrace the concept of parental choice regarding testing and monitoring, and many will provide help if you wish to pursue a drug-free childbirth. Most midwives are in the business because they embrace the philosophy that childbirth is a natural process requiring only assistance, not intervention. However, it is possible to run into midwives whose personalities and philosophies do not mesh well with yours. If you are not already sure which category of practitioner you prefer, it is a good idea to investigate the facilities available in your community, to get information on their philosophies, and most important, to ask women and their partners what their experience has been.

FAMILY PHYSICIANS

These medical doctors have three years of family practice residency, including a minimum of three months in the specialty of obstetrics and gynecology. Again, the likelihood of a family physician respecting your choices regarding prenatal care and childbirth will be influenced by the medical school he attended. Some family physicians will be more oriented toward a medically directed hospital birth than others. However, it is interesting to note that the American Academy of Family Physicians has issued a statement encouraging birthing as a family event that can be safely experienced in a variety of settings, including the home.

MIDWIVES

There are several kinds of midwives. Certified nurse midwives (CNM) are registered nurses with two years of advanced practice in caring for pregnant women and delivering babies. They are certified by an independent accrediting agency in cooperation with the American College of Nurse Midwives (ACNM). Certified nurse midwives usually work under the supervision of a physician and deliver babies in hospitals or birth centers. Some attend home births. There has been a tremendous increase in CNM-attended hospital births in recent

years and research has shown that midwife-attended births have outstanding outcomes.

Certified professional—or "direct entry"—midwives (CPM) are trained through an independent midwifery school or apprenticeship. They are certified by the North American Registry of Midwives (NARM) in cooperation with the Midwives Alliance of North America (MANA). Although many CPMs have college degrees, college education is not required for certification. However, advanced practice experience with pregnant women, delivering babies and postpartum care is required. Direct entry midwives work independently, in consultation with physicians rather than under their supervision and they usually deliver babies in birthing centers and at home.

Licensed Midwives (LM) are CNMs, CPMs or independent midwives who meet the requirements for midwifery licensure established by a particular state and have usually completed a rigorous written and practical examination. About 25 percent of all states provide midwifery licensure at this time, and midwifery licensure bills are currently pending in several states.

Midwives attend about 6 percent of all births in the United States. In states like New Mexico, where Licensed Midwives have been available since 1978, nearly 25 percent of all births are attended by midwives. By comparison, midwives attend about 75 percent of all births worldwide.

This is your birth experience, and you want to find a birth attendant who shares your philosophy about childbirth. Although there are certainly exceptions with individual practitioners, for the most part the midwifery model for childbirth is radically different from the medical approach. Throughout the ages, women have always helped each other give birth. The midwifery profession grew out of that tradition. Rather than viewing pregnancy as a medical condition with corresponding stresses on the mother and risks to the mother and child, the midwifery model approaches pregnancy as a healthy and entirely normal condition. Obstetricians, on the other hand, are surgeons; specialists trained to deal with complicated deliveries.

In spite of the comparatively low number of midwives in the United States, midwifery has an impressive safety record. Several well-documented studies have reported that, compared to physician-attended births, midwife-attended births rely much less on pain medication and have much lower rates of Cesarean delivery and other inter-

Finding a "Mother-Friendly" Place of Birth

In the mid-nineties, the Coalition for Improving Maternity Services issued a set of guidelines for hospitals, birth centers, and homebirth caregivers to follow, constituting a model of ideal childbirth. To be designated mother-friendly, a birthing setting or caregiver must:

1. Offer all birthing mothers unrestricted access to the birth companions of her choice, including fathers, partners, children, midwives, and doulas.
2. Provide accurate statistical and descriptive information to the public about its practices and procedures.
3. Provide care that is sensitive and responsive to the mother's beliefs, values, and customs.
4. Provide the birthing mother with the freedom to walk, move about, and assume the positions of her choice during labor and birth.
5. Have clearly defined policies and procedures for working cooperatively with other maternity and community services before, during, and after birth and for breastfeeding.
6. Avoid routinely employing practices and procedures that are unsupported by scientific evidence, such as shaving, enemas, IVs, early rupture of membranes, electronic fetal monitoring, episiotomy, etc.
7. Teach and provide primarily non-drug methods of pain relief.
8. Encourage all mothers and families, including those with special-care newborns, to touch, hold, breastfeed, and care for their babies.
9. Discourage non-religious circumcision of the newborn.
10. Promote exclusive breastfeeding.

To learn more or to find out about mother-friendly childbearing centers and services in your area, contact The Coalition to Improve Maternity Services (CIMS), listed in the resources at the end of this book.

---

ventions such as forceps and vacuum extraction, as well as significantly lower incidences of low birthweight babies (suggesting better prenatal care). One of the largest studies to date, a twelve-year study of 30,311 nurse-midwife-attended births at the Normal Birth Center at the University of Southern California Women's Hospital, reveals no maternal or fetal deaths.

Midwives are trained to serve as a companion and guide to the pregnant woman, not only performing customary prenatal monitoring, but also counseling women on nutrition, emotional adjustments, and preparation for labor and birth. Because many midwives are experienced mothers themselves, they are able to give sympathetic woman-to-woman advice. Women seem to feel particularly comfortable sharing their concerns with midwives.

Midwives spend a significant amount of time with their clients during prenatal visits, and provide continuous, hands-on care during labor, birth, and postpartum. In contrast, most obstetricians work in a group practice; you may see any one of the doctors for your prenatal visits and birth. Also, you will spend most of your laboring hours with a hospital nurse with whom you have most likely had no previous contact; the doctor will check on you periodically and then be present only for the actual delivery.

Because midwives believe strongly that birth is a normal process, they avoid the use of routine obstetric interventions. They are trained to recognize complications and to intervene only rarely. They support the event as it unfolds instead of trying to manage the birth according to hospital-imposed timetables or rules.

Although women who have had a less-than-satisfactory birth experience can point out, and rightly so, that a healthy baby is what really matters, a midwife can help a woman cherish the process of the birth as well as the outcome.

Place of Birth: Home, Hospital, or Something in Between

The best place for you to give birth is wherever you feel safest. It is really that simple. You can have your baby in a hospital, in a birth center, or in your home. Wherever you feel least inhibited to act according to your own instincts—to make as much noise as you like, to assume any position that feels right—is where your labor will proceed most smoothly. We are, after all, animals, and our bodies, when left to their own devices, know what to do.

HOME BIRTH

Although the vast majority of births in this country take place in a hospital, there is no evidence that hospital births are any safer than home births. A number of studies have shown home births to have equal or lower infant or maternal mortality rates and significantly fewer interventions than hospital births. And no study has ever shown that, among low risk women, planned home births with trained attendants have any higher perinatal mortality rate than hospital births. According to a 1992 survey cited in the *British Medical Journal*, 91 percent of women who had their last baby at home said that they would prefer to have their next baby at home. And, among women who have experienced both homebirth and hospital birth, 76 percent preferred giving birth at home.[2]

Again, it is important to keep in mind that birth is a normal process, not a medical event. Most complications that would require medical attention show up during prenatal care, or in the first stage of labor, when there is still plenty of time to transfer the laboring woman to a hospital.

Even among women labeled high-risk, there is some evidence that home birth is a viable option. Studies from the Netherlands and Britain—where a high percentage of women choose home birth—show that perinatal mortality among high risk women is higher in hospital births than in home births. This surprising statistic may result from the much higher rate of interventions in hospital births. For example, electronic fetal monitoring, because it inhibits the laboring woman's movement, can stall labor. The use of drugs to augment a stalled labor can lead to overwhelming, painful contractions, which may necessitate an epidural. An epidural may prolong the pushing stage because a woman can no longer feel or work with her contractions. Often, a Cesarean delivery, with its greater risk of complications, is the result.

You need to weigh the relative risks: the risk of an emergency in a home birth (which may or may not have a better outcome in the hospital), versus the risk of infection and a higher rate of interventions in the hospital.

Christine

A few months ago, I gave birth to my second child in the upstairs bedroom of an ordinary house on a quiet and leafy suburban street. I had no bright lights, no steel bed, no electronic monitors, no needles, no drips, and no charts. I had, instead, the understated comforts of anyone's corner room—books, family photographs, and well-used furniture—augmented only by a stack of clean linens and one small satchel of medical equipment.

I labored by lamplight, first in a broad, soft chair and then on a bed piled with pillows. My attendants were neither shift nurses nor the on-call obstetrician, but rather my husband, two friends, and two midwives. I did not have to wonder if my older child missed me, for I knew she was peacefully asleep in the next room.

Christine Hale, "Birth at Home: An Immanent Power," *Mothering,* Spring 1991.

If you are thinking of choosing a home birth, you should:
- Read all you can about home births.
- Ask friends who have had home births what their experience has been; get recommendations for birth attendants.
- Interview potential birth attendants using the questions below. Specifically, be sure the attendant you choose has experience with emergency procedures and equipment and that you or she has the appropriate medical back-up with an obstetrician and a hospital.
- Make sure the attendant you choose is someone you trust to give you good advice but who will allow you to make choices during the birth.
- If you know you have twins, or your baby is in the breech position—especially if either of these situations accompanied your first pregnancy—you will probably want to rule out home birth. Most midwives no longer deliver vaginal breech or twin births. For more on breech or twin births, see Chapter 3.

Questions for birth attendants at home.
- What is your emergency procedure?
- Under what circumstances do you transport to the hospital?
- What hospital back-up or doctor back-up do you use or recommend?
- Are you trained in CPR?
- What emergency drugs do you have on hand, and for what purposes?
- What emergencies have you handled?
- What equipment and supplies do you bring to a birth?
- What is the procedure for checking progress during labor? blood pressure? fetal heart rate?
- Do you have preferences for position at birth?
- How do you feel about having older children attend the birth?
- Is a newborn exam done at birth? What does it consist of?
- How long after the birth do you remain with the mother and child?
- How often do you follow up to check on mother and child?

HOSPITAL BIRTH

If you are not comfortable with the home birth option, or if your home situation is not conducive to a pleasant childbirth experience, you can achieve the kind of birth you want in a hospital setting. Small community hospitals tend to use fewer interventions than large urban hospitals and university or teaching hospitals. However, thanks to customer demand, many larger hospitals have moved away from giving enemas, shaving pubic hair, and automatically using an intravenous unit to maintain blood glucose levels. Some have incorporated homelike birthing rooms where women can labor and deliver without being transferred to delivery rooms that look and feel like operating rooms. Some even offer Jacuzzis, rocking chairs, and CD players.

Keep in mind that a large hospital—even one with a homey environment—is still a hospital, staffed with medical personnel trained to view birth as a medical event. To find out if your local hospital is a place where you would feel comfortable delivering your baby, you will need to talk at length with your ob/gyn doctor and to take a care-ful tour of the hospital maternity center, asking many direct questions. If you do not like what you see and hear, then it is time to look at local birthing centers. Most health plans will transfer benefits to qualified birthing centers.

Among the most important questions you should ask both the obstetrician and the hospital representative are: What percentage of babies are delivered by cesarean section? At what stage are you likely to induce labor or try to speed labor with the use of drugs? And, what percentage of births are—medicated—that is, what percentage of laboring mothers are given pain-killing drugs? You want to find out whether the prevailing philosophy is to rush labor or to allow it to take its natural course, and whether pain-killing drugs are given routinely or only as a last resort at the request of the laboring mother.

These questions are especially important because recent studies reveal that some hospitals have much higher incidences of Cesarean sections than others do, indicating that they use procedures that influence the outcome. For example, inducing labor increases the likelihood that it will end in Cesarean. Or, if using pain-killing drugs is the norm and you will be considered unusual for requesting a drug-free birth, you are more likely to be offered drugs at moments when you are not in good condition to refuse.

Many obstetricians are willing to work with you in preparing a birth plan that you, the doctor, and your birth partner can all sign. If you take a copy of the birth plan with you to the hospital, you will be more successful at being allowed to make your own decisions regarding drugs, IVs, monitors, and induction than if you go without such a plan. It is vitally important that your birthing partner and/or labor doula go into the hospital as your advocate, someone who understands your desires and who can vouch for them if you become too weary or too emotional to speak for yourself.

Another important consideration with a hospital birth is how the period following the birth will go. Some mothers are taken by surprise when their baby is whisked away to a hospital nursery immediately after the birth. Few tests and procedures are actually necessary in the hours immediately following the normal delivery of a healthy child. And all of those that are essential can be done right in the room where the baby is delivered. Studies regarding the ability of a child to begin breastfeeding right away and theories about the importance of immediate bonding with the mother indicate that the healthiest place for the newborn child is in your arms.

Questions for the doctor or midwife in the hospital maternity ward.

- Do you induce labor? Under what circumstances?
- Will I labor and deliver in the same room? Are birthing rooms available?
- Are enemas and pubic shaves done in the hospital?
- Is moving around encouraged during labor?
- Are IVs routinely started on laboring women?
- Are electronic fetal monitors routinely used?
- Is eating and drinking during labor allowed?
- What percentage of your births are Cesareans? forceps deliveries? vacuum extractions?
- What is the newborn test procedure?
- Is rooming-in available?
- How soon after birth will I be with my baby? Does my baby have to go to the nursery?
- Are supplements routine in the nursery? Can my husband room in as well?
- Can older children be present at the birth?
- How long is the average hospital stay after childbirth?

BIRTH CENTER

During the last twenty years, birth centers have been established in all major cities and in many suburban and rural areas. Some birth centers are free-standing; some are affiliated with a hospital. They have the advantage of offering skilled clinical care and access to emergency equipment in a homelike, private setting. Most birth centers look like friendly country inns, with quilts on the beds, wallpaper, and lots of plants.

The staff at birth centers are usually committed to helping a mother labor in whatever way makes her the most comfortable, and they are usually especially attuned to the possibility of drug-free births. Birth centers encourage women to move around freely, eat and drink during labor, and use the tub or shower to ease labor pain. Family participation in the birth is usually an option. Mothers and babies are kept together after birth, and breastfeeding support is given right away.

Birth centers encourage women to take responsibility for themselves during prenatal exams, by monitoring their own charts, taking their own urine samples, and asking questions if something seems wrong.

As with home birth, birth centers have a documented safety record. Large-scale studies have shown birth centers to have as low or lower an infant mortality rate among low-risk births as hospitals and, importantly, they have half the Cesarean rate.[5] Birth centers generally offer lower fees than hospitals, and in the majority of states, costs are covered by health insurance.

Questions for all potential birth attendants.

- What kind of childbirth preparation classes are offered where you practice?
- How are fathers involved in prenatal visits and the birth?
- Do you work with partners? What is the likelihood you will be the one to attend my birth?
- Will my requests (birth plan) be in my records so your partners will be aware of them?
- What percentage of your clients have unmedicated births? Cesareans? episiotomies?
- Is nutritional counseling a part of your practice? What are your views on weight gain, exercise, and alcohol?
- Do you recommend breastfeeding? What percentage of your clients breastfeed?
- What does prenatal care consist of? What things are checked? How often? What equipment do you use?
- What is the cost of your care? What amount has to be paid in advance? Does my insurance cover it?

Birth Education: Physical and Emotional Preparation

As you consider where you want to give birth, you should begin the process of learning about and preparing yourself for childbirth. Most hospitals and birth centers offer birth education classes for mothers and their partners who are planning to deliver on site. Some birth education classes espouse a particular philosophy and technique, like the Lamaze, Bradley, or Birthing Within methods. Many, however, incorporate a number of different techniques. The main focus in such classes is almost always on relaxation and breathing techniques designed to help you remain relaxed through contractions, optimizing the possibility of a drug-free, stress-free, enjoyable birth experience. Look for a teacher who has a positive approach to childbirth and whose philosophy leans toward minimal medical intervention during labor and delivery. Research shows that the biases of childbirth educators can encourage or discourage parental decision making and can strongly influence such things as whether or not a woman uses pain medication or chooses to breastfeed.

Birth education need not take place in a formal class. You can educate yourself about the anatomy and physiology of birth and learn relaxation techniques through yoga, meditation, and bodywork. For more on childbirth education, see Chapter 3.

YOGA

Yoga is excellent preparation for childbirth because yoga postures teach you to relax your entire body at the same time that one part of your body is in tension, which is exactly what you will need to do in labor. The gentle stretching loosens tight ligaments that are performing double duty during pregnancy and helps your pelvic area to open up for childbirth. Yoga gives you strength and muscle tone to help you handle a long labor. And regular yoga practice can give you energy and a sense of emotional and spiritual balance that can enable you to remain centered on the positive aspects of childbirth.

Many communities now have yoga centers, and you can ask for a prenatal yoga class where you will have the added benefit of meeting other mothers-to-be. A number of high-quality video tapes are available that offer yoga instruction. If you are practicing on your own, be sure to get a videotape specifically for prenatal practice, as there are some yoga postures that are not recommended for the expectant mother.

MEDITATION

Birth is a spiritual, transcendent experience. The habit of mindfulness learned in meditation can serve you well when you are in labor. Meditation, as well as the breathing techniques taught in childbirth classes, helps you develop the ability to focus at will and to stay in the moment during contractions. Any other endeavor that heightens mental awareness and enhances your ability to release tension—such as hypnosis, visualization, and some of the martial arts—can also be helpful.

BODYWORK

It is not often enough that you find time to pamper yourself, but pregnancy provides you with a wonderful excuse. Massage, reflexology, and other forms of bodywork such as rolfing (a version specially modified for pregnancy), Jin Shin Jyutsu, Feldenkreis movement, craniosacral therapy or Watsu all help you get in touch with your physical self at a time when you need to be most aware of how your body is changing to accommodate the baby within you. These techniques, which may be new to you, also enhance your ability to relax, which is so important both in childbirth and in mothering. Choose methods and practitioners with whom you feel safe and comfortable.

Sara

When I found out I was pregnant, one of the first people I told was my massage therapist. Massage had always been a physical release for me; now it became an emotional release, as I gave in to the overwhelming feelings surrounding this new development.

Throughout my pregnancy, massage was an important component of my well-being. Lying on a foam massage table, I could relax completely as strong hands soothed my tired legs, feet, and back. My new shape made me feel awkward and off-balance, but on the massage table I felt floating and cocooned. The baby responded, too, with happy little movements while I was rubbed.

CELEBRATING YOURSELF

The traditional function of the baby shower is not simply to provide the necessary clothing and equipment a new mother needs, but to invite all the members of a community to support the new mother with their energy. When you approach a baby shower with this support function in mind, you invite the participation of your circle of friends in your baby's birth and upbringing. Another way to celebrate during your pregnancy is to make a gift for your child. Whether it is a crib or a pair of booties, this act of devotion focuses your thoughts on the baby and by making the baby more of a reality, helps you to feel ready for the birth.

A pregnancy journal celebrates the transition you and your partner are making together. By recording your thoughts about and dreams for your baby, you remain conscious of your own emotional growth. While having a baby is serious business, taking it too seriously, however, can be counterproductive. Balance this thoughtful preparation with a sense of playfulness, with singing and laughing. Playfulness keeps you hopeful and develops your intuition. Singing and laughing, for example, relax your whole body. Try relaxing the muscles of your face and jaw and notice how your vaginal muscles relax. So laugh, sing, and smile.

Thin Is Not In

Pregnancy is the time to nourish your body with wholesome foods. While during the period of preconception you made your body strong and welcoming, now you need to eat more to sustain two lives. Gone, thankfully, are the days when women were counseled to strictly limit the amount of weight they gained during pregnancy. Current guidelines from the Food and Nutrition Board call for a minimum weight gain of fifteen pounds for women who are somewhat overweight to begin with, and up to forty or fifty pounds for underweight women. The important thing to remember—more important than the number you see on the scale—is that the quality and quantity of food you eat have a direct impact on your baby's health. Weight gain, especially during the second and third trimesters, is necessary to prevent low birthweight babies.

As you prepare and eat food during your pregnancy, focus on why you are eating, and enjoy watching the pounds go on. Imagine your child resting on your soft body. Mothers are meant to be soft. Rather than worry about the future and how you will lose the weight, think about doing the best job you can of taking care of your baby right now. Follow the preconception and pregnancy diet suggestions in Chapter 1.

Natural Soothers for Pregnancy Complaints

As your body goes through all of the changes necessary to create a new life, you most likely will feel a little off-balance at times. But if you view the discomforts of pregnancy as the side effects of a natural process rather than as symptoms of an illness, you will be much better equipped to handle them without potentially harmful medications. Here are some gentle remedies for treating some of the common complaints of pregnancy.

MORNING SICKNESS

Despite its name, the nausea that affects more than 75 percent of all pregnant women can occur at any time of the day, usually between the second and eighth week of pregnancy. Morning sickness may result from an increase in hormone levels or by a natural process that slows the action of the digestive tract to allow your body to absorb more nutrients. Both the increased hormone levels and slower digestion are actually signs of a healthy pregnancy—in fact, women who experience morning sickness have lower miscarriage rates than those who do not. Try these remedies when nausea strikes.

Diet. A low blood sugar level contributes to morning sickness. Try small, high-carbohydrate and high-protein snacks such as nuts, dried fruits, and whole-grain crackers throughout the day, and a yogurt or a fruit smoothie before bed or first thing in the morning. Papaya enzyme tablets taken with meals and acidophilus-containing foods such as yogurt and kefir can decrease digestive upset.

Vitamins. Vitamin B6, found naturally in yeast, blackstrap molasses, wheat germ and bran, and organ meats, has been shown to provide relief in clinical studies. Try adding brewer's yeast and blackstrap molasses to a smoothie, or take a Vitamin B6 supplement. One hundred milligrams three times a day is the recommended dosage during pregnancy.

Herbs. Ginger is one of the best antinauseant remedies around. You can nibble on it in crystallized or fresh form, or in the pickled variety that accompanies sushi, or take it as a tea or powder.

Aromatherapy. Some doctors dismiss morning sickness as being a psychological problem: all in a woman's head. But it may be more in her nose. Your sense of smell is heightened during pregnancy, and certain odors—strong perfume, overbrewed coffee, cooking grease—can make you sick to your stomach. Try waving a lemon under your nose, or take a whiff of lavender or peppermint. For more on aromatherapy, see Chapter 12.

Homeopathy. Homeopathic remedies are safe to take during pregnancy. For advice on using homeopathy, see Chapter 12. Homeopathic remedies for morning sickness include Sepia, Ipecac, and Nux vomica.

Acupressure and acupuncture. Pressure on certain points can sometimes help at the beginning of a queasy spell. Try deep, probing pressure with your fingers for a few minutes on a point two thumbs width below the wrist crease on the inner surface of your wrists, directly in line with the middle finger. You can also buy motion sickness wristbands designed to put pressure on this point. Acupuncture, administered by a licensed practitioner, can also be very helpful for morning sickness.

INSOMNIA

Difficulty sleeping is a common complaint in the third trimester of pregnancy when it is hard to find a comfortable position to sleep in. Here are some remedies that may help.

Herbs. Herbs high in calcium, such as skullcap, oats, and raspberry leaf, soothe the nerves, promote restful sleep, and ease muscle cramps. To help yourself relax, try floating a cloth bag full of chamomile and lavender blossoms in a warm bath; after your bath, drink a mug of raspberry tea.

Aromatherapy. Neroli and sandalwood are soothing to the mind and emotions. Sprinkle a drop or two on your pillow, or drink a spoonful of orange flower water, which contains neroli oil, in a cup of warm milk before bed.

Do-It-Yourself Pregnancy Soothers

Follow these recipes for natural pregnancy soothers you can make on your own. You can find the ingredients at natural foods stores.

Cocoa butter cream

Use this rich cream all over your body to relieve itchiness, keep your skin soft, and possibly reduce stretch marks.

　¼ cup grated cocoa butter
　1 teaspoon almond oil
　1 teaspoon light sesame oil
　1 teaspoon vitamin E oil

Gently heat all the ingredients together in the microwave for thirty seconds or in a double boiler on the stove over low heat. Stir to mix, and pour into a clean jar. Store in a cool, dry place. The recipe can be doubled.

Peppermint leg gel

Massage this light, non-greasy lotion into your legs and feet for an instant pick-me-up.

　½ cup aloe vera gel
　1½ teaspoons cornstarch
　1 tablespoon witch hazel
　3–4 drops peppermint oil

Heat the first three ingredients together on the stove over low heat, until the mixture forms a clear, thick liquid the consistency of honey. Let it cool, add peppermint oil, and stir to mix. Pour into an airtight container.

Homeopathy. Coffea, Pulsatilla, Arnica, and Chamomilla are most often recommended for sleeping difficulties. See Chapter 12 for more on homeopathic remedies.

HEMORRHOIDS AND VARICOSE VEINS

Abdominal pressure and increased blood volume can cause these discomforts. Try the following strategies.

Diet and vitamins. Make sure you eat plenty of fiber—fruits, vegetables, and bran—to soften your stools. Vitamin B6 is often recommended to help reduce varicose veins and fluid retention, and vitamin E helps prevent varicose veins and blood clots. Vitamin C can strengthen the venous walls, while garlic improves circulation. Get these vitamins from food sources (see Chapter 1) or supplements.

Herbs. Comfrey, calendula, and yarrow, in a salve or a sitz bath, can help soothe hemorrhoid discomfort. There are several commercial blends available at health food stores. Nettle leaf, taken as a tea or a tincture, can reduce hemorrhoids by improving the elasticity of the veins.

Aromatherapy. For varicose veins or swelling, try elevating your feet and gently massaging from the ankles upward with cypress, lemon, lavender, rosemary, or geranium oils (during pregnancy or anytime, always use essential oils that have been diluted as undiluted oils can be too potent—for more information, see Chapter 12). Cypress and lemon oil can also help soothe hemorrhoids; apply these oils, diluted in a carrier oil such as almond, grapeseed or safflower, directly to the area. You also can use them in a sitz bath.

Homeopathy. Remedies include Nux vomica, Belladonna, Aloe, and Pulsatilla. See Chapter 12 for more information.

When Something Goes Wrong

Although miscarriage occurs in one out of five pregnancies and is usually the result of a malformed fetus, those facts do not make it emotionally any easier when your pregnancy ends abruptly.

You are likely to feel sadness and anger at your loss. Give yourself time to experience these emotions, and seek the help of friends or a support group. Guilt is another common response to miscarriage. Instead of spending unnecessary time punishing yourself, you can channel your feelings of guilt into healthy questions about why the miscarriage occurred. Spend time with your birth attendant examining why you might have miscarried. If you can learn the real reason, you will alleviate any sense of personal failure on your part. However, be aware that there may be no clear explanation forthcoming.

You may wish to see your baby. This is your right. A well-meaning friend or relative may admonish you not to consider a miscarried fetus as a real baby in order to help you avoid grieving. But most parents who go through the grieving process and call it grieving find that acknowledging their grief is exactly what they needed to do. Some parents have found it emotionally helpful to name the baby and to plant a tree or contribute to a cause for children in the baby's memory.

Some miscarriages are over within a few hours, while others can cause bleeding, discharge of the placental tissue, and cramping for a month or even two. Even with a prolonged miscarriage or a stillbirth (miscarriage after the twenty-fifth week) you can remain safely at home under the advice of a trained birth attendant. If heavy bleeding or signs of an infection are apparent, you may need a D and C (dilatation and curettage, or scraping of the uterine lining).

Some suggested herbs to speed up the healing process are collinsonia (to increase pelvic circulation), helonias and squaw vine (both tone the uterus; helonias should not be taken during pregnancy), pipsissewa (lymphatic cleanser), and raspberry leaf (muscle toner). You may want to combine these herbs into a tea. Wild yam root is a safe preventative in the case of a threatened miscarriage. Drink two cups of this tea a day to ease cramping.

The homeopathic remedies Sabina and Viburnum opulus are used to treat the threat of miscarriage. Bacillinum is used as a preventative if a mother has a history of repeated miscarriages. With all homeopathic remedies, please consult a trained homeopathic practitioner.

CHAPTER 3 Natural (Drug-Free) Childbirth

Childbirth is a peak experience. It is likely to be a greater challenge than we anticipate, but it need not be more than we can handle.

Childbirth is transformative. How you labor can reflect your basic personality and it can change you for the better. If you are someone who embraces the unknown, you will probably welcome the challenge of childbirth. If you tend to blame others and feel victimized when things go wrong, you can begin early on to take responsibility for yourself during pregnancy and to focus on your strength during labor.

Childbirth is an initiation. Giving birth means stepping beyond the familiar into unfamiliar territory. A woman who experiences labor relying on her own inner resources knows she is strong. Approaching birth in this way can mean giving birth to a new version of yourself.

Pain in Labor

We have all heard the horror stories and seen the television depictions of excruciating labor. Although childbirth need look nothing like these dramatizations, the reality is that it usually is painful. How could it be otherwise when the cervix, pelvis, and vagina stretch to accommodate a head the size of a grapefruit while the muscles of the uterus contract powerfully to push the baby out? But, childbirth pain, unlike other physical pain, is pain with a purpose—not pain as a warning sign.

If the degree of pain two women have during labor is measured with biofeedback, the results will typically show it to be similar. Yet different women experience labor pain differently. Some women—a lucky few—report painless labor. Others describe the pain during labor as the most intense sensation they have ever had. So the important question seems to be not whether there will be pain, but whether we can trust in our ability to cope with it. Labor pain is healthy pain—part of a normal process—and the pain is nothing that will damage us. Women are designed for childbirth. We have all of the inner resources we need to cope if we trust in ourselves enough.

Why women experience labor pain differently is a matter of debate. Some birth attendants speak vaguely of the notion that different women naturally have different thresholds for pain. But there is plenty of evidence to suggest that the point at which an individual woman reaches her pain threshold is not a factor of her particular body type or biological makeup, but is dependent on factors present in the specific situation. For example, if medications are used to induce or speed up labor, contractions will almost certainly be more intensely painful. Even something as simple as bright lights in the delivery room can make labor seem more painful because they make it more difficult for a woman to relax.

In addition, a woman's perception of pain is influenced by her personal beliefs about pain and her culture's expectations regarding pain management. Dealing with labor pain effectively requires that we change our relationship to pain, its physical sensation in our bodies and its accompanying emotional response. Our previous conditioning associates pain with danger. Women, therefore, are vulnerable to the cultural suggestion that labor is dangerous and requires external "relief" rather than welcoming labor pain as a healthy, powerful transition to birth. These cultural attitudes and beliefs about pain in general and birth in particular are translated into personal fears, doubts, and insecurities about ourselves, our bodies, and our abilities to manage labor. Freely expressing these inevitable fears and anxieties with your partner and close friends helps to transform them into inner strengths that you can call upon during labor.

Fear and anxiety are known to contribute to the experience of more intense pain in labor. A woman's ability to relax is known to contribute to the experience of less intense pain. One goal of natural childbirth is to minimize the factors that might lead a woman to experience childbirth pain more intensely and to maximize the factors that help a woman to labor with confidence and to trust in her ability to relax.

The Fear Factor

To understand how natural childbirth can reduce stress and pain, it helps to understand the physiology of birth. Think about how other mammals give birth. If an animal is safe while giving birth, there will be low levels of adrenaline present in her body. If she is threatened while she is giving birth, adrenaline levels rise quickly, which stalls her labor and gives her time to fight or flee. If her young's head is already engaged, however, the added adrenaline enables her to give birth quickly and to have the energy to protect her newborn.

The uterus is the only muscle in the body that contains two opposing muscle groups—one to contract and open up the cervix, and another to close and tighten the cervix to stop labor. When the birthing mother becomes afraid—and many women are afraid as they go into the unknown territory of labor—adrenaline creates the fight or flight reflex, causing her cervix to tighten at the same time that her uterus is continuing to push the baby toward the cervix with each contraction. The result is the very real pain of two powerful muscle groups pulling in opposite directions.

This chain of events is what obstetrician Grantly Dick-Read, author of *Childbirth Without Fear,* called the fear-tension-pain syndrome. In effect, fear causes a woman's labor to be more painful, because her body is fighting itself.

In labor, a woman's body needs to relax entirely to allow her cervix to open up completely. For her to relax, her adrenaline levels must be low. Once the cervix is fully dilated, an unmedicated woman will experience a surge of adrenaline and an overwhelming urge to push, making the final stage of labor easier and less painful.

Why Drug-Free?

If labor is painful, why go through it without pain-relief drugs? Perhaps the most important reason is that birth is a normal process that occurs most easily when it is allowed to proceed naturally. Once a medical intervention is introduced, it tends to lead to another—and another—in an escalating spiral. For example, electronic fetal monitoring inhibits a laboring woman from moving around, which can cause contractions to feel more painful, leading to a greater use of epidural anesthesia—injection of an anesthetic into the lumbar area of the spine in the space between the spinal cord and the dura; the procedure is commonly called "an epidural." When Pitocin (an artificial version of the hormone oxytocin used to augment labor) is given to speed up labor because it is not proceeding according to prescribed timetables, it tends to cause overwhelming, back-to-back contractions, again generally leading to an epidural. An epidural, on the other hand, can prolong or stall labor, often resulting in a forceps or vacuum extraction, episiotomy or, in many cases, a cesarean delivery.

HOW SAFE ARE DRUGS GIVEN IN LABOR?

The World Health Organization guidelines call for avoiding the routine use of pain-relief and anesthetic drugs, and for inducing birth only when medically indicated. Yet, 75 to 90 percent of all laboring women in the United States today receive an epidural, and about one-third of all births are induced or augmented with Pitocin.

Most women receiving an epidural do not know what drugs are being used or what the safety implications might be for themselves or their baby. A lumbar epidural is a regional anesthetic administered through a long needle inserted into the spine. It gives pain relief by partially or totally numbing the body from the ribs to the toes. A woman remains curled on her side without moving during the procedure, which takes effect in twenty to thirty minutes. If an intravenous line is inserted for continuous administration of IV drugs, she must remain on her back for the rest of her labor, which can inhibit her ability to push (since the supine position is the worst position for pushing) and may lead to a need for a Cesarean delivery.

The drugs used in an epidural are Caine-derivative anesthetics. The Caine derivatives we are most familiar with are Novocain and cocaine. Additional drugs, such as morphine, may be added.

We now know that any drug ingested by or injected into a pregnant woman's body crosses the placenta to the baby. When a drug is given during labor, the dosage is determined by the mother's weight, which is approximately twenty times that of the baby, meaning that a large dose of drug is entering the baby's system. The newborn must metabolize these drugs through the liver, increasing the likelihood of jaundice. Babies born to mothers receiving an epidural have less muscle tone and strength, and so many have difficulty sucking, complicating the first days of breastfeeding. In addition, they score lower in motor skills on the Neonatal Behavioral Assessment Scale in the first month of life.

In a well-designed case control study at the Karolinska Institute in Stockholm in 1990, researchers compared children exposed to pain relieving drugs in labor with those who were not and discovered an increased risk of drug addiction later in life.[1] Researchers suggest that the use of opiates, barbituates and nitrous oxide in labor causes imprinting in the babies.

Mothers report side effects from epidurals as well, including severe headache, backache, fevers, urinary retention, and numbness or weakness in arms and legs. Twenty-three percent of women who receive epidurals have complications such as these.

The 1996 Physician's Desk Reference cautions that "local anesthetics [the type used in epidural anesthesia] rapidly cross the placenta...and when used for epidural blocks, anesthesia can cause varying degrees of maternal, fetal, and neonatal toxicity." Epidurals have been linked to an overall increase in operative deliveries: cesareans, forceps deliveries, and vacuum extractions.[2] In fact, a woman who receives an epidural has a four times greater risk of forceps delivery and vacuum extraction and at least a two times greater risk of cesarean than a woman who does not. A 1997 *Time* magazine article noted that a mother's temperature may become elevated with the use of epidural anesthesia, resulting in the infant being given a "full work-up" for possible infection. This work-up may include extensive blood work and a spinal tap.[3]

THE DANGERS OF INDUCTION

We are only just beginning to understand the complex processes involved in the onset of labor. Current research suggests that it may be the baby's brain that initiates birth by prompting the baby's endocrine system to secrete a hormone that triggers a response in the mother. The problem with artificially inducing labor is that determining when a baby is ready to be born is, at best, an imprecise science.

Doctors today pinpoint a specific day as a woman's due date by calculating from the date of her last menstrual period or by using a sonogram. If they rely on counting from the last menstrual period, they assume that she has a twenty-eight-day menstrual cycle (which most women do not) and that she can recall exactly the first day of her last period. As it turns out, this method is only 85 percent accurate in determining a due date, plus or minus two weeks. Factors as diverse as the mother's age, whether it is her first pregnancy, and how much caffeine she has consumed, can affect the length of the pregnancy. Even ultrasound is only 85 percent accurate in predicting a due date, plus or minus two weeks.

Despite the imprecise nature of predicting gestational age, many doctors routinely recommend induction when a woman is past her due date, and many women, having anticipated the big day for nine months and feeling mentally ready to have a baby, go along willingly.

As mentioned before, Pitocin—an artificial form of the hormone oxytocin—is most commonly used to induce or augment (speed up) labor. Despite the fact that the Food and Drug Administration (FDA) has never approved Pitocin for the augmentation of labor—and removed its approval of Pitocin for the elective induction of labor in 1978—it is routinely used today to induce labor in mothers who are past their due date, afraid of having a "too-big" baby, or just tired of being pregnant.

Pitocin, administered through an IV drip, causes long, strong contractions that are described as much more painful than natural labor by women who have experienced both. Most Pitocin-induced mothers require pain-relief medication. Pitocin requires continuous fetal monitoring, restricting the mother's mobility. The effect on the baby of strong, back-to-back contractions is like being pushed underwater before having time to catch his breath. We do not yet know what long-term effect this decreased oxygen supply has on the baby's brain. We do know that Pitocin can in rare cases cause fetal seizures, hemorrhage, and brain damage.

THE BONDING PERIOD
Many drugs given during labor interfere with the ability of both mother and child to form the bond that nature intends for them to form. Without interference, during the last contractions, the fetus releases a high level of adrenaline, emerging from the womb alert and wide-eyed. When a baby is put immediately in his mother's arms, the baby will gaze into her eyes unblinkingly. In most women who experience drug-free birth, the body produces very high levels of the hormone oxytocin—sometimes referred to as the love hormone because it induces maternal behavior and is present during lovemaking. Given the baby's natural alertness and the mother's infusion of oxytocin, if the two are allowed skin-to-skin and eye-to-eye contact, the first, critical bonding between mother and child is established.

A woman who has been given drugs to alleviate labor pain does not experience the rush of oxytocin that women do who have not been medicated. Because all drugs cross the placenta, a baby exposed to drugs may not experience the rush of adrenaline and may not be alert enough to engage with her mother until several hours or even several days after the delivery.

CHILDBIRTH AS A RITE OF PASSAGE
A more subtle argument for drug-free childbirth is the transcendent quality of the experience itself. Going through childbirth without drugs can put a woman in touch with an inner part of herself that she may have never known existed. She may discover a newfound sense of strength that will change the way she approaches future challenges. A woman who feels as though she was in charge of her birth experience may go into motherhood more confidently and be more willing to make choices that are in the best interest of her child, even if they buck current trends. The greatest reward for having experienced a drug-free childbirth may well be that feeling of having met a challenge and discovered what the mind and body are capable of doing.

Jane
My husband joked through my pregnancy that natural childbirth sounded about as appealing to him as natural root canal, but I knew instinctively that I wanted my labor to be drug-free. There are very few events in life that force us to be powerfully present. I wanted to fully experience the birth of my child, with all its pain and joy and intensity.

As an athlete, I was used to pushing beyond my pain threshold, but that still didn't prepare me for the overwhelming, inevitable force of labor. I felt as if I were simply a vessel through which this new life was being brought into the world. Although I cried out in agony for it to stop, five minutes after a perfect child was placed on my chest, I would have joyfully done it all over again. I later told my husband that I felt sorry that he would never get to go through an experience as profound as childbirth.

Preparing for Natural Childbirth

Birth is normal, but it is never the same—each birth is different. You can do everything "right," read all you can on childbirth, and prepare yourself to the best of your abilities, but you still cannot control the outcome. Birth is unpredictable by nature. Perhaps the best way to prepare for birth is to become skilled at handling the unexpected. The kinds of things you learn in an Outward Bound–type surrender experience—relying on your inner resources, trusting your body's responses, developing quick and decisive thinking under stress—may be the best way to develop confidence in your ability to rise to the challenge of childbirth.

More conventional childbirth preparation includes classes in childbirth methods such as Lamaze and Bradley. Lamaze, however, has come to be a catchword for all childbirth education classes. The actual Lamaze method teaches several altered-breathing techniques as well as other labor soothers. The Bradley Method emphasizes deep, rhythmic, abdominal breathing, encouraging women to visualize their bodies opening up with each contraction. In the Bradley method, partners also learn guided relaxation and massage techniques to help the mother relax. Both approaches are successful at enabling women to have an unmedicated labor, Bradley perhaps more so than Lamaze. Because of its focus on drug-free births and the pain management techniques it teaches, the Bradley method is over 90 percent effective in facilitating unmedicated births, according to its originator Dr. Robert Bradley.[4]

The danger with any childbirth preparation method is that it can make birth seem more predictable than it is. By stressing techniques for "managing" pain, contemporary childbirth education classes imply that labor can be controlled and pain minimized if we practice diligently enough. The fact is that labor is uncontrollable. Many women go into labor ill-prepared for the overwhelming, powerful sensations they experience; as a result, they panic.

To avoid that panic, it is important to educate yourself about childbirth, to understand what happens when you are in labor, and to know how to help yourself. Get in touch with yourself through body awareness techniques such as yoga or dance, and mind awareness techniques such as meditation and visualization. For more on childbirth education, see Chapter 2.

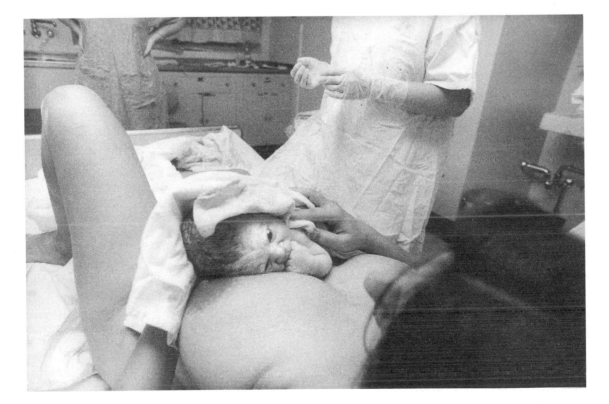

Sample Birth Plan

We are looking forward to a natural childbirth and have planned, prepared, and practiced for this birthing experience. We would like to be informed about any procedures or tests before they are performed. In the case of an emergency, we would like to be told of our options so that we may make appropriate decisions.

We prefer:
- Partner (husband) and birth attendant present throughout
- Option to have children present
- Freedom to move about and change positions
- Freedom to eat and drink throughout
- Freedom to use shower or tub
- Massage and stretching of perineum to avoid tearing
- Gentle and controlled pushing stage in squatting position
- Quiet room and dim lights for delivery
- Baby placed on mother's chest immediately for breastfeeding
- Placenta allowed to be delivered spontaneously
- Cord not clamped or cut immediately

- Baby and mother left undisturbed for the first hour
- Any newborn procedures delayed until after the first hour
- Cleaning of vernix delayed or avoided
- Oral form of vitamin K for baby
- Antibiotic ointment or no eye treatment at all for baby
- PKU screening delayed until baby is five days old
- Rooming-in for baby and partner

We prefer to avoid:
- All medication (please do not offer; we will ask for it if needed)
- Shaving, enema, or IV
- Electronic fetal monitoring
- Vaginal exams (keep to a minimum)
- Stripping of membranes or breaking of bag of waters
- Time limits imposed on labor
- Supine position for pushing stage
- Episiotomy
- Use of forceps or vacuum extraction
- Any supplemental bottle-feedings
- Circumcision

PAIN RELIEF WITHOUT DRUGS

We have already discussed how interventions in the natural process of childbirth can actually lead to a more painful experience, making it more likely that pain-relief drugs will be used. Natural childbirth techniques can lead to a less painful experience because working with your body and allowing it to birth the way it knows best usually results in a quicker, more efficient labor. Still, natural childbirth advocates can not promise a pain-free experience. Coupled with an overall positive attitude toward childbirth as a natural process are many techniques for managing pain that offer relief without drugs.

Remember, too, that the most painful part of labor is the shortest. The most cervical dilation occurs rapidly just before the baby is born. This stage is the point at which many women feel they cannot go on—similar to a marathon runner "hitting the wall"—but it means birth is imminent.

These are some time-honored natural pain relief techniques.

Sit, stand, or squat. Get on your hands and knees. Lying down is just about the worst position to give birth in. In traditional societies, women have always chosen to give birth in upright postures. Only in the twentieth century did anesthetized birth and the supine posture became the norm.

Birthing upright can make labor shorter and less painful, because gravity assists the process. Squatting widens the pelvic outlet by as much as 25 percent. An upright woman can also use her abdominal muscles to push more effectively. Lying down, on the other hand, puts the weight of the uterus on the vena cava—the main vein that returns blood to the heart—thereby cutting the blood and oxygen flow to the baby. To avoid this decrease, pregnant women are cautioned not to lie on their backs for extended periods of time during the last trimester of pregnancy.

There is no right position for labor—you may choose to give birth sitting up in bed, on your hands and knees on the floor, standing and leaning on a helper or a bar, or in a supported squat, with a helper holding you up from behind.

Move around. Any kind of movement helps the passage of the baby through the birth canal. Often just getting up and walking around can jump-start a stalled labor. So walk, sway, rock in a rocking chair, sit and rotate on a big rubber ball—whatever feels right.

Get in warm water. A tub or shower can do wonders for your mood. Warm water feels particularly good for back labor. Have your helper or partner get in with you and apply massage and counter-pressure.

Try aromatherapy. Your favorite scents, along with soft candles and soothing music, can set a mood that will help you relax and produce endorphins, your body's natural pain-killers. Try diluting a few drops of essential oils in a bath, on cool or warm compresses for your forehead or lower back, or blended in massage oil for massaging your back or feet. Use lavender or clary sage (not sage, which should be avoided in pregnancy) or make the blend described in the sidebar.

Try homeopathy. If you have some experience with homeopathy, or have a homeopathic practitioner available during your labor, you may want to try a remedy to speed a stalled labor or to relieve pain or exhaustion. Homeopathic remedies are chosen based on a specific set of symptoms. When the right remedy is chosen, it can stimulate the body to balance itself, and because homeopathic remedies are made of natural substances diluted many times, they pose no danger to mother or child. (For more on homeopathy, see Chapter 12.)

Remedies for labor, depending on individual symptoms, include black or blue cohosh for stalled labor; Pulsatilla or Chamomilla for slow labor; Aconite for fear, and Arnica for fatigue.

Consult a homeopathic manual (see Resources) for more information.

Massage Oil for Pain and Tension in Labor

¼ cup sweet almond oil or pure vegetable oil
10 drops lavender
6 drops clary sage
4 drops geranium
2 drops jasmine
3 drops rose

Combine, and store in a plastic bottle away from light.

Try nipple stimulation. Nipple stimulation releases oxytocin, the hormone responsible for starting and maintaining uterine contractions. Midwives have long suggested manual self-stimulation (or partner stimulation) of the nipples to speed up a slowed labor. Lovemaking, which releases oxytocin as well as labor-inducing prostaglandin (via the partner's sperm), can also be used in early labor to stimulate contractions.

Eat and drink. Most hospitals routinely forbid anything by mouth once labor has begun, because of fear of aspiration, should general anesthesia be necessary. However, studies have shown that aspiration is linked to the anesthesiologist's techniques rather than the mother's food intake, and that dehydration and low blood sugar can be more dangerous to the laboring woman than any risk of aspiration. Just as in a marathon or any other event as physically demanding as labor, many women find that they feel better if they eat and drink light, complex-carbohydrate, easily digestible foods and fluids.

Do your exercises. A woman in good shape will have more strength and endurance for labor than someone who has had a sedentary pregnancy. Besides aerobic activities like walking or swimming, practice pregnancy-specific exercises such as Kegels, pelvic rocking, and squatting—all taught in good prenatal exercise and childbirth classes.

Relax. Go with the flow. Remember that labor works best when you work with your body. Using your relaxation training from childbirth classes, yoga, or meditation, breathe through each contraction. Visualize your body opening up to let your baby through. Assume any position that feels right and allow yourself to make noise, if it feels good. Surrender to the process.

Do what you need to feel protected and secure. During labor, a woman enters a primitive state. Any stimulation, such as asking her a question or switching on a bright light, can disturb her. This heightened sensitivity is why animals seek out a private, safe place in which to give birth. For you, this place may be your home, a birth center, or a mother-friendly hospital. For more on choosing a birth place, see Chapter 2.

Have a doula. The presence of a doula, a woman specifically trained to help in labor and newborn care, may shorten your labor and reduce your need for pain medication, just by making you feel secure. The doula can suggest changes of position, give you massage and counter-pressure where you need it, and offer you reassurance when you begin to fade.

Women in labor are vulnerable and susceptible to suggestion. Labor and delivery nurses in hospitals are usually trained to focus on monitoring and recording vital signs rather than on giving women coaching. Offering pain-relief medication has become a reflex, when most of the time a woman just needs some help getting through her fear. A doula or other experienced birth support person can help you work through that fear and find your own inner strength.

AVOIDING AN EPISIOTOMY

Episiotomy—a surgical cut made in the perineum, the area between the rectum and vagina, to enlarge the birth opening—has become common-

Dads and Doulas

It is clear that labor proceeds best when allowed to take place naturally. For this to happen, the laboring woman needs to feel safe, secure, and supported. In our society, that support is most commonly provided by the baby's father. However, it may be a mistake to assign the "coaching" role to a husband or partner.

Up until the 1960s, fathers were usually relegated to pacing the hospital halls during their children's birth. The advent of childbirth methods such as Bradley and Lamaze gave husbands a new role. Borrowing from sports terminology, armed with stopwatches and charts, fathers became "coaches."

The problem with this approach is that it implies that fathers should be doing something to make childbirth easier, when what the laboring woman really needs is to simply let go and let the process happen. It is hard for any man, who has no point of reference in childbirth, to relate to what his wife is feeling. Taking on the role of questioning medical interventions and making sure the birth plan is adhered to can put the father into an adversarial relationship with the birth attendant—a role that most men are not particularly experienced at or comfortable with. Perhaps most importantly, fathers need to be allowed their own transformative experience of witnessing their newborn child's birth; that experience can be diminished by needing to act as coach.

In most non-industralized societies, men have birth customs of their own, called "couvade," in which they manifest some of the symptoms of pregnancy and act out their own version of labor. They often have a special role to play once the child is born, acting as the child's spiritual guardian. Perhaps we can learn from these cultures that men need to create their own birth rituals.

If the father does not act as your support person, who will? Many women find the help of a doula invaluable in this capacity. A doula (from a Greek word meaning woman helping woman) offers comfort to the laboring woman, support for the woman's partner, and helps communicate the couple's needs to the birth attendants. Research has shown that the presence of a doula reduces the length of labor, use of pain medication, and number of cesarean births significantly.

place, despite the fact that the American College of Obstetricians and Gynecologists recommends against its routine use. Episiotomies were originally given when women began to be anesthetized for birth, making the use of forceps necessary. The rationale for most episiotomies is that an incision may heal more quickly than a tear, although research has shown the opposite to be true.

The downside to an episiotomy is a painful recovery period. It can be difficult to sit down for a few weeks and intercourse may be uncomfortable for several months. And, the stitches can get infected, requiring antibiotics.

As always, keep in mind that women are designed to give birth without surgery. In most cases, an episiotomy can be avoided by taking the following steps.

Choose a birth attendant and place of birth with a low episiotomy rate. If your doctor or birth attendant performs episiotomies as a matter of course, the following preparations for giving birth without one will go for naught. As many as 80 percent of first-time mothers giving birth in a hospital receive an episiotomy, as opposed to 10 to 15 percent of mothers birthing at home or in a birthing center under the care of a midwife.

A skillful birth attendant who is committed to helping you avoid an episiotomy will encourage you to slow down during the pushing stage and will continuously lubricate and support your perineum by using hot compresses and counter-pressure during the delivery.

Eat well throughout your pregnancy. Good nutrition helps the perineum become elastic to stretch for childbirth. Particularly important are vitamin E, protein, and short-chain fatty acids, found in nuts and seeds, cold-pressed oils, and cold-water fish such as salmon and tuna.

Practice Kegels. The Kegel muscle makes up the floor of the pelvis, and is critical in bladder function and sexual enjoyment. A strong Kegel muscle will stretch to its maximum during childbirth and then bounce back again. Using the same squeezing motion that you would use to stop the flow of urine, flex this muscle tightly and deeply while you relax the rest of your body. The doctor for whom the exercise was named recommended 300 flexes a day. Practice Kegels when you are sitting at your desk, stopped at a stoplight—any time you think of it.

Avoid an epidural. Episiotomies are much more commonplace in a medicated birth. It is harder to push effectively if you cannot feel your body's natural urges and if you are unable to stand or squat.

Cesarean Sections—Lifesaving Surgery or Unnecessary Epidemic?

The World Health Organization recommends that Cesarean sections be performed in no more than 10 to 15 percent of births. Yet, the Cesarean rate in the United States is over 20 percent. There are certainly instances in which a Cesarean is a necessary, life-saving procedure. However, the number of Cesareans performed in the United States has quadrupled in the last twenty-five years, mainly because doctors, wary of malpractice suits, are much more apt to perform a Cesarean section than to let a prolonged and possibly complicated labor run its course. And, also because women who have had a previous Cesarean birth, or who are giving birth to a breech baby or to twins, are routinely delivered by Cesarean.

AVOIDING A CESAREAN BIRTH

The most reliable way to decrease your chances of having a Cesarean is to choose a birth attendant who is committed to avoiding unnecessary Cesareans. Studies have shown that Cesareans are 2.5 times less likely to be performed on women cared for by midwives, as opposed to obstetricians. When choosing a doctor or midwife, be sure to ask about their Cesarean rates. The reaction to that question may be revealing.

In addition, use the suggestions recommended in the section on Pain Relief Without Drugs above. Different birthing positions, relaxation techniques, and a supportive environment can all help your labor to progress. Try to avoid any kind of medical intervention in labor—remember that one intervention tends to lead to another, often resulting in a surgical birth.

IF YOU HAVE A CESAREAN

Most Cesareans are called for during labor, when the birth attendant feels that either the mother or baby is threatened. But some women schedule a planned Cesarean, because of a breech-positioned baby, or pregnancy with twins or other multiples, or for other medical reasons. If you have to have a planned Cesarean, there are some things you can do to feel more in control of the birth experience.

Ask your doctor if you can wait to go into labor naturally. Many doctors will want to schedule a Cesarean, but some are willing to let you go into labor first. This way you will get to experience the excitement of early labor, and you will know that your baby went full-term.

Make the operating room as much like your own environment as possible. Some hospitals may not be willing to let you play music in the operating room or burn an aromatherapy candle, but it does not hurt to ask. This is your birth experience.

Participate in the birth as much as you can. Most obstetricians place a screen over the mother's abdomen during a Cesarean. If you are not squeamish, you may want to ask to have the screen lowered so you can watch the baby being taken out. If you are under general anesthesia, someone can take pictures or a video so that you do not feel later that you were entirely removed from the process.

Do whatever you can to bond with your baby right away. As soon as possible after the baby is examined, have someone place the baby on your chest, skin to skin. Try to nurse on the operating table (you will need help positioning the baby, since you will be lying down). Delay any procedures you can that would take the baby away from you. Keep the baby in the room with you during your hospital stay, and have your husband or other helper stay with you too, so you can focus on the baby while they tend to your needs.

Erin

My body had always been able to accommodate my requests. I was used to hiking 1400 foot peaks, skiing, and scuba diving without a problem. So when I learned at my thirty-six-week check-up that my baby was breech, I was devastated.

Once I let go of the feeling that my body had somehow let me down, I decided to focus on creating a birth experience as close as possible to the one I had envisioned.

My husband and I made a deal. I felt strongly about bonding in the delivery room. Since I would not be able to hold our newborn for long, the bonding would be up to him. We kept the scheduled Cesarean date a secret from family and friends. We had planned to walk our favorite trail during labor—we went ahead and walked it before driving to the hospital. We chose the music for the operating room. I requested that I be allowed to walk into the operating room, rather then ride in a wheelchair. I don't think the birth could have been any more euphoric.

As the doctors stitched me up, I was scared and felt alone. I wanted my husband's hands on my forehead telling me it would be all right, but his touch was needed elsewhere. Every time I watch the video and see his hands on Grace's tiny head, welcoming her into the world, I know that was all that mattered.

RECOVERING FROM A CESAREAN

There is a common misperception that having a Cesarean is easier than going through labor. But a Cesarean is major surgery, and the pain of childbirth comes afterward. Some women say after a Cesarean that instead of feeling like a mother, they feel like they want one.

So mother yourself. Be kind to yourself. You will probably need someone—like your mother, or a doula—to take care of you for the first week or so. Perhaps the best advice is to stay in your nightgown for a week—get out of bed and move around, but do not try to do anything around the house or go anywhere until your incision begins to heal. It may be difficult to find a comfortable nursing position at first. Try holding a pillow over your incision or using the "football hold" (baby held along your side, resting on your forearm). Nursing will get easier with time. It may take six to eight weeks for you to recover fully.

VBAC: ONCE A CESAREAN, NOT ALWAYS A CESAREAN

While the number of women who have a vaginal birth after a Cesarean (VBAC) was once very small, the rate has climbed to a high of over 35 percent today.

There are many reasons to attempt a VBAC. The recovery period is much quicker and the risk of complications—including infection and hemorrhage—is much smaller with a vaginal birth. Babies born by Cesarean, even elective Cesarean, generally have more problems initially than babies born vaginally, including lower Apgar scores (a measure of the baby's condition at birth) and a higher likelihood of needing intensive care or breathing support. The reason vaginally born babies have fewer problems is that during labor, the uterine contractions literally massage the baby's skin and stimulate the nervous, respiratory, cardiovascular, gastrointestinal, immunological, and endocrinal systems. Babies born by Cesarean miss all that stimulation. They are also more likely to be premature and low-birthweight, since many Cesareans are scheduled early.

A Cesarean can also upset the bonding period designed to take place after birth. Pain and disorientation from major surgery can make it difficult for a mother and baby to connect in the same way that they would in an unmedicated vaginal birth. Hormones that facilitate the bonding process and are secreted during the final stages of labor, such as oxytocin and adrenaline, are often lacking in a Cesarean birth that has not been preceded by labor. Breastfeeding may get off to a poorer start because of the more limited bonding time in the first few days and pain from the incision when nursing.

Once you decide you want to have a VBAC, you need to commit yourself to the idea wholeheartedly. Lingering fears and doubts will only get in the way, as will naysayers, so surround yourself with positive thoughts and people. Support will be expecially important to help you stay commit-

ted in labor, so find a doctor or midwife who is enthusiastic about VBAC and consider the help of a doula.

SPECIAL CIRCUMSTANCES—BREECH BIRTHS AND TWINS

A baby who is breech (positioned buttocks- or feet-first) can sometimes be turned head-first before the onset of labor through the use of external manipulation, by hands-and-knees pelvic rocking, or by lying in a tilt position, with your head, shoulders, and feet on the floor and your pelvis raised off the floor on pillows. Some practitioners have even been effective at turning breech-positioned babies through music, acupuncture, or hypnosis.

If turning is not effective, a Cesarean section is usually scheduled, in spite of the fact that research shows that vaginally born breech babies are at no higher risk than breech babies born by Cesarean. As recently as the 1970s, 90 percent of breech babies were delivered vaginally. However, because doctors fear they will be sued for malpractice if they do not intervene in the case of a breech presentation, breech extraction is rarely taught in medical schools or even to midwives any more, and this procedure is almost never covered by insurance.

Doctors are increasingly reluctant to deliver twins vaginally because they are afraid one or both twins will be in the breech position. However, as with single breech births, research bears out the fact that twins can be safely born without surgery. There are a handful of doctors and midwives who specialize in the vaginal delivery of single and multiple breech babies. For information on getting in touch with one of them, see Resources.

Handling Disappointment—When the Birth Is Not What You Expected

We plan for childbirth. We make decisions designed to create an atmosphere and an experience that we will remember with joy for the rest of our lives. We make decisions designed to ensure that our babies will get the healthiest start in life. Yet the fundamental truth about childbirth— that it is a natural process—means also that it is an unpredictable process. You can control the birthing process only up to a certain point.

You can engage the practitioner who is most likely to honor your wishes; you can choose the site for the birth that makes you most comfortable; you can bring your partner and a doula who will give you maximum support; you can take optimum care of your body and learn the most effective techniques for natural childbirth. However, you will come to realize that beyond taking these important steps, there is still an element of the unknown and unknowable in every birth. We speak of "our" births, but they are really our babies' births. In the end, all you can do is surrender to the event and let nature take its course.

Looked at in a positive light, this learning to surrender is one of life's greatest lessons. But for many women, when childbirth does not go the way they had planned, they become hard on themselves, their partners, or their practitioners. They second-guess their choices and spend many unproductive hours, days, or weeks wishing they had done something differently. They blame themselves for "failing" in childbirth.

It is important to have high ideals and clear goals regarding your birth experience. It is also important to have realistic expectations. Most important of all is to realize that your baby's birth is the beginning of your life as the mother of that child. Life with your child will contain both exhilaration and disappointment. You can do your best and make all the right decisions given the information you have, and yet you will eventually know that the whole experience of parenthood is not within your control.

If you are disappointed with your birth experience, it can help to tell your birth story to sympathetic friends. Many communities have support groups for women who have had Cesareans or disappointing births. Some women have found that it helps to imagine the birth happening a different way. In your imagination, you can sometimes tie up the loose ends psychologically. Think about what might have happened differently, what you would do the next time. If you are severely disappointed, then you need to heal, and the healing may take some time. But the time will come when you can forgive yourself and others for any real or imagined failings and move on.

Although most of us will not have a lot of chances to finally "get it right" with birth, we will have thousands of moments with our children. Birth is right no matter how it happens, because it is, after all, the beginning of our baby's life.

Older Siblings at the Birth: A Family Affair

It was not long ago that men were excluded from delivery rooms; now it is a rare father who is not present at his child's birth. Perhaps at some point, the idea of older children witnessing the birth of a sibling will not seem so unusual.

There are many reasons why parents want to include their older children in the birth of a sibling. Some do not want a young child to associate the birth with separation from their parents—having Mommy and Daddy leave, perhaps in the middle of the night, in the case of a hospital birth; or being taken away themselves, in the case of a homebirth. Others hope having the older siblings there at birth will foster a special closeness between siblings. Still others simply feel it is an event that affects the whole family, and they want their children to be there.

Children, even young children, may be better equipped to handle the powerful experience of childbirth than we think, but only if they are well-prepared. If you are concerned about shielding your children from the possible trauma of witnessing a difficult birth, remember that children's fantasies about what might have happened are usually more alarming than reality.

The question of whether your children are ready to witness a birth can be answered only by you. Age is not really a factor as much as your perception of your child's readiness. Some parents have children as young or younger than two present at a birth—even though they may not understand or take much interest in what is going on—simply to avoid separation. If you are considering having siblings attend your birth, consider the following questions for each of your children:

- How do they handle seeing someone they love in pain?
- Are they frightened by the sight of blood?
- Are they comfortable with nakedness?
- Have they been through any traumatic events recently that might affect their ability to handle the birth?
- Most importantly, do they want to be there?

You must also ask yourself if you feel comfortable birthing naturally, making noises, and letting go completely in front of your child. If the answer is no, it is probably not in anyone's best interests to have your child present.

If you decide that a family birthing experience is for you, you will need to find a place of birth that welcomes children. Many hospitals do not; most birthing centers do as long as you bring a support person along who can leave the labor room with the child if necessary. One of the reasons some women choose a homebirth is because they want their children to see birth as a normal, nonmedical process.

These are several things you can do to prepare for including your child in a sibling's birth.

- Let your child know as soon as possible about your pregnancy.
- Bring your child to prenatal visits; let the child listen to the baby's heartbeat.
- Involve the child in picking out the baby's clothes and thinking about names.
- Try to find a childbirth preparation class for siblings; show your child pictures and movies about birth; explain the process in terms your child can relate to.
- Discuss ways that your child can help in labor—bringing you cool washcloths or drinks, rubbing your belly, playing requested music, or taking pictures.
- Allow your child to wander freely in and out of the room where the birth is taking place; to play, take naps, and eat. If the birth is at a hospital, you may want to arrange to have your child arrive just when the birth seems imminent.
- Make sure to reassure your child as soon as possible after the birth, and spend some special time together.

- Most importantly, whether you are at a birthing center or at home, assign a friend or relative to take care of your child during the birth. You and your husband will be preoccupied with your own roles; your child needs someone to focus solely on his needs.

For some children, witnessing the birth of a sibling can be exciting and awe-inspiring. But do not be disappointed in your young child if he or she fusses, needs cuddling, or seems merely uninterested.

Many families describe the experience of sharing a birth together as one of their closest moments. Perhaps as children become more accepted as participants in childbirth, they will learn to view birth as a natural, normal process, and be better prepared for the birth of their own children.

> ### Dori
> I could tell by the look on four-year-old Ben's face that the baby's head was indeed out. I had never seen his eyes so wide. He knew there was a baby inside me, and he knew how it was going to come out, but I don't think he really grasped the concept until he saw the baby with his own eyes.

Your Baby's First Few Days

The hours following your baby's birth constitute a critical bonding period. Researchers have found that mothers who have close physical contact with their babies in the hours after birth tend to be more responsive to their babies' needs later on, and more successful in breastfeeding.[5] Research by Marshall and Phyllis Klaus also shows that, left to his own devices, a newborn has the amazing ability to find his way to his mother's breast and begin suckling within the first hour or so.[6] Because this initial bonding is so important, try to have any newborn test or procedures put off for a few hours, or done with your baby in your arms. Certain procedures that are required by state law can be administered in a such a way that they cause a minimum of mother-child separation and trauma to the newborn. You will need to discuss your wishes about these tests when you interview birth practitioners. And you need to include your wishes in your birth plan, so if the practitioner you have chosen is not present for some reason, you can still insist that your wishes be honored. Even if hospital procedures are required by state law (and many nurse-midwives must follow the same regulations even in home births), you can request that they be performed differently. You can also refuse any procedure. You may be required to sign a waiver, and you should be sure that you have researched the issue thoroughly and feel comfortable with the risk factors involved.

Some of the procedures you can expect are described below.

VITAMIN K

NEWBORNS MAY RARELY BE BORN WITH A DEFICIENCY IN VITAMIN K, WHICH AIDS IN BLOOD-CLOTTING

Vitamin K injections for newborns are mandated in most states, but the vitamin is administered orally in many European countries. Several studies have indicated a link between vitamin K injections and childhood cancer.[7]

Some parents feel that the potential benefits of vitamin K injections are outweighed by the risks. Other parents object to giving their babies a shot immediately following birth. Oral Vitamin K is still pending FDA approval in the United States, but you can request that your hospital administer the vitamin orally. The oral dose is usually two times the injected dose. The best way to give it is in the corner of the baby's mouth during nursing. Some midwives offer an herbal form of vitamin K for the baby, or offer the mother alfalfa tablets, which are high in Vitamin K that can be passed on to the newborn in breastmilk.

PKU SCREENING

Phenylketonuria (PKU) is a rare inborn error in metabolism that, if left untreated, can cause mental retardation. The condition can be averted by immediately putting the baby on a special diet low in animal protein.

Most PKU screening is done by pricking the infant's heel to obtain enough blood to fill three circles on an absorbent card. The testing is usually done in the hospital before discharge, and again at a one- or two-week check-up. However, the infant must have consumed three or four days of breastmilk or formula before phenylalinine shows up, and many families are discharged from the hospital within twenty-four hours. The optimal time for testing appears to be five or six days after birth. Brain damage can occur as early as ten to fourteen days after birth.

Because of the high false-negative rate of doing the test within the first two hours and the trauma of the procedure, some parents choose to wait to have the test done at five days to a week postpartum. Warming the baby's foot with a hot washcloth gets the blood flowing and may make it unnecessary to jab the heel repeatedly. It is also important to know that babies who test positive do not have to be put on special formula—they can still be breastfed, provided the mother follows a low-phenylalinine diet.

EYE DROPS

Babies are given silver nitrate drops or antibiotic ointment in their eyes to prevent them from contracting an eye infection caused by gonorrhea bacteria in the birth canal. Most hospitals require the treatment within the first hour or two of birth, and many nurses will want to do it right away.

Unlike the silver nitrate drops, the antibiotic ointment does not burn the baby's eyes. But it does temporarily blur the baby's vision, and if it is given during the alert period immediately following the birth—when the infant is usually intent upon nursing and gazing into his mother's eyes—the treatment can disrupt the bonding process. You can ask that the eye treatment be done after an hour or two, when the baby usually begins getting sleepy, or you can refuse this procedure.

CLEANING THE VERNIX

When babies are born, they are covered in vernix, a thick, waxy substance that protects their skin. Many hospitals give the baby a sponge or water bath right away to wash away the vernix. This procedure, again, disrupts the bonding process, and can cause the baby's temperature to drop, which may lead to a stint under warming lights.

It is not necessary to clean the vernix off. You can rub it right into the baby's skin as you hold the baby on your chest. (Some midwives call it 'baby cold cream'!)

Frederick LeBoyer, author of *Birth Without Violence*, recommends easing the newborn's transition into the world by immediately immersing the baby into a tub of warm water.[8]

While this can interrupt the bonding period, you may request to have a "LeBoyer bath" set up at your bedside a few hours after the birth where you and your partner—and other children—can give the baby her first gentle bath.

After the Birth—Taking Care of You

Many cultures have their own customs for honoring new mothers and welcoming their babies into the world. The ancient Hindu Ayurvedic tradition of medicine encourages new mothers to stay home with their babies and be pampered for the first twenty-two days after birth. Few visitors are allowed, and special foods are prepared for the mother. In Southeast Asia, the traditional post-birth lying-in period is known as Mother Roasting. As soon as the baby is born, a ceremonial fire is built and tended near the bedside, and mother and baby lie nude by this fire for up to a month while being taken care of by family members. The sauna-like atmosphere seems to help the mother and infant recover quickly from birth, and nudity facilitates skin-to-skin bonding and breastfeeding on demand.

We could learn something from these cultures about the importance of the postpartum period. Most new mothers in our society are sent home from the hospital after one or two days and are expected to take up the demands of motherhood, usually without the benefit of their own mothers or other relatives nearby to offer guidance or support.

You can expect to be overwhelmed by the experience of new motherhood, even if it is your second or third child. Your body is busy recovering from the demands of childbirth—your uterus is shrinking to its pre-pregnancy size, your bones

and muscles are beginning to realign, and the placental site, and possibly an episiotomy or Cesarean incision, are healing. Your body is also making colostrum and milk for your baby.

Hormone levels, which have been at an all-time high during pregnancy, plummet within hours of birth. On top of this, you will probably be sleep-deprived from the round-the-clock demands of feeding and caring for a newborn. It is not until four to six weeks following an uncomplicated vaginal delivery, and six to eight weeks after a complicated delivery or Cesarean, that you will feel like your old self again.

At the same time that you are recovering physically, you need to take time to bond with your new baby and redefine your family now that this baby is in it. Even if you already have children, the birth of each new baby means the birth of a new family, and each family member must readjust his or her role. During this time, it is critical for you to be able to focus on caring for your baby without distractions from the outside world or even from within your own family.

Jan

I was speaking to a wise friend of mine a month after my third child was born, explaining that my two older children were feeling neglected. I told her that I was thinking of hiring a sitter once a week so that I could spend some time alone with them, without the baby always interrupting us. "Why?" was her response. "Your children need to understand that the baby needs you constantly now, just as they needed you when they were infants. You can still give them lots of love and attention, but you do not need to do anything artificial. They will find their new place in the family soon enough."

As you readjust to life with your new baby, it is natural to go through a seclusion period. Both you and your baby will benefit from a peaceful time of discovering each other. It is easier to concentrate on each other if you make it clear to relatives and friends during your pregnancy that you want to spend some time alone as a family before receiving visitors. If friends do call or drop by unannounced in the first few weeks, you can explain to them that you will be delighted to share your baby with the outside world once you both have had time to get to know each other.

DOULAS—MOTHERING THE MOTHER

It would be nice to have the support network in place to allow you to just focus on your baby, but unfortunately most people do not have family close by or friends who can drop everything for them. Just as a doula can be an invaluable support during labor, a doula or mother's helper postpartum can take care of you so you can take care of your baby. Doulas usually come into the home ten to twenty hours a week following the birth, and help with childcare for older children, cooking, shopping, and other household chores. Trained doulas also provide breastfeeding support and newborn care advice. In some other countries, such as the Netherlands, a home nurse who provides these services during the postpartum period is considered an integral part of the health care team.

REGAINING YOUR STRENGTH

Do you know women who seem to recover from childbirth within days? Do you know others who still seem weak and pale two or three months after their baby is born? Recovery periods vary based on psychological and attitudinal factors, genetic factors, cultural factors, and the general health of the mother. Given all these variables, however, you should not feel weak beyond six weeks after a vaginal delivery. To speed your physical healing, there are several things you can do for yourself.

Exercise. Somewhere between two to six weeks postpartum, you should be able to begin light exercise. Walking is ideal, with your baby held snugly in a front carrier. Yoga can help you gradually get your muscles back in tone and your body realigned; it also helps stimulate your circulatory and respiratory systems, and can give you energy. Begin doing poses at home, and when you are ready to venture out into the world, join a postpartum yoga class where you can bring your baby and meet other mothers.

Get a massage. Just as during pregnancy, massage following the birth is a great way to nurture yourself. It is also a vital healing technique, helping to restore your circulation and to speed musculoskeletal recovery.

Rest. In most nonindustralized cultures, women spend twenty-four hours a day with their newborn child, napping when the baby sleeps and feeding the baby on demand throughout the night. If you take time out of the day to nap with the baby, you are much less likely to feel resentful when you are awakened at night.

Eat well. If you are breastfeeding, you need to drink plenty of fluids and eat wholesome, nourishing foods to keep your energy up. The postpartum period is not the time to worry about losing weight—it can take a year for your body to return to its pre-pregnancy size, and your baby's nourishment depends on your getting enough to eat and drink. Many women find that with breastfeeding, they lose weight gradually anyway, even though their appetite has increased.

COPING WITH POSTPARTUM BLUES

It is normal to feel tired, anxious, and occasionally weepy in the first few weeks after you give birth. If, however, these symptoms begin to worsen—if you feel out of control or panicked—you may be one of the estimated 10 to 20 percent of all women who experience postpartum depression, or PPD.

In recent years, PPD has begun to be recognized as the most common complication of childbirth. Its effects can be debilitating on a woman and her family. It is caused by a combination of biochemical, psychological, and societal factors. The major hormonal shifts that occur after childbirth, and again when menses is resumed, can alter the brain chemistry in a way that triggers mental illness. A woman who has a history of depression or who is under stress from other life changes besides the birth of a child can be at risk for PPD.

Treatment for severe cases often involves antidepressant medication and, sometimes, hospitalization. If either of these courses are recommended, it is critical to try to preserve the bonding and breastfeeding relationship between mother and baby. Investigate hospitals that allow you to keep your baby with you, and look into drugs that allow you to continue to breastfeed. (See Chapter 4 for more on drugs contraindicated during breastfeeding.) Above all, try to find a psychiatrist who understands the importance of the mother-infant bond.

Some women who do not have severe symptoms have been successful in overcoming PPD without drugs, by using a combination of nutritional remedies (vitamin B6 seems to be particularly helpful), herbs, and meditation. With any approach, counseling is critical for the whole family, as is a strong support network of people who are available and will check in on you during your vulnerable times.

Most importantly, seek out help—you cannot get through something like this alone. Trust that you will not always feel this way. Know that you are not at fault, that you are a good mother, and that in time, motherhood will live up to your hopes and expectations.

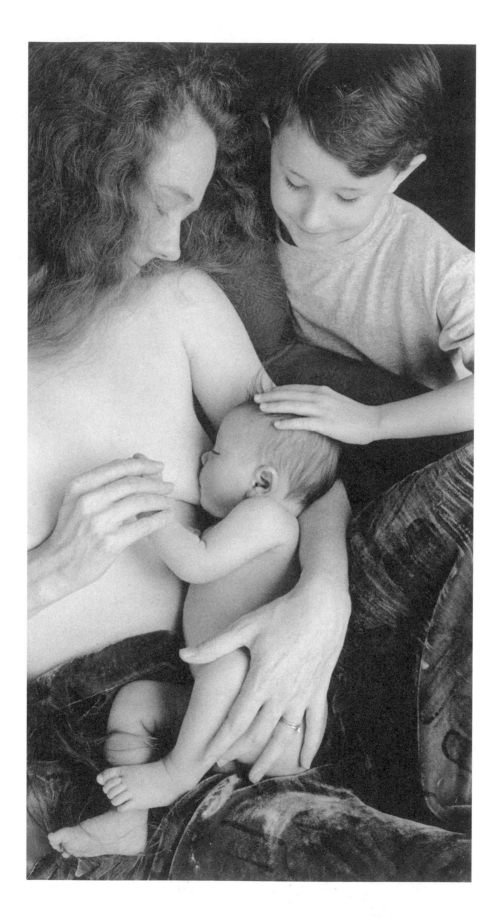

CHAPTER 4 # Breastfeeding

If someone told you there was a pill you could give your baby that contained antibodies to all the specific viruses and bacteria he or she would be exposed to throughout infancy, would you want to know more about it? What if they told you this pill would significantly reduce your child's risk of childhood ear infections and even childhood cancer? That it could improve your child's vision—even make your child smarter? Not only that, they might add, but giving your child this pill would also reduce your own risk of breast cancer. And the cost of this pill? Absolutely free.

This "pill," of course, is breastmilk. Every year, researchers learn more about this complex and amazing substance. Breastmilk contains all the nutrients vital for a baby's nourishment. Its composition changes from feeding to feeding, and even during feedings, according to what the baby needs most at that moment. The amount of milk produced at each feeding is triggered by the mother's hormonal response to the baby's suckling, so that the mother's breastmilk supply is regulated by the baby's demand.

But breastmilk is much more than simply food. It is a living substance that provides antibodies, protective bacteria, and other elements that help prevent a baby from getting sick, while encouraging the baby's immune system to mature. A mother's breastmilk forms antibodies specific to the bacteria and viruses she and her baby have been exposed to, within a few hours of that exposure. Colostrum—the nutrient-dense first milk a mother produces in the days immediately after childbirth—contains most of the immunities a baby needs in the initial few weeks of life. It is easy to see why infant formula companies have never been able to synthetically duplicate the myriad properties of breastmilk.

Advantages to Breastfeeding

Besides its nutritional and protective benefits, breastfeeding is best for mother and child for many other reasons. These are some of the advantages to breastfeeding.

HEALTH BENEFITS FOR THE BABY

Breastfed babies have one-quarter the risk of ear infections—the number one cause of childhood doctor visits—as babies who are fed formula. Breastfed babies also have lower incidences of allergies, asthma, diabetes, pneumonia, respiratory infections, meningitis, and lymphomas (childhood cancer).

HEALTH BENEFITS FOR THE MOTHER

Breastfeeding provides significant protection against breast and ovarian cancer. The amount of protection increases with the total number of years a woman nurses her babies—for example, women who breastfeed for two years reduce their chances of breast cancer by 40 percent; women who breastfeed for a lifetime total of six years reduce their incidence of breast cancer by two-thirds.[1] Breastfeeding mothers experience less osteoporosis later in life, because their bone density increases with each child nursed, thanks to the hormones produced by breastfeeding.

INTELLIGENCE

Breastmilk is now being recognized as the perfect "brain food." Babies fed breastmilk consistently score higher on IQ and vision tests than formula-fed babies. The difference has been isolated to components in the breastmilk itself, rather than environmental factors surrounding infants who are breastfed.[2] During the first year of life, when the child's brain is doubling in size, breastmilk provides DHA, an omega-3 fatty acid, which is critical to eye and brain development.

CONTRACEPTION

Most women in the United States have been led to believe that breastfeeding is not effective birth control. It can, however, be a reliable method if practiced a certain way.

In developing countries women have long relied on breastfeeding to prevent pregnancy. Women in these countries generally nurse their babies frequently throughout the day and night. By contrast, in the United States women are encouraged to nurse on three- to four-hour schedules, to give supplemental bottle-feedings, and to "train" their babies to sleep through the night—without needing to nurse—as soon as possible. Frequent, on-demand breastfeeding, however, almost always causes amenorrhea (suppression of menstruation).

For the first six months after the baby is born, breastfeeding is more than 98 percent effective in preventing pregnancy, if the mother nurses her baby at least five or six times in a twenty-four-hour period, including during the night.[3] This is a better effectiveness rate than that of most birth control methods. Once a baby turns six months and begins to eat solid foods as well as sleep longer stretches at night—thereby nursing less frequently—the mother often begins menstruating again, and fertility returns.

WEIGHT LOSS

Many women find they lose their pregnancy weight easily when nursing, even though they are eating more than they did before they got pregnant. Breastfeeding requires an additional 500 to 1,000 calories a day to produce adequate milk. Two-thirds of this comes from the food you eat, while another third is taken from the fat stored for this purpose during pregnancy. Restricting your calorie intake while breastfeeding can decrease your milk supply.

Most nursing women find that by eating a balanced diet of at least 1,800 calories a day, and exercising moderately (walking with the baby, for example), they lose their pregnancy weight within a few months to a year. (One theory is that it takes nine months to put the weight on and another nine months for it to come off.) In addition, hormones produced during nursing help the uterus contract and shrink quickly to its pre-pregnancy size, allowing you to regain your pre-pregnancy figure more quickly.

BONDING

Breastfeeding is designed to encourage mother-infant bonding. When your baby nurses, you produce prolactin and oxytocin, hormones that induce maternal feelings. No wonder many women report "falling in love" with their babies each time they nurse.

Nursing necessitates holding your baby closely, skin-to-skin. Many mothers will gaze at their babies as they nurse, and stroke them gently or play with their little fingers and toes. Nursing forces you to take time out for a cuddle together, several times a day. You can certainly do the same while bottle feeding, but it is all too easy to put a baby in an infant seat and prop a bottle in her mouth while you get something done around the house.

COST AND CONVENIENCE

Breastmilk is always available in the right quantity and at the right temperature. It requires no mixing, sterilization, or equipment, and is safe regardless of the quality and availability of water. And it is free.

The Politics of Breastfeeding

Breastfeeding is not simply beneficial for babies; it is a national health care issue. The World Health

Organization (WHO) recommends breastfeeding for at least two years. Yet, only 14 percent of babies in the United States are breastfed for one year. Compliance with the WHO infant feeding guidelines worldwide could save the United States an estimated $1.5 billion annually in healthcare costs.

There are many ways that women are subtly and not-so-subtly discouraged from breastfeeding in the United States. Nursing in public is far from accepted here, and there are rarely appropriate places provided for women to nurse discreetly in public settings—chairs in women's restrooms, for example. Images of women breastfeeding seldom appear in the popular media. Instead, bottles have become the "logo" of babyhood.

More importantly, women are expected to go back to work as soon as six weeks after a baby is born, before their breastfeeding technique and breastmilk supply have been firmly established. Only a very few workplaces make it easy for nursing mothers to express milk, by providing breaks in the daily schedule or a comfortable place in which to pump.

Babies born in hospitals often get off to a poor breastfeeding start. Many hospitals keep babies in a nursery for at least part of the time, where they have limited contact with their mothers, undermining the critical importance of early and frequent suckling to establish a good milk supply. Supplemental bottles and pacifiers are often given to babies by well-meaning nurses. When a baby is introduced to a rubber nipple while he is still learning the mechanics of breastfeeding, "nipple confusion" can result, leading to breastfeeding failure.

Formula companies ply women with free samples, and using them can effectively end breastfeeding before it is established. A baby quickly becomes used to the bottle because it delivers milk more rapidly than the breast does. The more bottles a baby takes, the less she will need to nurse. Because supply is regulated by demand, if a woman's breasts are unstimulated by nursing, her milk will soon dry up.

Worldwide, these practices have tragic implications. Fewer than 50 percent of infants in the developing world are exclusively breastfed. Women in developing countries often go home from the hospital with their babies on formula that costs more than a week's wages. They simply want to do the best for their babies, and follow the cues given to them by the medical establishment, which often unknowingly promotes formula as better than breastmilk. Bottle-fed babies in developing countries can die from formula mixed with unsafe drinking water; or, fed diluted formula because their families cannot afford adequate supplies, they starve to death. Reduction of formula feeding and improved breastfeeding practices could save an estimated 1.5 million children's lives a year.

To halt this trend, UNICEF and WHO launched the Baby-Friendly Hospital Initiative in 1991. It calls for hospitals to adopt Ten Steps to Successful Breastfeeding (see sidebar). To date, 14,000 hospitals worldwide and 15 in the United States have made a commitment to abide by the Ten Steps.

Ten Steps to Successful Breastfeeding

Every facility providing maternity services and care for newborn infants should:

1. Have a written breastfeeding policy that is routinely communicated to all health care staff.
2. Train all health care staff in skills necessary to implement this policy.
3. Inform all pregnant women about the benefits and management of breastfeeding.
4. Help mothers initiate breastfeeding within a half-hour of birth.
5. Show mothers how to breastfeed and how to maintain lactation even if they should be separated from their infants.
6. Give newborn infants no food or drink other than breastmilk, unless medically indicated.
7. Practice rooming-in to allow mothers and infants to remain together twenty-four hours a day.
8. Encourage breastfeeding on demand.
9. Give no artificial teats or pacifiers (also called dummies or soothers) to breastfeeding infants.
10. Foster the establishment of breastfeeding support groups and refer mothers to them on discharge from the hospital or clinic.

Closer to home, in 1997, the American Academy of Pediatrics issued a report recognizing breastmilk as the foundation of good infant nutrition. The new AAP guidelines recommend breastfeeding for at least a year, with no other food or vitamin supplements for the first six months. The guidelines call for breastfeeding to begin as soon as possible after birth, preferably within the first hour. They stress that newborns should be nursed whenever they show signs of hunger—at least eight to twelve times every twenty-four hours; for at least ten to fifteen minutes on each breast.

Hospital procedures are beginning to change as a result of the new AAP guidelines. The guidelines recommend rooming-in—keeping mother and baby together throughout the hospital stay—and postponing any procedures that interfere with breastfeeding. They advocate eliminating supplements to breastfeeding, including water or formula, during the hospital stay. They call for an end to hospital discharge packs containing free infant formula. The guidelines even urge that breastfeeding be continued if mother or baby needs to be hospitalized, and emphasize that breastfeeding may need to be halted only temporarily if the mother must take medications that are unsafe for the breastfeeding child.

The AAP guidelines have already had a major impact on breastfeeding rates in the United States, which have reached a thirty-year high. About two-thirds of mothers breastfeed their babies currently, with more than a quarter continuing past six months. Interestingly, there are wide regional variations in breastfeeding rates. Seventy percent of new mothers breastfeed in the Pacific and Mountain states—almost double the rate of mothers breastfeeding in the South. Cultural attitudes and the promotion of breastfeeding by the medical establishment have contributed to the high breastfeeding rates in the West.

Getting Started Breastfeeding

Breastfeeding is the most natural and maternal of acts. Consider the lovely symmetry of the word "mammal"—from the Latin "mamma," meaning both "breast" and "mother."

Breastfeeding works. There should not be anything difficult or painful about it. If this were not true, our species would have died out long ago.

However, most women in our culture do not have the benefit of learning the womanly art of breastfeeding from their mothers or other relatives. Health professionals are often misinformed about breastfeeding. As a result, some mothers get off to a poor start and lose their confidence in the process or decide that it is not worth the trouble. If you have trouble breastfeeding, find health professionals or lay counselors who are really knowledgeable about breastfeeding. When women "can't" breastfeed, it's not their fault. The medical community failed them by not providing the best advice.

Breastfeeding is worth any initial trouble, and when done the way nature intended, it is the easiest, most convenient way to feed your baby. The key to successful breastfeeding is getting off to a good start. Here are some tips to keep in mind during the first few days:

MAKE SURE THE BABY IS LATCHED ON CORRECTLY

If the baby is positioned correctly on your breast, you should not feel pain while nursing. Proper latch-on means the baby's mouth is over the areola (the darker area surrounding the nipple) and not just the nipple. To ensure this, hold the baby on her side so you are tummy-to-tummy. Cupping your breast, lift it and lightly tickle the baby's bottom lip until she opens her mouth as wide as a yawn. Then pull her close so that the tip of her nose touches your breast.

If your nipples are sore, it is probably from improper positioning or latch-on. Check with your midwife, doula, a La Leche League leader (see "Social Support for Breastfeeding," page 56), or a lactation consultant to make sure the baby is positioned right.

NURSE FREQUENTLY IN THE FIRST FEW DAYS

The key to establishing your milk supply is nursing right away, and continuing to nurse frequently in the first few days. A healthy newborn, when put on his mother's chest, will usually find his way to her breast within the first hour and begin nursing. These first feedings give the baby the colostrum that is so vital in developing his immunities. At the same time, the baby's early nursing stimulates uterine contractions to help the mother deliver the placenta and lessen blood loss.

Although it appears that the baby is not getting much liquid in the first few days, frequent sucking helps to regulate your milk supply and to prevent your breasts from becoming engorged—swollen with milk and fluids. It also gives you both practice at nursing before your milk "comes in."

At about three or four days postpartum, your breasts will probably feel fuller and more tender, as you begin to produce greater quantities of mature milk to replace the initial colostrum. At this point it is especially important to nurse frequently to avoid engorgement. When the breasts become engorged with milk, blood, and lymph fluids, they can get so hard that it is difficult for the baby to nurse. Expressing a little milk by hand or with a breast pump can soften the breasts just enough to allow the baby to latch on. (For more on engorgement, see Overcoming Difficulties below.)

It is not unusual for a newborn to want to nurse every hour, or for hours at a time, in the first few days. For this reason, keep the baby with you as much as possible. Even if you have had a Cesarean or if the baby needs to have special care or monitoring, the more you can be together, the more likely you are to begin a good breastfeeding relationship.

AVOID SUPPLEMENTS

Many hospitals routinely recommend giving newborns supplemental bottles of water to keep them from getting dehydrated. When babies are given a bottle in the immediate postpartum period, just as they are learning to nurse, they can get nipple confusion and refuse the breast. A baby who is filled up with glucose water or just plain sterile water in between feedings will be less hungry and less willing to nurse. A baby who is nursing frequently is getting all the fluids she needs, and does not need supplements. Even in the first few days, when the baby does not seem to be getting much liquid from your colostrum, there is no need to supplement. Colostrum is

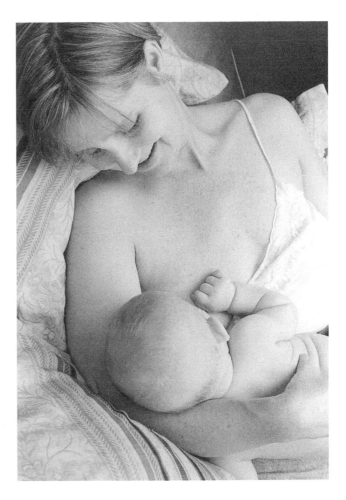

nutrient-dense food, designed to be consumed a little at a time.

Pacifiers are not a good idea either. Several studies have shown that pacifiers can lead to incorrect sucking technique, early weaning, and breastfeeding failure. Remember that breastfeeding works by supply and demand. The more the baby nurses; the more milk is produced. Pacifiers can upset this delicate balance.

FIND A SUPPORT NETWORK

Even though breastfeeding is one of the most natural things in the world, it can be a challenge in the postpartum period when you are still recovering from the birth and getting used to your new baby's cues. Take advantage of your midwife, baby nurse, doula, lactation consultant, or La Leche League leader to help you find the most comfortable nursing position, particularly if you have had a Cesarean. It helps to have someone who is more experienced at breastfeeding to remind you that afterpains while nursing are just nature's way of shrinking the uterus back to its normal size; that the tingling, pin-pricking sensation you feel as you start to nurse is your milk letting down; that your baby really is getting milk from your breasts. If you are not finding the support you need from your birth attendants (and many medical professionals are misinformed about breastfeeding), get in touch with a local breastfeeding support group such as La Leche League (see "Social Support for Breastfeeding," page 56).

Nursing on Cue Versus Scheduled Feedings

Once you have made it through the first week of breastfeeding and are beginning to settle into a rhythm, your biggest challenge will probably be figuring out how often to nurse. One notion popular in the 1960s and recently reintroduced by the best-selling child-rearing book *On Becoming Babywise,* advocates putting infants on a strict three- to four-hour feeding schedule and cutting out night feedings at four to six weeks. The theory is that keeping babies on a schedule will regulate their metabolism and teach them to find ways to comfort themselves in between feedings.

It certainly would be more convenient for parents if babies could be fed according to a timetable. But there are dangers with this approach. The biggest problem with feeding schedules is that the concept was designed for bottlefed babies. Breastmilk is more easily and quickly digested than formula—which means that breastfed babies get hungry more often. According to La Leche League, newborns need to nurse eight to twelve times a day. Because of their frequent feedings, breastfed babies are sometimes viewed as "fussier" or more demanding. Their "fussiness" or cries may be nature's way of ensuring that they eat as often as they need to.

Putting your baby on a feeding schedule can damage the trusting relationship you are trying to build with your child. When your baby, who was fed continually in the womb and has never known hunger, cries out to be fed—and is ignored because it is not time—he begins to learn that the world is not a very comforting, warm, or safe place. The more you harden yourself to your baby's cries, the more you lose your ability to communicate with him by reading his cues.

A more tragic implication of schedule feeding can be failure to thrive—slow weight gain that can be a serious threat to the baby's health—and in extreme cases, starvation. There has been at least one documented case of a baby starving to death while her parents, thinking they were doing the best thing for her, listened to her cries.[4]

Proponents of schedule feeding argue that babies need to learn to comfort themselves; that if you nurse them when they cry, you will not know whether they were hungry or just wanted comfort; and that they are manipulating you if you respond every time they cry.

Babies are born vulnerable and trusting. For the first six months or so, you are your child's sole source of comfort, and the only way he has of communicating with you is crying. If what your baby needs is comfort, and he gets that comfort from nursing, is that any less important a need than food? Do you really believe that your baby is trying to manipulate you? If your baby communicates a need, and you respond, you are building a trusting relationship.

It is also not in your baby's best interest to try to "drop" night feedings to get your baby to sleep through the night. Because breastmilk is easily digested and babies are growing quickly, breastfed babies may need to feed during the night for up to, and maybe even beyond, the first year. A study of nursing mothers showed that babies as old as ten months got at least 25 percent of their intake of mother's milk during night feedings.[5] Ignoring your baby's nighttime cries, even though it is commonly recommended by some popular baby books, particularly Richard Ferber's *Solve Your Child's Sleep Problems,* can have profound implications for your child's development of trust. But nighttime nursing does not have to spell sleep-deprivation—you can bring your baby to bed with you in the middle of the night or put a cot in your baby's room where you can lie down and nurse without fully awakening. For more on night waking, see Chapter 8.

Elizabeth

I nursed my first child every forty-five minutes. Luckily for my son's sake, I trusted those darn instincts I didn't think I had, and I let him just nurse and nap in my arms whenever he wanted to by day, and nurse and sleep beside me whenever he wanted to at night. My instincts told me that if he was happy in my arms, then that is where he needed to be.

Demand nursing, as I saw it, was no different from caring for a family member who has been rendered powerless. Would we refuse an incapacitated father a meal because it was "not time"? Or leave a paralyzed spouse alone in a room to "cry it out"—checking in every ten minutes to say, "It's OK"—without trying to find out what is wrong and doing something about it? If he or she only wanted to be held, would we refuse, for fear of spoiling someone we love?

Trust your baby to know how often he needs to eat. Every baby is different—some want to nurse every hour, others go four hours in between feedings, others have no regularity at all to their timetables. The main thing is to watch the baby, not the clock. No one can tell you when your baby is hungry or needs to nurse except your baby.

Worries About Milk Supply

Many new mothers worry that they do not have enough milk to feed their babies. The fact is, every woman has enough milk, except for the very rare woman whose milk ducts never developed. Common practices, however, such as putting babies on a feeding schedule, giving supplemental bottles, or using a pacifier can decrease milk supply.

Putting your baby on a feeding schedule can wreak havoc on your milk supply. This is because frequent, short bouts of nursing are much more effective at keeping up your milk supply than nursing at longer intervals, even if the baby feeds for long periods of time. If your milk supply dwindles, the baby will not be satisfied, and her weight gain may be slow. Your baby's doctor may advise you, or you may be tempted, to supplement with

formula. The more you supplement, the less milk you will produce (since supply is regulated by demand), and so on, in a vicious cycle.

Limiting your baby's time at each breast can affect your milk supply as well because the composition of your milk changes throughout the course of a feeding. The "foremilk" produced at the beginning of a feeding is high in fluids and low in fat, while richer, higher-calorie "hindmilk" is produced at the end of a feeding. Letting your baby make the call about when to switch breasts (which he will indicate by coming off the breast or falling asleep) ensures that your baby is getting the right amount of calories and fluids in each feeding. If you switch breasts according to an arbitrarily determined timetable, your baby may be filling up on low-calorie foremilk and may gain weight slowly—again leading to the vicious cycle of supplementation and decreased milk supply. If your baby is difficult to awake after filling up at one breast or is uninterested in nursing on the other side, you can simply alternate breasts with each feeding rather than switching during each feeding.

Another argument for following your baby's cues rather than the clock is that babies go through growth spurts, during which they may nurse voraciously for a day or two. These high-frequency days serve to increase your milk supply to accommodate your growing baby. If you are feeding according to a schedule, you will not be able to respond to your baby's attempt to boost your milk supply.

An important point to keep in mind about weight gain is that infant growth charts are based on data collected from babies who were mainly formula fed. Breastfed babies may gain weight more slowly than these charts indicate, leading doctors to label them as "faltering." More important than any number on a growth chart is whether your baby is consistently gaining weight.

The other indication of whether your baby is taking in enough milk is watching what comes out. The more often and efficiently a baby feeds, the greater the number of wet and soiled diapers she will produce. Expect about six to eight wet cloth diapers a day, or five to six disposable diapers (disposable diapers stay dry longer because of the water-absorbing chemicals they contain).

There may be instances when an insufficient milk supply can not be alleviated by simply nursing more. In that case, you need to look into other factors. Stress, fatigue, anemia, and cigarette smoking can all diminish a mother's milk production. If your milk supply seems to have dropped sharply, try to slow down, get more rest, and drink plenty of fluids. You may want to try taking some herbs that increase milk production, including fenugreek, red clover blossoms, nettles, red raspberry leaf, blessed thistle, alfalfa, borage, fennel, and hops. (For more on herbs, see Chapter 12.)

Overcoming Difficulties

Pain during breastfeeding is a sign that something is wrong. If you are experiencing pain other than the normal pins-and-needles sensation of letdown, get some help quickly. A problem that goes untreated can develop into an infection. Here are some things to watch out for:

SORE NIPPLES

Improper positioning or latch-on can cause sore, chafed, cracked, or even bleeding nipples. Find a leader from your local La Leche League or a lactation consultant who can observe you breastfeeding and help you correct the problem.

The best treatment for sore nipples is breastmilk itself. Because of its amazing anti-bacterial properties, breastmilk is used to treat skin irritations in many parts of the world. Just express a few drops of milk and rub it into your nipples, letting them air-dry. You can also try a salve of calendula or comfrey.

If the pain is accompanied by itching or burning, you may have thrush, a yeast infection. The baby may also have thrush, which appears in white patches inside the mouth. The usual treatment is nystatin, an anti-fungal cream available by prescription, for both you and your baby. You can continue to nurse throughout the treatment.

ENGORGEMENT

Engorgement—a painful swelling of the breasts—can occur if the baby is not nursing frequently. Once the breasts become engorged, the baby may have trouble latching on. Try applying warm, moist compresses to your breasts before nursing to stimulate let-down, or express a little milk to soften your breasts enough for the baby to nurse. A hot shower is a good remedy too. The best remedy is long, frequent nursing. If left untreated, engorgement can develop into mastitis.

MASTITIS

Mastitis is breast inflammation from an infection or plugged milk duct. It usually causes a low fever and achy, flu-like symptoms. The breast feels hot and swollen. Mastitis may be caused by infrequent nursing, a too-tight bra, stress, or fatigue.

Again, the best treatment is nursing. Begin on the affected breast to help drain it (remember, your baby is already receiving antibodies from your breastmilk that will protect her from infection). Try different nursing positions to find one that is more comfortable. Apply heat to the breast and massage the area while it is warm. Rest is essential.

If the fever persists for twenty-four hours, it may be necessary to take an antibiotic. Most antibiotics are compatible with breastfeeding (see Drugs and Breastfeeding below).

Drugs and Breastfeeding

If you need to take a prescription drug for a medical condition while you are nursing your baby, chances are that you can continue to breastfeed. There are very few prescription drugs that are contraindicated during breastfeeding. In the rare case that there is no breastfeeding-compatible form of the drug you need to take, you can still "pump and dump"—express your milk and discard it while you are taking the medication—and use formula to feed your baby.

However, it is best to limit the drugs you take to those that are absolutely necessary, since anything you ingest has the potential to reach your baby's milk supply. Drug-free milk is particularly important in the first few days of your baby's life, especially if your baby was premature, since a newborn's liver is not mature enough to metabolize drugs.

Drugs that are contraindicated during breastfeeding are:

bromocriptine (Parlodel)
cocaine (Crack)

cyclophosphamide (Neosar, Cytoxan)

cyclosporine (Sandimmune, Neoral)

doxorubicin (Andriamycin)

ergotamine (Wigraine, Cafergot, Ergostat, Ergomar, DHE-45)

lithium (Lithobid, Eskalith)

methotrexate (Folex, Rheumatrex)

phencyclidine (PCP, Angel Dust)

phenindione (anticoagulant)

Certain antidepressant and anxiety drugs may have an effect on nursing infants; check with your doctor to find an alternative drug that is compatible with breastfeeding. Aspirin is questionable; acetaminophen (Tylenol) is a better choice, or better yet, try a nonpharmaceutical approach to pain relief. Herbal remedies for some common complaints include:

- rosemary tea for headaches and cramps
- fennel tea for indigestion
- echinacea for colds
- wild cherry bark for coughs
- St. John's wort for anxiety and depression

(See Chapter 12 for more on herbs.)

Drugs of abuse that are contraindicated during breastfeeding are amphetamines, cocaine, heroin, and nicotine. Cigarette smoking is a bad idea whether you are breastfeeding or not, since smoke inhaled by the baby can cause respiratory infections, vomiting, and nausea. Smoking also can decrease your milk supply. Caffeine, consumed in large amounts (five cups or more a day), can cause restlessness and irritability in the nursing baby. Alcohol has not been shown to have negative effects on the nursing infant, except in large quantities (a six-pack or more of beer a day).[6]

When evaluating the safety of a drug prescribed during breastfeeding, you should consider the following questions:

- Has the drug been given safely to babies?
- What side effects have been seen in babies who have taken this drug?
- Will the drug affect my milk supply?
- Is there an alternative with fewer side effects?
- Do I really need to take this drug?

If you need to take a drug during breastfeeding, take it immediately after nursing to allow

---

The Breastfeeding Father

While a father cannot nurse his child, he can still play a critical role in the breastfeeding relationship. A nursing mother needs a lot of support. The baby's father is usually the primary support person. He can help create a home environment conducive to successful breastfeeding.

Support means more than simply being encouraging; it means cooking, doing the laundry, going grocery shopping, taking care of visitors—whatever the new mother needs so that she has time to nurse. Most fathers would rather do any of those jobs than get up in the middle of the night to fix a bottle.

Here are some other things the father of a nursing baby can do:

Support your wife unconditionally in her decision to breastfeed. Educate yourself about the benefits to mother and child, and remind your wife of them if she begins to question her decision.

Learn your own special ways to comfort the baby. Fathers may feel left out of the nursing relationship, and while it is true that nursing babies need their mothers, they can quickly come to associate their fathers with different kinds of comfort. Rock the baby, dance with the baby, sing, drive around the block, develop your own "daddy hold" (the neck nestle—baby cuddled on your chest, head tucked under your chin—is a favorite). You can also help by bringing the baby to Mama in the middle of the night.

Remember that nursing babies need to be with their mothers. As tempting as it may be to plan a night or weekend away with your wife, your baby's needs take precedence right now. Wait until the baby is old enough to be nursing less frequently, or bring the baby along.

Take over if your wife needs some time off. It can be overwhelming to be needed the way a nursing mother is. If your wife needs a break, volunteer to take the baby for a couple of hours so she can take a nap, take a walk, get a massage—whatever she needs to rejuvenate herself.

your body to absorb it before the next feeding. You should try to discontinue treatment as soon as it is safe to do so. But keep in mind that many women have breastfed successfully while on extended drug therapy.

Sex and Breastfeeding

There is no denying the fact that breastfeeding can have an effect on your sex life, and the mother's diminished interest can be hard on your relationship. It helps to know that there are biological reasons for a woman's sex drive to take a dive while she is breastfeeding, and to remember that this, too, will pass.

Like everything else about breastfeeding, the hormonal changes it causes in the mother are remarkable. There are two somewhat separate, yet overlapping, sets of hormones present in the mother: reproductive hormones responsible for ovulation and the desire for procreation; and lactation hormones that arouse maternal feelings. The lactation hormones of prolactin and oxytocin in a breastfeeding mother seem to overwhelm the hormones responsible for sexual desire. This effect can continue as long as ovulation is suppressed— anywhere from six to twenty-four months in a mother who is breastfeeding frequently.

At the same time, the lactation hormones work very similarly to the sexual hormones. Oxytocin, which is released during breastfeeding, is also present in all aspects of friendship and love, including lovemaking. For this reason, breastfeeding can be a sensual experience. It arouses pleasurable, deep, almost spiritual feelings of closeness between a mother and child. A breastfeeding mother may have all her need for human contact fulfilled by nursing and holding the baby. Many nursing mothers feel "touched out" at the end of the day.

The wise couple will handle this temporary phase in their relationship by seeking out other forms of intimacy until the woman's sexual desire returns. These may include:

TOUCHING
Having children teaches us that much of our sexual desire is a longing to touch and be touched.

Now is the time to rediscover hand-holding, hugging, kissing, "spooning" in bed—not as foreplay, but as intimate moments fulfilling in themselves.

MASSAGING
The partner who is most tired gets the massage; the one least tired gives it. If erogenous zones are too sensitive, hand and foot massages still feel wonderful.

SHARING SENSUAL MOMENTS
Discover the sensuality in a wonderful shared meal, classical music by candlelight, or an aromatic bath. Add special new touches of tenderness and mystery to your time alone together.

APPROACHING LOVEMAKING GENTLY
Intercourse will probably feel different during breastfeeding. The breastfeeding hormones can cause vaginal dryness, so some lubrication may be necessary. A woman may feel sore for some time after the birth, especially if she has had an episiotomy. (Intercourse is not recommended until bleeding has stopped—about four to six weeks after the birth.) A nursing mother may not want her breasts touched, and they may leak or spray milk when she is aroused. Try to be sensitive to these changes as a couple and to communicate openly and with a sense of humor.

Social Support for Breastfeeding

No matter how committed you are to breastfeeding, there will inevitably come times when your commitment is challenged—when your well-intentioned friend admonishes that you are feeding the baby too often; when your mother-in-law criticizes you for nursing in public; when your employer makes it clear that operating a breast pump in the employee lounge is frowned upon. At these critical moments, it is helpful to know about breastfeeding support organizations that can reinforce your decision by supplying needed information, advice, and advocacy.

One of the most well-respected support groups is La Leche League International, founded in the 1950s by a group of breastfeeding mothers. Today the organization provides mother-to-mother support through 8,000 volunteer leaders. You can attend nursing support meetings throughout the country and internationally, receive phone counseling twenty-four hours a day, and access an extensive information library. (See Resources.)

The International Lactation Consultant Association (ILCA) is an organization of health care professionals who help women solve breastfeeding problems. Lactation consultants may work in the hospital and can visit you in your home. To find a lactation consultant near you, see Resources.

Breastfeeding in Public

A hungry baby needs to eat, whether you are at the shopping mall, in a restaurant, or in an airplane. The wonderful thing about breastfeeding is that you never have to pack formula or warm bottles when you are out and about. As soon as you and your baby are a happy nursing pair, there is no reason not to nurse wherever you happen to be.

Breastfeeding in public can be done very discreetly. With your baby cradled in one arm against your breast, all you should be exposing to a passerby is the back of your baby's head. Just be sure to wear clothing with nursing access when you go out. If you are wearing clothing that does not allow for discreet nursing—a bathing suit, for example—you can always drape a towel or blanket over your shoulder and the baby while you nurse. When you carry your baby in an over-the-shoulder fabric sling, you can breastfeed on the spot—even standing in line at the grocery store! (For more on "babywearing" in a sling, see "The Art of Babywearing," page 109.)

If you encounter any curious or hostile stares, smile benignly back, knowing that you are contributing to the health of the next generation, and that you are setting a beautiful example for other women, young girls, and expectant fathers. Fortunately, fewer people raise an eyebrow at nursing mothers today—in fact, a woman's right to breastfeed in public is protected by law in many states. Perceptions are changing, as people become educated about the health benefits of breastfeeding. With continued awareness, perhaps breastfeeding in public will become as accepted as smoking in public is now frowned upon.

Breastfeeding at Work

There is a reason that the United States has one of the lowest breastfeeding rates in the world, and that most women do not breastfeed past three months. It is because the majority of women go back to work six to twelve weeks after having a baby.

Breastfeeding and working don't have to be incompatible. In fact, if you are working outside your home, you will probably find it even more important to maintain the special closeness that breastfeeding allows. Nursing your baby when you get home from work forces you to focus on what is most important at that moment, rather than worrying about getting dinner or the laundry started. A pre-dawn nursing session can be a peaceful start to your morning, and the calming hormones it produces can help carry you through the rest of a hectic day. Breastfeeding becomes especially important if you are leaving your baby in a day care setting, because breastmilk will provide immunities to help keep your child from getting sick.

Here are some tips for the nursing working mother:

FIND A CAREGIVER WHO IS SUPPORTIVE OF BREASTFEEDING

Before the baby is born, or shortly after, you will probably need to begin investigating child-care options. Whether you choose in-home care or a day care setting, your caregiver needs to be committed to your breastfeeding as well, or at least understand your commitment to it. She must be willing to treat your expressed milk as liquid gold (breastmilk should never be microwaved, for example, or refrozen after it is thawed) and to hold off feeding a hungry baby until you get home.

BEGIN EXPRESSING MILK BEFORE YOU GO BACK TO WORK

For the first three to four weeks of your maternity leave, try not to think about going back to

work. Enjoy your new baby and luxuriate in long, frequent feedings to build up your milk supply.

After the first month you should begin to practice expressing milk. Borrow or rent a breast pump if you can, to find one that works for you. Some women prefer manual pumping, but for a working mother, a double electric pump is definitely the most efficient way to go. Begin to practice pumping before your baby nurses, when your breasts are most full. Be sure to freeze any milk you collect—your baby will need it once you go back to work. Try to pump at around the same times each day—ideally during the hours that you will be pumping at work. This will build up your milk supply at these times of day. Even if your baby is nursing very frequently, once you begin pumping in addition to nursing, you will build up your milk supply and have milk to store.

At six or eight weeks, have your husband or someone other than yourself give the baby a bottle of expressed milk. Giving a bottle before this can lead to nipple confusion; if you wait until after two or three months the baby may refuse

the bottle. Before you go back to work, have your caregiver try giving the baby a few bottles.

EASE YOUR TRANSITION BACK INTO WORK

If you can, go back to work midweek so you will have only a few days of separation until the weekend. For the first few weeks, cancel all activities except working and being with the baby. Get help with the grocery shopping, cooking, and housework. Go to bed early, eat well, and drink plenty of fluids.

CONSIDER SLEEPING WITH THE BABY

For working mothers especially, sharing sleep with the baby can be a lifesaver. You will get more sleep, and nighttime feedings will boost your milk supply. Many working mothers find that the baby begins to feed less during the day once they go back to work, holding off until Mom is home. Cherish the special closeness you and your baby can have at night.

Gale

No matter how stressful my day has been, it all disappears the moment my baby and I sit down to nurse. Breastfeeding means there is no getting-to-know-you-again period at the end of the day. We are immediately a couple again, and the day's separation is completely erased. It makes me feel more secure in my place at the center of his world, because nursing is the one thing that only I can do for him.

SOLICIT THE SUPPORT OF YOUR EMPLOYER

In order to continue nursing once you go back to work, you need a clean, private place in which to pump your breastmilk and time for pumping breaks, ideally in the morning and afternoon. Your employer should be able to accommodate you on both counts. If you encounter opposition, gently remind your employer that supporting nursing moms is good for the bottom line: Breastfed children get sick less often than formula-fed children, so you will not need to take as many sick days to care for your child.

Allowing nursing mothers to pump at work is not just politically correct, it may soon be the law.

Legislation is pending that would guarantee nursing mothers pumping time at work, give tax credits to companies that provide lactation support, and prohibit discrimination against nursing mothers in the workplace.

Special Circumstances

Many mothers encounter bumps along the road in their nursing relationship with their baby. Some mothers, however, face particular challenges that tempt them to give up. But it is often in these challenging situations that breastfeeding becomes more important than ever.

It is certainly possible to nurse multiple babies, adoptive babies, premature babies, even babies with a cleft palate—if you are committed to breastfeeding. Here are some special circumstances you might encounter:

THE ILL BABY

If your baby is sick with a fever, diarrhea, or vomiting, there is no reason to take him off the breast or give supplements. Your baby is receiving all the fluids and electrolytes he needs from your breastmilk. The antibacterial properties in breastmilk will help your baby get better quicker than any supplement would.

THE ILL MOTHER

If you need to be temporarily on medication or hospitalized, there is no reason to wean your baby. Very few medications are incompatible with breastfeeding (see "Drugs and Breastfeeding," page 54). (Also, see Resources for books that list the effects of specific drugs on breastfeeding.)

An extended hospital stay can cause a traumatic separation between a mother and her nursing baby. Find out if your hospital allows rooming-in for nurslings, or at least daily visits (sometimes the rules will state otherwise, but you may be able to bend them). Secure a pump as soon as possible (preferably a double electric pump) and express milk frequently throughout the day and night to boost your supply and keep your baby well-fed.

It may take time for a young child to reconnect with you after an absence for a hospital stay. Nursing can help quickly reestablish your bond.

Do not be surprised if your baby wants to nurse almost constantly once you are reunited. If you are having difficulty with your baby's sudden increase in nursing frequency, it may help to think of your baby in terms of a newborn, and recognize that you may have to start your nursing relationship all over again.

THE PREMATURE BABY

Fewer than 50 percent of premature babies are breastfed. Breastfeeding becomes more critical than ever, however, when a baby is born prematurely, because the colostrum the mother produces is extra-rich in antibodies and other anti-infective agents to help protect the vulnerable infant.

Even if your premature baby is not strong enough to nurse at the breast, you can still give him expressed breastmilk. Before premature babies are big enough to nurse, they can be fed expressed breastmilk through a tube or cup rather than a bottle, to avoid nipple confusion. Studies have recently found that preemies can nurse earlier than is generally believed.

> ### Susan
>
> The pace of having four infants the same age is so great that I don't think I would have been able to sit so quietly and be with each of my children so intensely if I had bottlefed them. Not that you can't nurture your babies while bottle-feeding—but with this many children, it is just too tempting to do a lot of bottle propping.

MULTIPLE BABIES

You must be doubly—or triply—dedicated to nurse twins or other multiples. It can certainly be done, however: mothers have successfully breastfed triplets, quadruplets, and more.

Milk supply is not usually a problem, since supply is regulated by demand, but finding the time and energy to nurse around the clock is! If you can synchronize the babies' feedings, so much the better. The most important thing is to have help from your partner, friends, and a doula or a nurse if you can afford it or your insurance covers it. Your husband or doula can bring the babies to your bed to nurse as soon as each one gets hungry, so you can sleep as much as possible, and can handle their care while you nap during the day. You will also need to eat a lot of nutritious food, so take friends up on offers to cook for you.

THE ADOPTED CHILD

Many adoptive mothers can successfully nurse. In fact, "wet nurses"—women whose occupation was caring for and nursing other people's babies—were extremely common in the nineteenth century.

Pregnancy is not a requisite for producing milk. Milk production is stimulated by suckling or expressing milk, as well as by the hormones of pregnancy. If you have advance notice of your adoption, you can begin preparing a month or two before by pumping your breasts with an electric breastpump. A few women have been able to build up a full milk supply this way, but many women find it takes suckling from the baby to produce more than a trickle of milk.

Once the baby arrives, just as in any nursing relationship, frequent suckling is the best way to build up milk supply. Most women find they have to supplement at least in the beginning, if not throughout the nursing relationship. The best way to do this is with a nursing supplementer—a bag that you hang around your neck, that provides a supplement through a tube for the baby to receive at your breast.

Even if your baby is getting very little or even no breastmilk, you can still provide warmth and comfort. The trick to happy adoptive nursing is distinguishing "nursing" from "breastfeeding."

The Advantages of Extended Nursing

The common reaction to the sight of a toddler nursing in our culture is discomfort or even disgust. The average age of weaning in the United States is three months. However, the average age of weaning worldwide is 4.2 years. The World Health Organization states that babies should be breastfed for at least two years; the American Academy of Pediatrics recommends breastfeeding for a minimum of one year.

Why is it that we find something perverse about breastfeeding a child who can walk and talk, yet we think nothing of two-year-olds who use a bottle, or five-year-olds who suck their thumbs or a pacifier? We are so used to women weaning their babies by the time they go back to work or shortly thereafter, that it disturbs us to see babies nursing beyond a year.

Many people feel that once a baby is eating a well-rounded diet of solid food, there is no reason to continue nursing. However, there are certainly benefits to breastfeeding past this point. They include:

NUTRITION

Breastmilk is the most nutritionally dense food available to a growing child. It is designed to be an important source of nutrition for the baby through the toddler years. Studies have shown that breastfed children over a year old take in significantly more energy and nutrients than non-nursers. Mother's milk can provide as much as a third of a toddler's calorie and protein needs, and the majority of a child's vitamin A, vitamin C, and iron.

Toddlers are notoriously picky eaters, and it can be difficult to ensure that they are getting enough high-quality nutrients. Given the opportunity, however, most toddlers are more than willing to nurse. Breastmilk can contribute significantly to a growing child's diet.

IMMUNITIES

The disease-protective factors in breastmilk do not diminish over time; in fact, they become more concentrated as the child matures. This concentration seems to be nature's way of protecting the older child as he becomes increasingly mobile and therefore is exposed to more sources of infection. The longer the duration of breastfeeding, the longer the period of immunity. Studies show that some of the immune-protection benefits of long-term breastfeeding may be lifelong. Nursing children receive day-to-day protection as well from the antibodies in their mother's milk.

EMOTIONAL BONDING

The release of strong mothering hormones every time a woman nurses can deepen the bond between mother and child. Nursing gives you a chance to cuddle with a toddler who may otherwise be too active for much physical contact. Nursing can be a powerful means of comforting a child, and many mothers are glad to be able to offer it when their older child is sick or hurt.

BENEFITS TO THE MOTHER

Your risk of breast and ovarian cancer and osteoporosis all decrease proportionally the longer you breastfeed.

Rosemary

When people were surprised to learn that I was still breastfeeding my three-year-old daughter, I admitted that I never really expected to be conversing with a child about "when she thought she might quit." I giggled and told them I might have to go off to college with her. I laughed while trying on bras in a dressing room as my daughter yelled in delight, "That's my nursie!"

But once she weaned herself just before she turned four, I felt satisfied and full. I had done a job well, and finished it completely. The lesson I had learned would not only serve me well in the childrearing years to come, but would last a lifetime.

Fears About Long-term Nursing

Despite all the benefits of long-term breastfeeding, our culture frowns upon it. Some people are afraid that the child will never grow up, or that nursing is somehow sexual, or that the mother is doing it to fulfill her own unmet needs. These fears are generally unfounded in reality. Here is a look at some of the common objections to extended breastfeeding:

IT MAKES CHILDREN TOO ATTACHED

Children need to be attached; children are dependent. It is only by having their needs met in a safe and loving environment that they can grow up into secure, independent adults. Children who are allowed to be dependent as long as they need to be will reach for independence once they are ready.

THE CHILD WILL NEVER GIVE IT UP

Most children, when left to their own devices, will stop breastfeeding sometime between fifteen months and four years. At that point, they simply lose interest, or peer pressure takes over.

THERE IS SOMETHING SEXUAL ABOUT IT

This argument has been used against breastfeeding mothers in custody cases, especially against mothers of boys. Young children have an intense need for intimacy and physical contact, and breastfeeding can fulfill that need. That does not mean that it is sexual, any more than are other expressions of affection for a child.

MOTHERS DO IT TO FULFILL THEIR OWN NEEDS

This belief implies that you can make a child nurse. A child, especially an older one, will simply not nurse if she is not interested. Although most nursing mothers do gain a lot of satisfaction from their relationship with their children, most of that satisfaction comes from knowing that their children's needs are well-met.

Tandem Nursing

Sometimes a mother who is committed to long-term breastfeeding finds that she is pregnant again and assumes that she has to wean her toddler. Although tandem nursing—breastfeeding an older child as well as a newborn—takes a lot of dedication, it can certainly be done safely. It does take a lot of energy as well, however.

If you do decide to try tandem nursing, there are some things you should know. Your milk supply may take a sharp decline during your pregnancy, sometime around the second or third month. This decrease should not be a worry for your toddler, since most nursing toddlers are not solely dependent on breastmilk for nourishment. You may also experience nipple soreness during pregnancy and want to cut back on nursing time. Try to establish some limits with your toddler.

Toward the end of your pregnancy, nursing can trigger contractions. This phenomenon may cause you some discomfort, but it will not induce labor on its own. (Nursing can, however, be a boon for jump-starting a slow labor!)

When your baby is born, rest assured that your newborn will receive the colostrum she needs, because your milk will automatically change to colostrum. It is a good idea to feed the newborn before the older child for the first week, to ensure that she gets enough colostrum. When your milk "comes in," your older child can be helpful in relieving engorgement.

Once your milk supply is reestablished, you need not worry about whether your infant is getting enough milk. Again, supply is regulated by demand, so whether you are nursing one baby or two, there will be enough for both of them.

It is not unusual for your toddler to want to nurse much more when a new baby comes along. Nursing is your toddler's form of comfort, and the birth of a sibling can throw a child off-balance. Many women can become overwhelmed from the stress of nursing two demanding children. It may be helpful, once your older child has adjusted somewhat to the new baby, to set some ground rules. You could let your toddler know that you can nurse him only in the morning and evening, for example, or that the baby gets the first turn.

Rose

There are times when Eric and baby Cliff and I are snuggled together nursing that I feel so warm and full of love. Each child is so unique and it feels so good to be able to give each what he needs. They like to play or hold hands when they nurse together. It's like the three of us share a special secret.

Child-led Weaning

When should a child be weaned? That is like asking when a child should walk, or speak in sentences, or learn to ride a bike. Each child has her own developmental timetable.

Rather than set any deadline for giving up nursing, consider the notion of child-led weaning. As with all other developmental milestones, if you allow your child to wean when she is ready— to remain secure in the nursing relationship until she is ready to move on—you are helping her to build a confident, trusting foundation for future independence.

Many women who nurse toddlers did not start out planning to do so—they simply didn't impose a limit on an activity that their child obviously needed and benefitted from. Although at times it may seem as if your child will be nursing through high school, children will eventually wean themselves. If you decide to let your child decide when to wean, here are some guidelines to follow during the process:

DEVELOP OTHER FORMS OF COMFORT
Nursing is a great source of comfort to a child, but it should not be an easy way out for you in place of other forms of soothing or stimulation. Your repertoire of soothers can include things like backrubs, special snacks, reading, and outings.

If you are trying to cut back on your child's nursing, be sensitive to the times and places that he associates with nursing. Avoid sitting in your special nursing chair, or have Dad try singing your child to sleep in place of you nursing the child to sleep.

It may help to make sure that your child is well-fed and rested—not only because a hungry, thirsty, or sleepy child will want to nurse more, but because a well-rested toddler is better able to cope with minor frustrations and hurts without needing to fall back on the comfort of nursing.

A basic tenet of child-led weaning is "don't offer, don't refuse"—breastfeed when your child asks to, but do not offer it otherwise. This approach may work for you, or you may want to impose some limits.

DISCUSS LIMITS
The advantage to weaning an older child is that you can talk about it and set limits. You might feel strongly about not nursing in public, and can tell your child that you need to wait until you are in a more private place. Many older children want to nurse mainly in the morning and at night, where you can do it in the comfort of your own home.

You may want to come up with a plan with your older child for giving up nursing. You may actually find that your child proudly announces that she is through before the deadline. (Try, though, to be flexible if your child is not ready when you are.)

EXPECT AN EBB AND FLOW IN YOUR CHILD'S INTEREST IN NURSING
You may discover that your toddler seems to be forging ahead toward independence—nursing only occasionally—and then suddenly wants to nurse like a baby again. Try to take these inconsistencies in stride, knowing that your child is demanding from you exactly what he needs at that time. You may find that the more you resist him, the more he wants to nurse, but if you simply relax about it, he will cut back on his demands.

Be cautious about "nursing strikes"—when a baby around a year old becomes easily distracted while nursing or refuses to nurse for a few days. Generally, a baby who has been exclusively nursed for the first six months will not be ready to wean this early. She may be ill, experiencing discomfort from teething, or just overly stimulated. Rather than interpreting it as a sign of readiness to wean, you can usually ease your one-year-old through a nursing strike.

TRUST YOUR CHILD
Child-led weaning means trusting your child and having confidence that your child knows what she needs. It means trusting yourself enough to ignore a society that claims to know your child better than you do. This weaning will be the first of many you will face with your child, and the way you approach it can set the tone for later child-rearing decisions.

We must trust our children to show us their needs, and trust our own ability to recognize and meet those needs.

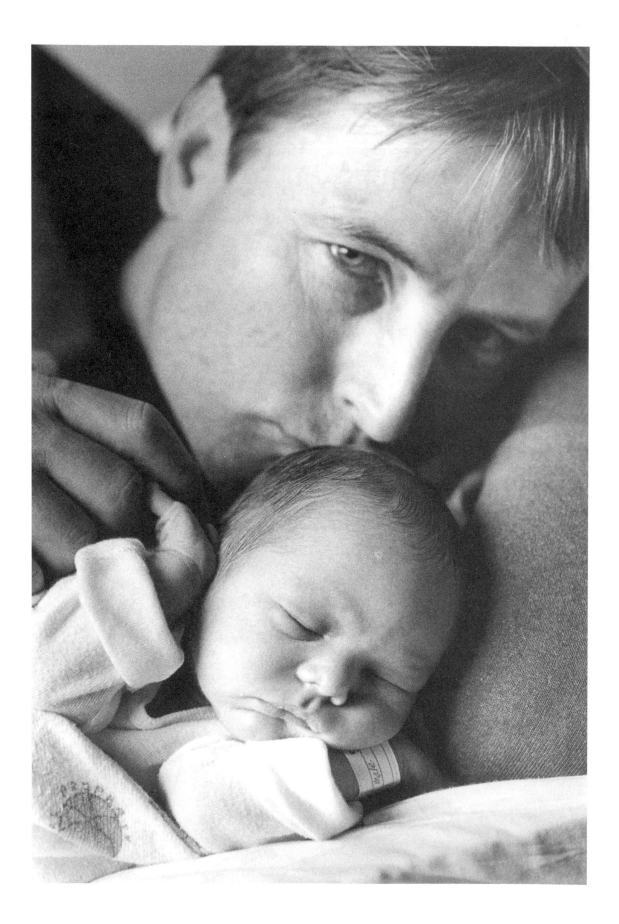

CHAPTER 5

Circumcision

The long-awaited day is here. Your child is born.

If you followed a natural parenting approach, you kept your body free of toxins during your pregnancy, took steps to make your baby's birth a gentle and non-traumatic event, and made the decision to breastfeed to provide the best nourishment for your baby.

Now, if your child is a boy, and you are like most Americans, you will hand him over to a doctor who will, behind closed doors and most likely without anesthesia, perform a painful and medically questionable operation on him—circumcision.

Circumcision is the most common surgery performed in the United States today. Forty years ago, 90 percent of American males were circumcised, and parental consent was not required. Today the circumcision rate in the United States has dropped to below 60 percent—and as low as 34 percent in the Western states, according to the National Center for Health Statistics of the United States Department of Health and Human Services. In 1999, the American Academy of Pediatrics decided, after analyzing almost forty years of medical research on circumcision, that the medical benefits are not sufficiently justified to recommend circumcision as a routine procedure.

Worldwide, only 15 percent of males are circumcised; most of them Muslims or Jews. Circumcision is almost unheard of in Europe, South America, and non-Muslim Asia. Canada and Australia both have a circumcision rate of under 20 percent. In Britain, where the circumcision rate used to be 90 percent, the rate has dropped to almost zero.

These widely varying rates throughout the world demonstrate that circumcision has become a cultural operation. If there were a strong medical argument for circumcision, it would probably be practiced more universally. Other than for religious reasons, there is no compelling rationale for it.

Circumcision was not common, except among Jews, until 150 years ago. In the Victorian era, doctors began performing circumcisions to try to prevent masturbation. This rationale is well-documented in medical literature dating from 1860 until as late as 1970.[1,2] Soon doctors were claiming that circumcision cured everything from bed-wetting to epilepsy to insanity.

Today these claims have been discredited, but a whole new set of medical rationales has been substituted. The fact is, however, that the current medical justification for circumcision developed after the operation was in wide practice.

What Is Circumcision?

Circumcision is surgical removal of the foreskin, the sheath of skin that covers the glans (head of the penis). At birth, the foreskin is attached to the glans just as a fingernail is attached to a finger. In circumcision, the foreskin is literally torn from the glans, like tearing a fingernail from a finger.

Most nonreligious circumcisions are performed in the hospital when the baby is less than forty-

Lauren

Dear Zachary: I am sitting on a small stool outside a doctor's examining room, tears filling my eyes, my milk beginning to flow in response to your agonized cries for mercy and help. I have never heard such screams. Should I run in and stop them? How long can you—can I—endure this? I feel so helpless as I recall your beautiful birth just eight days ago. I pushed you out into your father's hands; then you were returned to my chest for soft-sweet suckling. We have shared comfort, security, and love with you. Now your gentle beginning seems to be turning to dust as your screams pierce my heart, telling me of this assault called circumcision you are now enduring.

Small, trusting person: Will I ever know what scars this brings to your soul? Suddenly I feel betrayed by generations of mothers! Why have I not been told of the agony, the choked screams, and the final defeated exhaustion you must endure while being strapped down to a barbaric device called a Circumstraint and then being cut, stretched, bled, and squeezed until outraged screams are transformed into inaudible wheezes?

After an eternity of separation, you are returned to my arms by your very pale father, who has witnessed this circumcision. Zac, can you feel my touch, my sorrow? Your eyes are clamped shut and you don't respond, as I quickly carry you away with tears falling down my face. You refuse to nurse, and I understand why you prefer to deny your worldly existence for a while. Sweet baby, will my love, warm milk, and gentle touch be enough to help you forget? I know that I never will forget this. I promise you, Zachary, that from this day on I will let nature be my teacher and love be my guide.

Lauren Freiderich, *Mothering,* Summer 1979.

eight hours old. The baby is strapped, spread-eagled, to a plastic device called a Circumstraint™. The doctor inserts a hemostat—needle-nose pliers—into the hole at the end of the foreskin and clamps the hemostat down, crushing the blood vessels in the top of the foreskin. A probe is then inserted under the foreskin and run circularly around the glans several times, ripping the inner foreskin from the penis. A bell-shaped device is placed on the fresh wound, and a thumbscrew device or a suture is used to squeeze off the blood supply until the foreskin is amputated. The foreskin is then cut away. This procedure is normally done without anesthesia, because of the risks involved in using painkillers on newborn babies.

Like all surgery, circumcision has inherent risks, including excessive bleeding and infection. The circumcision wound is larger than most people imagine. The wound is not just the circular point of union between the outer and inner layers of the remaining skin. When the foreskin is torn from the head of the penis, a large, open area of raw flesh is created. Until it heals, this wound is in continual contact with urine and feces in the diaper.

Skin tags and bridges can form from shreds of foreskin left on the glans, or pitting and scarring may result when pieces of the glans are torn off with the foreskin. Depending on the amount of skin cut off and how the scar forms, the circumcised penis may be permanently twisted or bowed. The contraction of the scar tissue may pull the shaft into the abdomen.

In extreme cases, part or all of the glans is accidentally cut off. There have been actual cases of sex change operations performed on babies because of a botched circumcision.[3] Death from circumcision is rare, but does occur.[4]

Circumcision Is Painful

Virtually all doctors agree on the fact that circumcision causes severe, persistent pain. Imagine having the most exquisitely sensitive part of your body amputated without anesthesia. We are only beginning to understand some of the long-term effects of that pain.

Surgery used to be routinely performed on infants without anesthesia, based on the assumption that they did not feel pain. We now know that newborns are perhaps more sensitive to pain than adults are. The American Academy of Pediatrics states that the centers of the brain necessary for pain perception are well developed by the third trimester. Recent studies have shown that early pain or trauma can have long-term consequences on sensory or pain behavior, extending into childhood or beyond. One well-documented study indicated that boys who are circumcised without anesthesia have a lower pain threshold than girls or uncircumcised boys.[5]

Circumcision can disrupt mother-child bonding and breastfeeding. Subdued, less interactive behavior is a common reaction to stress in newborns. In response to unbearable pain, circumcised babies sometimes withdraw into a state of prolonged, unrestful sleep that can last several days or more. They breastfeed less frequently and are less available for interaction. This withdrawal may lead to early breastfeeding failure (see Chapter 4).

Circumcision has been performed without anesthesia as much as 90 percent of the time for two reasons: anesthesia is risky to use on newborns, and it is not very effective in circumcision, anyway. American Academy of Pediatrics guidelines, revised in 1999, now call for the use of pain relief during circumcision.

EMLA, a topical cream, is the anesthetic most commonly used in circumcision. However, EMLA is now contraindicated in babies younger than one month because it can have severe side effects.

Dorsal penile blocks and penile ring blocks—anesthetizing injections into the penis—are effective at reducing circumcision pain about 60 to 80 percent of the time, when administered correctly.[6] However, these injections do not numb the penis completely because they do not reach the sensitive frenulum nerve. Multiple injections into the penis are, themselves, painful. There can be potentially life-threatening side effects from the anesthesia. Pain returns once the anesthesia wears off, for the week to ten days that it takes for the circumcision wound to heal.

Other time-honored pain-relief techniques for circumcision include giving the baby a finger dipped in wine or a pacifier dipped in sugar to suck on. Common sense suggests that sucking on wine or sugar during an amputation, with no other form of anesthesia, does little to alleviate the pain.

Anonymous

Our son Jesse was born at home last summer, and it was a lovely experience. I had read and studied all aspects of pregnancy, childbirth, and newborn care, and had spoken with many childbirth education professionals before Jesse was born.

The circumcision decision was a hard one—my husband and I are Jewish. I cried the night before and had misgivings, but it seemed silly to cancel it.

Jesse did not scream or seem to be in pain, but I was horrified at what I saw. The mohel cut off the very end of Jesse's penis! From there, things got worse. He got sepsis (a deadly blood infection) and was hospitalized at the age of ten days, for ten days. I stayed with him constantly and nursed him and held him, as did my husband. It was as close to hell as I ever want to get!

My son has a healthy penis; the urinary tract was not damaged. Cosmetically, he has a slope on one side instead of a rounded penis, but the doctors say he has total use and function. They also tell me horror stories about little boys who were not as lucky as Jesse.

We regret the insufficient research we did on circumcision. Our son's experience shocked us into the immense responsibilities of being "good" parents.

Anonymous letter, *Mothering,* Summer 1979.

What Is the Foreskin?

Millions of years of evolution have fashioned the human body into a model of refinement, elegance, and efficiency, with every part having a function and purpose. Evolution has determined that mammals' genitals should be sheathed in a protective, highly sensitive foreskin.

The foreskin is specialized tissue, rich with blood vessels and nerves. It is a many-layered organ, covering and extending beyond the glans (head) of the penis before folding under itself and attaching just behind the rim of the glans. The inner surface of the foreskin is a mucous membrane similar to the underside of the eyelid or the inside of the cheek, that secretes lubri-

cants and protective antibodies. The frenar band (lips of the foreskin) tapers past the tip of the glans. The frenar band is a highly sensitive structure consisting of tightly pleated concentric bands that allow the foreskin to be retracted, exposing the glans.

The inner foreskin is attached to the glans by another particularly sensitive ligament called the frenulum, similar to the frenulum that secures the tongue to the floor of the mouth. The penile frenulum helps return the retracted foreskin to its usual forward position over the glans.

Because it is an organ with two surfaces, the foreskin's true length is twice the length of its external fold. It comprises 80 percent or more of the penile skin covering, or at least 25 percent of the length of the flaccid penis.[7]

Just as the eyelids protect the eyes, the foreskin moisturizes and protects the glans. It main-

tains the glans as an internal organ, protecting the urinary tract from contaminants. The foreskin also contains glands that secrete antibodies to defend against infection.

The Medical Pros and Cons

Fifty years ago, doctors believed there were sound medical reasons for performing circumcisions. Today, the medical rationales have been disproved. The American Academy of Pediatrics (AAP) states in its 1999 circumcision policy that the medical justification for circumcision is not significant enough to recommend it as a routine procedure. Here is a look at some of the diseases circumcision was once thought to prevent.

URINARY TRACT INFECTIONS
Some well-publicized studies have indicated that intact men (men who have not been circumcised) have a greater risk of urinary tract infections (UTIs), because certain bacteria can adhere to the foreskin. Whether the risk of UTIs is significantly higher is debatable. The AAP points out that several of these studies, which were conducted at United States Army hospitals, may have been flawed. Other research has found that most UTIs are a result of urinary birth defects.[8]

These studies aside, UTIs are relatively rare (approximately 1 in 100 male infants). There is evidence that breastfed babies have a lower incidence of UTIs. Besides, UTIs are usually treatable with antibiotics, so it is hard to justify a surgical procedure—with its own risk of infection—to lower the risk of urinary tract infection.

SEXUALLY TRANSMITTED DISEASES
Some early studies suggested a lower risk of syphilis and HIV among circumcised men. However, the AAP points out that these reports were flawed, and the Journal of the American Medical Association and other researchers have found that circumcised men actually have a higher risk of gonorrhea, certain types of herpes, human papilloma virus, and chlamydia. The AAP concludes that using condoms and limiting sexual partners is far more effective than circumcision as a defense against sexually transmitted diseases.

CANCER OF THE PENIS

In several major studies of American men with cancer of the penis—most done in the early 1900s—none were circumcised. This finding led some researchers to claim that circumcision was effectively an immunization against penile cancer.

However, other studies have since turned up cancer of the penis in circumcised men. Japan, Denmark, Finland, and Norway, where boys are not circumcised, all have lower rates of penile cancer than the United States.[9] Recent studies seem to indicate that penile cancer is closely associated with poor hygiene, and that certain sexually transmitted diseases predispose a man to getting penile cancer.[10]

More importantly, cancer of the penis is extremely rare—less than one case per 100,000 men in the United States. Breast cancer is much more common, yet we do not remove girls' breasts as a precautionary measure. In fact, the risk of complications from circumcision surgery—which ranges between .5 and 2 percent—is much higher than the incidence of penile cancer.[11] And the American Cancer Society has stated that the fatality rate from circumcision accidents is similar to the mortality rate from penile cancer.

CANCER OF THE CERVIX

Cervical cancer used to be practically unheard of in Jewish women; therefore it was assumed that circumcision in a partner was an effective guard against cervical cancer. This theory has since been disproven. The American Academy of Pediatrics states that "evidence linking uncircumcised men to cervical carcinoma is inconclusive. The strongest predisposing factors in cervical cancer are a history of intercourse at an early age and multiple sexual partners."

PHIMOSIS

Phimosis—a tight foreskin that will not retract—is the most common abnormality of the penis. However, it can not be diagnosed at birth, because the foreskin does not usually retract naturally until sometime between three years and puberty. Therefore, it is not justification for circumcision.

If a boy is diagnosed with phimosis, it does not mean he needs to be circumcised later on. There are a number of new nonsurgical treatments available for phimosis, including stretching and steroid creams.

BALANOPOSTHITIS

Balanoposthitis is an infection of the foreskin. While it would seem that circumcision would guard against balanoposthitis, it can occur in circumcised as well as intact men, since circumcision leaves a foreskin remnant. Proper hygiene is the best protection against infection.

Circumcision and the Medical Establishment

In 1971, the American Academy of Pediatrics (AAP) came out in public opposition to circumcision, which was at that time performed almost universally in the United States. In 1975, the AAP reinforced this position, issuing a statement that "there is no absolute medical indication for routine circumcision of the newborn." Both the AAP and the American College of Obstetrics and Gynecology reiterated their opposition in 1983. As a result of these statements, circumcision rates dropped from higher than 90 percent to just over 50 percent in the early 1980s.

In 1989, however, the rate began to climb again, when the AAP issued a new report, stating that "newborn circumcision has potential medical benefits and advantages as well as inherent disadvantages and risks." These "potential medical benefits and advantages" refer to a slightly higher risk of urinary tract infections in uncircumcised babies. However, the overall risk of such infections in baby boys is less than one percent, and such infections in infancy are often associated with underlying anatomical anomolies. The "inherent disadvantages" refer to the pain of the procedure and its long-term impact. In 1999, the AAP issued a new recommendation stating that "the benefits are not significant enough for the AAP to recommend circumcision as a routine procedure." For the first time in AAP circumcision policy history, the new recommendations also indicate that if parents decide to circumcise their infant, it is essential that pain relief be provided.

Other countries have been clear in condemning circumcision for many years. Canada, Australia, and Britain all have position statements opposing circumcision. The Canadian Paediatric Society, Fetus and Newborn Committee, says it "...does not support recommending circumcision as a routine procedure for newborns." The Australian College of Pediatrics says "Neonatal male circumcision has no medical indication. It is a traumatic procedure performed without anesthesia...." The British Medical Association Guidelines state, "To circumcise for therapeutic reasons where medical research has shown other techniques to be at least as effective and less invasive would be unethical and inappropriate."

Circumcision and Sex

The foreskin is the most erogenous zone in the male body, containing a greater concentration of specialized nerve receptors than any other part of the penis. Circumcision cuts off more than three feet of veins, arteries, and capillaries; 240 feet of nerves, and more than 20,000 nerve endings.[12]

The foreskin is a moveable skin sheath that provides natural lubrication during intercourse. It glides freely and smoothly over the shaft of the penis, allowing the penis to move nonabrasively in and out of the vagina inside its own slick covering of skin.

Circumcision desensitizes the penis radically. When the glans, normally an internal organ, is externalized, it becomes dry and tough. Circumcision severs all the nerve receptors in the foreskin. It almost always damages or destroys the highly erogenous frenulum. Although circumcised men certainly are able to climax and enjoy sex, men who have had to be circumcised as adults report that their sexual pleasure is drastically compromised after circumcision.[13]

Women in Britain overwhelmingly prefer sex with an uncircumcised partner, according to a recent survey of 138 English women who had had intercourse with both circumcised and intact partners. The women in the study reported more vaginal discomfort, shorter duration of intercourse, fewer vaginal orgasms, and fewer multiple orgasms during sex with circumcised men.[14]

Care of the Intact Penis

One of the most common myths about circumcision is that it makes the penis cleaner and easier to take care of. Eyes without eyelids would not be cleaner, neither is a penis without its foreskin. The externalized glans and urethral opening of the circumcised penis are constantly exposed to abrasion and dirt. The loss of the protective foreskin leaves the urinary tract vulnerable to bacteria and viruses.

A child's foreskin, like his eyes, is self-cleansing. Just as it is inadvisable to lift the eyelids and wash the eye, you should not retract a child's foreskin and wash the glans. Immersion in plain water during the bath is all that is needed to keep the intact penis clean.

Sometime between birth and puberty, a child's foreskin should separate from the glans, and he will discover that the foreskin retracts. No one should ever force the foreskin to retract before it does so on its own. Forcibly retracting and washing a baby's foreskin destroys the beneficial bacterial flora that protect the penis from germs, and can lead to irritation and infection. The best way to care for a child's intact penis is to leave it alone.

The white emollient under the foreskin is called smegma. It is a beneficial and necessary substance that moisturizes the glans and keeps it smooth and soft. Its antibacterial and antiviral properties keep the penis clean and healthy. Smegma appearing in an infant's penis indicates that the foreskin is sloughing off dead skin cells and preparing to retract. The smegma can simply be wiped away.

Once a boy reaches puberty, if his foreskin has retracted, he can gently slip the foreskin back and rinse his glans and inner foreskin with warm water. Soap is not necessary. As your son reaches this point, you can speak to him about proper genital hygiene. But he will most likely have figured it out himself by then.

Deciding to Circumcise

If you decide to circumcise your son, you do not need to have it done right away. You may want to wait until he is six months old, when breastfeeding and bonding are firmly established and he can

undergo the procedure under general anesthesia. Circumcision is definitely not safe for a premature infant, at least until he is ready to be discharged from the hospital.

It is important to rule out any genital abnormalities before a circumcision is performed, because the foreskin may be needed later for surgical correction of anomalies. If your son's penis is very small, he may have "hidden penis," which is a contraindication for circumcision, since circumcision would necessitate removing too much skin. You should also know if your family has a history of bleeding disorders, which would put your child at risk during the surgery.

Discuss anesthesia with your child's doctor. Dorsal penile block and penile ring blocks have been shown to be the most effective methods. Be sure to have an experienced surgeon carry out the operation. Circumcision, although common, is not minor surgery.

You should also know that there are alternatives to removal of the entire foreskin, including keeping some of the inner foreskin, especially the frenulum. You may want to investigate these options to allow your son to retain as much sexual sensitivity as possible.

The Rights of the Child

Circumcision causes the loss of a normal, functioning body part, and leaves a scar. It violates the right that any patient should have to refuse treatment or seek alternatives. An infant is obviously too young to consent to anything, but he is the one who must live with the consequences of the procedure. Informed consent by one or both parents is now required by law, but rarely are parents truly informed of the traumatic nature of the operation or given all the current medical arguments.

Your child is born whole, intact, and perfect. He trusts that you will make the right decisions for him and protect him from harm. When given a choice, most men value their wholeness and keep their foreskins, for the same reasons that they would keep their other organs of perception. When you choose to let your son remain intact, you are letting him know that you respect him, his body, and the man he will become.

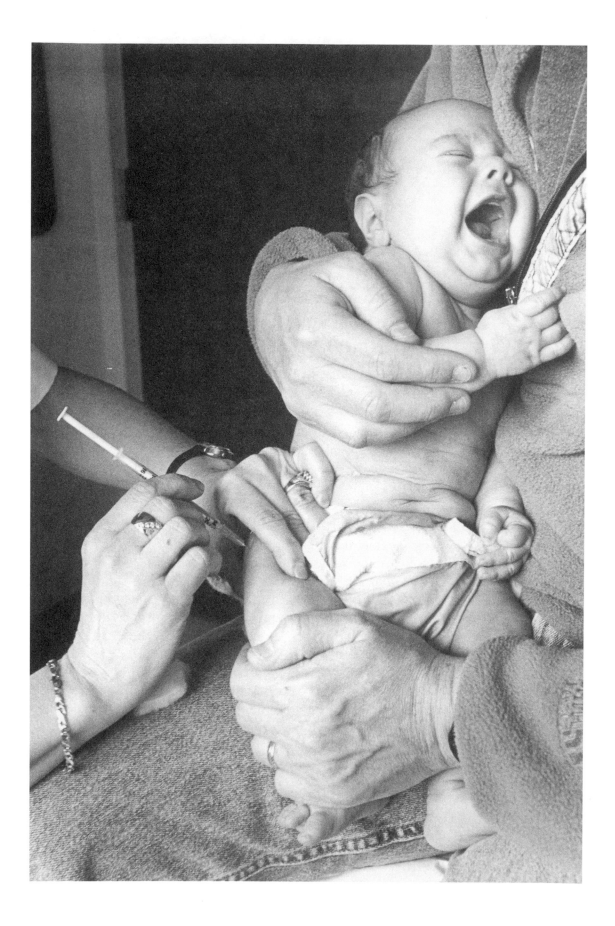

CHAPTER 6 Vaccinations

Forty years ago, when universal vaccination of children was begun in the United States, vaccines were hailed as wonder drugs. Before the introduction of the polio vaccine in 1962, parents feared that their children would contract polio from swimming pools and puddles. Diseases like diphtheria had a death rate of one in ten. One out of 100 who contracted whooping cough did not survive.

Today, however, due to a combination of improved sanitation, better nutrition, and vaccinations, many of these diseases have all but disappeared. There were only four cases of diphtheria in 1992—compared to 206,939 cases in 1921—and there is no live poliovirus today in the Western Hemisphere, although there are five to seven cases of vaccine-induced polio a year in the United States.

As the diseases have declined, and new research has suggested that there may be a down side to vaccinations, some parents are questioning whether the benefits of vaccinations outweigh the risks. They are challenging the growing number of vaccines, some of which seem excessive. And only now do we have enough data from universally mandated vaccinations to examine long-term effects.

While many parents would never think of questioning vaccinations, others have sound philosophical, religious, medical, or health-related reasons for conscientiously objecting to vaccinations.

Vaccination Concerns

The dilemma regarding vaccination reflects a fundamental difference between the parents' and the health professionals' points of view. For parents, the small but very real risk of some vaccines can cause serious concern. All we as parents really care about is: Can adverse side effects happen to our child? We are not willing to sacrifice our child for the good of the many. From the health professionals' point of view, vaccines have greatly reduced death and complications from disease, and a few debilitating or fatal reactions to a vaccine are a small price to pay for the protection they afford to the majority.

Health professionals also witness more of the death and devastation from disease than does the average parent. Those health professionals and others who don't favor giving parents free choice regarding vaccines fear that children—who, of course, can't choose for themselves—will die or suffer the complications from disease because of their parents' bias against vaccines.

Risks and Adverse Effects of Vaccinations

Common side effects of vaccines include soreness and redness at the site of the vaccination and perhaps a low-grade fever. However, occasionally there are more serious vaccine-related injuries.

The National Childhood Vaccine Injury Act of 1986 established the National Vaccine Injury Compensation Program (NVICP), effective October 1, 1988. The law was passed in a climate of increasing lawsuits by consumers against vaccine manufacturers, threats by manufacturers to discontinue vaccine production, and dwindling vaccine supplies.

The NVICP gives compensation for injuries from any one of the following vaccines: diphtheria, tetanus, pertussis, measles, mumps, rubella, polio, hepatitis B, Hemophilus influenzae type B (HiB), and varicella (chicken pox).

Since its inception, the program has received over 5,000 claims for compensation; 85 percent of these claims were for vaccines administered before 1988. Of those 5,000 claims, over 1,100 awards totaling $800 million in compensation have been made to individuals or families.

Between 1989 and 1994, the Institute of Medicine (IOM) carried out mandated reviews of all scientific evidence concerning the possible adverse effects of the vaccines covered under NVICP. The National Academy of Sciences chartered the Institute of Medicine in 1970 to enlist distinguished members of the appropriate professions in the examination of health policy matters.

In 1991, the IOM published *Adverse Effects of Pertussis and Rubella Vaccines*, and in 1994, *Childhood Vaccines, Evidence Bearing on Causality*. During its attempt to find evidence regarding vaccine injuries, the IOM identified the need for further research into and surveillance of adverse events associated with vaccinations. Their published works, however, do indicate evidence suggesting a cause-effect relationship between the following vaccinations and adverse events:

- Diphtheria, Tetanus Toxoids, MMR (Measles-Mumps-Rubella) Vaccine, DPT (Diphtheria-Pertussis-Tetanus) Vaccine, Hepatitis B Vaccine, Measles Vaccine and anaphylactic shock (a severe allergic hypersensitivity reaction).
- Measles Vaccine and death from measles-strain viral infection
- MMR Vaccine and thrombocytopenia (low blood platelets)
- Oral Polio Vaccine and poliomyelitis in the person who receives the vaccine or someone they come in contact with—usually an immune-compromised person
- DPT Vaccine and protracted, inconsolable crying, shock, unusual shock-like state, and acute encephalopathy (brain dysfunction)
- Rubella Vaccine and acute or chronic arthritis
- Diphtheria, Tetanus Toxoids, Oral Polio Vaccine, Injected Polio Vaccine and Guillain-Barre syndrome (an uncommon, usually temporary form of polyneuritis that can cause loss of muscle strength, loss of or altered sensation, and sometimes, paralysis)

Knowing that these vaccine injuries can occur and that they are compensated for by the federal government gives us pause as parents. While you can compare the complications and fatalities of a disease with the risks of adverse events from the vaccine for the disease (See "Risks and Benefits of Diseases and Vaccinations"), doing so can be misleading. Some vaccines do have more of a history of adverse events than others do, but this fact does not necessarily make the other vaccines less dangerous. There are also unknown risks because the possible adverse effects of vaccination may be cumulative and chronic rather than immediate and acute.

The DTP vaccine of the 1980s was involved in the greatest number of lawsuits before the formation of the National Vaccine Injury Compensation Program. It has historically been associated with more fever, fretfulness, drowsiness, or soreness in the leg at injection site than have other vaccines. Serious reactions include limpness, pallor and/or convulsions, severe brain problems, and permanent brain damage. With the introduction of the acellular (DTaP) pertussis vaccination in the last five years, the more serious of these reactions have significantly decreased.

Only a large-scale and long-term study comparing vaccinated to unvaccinated children would accurately describe vaccine benefits and/or side effects. Vaccines that have fewer side effects are not necessarily safer.

The vaccine toxin itself, the culturing medium on which the vaccine is grown, additives and preservatives, and the sensitivity of the person receiving the vaccine can all contribute to an adverse reaction. The culturing medium (usually egg protein) and additives such as neomycin can cause allergic reactions in susceptible individuals. The mercury compound, thimerosal, used as a preservative in hepatitis B, diphtheria, pertussis and accelular pertussis, tetanus and HiB vaccines, can cause a local hypersensitivity.

In July 1999, a joint statement by the US Public Health Service and the American Academy of Pediatrics called for the elimination of mercury content in childhood vaccines. The cumulative effect of mercury can cause brain damage. Thimerosol has been used as an additive to biologics and vaccines since the 1930s because it is very effective in killing bacteria used in several vaccines and in preventing bacterial contamination. The Food and Drug Administration Modernization Act of 1997 called for the review and assessment of all mercury-containing food and drugs. In June 1999 the FDA notified vaccine experts that if infants younger than six months receive a number of thimerosal-containing vaccines at the same visit, the thimerosal levels in these babies could temporarily hit the Environmental Protection Agency's precautionary level on mercury exposure. Efforts are now underway to manufacture thimerosal-free vaccines.

Certainly, the individual's constitution must play some role in any reaction. Most vaccines are given in several doses over time. A history of bad reactions from a previous dose or a reaction in older siblings is a definite warning sign. The most severe brain injury occurred in infants who had had a previous bad reaction to the DPT shot.

The medically-accepted time period for determining whether a child has had a reaction to a vaccine varies with each vaccine, but ranges from a few hours to a few weeks. It is impossible to realistically place a time limit on vaccine reactions, however Mark Geier, MD, PhD, codirector, Genetic Consultants, and director, Institute of Immuno-Oncology, says that 79 percent of all infant deaths under one year of age occur within twenty-eight days of vaccination. Neurological reactions and autoimmune reactions may develop unnoticed for weeks before their symptoms appear. It is possible that acute and chronic reactions to vaccines exist in a continuum in which the obvious symptoms are just the tip of the iceberg.

If you suspect your child has had an adverse reaction to a vaccine, notify your child's healthcare provider, so that he or she can report the reaction and reconsider future vaccinations.

Vaccine Effectiveness

Public health measures such as improved nutrition and sanitation have contributed to the decline in many diseases and the virtual elimination of pandemics of diseases such as the plague in medieval Europe and influenza outbreak in twentieth-century America. All vaccine-preventable diseases have further declined since vaccines were introduced, some quite dramatically. The FDA requires effectiveness studies before approving a new vaccine, but does not require long-range safety studies.

Most vaccines are about 90 percent effective, so approximately 10 percent of those vaccinated will not develop immunity. Two to 15 percent of vaccinated kids will get sick during an outbreak of disease such as measles or whooping cough while 70 to 95 percent of unvaccinated kids will. A child with actual immunity—whether naturally acquired from the disease, artificially acquired from the vaccine, or passively acquired from the environment—will not get sick.

Natural and Artificial Immunity

Natural immunity acquired by recovery from acute illness such as measles is ordinarily absolute and lifelong, such that the risk of reinfection is practically zero. The ability to mount a vigorous immune response—to respond acutely and to recover from an acute infection—is the chief stimulus for the maturation of a healthy immune system. Some vaccine critics say that artificial immunity limits the immune system's opportunities to fight off acute disease.

Artificial immunity is not true immunity, and some suggest that vaccines may achieve protection from acute diseases at the expense of increased susceptibility to chronic disease. New research suggests an alarming increase in chronic disease in children that parallels the increase in the mandatory vaccination of children.

Unlike the acute, natural infections they are designed to prevent, vaccines produce no massive immune system response, but remain active in the antibody-producing cells of the body more or less indefinitely. Vaccines work by rendering the body less likely to respond acutely to acute measles, for example, because it is already fighting off chronic measles on an ongoing basis.

Increase in Chronic Disease

While the death rate in children under seventeen has dramatically declined since 1900, the rate of disability from chronic disease is 3.7 times higher than it was in 1960. From 1960 to 1981, the number of chronically disabled children doubled, and it has nearly doubled again since 1982. In 1960, the incidence of asthma, allergies, autism, and other disabling conditions in children was 1.8 percent; in 1994, it was 6.7 percent. The five most common childhood disabilities are, in order: learning disability (29.5%); speech problems (13.1%); mental retardation (6.8%); asthma (6.4%); and mental or emotional disorders (6.4%).

Michel Odent, MD, and fellow European researchers showed that the incidence of asthma is five times greater and of earaches is two times greater in children who have received the whole-cell pertussis vaccination than in those who have not.[1] Denver physician Philip Incao, MD, reports that 50 percent of the children in his family practice are vaccinated, and 50 percent are unvaccinated. He has observed that unvaccinated children usually have an immune system that reacts more responsively and vigorously to acute infections than that of vaccinated children. According to Incao, unvaccinated children also have fewer allergies and chronic conditions than their vaccinated friends, due, in his opinion, to natural exposure to the vaccine-preventable diseases of childhood.

Recent research suggests that vaccinations and antibiotics could result in increased allergies and asthma in children. Thirty-one percent of all children have some chronic condition such as respiratory allergies, repeated ear infections, asthma,

eczema or skin allergies and, in adolescents, frequent or severe headaches.[2,3] Eighteen percent of children have special health needs and require health and related services of a type or amount beyond that required by children generally.[4] One in 500 children (0.2 percent) need assistance or special equipment for activities of daily living like eating, dressing, bathing, etc., because of a chronic physical or mental condition.[5]

While other factors such as environmental pollution, the effects of poverty, and lack of access to health care and proper nutrition—as well as increased screening for chronic diseases—may also contribute to this increase, more research is needed into the possible relationship between vaccinations and chronic illness.

The research of J. Barthelow Classen, MD, staff fellow at the Laboratory of Immunology at the National Institutes of Health (NIH), indicates a relationship between vaccines and autoimmune diseases. He cites New Zealand research showing that the incidence of diabetes in children has increased by 50 percent since 1988 when hepatitis B vaccine was first given to children under the age of one.[6]

According to research led by Andrew Wakefield, MD, the MMR vaccine may cause gastrointestinal problems that can lead to autism.[7] These researchers have called for an end to the combined MMR vaccination until further research can be done. An independent panel set up by the Medical Research Council in Britain is organizing an investigation into the possible MMR-autism link, but no link has been found to date. Wakefield and his colleagues caution that they "did not prove an association" between the MMR vaccine and the behavioral and gastrointestinal abnormalities seen in their subjects. However, rubella infection is a known risk factor for autism, and several other researchers have tentatively linked MMR vaccine to cases of autism.[8]

Risks and Benefits of Diseases and Vaccinations

The following is a brief overview of the risks and benefits of vaccines for eight of the ten diseases on the American Academy of Pediatrics immunization schedule. The chickenpox and Hepatitis B vaccines, the latest—and controversial—additions to the schedule, merit a special look. Such an overview oversimplifies the vaccine decision, but can be helpful in formulating your own opinions.

DIPHTHERIA

Diphtheria is a disease caused by a toxin that is released by a bacterium. The toxin causes a membrane to form on the mucous surfaces of the body and occasionally on the skin. The complications of the disease include respiratory distress, heart failure, and paralysis. One in ten die.

The greatest number of cases of diphtheria were in 1921 when 206,939 contracted the disease. In 1992, there were only four cases.

The diphtheria vaccine is usually given in combination with pertussis and tetanus as the DTP or DTaP vaccine, but it can be given individually. It is 95 percent effective and the side effects, which are minor, include soreness at the injection site, and slight fever within the twenty-four hours following the vaccine.

Possible contraindications or conditions that may make the diphtheria vaccine inadvisable include moderate or severe illness at the time of the proposed vaccine or a serious reaction to previous doses of the same vaccine.

MEASLES

Measles is caused by a virus and was a common childhood disease until a few decades ago. In 1941, there were 894,134 cases of measles; in 1992, that number had dropped to 2,200.

The symptoms of measles include small spots like grains of sand in the mouth and inside the cheeks; blotchy, itchy rash with raised spots; high fever; runny nose; and red, watery eyes sensitive to light. Measles lasts from one to two weeks and is often a mild illness in children.

Complications of the disease include ear infection and pneumonia in one in ten, and encephalitis (brain dysfunction) in one in 1,000. Measles has a death rate of one in 5,000. The vaccine is usually given in combination with mumps and rubella, but can be given individually. It is 90 percent effective unless given before twelve months.

Earlier than this, the vaccine may not be effective if the child still has natural immunity from the mother.

Side effects of the vaccine include rash and a slight fever. Encephalitis can occur in one out of every 2,500,000 vaccinations.

The vaccine is contraindicated if one has a moderate or severe illness or cancer, has had a previous reaction to the MMR vaccine or a previous severe allergic reaction to egg protein (a vaccine ingredient), or if one is taking medications that reduce resistance to infection.

MENINGITIS (HAEMOPHILUS INFLUENZAE TYPE B)

Meningitis is a serious illness, especially in infants under one year of age; it can cause death in one out of 20 and permanent brain damage or deafness in one out of four. Haemophilus influenzae type B is a bacteria that is a common cause of bacterial meningitis.

The greatest number of cases of meningitis was in 1987 when there were 12,000 cases. In 1993, just a few years after the vaccine was introduced, only 17 cases occurred.

The symptoms of the disease can be misleading as they include cold, fever, and ear infections. More advanced symptoms include lethargy, bulging fontanel, neck stiffness, and eating difficulty. Swift medical attention is imperative. The disease lasts one to two weeks.

The HiB (Hemophilus influenzae type B) vaccine is 90 percent effective. Side effects include fever above 101 degrees F. in one in fifty, and redness and swelling at the site in one in 100.

Possible contraindications to the vaccine include moderate or severe illness, and previous serious reaction to the mercurial preservative, thimerosal.

MUMPS

Like measles, mumps is caused by a virus and was a common childhood disease until the seventies. The greatest number of cases was 152,209 in 1968. By 1992, the number of cases had dropped to 2,460.

The symptoms of the disease include fever, headache, and inflammation of salivary and possibly other glands. This inflammation causes the cheeks to swell.

One in ten can develop mild meningitis from having the mumps; four in 100 can develop encephalitis, and deafness can occur in six out of 100. About 25 percent of adolescent males or men with the mumps will experience painful testicles, but this has no long-term effect. Few die from the mumps—one to three in 10,000.

The mumps vaccine is usually given in combination with measles and rubella and is 90 percent effective if given before fifteen months.

The vaccine can occasionally cause mild swelling of the salivary glands, rash, and a slight fever in one out of 6.5 to one out of 20.

Possible contraindications to the mumps vaccine include moderate or severe illness or cancer; previous severe reaction to the MMR vaccine; severe allergic reaction to egg protein; and a personal or family history of seizures.

PARALYTIC POLIOMYELITIS (POLIO)
Polio is caused by a virus. The greatest number of cases of polio was 21,269 in 1952. The disease has a 76 percent fatality rate in children under two, and a 7 percent fatality in those over two.

There is, however, no live poliovirus today in the United States, and the World Health Organization considers live poliovirus to be eradicated in the Western Hemisphere. Each year, however, there are five to seven vaccine-related cases of polio in the United States.

Polio is a viral disease with flu-like symptoms. Its most serious complication is permanent crippling, but for 90 percent of those who contract it, polio manifests as a flu-like illness without serious complication. Most people who become infected with natural polio never get sick. Others will have a sore throat, cough, fever, stomach pain, vomiting or stiff neck and headache. About one out of every thousand people who get natural polio infection will be paralyzed.

The vaccine for polio is either an oral or an injected polio vaccine (OPV, IPV, or eIPV), and the rate of effectiveness varies from 80 to 95 percent. Paralysis occurs as a side effect of the vaccine in one out of 520,000 first doses.

Possible contraindications to the polio vaccine include moderate to severe illness; previous severe reaction to OPV or IPV; immunosuppression or living with someone who is immunosuppressed; pregnancy; and allergy to the additives neomycin or streptomycin. Contraindications to the oral polio vaccine only are the use of long-term steroids, cancer, radiation therapy, or AIDS.

PERTUSSIS (WHOOPING COUGH)
Pertussis is caused by a bacterium and can be a serious, long-lasting disease. The disease starts with a slight fever, runny nose, and loose cough and can develop into severe coughing spells that interfere with eating, drinking, and breathing. Pertussis can last from three to twelve weeks.

The greatest number of cases of pertussis, 265,269, occurred in 1934. By 1992, there were 3,359 cases, 70 percent of which were in children under five.

In infants under six months, pertussis can cause hospitalization in three out of four cases, pneumonia in one out of five, and convulsions in one out of forty. One out of twenty infants under six months with pertussis requires intensive care. One out of 100 die.

Until recently, side effects have occurred more often with the DPT vaccine, of which pertussis is one component, than with other vaccines. The whole cell pertussis vaccine (DTP) is 36 to 83 percent effective, while the acellular pertussis vaccine (DtaP) is 84 to 95 percent effective and has fewer side effects.

A temperature above 102 degrees F. is quite common after a DTP vaccine. Persistent crying, even cephalic (high-pitched) crying is present in one out of 100 babies vaccinated for DTP. Limpness, pallor, and convulsions are present in one out of 1,667 vaccinated with DTP, but are not present with DtaP, the acellular pertussis vaccine. Severe brain problems can occur with the DTP vaccine in one out of 10,000 cases, and permanent brain damage in one out of 310,000.

Possible contraindications to the vaccination include moderate to severe illness; previous reaction to DTP, DPT or DTaP vaccine; undiagnosed seizures; sibling or parent with seizure disorder; any brain or central nervous system problem.

RUBELLA

Like measles and mumps, rubella is caused by a virus and was a common childhood disease until twenty years ago. The greatest number of rubella cases was 57,686 in 1969, and between 1964 and 1965 there were 20,000 cases of congenital rubella syndrome, a disease that a baby can get in utero from a mother who contracts rubella. In 1992, there were 148 cases of rubella and 9 cases of congenital rubella syndrome.

With rubella, there is a slight fever, a faint, pink rash, and mild swelling of the neck, underarm, and groin glands. The disease usually lasts about three days.

The death rate for rubella is low: one in 5,000. Joint swelling occurs in one out of three adult women who contract the disease, and purpura (a temporary bleeding disorder) as well as encephalitis can occur in one in 6,000 cases.

The most serious complication of rubella is miscarriage or birth defects in pregnant women who contract the disease. These occur at the rate of about one per 50,000 or about sixty infants per year.

Because of this pregnancy complication, it is particularly important for girls to develop immunity to rubella. The vaccine is 90 percent effective if given before fifteen months, but its immunity can wear off before adolescence. Natural immunity to rubella, achieved by exposure to the disease, is the most reliable source of immunity.

Side effects of the rubella vaccine include a rash and slight fever in one out of 6.5 to one out of 20 who receive the vaccine. Mild swelling of the neck glands and a rash occur in one out of seven. Aching joints occur in one of 100 adults who are vaccinated, and temporary joint swelling occurs in one out of forty adults.

The most serious side effect of the rubella component of the MMR vaccine is acute or chronic arthritis in one out of fifty. This reaction is most common in adults who are vaccinated and is seldom seen in children.

Possible contraindications to the vaccine include moderate or severe illness; previous severe reaction to the MMR vaccine; severe allergic reaction to egg protein; cancer; leukemia; lymphoma; medication that reduces resistance to infection; pregnancy; and immune globulin or blood transfusion in the last few months.

TETANUS

Tetanus is a disease caused by a bacterium found in the soil and is fatal in four out of ten cases. Unlike the other diseases for which we vaccinate, tetanus is not contagious. Its symptoms include serious, painful spasms of all muscles, and its complication is lockjaw.

Tetanus bacteria can enter the body through a cut or puncture wound, particularly one that does not bleed freely. As an anaerobic disease, it can grow only in the absence of oxygen.

The greatest number of tetanus cases occurred in 1923 when there were 1,560 cases. In 1992, there were 42 cases.

The tetanus vaccine, which is 95 percent effective, is usually given in combination with diphtheria and pertussis in the DTP or DTaP vaccine, but it can be given alone.

Side effects of the tetanus vaccine include mild soreness at the site and a slight fever.

Contraindications to the vaccine include moderate or severe illness or a previous severe reaction to the vaccine.

Chickenpox and Hepatitis B Vaccination: Necessary or Not?

The recent introduction of varicella (chickenpox) vaccine and the hepatitis B vaccine has stretched vaccine credibility for many parents. In March 1995, the FDA approved the licensure of a live attenuated varicella (chickenpox) vaccine. Chickenpox is an infection caused by the varicella virus. In May 1995, the American Academy of Pediatrics announced that it should be given to all children ages one to eighteen years old. The vaccine was first developed almost twenty-five years ago.

The approval of the chickenpox vaccine was driven more by the economic costs of work time lost to parents when children contract chickenpox than by the complications of the illness itself. Chickenpox accounts for fifty-six deaths and 11,000 hospitalizations annually in the United States.

One concern about varicella is that the vaccination may be effective only for a limited time, which could cause more outbreaks of chickenpox among adults, for whom it can be a more serious condition. Phillip Brunnell, head of pediatric infectious disease at Cedars Sinai Hospital in Los Angeles, questioned in a 1993 *New York Times* article whether it was necessary to give a vaccine with unknown side effects to prevent a very mild disease. Some experts recommend chickenpox vaccination for those children who reach age eleven without naturally acquired immunity.

Hepatitis B is one of a number of viruses that can cause hepatitis (inflammation of the liver) and is primarily a blood-borne adult disease. At highest risk are intravenous (IV) drug users, their sexual partners, and people with multiple sex partners, although 64 percent of transmissions in children and adolescents have no known risk factor. In 1991, the Centers for Disease Control and Prevention (CDC) recommended that all infants receive the first dose of hepatitis B vaccine before discharge from the hospital, even though the only newborns at risk for hepatitis B are those born to infected mothers.

Ironically, only fifteen states require mandatory hepatitis B screening of all pregnant women, while thirty-five require children to have three doses of hepatitis B vaccine for admittance to day care or school.

Recently the National Vaccine Information Center (NVIC), formerly called Dissatisfied Parents Together (DPT), released figures on an alarming number of hepatitis B vaccine-associated adverse reactions. Independent analysis of raw computer data generated by the government-operated Vaccine Adverse Event Reporting System (VAERS) confirms that in 1996, there were 827 serious adverse reactions reported to VAERS in children under fourteen who had been injected with the hepatitis B vaccine. The children were either taken to a hospital emergency room, had life-threatening health problems, were hospitalized, or were left disabled following vaccination. During that same period, in contrast, the number of actual hepatitis B cases in children under fourteen in the United States was 279. Even before the introduction of the hepatitis B vaccine, the United States has historically had one of the lowest rates of hepatitis B disease in the world.

Some experts worry about the effects of the genetically engineered recombinant DNA hepatitis B vaccine in the United States. Bonnie Dunbar, PhD, a Texas cell biologist and vaccine researcher, says it takes weeks and sometimes months for autoimmune disorders such as rheumatoid arthritis to develop following vaccination. No scientific research or controlled long-term studies into the side effects of this vaccine have been conducted on American babies, children, or adults.[9]

The Centers for Disease Control and Prevention (CDC) contends that the hepatitis B vaccine is safe. To learn more about their viewpoint, call 800-232-2522 or see their Web site (*http://www. cdc.gov/nip/vacsafe/fs/ghepb.htm*). Of special interest is a report entitled, "Questions and Answers about Hepatitis B and the Vaccine that Protects You."

On May 18, 1999, Representative John Mica (R-FL) chaired a congressional hearing on the hepatitis B vaccine in response to parents' phone calls. "Hepatitis B Vaccine: Helping or Hurting Public Policy" was heard by the subcommittee on Criminal Justice, Drug Policy, and Human Resources. Testimony was heard from scientists, doctors, hepatitis B vaccine-injured children and adults, government health officials, members of the Federal Drug Administration and Centers for Disease Control and Prevention.

In July 1999, less than two months after the hearing, the Association of American Physicians and Surgeons (AAPS) issued a statement calling for an immediate moratorium on mandatory hepatitis B vaccines for *schoolchildren* pending further research into serious side effects. "Children younger than fourteen are three times more likely to die or suffer adverse reactions after receiving hepatitis B vaccines than to catch the disease," says Jane M. Orient, MD, executive directors of AAPS.

At the same time, a joint statement by the US Public Health Service and the American Academy of Pediatrics called for a roll back of the universal recommendation that all *newborn infants* receive hepatitis B vaccine at birth and for a delay in vaccination of premature or underweight babies. Additional congressional hearings on vaccine safety are expected to be forthcoming.

MORE VACCINES?

Forty years ago, the diseases we vaccinated against were ones everyone feared. Today, we are faced with vaccine decisions regarding diseases we are not particularly afraid of, such as chickenpox and measles, as well as vaccines that can be particularly reactive, such as pertussis and hepatitis. In addition, many new vaccines are under development. On August 31, 1998, the US Food and Drug Administration (FDA) licensed the rotavirus vaccine and in November, the American Academy of Pediatrics (AAP) recommended that the vaccination be given to infants at two, four, and six months of age. The vaccine is also recommended by the CDC's Advisory Committee on Immunization Practices (ACIP).

However, Theodore Ganiats, MD, of the American Academy of Family Practice (AAFP) opposes the rotavirus vaccine mandate. Ganiats said that the recommendation "could necessarily override patient preference by promoting use of a vaccine that does not produce herd immunity and for which the cost is not yet determined."

Drug trials in the US, Finland, and Venezuela have shown the vaccine to be 48 to 68 percent effective against rotavirus and 80 percent effective against the severe illness associated with rotavirus. Rota Shield is a rotavirus vaccine, not a diarrhea vaccine. Children will still get diarrhea, but the most severe cases of diarrhea are those associated with rotavirus. The rotavirus vaccine can be given in conjunction with other vaccines such as DtaP (or DTP), HiB, hepatitis B, or polio vaccines.

On October 24, 1999, the CDC withdrew its approval of the rotavirus vaccine. Earlier that week, the vaccine manufacturer American Home took RotaShield off the market. This is the first time a vaccine has been withdrawn from the US market for safety concerns. An estimated 1.5 million doses of rotavirus vaccine have been administrated to infants since it was licensed. As of July 7, 1999, the Vaccine Adverse Event Reporting System (VAERS) has received fifteen reports of bowel obstruction (intussuspception). Symptoms include persistent vomiting, bloody stools, black stools, abdominal bleeding, or severe colic pain.

Some of the more than 200 viral and bacterial vaccines currently under development include: chlamydia, cholera, cytomegalovirus, dengue virus, E. coli, Epstein-Barr virus, gonorrhea, group A streptococcus, group B streptococcus, hepatitis C virus, hepatitis D virus, hepatitis E virus, herpes simplex virus type 1 and 2, HIV-1 (44 different kinds), HIV-2 (seven different kinds), human papillomavirus, influenza virus (seven different kinds), Japanese B encephalitis virus, Legionella pneumophila, mycoplasma pneumonia, toxoplasma gondii, and tuberculosis.

In 1998, the *Journal of the American Medical Association* reported on surveys of physicians that indicated that 20 percent of physicians object or express concern about giving three injections, and even more object to four injections, at a single visit.[10]

Vaccines and Big Business

In the last twenty years, vaccine manufacture has become big business. In 1969, biological weaponry was outlawed internationally, and the United States Medical Research Institute of Infectious Diseases changed its mission from biological weaponry research to the development of protective vaccines and the control of lethal microorganisms and infectious diseases.

Worldwide revenues from vaccine development are nearly $3 billion and are expected to more than double to $7 billion over the next five years. Vaccine industry revenues are estimated at more than $1 billion a year in the United States alone, up from $500 million in 1990. The cost to fully vaccinate a child has risen from $107 in 1986 to $367 in 1996, a 243 percent increase over ten years.[12]

Some parents fear that the profits from vaccinations could be fueling the push to develop new ones and that the government involvement in the development of vaccines influences medical recommendations.

What Are Vaccines?

Vaccines are fragments of bacterial or viral material that are injected directly into the bloodstream. They fool the immune system into thinking that there is an ongoing infection and it responds by producing antibodies against the disease—antibodies that can be measured in the blood over a long period of time. The immune system may not produce the same amount or type of antibodies as in a natural infection, but immunity does occur, although it is not always permanent.

Vaccines can be one of two types: killed—that is, totally inactivated—or live, wherein the organism has been damaged so that it cannot cause infection but is still not completely dead. Vaccines contain preservatives and other chemicals.

A Short History of Vaccines

The search for vaccines, which led incidentally to the discoveries of the germ theory of disease and the immune system, began in ancient China in response to smallpox, a native Asiatic disease that spread to Europe with the opening of the trade routes. As a result of the unsanitary living conditions created by the Industrial Revolution, this rare disease became a leading killer. Even though 75 percent of those who contracted smallpox survived, over a million Europeans alone died of smallpox every year.

The early vaccination practices used in ancient China look barbaric today: Smallpox scabs were dried, pulverized, and blown into the noses of healthy individuals through special bone inoculation tubes. This exposure usually resulted in a mild case of smallpox, which, in effect, immunized the patient against severe future cases.

In some cultures in Asia Minor and Africa, healthy people were induced to swallow the scabs or pus of infected persons. In others, native healers opened veins or scratched healthy skin with needles and rubbed infected pus into the wounds.

In 1796, Edward Jenner, an English country doctor from Berkeley, Gloucestershire, noticed that dairymaids who contracted the mild disease cowpox were subsequently immune from smallpox. When he brought this connection before his professional colleagues, he was attacked and threatened with professional expulsion.

Jenner nonetheless persisted, and without understanding the scientific basis of his results, was successful in establishing scientifically that cowpox inoculation rendered the subject immune to smallpox. Jenner named his discovery vaccination from the Latin word *vaccinus*, relating to cows.

In the United States, from 1820 to 1875, smallpox epidemics hit every major city, all of which were crowded and lacked sewage disposal systems and clean water. Efforts to improve living conditions in cities helped to effectively slow the spread of communicable diseases. American cities were slow to adopt universal vaccinations, and until the mid-twentieth century, the United States had the highest rate of smallpox deaths of any country in the Western Hemisphere.

French chemist Louis Pasteur (1822-1895) was one of the first to understand the implication of the germ theory of disease. He discovered a weakening process called attenuation in which an "aged" live disease culture is inoculated into a living organism and will not produce the disease, but will, in most cases, produce resistance to it

Following Pasteur's demonstration that attenuation of harmful microbes transformed some germs into vaccines, the international scientific community rushed to identify and convert into vaccines the leading causes of death in the industrial world at the time: tuberculosis, pneumonia, cholera, dysentery, diphtheria, meningitis, influenza, typhoid, childbed fever, and sexually transmitted diseases.

Many of the world's top scientists worked during the early decades of the twentieth century to discover a polio vaccine. Swedish research correctly discovered that polio invades the gastrointestinal tract through food and water. It usually causes a mild, generally unnoticeable infection, giving the body time to develop natural immunity to subsequent polio infections.

In 1935, two scientists who had earlier developed an effective diphtheria vaccine pioneered a killed-virus poliovirus vaccine and an attenuated live poliovirus vaccine. Ten thousand children were injected with the killed-virus vaccine and 12,000 with the live vaccine. Tragically, some children contracted polio from the vaccines and some died.[11]

Between 1952 and 1954, Dr. Jonas Salk, of the University of Pittsburgh, revised the killed-virus formula of the earlier scientists and developed strains of vaccines cultured on monkey kidney tissue.

Salk's vaccines worked well in clinical trials until 1955, when reports of vaccine-associated poliomyelitis started. Of the 204 cases that occurred, 79 were in vaccinated children, 105 were among vaccinated children's family members, and 20 were among contacts in the community. Seventy-five percent of the cases were paralytic poliomyelitis, and eleven people died. Investigation revealed that in seven lots of the vaccine, the poliovirus had not been killed.

Vaccine production was halted and a complete political shake-up hit the United States Health, Education, and Welfare Department (HEW). The secretary of HEW, the secretary of the National Institutes of Health, and several other officials resigned. The polio vaccine was restarted after screening procedures were tightened.

In 1954, the National Foundation for Infantile Paralysis gave Dr. Albert Sabin a grant to develop a live poliovirus vaccine. Sabin realized that the advantage of a live vaccine is that it more closely resembles the natural infection route. The live virus vaccine was tested internationally, and in 1962, the Sabin trivalent was licensed and used to vaccinate millions of adults and children in the United States.

The first successful measles vaccine—the Edmonston live measles virus vaccine—was licensed in the United States in 1963. In 1966, doctors at the Federal Bureau of Biologics developed an attenuated live rubella virus vaccine. The Hilleman mumps vaccine was licensed in 1968. Maurice Hilleman and his Merck Institute colleagues also developed the hepatitis B vaccine in 1969 and tested it among the New York City homosexual population in 1978, where it was shown to be 92.3 percent effective. In the mid-1980s, a vaccination for Hemophilus influenzae type B meningitis was developed.

Vaccination and Parents' Rights

Self-determination and autonomy in decisions about one's health have been recognized as fundamental moral values in United States law for almost a century. The American College of Obstetricians and Gynecologists, the American Hospital Association, and the International Childbirth Education Association all have doctrines of informed consent.

Informed consent means that a health practitioner must disclose all information, including risks and benefits, that a reasonable person would need to know in order to make a decision. It also means that the one consenting must do so voluntarily and without coercion. Implicit in these doctrines of informed consent is the right to decline.

In regards to vaccinations, informed consent, or informed choice, means that your doctor must talk to you about the risks and benefits of vaccinations before asking your permission to vaccinate your child. All states offer exemptions to vaccinations for medical, religious, or philosophical reasons. These exemptions are obtained from the state health department and filed with the child's day care or school in lieu of vaccination records.

Some consider those who refuse vaccinations as selfish and lacking in community spirit. Advocates of universal vaccinations see philosophical exemptions as a risk to the "herd immunity" that they believe is achieved by vaccinations.

Successful vaccine programs, according to Eugene D. Robin, MD, active professor emeritus at Stanford University School of Medicine, require participation by a substantial portion of the population for the highest level of immunity. Accurate assessment of the risk and benefit ratio of each vaccine by means of a prospective, randomized, controlled clinical trial should be obligatory. An educational process involving the public should be mandatory, in which the risks and the uncertainties are described, as well as the potential benefits.

According to Robin, a cross-over point will be reached, where the rate of adverse effects from the vaccine for individual patients will be higher than the adverse effects of the disease. At this point, for individuals, the wise thing might be to refuse the vaccine. However, for society it might be useful to continue vaccination to prevent resurgence of the disease in the general population.

Making the Decision

There is no right answer to the vaccination dilemma except the one that is right for you and your family. Your responsibility is to make informed and educated decisions regarding their health. The decision-making process regarding vaccinations may be challenging and even troubling for doctors and parents, but it is important that parents actively participate in decisions affecting their child's welfare.

You need to evaluate whether vaccination represents a significant threat to your child's health, in which case you may decide not to have your child vaccinated. You may decide that vaccinations will help your child to ward off epidemic diseases and choose to have all the vaccinations that are available. Or, you may fall somewhere in between, appreciating the benefits of some vaccines while being concerned about others, especially when the risks from the disease are minimal. In that case, you may decide that some vaccines are unnecessary or risky while others are valuable.

Most parents want to comply with the Centers for Disease Control (CDC) and American Academy of Pediatrics (AAP) recommended vaccination schedule, and most do. Those who conscientiously object to vaccinations amount to a very small percentage of parents. They do not consider themselves to be a threat to universal compliance or to "herd immunity" because they believe that one's susceptibility to disease has more to do with the overall health of the person than with the presence of germs. Therefore, they are interested in providing a wholesome diet and practicing preventative medicine to keep their child's immune system strong and better able to fight off disease.

British homeopath Miranda Castro, who regularly counsels parents making vaccine decisions, offers the following suggestions to parents:

- Weigh the pros and cons of each vaccination, gathering information from both sides. It is sensible to do this when pregnant rather than to wait until the baby is born. Parents are more vulnerable after the baby is born and may find it hard to resist persuasion. Ideally, partners need to be involved in the decision-making process together.
- Seek out medical providers who are sympathetic to your needs and wishes. Parents deserve doctors sympathetic to their needs, especially their wish to make informed choices about every aspect of their child's health care, including vaccination.
- Ask yourself whether you are prepared to nurse your child through an illness such as whooping cough. And, consider how you would feel if your unvaccinated child died from a disease such as meningitis for which there is a vaccination. Likewise, you will also need to ask yourself how you would cope if your child had a reaction to a vaccine or became chronically ill or died as a result of a vaccine.
- If you decide to vaccinate, work with your healthcare practitioner to decide which vaccinations can be delayed until your child is six months or older. Vaccines are administered beginning at six weeks because this schedule ensures a higher rate of compliance from the public. However, vaccines also cost less when administered to infants and some vaccine-preventable diseases, notably HiB and whooping cough, are clearly more severe in young infants.

For a healthy, breastfed baby cared for at home, delaying certain vaccinations may be reasonable because breastfeeding affords the infant some of his mother's antibodies. Breastfeeding does not, however, protect the infant from airborne germs. Infants cared for outside of the home or routinely exposed to large groups of strangers may have more risk of disease.

If your child was small for gestational age or was born prematurely, consider waiting even longer. The immune system matures at two years of age.

- Do not allow your child to be vaccinated if she has been ill or has had a cold or runny nose within the last forty-eight hours. An immune system that is already taxed may be more likely to react badly to vaccinations.

- Ask your doctor to administer one vaccine at a time; because we do not contract more than one disease at a time, it makes sense to have only one vaccine at a time. This way, if an adverse reaction occurs, you and your doctor will know which vaccine is the culprit.

- If you have a family history of central nervous system disease, deafness, blindness, convulsions, or life-threatening allergies, the pertussis vaccine may be contraindicated for your child. The new acellular pertussis vaccine is less reactive than the previous whole-cell one.

- If one child in your family has had a serious reaction to the pertussis vaccine, the child's sibling should probably not receive that vaccine.

- If your child exhibits a severe reaction to any vaccine, immediately report it to the Vaccine Adverse Effects Reporting System (see "Resources"). Reconsider future doses of the same vaccine.

- Ask your physician to report the severe reaction to the Centers for Disease Control and Prevention (CDC).

- Always write down the batch and number of any vaccine that your child is given. Be sure to look carefully at the vial whenever your child receives a vaccination to be sure the doctor or nurse is administering the correct vaccine.

- If for any reason your child becomes ill enough to be hospitalized within two weeks following a vaccination, fully describe the course of the illness to your healthcare provider or health clinic immediately.

- After your child receives the oral polio vaccine, keep him away from anyone who has an immune deficiency, for that person's own protection. Because the poliovirus is shed in your baby's saliva and stool for days and months after he receives the oral polio vaccine, it is especially important to keep people who have

an immune deficiency away from your baby's diapers. The oral poliovirus is shed in the stool for four to six weeks after the first dose; for two weeks after the second dose; and for ten days after the third. An effective injected poliovirus vaccine is now available and will be the vaccine of choice after the year 2000; these precautions will then be unnecessary.

A child who has recently received the oral poliovirus vaccine poses no real threat to healthy children, though he may accidentally vaccinate his unvaccinated classmates. We do not need to keep our kids away from each other.

Schools keep nonvaccinated children home during an outbreak of disease to protect them, and to slow the progress of the disease, as they are more likely to contract the disease. During an outbreak of whooping cough (pertussis), it is especially important to take extra care of the unvaccinated child. Early detection and a prophylactic course of erythromycin can temper the disease.

Make your peace with the fact that choosing whether or not to vaccinate your child is a difficult decision and that either choice has risks. Your goal is to make sure that the risks are minimized.

Your decision will ultimately be a leap of faith. Take your time, talk to as many people as is helpful, read, and think things through. Talk together as a couple. Check out the Resources section at the end of this book. There are several national organizations and a growing number of state vaccine groups you can contact for more information.

Respect the opinions of others. If we appreciate our civil liberty of informed consent, then we must respect other's right to choose, whatever that choice may be regarding vaccination. Remember that twenty years from now, you may not remember your doctor's name or the name of this book, but only you will have lived with the fruits of your actions with your young children. Be gentle on yourself as you make this difficult and very personal decision.

CHAPTER 7

Crying

Why do babies and young children cry so much? And why does their crying bother us adults so much?

Because crying *does* bother us, the message we so often send to our children is that it is not all right to cry. If a baby crying at the mall can not be quickly calmed, her mother may leave at once. When a four year old falls on the sidewalk, his father may say to him, "C'mon now, don't cry. It's not that bad." We attempt to distract our children from their tears or send them to their rooms to cry so that no one will be disturbed by the sound. At the same time, we resist crying in front of our children, fearing that it will upset them.

In fact, of course, there is nothing wrong with crying. A good cry, whether for a child or an adult, is a relief. The positive outcome of crying is a release of pent-up emotions and stress. The negative outcome of *not* crying when crying is called for is that suppressed tears can lead to suppressed emotions. When we experience extreme emotion but cannot release tension through crying, our feelings may overwhelm us, leading to depression and even despair.

William H. Frey II, author of *Crying: The Mystery of Tears*, says, "It is difficult to feel very sad or hurt without crying, and we soon learn that it is easier not to cry if we do not allow ourselves to feel strongly in the first place.... Individuals who learn to hide their emotions from others may eventually hide them so well that they no longer know what or how they feel."[1] Realizing that he had not shed a tear since childhood, Frey himself made a conscious effort as an adult to express his feelings and was eventually able to cry when moved or upset.

The Physiology of Tears

Crying is more than an emotional release—tears may actually be necessary to rid the body of certain chemicals. Biochemist William H. Frey II studied the chemical composition of tears, distinguishing between irritant tears (the kind that result when you cut an onion, for example) and emotional tears. He found that emotional tears contain a significantly higher concentration of detoxifying proteins than do irritant tears, and that they also contain endorphins that reduce pain sensation, as well as a hormone typically released in response to stress. "Crying it out," then, may be more than a figurative expression; it may be what literally happens as the body rids itself of stress-induced chemicals. Holding back tears, on the other hand, may inhibit the body's ability to handle stress. Frey says, "When we teach children to suppress their feelings and not to cry, we do them a great disservice by robbing them of one of nature's adaptive responses to emotional stress."[2]

Crying is not only a way to relieve stress; it also is a critical step in coming to terms with grief or depression. Many therapists report that clients who cry frequently in psychotherapy show significant improvement, compared with those who do not express their feelings. After clients cry in a therapy session, they exhibit lowered blood pressure, pulse rate, and body temperature, as well as more synchronized brain-wave patterns.[3] During the most intense phase of a depression, crying may not occur. Because a diminished ability to feel is a hallmark of depression, crying—acknowledging one's feelings—may be the first step in alleviating depression.

Why Crying Makes Us Uncomfortable

What if, even though you know that crying is healthy, your baby's cries make you anxious and tense? There are plenty of possible reasons for your reaction. Perhaps hearing your child cry brings back memories of your own childhood, when you might have been left alone to cry it out. Or perhaps your parents became overtly distressed when you cried. Or perhaps you feel guilty and ask yourself, "What am I doing wrong that makes my baby cry every single night—or every time she is frustrated? What can I do differently? Am I a bad mother if my baby cries?" Our society reinforces this "bad mom" message by giving a mother disapproving looks if her child cries. Later, as our children get older, we pass on to them the message that crying is socially unacceptable, a sign of weakness.

Researchers have found that most of us respond to babies' cries in either an egoistic or an altruistic manner. Egoistic responses are motivated by concern with self—we want to stop the baby's crying because it is irritating. Battering is an extreme example of an egoistic response. Altruistic responses stem from empathic discomfort—we want to alleviate the baby's suffering. Probably some element of both factors is present each time we respond to our babies. The problem with an egoistic response is that because it grows out of our needs rather than the baby's, it is unlikely to comfort the baby. An altruistic response, on the other hand, is much more likely to be in tune with what the baby needs. Prolactin and oxytocin—the "mothering" hormones stimu-lated during breastfeeding—have been shown to prompt an altruistic response to crying.

A baby's cry is *supposed* to invoke a physiological response in those who hear it. Rooted in a baby's survival instinct, crying is a way of ensuring that his needs will be attended to. Research indicates that we may have an innate response to a baby's cries. Several experiments with one-day-old babies showed that they became distressed when they heard another infant's cry, suggesting that our reaction to an infant's wails may be something we are born with.[4]

Crying Is Your Baby's First Language

While crying can be a healthy release for children and adults, it is even more important for babies because it is their only means of communicating—their only resource. As your baby's range of communication becomes more sophisticated, she will cry less, but for now, crying is her way of reaching you.

Well-meaning friends and relatives will typically inquire about your newborn, "Is she a good baby?" What they mean is, of course, "Is she a baby who cries very little?" This question reveals a basic misunderstanding of a baby's behavior.

Your baby cries when she wants something—that something might be food, a diaper change, a cuddle, or simply relief from some stress in her environment. Until she can communicate better, your baby's wants and needs are the same. If she cries out for you, it is because she needs you. Yes, she is "manipulating" you. Babies are biologically designed to manipulate their parents—to communicate their needs and have those needs fulfilled—in order to ensure their survival.

Responding to Our Children's Cries

Raised in a society that prizes independence and self-reliance, we may fear that responding to our babies when they cry will lead to spoiled, clingy children. Studies indicate that the opposite is true. Researchers Steve Bell and Mary Ainsworth found that infants whose cries are promptly answered in the first six months of life cry less frequently and for shorter duration, for the next six months and beyond, than do babies who are not responded to as quickly. The same researchers found in a sample of American mothers that the mothers deliberately ignored their babies' cries 46 percent of the time in the first three months.[5]

The more you nurture the bond between yourself and your baby by responding to his needs, the more in sync with your baby you will be and the better able to read his subtle cues. Ignoring your baby's cries distances you from your child. As you harden your heart to his distress, you become more emotionally detached.

In many non-Western cultures, mothers are adept at reading their babies' signals—the body movements and facial expressions that precede crying—and are able to respond to their babies *before* they cry. Mothers in these cultures are usually in continuous contact with their babies: They hold them most of the day in a sling-type carrier, sleep with them at night, and nurse them on demand. This close contact leads to a highly developed sensitivity to their babies' communication.[6]

The key to interpreting your child's cries is good listening. The more you listen to your child, the better you will understand him. The important thing is taking the time to figure out what your child has to say.

Why Your Baby May Be Crying

Your baby cries for many different reasons. Most parents can distinguish a cry of pain from a fussy cry, but their ability to sense subtle differences in their baby's communication stops there. You can tell a lot by observing your baby's behavior, by being aware of her schedule, and by simply listening closely. It may take practice at first, but the more you are attuned to your child, the better you will become at understanding her cries. Here are some of the most common reasons why babies cry:

HUNGER
Hunger cries are rhythmic, brief cries that get more and more intense until they quickly turn into full-blown cries of pain. Baby may root around for a breast or bottle, or suck her fingers. You can minimize hunger cries by letting your baby establish her own feeding schedule. Allow her to nurse longer and more frequently, and to get her fill at each breast so she takes in enough rich hindmilk (see Chapter 4 for more on breastfeeding).

OVERFEEDING
Frequent spit-ups and cries of discomfort soon after meals may indicate overfeeding among formula-fed babies. Because babies cannot regulate their own formula intake until the second month, they will suck a bottle until it is dry. If your baby spits up and seems uncomfortable after each bottle-feeding, try smaller, more frequent feedings. If he seems to have swallowed air, try burping him.

Most breastfed babies do not need to be burped routinely, because they will take in only as much milk as they need. Even if your baby wants to nurse frequently, you need not worry that he is getting too much to eat. Spitting up after nursing is common (due to the baby's immature digestive system and swallowing reflex) but do not be concerned unless it appears to be projectile vomiting—spit-up that shoots out of the baby's mouth, sometimes as far as a few feet away. If your baby spits-up a lot, try offering one breast at a time for feedings and alternate breasts from feeding to feeding.

TIREDNESS OR OVERSTIMULATION
A fussy cry is sporadic and sometimes half-hearted. The baby may rub her eyes and bat at her ears, or toy with her hair. She turns away from adults and resists soothing attempts. If your baby is overstimulated, try taking her to a quieter room. Help her to fall asleep by nursing her, rocking her in your arms, or rubbing her back.

LONELINESS OR BOREDOM
The coos and gurgles of a three month old can turn into protests and wails when she is left alone too long. The bored cry is "fake" sounding, with low, throaty noises followed by a crying sound and more moans. Babies crave human contact even more than they need food. Consider studies done with other primates: Infant monkeys taken from their mothers preferred a cloth-covered mother substitute that they could cling to, rather than a wire form containing a bottle of

milk that they could suckle on.[6] Your child is probably happiest when he can touch you. Other cultures around the world recognize this need, and mothers keep their babies constantly with them in sling-type cloth carriers or backpacks.

You can wear yourself out trying to entertain your baby with mobiles or mirrors, or you can "wear" your baby in a sling or front carrier, and let her entertain herself by seeing the world on your level, content in the comfort of your touch. (For more on "babywearing," see "The Art of Babywearing," page 109.)

HEAT

If your baby is overheated, he may whine and fuss, appear flushed, have a sweaty scalp, and act sluggish or breathe rapidly. Red dots—prickly heat—may appear on his face, neck, or shoulders. First, check for fever if he seems sick. If you have no reason to suspect an illness, he may just be too hot. After the first few weeks, your baby will be comfortable in the same temperature range you are in. His skin should be warm to the touch, but not hot, under his coverings. If your baby is too hot, remove some blankets or clothing, or give him a cool sponge bath.

COLD

Your baby may startle or scream when undressed or placed on a changing table; she may shiver or appear bluish around the lips. After the warm security of the womb, infants hate to feel uncovered and vulnerable. Swaddle your baby securely in a light blanket and undress her one part at a time rather than exposing her completely. Put a soft sheepskin or towel on the changing surface. Clean her with warm sponge baths under a blanket, putting off baths until she is older. Keep booties and a cap on her if she appears cold even in a blanket.

INTERNAL PAIN

A cry of pain is loud and long, followed by a long pause in which the baby seems to hold his breath. Then another alarming scream is sounded. The baby's mouth is wide open, and his tongue is arched; his hands and feet are drawn up or circle in agitation.

Your baby's screams may be due to his immature digestive system, teething pain, or an ear infection. First, try soothing techniques like nursing, rocking, or taking him in the tub with you. The pain may also be caused by diaper rash. Apply a healing salve and let his bottom "air out" without a diaper. If the crying lasts or you are concerned, call your healthcare practitioner.

CONSTIPATION

If the baby turns red and seems to squirm or strain to pass a bowel movement, he may be constipated. (Constipation is unusual in breastfed babies.) Occasional constipation should not be a cause for concern, but if your baby cries out in pain during a bowel movement or strains at urination, you may want to take him to the doctor to check for a constricted anus or urinary passage.

EXTERNAL PAIN

Piercing screams or sudden, intense cries for no apparent reason suggest that something in your child's environment is causing her pain. Check for tight bands on her clothing, scratching from Velcro diaper cover closures, an open diaper pin, or irritating fabrics. Look at her fingers and toes to see if a strand of long hair or a loose thread is cutting off circulation.

Vimala

I was standing in line at a department store recently, and a baby in a stroller began to cry. Several people nearby became uncomfortable; some scowled and whispered. The baby's mother picked him up and turned with a warm smile to the others standing in line. "He has a lot to say!" she called out. Instantly everyone smiled and relaxed.

Vimala McClure, "Crying: Good for You, Good for Baby!" *Mothering,* Winter 1996.

Ways to Soothe a Crying Baby

Even if you can not figure out what is making your child cry, you can still try to comfort her. Here are some time-honored infant soothers:

SUCKING

Babies have a strong need to suck. Often simply nursing your baby will calm her. But you may be tempted to give her a pacifier if you feel that she is using your breast for comfort rather than food. Remember that babies need comfort as much, if not more, than they need food. A rubber nipple cannot provide the security that your warm body and loving touch can.

ROCKING

The soothing motion of a rocking chair can lull your baby—and you—into tranquility.

MASSAGE

Massaging your baby puts you literally in touch with him, making you more sensitive to his nonverbal signals. Massage has been shown to help premature babies gain weight, asthmatic children improve breathing, and diabetic children comply with treatment.[7] "Touch is as important to infants and children as eating and sleeping," says Tiffany Field, PhD, professor of pediatrics, psychology, and psychiatry, and director and founder of the Touch Research Institutes at the University of Miami School of Medicine.[8]

To massage your baby, remove all his clothes and diaper, then place him on his back on soft towels in a warm room (put a diaper or cloth over him; keep him covered with a light blanket if he seems cold or uncomfortable). Rub a light, nongreasy oil such as almond oil on your hands, just enough to help your hands glide more freely. With gentle but firm strokes, using your whole hand, massage his shoulders, each arm, and each leg. Rub each foot and hand with your thumb and fingers. Turn your baby over onto his tummy and massage his back and buttocks.

HOLDING

Usually, what your baby craves most is human contact. Our consumer-driven culture encourages new parents to spend small fortunes on gadgets to swing, bounce, and lull their babies—complete with recorded sounds of the womb. But all your baby really wants is to be held close to you, to hear the reassuring beat of your heart, and to feel your warm touch. A study of newborns found that those who were carried over four hours a day, even when they were contented or asleep, cried

---

Catherine

Although my oldest child is almost twenty now, I still have the chair in which I rocked him and my other babies. What a trove of memories that rocker holds. I can sit down in that beat-up old chair and be flooded instantly with absolute calm. What, after all, is more peaceful than a sleeping infant?

When babies sleep, they snuggle tight into your shoulder. Their warm, milky scent tickles your nose—the ultimate aromatherapy. Tension is pulled from your body like the moon pulls the tides out to sea naturally, inexorably. Swaying back and forth with your tiny tranquilizer eases everything but the satisfaction of the moment.

Catherine C. Leonard, "Rocker Therapy," *Mothering,* November/December 1998.

almost 45 percent less than those who were not carried as much.[9] So go to your baby, pick her up, hold her, and cuddle her. Get into a warm bath together. Put her in a sling or front-carrier, and take a walk together, or keep her with you while you do chores around the house. Each time you reach out to your baby, your mothering hormones will surge, and the bond between the two of you will deepen.

A Good Cry

Responding to your baby's cries does not always necessarily mean stopping your baby's cries. Sometimes babies and children, like adults, need a good cry. Infants have to make the transition from the womb to the outside world, and often crying is their only way of letting off steam after being bombarded with external stimuli all day long.

As mentioned earlier, mothers in many non-Western cultures, because of their constant contact with their babies, are sensitive to their babies' signals and are able to respond to them before they cry. The mothers' responsiveness, however, does not mean that their babies never cry. Researchers have observed in nonindustrialized societies that although infants rarely cry during the day, it is common for them to cry for long periods in the evening. Adults know this is release crying and accept it. Sandy Jones says in *Crying Babies, Sleepless Nights,* "There's a difference between not responding, and responding and allowing, in which you've used your judgment about what your baby seems to need."[10]

Ignoring your child's cries is never a good idea. But sometimes it can be reassuring to your child to be allowed to cry in the safety of your loving arms. Just as our own tears are easier to bear when we are held by those we love, the same is true for our children. Try holding your baby during these episodes of release crying. You may find that the crying subsides, or you may conclude that your baby needs to cry to release stress. Either way, you are offering your baby the comfort of your touch.

If your baby is truly inconsolable, see "Tips for Colic" below.

Tips for Colic

If you are wondering if your baby has colic, he probably does not. When you have a colicky baby, you know it. A colicky baby is one who cries more than three hours a day, usually in the evening hours, at least three days a week. The colicky baby cries intensely and appears in agony. He may have a flushed face, and a rigid, distended abdomen. He cries with legs drawn up and hands clenched.

Colic peaks at six weeks and usually disappears by the time the baby is three or four months old. It affects 10 to 25 percent of all babies. No one knows for certain what causes colic, although it is thought to have something to do with the baby's immature digestive system.

Although there is no known "cure" for colic, many things may ease it. Here are a few tips for getting through this difficult period:

RULE OUT AN INTERNAL DISORDER

Extended crying may be caused by an inner ear infection, urinary tract infection, or numerous other ailments. Keep close track of your child's other symptoms, and take him to a healthcare provider if you are concerned that he is experiencing internal pain.

TRY CHANGING YOUR BABY'S DIET

If you are breastfeeding, following this advice means changing your own diet, of course. Some babies are particularly sensitive to certain foods. Dairy products seem to be the number one culprit; studies have shown that many cases of colic quickly disappear when breastfeeding mothers stop eating dairy products. Other offenders include eggs, soy, wheat, corn, nuts, citrus, and tomatoes. Cruciferous vegetables such as cabbage, broccoli, turnips, radishes, cauliflower, and leafy greens can cause intestinal gas in you and your baby. Junk food with artificial colors and flavors can be hard for babies to digest, as can caffeine, alcohol, and chocolate. Look at your diet to see if it is high in any of these foods, and try reducing or eliminating them.

If your baby is bottle-fed, you can try switching formulas, although this has not proven to be very effective. By all means, do not switch from breastfeeding to formula-feeding—your baby needs the closeness of nursing, and you need the let-down of mothering hormones that breastfeeding induces to help you through this frustrating time.

Nancy

My son, Nicholas, had colic that started when he was two weeks old. Although Nick would nurse contentedly throughout the day, every night from 8 p.m. until 2 A.M. he would try to nurse, then arch back and scream. Our pediatrician diagnosed colic, which was good news because this meant there was nothing physically wrong with him. It also meant that my husband and I could expect to face an inconsolable infant every night for about six hours for the next two or three months.

It was clear to me that Nick was reacting to my milk. After a week of eliminating one food or another from my diet, I began to think in terms of what I could eat instead of what I couldn't. The list of allowed foods was dishearteningly small: oatmeal, quinoa, millet, a seed oil (such as canola), bananas, boiled chicken, and salt. I drank water. Nothing else.

It worked. The first night was remarkably easier. By the second night, Nick's colic was gone. I ate like this for six weeks. Then I started adding one food at a time every few days to see if Nick would react. During these six restricted weeks, I lost ten pounds, came down with two colds, and noticeably lacked energy. But the colic was over, and everything else was an insignificant price to pay. Many people complimented me on my willpower to eat such a limited diet, but as any mother of a colicky baby knows, willpower had nothing to do with it. No craving in the world can match the threat of a night of colic.

Nancy Morgan, "Strategies for Colic," *Mothering,* Summer 1997.

TRY CHANGING YOUR FEEDING ROUTINE

Offer smaller, more frequent feedings, for example. Feed your baby before the crying spell usually begins. Burp him often. Try keeping the baby in an upright position while you feed him.

One Australian study found that mothers who tried to nurse only on one side per feeding significantly reduced their babies' colic—perhaps because the babies got more high-fat hindmilk. (The mothers were encouraged, however, to feed their infants whenever they were hungry, and to offer the other breast if the baby still was not satisfied.)

REDUCE STRESS IN YOUR BABY'S ENVIRONMENT

Try to decrease any anxiety you are communicating. Slow down your pace. To eliminate as much overstimulation as possible for both your baby and you, provide a low-key atmosphere, with soft music and no startling noises.

MASSAGE YOUR BABY

Massaging the stomach can aid digestion. A half-hour or so after a feeding, using the technique described in "Ways to Soothe a Crying Baby," page 91, massage your baby's stomach in a clockwise motion with your fingertips. Repeat this circling motion several times, folding the baby's legs up to his stomach. Your efforts may be rewarded with a release of gas. Continue with an all-over body massage.

TRY THE "COLIC CARRY"

Place your baby on your forearm, with your hand between his legs and his head supported in the crook of your arm. His head will be slightly higher than his feet, and his stomach will be resting on your forearm. Rock him gently back and forth as you hold him securely in this position.

TRY HERBAL REMEDIES

Fennel, dill, catnip, and chamomile have all been reported to help colic. Make a tea of these herbs, alone or in combination, and take it yourself before nursing, or give your baby ten to twenty drops of the tea with an eyedropper.

TRY HOMEOPATHIC REMEDIES

Many colic cases have been resolved very quickly with the right homeopathic treatment. Some common homeopathic remedies for colic include colocythis (bitter cucumber), magnesium phosphorica, and dioscorea villosa (wild yam). See Chapter 12 for more on homeopathy.

TRY CHIROPRACTIC REMEDIES

Chiropractors have found a high incidence of abnormality in cervical and thoracic spinal joint function in colicky infants. If an infant has a spinal disturbance, caused by birth trauma, chiropractic treatment has been shown to resolve or minimize colic.[11]

COMFORT YOUR BABY

Try the suggestions in "Ways to Soothe a Crying Baby" on page 91, including holding your baby, rocking her in a rocking chair, carrying her in a sling, and getting in a bath together.

Take colic seriously. Do not let anyone trivialize the very real pain you, your child, and your family are experiencing. Take care of yourself. Accept offers from friends or family to help out, so you can take a night off once in a while. Nap when you can.

Do not take the baby's behavior personally. Although some people may try to blame you by suggesting that the baby is reacting to nervousness on your part, no correlation has been shown between babies with colic and anxious parents. If you are tense, it is probably a result of dealing with a colicky child rather than a cause of it!

Above all, resist the temptation to label your baby "difficult." You have a very sensitive child. Give your child the latitude to adjust to the world with the reassurance of your love. Although it may not seem like it at the time, three months—the usual course for colic—will go by quickly.

Crying in the Older Child

Even though children can communicate in ways other than crying as they grow, they are still limited in their range of expression and may resort to crying. Children, like babies, need to cry occasionally. The best thing you can do for your crying toddler or older child is to listen to what she is telling you (or not telling you) and offer her reassurance.

To just sit with children and hold them while they cry can be difficult. Our almost automatic reaction is to try to get them to stop—as though to stop crying is to stop hurting. Another common response to children's crying is to send them away, to a time-out chair or to their room. The message comes through: I don't want to hear you in pain. Go away with your hurt, and come back when you are well again.

Crying calls attention to pain and loss. Attending to the crying helps heal the hurt. By listening to our children's distress with compassion, we encourage them to share with us the stresses and demands of growing up and surviving disappointment. By accepting their hurt and not succumbing to the urge to "fix" the cry or get them to stop, we are reassuring them that adults are not panicked by crying. The message emerges loud and clear that we welcome their feelings, that we can be sympathetic and supportive, and help them weather their difficulties. With practice, children begin to notice their hurts earlier, and put them into words. In time, they may seek us out to share their pain before they feel overwhelmed.

Living in a big world offers challenge, excitement, hurt, and frustration to a little child. Children lose control when they face feelings that overwhelm them. When a child can face these feelings wrapped in his mother's arms, the world does not seem such a scary place.

Here are some tips for responding to your toddler or older child's cries:

REMEDY ANY PHYSICAL HURT

As calmly as you can, remove a pinched finger from a door or take out a splinter, then hold and soothe your child until she stops crying. Do not dismiss a hurt. Give her time to recover from it.

LISTEN CAREFULLY TO YOUR CHILD

Hold her close and listen to what she has to say, both in her words and her body language. Listening means just that—not offering solutions, but simply allowing her to express her feelings.

DO NOT PASS JUDGMENT

Saying to a child, "That didn't hurt," or "You shouldn't let that bother you," does not help. Feelings exist; they are neither right nor wrong. They cannot be intellectualized away.

OFFER REASSURANCE

You cannot make your child's hurts disappear, but you can provide comfort. You do not need to say anything; your touch and loving eye contact will communicate more than words. If your child is fearful, reassure her that you will be there to keep her safe.

ALLOW TIME FOR THE EXPRESSION OF FEELINGS

Often a child will start crying about a recent incident and then move on to cry about an earlier, more significant event. Do not rush your child; it may take time for her to work through her feelings.

Your goal is to provide comfort and a safe haven for your child to express her feelings and work through traumas. You do not want to minimize her hurts, but overreacting will not help, either. Especially with a toddler who is prone to the bruises and tumbles that accompany newfound mobility, you can downplay your child's reaction by keeping your own in check.

Katie

Marie started walking the day she turned ten months old. We knew there would be a lot of crashes and boo-boos in the weeks to come. However, as Marie wobbled along, we learned how to encourage rather than frighten her.

After each tumble, Marie would look to us first before really reacting. Instead of looking horrified when she fell, we would clap our hands and cheer, yelling, "Yippee, look how far you got!" Marie was delighted by all the positive hoopla and would pull herself up, ready to toddle off once again.

If Marie actually did scare or hurt herself, her tears were immediate and genuine. And, of course, our support was just as immediate. She never became totally distraught by routine falls because she understood that they required little fuss and that real accidents were met with real responses.

Katie Engen, "Look Before You Leap," *Mothering,* March/April 1998.

It's Okay for You to Cry, Too

Finally, do not be afraid to cry yourself, especially in front of your children. You need not worry that your tears will frighten them—deliberate withholding of your feelings, which even toddlers can sense, will probably upset them more. Allow yourself to cry. Watching you, your children will learn how to take care of themselves when they are upset. They will learn that tears are normal. They will learn that it is all right—that it is ultimately human—to express your feelings in an atmosphere of love and support.

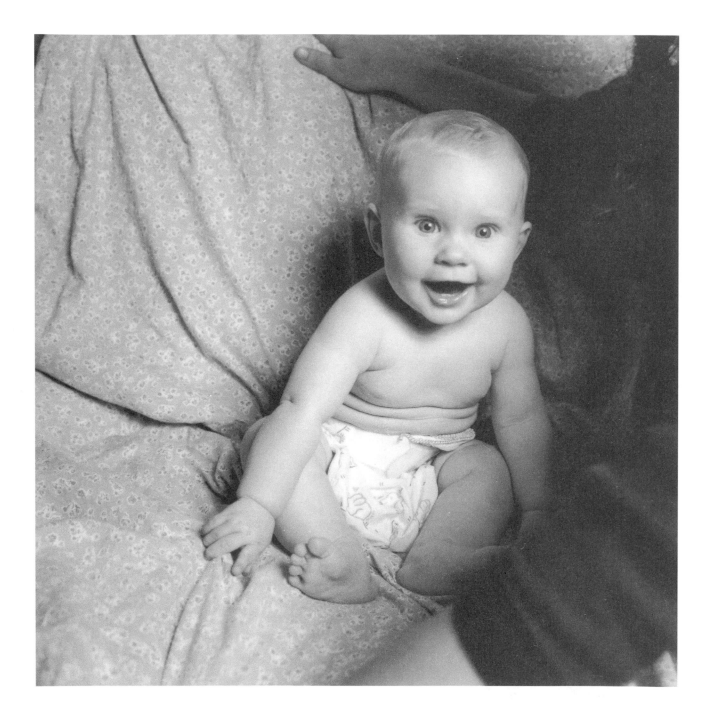

CHAPTER 8

Night Waking

"Sleep as much as possible now—while you can." The common warning to parents expecting their first child sends a clear message: When a new baby comes along, you do not sleep. It is, of course, true that babies and young children wake in the night and, more often than not, they need the comfort of our presence to soothe them back to sleep.

Some children are natural-born all-night sleepers, and they are a marvel to the majority of us whose children are natural-born night wakers. Among night wakers, there are those who awaken once a night to nurse for ten minutes, those who wake every forty-five minutes, and those who exhibit every pattern in between. We can be grouchy about it and jealous of those parents who sleep blissfully through the night from the beginning. But there is another way to look at night waking: It is a natural part of a child's daily life, and it presents one more opportunity to bond, to nurture, and to meet our child's needs.

One popular, logical sounding approach to night waking that is blindly embraced by some parents suggests that leaving a baby or toddler to his own devices in the middle of the night will enhance his ability to be independent and self-reliant, both considered desirable traits in our culture. Put another way, this theory implies that to nurture a child through his wakeful periods during the night is to foster dependence and weakness of character.

We would like to stand this theory on its head, first because our culture does not suffer from a lack of independent, self-reliant people. If anything, we suffer increasingly from a shortage of people who have been nurtured enough—and are secure enough—to nurture and embrace others in their times of need. Psychologists know that we often continue as adults to long for what we missed in childhood. If we did not feel nurtured as children, we will constantly seek nurture—sometimes in unhealthy ways—but we will not be good at offering it to others.

Independence cannot be taught—it is a stage that children reach only after their dependency needs are fulfilled. Insisting that a child alter her instinctual need for nurture to fit a set timetable is not the way to encourage independence. Since every baby is born with a unique pattern for sleeping and waking, it seems more logical to assume that trying to "break" that pattern can leave her with the sense that her own way of doing things is "wrong," which is not a recipe for self-reliance.

Psychological issues aside for the moment, when we consider the subject of our night waking children, we usually think first of a more immediate and concrete concern: our own desperate need for sleep. Baby or no baby, many of us must continue to get up, make breakfasts and lunches, get older children to school, and then face the day as productive people. Understandably, we are eager to conform our children's schedules to ours so that we can get back to a "normal" life with our eyes wide open.

Deborah

I have two daughters. With the first, I accepted the notion that she needed to learn how to get herself to sleep. At the end of the day, she was never ready to let go. It was as if her brain just would not slow down and let her relax. My husband and I took the advice to let her cry alone in her crib—for as long as twenty minutes—and it worked. We weren't cruel about it. We provided lovely, sweet routines including songs and books. But beyond that, by golly, we knew what she needed was sleep, and we were not going to give in to requests for more attention.

So for the first year of her life she cried and screamed, my husband and I got used to it, and she always fell asleep within the prescribed twenty minutes. Then, at the time when the books said she should be able to sleep through the night, we used the same method, ignored her night waking, and eventually she did not call out to us anymore. Everything seemed to work just the way the books said it would.

That daughter is thirteen now, and she still cannot fall asleep without a production. I have a joke with her that since she learned to talk, twelve years ago, I have never been able to walk out of her room after the last kiss without her calling, "Mama, I just have one more thing to tell you." That, I tell her, is 4,380 nights I have stood in the door and heard one last story, and then, most nights, have had to walk out on her and shut the door to prevent the "one last story" from stretching into more.

Now I know that what she is really saying is, "Mama, stay with me; I'm not ready to see you go yet. I just can't get enough of you." I knows she lies awake for a long time before dropping off. I think she is still, in a way, crying herself to sleep.

Circumstances led us to handle our second daughter differently. I was sick during much of her first year. I couldn't stand to hear her cry herself to sleep, and I brought her into bed with me much more often than not. When she woke in the night, I didn't want her to wake her older sister, who shared her room, so I lay down with her then, too. Now, at age ten, she still kisses me sweetly every night and with no fanfare drifts calmly into a sound sleep.

But we have had years to adjust to the workaday schedule. Babies—and even toddlers—are still operating on a primitive assumption biologically designed to keep them alive. They need to be picked up and carried when they cry. Babies are not supposed to conform to our twenty-first century sleep schedule, and they will not conform without a fair amount of manipulation of their natural internal clocks. We can impose our will on our children, but we cannot guarantee that their submission will not lead to alienation and rebellion. We fool ourselves if we think that babies who have given up on crying out for nurture have really learned to soothe themselves.

The challenge to parents who want to take their children's natural growth and development into account is to consider the inconvenience of night waking as part of their job description as parents. By learning the principles of sleep and sleep patterns, and by thinking creatively about ways to nurture a wakeful child instead of how to escape from those middle-of-the-night demands, parents can develop an attitude toward their children's patterns that will, in the long run, help everybody sleep better.

Instinct for Survival

Babies' cries are an instinct and a resource. The reason it hurts in our bellies when we hear a baby cry is because we are not supposed to be able to endure a baby's cry. That reaction is what ensures a baby's survival. When the baby suffers, we suffer. When it comes to night waking, it is natural for it to hurt more to stay in bed and ignore the cries than to get up and nurture the child.

It is not just physical survival babies seek. Child development theorist Erik Erikson wrote that the crisis of the first year is trust versus mistrust. If a child does not learn to trust others and the environment enough to enjoy a healthy psychological attachment, he will learn mistrust. Trust is learned if there is adequate warmth, touching, love, and physical care. Trust inspires faith in people and

Carol

When Paul turned ten months old, my husband and I became so concerned about wakeful episodes a few times each night that we scheduled an appointment with our pediatrician. He informed us, almost jovially, that the definitive cure would be to let Paul "cry it out." My insides rebelled. I felt an anticipatory wave of depression at the thought of abandoning him.

I suggested a second consultation. This time I selected a pediatric authority who had written several books avidly applauding the importance of catering to a baby's needs. When we met with Dr. Lee Salk, he almost pleaded with us not to let Paul cry. He told us that the most important development in a child's first year of life is the sense of trust. I asked feebly, "But what about his resources? I've heard that comforting babies will prevent them from using their own resources."

He answered without hesitation, "But crying is his resource."

Carol Smaldino, "Tossing and Turning Over 'Crying It Out,'" *Mothering,* Spring 1995.

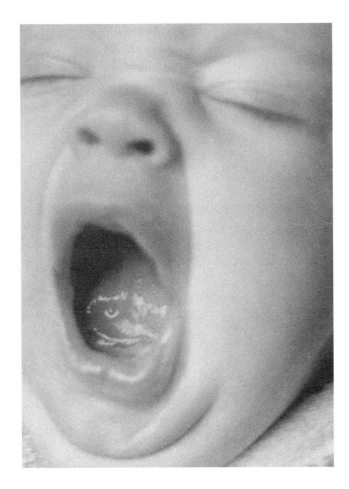

faith in the environment. This aspect of our future approach to relationships is laid down in infancy.

New research results publicized in the last two years underscore Erikson's emphasis on the importance of touch, direct attention, and communication during the first three years of life. The research shows that a child's intellectual and emotional well-being are as dependent on sufficient physical contact with nurturing adults as they are on sufficient nourishment.

So, though many child development experts argue that a baby who is well fed and dry has no business being up in the middle of the night, we argue that your child may well have important reasons for calling out to you. She may be about the business of soliciting your warm touch for the sake of feeding her soul—and her brain.

Child Development and Night Waking

To suggest that we can teach or discipline an infant to sleep in a prescribed way assumes a psychological sophistication that the human infant simply does not possess. The human infant does not yet engage in self-reflection, and so will probably not associate a "punishment" with an "offense." Even if the infant can make the association, it is questionable whether he will remember it the next time the same situation occurs. And even if he does remember, he has only minimal self-control. The only way to regulate sleep habits, therefore, is through behavior modification, a method we usually reserve for the socially miscreant.

Children do begin very early to develop a style for handling interactions between themselves and others. Using behavior modification can set up an adversarial relationship between parent and child, because rather than honoring the special integrity of each child, it suppresses the child's will. Parents who desire a future cooperative relationship with their children begin by acknowledging a child's natural developmental schedule and working within it. Ironing out the developmental "kinks" requires loving patience, not harsh methods.

Melvin Konner asserts in his book, *Childhood*, that our modern methods of letting babies "cry it out" would be considered child abuse in most traditional cultures. He writes of the !Kung children in southern Africa who, "despite their intense early dependency," grow up strong, independent, and deeply committed to their extended family bands. Upon hearing a translation of Dr. Spock's suggestion for unspoiling a child by leaving him to cry until he figures out crying is not going to get him anywhere, a !Kung mother replied: "Doesn't he understand he's only a baby, and that's why he cries? You pick him up and comfort him. Later, when he grows older, he will have sense, and then he won't cry anymore."

"The !Kung," Konner points out, "bet on maturation—and they have never yet had a child who didn't outgrow crying."[1]

The Family Bed

If you ask an Italian or Japanese or African mother whether her baby sleeps through the night, she won't know how to respond to the question. That is because in two-thirds of the cultures around the world, babies sleep with their mothers, who instinctively soothe them back to sleep before either mother or child has fully awakened. The United States is one of the few societies in the world in which babies are left alone to sleep in their own rooms.

In other cultures, family sleeping is not just a product of a lack of adequate space. In Japan, for example, where babies sleep with parents and older children sleep with grandparents, siblings, and other relatives, the practice reflects the strength of family bonds, and children's sleeping with parents expresses a strong cultural emphasis on the nurturant aspects of family life.

To mothers around the world, sharing a family bed has many advantages. Everyone sleeps better: Parents don't have to get out of bed in the middle of the night to put a baby back to sleep, and babies are not left alone to cry long enough to awaken. There are no drawn-out bedtime rituals. Children do not view bedtime as something to be fought, but can go to sleep peacefully in the security of knowing that they are not alone in the

middle of the night. Children are more securely attached, and parents are more well-rested.

Despite these advantages, however, attitudes against co-sleeping are highly ingrained in American culture. Meredith Small, in her 1998 book, *Our Babies, Ourselves* points out that 88 percent of American pediatricians recommend that babies sleep in a crib in their own room, and 65 percent believe that babies should not receive any parental contact in the night. The message from the medical establishment is that it is somehow unhealthy or improper to sleep with your children. The idea is promoted that children who are allowed to sleep in bed with their parents will never learn to sleep alone. On September 29, 1999, the Consumer Product Safety Commission (CPSC) warned against placing babies in adult beds, based on a retrospective study that reviewed 2,178 case summaries from CPSC Death Certificate File.

This study was met by strong international criticism for relying on an incomplete, anecdotal and unreliable database. In most of the reported cases where a baby died in an adult bed, there was no indication of whether an adult was actually present in the bed at the time of the infant's death. Neither was critical information given regarding the infant's sleep position, maternal smoking, maternal breastfeeding, or the reasons for bedsharing.

Twenty other peer-reviewed scientific papers, including research in Great Britain and New Zealand, have demonstrated the safety of intentional bedsharing.

In fact, co-sleeping may be a factor in preventing Sudden Infant Death Syndrome (SIDS). Sleep researcher James McKenna suggests a link between solitary sleep and SIDS, pointing out that the SIDS rate in Asian populations, where co-sleeping is the norm, is a fraction of that in Western societies. Observing mother-infant pairs as they slept in the same bed in a "sleep lab," he noted that co-sleeping mothers constantly cuddle, reposition, and comfort their babies, without even being conscious. "One possible consequence of solitary infant sleeping is that infants will sleep too much—too long and too hard," says McKenna. "The sensory intrusions of co-sleeping partners (a sudden nudge, noise, touch, or sleep movement) provide the infant with practice in arousing within his or her natural ecology, and thus serve the infant should some internal respiratory mishap require a quick and efficient awakening."

Many advocates of the family bed believe that the practice is more common in the United States than most people are willing to admit. Tine Thevenin, who wrote *The Family Bed: An Age-Old Concept in Child Rearing* in 1986, asks, "Why, in the span of four or five generations, have we come to believe that separate sleeping is the only 'right' thing to do and that sleeping together leads to all sorts of horrible consequences?"

Parent Development and Night Waking

Once we become parents, it is easy to blame ourselves when our children's behavior seems out of our control. The pervasive idea that we should be able to control sleep habits leads us too quickly to call night waking a "sleep disorder" and to wonder what we are doing wrong to cause it. Research gives no indication that anything parents do causes night waking. Babies whose cries are responded to rapidly are not more prone to it. Assuming that there is some method out there to treat sleep "disorders" undermines a parent's confidence. Despite the notion that "healthy, normal" babies sleep through the night, surveys of parents show that most babies do not sleep through the night, at least not until all their teeth are in.

Social worker Carol Smaldino worries about the possibility that parents who follow the prescription to let their children "cry it out" must necessarily distance themselves from their own feelings, "perhaps unaware of just how far from compassion people can go as they become isolated from any awareness of their emotions." Becoming "hard hearted" toward night waking children—which is Dr. Spock's term for the process—is not a positive developmental shift for parents to make if they want to cultivate a family whose relationships are based on trust, integrity, and emotional soundness.

While waiting for our children to develop physically and emotionally to the point where they can realistically soothe themselves to sleep, we need to work on our own development toward tolerance, patience, and acceptance of those aspects of parenting that are beyond our control. What remains in our control is the ability to continue to care for our children even though they are keeping us awake at night; to continue to hold on to our own integrity as feeling people.

To embrace a philosophy that takes into account the individual needs of each child is not to ignore the unfortunate reality that we need sleep. We need to nurture ourselves in this process of raising children. The key to tolerance, and a natural passage through the night waking years, is to observe, accept, and work with your child's own inner rhythms and timetables, which can lead to the understanding that nurturing your child and nurturing yourself are not mutually exclusive enterprises.

Why Babies Wake at Night

Sleep is an instinct and a need, not a skill or a habit. It is not something we can try to do. We can try not to sleep, but eventually it will overcome us. Studies have determined that infant wakefulness is not simply a function of hunger, but that there may be pre-existent, sleep-wakefulness rhythms in newborns that varies greatly from child to child. Each baby is born with individual sleep patterns already established, and each gradually develops new patterns depending on the maturity of the central nervous system along with the child's personality, need for sleep, and sensitivity to her surroundings. As with talking, walking, self-discipline, and toilet learning, each child develops a mature approach to sleep at her own pace.

Many pregnant women have noticed that when they slow down and/or sleep, especially in the last trimester, their baby will stretch and/or readjust his position. Pregnant women have also reported that after they get up to urinate in the early hours of the morning, their babies get active. Thus, many babies' night waking patterns begin even before birth.

A Swiss pediatrician named Stirnimann found that infants' sleep patterns (early risers or late nighters) were directly related to the mothers' sleep habits during pregnancy. Early rising mothers bore early rising babies, and vice versa. Stirnimann showed that unborn babies can adjust their rhythms to their mothers' with great precision.[2]

Further studies suggest a strong connection between the length of labor and state of the baby upon delivery and the child's sleep needs.

As an infant grows, all the different systems of the body mature, but it really takes about two years for the nervous and immune systems to mature enough to foster the ability to sleep through the night on a regular basis. Many growth-related processes can interrupt sleep—teething, growing pains, an increased perception and awareness. Expecting a child to learn not to wake up, with all that is happening inside him and around him, is just not realistic.

Some of the common causes for wakefulness that are listed below can, if recognized, be prevented. Others are an inevitable part of growing and developing, and they require our understanding and compassion.

HUNGER

Having been constantly nourished in the womb, a newborn experiences hunger for the first time. During the first few months of life, an infant must wake to nurse, since human milk is low in fat content. Later, growth spurts will lead to sudden increases in the amount of food a baby needs. In the first year of life, a baby triples her birth weight; a growth phenomenon that will not be equaled at any other time. It is common for a baby who has slept through the night for several weeks to suddenly go through a period of night waking in order to eat more than before and increase your milk supply. (See Breastfeeding, Chapter 4.)

Allan

Mark complains often, after he has gone to bed, that his legs hurt. We have concluded, since my daughter and many of her friends experienced the same discomfort, that it is "growing pains." I used to put Tiger Balm on my daughter's legs until I started using homeopathic remedies. Now I give them a dose of Calcarea Phosphorus when they need it, the pains go away and they sleep through the night. I was interested to learn that the remedy is made from calcium and phosphorus; which is what bones are made of.

ENVIRONMENTAL FACTORS

A room that is too warm or too cold, or clothing that is too confining can all wake a child. We often dress our children more warmly and wrap them more tightly for sleep than is reasonable. The rule of thumb is to dress your child for bed the same way you dress yourself. If you are wearing loose cotton pajamas and sleeping under a sheet in warm weather, that is probably just what your child needs. If you are under a thick, down-filled duvet with flannel pajamas, dress your baby accordingly.

OVERSTIMULATION

Just as adults have trouble falling asleep or staying asleep when overstimulated, babies become overstimulated by their environment. Children who feel, see, and hear things more acutely than others—those who have low sensory thresholds—are often night wakers. If your baby or toddler is waking during the night, keep a record of what sorts of stimulation he is receiving during the day. A trip to the mall, an afternoon with older, rowdy children, an evening of roughhousing—all can lead to overstimulation and night waking.

TEETHING

It has been said that, short of childbirth, teething is the most painful experience any of us will endure in the normal course of events. New teeth are as sharp as little needles. First they must descend through, and thus cut, the gums; then, the sharpness needs to be planed with biting down and teeth grinding—if in fact other teeth are in place to serve as grinders. The process of getting new teeth, for many babies, upsets their whole system. Constant drooling is the norm along with fretfulness, agitation, and sometimes even sickness because the immune system is more vulnerable.

ILLNESS

Babies and toddlers are often fretful at the onset of illness before any other symptoms present themselves. Some babies naturally sleep with their mouths closed; if they have a cold they may wake continually because their nasal congestion means they cannot breathe. Constipation and other digestive difficulties will cause pain hours before you can figure out what is bothering your baby, and earaches and ear infections are more painful than most adults realize.

BUG BITES AND PINWORMS
Even the cleanest houses are prone to mosquitoes, fleas (if you have pets), and the occasional tiny spider. If you are getting bitten by fleas and mosquitoes, you can be sure your baby is, too. Keep corners and crevices vacuumed. If an older child gets a painful case of worms, be sure to check the baby for worms, too.

DREAMS AND NIGHT TERRORS
Falling asleep can be frightening for one reason or another. Dreams and nightmares are very real to children and can be intensified by TV, stories involving monsters and death, and other outside influences. Night terrors are physiologically different from nightmares. Terrors happen during deep sleep and may be the result of an immature central nervous system. The child screams or cries, and does not wake, but seems almost to be hallucinating. Heart and respiratory rates are elevated. Night terror can be a frightening, wrenching experience for parents unfamiliar with the phenomenon because the child may continue to scream or cry without waking up. Night terrors are not uncommon, especially in two-year-olds. But if they continue for more than a week, consult your doctor or healthcare practitioner.

SLEEPWALKING AND TO THE MOON
Sleepwalking also occurs in deep sleep and is more prevalent than we realize. Children who sleepwalk often share a common thread: The episodes occur during a full moon—with the child walking toward a window facing the moon. One theory is that the moon's rays are a strong energizer. There is even a homeopathic remedy for sleepwalking called Luna (naturally). The full moon phenomenon is fairly common, but many people are embarrassed to admit it happens to their child.

OVERTIREDNESS
Many sleep experts agree that depriving a child of a needed nap will not help the child fall asleep or sleep for a longer stretch at night. A child who misses her nap may actually have more trouble sleeping at night. Similar to being overstimulated, her brain continues to work at a high level, though her body may be craving sleep. Simple physical exercise like running and playing outside are rarely overstimulating.

SEDENTARINESS
Lack of exercise and fresh air may inhibit sound and refreshing sleep. Finding a balance between enough exercise and too much stimulation is sometimes difficult, especially since a child's needs and sensitivities in these areas are constantly changing.

DIET
Diet definitely affects many children and their ability to fall asleep and stay asleep. Some children are more sensitive than others to sugar, food additives (especially artificial colorings), caffeine, citrus, apple juice, and other foods. Caffeine is transmitted to nursing babies in breast milk. Raw broccoli and onions are believed to cause stomach acid in nursing infants. Because every child is different, diet is an area where observation is important. If you notice that every time you eat certain foods, your nursing baby wakes in the night with colic, then your solution to that period of night waking is easy to see.

David
One night our two-year-old daughter woke every fifteen or twenty minutes all night long. She was miserable; desperate for sleep but unable to keep her mind still. My wife and I were beside ourselves with worry and our own exhaustion. Before we called the doctor in the morning, my wife suddenly remembered something about the potluck dinner we had attended the night before. Iced tea had been served, and our daughter, who had become an inveterate moocher, almost certainly had charmed any number of people into sharing their drinks with her. Lots of children we know drink caffeinated drinks and have no ill effects. But we have since learned that even a little chocolate or a cola will set our daughter off on a caffeine high for hours.

ACTIVE, BRIGHT, DETERMINED YOUNG WORKAHOLICS

You know how you feel when you start a new project and are full of ideas about how to go about it. You lie awake, thinking of strategies and even get up to jot down your ideas before they are lost. A lot of babies practice in their sleep their newest accomplishments and challenges, from rolling over to crawling and walking, and often these activities wake them up. When toilet learning begins, toddlers are particularly prone to wake up either just before or just after they urinate.

OTHER POSSIBILITIES

There are, of course, medical reasons for night waking that should be looked into when all else fails. Low sensory thresholds that relate to inadequate levels of cortisone can be a cause of night waking. Another more obscure cause is Cerebral Allergy or Allergic-Tension Fatigue Syndrome. Some children have low blood sugar or experience a severe drop in blood sugar when they sleep. Others may have an imbalance in their central nervous system, or a glandular or mineral imbalance. Mold in mattresses, petrochemicals, a down comforter, or a sleeping bag can be an irritant that interferes with relaxing sleep. Talk to

your healthcare practitioner if you suspect a systemic cause for night waking.

If you can discover what is causing your baby to wake up at night, even if you can't make the situation better, you are much more likely to accept and tolerate the behavior. If you can solve the problem—warm up the room, remove some layers, quit serving chocolate desserts, stop wrestling with the kids right before bedtime—consider yourself lucky. If teething, illness, those six mosquito bites he got at the picnic, or a two-week growth spurt is the problem, then you probably will save your sanity best if you take the attitude that you cannot control this situation, and let nurturing your child through these rough patches be your reward for lost sleep.

Very often, however, there is no identifiable "cause" for night waking—it is simply a normal pattern for children. Recognizing this, you might try some of the following techniques for helping yourself and your child make the best of those middle-of-the-night-encounters.

How to Nurture a Child in the Wee Hours

Despite our best efforts at anticipating the cause of night waking and cutting it off at the pass, almost every child goes through several periods of wakefulness in the first few years of life. The crux of the issue, then, is how we choose to deal with the situation. To keep the family in balance, we think first of comforting and nurturing the child, and then, but no less important, of nurturing ourselves. Following are some suggestions:

FEED THE HUNGRY BEE

A catch phrase during the 1960s, "feed the hungry bee" means: When someone is in distress, don't ask whether or not he has a good reason to be in distress, or whether he deserves to be bothering you with his problems, just go over there and feed him—with real food, hugs, a sense of belonging, or whatever he needs to feel better.

Go to your baby when she is crying. Pick her up. Reassure her that you are always with her and that you are there to meet her needs. Do not worry that you are teaching her to be dependent. Believe that you are teaching her that she has a certain amount of control over her environment; that she should trust in her ability to get results; that it is all right to ask for help; that when she asks for help, she will not be rejected; that the resource she has at her disposal, whether it be crying or calling out your name, is a useful resource for effecting change.

Don't worry that she will become selfish or will always use crying to get what she wants. She will soon enough abandon crying when her range of resources becomes more sophisticated.

Nancy

Night calls. My husband gets them every sixth night because he's a doctor. I get them nearly every night because I'm a mom. It's part of my job. I can choose to love it or hate it. So I love it and hate it. I hate feeling tired the next day, but I love sharing the stillness of the night with my children. For a few minutes, I can pretend there's me and them and no one else. All too soon, friends and activities and school and teachers will come into our circle of love, and I will miss my night calls.

Nancy Sleeth, "Night Calls," *Mothering*, Winter 1992.

Jane

When each of our children were babies, we brought them to bed with us so I could nurse throughout the night. Once they weaned, however, I thought they should be sleeping in their own beds, and moved them down the hall.

Bedtime became a major production, and middle-of-the-night wakings were the norm. More often than not, my husband would end up in one of the children's beds for the duration of the night after soothing them back to sleep. Or all three children would crawl in with me, crowding my husband out into another room.

Finally, we put a futon on the floor next to our bed. Instead of making the children start out in their own rooms, we surrendered to letting them sleep together on the "little bed" each night. They slept soundly and securely, and we got to cuddle with each other again. My husband, who resisted the idea at first, now says he loves to lie awake in the middle of the night and listen to the quiet breathing of his four favorite people in the world.

CONSIDER THE FAMILY BED

Taking your cue from other cultures, try bringing your children to bed with you. There is no one way to do it—whatever arrangement works best for your family is the one that is right for you. You can start your baby out in your bed, lying down with her at bedtime until she falls asleep. You can put her bassinet or crib at the foot of your bed and bring her into your bed to nurse when she awakens in the middle of the night.

Once you have more than one child, if your bed starts to get crowded, you can invest in a king-sized bed, push twin beds into place beside your bed, or put a futon or mattress on the floor next to your bed.

Some parents worry that their sex lives will suffer if they bring the children into their bed. Remember that bed is not the only place for intimacy. Stolen moments in other rooms can sometimes be more spontaneous and romantic. If your children start out in their own beds, you can make love before their middle-of-the-night wakings, or if they are heavy sleepers, you can be quietly intimate while they slumber on the futon. There are many ways to be creative about your relationship and to nurture your children at the same time.

MAKE NURTURING YOUR CHILDREN EASY ON YOURSELF

The easiest way to nurture your baby in the middle of the night is simply to roll over and offer her your breast. Start your baby out in your bed, and you will both sleep better.

Some parents keep a bed or pallet made up and ready in their baby's room, so that they can crawl in with the wakeful child and go back to sleep with very little disturbance. Nursing mothers find the extra bed invaluable. If you take a few minutes to get situated, you can fairly quickly go back to sleep with the baby nursing herself to sleep soon after.

Practicing relaxation techniques while nursing or holding a wakeful child not only enhances your own ability to go back to sleep, but many mothers and fathers report that their own deep breathing or meditations seem to transfer a sense of calm to the child. If you yourself have trouble sleeping while holding or nursing your child, then have available a warm wrap, sit or lie in a comfortable position with the child resting against your heart or on your shoulder, and begin, first, to breath deeply and rhythmically. With your eyes closed, focus on your breath by counting slowly as you inhale and exhale, trying to make each breath equal in length. This is an excellent time to practice the meditations you always wish you had more time for.

Many a father has discovered, to his complete surprise, the joys of snuggling with a child in the stillness of the night. When the need to nurse is not the issue, fathers report that the experience of going to a small child in a dimly lit room and falling asleep with him in the spare bed, with perhaps a lullaby or two on the tape, is a deeply enriching experience.

LET GO OF THE IDEA THAT YOUR CHILD IS TRYING TO MANIPULATE YOU

Just let it go.

GET YOUR SLEEP WHEN YOU CAN; IT WILL BE ENOUGH

There is nothing fun or romantic about sleep deprivation. It can make you grouchy, ineffective, and more susceptible to stress than usual. Though parents who are well out of the night waking years report that the time when they were dealing with sleep deprivation seemed like a short time, parents who are in the thick of it report that a few weeks with night waking children seem like a lifetime. They can't remember what it is like to feel "well rested."

Sleep experts have found that replacing lost sleep need not be an hour-for-hour proposition. The early "delta" sleep that we need to rejuvenate our bodies is not lost in the typical night waking scenario, but parents with wakeful children are often deprived of rapid-eye-movement (REM) sleep, the later, "dream" stage that creative people and problem solvers particularly need. However, when someone has been deprived of REM sleep, research shows that he or she gets to that level of sleep more quickly the next time and spends more time there.

The foremost and best advice to parents of a baby is, "sleep when the baby sleeps." No matter what time of the day or night that happens to be,

Dave

When my daughter was born, I discovered that I knew lullabies. I love to sing, though I'm not all that good at it. These lullabies just came up out of some deep well of memory, and eventually I learned more from my wife and our friends. When the baby didn't need to nurse, especially when she got a little older, I loved nothing more than sitting in the rocker beside her crib in the middle of the night, holding her ear next to my chest while I sang low enough to avoid waking my wife. My daughter never minded if I was slightly off-key. And I knew it was the deep vibrations of my singing that soothed her back to sleep. I will never forget that feeling. I was in heaven.

allow yourself to fall into restful sleep with full knowledge that the baby is safely asleep.

The concept of "the power nap," formerly known as "the cat nap," is popular with everyone from business executives to graduate students, and it is an excellent resource for parents. Most health practitioners report that falling asleep for ten minutes is far more refreshing than sleeping for an hour or two to make up for an hour or two missed the night before. One mother reports that no matter how tired she is, all she needs to do is reach that level of "unconsciousness" for a minute or two, and she wakes feeling absolutely rejuvenated.

Working mothers and fathers find time for the power nap at their desks, or, if privacy is an issue, many go to their cars during lunch and close their eyes there. Riding the bus or train home is also an excellent place for that moment of "unconsciousness." Some work-sites have a lounge with cots available, and in some states, if such a space is requested, employers must provide it.

At-home mothers and fathers frequently speak of the mid-morning television programming for toddlers as a godsent time for power napping. By first making sure that their children are paying rapt attention to what's on the screen, that the room with the television is childproofed, and that their children cannot open the door to the rest of the house, they doze blissfully, if briefly, and find their dreams are pleasantly permeated with the songs of Big Bird, Elmo, and Mr. Rogers.

TRY NOT TO KEEP TRACK OF HOW MANY HOURS OF SLEEP YOU'VE SLEPT

It is best to avoid looking at the clock each time you get up. If you find yourself saying every day, "I only slept four hours last night," you will probably feel more tired than you would if you can't really say exactly how much you slept—or didn't sleep.

Janet

With one child waking, I learned to accept interrupted sleep, but with three children waking, I've learned to accept less sleep. I've survived, and actually, survived quite well. In the process I've realized that eight hours of uninterrupted sleep is a myth. After all, several presidents coped with the stress of their job by taking numerous cat naps. Good chunks of sleep are sometimes necessary, but I can function well on a steady diet of small stretches. When my intellectual and physical resources were exhausted, I found that prayer worked wonders—prayers for the children to sleep better and prayers for the physical and emotional strength to carry on.

Janet Jendron, "The Case of the Night Wakers," *Mothering* Publications, 1983.

GO FOR THE NURTURE

Parenting is not a 9-to-5 job. Your role as a nurturing parent does not end once the lights go out. Many parents who set out to wean their children at three months of age and are determined to let them "cry it out" at night until they get over it, find themselves still nursing their children a year later. Said one mother, "Our pediatrician tells us it's bad to nurse beyond one year and it's best to let our children put themselves back to sleep at night. Our hearts, however, tell us it's wrong to let them cry it out."

THIS, TOO, SHALL PASS

Tailor your night waking solutions technique to your own level of comfort, remembering always that your babies are not trying to manipulate you; that meeting their needs is a way of ensuring they will not grow up needy; that by nurturing them you can nurture yourself; that you can recoup some lost sleep; and that this, too, like all other phases of your children's brief time with you, shall pass.

CHAPTER 9

Attachment Parenting

Babies in Bali are considered divine. They are held in arms day and night—attached, in effect, to their mothers' bodies—for the first six months of life, and they are literally not allowed to touch the earth until a ground-touching ceremony takes place on their half-year birthday.

Even if you do not know what attachment parenting is, you may be doing it. Like those mothers in Bali, people around the globe have practiced attachment parenting without ever having heard of it. Coined in the early Nineties, the phrase "attachment parenting" describes what is actually the oldest form of child-rearing, the form practiced by most cultures around the world. The fact that we have had to invent a phrase for it tells us how far our American society has diverged from this style of parenting.

What Is Attachment Parenting?

Attachment parenting—or "responsive," or "in-arms" parenting—recognizes the strong attachment babies have to their mothers and encourages close physical contact between children and their mothers until the children are ready to become more independent.

In practice, attachment parenting means carrying your infant for much of the time during the first six months, breastfeeding on demand, and bringing your child into bed with you at night. Adopting this approach means responding to your child's needs to be held and to be near you, with-

out fear of spoiling the child. It means allowing your child to decide when she is ready to wean from your breast and your arms.

Although attachment parenting may sound like an all-consuming approach to parenthood, it is, in many ways, the easiest, most natural way to raise children. The more contact you have with your child, the more adept you become at reading his body signals, and the more responsive you can be to his needs—often before he even articulates those needs. The more your child is held, the happier he will be, and the more you will want to be around him. The more you hold your child and nurse him on demand, the higher your levels of prolactin and oxytocin—the "mothering" hormones—will soar, reinforcing your commitment to this style of parenting.

Attachment parenting is instinctive parenting. You do not need a book to tell you how to do it—your instincts will tell you what you need to know, and if they do not tell you right away, your child will guide you with her demands. Babies are biologically programmed to let us know what they need, if we just listen to them.

The Art of "Babywearing"

The key to getting attached is "wearing" your baby—carrying your baby in a sling, backpack, or front-carrier. In most developing countries, women have devised cloth wraps to hold their babies securely against their bodies as they go about their daily business. In American culture, we isolate our babies in strollers, infant seats, battery-operated swings, and cribs, when what they crave most is simply the comfort and protection of their mothers' warm, available bodies.

A baby carrier enables you to keep your baby in contact with you as much as you like while you get housework done, talk on the phone, and run errands. The advantage to a sling, as opposed to a backpack or front-carrier, is that it allows for a wide variety of carrying positions, accommodating newborns to toddlers. Another advantage to a sling is that it slips easily over your head, with no snaps or buckles, allowing you to use it on and off throughout the day. You can also breastfeed your baby while she is in the sling: It functions as a cover-up, allowing you to nurse discreetly, hands-free, whenever and wherever your baby needs it. However, a front-carrier or backpack will still accomplish the same goal of keeping your baby in contact with you.

The basic sling design is a rectangular piece of fabric, with a tail at one end and rings at the other end to loop the tail through. You slip it over your head and one arm, and position the baby so that he is cradled in the fabric of the sling. There may be a cushioned shoulder pad for comfort and padded edges for added security. You can make your own fabric sling, or buy one in baby stores or through one of the sources listed in Resources.

The Benefits of Babywearing

Pediatrician William Sears, father of eight children and author of ten books on attachment parenting, originated the term "babywearing" after observing women in other cultures carrying their babies all day in a sling. When he asked these mothers why they carried their babies, they cited two reasons: It makes the baby happier, and it is easier for the mother. What more could you ask for? Here are some of the other benefits to babywearing.

CARRIED BABIES CRY LESS
Being carried in a sling eases a baby's transition from the womb to the outside world. As you move about, your motion and the sound of your heartbeat are familiar and comforting to your baby. Car-

ried babies do not need to cry because their needs are met instantly. Mothers who carry their babies become sensitive to their baby's cues and can anticipate their needs even before they cry.

CARRYING HELPS BABIES THRIVE
Sears believes carried babies thrive better because a baby who uses less energy for crying has more left over for growing. Babies who expend tremendous energy to get the attention they crave, he feels, do so at the expense of their development.

CARRYING HELPS BABIES LEARN
Being carried may be more than just soothing to a baby—it may be essential for his brain development. The cerebellum—the part of the brain that is involved in emotional behavior and that regulates muscle coordination—is the only part that continues to develop long after birth. According to neurologist Richard Restak, optimal development of the cerebellum is stimulated by motion. Restak states that "physical holding and carrying of the infant turns out to be the most important factor responsible for the infant's normal mental and social development."[1]

Babies who cry less spend more time in a state of quiet alertness—the state in which a baby is most receptive to learning. A baby in your arms or a sling sees the world from your perspective, and she gets to absorb all the fascinating sights, sounds, and smells of the world from your level. You do not need expensive developmental toys or infant stimulation classes to give your child a head start in intelligence—all you need is to lift your baby into your arms and let her experience what the world has to offer.

CARRYING HELPS BABIES DEVELOP MOTOR SKILLS
Contrary to what you might think, babies who spend most of their first six months in arms are not stunted in their motor development. Quite the opposite is true. Your in-arms baby gets to passively participate in your motion, preparing him for the next stage when he is ready to crawl. Carried babies actually demonstrate better motor development skills than babies who are not carried, according to Sears, perhaps because their energy is directed toward growing rather than fussing.

BABYWEARING HELPS BUSY MOTHERS

By carrying your baby in a sling, you are able to continue your daily routine with your baby in tow. Rather than feeling overwhelmed by your infant's demands and frustrated at your inability to get anything done, you can attend to your baby's needs while you prepare meals, clean the house, go out with friends, even work. Babywearing allows you to truly "have it all."

Getting Started Babywearing

Instead of putting your baby down for most of the day, get used to carrying her in the sling as you go about your daily activities. When she falls asleep, you can either continue to carry her, or lay her down—still in the sling—and slip yourself out of it. When you go out for a walk or to run errands, carry your baby in a sling rather than a stroller, where she can touch and see you. When you meet a friend for coffee, instead of lugging a heavy infant seat out of the car, transfer your baby into the sling, where she can join in your conversation and nurse when she needs to. You may soon find you get used to taking your baby with you wherever you go—to the store, out to dinner, to the movies or a museum (your baby should not disturb anyone because you can nurse her before she fusses).

Most slings come with drawings and descriptions of the many different carrying positions possible. Newborns like to be cradled in the security of the sling or snuggled face-first against your chest. As your infant develops more neck control, you can place her with her head resting on the padded edges of the sling, so she can see more of the world. The "kangaroo-carry" positions your baby facing out, with her back against your chest, held securely in the pouch of the sling. A toddler can ride on your hip or on your back, with her bottom resting in the sling and her legs dangling out.

Once you have become accustomed to carrying your baby in a sling, you may begin to develop a new mindset about what is natural for babies. Rather than leaving your baby in a crib, infant seat, or swing for long periods of time, to be picked up only to be fed or played with, you can begin to make the shift toward carrying your baby with you most of the time, only putting her down for short intervals. You may find that the more you carry your baby, the more natural it feels. Many mothers who become used to having their babies close to them say that they feel "naked" without them.

The Nature of Dependency

Human babies are the most dependent of all mammal newborns. We have the largest brains in the animal kingdom, with the majority of our brain growth occurring outside the womb—otherwise our heads would never fit through the birth canal. Thus we are born undeveloped, with our nervous system still in the process of growing—a process that takes three more years. Some researchers refer to the total gestation period of a human baby as eighteen months: nine months in the womb, and nine months out of it. Just as your baby was rocked constantly and fed continually in your womb, he will be happiest when held in your arms and nursed on demand at your breast during the development period outside of the womb, for at least the next six to twelve months.

Because babies are born helpless, they are hard-wired for survival. In prehistoric times, infants who were kept near their parents survived despite predators. As a result of our millions of years of hunter-gatherer inheritance, babies have a built-in alarm that signals anxiety when they are separated from their primary caregivers. We are born thinking saber-tooth tigers are still out there.

Americans, however, have a cultural bias against dependency. Our culture teaches us that children need to sleep in their own beds to develop independence; that carrying a baby too much will produce a clingy child; that child-rearing "experts" are best qualified to tell us when our children should sleep through the night or wean from the breast.

Children do not need to "learn" independence; it cannot be taught. Independence is a natural state that children grow into, just as they move from crawling to walking, from babbling to talking. A child can only become independent after she has had an opportunity to experience and outgrow dependency. Begrudging dependency because it is not independence is like begrudging winter because it is not yet spring. Dependency grows into independence in its own time.

Researcher Mary Ainsworth has confirmed that the indulgence of early dependency leads to independence. She found that maternal responsiveness and close bodily contact are associated with the unfolding of self-reliance, and that the reduced anxiety levels that result when attachment needs are met—a phenomenon she refers to as the "secure base effect"—enable the child to explore his environment with confidence.[2]

Allowing our children to be dependent for as long as they need to be means respecting their inner timetables. Led by society to believe that our children "should" achieve developmental milestones within a prescribed time frame, we lose sight of each child's individual needs. Your child is the only one who knows when she is ready to be put down, to wean, to sleep in her own bed, to use the toilet on her own. Your baby will "let" you put her down when she becomes interested in other things, which will happen soon enough. She will wean from your breast

Linda

My first two boys had demanding temperaments as infants. The older one breastfed in a somewhat scheduled manner, and I weaned him at nine months. I never let him cry for too long, but it usually took me a while to figure out why he was fussing, and I did not automatically put him to the breast. He slept in a crib down the hall from our room, and although we never let him "cry it out," he had to cry long enough for us to awaken and hear him. Even though I loved to hold, touch, and cuddle him, I used a baby swing, walker, and playpen, even if he fussed. After all, everyone warned me not to spoil him or let him rule the family!

My second son nursed with fewer restrictions and weaned naturally at thirty-three months. It was during his infancy that I learned about family co-sleeping, and although he started out in the crib, he soon spent more time in our bed. I carried him more, leaving the baby paraphernalia unused, and left him with sitters less frequently and for shorter time periods than his older brother. He was a much fussier and clingier baby, and I realize now that maybe the more responsive mothering that he received enabled him to more freely express his needs.

With my third child, I hope that I may heed my own instincts when my fussy, dependent toddler demands my last ounce of patience, and that I may look on it as a privilege to have a baby who demands the very best I have to give.

Linda M. Caplan, "High-Need Mothering," *Mothering*, Winter 1988.

when she no longer needs it. The truth is that you cannot "make" babies or children do anything without overpowering them, and when you do that, you set up an adversarial rather than a cooperative relationship.

Yes, securely attached children may seem more dependent—even needy—than children who are parented in a less responsive way. They get held more and nurse longer because they demand exactly what they need. Those demands are entirely appropriate for a young child. Because their needs are completely fulfilled at each stage of development, they can move on to the next stage with confidence. Only by having their dependency needs met do children grow into independent, confident, secure adults.

Responding to Your Child's Needs

The first three years of a child's life are critical in his development of trust, empathy, and affection, according to Elliot Barker, MD, editor of *Empathic Parenting*. Children whose early needs are gratified in a responsive environment—whose innate desire to be close to their parents day and night is recognized—can internalize the empathy of their parents, and grow into affectionate, sensitive adults. If the child's emotional needs are not met during the early years, his capacity to form secure, attached relationships later in life may be compromised.[3]

A 1998 study confirms the positive effects of responsive parenting. Researcher Steve Bell, PhD, an associate professor of psychology at Berry College, attempted to measure the long-term results of attachment parenting among a group of grown children who were raised according to a responsive, or attachment, parenting philosophy.

For his sample, Bell used fifty-one young adults whose mothers had adhered to the philosophy of responsive parenting, based on allegiance to the principles of La Leche League, an international organization of women who support good mothering through breastfeeding. These grown children had been breastfed as infants on demand for an average of two and a half years, and half of them had slept with their parents for at least the first six months. He compared them to a control group of twenty-nine young adults raised by non-La Leche League participants. The control group of parents did not nurse their children for the most part (less than 30 percent attempted nursing, and the average age at weaning was three months); did not have their babies sleep in bed with them; and were five times more likely to work outside of the home when their children were young.

Bell gave the two groups of young adults three adjustment tests: the Defining Issues Test, which measures moral reasoning; the Psychap Inventory, which measures personal happiness; and the Quality of Life Test, which examines such factors as physical well-being, parent-child relations, and marital relations. He found that the children who were responsively parented were happier and had significantly higher Quality of Life scores than the control group. The responsively parented group also had a higher level of moral reasoning—basing their moral decisions on the needs of others and society—than the control group, who tended to reason according to a personal reward orientation. Though recall bias may have influenced the results, the differences in the two groups were significant.[4]

What Happens When You Do Not Respond

Parents who do not respond to their children's needs—who leave them to soothe themselves in infant seats or swings for long periods of time, or who let them cry it out at night—may feel that their children are well-adjusted because they appear quiet and compliant. What may happen, however, is that children who continually fail to elicit a response give up and learn to accept a lesser level of care. They may become attached to objects—pacifiers or blankets—rather than people; they may stop crying, which is their only means of communication; and they may withdraw into themselves. All of these reactions may be interpreted in our society as independence, when they may actually be evidence of resignation. Psychologist Paul F. Klein, PhD, says, "For a child whose attachment needs are chronically frustrated, anxiety and depression will diminish when attention to the need diminishes. The cost, however, is exorbitant; loss of the ability to trust, loss of the capacity for intimacy, and a diminished ability to empathize with oneself and others."[5]

The societal cost of not parenting responsively may be great. Klein notes that studies confirm the existence of attachment deficiencies in the backgrounds of people with agoraphobia, depression, alcoholism, antisocial personality disorder, and borderline personality disorder. Psychiatrist Elliot Barker, who has done extensive work with

psychopaths, feels that the root of the psychopath's lack of remorse, inability to understand affection, and negative view of other human beings may stem from inadequate nurturing and attachment in early childhood.[6] "In the final analysis," concludes Klein, "the farther we stray from meeting children's attachment needs, the more likely we may be to produce a population skewed toward depression, anxiety, and relationship disorders."[7]

What About Spoiling?

We all love our children and want to do what is best for them. It is the rare mother who lets her child cry or ignores her child's needs because it is simply inconvenient to respond. Instead, in an effort to do "what's best" for our children, we may deliberately ignore them. Why? Because we're afraid of spoiling them. Your friends and relatives will advise you, "Put that baby down—you're spoiling her!" or "You have to let that child cry once in a while so he knows who's the boss!"

Babies are born innocent and trusting. A baby takes it for granted that all his needs will be taken care of from the moment of birth. Responding to your baby's needs will not "spoil" your child—perhaps the only way for a child to "spoil" is through neglect. Babies whose needs are fulfilled in a loving, sensitive environment grow into happy, well-adjusted children who are a pleasure to be around.

Responding to your child's needs doesn't mean making your child the center of your universe. In fact, the opposite is true—for the first few years, at least, your child's universe centers around you. Attachment parenting means honoring your child's needs for closeness—it does not mean giving up your own life. Wearing your baby in a sling allows you to keep your baby with you while you carry on with your daily tasks; bringing your baby in bed with you at night allows you both to sleep peacefully without nighttime struggles and crying.

Brenda

We had been home with our newborn daughter, Grace, four days before our relatives began arriving, descending upon us with gifts and praise, admiration and advice. I was soon told that holding Grace all the time and never letting her "cry it out" would make her "spoiled rotten."

I've always disliked that phrase. Is a "spoiled rotten" baby happy or unhappy? Grace is happy when being held, but I'm told that this spoils her. The belief among my relatives is that if Grace is held and loved "too much," she will become a clinging, dependent prima donna.

Isn't it ironic that a new parent is more likely to be criticized for giving a baby "too much" love than too little?

Brenda Ferguson, "Spoiled Rotten," *Mothering*, Fall 1981.

The Roots of Attachment Parenting

Attachment parenting has its basis in biology. There are two kinds of mammals in the animal kingdom: the "caching" species and the "carrying" species. Caching animals, such as deer, hide their young to protect them while the parents forage for food. The young must remain silent for long periods, so as not to attract predators, and they have internal mechanisms that control their body temperature in their mothers' absence. Mother's milk in the caching species is high in protein and fat because feedings must be widely spaced, and the infants suckle at a very fast rate.

In carrying species, babies are born helpless, without the ability to regulate their bodily functions. They need to be in constant contact with their mothers for protection. The milk of a carrying species is low in fat and protein, designed for continuous, on-demand feeding. The babies of a carrying species suckle slowly, and they cry when out of contact with their parents. Humans, like all higher primates, are a carrying species.

As we have evolved into an industrialized society, we have become distanced from our biology and instincts. But a look at more indigenous cultures reveals that attachment parenting is still the norm throughout most of the world.

Psychotherapist Jean Liedloff, who was one of the first to reintroduce the concept of what she called "in-arms" parenting to the Western world, spent several years in the South American jungle with the Yequana Indians, a Stone Age tribe. She observed that the Indian infants were carried constantly by their parents or siblings and that they napped peacefully while the adults or children carrying them ran, danced, and paddled canoes. She also observed that these were the happiest people she had ever seen. The children were obedient and well-behaved, and almost never cried or fought with each other. The adults were serene and centered.[8]

Jean-Pierre Hallet lived among the Efe Pygmies of Zaire's Ituri Forest on and off for sixty years, and he has lectured and written extensively about them. He describes the bond between child and mother as "like a fruit to its branch." Mothers and their babies are never separated for the first year. Babies are carried naked on the mother's bare chest or back, maintaining skin-to-skin contact. The babies nurse continually, weaning at about five years. Young children sleep between the father and mother.

The Pygmies show a great deal of physical affection for each other. Children are not criticized and do not need to be controlled—they simply follow their elders' lead. The Pygmies are self-respecting and totally secure. They lead a cooperative, joyful lifestyle that is wholly free of aggression. Hallet believes that the Pygmies are the living evidence of our innate goodness—that these forest people demonstrate that when we gently nurture and guide our children without repressive controls, human beings can live together in harmony.[9]

Several groups of researchers have tracked the !Kung San of the Kalahari Desert (better known to most Westerners as "Bushmen," although this is a derogatory colonial term), because they offer a revealing glimpse into our hunter-gatherer past. The !Kung indulge their infants' needs without reservation. Babies are carried in a sling and nurse more or less continually—about four times an hour. Mothers have an empathic understanding of their children and can anticipate their hunger, waking, and defecation. During the first year, the average amount of time an infant fusses before his mother responds is about six seconds.

The infant initiates separation from his mother, beginning to explore his environment by crawling, while the mother remains in sight as a secure home base to return to. Children wean at around three years and continue to get their mothers' almost exclusive attention for about another year.

!Kung children are much more independent than children in industrialized countries. Comparisons between the !Kung and industrialized cultures reveal that !Kung children under five will venture farther away from their mothers and engage in more interactions with other children. A fourteen-year-old !Kung boy can drive a lion away from an antelope carcass with a stick; a young !Kung woman will go out into the desert to birth her baby alone. They are confident, resourceful people.[10]

Giving It a Name

Although this "in-arms" style of parenting has always been the most common way of child-rearing around the world, Western culture has, in the last 200 years, diverged from attachment parenting. It was only 200 years ago that the crib was introduced in Victorian society—up until then, all babies slept with their parents. Anthropologist Meredith Small, who writes about how other cultures parent, says, "…parenting styles in Western culture—those rules we hold so dear—are not necessarily best for our babies. The parental practices we follow in the West are merely cultural constructions that have little to do with what is 'natural' for babies."[11]

After spending years in the jungle with the Yequana tribe, psychotherapist Jean Liedloff developed what she called "the continuum concept"—the idea that the "mother-child continuum" established in the womb needs to continue after birth. The principles of the continuum concept include maintaining constant contact between mother and baby while the mother goes about her business; immediately responding to the baby's needs without showing undue concern or making him the center of attention; and treating the child as welcome and worthy. When the continuum is maintained, Liedloff contends, both mother and child feel "right." In contrast, she argues, children in Western cultures develop a sense of wrongness and shame about their desires when they are excluded from normal adult activities, and their cries are ignored.[12]

Pediatrician William Sears adapted Liedloff's concept to contemporary parenting styles, and, as mentioned earlier, popularized the terms "attachment parenting" and "babywearing" in the 1980s. The term "attachment" was actually first used to describe the mother-infant bond by British psychiatrist John Bowlby in the 1950s. Bowlby studied children under three who had been separated from their mothers during short or prolonged hospital stays. He was struck by the depth of their attachment to their mothers and their misery upon separation. From his observations, he concluded that even brief maternal separations can be psychologically damaging to young children, and that from the young child's viewpoint no one, not even Dad, can substitute for Mom.[13]

Separation Anxiety

Bowlby found that children go through three phases during prolonged separation from their mothers. At first they will protest the separation with tears, unhappiness, and constant vigilance for their mothers' return—all the typical signs of "separation anxiety." The next stage is marked by despair. Fortunately, most mothers return from their aerobics class or night out on the town before this stage is reached. If, however, Mom has gone away for a week alone with Dad, leaving her eighteen-month-old with his grandparents, the child may appear anxious, listless, and depressed as the separation wears on.

The third stage that Bowlby identified is detachment, which, he contends, can occur within several days to a week of separation. The child, resigning himself to the fact that his mother is gone, no longer seeks his mother, and acts as though he does not recognize her upon her return. Most children never get to this point because the substitute caretaker succeeds in reassuring them with loving care. But some mothers have found after short separations from their young children that the children turned away and refused to acknowledge them for hours or even days after their return.

The effects of separation can be long-term, according to Bowlby. Because the first three years of a child's life are so critical in terms of developing the capacity for affection and trust, prolonged maternal separation during this period can impair a child's ability to form secure, loving relationships later in life, and can lead to chronic withdrawal and depression.[14]

Even brief separations can lead to a deep sense of loss for a child too young to understand the passage of time. In a child's eyes, Mother is not merely absent; she is gone forever. "Most people think that it does no harm to go away and leave a very young child, because they feel the baby does not know the difference. This is not true," says Dr. Lee Salk, author of *What Every Child Would Like His Parents to Know.* "In fact, the opposite is true. The very young child does know, vividly. Because he has very little concept of 'now' and 'later,' a baby does not understand that if you go away you will ultimately come back. . . . If he cannot see you, you are no longer there; in fact, you don't exist."[15]

Separation anxiety is actually a healthy sign, according to researchers who followed ninety-eight mother-child pairs as the children grew from three months to three years old. The researchers concluded that tantrums or clinginess in children whose mothers leave them briefly are healthy expressions of emotional distress, reflecting sound psychological growth. They also concluded that mothers who respond to these outbursts with immediate gestures of comfort help promote a secure relationship and foster their children's later ability to express sadness and anger in appropriate ways. In contrast, mothers who ignore or downplay their children's cries may be contributing to insecure maternal links and eventual problems in coping with volatile emotions.[16]

Limiting any separations from your child in the first few years may make your child better able to deal with separations later on. The same researchers found in their study of ninety-eight children that as three year olds, the children with secure maternal attachments were visibly distressed at their mother's departure, yet able to approach challenging tasks with confidence and motivation during her absence. Those with insecure maternal relationships were more apt to tolerate the separation well, but expressed anxiety, discomfort, and withdrawal in their play. Insecure youngsters who learn to suppress distress responses, say the researchers, may pay an emotional price later on.[17]

Some separation from your child is necessary, of course. But adopting the mindset of taking your baby with you wherever you go can do wonders for your bond with your child and your child's sense of security. There will be time later, when your child is older, for getaways on your own.

Work, Childcare, and Choices

If even brief separations can be traumatic to the mother-child relationship in the early years, then this begs the question, what about going back to work?

Honoring the mother-child attachment does not necessarily mean giving up working when you have a child. Women in all societies have always worked. In tribal cultures, women might gather food or weave baskets, with their babies either carried with them in a sling, or cared for by other members of the village. It is only in Western culture that the notion of women going to work usually means leaving the children behind.

Every mother is a working mother. In looking at your options, it may help to expand your view of "working." Here are some choices you may want to consider.

WORK FROM HOME
Writing, design work, consulting, and sales are just a few of the kinds of jobs you can do from home. In the interest of streamlining, many companies are cutting back on full-time employees and using self-employed freelancers to do work once done solely in offices.

TAKE YOUR BABY TO WORK WITH YOU
Many outside jobs, including selling real estate, shopkeeping, and cleaning houses, allow you to "work and wear"—to wear your baby in a sling while you work.

WORK PART-TIME
Look for a company that is receptive to job-sharing arrangements, or that allows working mothers to cut back their hours or work from home part of the time. Be creative—some moms work odd hours (a nurse might work the night shift at a hospital, for instance, or a pastry chef, the predawn hours in a bakery).

REEXAMINE YOUR FINANCIAL SITUATION
Some families feel they cannot get by without a dual income. For a single mother, certainly, working is a necessity. But many families can live on one income if they simplify their lifestyles. Our consumer culture drives us to provide our children with material objects at the expense of giving them our time. Perhaps you will not be able to afford a new car, or even set aside savings for your children's college education if you cut back

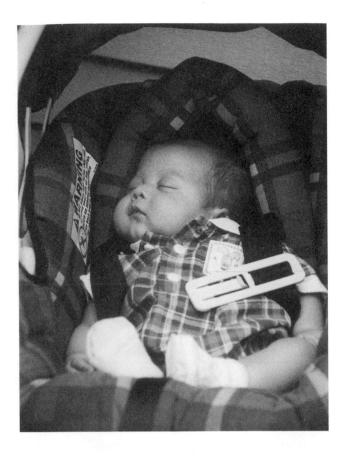

ships, according to Zero to Three, the National Center for Infants, Toddlers, and Families.

Finding a relative or friend to care for your child is ideal. An au pair—a young woman, usually from Europe, who comes to the United States via a government-regulated program to provide live-in childcare for a year—can be an affordable option, but you cannot meet applicants ahead of time. An experienced nanny is the best—and most expensive—choice.

Putting your child in daycare is far from optimal. The high turnover rate among day care staff—second only to that of parking lot and gas station attendants, according to Marcy Whitebook, director of the National Child Care Staffing Study—as well as the minimal, if any, training, and low staff-to-infant ratio mean that your child will most likely get only a fraction of the attention she needs. Moreover, it is hard on a child to be rushed out of the house first thing in the morning to spend all day in an environment that is not home, where she must compete for attention with numerous other babies.

on working. But you will be able to give your children the most important thing you can offer them right now—a head start in life.

When you look at your income, keep in mind the additional expenses you will have to incur in clothing and transportation to work outside of your home, as well as what you have to pay someone else to do while you are working, including childcare, housecleaning, and maybe even laundry. These costs can add up. When you consider that these expenses must, in most cases, be purchased with after-tax dollars, recognize that your pretax income needs to be approximately 30 to 40 percent more than the cost of these services.

IF YOU MUST WORK FULL-TIME, FIND AN IN-HOME CHILD CARE PROVIDER

Ideally, a child needs his mother's attention for the first few years; if that is not possible, the next best thing is the attention of a consistent, in-home caregiver. Having too many caregivers before age three can slow a child's development and leave children reluctant to form new relation-

PUT OFF GOING BACK TO WORK

You cannot possibly learn to be a parent in six to ten weeks. Yet that is when most maternity leave policies end, and women go back to work full-time. Your child's needs are deceptively simple during the first year; you may think that a childcare provider can attend to these needs as well as you can. But the mother-child attachment is particularly important in the early years, and critical in the first six months.

If you can put off going back to work full-time until your child is at least a year old, do. At least for the first three to four months, when you are establishing a strong bond with your baby, it is best not to work at all. "Each extra month of mothering is like money in the bank for both mother and child," says T. Berry Brazelton, MD, author of *Touchpoints*.[18]

QUIT "WORKING"

How can we say that a full-time mother is not working? Is caring for a child "playing?" And how did the most important job in our culture—the duty of raising future generations—get granted such low status? Maybe there will come a time in our society when a woman is looked upon as a better person for devoting herself full-time to nurturing her children. In the meantime, you can derive your own satisfaction from doing the best job you know how at the task of raising your children.

Finding Fulfillment as a Mom

Economics is not necessarily the driving force behind many mothers' decision to work outside the home. One-third of the women who are juggling career and family say they are not working to alleviate financial hardship.[19] Instead, many women maintain their careers once they have children because working brings them personal fulfillment.

It is easy to believe that you will fall off the career ladder or become less "marketable" if you take time off to raise your children. But marketability can be regained; a childhood cannot. Remember when you consider your lost career "potential" that your potential as a mother will never again be quite as profound as it is during your child's first few years. Your career may span forty or more years. Your children will probably live with you for eighteen years; they may only be home for five years before full-time schooling begins; and you will be the center of their universe for only the first three years or so. Three or six or seven years is not a lot of time to take out of an entire career. If you feel that you cannot turn down a job because it seems a once-in-a-lifetime opportunity, consider that parenting is truly a once-in-a-lifetime opportunity.

And yet, staying at home has its challenges also. You have to learn to value yourself for who you are, not for what you do. You have to learn to manage your time yourself (although your kids will do a fine job of teaching you that!). And, you have to realize that although mothering doesn't bring in a paycheck, if you paid someone to do all the things you do, it would cost over $36,000 a year. Some things, however, really cannot be quantified.

Sometimes mothering may feel like a thankless task. Your children expect you to give them the highest quality of care—but you do not get any recognition for it. You may feel taken for granted or undervalued by society. Yet there is no substitute for the quiet, ordinary, irreplaceable moments between a mother and her child.

Staying at home to raise your children does not have to mean giving up personal fulfillment. There are many ways to maintain a career or outside interests from home. As tribal cultures demonstrate, children do not need to be the center of attention to be well-adjusted—they simply need to be kept close and integrated into the activities of their parents. According to Jean Liedloff, young children are uncomfortable when adults are focused on them; rather, they need to be the observers in order to absorb and learn as the adults around them go about the business of daily life.[20]

The Myth of Quality Time

It is tough to fit parenting into neat evening and weekend time slots. "Quality time" cannot make up for quantity time. "Quality time" is a convenient way to rationalize combining career and children. True quality moments happen when you and your child are sharing a peanut butter sandwich or chasing butterflies through the yard, not during a

Ed

My children may never know, and don't need to know, that in recent years, I have been getting out of bed at 5:00 or 5:30 most weekend mornings. That is my time. There is no better time for me to write.

When they roll out at 8:00 or 8:30, it's time for me to stop writing, for they will have something to ask me or tell me. Their energy and enthusiasm will keep them darting past me every twenty-three minutes or so all weekend long. No way can I respond if I'm absorbed in my writing or if I'm engrossed in other favorite projects. Anticipating real quality moments, on a child's terms, means knowing some of that time is their time—literally, on a moment's notice.

Ed Wojcicki, "Forget About Planning Quality Time," *Mothering,* Summer 1992.

scheduled two hours at the park on Saturday morning. Memorable moments defy scheduling. When a child comes home from school with exciting news, it somehow loses its urgency when it has to wait until six o'clock. Toddlers are even less adept at waiting for anything; they need to have their ideas and questions attended to immediately.

True quality time is not a chunk of uninterrupted time set aside by adults to specifically spend time with their children. Rather, quality time is all the moments throughout the day when your child needs you, is receptive to you, or is playing, singing, or talking to you, on her timetable, according to her need. Relationships need quantity time to have quality time.

Moreover, our expectations of "quality time" can be so high that the reality often falls flat. When things don't go according to plan, we may feel resentful or angry—and a planned "quality" moment turns into a disaster. "American parents try to crowd too much emotion into a short span of time," says child psychologist Bruno Bettelheim. "The one thing they cannot do is relax and be themselves, and since they want their emotions at these times to be exclusively positive, they suppress more complex emotions and their relationships with their children become shallow."[21]

Parenting Is Not a 9-to-5 Job

Raising a child demands the best that you have to give. It takes personal sacrifice, a phrase we don't hear much anymore. When you decide to bring a child into the world, you are signing on for a lifetime commitment.

Mothering means being on call twenty-four hours a day, seven days a week, with no vacation time and no sick leave. There are no promotions and no performance bonuses. It is the most all-consuming, frustrating, rewarding, and important job you will ever do. May you give it an effort worthy of your children.

CHAPTER 10

First Food

Your baby is a few months old, and you have established a comfortable breastfeeding rhythm. Then comes the inevitable call from your mother. "What are you feeding that child?" she wants to know. Suddenly you begin to question whether your milk alone is enough for a growing baby. When do you need to start thinking about feeding solid food?

Solid food should not be introduced until your child shows a readiness for it—usually sometime between six months and a year old. Breastmilk is the most nutritionally complete first food you can give your baby. The current American Academy of Pediatrics guidelines recommend that breastmilk be a baby's primary source of nutrition for the first year and that solids not be introduced until a baby is at least six months old.

Solid-Food Myths

You are likely to encounter pressure from everyone from your mother-in-law to your next-door neighbor to feed your baby solids before six months. The reasons that people want to give a baby solid food as soon as possible are often based on misperceptions.

SOLID FOOD DOES NOT HELP A BABY SLEEP THROUGH THE NIGHT

Many people believe that "filling a baby up" on cereal will enable him or her to sleep for longer intervals. One loophole in this argument is that babies wake up for many reasons besides hunger, including a need for comfort and cuddling (see Chapter 8 for more on night waking). A full baby is not necessarily a sleepy baby.

For some babies, the introduction of solid food does coincide with sleeping through the night; but, for others, there is no such correlation. In one study of breastfed and formula-fed six-week-old infants, the babies who were given rice cereal before bed showed no difference in sleep habits compared to those who were not. The researchers did find, however, that the majority of babies in the study—regardless of whether they were given cereal—increased their nighttime sleeping over the course of the fifteen-day study.

Because breastmilk is easily digestible, breastfed babies often wake up at night hungry. However, evidence suggests that night waking is a normal pattern for babies and that waking at night may be necessary for a baby's optimal development. For tips on coping with your child's night waking, see Chapter 8.

SOLID FOOD DOES NOT HELP A BABY GAIN WEIGHT

A breastfeeding mother who is concerned that her baby is not gaining weight quickly enough may think that supplementing with solid food is the answer. However, breastmilk is designed to meet all of a baby's nutritional needs for the first year, with no need for any kind of supplementation.

It is extremely rare for a well-nourished mother not to have enough milk to feed her baby. Because milk supply is regulated by demand, simply nursing longer and more frequently is the way to boost a mother's milk supply and increase a baby's weight gain (see Chapter 4 for more on breastfeeding).

When evaluating your baby's weight gain, keep in mind that the infant growth charts used by most doctors were developed using formula-fed babies. The growth pattern of a breastfed baby may deviate quite a bit from these norms. The most important indicator of your baby's weight gain is his robust appearance.

BREASTFED BABIES DO NOT NEED THE ADDITIONAL IRON IN SOLID FOOD

Infant formula and baby cereals are fortified with iron, leading many parents to conclude that babies need supplemental iron. In fact, most breastfed babies who do not eat solid food for the first year will get all the iron they need from breastmilk. Even though the iron content of breastmilk is low, it is very well-absorbed by the body (50 percent of the iron in breastmilk is absorbable, as opposed to 4 to 10 percent in iron-fortified formula).

The irony is that when babies begin eating solid food, the iron in breastmilk is no longer as well-absorbed. Once a breastfed baby starts solid food, she will need additional iron—either from food sources or from iron supplements such as ferrous sulfate or herbal iron. Baby cereals are fortified with iron, but the form of iron used is so poorly absorbable that it is not a reliable source of iron supplementation. Foods that are naturally high in iron are the best choice. Whole grains are rich in iron; buy or make your own whole grain baby cereal (see recipe, below). Add a sprinkle of iron-rich sea vegetables such as kelp or dulse (available in the Asian foods section of your grocery store) to your baby's food. Other foods high in iron include apricots, peas, and tofu. Cooking foods in a cast-iron skillet can boost their iron content considerably. Foods high in vitamin C enhance the absorption of iron, but a diet high in dairy products can inhibit the absorption of iron.

MY MOTHER THINKS I SHOULD FEED THE BABY SOLIDS

Your mother or mother-in-law is apt to encourage you to feed your baby solids as soon as possible, since it was common wisdom a generation ago to give babies rice cereal starting at about six weeks. (Remember, this generation also believed that formula was superior to breastmilk.)

We now know that a baby's digestive system is not ready to handle solid food before six months, and that breastmilk is the most nutritionally superior food you can give your baby for the first year, according to the American Academy of Pediatrics.

Solid food is more important for formula-fed babies, since formula cannot meet all of a baby's nutritional needs after six months. But for breastfed babies, there is no nutritional reason to introduce solid food earlier than a year.

No Need to Rush

Here are some of the advantages to waiting until after six months to give your baby solids:

DELAYING SOLIDS DECREASES YOUR CHILD'S RISK OF DEVELOPING FOOD ALLERGIES

The earlier a baby is exposed to any food other than breastmilk, the higher the likelihood that he will develop food allergies.[1] A baby younger than six months has an immature digestive system that is not yet ready to handle solid foods. Food given earlier than this can cause adverse reactions. After about six months, a baby begins producing enough digestive enzymes and antibodies to handle solid foods without as high a risk of food allergies.

INTRODUCING SOLIDS TOO EARLY CAN INTERFERE WITH YOUR CHILD'S GROWTH

No solid food can compete with breastmilk as a source of nutrition for the first year. Filling your baby up with solid food prior to age one simply means that she will get less breastmilk. Common first baby foods—cereals, fruits, and vegetables—are low in calories, but high in carbohydrates. These foods can make a baby feel full—causing her to nurse less—without giving her enough calories to maintain proper growth.

Solids can also tip the scales in the other direction: Because it is easy to overfeed solid food to a young baby who cannot let you know when she has had enough, the early introduction of solid foods can lead to obesity later in life.[2] Breastmilk is the perfect food for a baby, containing no empty calories.

WAITING TO INTRODUCE SOLIDS IS MORE CONVENIENT FOR YOU

You may think that life will be easier when your baby begins a diet of solid food, since you will be able to cut out a few nursing sessions. Giving your baby solids is not necessarily more convenient than breastfeeding, however.

Because breastmilk is a baby's best source of nutrition for the first year, you should still continue to offer your baby the breast before each meal of solid food—so in reality you will not be cutting back much on nursing.

The longer you wait to give your baby solids, the less careful you will have to be about what you feed your baby, since an early introduction of solids can lead to food allergies. If you give your

baby's digestive system a chance to mature, it is more likely that you will be able to feed your baby whatever the rest of the family is eating rather than having to prepare special meals.

Your baby will also be better able to feed himself as he gets older. Spoon-feeding a baby is a messy, time-consuming affair, requiring that you prepare or buy special foods. Breastfeeding is transportable, it costs nothing, and you can nurse your baby while you eat dinner with the rest of the family. Why not enjoy the convenience of exclusive breastfeeding for as long as you can?

When Is Your Child Ready for Solid Food?

As with all other developmental milestones, readiness for solid food depends on the baby. Just as with weaning and sleeping through the night, it is best to let your child make the call about when he is ready for an expanded diet. Sometime between six and twelve months, your baby will probably begin to indicate a readiness for solid food. Look for the following signs:

PHYSICAL READINESS

Until a baby shows certain signs of physical development, his digestive system is probably not ready for solids. Sometime between four and six months, a baby loses the tongue-thrusting reflex. Trying to feed him solid food before this reflex is gone will result only in the food being spit back out. The tongue-thrushing reflex seems to be nature's way of protecting the baby against food that he may choke on or that his digestive system is not mature enough to handle.

Signs of readiness for food include the ability to sit up—which can be helpful in swallowing—and the manual dexterity to pick up food and put it in the mouth. The appearance of teeth is sometimes seen as an indicator that a baby is ready for solids. However, teeth are not necessary for chewing food; chewing is done by the molars, which often do not appear until the second year. Babies do very well gumming their food before the molars come in.

HUNGER

A sudden increase in appetite does not necessarily mean your baby is ready for solids; he may simply be going through a growth spurt. If your baby is older than six months, however, and still appears hungry after unrestricted nursing for four to five days, he may be ready to try something new.

INTEREST IN FOOD

Your baby will almost certainly let you know when he is ready for a bite of whatever you are having. Sometime after he can sit up and chew, a baby who previously showed no interest in food will suddenly start watching intently as your spoon goes to your mouth, and he may try to grab food from your plate. This "mooching" is your signal to expand your menu offerings.

Getting Started

First feedings should be small. Until your baby is a year old, food should be viewed as a way to accustom your baby to new tastes and textures and to joining in at mealtimes—not as a source of nutrition. Think of solid food as a condiment rather than as the main course.

Keep foods simple for at least the first few months, to enable you to detect any food sensitivities your baby may have. Introduce each new food alone, rather than in combination with other foods. Feed each new food for three to five days, just a spoonful at a time, and watch for any reaction. Allergic reactions might include a rash around the mouth or bottom, congestion, coughing, wheezing, red eyes, ear infections, constipation, or diarrhea. A mild reaction means you should hold off on serving that food for a few months. A severe reaction should be discussed with your health practitioner.

Foods should be mashed with a fork or put through a food mill until still chunky. A baby who is six months or older should not need to have her food pureed or liquefied. Once your baby is able to pick up small objects between her thumb and forefinger, give her finger foods; just be sure the pieces of food are small enough that they will not present a choking hazard (see "Foods Babies Can Choke On," page 128). And do not ever leave your baby alone while she is eating, in case she does choke or gag.

Continue to breastfeed your baby as much as she wants. Offer your breast before meals, so that she gets most of her calories from breastmilk.

First Foods

Start with foods that are low in protein and easy to assimilate, such as:

FRUIT

Fruits are a good first choice because most babies will be attracted to their sweetness. Bananas are perfect—you can mash them up for a child under nine months, and cut them into small pieces for an older child. Apples and pears can be served stewed and pureed, or grated in small pieces. Peaches and apricots can be mashed or diced. Bits of melon and blueberries make good finger food. Wait until your child is over a year old to serve citrus fruits, as they can be allergenic. Dried fruits such as raisins should be avoided, since they can cause choking and can get stuck between the teeth and cause cavities.

VEGETABLES

After your baby has gotten accustomed to a few fruits, try serving vegetables. Start out with the sweeter, orange varieties: sweet potato, carrots, and winter squash, cooked and mashed. Potatoes, peas, and green beans can be served mashed or diced. Avocado is one vegetable you can serve raw. Wait until your baby is a year before offering corn and tomatoes, as they can be allergenic.

GRAINS

Rice cereal is typically given as a baby's very first food. Few babies gulp it down with much gusto, however: All of the taste and texture have been refined out of it, leaving only bland carbohydrates. Whole grain cereals, on the other hand, contain protein, fat, fiber, vitamins, and essential minerals, as well as a hearty flavor and aroma. After your baby is tolerating fruits and vegetables well, you can introduce whole grain cereals, starting with a single grain at a time, and later mixing grains. Oatmeal, brown rice, barley, quinoa, and millet are good grains to start with. Wait on wheat; it is a common allergen. Buy commercially prepared single- or mixed-grain baby cereals, or make your own (see "Homemade Versus Prepared Food" on page 128).

You can serve cooked brown rice, whole grain toast, dry breakfast cereals, and whole grain pasta to an older baby. You may want to start with varieties of bread, cereal, and pasta made from spelt, millet, amaranth, and other grains, as wheat can cause allergies.

Teething biscuits, even the natural varieties, are not a good idea, as they can sit in a baby's mouth and cause tooth decay. Offer a damp cotton rag for teething on instead.

NUTS AND LEGUMES

While your child is breastfeeding, he does not need a lot of additional protein. After a year, however, when solid food begins to make up more of his diet, good sources of protein include tofu, beans such as chickpeas and pinto beans, legumes such as split peas, hummus (chickpea and garlic paste), and seed and nut butters such as tahini (sesame seed butter), and almond butter. Peanuts are one of the most allergenic foods; although peanut butter is a perennial children's favorite, it should not be given to children before they are two or three.

MEAT, CHICKEN, FISH, AND EGGS

Animal proteins are the most difficult foods to digest. They are probably not necessary until a child is walking and making more physical demands on himself; some people feel they are unnecessary, period (for more on vegetarian diets for children, see page 141, "The Vegetarian Family"). If you do serve meats or fish, they should be boiled or cooked until very soft, then chopped or flaked finely. Because egg whites can be an allergen, do not give them to your baby until he is over one year old.

DAIRY PRODUCTS

Cow's milk should never be given to a child under a year old, as it is high in protein and minerals, which can put a strain on an infant's immature kidneys. It is also highly allergenic. For more of a discussion of cow's milk, see "Cow's Milk: Good for Calves, Bad for Children?" on page 139.

Yogurt can be fed to infants, as it contains bacteria that make it easier to digest.

SUGAR AND SPICE

Babies naturally have a taste for sweet foods, since mother's milk is sweet. A baby's unspoiled palate can appreciate the subtle sweetness in fruits, vegetables, and grains, with no need for additional sweeteners. Refined sweeteners—including sugar, glucose, dextrose, sucrose, even molasses and brown sugar—can overwhelm and seduce baby's senses, causing her to develop a taste for artificially sweetened foods. Sugar is a prime source of empty calories, filling a child up and displacing more nutritional foods. There is no need to add sweeteners to your baby's food. (Honey should never be given to a child under one, as it may contain botulism spores that a baby's immune system cannot handle.)

Salt is unnecessary as well. Foods in their natural state contain all the sodium the body needs. Adding salt to a baby's food can skew his tastes toward heavily salted foods and can place stress on his immature kidneys.

Chemical additives are also best avoided: The effect of artificial sweeteners like saccharin and aspartame, artificial flavors and colors, and additives like MSG is not entirely known in children. Read food labels so you can avoid these unnecessary flavor-enhancers.

DRINKS

A breastfed baby needs no additional liquids for the first year. After your baby is a year old, you can offer him liquids in a trainer cup with handles and a lid. Good beverage choices include water, heavily diluted fruit juices, and weak herbal teas. You may want to continue to hold off on milk for a few years, because it causes reactions in so many children. See page 140 for dairy alternatives.

Common Allergenic Foods

Wait until your baby is at least a year old—two to three years old if allergies run in your family—before introducing these foods:

milk	citrus
wheat	tomatoes
egg whites	chocolate
soy	nuts, especially peanuts
corn	

Foods Babies Can Choke On

apple chunks or slices	potato chips
dry cereal	raw carrot sticks
hard candies or cookies	rice cakes
hot dogs or tofu dogs	whole corn kernels
meat chunks	whole nuts
peanut butter	whole berries or grapes
popcorn	

Your Budding Gourmet

When your baby is nine to eighteen months old, if she has been handling simple, single-ingredient foods well for a few months, you can begin mixing and matching. There is no reason to rush to add variety to your baby's diet—she is probably happy keeping it simple, and the longer you wait, the more you give her digestive system a chance to adapt to new foods. You need not worry about creating a picky eater; in fact, breastfed babies seem to readily appreciate a variety of tastes, since the flavor of breastmilk varies with each feeding, depending on what the mother has eaten.

The day will come—sooner, rather than later, if your baby seems to tolerate new foods well and you have no history of family allergies—when you can feed your baby whatever the rest of the family is eating.

Lisa

One night when Gemma was nine months old, we went to the Chez Panisse Cafe. Gemma's dinner from our plates would have made her the envy of any gourmand: crusts of good bread followed by some nice, ripe pear; warm goat cheese; perfect little roasted carrots, potatoes, and turnips, lots of garlicky white beans, some filet of sole, and grilled sardine.

She eats braised rabbit with abandon, teethes on artichoke leaves and octopus with zeal. I imagine her one day sitting around with her friends as they brag about favorite dishes their parents cook.

"My mom makes the most delicious brandade," Gemma might say rapturously.

"What's that?" her friends would ask.

"Ummmm! Salt cod, potato, and lots of garlic all mashed up with olive oil, then gratineed and eaten on croutons."

"Ewww!" the other kids would scream. And they'd never accept another invitation to eat lunch at our house.

Lisa Hanauer, "Baby Food is Whatever I Feed My Baby," *Mothering*, Fall 1997.

Homemade Versus Prepared Food

Some mothers never let a spoonful of commercially prepared baby food pass their babies' lips, swearing by the freshness and affordability of homemade baby food. Others roll their eyes at the thought of playing chef to the under-one set.

Actually, whipping up your baby's meals yourself does not have to be a complicated endeavor, and it has several advantages. Commercial baby food often contains starchy fillers such as tapioca and rice flour. Fruits and vegetables lose some vitamins, minerals, and taste when processed. Why not cultivate your baby's taste for fresh foods while she is still impressionable? Making your baby's food will certainly save you money—the cost of those little jars of baby food adds up. Serving homemade food is simply a matter of taking a little of the fresh food you are eating yourself, and pureeing it for your baby. Here are some ideas to get you started:

- Keep a baby food grinder at the table and grind foods from your plate that are appropriate for your baby.
- Steam fresh fruits and vegetables (no need to add more salt or sweeteners) and puree to the desired texture in a food processor or blender. Because fresh baby food will keep for only a few days in the refrigerator, freeze individual portions in ice cube trays or recycled small jars and defrost one serving at a time.
- Make your own whole-grain baby cereal by toasting a grain like brown rice, millet, or quinoa in the oven or a skillet. Grind the grains in a food processor or coffee grinder reserved for that use, immediately before serving them (grains begin to lose nutritional value within a day or two of grinding). To make cereal, simmer a few spoonfuls of ground grains in a half-cup of water. For older children, dress the cereal up with sliced fruit, yogurt, or maple syrup.
- Consider leftover rice a natural baby food. Stir in a little breastmilk, or heat it with a little chicken stock.
- Make polenta for the family, topped with tomato sauce and cheese, and serve the baby's plain.
- Oven-roast zucchini, potatoes, yams, and carrots with a little olive oil until soft.
- Mash sweet potatoes mixed with quinoa—a soft grain—for a nutrition-packed meal for a baby or toddler.
- Reserve some vegetables such as carrots, potatoes, lentils, or parsnips to puree for the baby when you are cooking stews, roasts, or soups for the family. For an older baby, you can puree a small portion of the stew or soup.
- Reserve some cooked grains for the baby when you make grain salads for the family.

Gretchen

At a time when many working parents can barely muster enough energy at dinner time to order Chinese take-out, cooking, pureeing, and serving homemade meals for our babies can seem overwhelming. Can the overscheduled—and/or the culinarily inept—really start whipping up healthful dishes for the little ones?

In the indelible words of my Aunt Rosalie, who fed six children while working full-time in the 1950s, "Sure you can darling. You just have to expand the meaning of the word cook." And she's right. Don't get trapped into thinking that "homemade" means exhausting rituals involving many boiling pots and virgin coffee grinders. Remember these simple words: If it's good enough for you, it's probably great for your baby. You don't need to make special baby cereal, for one thing, unless you wish to. You can simply cook oatmeal, then cool and mash one small portion for the little one. Ditto for pancakes. You may also discover that your child introduces you to a favorite dish or two. I'd forgotten how satisfying Cheerios can be until I bought a box for my son to use as finger food. Now he merrily drops them in a heap on the floor while I munch a bowlful for breakfast.

Gretchen Reynolds, "Reality Check," *Mothering,* November/December 1998.

Going Organic

As you look over the produce at the grocery store, you may wonder if organic food is necessary for your baby, given that it is usually more expensive. In answering this question, consider that pesticides are poisons—to pests and almost certainly to humans. Although Congress passed a Food Quality Protection Act in 1996 that

requires all pesticides to be safe for infants and children, a recent study done by the Environmental Working Group found that between five and 25 percent of the fruits consumed in the United States by children under age six contain unsafe levels of toxic chemicals. Peaches, apples, pears, and grapes were the worst offenders. In addition, the report found detectable pesticide levels—including several carcinogens and neurotoxins—in samples of Gerber, Heinz, and Beechnut baby foods.[3]

Organic food is particularly important for children, because their nervous system and organs are still developing, and their immature kidneys have a harder time ridding the body of toxins. Children tend to eat more fruits than adults, pound for pound, especially when you consider their small size relative to adults.

Organic fruits and vegetables are important for what they contain as well as what they do not. Because organic produce is grown in soil that has been replenished with organic materials, it is richer in many nutrients and contains more trace minerals and micronutrients than conventionally grown produce.

Consider buying seasonal produce from your local farmer's market. As fruits and vegetables ripen on the vine, they form phytochemicals—the substances in plants that prevent cancer and other diseases. Produce that has to be shipped to market is usually picked before it is ripe, before it has had a chance to form these phytochemicals. Organically grown, vine-ripened produce also tastes better; there is a world of difference between a tomato or peach from your local farmer's market and the flavorless, conventionally grown varieties at the supermarket.

Supporting organic farmers means investing in a more sustainable world for your children, since organic farming methods enrich rather than deplete the soil. Buying organic food is an investment in your child's future.

Fostering a Healthy Attitude Toward Food

Your child's first feedings are not only training her tastebuds—they are setting a pattern for her lifelong attitude toward food. If you offer her a variety of fresh, healthful choices and allow her to go at her own pace and develop her own tastes, you will be taking the first step in encouraging healthy eating habits for the rest of her life.

CHAPTER 11 Healthy Eating for the Whole Family

You may be looking forward to the day when your toddler is eating solid food with gusto. You might even imagine shared family meals that are as memorable for the conversation as for the cuisine. The question is: How do you serve wholesome foods that your child will actually eat—and avoid turning the dinner table into a battleground?

Food is much more than fuel to nourish our bodies. It is a symbol of love between parent and child, an expression of a parent's morals and values, and a powerful weapon used by both parents and children. Mothers pour their hearts into cooking for their children, then feel rejected when they refuse what is offered. Parents pass on their values to their children through food. Statements like "There are starving children in Africa who would be happy to eat what you've left on that plate" turn a child's eating habits into a moral issue. Parents attempt to discipline children over their eating habits, and children rebel. The result can be long-term obsessions with food, including weight problems and damaging eating disorders.

Trusting Your Children's Eating Habits

The key to avoiding mealtime conflicts is to trust your child's appetite. Several studies have shown that, when left to their own devices, children will make healthful food choices. Clara Davis of Children's Memorial Hospital in Chicago studied fifteen infants ranging from six to eleven months old, who were breastfed and had never been given any supplemental food. Offering them a wide variety of unprocessed, natural foods at each meal, she found that they ate well-balanced meals, according to nutritional standards, and even corrected their own deficiencies by choosing the foods that they needed most. The children in the study, who participated in the research up to age four, were extremely healthy.

Another study, conducted in 1991 at the University of Illinois, followed the eating habits and growth patterns of children age two to five. The children were given a variety of foods—including some sweets—at fixed times and in quantities that doubled the estimated daily requirements. Despite highly erratic eating habits, the children's daily calorie intake remained constant.

It seems that children have an innate ability to choose a healthy diet for themselves. Trusting your children on this issue, however, may require a leap of faith. Knowing the importance of a healthy diet, you may find it hard to relinquish control of your children's eating habits. You may feel that you are to blame if your children do not eat what is served, or if they want to snack before dinner and then are picky at mealtimes.

Food should be a shared pleasure, not a source of conflict. Here are some tips for taming the food battles. (These ideas may be particularly helpful with children over five; before that you may find that you need to give your children more guidance in their food choices.)

LET YOUR CHILDREN MAKE THEIR OWN FOOD CHOICES

Trusting your children's eating habits means offering them a wide variety of healthful foods, and letting them make their own choices. (Letting them choose can only be done within reason, of course—after all, you are not a short-order cook.) Allow your children their own choices for breakfast, lunch, and snacks. For dinner, serve the same meal to the whole family, but let your children decide what and how much they want to eat from their plates. Later, if they are still hungry, they can choose a before-bed snack.

The key to this approach is having a wide variety of wholesome foods on hand, so that every choice your children make is a healthy one. See "Food, Fun, and Children," page 142, for healthy snack and meal ideas.

RECOGNIZE THAT CHILDREN HAVE ERRATIC EATING PATTERNS

It is natural for children to go through growth spurts where they eat voraciously, and then to plateau, eating so little that you think they will starve. Often parents who worried that their children ate almost nothing at three and four suddenly have the opposite problem—worrying that their child is eating too much!—at seven or eight.

Learn to observe not just what your child eats at each meal or even throughout each day, but over the course of a few days or a week. You may be surprised at how your children actually balance their nutrient intake when they are allowed to be self-regulating.

CONSIDER SERVING ONE HOT MEAL A DAY

If you are accustomed to the idea that a healthy diet consists of three well-balanced meals a day—as most of us are—it is hard to let go of this approach. Young children, however, need to eat about every four hours, and usually prefer a little smorgasbord of snacks to a big meal. Children have relatively simple tastes and typically ask for a single item—a bowl of cereal, a smoothie, or a sandwich, for example. Rarely does a hungry child want a three-course meal. Remember, too, that a cold meal can be just as nutritious as a hot

meal—in fact, cooking food often reduces its nutritional value.

Consider having a variety of foods on hand—foods that you can easily give your children or that they can help themselves to throughout the day—and cooking just one hot meal a day. One mother describes her philosophy this way: "When I put the hot meal on the table, I call everyone together for 'family hour,' and they choose something to eat from what I've prepared, or else they just sit with us. Whoever is not hungry is not forced to eat."

You may need to reconcile this approach with your own notions about square meals, and eventually work toward having your children eat at more conventional times, if that is important to you. The main thing is to be flexible with young children and to recognize that their appetites may differ from yours.

START OUT WITH SMALL PORTIONS

Children can be overwhelmed by a plate heaped with food. It is much better to start with small portions and offer seconds.

LET GO OF THE IDEA THAT YOUR CHILDREN MUST CLEAR THEIR PLATES

Forcing children to eat everything on their plates is counterproductive because your insistence will lead only to resentment. A child simply may not be hungry at the time, or may truly dislike a particular food.

Instead, encourage your children to taste everything on their plates, but do not insist on it. Children's tastes change, and a food that a child did not like a year ago may suddenly gain favor this week; or they may like something raw that they did not like cooked. You may need to offer a food to a child many times before she decides that she likes it. Then again, she may never like it. Children have more acute taste buds than adults do and may reject foods that taste bitter or spicy or unpleasant to them.

DO NOT WORRY ABOUT UNCONVENTIONAL FOOD CHOICES

So many of our notions about food are based purely on convention. Why are donuts and sugary muffins considered acceptable breakfast fare, when apple pie is not? The Japanese eat fish, rice, and sea vegetables for breakfast, while Scandinavians start the day with a smorgasbord of meats and cheeses. Free of conventions, children may make seemingly bizarre food choices that actually satisfy their daily requirements. If your child wants to start the day with chocolate pudding and green beans, rest assured that an infinite possibility of food combinations can make up balanced diet.

Eda

When my husband was in the army in Fort Smith, Arkansas, and our daughter was about two years old, some nights were so unbearably hot that we would all wake up in the morning tired, listless, and lacking in appetite. I found the perfect solution for Wendy—an ice cream cone! If she had eaten cold cereal with a little cream and sugar, the nutritional value would have been similar. When we moved to a colder climate, she was happy to eat more traditional breakfast foods.

When Wendy was about eight, she stayed at a friend's house overnight. The next day she told us, "They have terrible breakfasts at Joan's house—hot cereal and bacon and eggs and blueberry muffins. I want a hamburger for breakfast tomorrow!" She had, on occasion, chili for breakfast when there was a snowstorm. Within reasonable limits, she had learned by then that one could be quite flexible about meals without ruining one's health.

Eda LeShan, "Taming the Food Battles," *Mothering,* Winter 1997.

LET HUNGER BE YOUR CHILD'S GUIDE

Young children have little tummies, and need to eat more often than adults. Forcing your child to avoid snacks "because they'll ruin your dinner" or to eat at mealtimes "because it's time to eat" disregards the cues your child's appetite is sending her. Conditioning your child to ignore her body's signals teaches her to eat for reasons other than hunger: because it is polite, or because the food tastes good or is forbidden, or for emotional reasons such as anger, sadness, or boredom.

Your child's natural rhythms may be different from yours. Begin to get a sense of her hungry times and offer her small meals around these times. Once you start to notice a pattern, you may be able to work slowly toward having her eat more at family mealtimes. If your child is hungry before dinner is ready, let her eat a snack. Imagine how you would feel if someone told you, "No hors d'oeuvres unless you promise to eat your whole dinner!" Remember, too, that eating a large meal just before bed is not necessarily the most healthful approach; children need fuel throughout the day, when they are expending the most energy.

DO NOT USE SWEETS AS A BRIBE

Telling your children that they can not have dessert unless they finish their dinner puts the focus on dessert as a reward. When a food is rationed out, children will naturally want more of it.

It may seem risky to trust your child's choices where sweets are concerned, but you could find yourself pleasantly surprised. Try leaving your child's favorite sweets on a shelf where she can help herself any time: Once a food is no longer forbidden, it may lose its special appeal and become just another food to be eaten in moderation (do the same thing for yourself, if sweets are an issue for you).

Instead of saving dessert as the reward for eating dinner, try serving a healthful dessert as part of dinner and letting your child decide in what order to eat his meal. Or offer a small treat after dinner that your child may help himself to if he is still hungry. Have wholesome cookies, fruit popsicles, and frozen yogurt on hand that your children can snack on during the day when they are in the mood for a sweet. In taking the emphasis off desserts, you will be allowing your children to make food choices based on their appetites rather than on unnatural cravings for "treats."

LET YOUR CHILDREN HELP PREPARE MEALS

Children will be much more interested in eating a meal if they had a hand in planning the menu or cooking it. Get some healthy kids' cookbooks (see suggestions in Resources) or experiment together. Even a young child can help stir or pour. Make it fun: Turn peach halves into Raggedy Anns with lettuce skirts and carrot peel hair. Make it instructive: Without being didactic, take the opportunity to talk to your children about how particular foods help them grow. Plan theme dinners around a country or custom, and research the theme together, extending it to the music and decorations. Your children will take pride in their creations and will look forward to mealtime.

DO NOT LET MEALTIMES BECOME BATTLES

You will have plenty of reasons to put your foot down with your children as they grow up. Save your energy for the things that you can control.

When children feel that they are trusted and their choices are respected, they become much more pleasant to be around. When there is no war, there is no one to fight with. Removing the relentless mealtime directives ("Eat this," "Don't eat that," "First your broccoli," "Three more bites if you want dessert") comes as a welcome relief. Instead of badgering your children about their eating, you can relax and enjoy the shared conversation and togetherness that family meals should be all about. The real payoff will come in seeing your children develop a comfortable relationship to both food and their bodies.

Jane

In the beginning stages of self-demand feeding, three-year-old Natalie asked me for applesauce, chicken, and vanilla ice cream for lunch.

"How do you know you can eat all that?" I asked her.

"I have lots of rooms in my tummy," she replied, pointing to three spots on her stomach where each food would go. She ate small amounts of all three items, in the order she chose, until she filled up her little "rooms." Today, she is an active, healthy, and attractive nine year old who remains quite self-directed in her eating.

Jane R. Hirschmann, "Raising Children Free of Food and Weight Problems," *Mothering*, Winter 1990.

Whole Foods Make Healthy Bodies

Recent research has highlighted the importance of a diet high in whole foods—unrefined grains, fruits, and vegetables—in maintaining immune system function and protecting against life-threatening diseases such as cancer and heart disease. Children, especially, need the nutrients from a diet high in natural, unprocessed foods to help their bodies develop and grow. One of the greatest gifts you can give to your child is to start him out at a young age developing a taste for foods in their most natural state. The main components of a whole-foods diet include:

WHOLE GRAINS

Whole grains are much more nutritious than refined grains. Refining a grain strips it of the germ and bran, which are rich in unsaturated fats, protein, carbohydrates, B-complex vitamins, vitamin E, and essential minerals, as well as fiber, leaving mostly starch and protein. Enriched white breads and cereals, in which vitamins and minerals are added back to a refined product, are not the same thing as a whole grain, whose nutrients and protective compounds work together synergistically.

Refined products are often disguised as whole grain products, requiring you to read labels carefully. If the first ingredient listed is whole wheat, oats, amaranth, barley, buckwheat, or millet, it is a whole grain product. If white flour—even unbleached or enriched—is the first ingredient, it is not a whole grain product. Sometimes a label will say "made with whole wheat" when the food item is mostly a refined grain product.

Begin introducing whole grain products to your family. Whole grain cereals are available in the natural foods section of your grocery store; mass-marketed brands include Grape-Nuts, Shredded Wheat, and Muesli. White rice has almost no nutritional value. Substitute brown rice, or experiment with cooked whole grains such as bulgur, quinoa, and amaranth, which are packed with nutrients and high in protein. Most pastas are made with refined flour. Try mixing in some whole grain pastas made from grains like amaranth, kasha, buckwheat, or spelt.

FRESH FRUITS AND VEGETABLES

Fruits and vegetables provide important vitamins, minerals, and enzymes for your growing child, and they are loaded with antioxidants and phytochemicals that play a role in preventing cancer and other life-threatening diseases. Fruits should be served raw, and vegetables served raw, steamed, or quickly stir-fried, to retain most of their nutrients. Juices are not a good substitute for whole fruits and vegetables, unless they are served immediately after juicing (see "A Cup of Apple Juice a Day?" page 140).

Organic produce does not contain potentially harmful pesticides, and it is richer in minerals and disease-fighting substances than conventionally grown foods (see "Going Organic," page 129, for more on organic foods). Turn going to the farmer's market with your children into an outing, or better yet, start a garden together. Even if you do not have room for a vegetable garden, you can grow a container of lettuce or a jar of alfalfa sprouts on a sunny windowsill. Children will be more motivated to eat their vegetables if they have grown them themselves.

ESSENTIAL FATTY ACIDS AND SWEETENERS

Children need adequate fat in their diets for the first two years. If you are breastfeeding, this fat will be provided by your breastmilk. After two years, you should not need to watch the amount of fat in your child's diet too carefully, provided she is getting mostly "good" fat. Good fats include olive, canola, peanut, sesame, and high-oleic safflower and sunflower oils, as well as the fats occurring naturally in nuts, seeds, and avocados. Organic butter and cream are also good sources of fat. Margarine contains trans-fatty acids, which may increase the risk of heart disease and cancer.

Although sugar is not necessary in the diet, most children have a sweet tooth and enjoy the occasional treat. The problem with refined sugars is that they create the roller coaster effect of a sugar high followed by a crash. The less refined a sugar, the longer it will take to be absorbed into the bloodstream, and therefore the less erratic its effect will be on blood sugar levels. Table sugar has been highly refined and stripped of all vitamins, minerals, fiber, and amino acids. Brown sugar is simply white sugar with a little molasses added for color and flavoring. Powdered sugar, turbinado sugar, and corn syrup are also highly refined.

The best choices for unrefined sugars include those derived from grains, such as brown rice syrup and barley malt, which contain complex carbohydrates. Unsulfured blackstrap molasses is also a good choice, because it is rich in minerals, especially calcium and iron. Sucanat—organically grown, dehydrated sugar cane juice—is better than table sugar, since it retains some complex sugars and minerals. Honey is sweeter than sugar, so it can be used more sparingly. (Honey should never be given to children under one, as it can be toxic to their immature immune systems.)

Many parents believe that sugar causes hyperactivity, but this suspicion has been disproved. Some children are more sensitive to sugar than others, but in general, it may be hunger, over-excitement, or even a food intolerance that causes a child to be hyperactive.

UNPROCESSED FOODS

The more processed a food is—the farther it is from its natural state—the less nutritional value it has. Junk foods add nothing to the body's reserves of vitamins and minerals, increasing its susceptibility to illness and infection. Occasional trips to McDonald's or special treats at Grandma's are fine, but when a child's diet consists mainly of processed foods that are low in nutritional value, his diet will not contribute to his overall good health.

Living in the Real World

Ideally, food should be eaten in its most natural state—unrefined, unprocessed, organically grown, in season. However, it would be wishful thinking to believe that your children will eat this well all the time. You may not have a good natural foods store nearby, or you may not like to cook. Even if you do a good job of preparing wholesome foods at home, your children will visit friends or relatives who eat differently, and they will be exposed to junk foods at school.

When your children are young, you can provide them with a variety of healthy choices to fuel their growth and encourage good eating habits. As they get older, however, their eating habits are out of your control. Attempts to control them will only result in rebellion. If you have laid the groundwork for a healthy attitude toward food, your children will be better equipped to make their own realistic choices. (However, it is never too late to make changes in your family's diet.)

Do your best to serve your family wholesome food without making it overly complicated. When food becomes oppressive, it is no longer enjoyable. Help your children understand why whole foods are better for them, but as in everything, maintain moderation in your approach to eating. Make mealtimes a memorable event by putting the focus on the joy of sharing good food together. Create your own food rituals for holidays and special events. Make food a source of pleasure for your family.

Food Allergies and Intolerances

If your child has a persistent stuffy nose or ear infections, appears hyperactive, or wets his bed frequently after he has learned to use the toilet, the culprit might be a food intolerance.

An allergic reaction to a food occurs when the immune system, mistakenly identifying a harmless substance as potentially harmful, produces antibodies in response. Allergic reactions include swelling of the mouth, face, or throat; hives; itchy eyes; coughing or wheezing; abdominal cramping; vomiting; and diarrhea. Swelling of the tongue may make breathing difficult; emergency care may be required.

Peanuts are the number one cause of fatal and near-fatal allergic reactions, although peanut allergies are relatively rare. Other allergenic foods include cow's milk, eggs, fish and shellfish, soy, and wheat. Many people eventually outgrow allergies to these foods, with the exceptions of nuts and fish. Children tend to be more allergic than adults.

True food allergies occur in only about five percent of all children. However, the number of children suffering from food intolerances is much greater. The symptoms are chronic, and are easily mistaken for other ailments. Symptoms of food intolerances and allergies may include:

PERSISTENT CONGESTION
Most healthy children will get between two and six colds a year. In between colds, your child's nose should be clear. If your child has continual nasal congestion, it may be caused by a food intolerance.

A cold will usually cause red, inflamed nasal membranes, with thick, yellow nasal secretions. If there is a cough, it will be loose and eventually productive. With a food intolerance, the nasal membranes will be pale, with thin, watery secretions; a cough, if any, will be dry and unproductive.

RECURRING EAR INFECTIONS
Food intolerances can also cause fluid to build up in the ears. Several studies have showed a link between ear infections and food allergies or intolerances.

FREQUENT HEADACHES
An allergic reaction causes tiny blood vessels to dilate so that fluid leaks out of the capillaries, causing swelling. When this swelling occurs in the brain, a headache results.

HYPERACTIVITY
Dr. William Crook, author of *Tracking Down Hidden Food Allergy*, conducted a five-year study of 182 hyperactive children and found that three out of four were made hyperactive by one or more common foods.

BEDWETTING
The bladder is covered by a smooth muscle, which can contract when a child eats foods he is allergic to. According to Dr. James C. Breneman, chairman of the food allergy committee of the American College of Allergists, food allergies are the number one cause of bedwetting.

MUSCLE ACHES
Nighttime leg cramps are commonly referred to as "growing pains" or blamed on too much or too little exercise. According to Dr. Crook, a much more common cause of muscle aches is food intolerance.

AN ANEMIC APPEARANCE

Children who are allergic may be pale, with dark, puffy circles under their eyes.

If you suspect your child is suffering from a food allergy, you can take him to an allergist for a skin test or blood test. Food intolerances are harder to test for. The best approaches for a suspected food intolerance are to follow an elimination or rotatation diet.

An elimination diet means completely removing the most common offenders—cow's milk, wheat, corn, eggs, soy, nuts, citrus, and chocolate—from your child's diet completely for five days. Then you can begin adding the foods back one at a time, waiting a few days between each addition to note any reactions. (For more on elimination diets, see Dr. Crook's book, *Tracking Down Hidden Food Allergy*, in Resources.) If you find that a certain food causes a reaction in your child, you should keep all traces of that food out of his diet. From time to time you can add a small amount back to test if the food intolerance persists.

A rotation diet means rotating foods so that your child is not eating the same foods until every third or fifth day. For example, if you gave your child pasta one day, you would wait three to five days before giving him another wheat product, and observe his reaction in the intervening time. Sometimes people with an intolerance to a particular food can handle it in small quantities; i.e., if it is only eaten every few days. Eventually children will outgrow most food intolerances if large quantities of the food are kept out of their diet when they are young.

Cow's Milk: Good for Calves, Bad for Children?

After children are a year old, parents are given the green light to feed them cow's milk—and they usually do so with gusto. Milk is a convenient source of calcium and protein for a growing child. Although there are other good calcium sources, geting a toddler to drink a glass of milk is easier than convincing her to eat a plate of spinach.

Does milk, as its boosters claim, really have something for everybody? For many people, milk is a source of digestive and other health problems. Dairy products are the number one cause of food intolerances, which can show up as frequent colds or ear infections, irritability and colic, rashes or itchy skin, and vomiting or diarrhea. People of Asian, African, or Native American descent are often lactose intolerant—meaning they have trouble digesting milk.

All mammal species, of course, produce milk as a complete food to nourish their young until they are weaned. After weaning, most mammals do not ever again drink milk. The exceptions are Hindus, Europeans, and Americans, who drink cow's milk throughout their lives. A sizeable majority of traditional cultures in the world do not drink milk, including most Asian and African populations.

If your background predisposes you to lactose intolerance, or if you feel unwell after eating dairy products, you might consider eliminating milk and dairy products from your diet while you are pregnant and breastfeeding as well as waiting to give your child cow's milk until he is a few years old. Infants can develop a milk allergy or intolerance before ever drinking it: When a pregnant or nursing mother drinks milk, undigested milk proteins pass into her womb through the placenta, and into her breastmilk.

Your child does not need to drink milk to get adequate calcium. The United States Recommended Daily Requirement (RDA) for calcium is 800 milligrams for children (1,200 for adults). However, the World Health Organization recommends a calcium consumption of only 500 milligrams across the board, and most populations around the world show no calcium deficiencies on calcium levels as low as 400 milligrams per day.

The difference lies in several dietary factors. First, a high protein intake, common in the United States, depletes the body's calcium stores.[1] Calcium absorption is also inhibited by a diet high in phosphates—found in dairy products, meat, and cola drinks—and refined sugars. On the other hand, magnesium—found in unprocessed foods, such as nuts, legumes, and whole grains—is vital for calcium absorption. Organically grown foods tend to be higher in calcium since the soil they grow in has not been depleted of minerals.

The bottom line is that your child does not need nearly the RDA for calcium if his diet is high in whole grains, organically grown vegetables, and unprocessed foods, and low in protein and refined sugars.

You and your child can get your calcium from the same place the cow did—the plant kingdom. Some of the best sources of calcium are:

- leafy green vegetables such as spinach, turnip greens, parsley, and broccoli (250 to 450 milligrams in one cup cooked vegetables);
- sea vegetables such as kombu, nori, and wakame (100 to 200 milligrams per tablespoon);
- sesame seeds (125 milligrams per tablespoon); blackstrap molasses (100 milligrams per tablespoon);
- nuts such as almonds and hazelnuts (100 to 200 milligrams per ¼ cup).

The easiest ways to insure your child is getting enough calcium are to sprinkle a mixture of dried seaweed, dried parsley, and toasted sesame seeds on foods; mix honey with blackstrap molasses and keep it in a squeeze bottle to use as a sweetener in foods; make sandwiches with almond butter or tahini (sesame seed butter); and serve lots of greens and tofu. (A child who is still breastfeeding should be getting all the calcium he needs from breastmilk.) If you remain concerned about your child's calcium intake, you can supplement with calcium magnesium citrate powder.

Your child need not miss dairy products; there is a wide assortment of dairy substitutes available at the grocery store, including calcium-fortified soy milk and rice milk, soy cheese, nondairy desserts such as Tofutti and Rice Dream, and rice milk puddings. A child who has trouble digesting milk may be able to handle yogurt, since it contains bacteria that make it more digestible. Look for yogurts that contain live acidophilus cultures. Goat's milk may also be more digestible than cow's milk for some people. You can make great-tasting, calcium-packed nut "milks" by liquefying a few tablespoons of almonds or hazelnuts in the blender with a cup of water and a spoonful each of honey and blackstrap molasses (you may want to strain the mixture after blending it or soak the nuts in the water overnight). Give this nut blend to your child to drink, or use it in place of milk in recipes.

If you do give your child milk, you may want to consider organic milk. Dairy cows are given recombinant Bovine Growth Hormone (rBGH) to increase their milk production. We do not yet know what the effect of rBHG is on humans, but many questions have been raised, including a possible association between growth hormones in dairy products and the early onset of puberty in girls in the United States. In addition, cows are more prone to infection when given growth hormones. The infections are treated with large amounts of antibiotics, which find their way into the milk. Organic milk does not contain rBGH or antibiotics. Virtually every dairy farm in the country that is not organic uses rBGH. Canada and Europe have banned the use of rBHG; the United States is the only large country to allow the hormone.

A Cup of Apple Juice a Day?

Most children have a drinking problem—that is, they drink too much juice. Parents may give their children juice, thinking it is the best way to satisfy their daily fruit requirement. However, unless a juice is freshly squeezed and served immediately, many of its nutrients are lost. Bottled or concentrated juices are mostly sugar. Even unsweetened juices contain concentrated amounts of fructose—the sugar that naturally occurs in fruits—as well as sorbitol, which can create gas, bloating, or chronic diarrhea. One study at the University of Connecticut Health Center found that children who drank as little as eight ounces of apple juice a day suffered from chronic diarrhea. The children improved immediately when apple juice was eliminated from their diets.

Children who fill up on juice may not be hungry for the foods that supply the nutrients they need. The best drink for children is pure water. If you do serve your child juice, it should be heavily diluted: one part juice to two parts water. If you invest in a juicer, you can make fresh, vitamin-packed juices at home, even mixing in vegetables. Many children who do not want to eat their vegetables will drink carrot juice, or an apple-celery-beet juice blend. Fruit smoothies made in the

blender from whole fruits (bananas, strawberries, peaches, and so on) with ice and yogurt are popular with many children. You can also try getting your child used to the taste of hot or iced herb teas such as hibiscus and chamomile, unsweetened or sweetened with a little honey (do not give your child honey until he or she is over a year, as it can be toxic to infants).

The Vegetarian Family

Your son suddenly announces one night at the dinner table, "I don't want to eat dead animals anymore." Whether your child has chosen solidarity with animals friends like Wilbur and Babe, or you have decided to raise your family vegetarian for health, ecological, or political reasons, you can rest assured that a vegetarian diet can provide all the nutrients a growing child needs.

A vegetarian diet is typically very low in cholesterol and animal fat—particularly if cheese and eggs are not eaten in excess—and high in complex carbohydrates and fiber, reducing the risk of heart disease, certain types of cancer, diabetes, and obesity. The trick with young children is ensuring that they get enough calories and nutrients from a vegetarian diet. Here are some areas to watch out for:

CALORIES

Children need plenty of calories to grow. Calorie-dense foods in a vegetarian diet include full-fat tofu and other soy foods; seeds, nuts and nut butters; dried fruits; and avocados. Because high-fiber foods can inhibit the absorption of calories, if your child is on a vegetarian diet, which is naturally high in fiber and low in fat, you might consider peeling your child's fruits and vegetables occasionally and using refined flour or cereal at times instead of whole grain products, or include eggs, cheese, and butter if you are not a vegan.

If your style of vegetarianism includes eggs and cheese, do not go overboard on them because they are high in saturated fat. Although children need fat in their diets, most doctors agree that they can still get plenty of fat and calories from plant sources.

PROTEIN

Most Americans—including vegetarians—get more protein than they need or can use. Although children require more protein per pound of body weight than do adults, even they can get abundant protein from a vegetarian diet. All foods contain protein. Fruit has very little, but vegetables, calorie for calorie, have quite a bit. Grains, beans, and soy foods like tofu and tempeh are more concentrated sources of protein.

If your child receives sufficient calories from a diet based on grains, beans, vegetables, and fruits, she can get adequate protein. To make sure, plan each meal around a simple, substantial, starchy food—like rice, pasta, or beans—and round it out with vegetables.

Practicing so-called protein combining, as espoused in the landmark book, *Diet for a Small Planet,* is not necessary. In real life, you "protein combine" every time you put peanut butter on bread or black beans on brown rice, or every time you give your child a glass of milk or soy milk to drink with a meal. But protein combining is not something to work at or worry about because we protein combine naturally in our diet.

CALCIUM

If you choose to be a vegan—a total vegetarian, eliminating dairy products and eggs as well as meat—your child can still get all the calcium she needs from plant sources. Besides, in following a vegetarian diet, she will not be getting excessive protein, which depletes calcium stores. For more on nondairy sources of calcium, see "Cow's Milk," page 139.

IRON

Vegetarians get plenty of iron from leafy greens, legumes, whole grains, and dried fruits. The type of iron found in meat has been deemed more usable by the body than from plant sources, but research does not indicate that this finding is a cause for concern. The only vegetarians who need to be cautious about iron are those who replace meat with too much cheese, since dairy products can inhibit the absorption of iron. For more on nonmeat sources of iron, see Chapter 10.

VITAMIN B-12

A plant-based diet consisting of fresh, unrefined foods easily provides every needed nutrient—with the probable exception of B-12, which is not reliably found in plant foods. Most vegetarians will probably get the tiny amount—2 micrograms a day—that is needed from microorganisms in their own bodies, but because B-12 is essential for proper functioning of the nervous system, it is best to be safe and supplement. You can give your child a 1,000-microgram tablet of B-12 once a week, or feed him cereal or soy milk fortified with B-12.

Planning vegetarian menus means rethinking the concept of "entree." Meals do not have to revolve around meat, chicken, or fish. Foods such as grains, starchy vegetables, beans and other legumes, and soy products such as tofu are hearty, satisfying, and versatile. The cuisines of the world are there to offer inspiration, too. If you have any doubt about the variety of vegetarian dishes, check out the meatless offerings at Chinese, Vietnamese, Thai, Indian, Ethiopian, Middle Eastern, and Mexican restaurants. For meatless meal ideas, see the menu suggestions below.

Food, Fun, and Children

Eating nutritious foods based around grains, fruits, and vegetables is a lot easier than it used to be, thanks to the proliferation of natural foods markets around the country. Here are some ideas to get you started cooking and eating wholesome, healthy foods:

SCHOOL LUNCHES

There are many other lunch possibilities beyond bologna. Try some of these ideas:

- Humus (chickpea spread) and lettuce or green or red pepper slices
- Peanut butter and sliced banana or apple
- BBQ beans: Puree canned black or kidney beans with barbecue sauce, and use as a spread.
- Smoked salmon on cream cheese
- Grilled cheese with tomato and alfalfa sprouts
- Veggie sandwiches: sliced cucumber, tomato, and alfalfa sprouts with mayonnaise and mustard, with or without cheese
- Mock chicken salad: crumbled marinated tofu mixed with mayonnaise or plain yogurt, chopped celery, salt, and pepper. (Marinate tofu in soy sauce, chopped or pressed garlic and grated fresh ginger.)

- Pita pocket: shredded carrots, sliced red peppers, cucumber, tomato, and chickpeas in a pita half; drizzle with a little plain yogurt or salad dressing
- Pigs in a blanket: chicken or tofu hot dogs wrapped in a whole wheat tortilla
- Hearty soups in a thermos, with breadsticks and carrot sticks
- Sushi rolls (vegetarian or cooked varieties, such as cucumber, avocado, crab, or shrimp) with rice cakes
- Rice or grain salads with chopped vegetables and nuts added

SNACKS

Keep healthy munchies or easy-to-prepare foods on hand for your children to snack on all day long.

- *Trail Mix:* Chopped dried fruit, nuts, pumpkin seeds, granola, dried coconut—let your children make their own favorite mix.
- *Ants on a Log:* celery sticks stuffed with peanut butter, with raisin "ants" marching along the top.
- *Super Power Protein Balls:* one cup peanut butter mixed with 3 tablespoons dried milk powder, ¼ teaspoon vanilla, and enough yogurt to moisten to a rolling consistency. Add carob powder, nuts, raisins, coconut, or oats, and roll in sesame seeds.
- *Corn cakes:* Toast 3 cups cornmeal and 1 cup rolled oats in a dry skillet, add ½ teaspoon salt, ¼ cup corn oil, and 3 cups water, and knead like playdough. Make flat, round cakes with your hands and bake at 350 degrees for about an hour.
- *Smoothies made from fresh or frozen fruit:* Use bananas, peaches, berries, and pineapple; juice or milk; and yogurt. Add tofu, soy protein powder, peanut butter, or almonds (chop well in the blender) for extra protein.
- *"Momsicles":* Yogurt, vanilla, and honey mixed with pineapple, apricot, or peach nectar, frozen in an ice cube tray with a stick in each cube.
- *Amazake:* creamy, sweet, brown rice milk (available in natural foods stores).
- *Veggie sticks with tofu dip:* Puree tofu, yogurt, lemon juice, and garlic in the blender.

- *Fruit salad:* Toss with plain yogurt, honey, and vanilla.
- *Fruit leather:* Cook 2 quarts ripe fruit (strawberries, plums, or whatever you like) over low heat in a large pot with a little honey, until fruit is soft. Cool and press through sieve. Spread softened fruit on an oiled baking sheet, and let it dry in the sun for a few days, or in a 200-degree oven for a few hours.

SWEETS

Make or buy wholesome treats that offer some nutritional value, instead of empty calories.

- Make wholesome cookies with vegetable oil in place of butter, and brown rice syrup in place of sugar; add rolled oats, dried fruit, and nuts for added nutrition.
- Instead of artificially flavored and colored birthday cakes, consider carrot cake with cream cheese frosting (cream cheese blended

with honey and vanilla), or homemade apple pie made with whole wheat or oat flour.

- Make fruit crumbles with sliced pears, apples, or peaches mixed with raisins. Top with rolled oats mixed with whole wheat or brown rice flour, cinnamon, vanilla, chopped walnuts or pecans, maple or brown rice syrup, and corn oil; bake.
- Substitute oat flour for wheat flour in cookies and pastries if wheat allergies are a problem.

VEGETARIAN ENTREES

Even if your family is not vegetarian, you may want to serve meatless meals a few times a week. Try these combinations:
- Black beans and rice
- Pasta with marinara sauce and three-bean salad
- Baked potatoes stuffed with beans, steamed vegetables, plain yogurt, or butter
- Stir-fried vegetables with tofu on brown rice
- Eggplant lasagne
- Hearty vegetable soups thickened with oat milk (puree oats with water in blender and strain); serve with crusty bread
- Winter squash stew: Saute sliced onions in oil until golden; add chunks of peeled winter squash and carrots, and saute until browned; add vegetable stock and chopped greens such as broccoli, kale, or watercress.

TOFU

Tofu is a perfect children's food: It is high in protein, with a soft texture and mild taste that absorbs other flavors well. It is easy to slip into dishes without your family even knowing it is there.
- Give your child cubes of marinated, baked tofu, which has a flavor similar to meat.
- Mix crumbled tofu with bread crumbs and/or rolled oats, chopped onion, minced garlic, an

egg, and Worcestershire sauce, and bake for meatless "meat loaf." Add brown rice or cooked lentils to the mixture if you like.
- Serve scrambled tofu for breakfast or dinner: Mash tofu with a fork, mix with chopped onion and tamari, and saute in oil until golden brown.
- Add whole wheat or oat flour and grated vegetables to the above recipe and shape into patties to fry or grill.
- Make tofu salad sandwiches from mashed tofu mixed with grated carrot, sliced scallions, cooked brown rice, rice vinegar, olive oil, and seasonings, and stuff into whole wheat pita bread.

SEA VEGETABLES

Seaweeds such as nori, dulse, wakame, kelp, and kombu are extremely high in iodine, phosophorus, potassium, and calcium (particularly important for vegetarians who do not eat dairy products). Many are also high in iron and protein. Here are ways to work these nutritious sea vegetables into your diet:
- Eat more sushi.
- Sprinkle dried seaweed in place of salt (seaweed is quite salty, due to its iodine content) onto rice, soups, and sandwiches. Buy a sea vegetable seasoning mix at an Asian or natural foods store, or make your own with crumbled, toasted seaweed and toasted sesame seeds.
- Make sea vegetable soup: Cook several sheets of toasted nori or wakame with a sliced onion in a stockpot full of water. Add a few teaspoons of miso for a flavorful stock. To complete the soup, add cubed tofu, sliced carrots, scallions, cubed potatoes, mushrooms, and other vegetables.
- Use agar, a seaweed derivative that works much like gelatin, in jams, jellies, and desserts.

PART 4 Natural Health Care

CHAPTER 12 Alternative Medicine and Family Health

Becoming a parent can give you a new perspective on many issues, including modern medicine. You fret at the first sign of discomfort in your children, but you also worry about what goes into their bodies: Are the medical remedies prescribed for your child safe as well as effective? Or, as the old saying goes, will "the cure be worse than the disease?"

Often people turn to alternative medicine for the first time once they have children. You may look into alternatives to conventional medicine because you question the need to use potent antibiotics or invasive procedures to treat non-emergency conditions in your child. You may believe that your child's own natural defenses will develop best if she is given a chance to fight off illness without too much intervention. Or you simply may want to investigate every possible option when illness strikes—a search that is very likely to lead you to alternative therapies.

Alternative medicine—with its emphasis both on addressing underlying causes of illness rather than symptoms and on strengthening the body's own ability to fight off disease—is well-suited to common childhood ailments. Children's natural vigor and untainted immune systems make them highly responsive to alternative therapies. Many alternative practices such as homeopathy, Ayurvedic medicine, and Oriental medicine center around the concept of a "vital force"—something that children seem to possess in abundance.

What Is Alternative Medicine?

The term "alternative medicine" refers to alternatives to standard medical practices used in the United States. This all-embracing term covers such disparate modalities as acupuncture, homeopathy, herbal medicine, and Ayurveda. Many practices labeled alternative are centuries old; others, such as sound and light therapy, are brand new.

Alternative practices are referred to as complementary or integrative when they are used in conjunction with conventional approaches. They are also sometimes referred to as holistic because they take into account a person's emotional, mental, and spiritual state as well as his physical condition. In contrast, conventional—or allopathic—medicine diagnoses specific pathologies or diseases and prescribes drugs or surgery for their treatment.

The Basic Principles of Alternative Medicine

Although the practices included under the umbrella term "alternative medicine" are quite diverse, some common basic principles set them apart from conventional medicine.

ALTERNATIVE MEDICINE EMPHASIZES "SELF-HEALING"

The core philosophy behind alternative fields of medicine is that healing should come from within;

that if the body (as well as mind and spirit) is supported and strengthened, it should be able to fight off disease without needing to rely on drugs or other interventions. Thus, alternative remedies do not work to treat a specific ailment as much as they work to support the immune system as a whole.

ALTERNATIVE MEDICINE TAKES INTO ACCOUNT THE "WHOLE PERSON"

Alternative practitioners treat the whole body rather than just the ill or injured part. In fields such as acupuncture and Ayurveda, the emphasis is on bringing the whole body into harmony, or balance, as a way to heal any problem, or imbalance. Often a corollary of the treatment is that other unrelated problems clear up once a state of balance is achieved.

An alternative practitioner may want to understand the patient's emotional and spiritual state as well as his physical condition in order to make a correct diagnosis. Also, factors such as diet, lifestyle, and environmental influences are usually carefully considered.

ALTERNATIVE MEDICINE FOCUSES ON PREVENTION

Conventional medicine is designed to cure disease. A common criticism of conventional medicine is that it does not emphasize prevention of disease.

The goal of alternative medicine is to make a person healthy by strengthening the immune system and bringing the body into balance, thereby preventing further illness. Alternative practitioners try to determine the underlying causes of an illness—whether they might be diet, environmental factors, or mechanical imbalances in the body—to prevent reoccurrence.

ALTERNATIVE REMEDIES ARE RELATIVELY GENTLE

Most alternative remedies—herbs, homeopathic remedies, massage, aromatherapy, and the like—are gentle and noninvasive and do not have unpleasant side effects. With the exception of some potent herbs and essential oils, overdosing on alternative remedies is difficult. For this reason, they are generally considered quite safe. The

biggest danger with alternative therapies is relying too much on them in severe illness, when the lifesaving ability of modern medicine is needed.

For a good example of the difference between alternative and conventional medicine, look at the treatment of ear infections, the number one cause of childhood doctor visits. Most pediatricians rely on antibiotics to treat ear infections; if the infections recur, a doctor may resort to an arsenal of different antibiotics as the child develops resistance to one type. The repeated use of antibiotics can suppress the child's immune system, leaving him susceptible to other infections. Eventually, if antibiotics are no longer effective, the pediatrician might recommend surgery, with its inherent risks, to place drainage tubes in the eardrums.

An alternative practitioner would probably start by recommending soothers to relieve the pain of the ear infection, such as warm herbal oil drops in the ear. He or she might then work on boosting the child's immune system to fight off the infection, via herbs or homeopathic remedies. At the same time, the practitioner would take a detailed history of the child's diet and lifestyle to investigate the underlying cause of the recurring infections. Depending upon the findings, the practitioner might recommend dietary changes to alleviate a food intolerance, or hands-on manipulation to correct a mechanical imbalance in the bones surrounding the ear. If the alternative practitoner's diagnosis is correct, he would achieve the same end result as the pediatrician—draining the ears—but without antibiotics or surgery.

Not Really "Alternative" After All

In establishing its Office of Alternative Medicine in 1992 at the National Institutes of Health (NIH), the United States government defined alternative medicine as that which is not taught in medical schools or covered by health insurance. The fact that this definition is now outmoded indicates how rapidly the field is changing. The majority of medical schools in the United States currently offer courses in alternative medicine, and an increasing number of insurance policies cover alternative therapies such as chiropractic and acupuncture.

Alternative medicine actually is not so "alternative." Worldwide, 70 to 90 percent of people use traditional medicine as their primary form of treatment, according to the World Health Organization. In the United States, the growth in alternative medicine has been exponential in the last decade. According to David Eisenberg's study, "Trends in Alternative Medicine Use in the United States, 1990–1997," 42 percent of the United States population had used some form of alternative therapy in 1997, up from 34 percent in 1990. The most popular therapies included herbs, massage, folk remedies, and homeopathy. Total 1997 out-of-pocket expenditures on alternative therapies were conservatively estimated at $27 billion, which is roughly equal to out-of-pocket spending for all United States physician services. As evidence of the field's growing legitimacy, the *Journal of the American Medical Association* devoted its November 11, 1998 issue to alternative medicine, stating in an editorial, "Alternative medicine is here to stay. It is no longer an option to ignore it or treat it as something outside the normal processes of science and medicine."

How Proven Are Alternative Therapies?

Although alternative medicine is increasingly accepted, some physicians still dismiss it because they do not know much about the field or because many alternative therapies have not been subjected to standardized testing.

Many parents do not care that alternative therapies have not been scientifically proven, however; all they care about is that they work. The efficacy of alternative therapies have been demonstrated anecdotally over and over and are now being recognized in medical journals. The November 11, 1998, issue of the *Journal of the American Medical Association* reported that, among other things, moxibustion (burning herbs to stimulate acupuncture points) was 75 percent effective in turning breech position babies in the womb, and yoga was more effective than wrist splinting in relieving carpal tunnel syndrome. In

November 1997, the National Institutes of Health reported that acupuncture is "clearly effective" for treating nausea during pregnancy, as well as the nausea and vomiting associated with chemotherapy and surgery.

More research is being done on alternative medicine all the time. The Office of Alternative Medicine (OAM), which was created in 1992 within the National Institutes of Health and was designated one of nineteen worldwide Collaborating Centers in Traditional Medicine by the World Health Organization, had its budget increased from $12 million in 1997 to $50 million in 1999. This increased budget allows OCAM to fund research into the effectiveness of alternative medicine.

Currently, thirteen alternative medicine research centers have been formed at universities around the country, including Harvard and Stanford. More than fifty alternative medicine research studies have been undertaken to date to analyze such issues as the effects of acupuncture on arthritis, St. John's Wort on depression, and shark cartilage on cancer.

However, alternative medicine is still a largely unproven, unregulated field, leaving the responsibility squarely up to the consumer to investigate the safety and effectiveness of alternative remedies and practitioners. Chapter 13 describes how to safely practice alternative care at home; for tips on how to find a qualified practitioner, see "Finding an Alternative Practitioner" below.

Following is a discussion of the main fields of alternative therapy. For information on treating common childhood ailments with these therapies, see Chapter 13.

Herbal Medicine

Herbs have been used by healers since ancient times and are the basis for 25 percent of the pharmaceutical drugs used today, including aspirin (from white willow bark). Herbal, or botanical, medicine refers to the use of tinctures, teas, capsules, salves, and poultices made from plants.

Herbs differ from drugs in that an herb is the complete form of the plant; drugs usually isolate the most active ingredient in the leaf, flower, seeds, or bark of a plant, then amplify it or synthetically reproduce it. For reasons that researchers still do not understand, the many components of a plant seem to work synergistically together, and the herb in its complete form seems to provide gentler therapeutic benefits than do synthetic drugs. For the most part, herbs can work as well as drugs in healing the body and strengthening the immune system, without harmful side effects. In addition, many herbs are naturally rich in vitamins, minerals, and other essential nutrients.

Just because herbs come from plants does not mean that they are all safe, however. Plants can be powerful medicine, and many herbs should not be taken by children or by pregnant or nursing mothers. Some herbs can have dangerous side effects or be poisonous if used in large amounts and/or over long periods of time—St. John's Wort, for example, can cause sensitivity to sunlight. In general, the bitter-tasting herbs are more potent medicinals, while pleasant-tasting herbs are safer. For a comprehensive discussion of the safety and side effects of most herbs, read *Herbs, Kids, and Health* or *The American Pharmaceutical Association Practical Guide to Natural Medicines* (see Resources).

Herbal medicines can be given as teas (dried herb leaves steeped in water; sweetened with a little sugar or honey if you like), or liquid extracts (administered with a dropper, given either straight or in warm water). Tinctures are herbs extracted into alcohol; glycerites are herbs extracted into glycerin. Special, sweet-tasting children's herb glycerites are available. Children should always be given alcohol-free herbal extracts. For a nursing baby, drink herbal extracts or teas fifteen minutes before nursing to give the baby the herb in your milk.

Herbs can also be given to children externally, to be absorbed through the skin. You can rub an herbal tea or extract on your child's feet, add a sachet of dried herbs to her bathwater, or even apply herb poultices (fresh or dried leaves pounded to pulpy mass) directly to her skin.

Make sure that you are getting herbs from pure sources. Look for organically grown herbs: You do not want to give pesticides to your children as medicine. "Wildcrafted" herbs are picked in the wild, but be warned, they are not necessarily purer than cultivated herbs. You can also grow your own herbs in your backyard. Peppermint, thyme, calendula, and comfrey are among the easiest herbs to grow and the most effective to use. Do not buy adult products thinking you can dilute the dose, as the herbs contained in the formula may not be intended for children. Remember, too, that reputable herbal companies do not make claims about an herb's medicinal value on the label, because doing so is illegal.

Here are some common herbs and their health benefits for children:

Aloe vera: heals burns and wounds (used externally).

Arnica: good for bumps and bruises (used externally).

Astragalus: strengthens the immune system.

Calendula: soothes skin irritations, burns, diaper rash (used externally).

California poppy: calming; used in children's nighttime formulas.

Catnip: calming, digestive aid; used for colic, sleeplessness, minor fevers.

Chamomile: a digestive aid and calming agent.

Comfrey: good for skin irritations, inflammations (should not be taken internally).

Echinacea: stimulates the immune system (best taken at the first signs of an illness).

Fennel: digestive aid; used for stomachache, gas, colic.

Feverfew: relieves fever and pain.

Garlic: antiviral, immune support (best taken raw).

Ginger: relieves nausea; anti-inflammatory.

Hops: sedative; hops flowers placed in a pillowcase make a good sleep aid for restless children.

Licorice: soothes sore throats, eases hay fever; antiviral.

Marshmallow root: immune support; demulcent (soothes inflamed mucus membranes).

Mullein: demulcent, expectorant; used for sore throats, coughs, asthma.

Peppermint: warming, digestive, antiviral.

St. John's Wort: antidepressant, antiviral; used externally on minor injuries and ear infections.

Thyme: expectorant, antibacterial.

Valerian: sedative; relieves insomnia, hyperactivity.

Wild cherry bark: treats coughs; used in many cough syrups.

Yarrow: anti-inflammatory, promotes sweating; relieves fevers, can be used in baths to relieve chicken pox or poison ivy.

Homeopathy

Homeopathy is one of the most widely used methods of alternative care around the world. It can be safely and economically self-administered, and it can have dramatic effects when the right remedy is chosen.

Homeopathy means "like cures like." The homeopathic system was formulated by a German physician, Samuel Hahnemann, toward the end of the eighteenth century. Hahnemann stumbled upon an idea that had been glimpsed by Hippocrates—that substances causing a certain set of symptoms in a healthy person can cure that same set of symptoms in a sick person. Hahnemann and his supporters recorded the symptoms caused by different substances by reviewing historical medical literature and by conducting "provings"—experiments in which they ingested small quantities of substances and noted the resulting physical and mental symptoms. Based on these records, they were able to prescribe homeopathically by matching the symptoms of a sick person with the remedy that would cause those symptoms.

Homeopathic remedies are made from over 1,000 plants and minerals. The raw material is "potentized"—serially diluted and shaken—resulting in remedies of various potencies, or degrees of dilution. The higher potency remedies are so diluted that they no longer contain molecules of the original substance—a fact that leads modern scientists to dismiss homeopathy. Yet, the fact that these highly diluted remedies do work is undeniable, at least to the millions of homeopathic prescribers and patients who have used them.

Homeopathic remedies are prescribed on the basis of a person's total symptoms, both physical and mental. The more a prescriber—whether physician or parent—understands a person's emotional and physical state, the more likely that the correct remedy will be chosen. For example, many remedies might be considered to treat a child's earache. The prescription is based not on the diagnosis "earache," but on the subjective experience of the child with the earache, depending upon his physical and emotional symptoms.

Because homeopathic remedies are so diluted, they can be safely self-administered with no adverse effects if the wrong remedy is chosen. Home remedy kits contain a variety of remedies for common childhood ailments, labeled according to the dilution factor. The higher the potency or dilution factor, the less often a remedy needs to be given. Generally, a remedy is given every fifteen minutes to every hour, for a few hours, until you see an improvement. At that point, the remedy should be stopped until the improvement stops. If the remedy is right, it will work, and you and the patient will know it is working. If the remedy is wrong, it will not cause any harm—it simply will not work. If there is no reaction after about six doses, the remedy should be changed.

Once parents become accustomed to homeopathic prescribing and familiar with which remedies work best for their children, many find homeopathic self-care to be very helpful for common childhood complaints. However, for those who are just starting out with homeopathy, or who are dealing with more serious complaints, seeing a homeopathic practitioner is helpful. Homeopathic prescribing is an art: There are over a thousand possible remedies, each matching a particular set of symptoms. Also, it can be difficult to be objective enough to notice important symptoms in a family member.

The homeopath's task is to recognize what is most unusual about your child and match the child's pattern to that produced by one of the homeopathic medicines. A homeopath will conduct an extensive interview with you and your child, taking into account your child's physical symptoms, temperament, sleep tendencies, food preferences, thoughts, fears, likes, and dislikes. To find a qualified homeopathic practitioner, see Resources.

Acupuncture

Acupuncture, the ancient healing system of Asia, is the most widely used therapy in the world. It is practiced extensively in the East, and its use is growing steadily in the Western world as more people discover its benefits.

The theory behind acupuncture is that the body contains a vital energy, called Qi or chi (pronounced "chee"). This Qi circulates through the body—just as blood flows through the blood vessels—along a system of pathways referred to as meridians or channels. There are fourteen of these meridians, each linked to an internal organ system.

According to Oriental medicine, if the flow of Qi is unbalanced, or blocked, illness will result. The acupuncturist seeks to restore balance to the body by stimulating the meridians by inserting slender needles into the skin, just below the surface, on acupoints along the meridian system. The goal of acupuncture is to relieve symptoms by helping the body rebalance itself.

Although modern science does not have a language to describe acupuncture, the fact remains that, in many instances, it works. Current research has described specific physiological shifts occurring after acupuncture, including beneficial changes in immune system function and hormonal activity. Acupuncture is used for children in treating everything from asthma to neurological disorders such as seizures, as well as milder complaints such as hay fever, constipation, and bedwetting. However, because some children object to needles, you may want to first try acupressure or shiatsu massage, which stimulate the meridians without using needles.

In treating your child, an acupuncturist will take into account her medical history and appearance, including her build, the shape and color of her face, color of her tongue, and quality of her pulses. The therapist may test for weakness along the meridians or in the muscles. The treatment usually lasts fifteen minutes to a half-hour, during which time the therapist inserts the needles, leaving them in for a few minutes if the child will lie still. With a young child, the treatment can be administered as the child is held in her parent's arms. In some cases, acupuncturists stimulate the needles with a weak electrical current, or heat them with burning herbs (known as moxibustion); however, these techniques are rarely used with children.

The treatment does not hurt; most people describe it as a mild tingling, leading to an overall sense of relaxation. Sometimes improvements are felt right away; other times it takes a number of treatments before the effects become apparent.

There are several kinds of acupuncture, including Chinese and Japanese. Chinese acupuncture is part of a complete system of Oriental medicine that also includes Chinese herbs, nutrition, and mind-body exercises such as Tai Chi and Qi Gong. Japanese acupuncture incorporates acupressure, sound therapy, and nutrition. To find a qualified acupuncturist or Oriental medicine practitioner, see Resources.

Naturopathy

Naturopathy is a field of medicine that utilizes various alternative therapies, including herbal medicine, homeopathy, acupuncture, and diet. Naturopathic doctors serve as primary care physicians for the whole family, referring patients to medical doctors or specialists when necessary. They receive the same medical training as MDs in medical school, as well as extensive training in nutrition and alternative therapies (see "Licensing and Education Requirements," see page 157).

Naturopathic medicine focuses on the body's inherent ability to heal itself and uses very safe, natural therapies. It is built around the following six principles, which have their roots in Hippocratic, Chinese, Ayurvedic, and Native American medicine:

1. Respect the healing power of nature and of the body to heal itself. Create a healthy internal and external environment.
2. Treat the cause rather than the symptoms. Symptoms should not be suppressed—they are signals of the body's attempt to heal itself.
3. First, do no harm to the patient. Methods used to suppress symptoms without treating the underlying causes are considered harmful.

4. Treat the whole person. Take into account physical, mental, emotional, environmental, and genetic factors that cause disease.
5. The doctor is a teacher and should educate the patient to take responsibility for his or her own health. The doctor is not a healer—it is the patient who accomplishes the healing.
6. Prevention is the best cure. The emphasis should be on building health, rather than on fighting disease.

If you are interested in exploring alternative health care methods for your children or yourself, talking to an experienced naturopathic physician in your area is a good place to start. See "Finding an Alternative Practitioner," page 156.

Chiropractic

Chiropractic medicine—the second largest primary health care field in the world—has become so mainstream that some no longer consider it "alternative." Many chiropractors are affiliated with hospitals, and the treatment is increasingly covered by health insurance.

Chiropractic centers around the belief that misalignment of the spine can cause pain and even disease, because all of the body's organs and tissues are connected by the nervous system to the spinal cord.

Chiropractors manipulate, or adjust, the spinal column to treat injuries, illness, or other disorders. The practice seems to be most effective in alleviating neck and low back pain, joint pain, muscle cramps, and sports injuries. It is a good alternative for those wanting to avoid surgery for injuries.

Chiropractic is used with children to treat respiratory problems such as colds, flus, and asthma, as well as ear infections, hyperactivity, and many other disorders. The subspecialty of chiropractic pediatrics believes that misalignments of the spine are common in children as a result of childhood tumbles and falls, and that spinal manipulative therapy is an important preventive measure in childhood to avoid more problems later on.

To find a licensed chiropractor in your state, see Resources.

Aromatherapy

Our sense of smell can trigger powerful emotional responses, perhaps because the nasal passages open directly onto the part of the brain that controls emotion. Aromatherapy—the therapeutic use of essential oils of plants—can change your mood, treat a rash or bug bite, or relieve a stomachache. Certain essential oils act as immune system stimulants or combat viruses, fungi, and inflammation. Above all, aromatherapy is a pleasurable treatment. Few children will complain about having lavender sprinkled on their pillow or eucalyptus rubbed into their chest.

Aromatherapy oils can be used many different ways: as a massage oil, in a bath, in compresses, in a steam treatment, or in an aromatherapy diffuser, which releases a mist of essential oils into a room. Essential oils should never be used undiluted on the skin—with the exception of lavender and tea tree oils, which can be applied directly to burns and bug bites. All other oils should be diluted in a carrier oil like almond or grapeseed by mixing just a few drops of essential oil into an ounce of carrier oil. Have your child sniff the oil—if he sneezes or objects to it, choose a different oil. You can also do a patch test by mixing a few drops of carrier oil with the essential oil, rubbing it onto a small area of your child's skin, and observing it for any reactions after twenty-four hours. Essential oils should not be used on babies under three months old.

Here are some of the safest and most helpful essential oils for children:

Tea tree: for first aid, bug bites, bug repellent; antifungal, anti-infectious.

Lavender: for first aid, burns, sunburn; antiviral and antibacterial, boosts immunity.

Peppermint: digestive aid; cools fevers; decongestant.

Eucalyptus: decongestant; for respiratory disorders, cools fevers; antiviral and antibacterial.

Chamomile: calming, digestive aid; good for ear infections; anti-inflammatory.

Sandalwood: for sore throats; sedative.

Bergamot: good for viruses, fevers; anti-parasitic, anti-inflammatory (can cause allergic reactions and sensitivity to light in some people).

Frankincense: good for infections or respiratory congestion.

Thyme: strong antibacterial; good for lung congestion.

Citruses (orange, grapefruit, mandarin, tangerine): mood-enhancing; can calm overstimulated children.

St. John's Wort: good for ear infections.

Rose: treats hay fever, asthma, and nausea; calming.

Sage: a decongestant; treats throat and mouth infections.

Bach Flower Remedies

Like homeopathic remedies, Bach Flower remedies are distilled from plant sources—in this case, flowers. The therapy is based on the belief that the emotions play a critical role in the health of the body, and that negative feelings and stress underlie physical illness. The flower remedies address a person's emotional state in order to help facilitate both mental and physiological well-being.

The Bach Flower Essences were developed in the 1930s by British physician Edward Bach, who was originally trained in conventional medicine and later turned to homeopathy in a quest to treat the whole person. Bach discovered and developed thirty-eight flower essences that related to the different "negative states of mind" that he had observed in his patients and that he felt to be the underlying causes of disease. These flower essences had the ability, he felt, to bring balance and harmony to the spirit in a safe and simple way, causing healing to begin from within.

Bach Flower remedies are gentle, nontoxic liquid preparations that are taken orally. It is impossible to overdose on them. They are generally taken four times a day, including first thing in the morning and at bedtime. They can be especially effective with children, who are unencumbered by cynicism and accept them with trust. Many younger children are captivated by the idea of taking "flower drops that come from the fairies."

Flower remedies can be chosen for children by matching the remedy description to the child's emotional state. For example, chicory is used for an overly clingy child; impatiens for the irritable or impatient child; and holly for the jealous child. Perhaps the best known Bach Flower Essence is Rescue Remedy, a combination of five flower essences that can provide almost instant calming in many emergency situations. For information on finding and using the remedies, see Resources.

Bodywork

Touch is as important to infants and children as eating and sleeping, according to recent studies by the Touch Research Institutes at the University of Miami School of Medicine and Nova Southeastern University. "Touch therapy triggers many physiological changes that help infants and children grow and develop," says Tiffany Field, PhD, director and founder of the Touch Research Institutes. "For example, massage can stimulate nerves in the brain that facilitate food absorption, resulting in faster weight gain. It also lowers stress hormones, resulting in improved immune function."

Clinical studies presented in November 1997 at the American Academy of Pediatrics annual meeting found that touch therapy can help premature infants gain weight faster, asthmatic children improve breathing function, diabetic children comply with treatment, and sleepless babies fall asleep more easily.

Here are some different types of touch therapy:

MASSAGE

Massage helps to reduce pain, soothe injured muscles, stimulate blood and lymphatic circulation, and promote deep relaxation. In doing so, it may arouse the body's own recuperative powers. The beneficial effects of massage on premature infants have been so well documented that massage is used regularly on preemies at many hospitals around the country.

You can easily practice massage on your baby or child at home, using the techniques described in Chapter 7, under "Ways to Soothe a Crying Baby," (page 91). For more information, see "Infant Massage," under Resources.

REFLEXOLOGY

The feet contain thousands of nerve endings, which in the practice of reflexology are believed to correspond to organs throughout the body. By massaging these reflex points, reflexologists attempt to stimulate healing processes in the body, as well as to improve circulation, increase relaxation, and ease pain.

You can safely practice reflexology on yourself and your children with the use of a reflexology chart, showing which reflex points correspond to which organ systems. For information on finding and using reflexology charts, see Resources.

SHIATSU

Shiatsu, which means "finger pressure" in Japanese, is an ancient Oriental medicine massage practice. A shiatsu therapist applies comfortable pressure to all parts of the body with the thumbs, palms, and elbows, and gently stretches the body to loosen joints and muscles. The therapy is used to reduce back, neck, and shoulder aches and pains as well as sleeplessness, digestive problems, and emotional stress. Shiatsu is meant to restore energy to the body and to stimulate the body's ability to heal itself. You can learn some simple shiatsu techniques to use on your family, or find a licensed massage therapist trained in shiatsu (see Resources).

CRANIOSACRAL THERAPY

Craniosacral therapy is light, hands-on therapy designed to enhance the functioning of the craniosacral system—the membranes and cerebrospinal fluid surrounding the brain and spinal cord. By removing restrictions in the craniosacral system, the therapy is believed to improve the functioning of the central nervous system and enhance the body's natural healing processes.

The field of cranial osteopathy is based on the belief that even a normal birth or a minor fall can cause trauma to the bones of the skull or sacrum, which can lead to colic or chronic ear infections, among other disorders. The cranial osteopath uses very gentle manipulation of these bones to relieve blockages in the flow of cerebrospinal fluid to alleviate these disorders.

Ayurveda

Ayurveda is a Sanskrit word meaning "the science of life." It is one of the most ancient healing sys-

tems, originating in India, and like many other alternative therapies, it seeks to restore balance to the body, mind, and spirit. Depending on an individual's body type, a combination of diet, herbs, and natural therapies is used to restore harmony.

According to Ayurveda, there are three body types (or *doshas*), known as *vata, pitta,* and *kapha,* that govern the actions and metabolism of an individual. Vata individuals are unpredictable, very active, and thin. Pitta types are perfectionists, intelligent, quick-witted, and strong, with a medium build. Kapha types are easy-going and slow-moving, with a tendency to be overweight. The three doshas make up seven body types in Ayurveda: mono-types (in which vata, pitta, or kapha predominate), dual-types (vata-pitta, pitta-kapha, or kapha-vata), and equal types (individuals in whom vata, pitta, and kapha exist in equal proportions).

The Ayurvedic doctor orders a treatment based on the person's body type, looking at the tongue, palpating the body, and listening to the pulse and intestines. Treatments may include diet changes, herbal mixtures, herbal sweat baths, yoga, meditation, and massage.

There is a separate branch of Ayurveda dealing with children, called *bala chikitsa*. Ayurvedic doctors trained in this specialty have had success treating children's respiratory disorders, ear infections, coughs, sore throats, digestive problems, colic, hyperactivity, sleeping disorders, and a host of other ailments, using dietary recommendations, herbal syrups, sweet herbal jams, and massage with Ayurvedic oils. Unfortunately, there are very few practitioners who are familiar with this specialty in the United States. You may be able to get started with Ayurveda for your child by contacting the National Institute of Ayurvedic Medicine to speak to a qualified doctor and by reading a good Ayurvedic self-care book (see Resources).

Anthroposophy

Anthroposophy is a philosophy based on the work of Austrian scholar Rudolf Steiner, the father of the Waldorf School movement. His life's work included contributions to the fields of literature, philosophy, history, natural science, theosophy, education, and the arts. Given his accomplishments, then, it is not surprising that at the heart of anthroposophy is a belief in the human spirit's enormous potential.

The medical practice of anthroposophy regards illness as a way in which the immune system can strengthen and develop. The patient is treated holistically, taking into account the body, mind, and spirit. Alternative remedies are used alongside conventional practices, nutritional therapy, rhythmical massage, hydrotherapy, art therapy, and counseling.

Humor and Faith

Finally, do not discount the healing powers of humor and faith. Dr. Lee S. Berk of the Loma Linda University Medical Center has found that laughter can decrease the hormones associated with stress and can improve immune response. In other words, the more laughter in your life, the less your overall stress response, and the greater your defense against illness.

Another study may demonstrate the effectiveness of prayer. San Francisco cardiologist Randy Byrd arranged for prayer groups to pray every day for half of the 393 patients in a coronary care unit, without telling the patients or their treating physicians. Those who were prayed for improved more and had fewer complications than those who were not. Recipients of prayer may have a sense that there is a community behind them; that they are not facing illness alone.

So pray with your child and laugh with your child—it may be the best medicine.

Finding an Alternative Practitioner

Here are some starting points for finding an alternative practitioner.

- Always try to start with a recommendation: either a referral from a friend or another patient, or from another health practitioner (your pediatrician, nurse-practitioner, or midwife). The professional organizations for each specialty usually screen their members to ensure that they have adequate training and experience, and can refer you to qualified practitioners in your area (see Resources).
- Check to see if a practitioner is state licensed. If licensing requirements for that specialty do not exist in your state (see "Licensing Requirements,"

page 157), the next step is to check with the professional organization for that specialty to see if the practitioner is a member.

Once you have located a practitioner, here are some good questions to ask:

- Where did you train; for how long; did you have clinical training? (Some degrees are mail order and basically meaningless.)
- How long have you been in practice?
- Do you have experience in dealing with children?
- Can you help my child? (The answer to this question should never be an outright yes; no

practitioner can guarantee that a therapy will work for a particular individual.)

- How do you approach treatment?
- How open are you to working in conjunction with conventional therapies?
- Have you dealt with this complaint before? Do you have a reasonable track record in helping people with this complaint? (You may want to ask about specific new research supporting the therapy's use for this complaint.)
- What are the advantages and disadvantages of the therapy? What are the risks, possible side effects, and expected results?
- How often will we have to visit? What is the overall length of the treatment?
- How much time do you spend with each patient during a visit?

Other things to look for:
- Does the practitioner's office appear to be a professional environment?
- Does the practitioner explain the treatment in terms you can understand?

- What is the cost of the treatment? Is it comparable to the cost of other practitioners? (You can call around in your area, or check with the professional association for that specialty.) Is the treatment covered by insurance? (Many alternative treatments are not.)
- Do you feel you could have a rapport with this person? Do you feel accepted, respected, cared for, and listened to? A relationship with an alternative care practitioner can be even more personal than a relationship with an MD, so you need to listen to your instincts about the person.
- Finally, do tell your child's primary health care provider about any alternative therapies you are undertaking. A study in the *Journal of the American Medical Association* revealed that more than 60 percent of those who use alternative therapies do not tell their doctors about them. Your child's doctor should know about any alternative therapies so they can be considered as part of your child's overall health care plan.

Licensing and Education Requirements

Naturopathic Doctors (NDs) are currently licensed in eleven states. To be licensed, an ND must attend a four-year graduate-level naturopathic medical school. Currently there are two such accredited schools in North America: Bastyr University in Washington, and the National College of Naturopathic Medicine in Oregon. Two are pending accreditation: The Southwest College of Naturopathic Medicine, in Arizona, and the Canadian College of Naturopathic Medicine, in Ontario.

At each of these schools, the ND receives the standard medical curriculum followed in medical schools, as well as extensive training in clinical nutrition, acupuncture, homeopathic medicine, botanical medicine, and behavior modification. The emphasis is on disease prevention and optimizing wellness.

Acupuncturists are currently licensed in thirty-six states. A Master's of Science degree in acupuncture or Oriental medicine is a four-year program with training in acupuncture, Oriental medicine, Chinese herbal medicine, and the health sciences. Curricula include anatomy and physiology as well as coursework and clinical training in acupuncture techniques and Chinese herbal medicine. There are about thirty such accredited programs in the United States. Some states allow acupuncturists to identify themselves as Doctors of Oriental Medicine, which simply means they have had the same training as a licensed acupuncturist.

Massage therapists have licensing requirements in twenty-six states, requiring 500 hours of massage coursework and hands-on training. Homeopaths are currently licensed in three states: Arizona, Connecticut, and Nevada. Chiropractors have licensing requirements in all fifty states. Ayurveda and herbal medicine are unregulated fields in the United States.

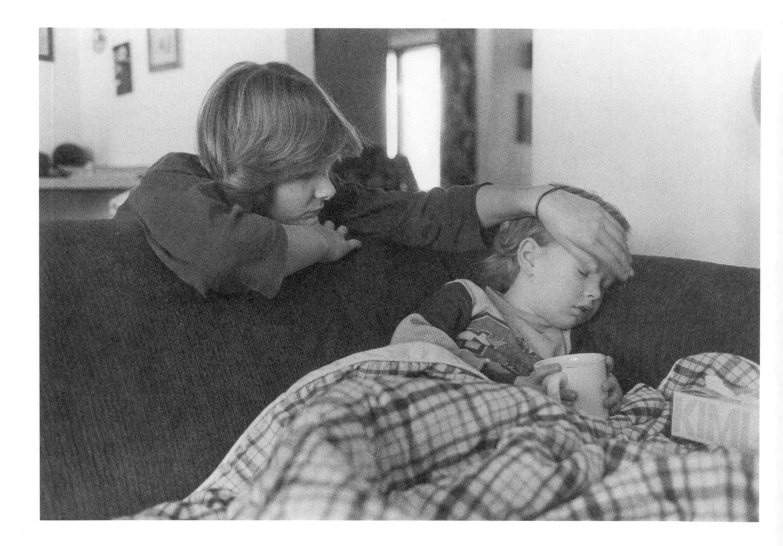

CHAPTER 13 The Natural Approach to Common Infant and Childhood Ailments

Children get sick—a lot. If you think about it, our children's being sick so often is actually healthy—it means that their immune systems are doing their job of developing resistance to the many viruses and pathogens they will come in contact with throughout childhood. Children also get hurt a lot, as they learn to walk, climb trees, and explore their world in the rough-and-tumble way that is so delightfully characteristic of childhood.

As a parent, you want to quell the helplessness you feel when your child is sick or hurting. Alternative remedies may be the answer. Because they are generally safe, you can administer them to your child at home without having to rush to a doctor or to rely on drugs for every malady. Keeping a repertoire of alternative remedies on hand will allow you to soothe your child through minor discomforts. Natural therapies, such as herbal medicine, homeopathy, aromatherapy, and Bach Flower remedies, and bodywork, such as massage, reflexology, and shiatsu, are particularly well-suited to home care. (For a description of each of these practices and information on how to get started with them, see Chapter 12.)

Alternative medicine is not a substitute for conventional medicine, but a collaborator with it. Certainly, some conditions do demand the disease-fighting capability of conventional medicine. But most often, children can fight off common ailments such as colds, ear infections, and scrapes with the help of some gentle soothers and an extra dose of cuddling and attention. Moreover, alternative remedies can be begun at a stage of an illness when drug therapy would not be indicated or useful. For chronic conditions that Western medicine has limited treatments for—including allergies, rashes, sleeplessness, and even behavioral problems such as hyperactivity—alternative therapies can be a godsend.

You Are the Expert

Using alternative medicine at home does not mean becoming your child's doctor. You should develop a relationship with at least one health care expert whom you can call upon for advice and treatment. But you should remember also that you are an expert when it comes to your child. No one knows your child better than you do; no one is better equipped to tell what is normal for your child and what is not.

Most parents bring their children in for doctor visits with a very good idea of what might be ailing them. Pediatrician (and father of eleven children) George Wootan found in his practice that most check-ups were unnecessary, what was needed instead was a little more parent education so that parents could make their own informed diagnoses of their children's health. As a result, he designed a pediatrics course for parents, covering how to do a physical exam, how to recognize a sick child, and how to treat common childhood illnesses at home. Parents

159

Elaine

When I was a young mother, my three-month-old son began having episodes of vomiting followed by unconsciousness. My husband and I went from one specialist to another, trying to find out what was wrong. No one seemed to know. Finally one doctor asked what I thought was wrong with the baby. I told him I believed it had something to do with food. He asked what made me think so, and I found myself producing evidence I didn't know I had.

Sometime later, when it had been demonstrated that our son did, in fact, have a rare type of food allergy, I told the doctor how amazed I was to find I had the information that could help my child and hadn't known it until he asked the right questions. He said the credit belonged to a medical school professor of his, who would say to his pediatric students, "If you don't know what's wrong with a child, ask the mother."

Elaine Heffner, "Staying in Charge," *Mothering*, Winter 1984.

who learn some simple home-care techniques are able to cut their doctor visits down considerably. And parents who are better informed get more out of each doctor visit because they ask the right questions.

When your children are ill, they are often not ill enough to necessitate going to the doctor's office—where they risk exposure to many different germs. A home-care remedy may be all they need, and you do not have to take a pediatrics course to be able to practice simple home-care with your children. You can start with the information in this chapter and Chapter 12, and perhaps read further in the books listed in Resources. With some knowledge, you can begin to take responsibility for your children's health, and, most importantly, understand what you do *not* have the expertise to handle at home.

Ideally, you should have a relationship with a doctor or health care practitioner who is accepting of home care and alternative therapies and open to telephone consultations. That way, you and the doctor can jointly determine whether a condition requires an office visit. (If your child displays any profound physiological or behavioral changes, you should not hesitate to get him to a doctor; see "When to Call a Doctor," page 173, for danger signs to watch for.)

Becoming steeped in the art of home care—as well as becoming a keen observer of your child's health—will only enhance your ability to recognize a serious illness. When conditions requiring medical treatment do arise, you will be better able to communicate with doctors about what your child might need, and better able to understand and welcome the lifesaving ability of modern medicine.

Keeping Your Children Healthy

Many people mistakenly believe that germs cause colds and other infectious illnesses. The state of our immune system, however, is what really determines whether or not we get sick. The specific bacteria or virus is not nearly as important as the medium in which it is allowed to flourish.

Boosting your child's immune system is critical to his good health—especially during the winter months, when children spend a lot of time indoors, breathing in germs. Alternative medicine works on the premise of bolstering the body's own natural defenses to enable the body to fight off illness. For this reason, natural remedies are safest and most effective when taken at the beginning of an illness, or as preventive measures. To best help your child, act at the first sign of malaise, before the condition becomes serious. A little help from nature is often all that is needed to jump-start the body's own defenses.

Here are some preventive measures to use during cold and flu season as well as at the first sign of illness, from Linda White, MD, coauthor of *Herbs, Kids, and Health* (Interweave Press):

SUPPLEMENT WITH VITAMINS AND MINERALS
Vitamin C plays a vital role in enhancing immune functions and tissue healing. During cold and flu season, give your child extra vitamin C: 250 milligrams of vitamin C four times a day up to 1000 milligrams. Overdosing on this water-soluble vitamin is not likely, and any extra will be excreted in

immune system because it stimulates the production of disease-fighting white blood cells. The key is to administer it liberally—a dropperful every few hours—at the first sign of a sudden chill, sore throat, or sneezing. Once an infection has already set in, echinacea is not as helpful. (Look for preparations that do not contain the herb goldenseal, as it can be strong medicine for children, and it has been overharvested almost to the point of extinction.) Often the timely administration of echinacea can prevent sneezing or a sore throat from turning into a full-blown cold. Echinacea should not be given on a continual basis, as that decreases its effectiveness.

Other good immune-boosting herbs for children include astragalus (good for treatment of stubborn respiratory infections; available in a blend with echinacea), licorice, marshmallow root, red clover, and bee products including bee pollen, propolis, and honey (bee products should not be given to children under a year old).

GO FOR THE GARLIC

Garlic is both a preventative and a remedy. Proven to destroy viruses and bacteria—including those responsible for colds, flus, and strep throat—garlic also effectively reduces fevers by inducing sweating, and it relieves coughs and colds by helping to expel mucus.

Garlic is most effective if eaten raw—in a tablespoon of honey (only for children over a year), in salad dressings, in hummus or tahini dips, mixed with plain yogurt and grated cucumber, or crushed with olive oil or butter to spread on toast. Use no more than one or two cloves. Raw garlic can, however, cause digestive problems for some people. Roasted or sauteed garlic cloves are still nearly as potent as raw garlic. Or make garlic and lemon tea: Pour a cup of boiling water over a crushed garlic clove; add the juice of a lemon and a few peppermint leaves. Brew for five minutes, and add honey.

To counteract the odor of garlic on the breath, eat raw parsley. Garlic capsules or extracts have not been shown to be nearly as effective as raw garlic. Garlic can also be administered externally: Mix crushed garlic with olive oil, apply a protective layer of olive oil to the bottom of your

the urine. Avoid a sudden decrease in dosage, which can cause increased susceptibility to infections. Taper off as illness wanes.

Zinc has been shown to protect against and help fight colds. High doses, however, can depress immunity. Give your child five to ten milligrams a day during periods of susceptibility to colds. (Zinc is best absorbed at the start of a meal, and drinking citrus juices for a half-hour before or after taking zinc inhibits its absorption.)

Vitamin A, beta-carotene, and the B-complex vitamins (B-1, B-2, B-6, B-12, biotin, niacin, pantothenic acid, and folic acid) also contribute to optimum immune functioning. Give your child a multiple vitamin that contains a balance of these vitamins as extra insurance against illness.

GIVE YOUR CHILD ECHINACEA AT THE FIRST SIGN OF ILLNESS

Echinacea (purple coneflower) has been shown in clinical studies to be a highly effective boost to the child's feet, followed by the garlic mixture, and bandage with a soft cloth, leaving it on for a few hours (undiluted raw garlic can burn the feet, so be sure to mix it with oil and check your child's feet periodically).

KEEP SWEETS AND PROCESSED FOODS TO A MINIMUM

Your child needs strong reserves of vitamins and minerals, which only a wholesome diet can supply, to fight infection. Foods with a high sugar content compromise the ability of white blood cells to fight bacteria.

CONSIDER AVOIDING DAIRY PRODUCTS, IF YOUR CHILD IS PRONE TO CONGESTION OR EAR INFECTIONS

Dairy intolerance is one of the most common and under-diagnosed childhood ailments. Dairy products can aggravate ear infections, respiratory congestion, and asthma. For more on milk intolerance, see Chapter 11.

GIVE YOUR CHILD PLENTY OF FLUIDS

Liquids can help loosen coughs and clear stuffy noses, as well as replace fluids that may be lost during vomiting, diarrhea, or fever. The best choices for liquids are water, weak herbal teas, diluted fruit juices, and, of course, breastmilk. And your mother was right: Chicken soup not only contains lots of nutrients, but it has been shown to lessen cold symptoms. Add chopped raw garlic to it for extra healing powers.

HUMIDIFY YOUR CHILD'S ROOM

A humidifier moistens the cold, dry air of winter, which can irritate throats and nasal passages, and increase vulnerability to infection. Be sure to clean humidifiers frequently to keep them effective. Children should not be exposed to tobacco smoke, which puts them at increased risk for respiratory infections.

SLOW DOWN YOUR PACE

Illness is sometimes a signal that life has become too hurried. At the first sign of illness, keep your child quiet and snug, and spend lots of time together reading, listening to music, and cuddling.

GIVE YOUR CHILD A MASSAGE

Massage can lower stress levels, stimulate circulation, relieve muscle aches, and provide overall soothing. You may want to avoid giving your child deep massage during a fever, as it can increase circulation and elevate body temperature.

PRACTICE VISUALIZATION

Have your child relax in a warm, quiet place. Then help her to imagine herself getting better, by envisioning her white blood cells as her favorite kind of animal attacking the germs, or by breathing in beautifully colored, healing air, and exhaling "bad" air.

TRY HYDROTHERAPY

The therapeutic use of water is a time-honored treatment for colds, sore throats, and flus. Healing herbs are absorbed very well in water through skin, as well as being inhaled in the ambient steam.

Give your child a hot footbath with a cold compress on the forehead to encourage sweating and rid the body of toxins. Or put your child in a hot bath to which herbs or essential oils have been added. After ten to fifteen minutes, wrap your child in towels and put him straight into a warm bed. A period of rest and sweating will maximize the treatment's effectiveness.

USE A EUCALYPTUS STEAM INHALATION

For respiratory infections, add three drops of eucalyptus oil or a bundle of aromatic herbs (eucalyptus, sage, thyme, rosemary, or wintergreen) to steaming water, and have your child lean over the steam, with a towel covering her head, to breathe in the inhalation. The eucalyptus inhalation will loosen mucus and fight infection. Afterward, you can pour the water into a warm bath, and let your child soak in it.

TRY A FOOT COMPRESS

To use this age-old technique for drawing out fever and toxins, soak a pair of cotton socks in cold water, wring them out, and put them on your child's warm feet (warm the feet up first if they are cold). Slip a pair of dry wool socks over the wet socks. As soon as the wet socks begin to warm up and dry out, repeat the process.

Despite your best efforts, you can not totally protect your child from getting sick. Home care tips for some common illnesses of childhood follow. For more information on using any of these remedies, see Chapter 12.

Fever

Fever is one of the most misunderstood childhood ailments. Fever is not a disease—it is a symptom of the body's attempt to fight off an infection. An increase in body temperature enhances the immune defenses, destroying viruses and bacteria.

Yet many parents automatically reach for acetaminophen (Tylenol) when their child's temperature goes above normal. Actually, suppressing fever interferes with the healing process and can prolong the illness. Instead, try to make your child comfortable, using the fever soothers listed below, and let the fever run its course.

Your child's temperature is not a reliable indicator of the severity of the illness. Young children can be very sick with a temperature of 100 degrees F. or less, or they can experience little discomfort and no danger with a temperature of 104 degrees F. Because even a temperature as high as 104 degrees F. may not need to be lowered, watch your child's behavior, not the thermometer. (See "When to Call the Doctor," page 173, for danger signs to be aware of).

Febrile seizures—which are triggered by a rapid temperature increase in response to infection and affect 3 to 4 percent of children between the ages of six months and three years—understandably worry parents. However, these convulsions are almost always the result of a predisposition or an underlying disease. A study in the New England Journal of Medicine reports that though febrile seizures are harrowing for parents, they do not cause any damage in most cases. Most children who have one seizure do not ever have another, and there is no connection between unsuppressed febrile seizures and epilepsy.

Sometimes doctors recommend that children who have had a febrile seizure be kept on phenobarbital. But a study at the University of Washington School of Medicine and the National Institute of Neurological Disorders and Stroke determined that children with a family history of epilepsy and a history of at least one febrile seizure who were taking phenobarbital showed lower IQ scores than those who were not on the drug. More importantly, the children on phenobarbital were just as likely to have another febrile seizure as their untreated peers.

Here are some things you can try when your child has discomfort from a fever:

HERBS

Herbs can increase comfort without interfering with the infection-fighting action of a fever. Elder flower and yarrow induce sweating and are helpful in managing hot fevers. Other herbs to use for fever in children include peppermint, chamomile, red clover, and rosemary. Make a tea of any or all of the above, sweetened with a little honey (never give honey to a child under a year old). Ginger is a warming herb to use when your child has a fever with chills. You can give your child a tea of

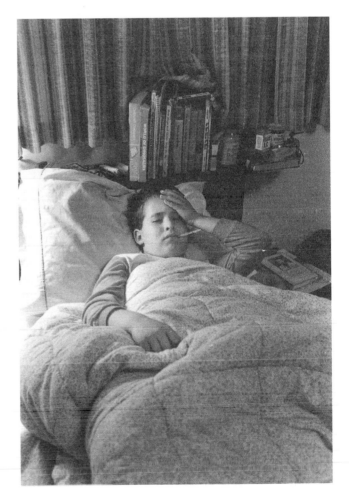

ginger and honey, or have him try a ginger foot bath. Grate a piece of fresh ginger and cover it with boiling water; let the water cool down, then soak your child's feet in it.

AROMATHERAPY

Lemon, lavender, eucalyptus, thyme, pine, rosemary, and sage are all scents that are soothing for fevers and contain immune-boosting properties. Give your child a bath with a few drops of any or all of these oils, or put them in an aromatherapy diffuser in your child's room. To cool a child down, put a cloth dipped in a cool tea of lavender on his forehead.

HOMEOPATHY

Aconite is often indicated in the early stages of illness. Belladonna is for fever with flushed cheeks and dilated pupils. Nux Vomica is for fevers resulting from overindulgences such as overeating or not getting enough sleep. Pulsatilla is for fevers that involve runny noses, tears, and clinginess.

HYDROTHERAPY

For mild fevers of 99 to 102 degrees F., a hot-to-tolerance bath or footbath will raise your child's body temperature. An "artificial fever" of this sort can theoretically break the fever and speed the healing.

To bring down a higher fever, you could try a tepid sponge bath. Never put your child in water so cold that he shivers, or so hot that it is uncomfortable.

LIGHT FOODS AND FLUIDS

Although feverish children are usually not hungry, they may be quite thirsty. Fruit juices and teas can help replenish lost fluids and nutrients. Try rose hip tea with a little honey, or hot lemonade—the juice of a lemon in a mug of hot water, sweetened with honey. (Again, never give honey to a child under age one.) A wonderful drink for strengthening the immune system is freshly squeezed carrot and red beet juice.

Once your child's appetite returns, raw fruits and vegetables will provide needed vitamins and minerals, stimulate digestion, and provide rough-

age to cleanse the system. Foods high in vitamin C (apples, berries, citrus fruits, carrots, broccoli, parsley, green peppers, tomatoes, cucumbers, rose hips, and honey) and carotenes (apricots, bananas, peaches, prunes, asparagus, avocados, broccoli, cabbage, carrots, pumpkin, spinach, sweet potatoes, tomatoes, yellow vegetables, and soy) will help fight the infection.

COMFORT

You are the best source of comfort for your feverish child. Stay home with your child and read, tell stories, rock, and sing to him.

Earaches

Earaches are the number one cause of pediatric visits. Fluid can easily build up in a child's tiny middle ear, creating pressure on the eardrum and causing intense pain. Most ear infections are painful, but not serious. If your child experiences more than two ear infections a year, you should look for underlying causes.

Over 90 percent of children suffering from ear infections are treated with a course of antibiotics. Antibiotics can cause harmful side effects and inhibit the immune system—possibly leading to recurring infections—by destroying good as well as harmful bacteria (see "Antibiotics: Out of Control," page 167).

Actually, the term "ear infection" is often inaccurate. Many inflammations of the middle ear are not caused by bacteria, and therefore are not infections. Antibiotics are effective only when bacteria are present—which is impossible to tell without taking an ear culture. One Dutch study of over 5,000 children found that 88 percent of children with otitis media (middle ear inflammation) never need antibiotics; other studies have found that 50 percent of middle ear infections resolve without prescription drugs.[1,2]

The middle ear drains through the eustachian tube. If the eustachian tube is blocked, the fluid in the middle ear stagnates, just as the water in a pond that has been dammed becomes stagnant. You could clear up the ears with antibiotics—just as you could clean the pond by dumping chlorine into it—or you could remove the blockage and get the fluid draining again. In the case of recurring ear infections, determining why the infections are happening is important so you can address the underlying cause while you relieve the child's discomfort.

There are several reasons why fluid might build up in the middle ear. They include:

ALLERGY

Many studies have suggested a link between food intolerance and middle ear problems. One study tested 104 children with recurring middle ear problems for food allergy and discovered 81 to be allergic. After eliminating the offending foods, 86 percent got better, and 94 percent got worse when the offending foods were reintroduced.[3]

The most common allergens are dairy products, wheat, egg white, peanuts, and soy. If your child suffers from recurring ear infections, you might first try eliminating dairy products from her diet, then the other common allergens.

NUTRITIONAL DEFICIENCY

Researchers have found that children with high susceptibility to ear infections are often deficient in zinc, iron, or vitamin A. One study found substances related to the improper intake of dietary fats in the middle ear fluid of children with otitis media. Eating trans-fatty acids—found in margarine as well as french fries, donuts, cake frostings, and other junk foods—can set the stage for inflammation.[4] Often children with recurrent earaches improve simply by switching to a more wholesome diet (see Chapter 11 for more on a whole foods diet).

MECHANICAL OBSTRUCTION

A blockage of the eustachian tube can occur as a result of swollen tonsils or adenoids, or from structural problems in the bones surrounding the ear. The biomechanics of these delicate bones can be disrupted by any physical trauma, including a fall or a difficult birth. Chiropractic adjustments or craniosacral therapy are often effective at resolving these problems and preventing recurring ear infections.

Although otitis media is usually not serious, it can occasionally lead to mastoiditis, an inflamma-tion of the bone just behind and below the ear; or meningitis, an infection of the membranes covering the brain. Symptoms of mastoiditis include thick pus discharging from the middle ear, redness and tenderness of the mastoid process below the ear, fever, and headache. Symptoms of meningitis include headache, stiffness of the neck, lethargy, loss of appetite, vomiting, fever, and chills, and in babies, a bulging fontanel (soft spot). Both mastoiditis and meningitis require immediate medical attention. They can occur even when a child is on antibiotics for an ear infection. Remember that you are the best observer of your child's condition, and be on the lookout for these warning signs.

Many children with recurring ear infections undergo tympanostomy tube placement—surgical insertion of drainage tubes in the eardrum. Tube placement is the most common general anesthesia-based procedure performed on children under two. However, many doctors themselves believe that the surgery is prescribed more than is necessary. A study of more than 6,600 children who had undergone tube placement found that almost 60 percent of the surgeries performed were unnecessary or had risks equal to benefits.[5] A five-year study reported in the *Townsend Letter for Doctors* (April, 1991) indicated that the procedure provides only temporary relief from ear infections and may, in fact, cause deafness. In ninety-eight children with tubes placed in one ear, there was a 21 percent higher incidence of deafness in the ears with the tubes.

There are many things you can do at home for childhood ear infections, short of resorting to antibiotics or tubes. If your child awakens in the middle of the night crying in pain, or appears feverish or congested, and complains that her ears hurt or pulls on her ears, you should suspect an ear infection. You can take the child to a doctor to confirm your diagnosis, or you can invest in a good otoscope and do the same thing the doctor does: Look in the ear to see if it appears red (this takes some practice). Or you can avoid both of these steps and trust your initial diagnosis. Either way, your course of action should be the same: to relieve the pain in the ear while bolstering the immune system to fight off the infection. Use the treatments recommended below, and watch your child for signs of the condition worsening. Most ear infections will clear up on their own in a few days.

If you do decide to use antibiotics, be sure to give your child immune boosters to counter the negative effects (see "Antibiotics: Out of Control," page 167). If your child suffers from recurrent ear infections, try to determine the root cause. If your doctor recommends tubes, be sure to get another opinion.

Here are some treatments to relieve the pain of earaches:

HERBS

Eardrops can help relieve the pain of an earache. A blend of mullein and garlic oil is a good choice because of its antiviral and antibacterial properties; St. John's Wort and calendula can also be added. You can buy herbal eardrops or make your own. To make garlic oil, add four crushed cloves of garlic to a jar with a quarter cup of olive oil, let stand one to three days at room temperature, strain, and store in the refrigerator for up to six months. Pure garlic extract that you purchase in a natural foods store— as opposed to garlic oil that you make in olive oil— can be irritating to the ear canal.

To administer eardrops: Run hot water over a spoon until it is warm, pour a few drops of oil onto the spoon to warm up, then put two to three drops in each ear while your child is lying down; plug the ear loosely with a cotton ball. Repeat two or three times a day for no more than four days.

AROMATHERAPY

Make an aromatherapy ear rub with several drops of lavender, tea tree oil, and chamomile in one ounce of olive oil. Rub the oil mixture around the outside of the ear and over the lymph nodes on the side of the neck, or dab a cotton ball in the oil, gently place it in the ear, and leave it in until the infection is gone, replacing it with a fresh cotton ball several times a day. Give your child a eucalyptus steam inhalation (see "Keeping Your Children Healthy," page 160).

HOMEOPATHY

Homeopathic remedies can be administered at home to relieve the pain of occasional earaches. If your child is angry, fearful, and sensitive to light and noise, consider belladonna, which is effective for earaches that come on suddenly, with severe, throbbing pains. Chamomilla is good for earaches associated with teething— the child may have one red cheek and be inconsolable, want to be carried, and act angry and intolerant. Children who need Pulsatilla tend to be weepy, sensitive, and clingy. Their cheeks will be pale, and there may be a thick, yellow-green discharge from the nose or the ear. Symptoms often come on gradually, frequently following a cold. Aconite is for the sudden onset of earache after a chill. The child may awaken in the night screaming with pain and appearing anxious and scared.

Recurring earaches also respond well to homeopathic treatment; consult a trained homeopath for help in choosing the right remedy.

Colds and Flus

According to Linda White, MD, colds are caused by viruses and can almost always be treated at home. The influenza, or "flu" virus, like a cold, causes stuffy noses, sore throats, and coughs, along with fever, muscle aches, and headache. The best approach with colds and flus is to make your child comfortable and support his immune system while allowing the condition to run its course. Cold and flu symptoms such as runny noses and phlegmy coughs have a purpose—to discharge the virus from the body—and suppressing the symptoms with cough suppressants, antihistamines, and fever-reducers like Tylenol may only prolong the condition.

Use the following home remedies to alleviate discomfort and bolster immunity. (Call your health practitioner if your child's condition worsens or does not improve in three to five days— possibly a sign that a cold has turned into a bacterial infection such as sinusitis, bronchitis, or pneumonia, which may need to be treated with antibiotics.)

Antibiotics: Out of Control

The overuse of antibiotics poses one of the greatest challenges to modern medicine: infections that are increasingly difficult to treat. Amoxicillin—which was developed to treat bacteria resistant to penicillin—has long been the drug of choice for ear infections. Because this antibiotic has been so widely used, more strains of bacteria have become resistant to it. Sulfa drugs and the other antibiotics that were developed to combat these resistant bacteria are also losing their effectiveness. The more that antibiotics are overused, the more dependent we are becoming on drug companies to develop new drugs, which are only marginally more effective.

An editorial in the September 17, 1997 issue of the *Journal of the American Medical Association* cautioned against the overuse of antibiotics and asked physicians to curb prescriptions of antibiotics. Physicians in focus groups say the major reason for overprescription is unrealistic patient expectations, and they report having too little time during the average appointment to discuss with patients why an antibiotic is unnecessary.

An antibiotic works by killing off bacteria in your child's system—good bacteria as well as bad. Because antibiotics diminish the number of beneficial bacteria in the bowel and intestines, the result can be diarrhea, parasitic infections such as Giardia, or an overgrowth of the yeastlike fungus Candida. More frightening is the fact that children who are treated repeatedly with broad-spectrum antibiotics tend to have antibiotic-resistant bacteria left in their system, making them—and the other children to whom they spread these bacteria—susceptible to bacterial infections such as ear infections, strep throat, and occasionally, meningitis. The more resistant the bacteria in a child's system become, the harder it is to treat them with antibiotics. After completing a course of antibiotics, a child is particularly vulnerable to a recurrence of the infection.

There are times when an infection is too strong for a child to fight without the aid of antibiotics. In these cases, welcome the lifesaving ability of antibiotics, and augment them with natural remedies to restore balance to your child's system and build his immunity. Use the following remedies during the course of antibiotics and for a full week afterward:

- *Acidophilus or bifidus:* These supplements restore friendly bacteria to the intestine and reduce the incidence of diarrhea and intestinal disorders. Find a good-quality brand at your natural foods store; give it to your child three times a day for a week.
- *Vitamin C:* Give a supplement daily.
- *Zinc:* Use a low-potency supplement several times a week.
- *Echinacea:* Give a dropperful several times a day to help support the immune system.
- *Astragalus:* This tonic herb is good for restoring vitality after a bout with infection.

HERBS

Linden and elder flower promote sweating and have an anti-inflammatory effect. Thyme dissolves mucus and acts as an expectorant. Make a tea of these, along with mullein, rose hips, peppermint, yarrow, wintergreen, or lemon verbena. The tea should be sipped as hot as possible to encourage sweating. For children who are kept awake by a stuffy nose, try the calming herbs chamomile and catnip.

An herbal footbath or bath can be particularly comforting for colds and chills. Steep a handful of thyme or linden and elder flowers in hot water for a strong infusion, strain, and pour into a hot bath or footbath. After ten minutes of soaking, wrap your child in towels or slip her feet into wool socks and put her to bed.

AROMATHERAPY

Eucalyptus helps relieve congestion. As a preventive measure, add a few drops of eucalyptus or tea tree oil to the bathwater each night during cold and flu season. Purify the air while your child sleeps by adding six to eight drops of eucalyptus oil to a diffuser or warm-air vaporizer.

A warm massage is very comforting to a child who is sick with the flu or a chest cold. To one ounce of carrier oil (grapeseed or almond), add a few drops of lavender, eucalyptus, and chamomile oils. Gently massage the chest, rubbing from the middle of the chest out toward the armpit to help loosen mucus. In addition to relieving discomfort, the anti-infectious properties of these oils can help your child get healthy.

HYDROTHERAPY

If a cold is not accompanied by a fever, you can support the body's fight against it by temporarily raising the body temperature. Put your child in a hot bath, shower, or, ideally, a sauna or steam shower, for no more than ten minutes. Essential oils of thyme, sage, or pine in the shower or sauna will help to relieve respiratory congestion.

Saline nose drops will loosen nasal congestion: Make your own with ¼ teaspoon of salt in ½ cup of warm water. At the onset of cold symptoms, take the preventive measures listed in "Keeping Your Children Healthy," page 160. If you treat a runny nose or a scratchy throat before it blossoms into something worse, you may be able to nip a cold in the bud.

Coughs and Sore Throats

Most sore throats are caused by viruses, for which antibiotics are ineffective. The remaining percentage are a bacterial infection, chiefly strep (short for streptococcal) throat. Signs of strep are a painful sore throat, a very red throat and tonsils with white patches, headache, greenish nasal discharge, and sour breath. The only sure way to determine strep throat, however, is to take your child for a throat culture. Strep throat is usually treated with antibiotics.

Coughs are typically caused by viruses following a cold or flu. They often start out dry and hacking, and become loose and phlegmy as the illness draws to its end. A productive cough should not be suppressed, but should be aided by expectorants that thin mucus and help to expel it. Call your health practitioner if your child develops a high fever, chills, rapid and shallow breathing, and chest pain (signs of pneumonia); greenish or brown phlegm accompanied by fever (signs of bronchitis), or a barking cough and wheezing (signs of croup). Linda White, MD, suggests the following remedies for coughs and sore throats:

LIQUIDS

Warm fluids help relax the airways and loosen mucus. Give your child warm apple cider spiced with cinnamon sticks, ginger, and cloves (a natural anesthetic); warm lemonade with ginger; apple cider vinegar (another natural anesthetic) and honey in hot water (if he's over age one); chicken broth; and plenty of healing herb teas.

HERBS

Licorice root is an herbal expectorant as well as demulcent (soothing to inflamed mucus membranes). To make licorice root tea, put a piece of licorice root in a cup of water, boil five minutes, strain, and sweeten with honey (for children over a year old). Let your child drink the tea and suck on the root.

Wild cherry bark inhibits coughing. Marshmallow root is both a demulcent and immune stimulating. Slippery elm bark tea or lozenges are soothing to the throat.

AROMATHERAPY

Massage your child's throat and chest with a few drops of eucalyptus, tea tree, and thyme oils in a carrier oil. Put a few drops of eucalyptus, lavender, clary sage, or sandalwood in a warm-air vaporizer or aromatherapy diffuser in your child's room. Or, give your child a steam inhalation with eucalyptus along with lavender, marjoram, or chamomile oil (see "Keeping Your Children Healthy," page 160).

HOMEOPATHY

Aconite is helpful for a child who wakes up in the middle of the night with severe pains and a fever, and acts restless, anxious, and thirsty. Belladonna is used to treat a child who acts demanding and difficult; the neck is tender and swallowing is painful. The Pulsatilla child is dependent and wants to be cuddled; the throat is dry and raw, and the child is not thirsty.

First Aid

Bug bites, sunburns, bruises, and bumps will hopefully be the most common ailments your child will face. With a few natural remedies on hand, you can alleviate your child's pain and speed the healing process.

Some cuts and falls require emergency care. Be sure to consult your health practitioner or get your child to an emergency room if:

- bleeding does not stop after 10 to 15 minutes of pressure.
- a laceration is ragged or deep.
- there is any foreign matter that cannot be removed from a cut.
- your child has a severe burn, appears in intense pain or injured after a fall, or has had more than a mild head injury.

Here are some good treatments to have on hand for general first-aid care:

ARNICA

Used for bruises, sprains, and sore muscles, this flower (*Arnica Montana*) is available in a cream or ointment, or can be given as a compress (apply a clean cloth soaked in a solution of one tablespoon of arnica tincture in one pint of water to the sore area). Homeopathic arnica can be given internally.

TIGER BALM

To treat muscle cramps and headaches, rub this salve on the affected muscle or temples, avoiding the eyes.

CALENDULA

This herbal remedy is anti-inflammatory, astringent, and antiseptic, and it inhibits bleeding. You can find it in salve form, often in combination with comfrey and other healing herbs. Use it for cuts, scrapes, rashes, burns, bruises, strains, and sprains.

ALOE VERA

Have this plant handy for wounds and all types of burns, including sunburns. Slice a leaf and apply the gel to the skin, or buy pure aloe vera gel.

LAVENDER OIL

Providing immediate relief for the sting or itch of insect bites, this remedy also helps in healing burns. Use lavender oil undiluted on the skin, or put a few drops in a lukewarm tub. For bruises, apply a compress dipped in equal parts cool water and apple cider vinegar with a few drops of lavender. Once the heat and swelling have subsided, massage the bruise with lavender and chamomile in a carrier oil.

TEA TREE OIL

Wash a wound with one part tea tree oil—a natural antiseptic—in ten parts water. For an insect repellent, fill a spray bottle with three ounces water, one ounce witch hazel or aloe vera juice, and twenty-four drops tea tree oil. Tea tree oil can also be applied to insect bites to stop the itching.

CHAMOMILE

This herb is an anti-inflammatory as well as a digestive aid. For diaper rash or other rashes, soak the affected area with a washcloth dipped in cool chamomile tea, or add chamomile tea to bath water.

ST. JOHN'S WORT

Herbal St. John's wort has anti-inflammatory properties and can be used topically on wounds and burns, or blended with oil to massage sore muscles. Homeopathic St. John's Wort (Hypericum) can be given internally after head injuries, puncture wounds, and animal bites.

WITCH HAZEL

A good topical treatment for bruises, bites, stings, and burns, it is also useful for leg aches accompanying growing pains.

RESCUE REMEDY

This Bach Flower remedy can given internally to ease feelings of shock or panic following a trauma.

TUMMY TINCTURE

Fennel and chamomile are soothing to an upset stomach. Put a few drops in water to take when tummyaches strike (add a few drops clove, caraway, or anise oil for a pleasing taste), or massage your child's tummy with chamomile and fennel in a carrier oil.

Healthy Teeth

Part of monitoring your children's well-being is making sure their teeth are healthy. Children can get teeth any time in their first year. To alleviate teething pain, try rubbing a little clove oil (diluted in a carrier oil) on your baby's gums, or massage along your baby's jaw and around her ear with warm chamomile oil (several drops of chamomile in one ounce of carrier oil).

Children's teeth should be brushed as soon as they get them, to establish good habits and prevent early tooth decay. Start with a soft toothbrush and no toothpaste at first. The best way to make sure your child is brushing thoroughly as she gets older is to get her a child's electric toothbrush. Your child's first visit to the dentist should be scheduled at age two or three, with twice-yearly check-ups thereafter.

Two issues you may want to check into further regarding your child's dental health are fluoride and mercury amalgam fillings. Fluoridation of community water supplies began in the 1940s, as a result of the discovery that fluoride in water could produce stronger, more cavity resistant teeth. Today, drinking water in about 60 percent of communities in the United States has fluoride added to it, and most toothpastes contain fluoride.

The problem is that too much fluoride can cause permanent stains on the teeth. More serious is the fact that fluoride is a poison, used in rat extermination. A single tube of toothpaste contains enough fluoride to kill a child.[6] Opponents of water fluoridation point to studies showing a correlation between fluoride and cancer, Down Syndrome, hyperactivity, nausea, headaches, and other ailments, as well as a weakening of the immune system.[7] They argue that a carcinogen like fluoride has no place in a community's water supply.

To find out the fluoridation level of your public water supply, contact your local water department. The safe fluoride content of drinking water is generally accepted to be one part per million (ppm), although, according to Dr. John Yiamouyiannis, author of *Fluo-*

ride: The Aging Factor (Health Action Press), it should ideally be .2 ppm or less. If you have your own well, you can get your water tested at a local laboratory, listed under your county health department. If you are concerned about your family's intake of fluoride, you can get a reverse osmosis water purification system to filter out the fluoride in your water, buy bottled water, or place your tap water under full spectrum lighting for one half hour before drinking.

You can look for salt-based toothpaste that contains no fluoride, or be sure that your children use no more than a pea-sized portion of toothpaste and do not swallow it. Instead of giving your children a chemical of questionable safety, you can keep their teeth strong by helping them to brush their teeth regularly and thoroughly, and by limiting their consumption of sugar, which has been proven to cause tooth decay.

If your child does develop cavities, he or she may be offered a silver filling composed of an "amalgam" of different metals, with mercury—a highly poisonous material—making up about half of the mixture. The theory has been that the mercury was bound up by the other metals in the filling, and therefore could not be harmful. However, current research has shown that mercury may be slowly released from the filling and absorbed into the body. Research teams at the University of Calgary and the University of Georgia reported on the damaging bioavailability of unexcreted mercury in humans in 1990, and Gregory Singleton, senior dental reviewer for the FDA, stated, "In light of emerging scientific data, the FDA needs to reexamine the use of amalgam." In Sweden, mercury amalgam fillings are banned.

You may want to consider asking your dentist to use a composite resin material or gold in your child's fillings rather than mercury amalgams, and you might even consider having your own fillings replaced if you plan to get pregnant, as raised mercury levels can cause birth defects and miscarriage.

Living with Asthma

Asthma is the most common chronic childhood disease, affecting four to five percent of all children in the United States. The most common approach to managing the condition is, however, through drugs. Many parents are uncomfortable with the constant intake of strong medications, and look for alternative treatments. Asthma is potentially life-threatening; for severe cases, don't abandon medication while you learn about alternatives. Here are some natural remedies that have been shown to be effective in treating asthma:

Diet Plenty of fluids—mainly water—will prevent the mucus in your child's lungs from becoming too dry and difficult to clear. Try cutting down on dairy products, sugar, and fried foods, which tend to increase mucus production. Certain food additives, especially sulfites—used by many restaurants on the fruits and vegetables in salad bars, as well as found in dried fruits—can be dangerous for a child with asthma. The artificial sweetener Aspartame (NutraSweet™), the flavor enhancer monosodium glutamate (MSG), and the food preservatives BHA and BHT may also cause problems for asthmatics. Eating a healthy, whole foods diet based on lean proteins, grains, and fresh fruits and vegetables is especially important for a child with asthma.

Supplements Essential fatty acids (EFAs) help to regulate the inflammatory response. Good sources are evening primrose oil or EPA (fish oil). Magnesium has a bronchodilating effect. Vitamin C has been shown to alleviate asthma symptoms. B-complex vitamin supports adrenal function and the nervous system. Vitamin B-12 may help to prevent asthma attacks. Discuss these supplements with a physician well versed in nutrition.

Massage In one study, asthmatic children who were given daily twenty-minute massages at bedtime by their parents for a one-month period had fewer asthma attacks and were better able to breathe. They also showed a decrease in anxiety and stress hormones.[8] Ashley Montagu, author of *Touching: The Human Significance of the Skin*, believes this is not only because the skin and the nervous system are related, but because emotions—including the need for comfort and reassurance—play a significant role in learning to relax and breathe correctly.

Eucapnic, or Buteyko breathing This method of breathing, developed by Russian doctor K.P. Buteyko, normalizes levels of carbon dioxide by controlling ventilation levels. Several unpublished studies in Russia and Australia found that children with asthma using eucapnic breathing improved after just ninety minutes of training in the method, and the majority were able to discontinue all bronchodilator medication. For additional information on eucapnic breathing, see Resources.

Herbs Astragalus is a Chinese herb that helps strengthen the lungs. Licorice root soothes the lungs and helps to strengthen adrenal function. Minor bupleurum formula is a Chinese herbal combination that is helpful in restoring and building the immune system. Picrorhiza korroa is used in Ayurvedic medicine for lung disease and other ailments. Other traditional remedies used for asthma include black haw bark, marshmallow root, ephedra, coltsfoot, yerba santa, wild cherry bark, gingerroot, peppermint, red clover, comfrey, nettle, parsley, and thyme. Consult a practitioner trained in herbal medicine.

Homeopathy Recommended remedies for the management of allergic conditions include Arsenicum album, Antimonium tartaricum, Chamomilla, Ipecacuanha, Nux vomica, and Pulsatilla. Homeopaths themselves advise parents not to treat symptoms of acute asthma with homeopathic remedies alone.

Acupuncture One study of children shows that acupuncture given twenty minutes before exercise will minimize the effects of exercise-induced asthma symptoms.[9]

Other natural therapies Yoga has proven beneficial in reducing the frequency of asthma attacks in adolescents.[10] Chiropractic spinal manipulation is used to treat asthma. Shiatsu has been effective for adults with asthma and may have benefits for children. Mind-body, relaxation, and visualization techniques are helpful in reducing anxiety, and therefore may be beneficial in reducing asthma attacks.

Practice prevention The most important thing you can do to prevent asthma attacks is to avoid common triggers. Limit your child's exposure to tobacco and other air pollutants. If your child is sensitive to animal fur, keep your family pet outside. Keep your child's room free of feather pillows, wool blankets, down comforters, and stuffed animals; encase your child's mattress and pillow in a plastic or vinyl fitted sheet; regularly change filters on all heating and air-conditioning units; and engage in a weekly clean-up campaign to reduce dust and mold in your child's room. Encourage your child to get regular exercise—particularly swimming in a pool that is not excessively chlorinated—to improve lung function.

Helping Your Child Cope with a Medical Experience

At some point in your child's life, he may have to be hospitalized or undergo a serious medical procedure. Although most hospitals are much more child-friendly than they used to be, a hospital stay is still a traumatic experience for a child.

The number one thing you can do to ease the trauma of hospitalization is to be with your child. Although that may sound like a given, as recently as the 1970s, parents' time with their children in the hospital was restricted to visiting hours, and still not all hospitals welcome parental involvement. You should know your rights as the parent of a hospital patient, and ask questions and make demands to ensure the best care for your child.

Here are some things you can do to ease your child's hospital stay:

INSIST ON STAYING WITH YOUR CHILD

It will help your child to relax and cooperate with the doctors, as well as heal much faster emotionally, if you are there to explain procedures and provide a familiar touch. With a young or nursing child, your being there around the clock is critical, so the child does not feel abandoned. Being there may mean taking a leave from work; getting help with your other children; and maybe even relocating temporarily to be with your child at a treatment facility distant from your home. Some hospitals provide housing where families can stay to be near their children. Many provide rooming-in for one parent; in others, you will have to grab what sleep you can in a waiting room chair. Try to determine ahead of time if your child's hospital is family-friendly, and investigate other options if it is not.

REASSURE YOUR CHILD IN AN HONEST WAY

Let your child know that you have asked lots of questions about what is going to happen and have made sure that only the necessary procedures will occur. Tell your child what is going to happen at each step of the procedure, and let your child know if it is going to hurt. When something does not go as planned, explain to your child the reason for the change. Even a young child who does not understand everything will be reassured by your tone of voice. Do not let the hospital staff lie to your child in an effort to minimize the situation, or your child will learn not to trust them.

BECOME YOUR CHILD'S ADVOCATE

You have a right to know the risks and benefits of all treatments given to your child and to participate in decisions about his medical care. Ask questions and take notes. Keep a log of all the medicines your child should be given. Find out when they should be administered, what the dosage is, and what the danger signs of overdose or allergic reaction are. Ask the nurse to explain the purpose of each piece of medical equipment, what the danger signals are, and what you should do in an emergency. Always question medications and procedures—some may be unnecessary. Most doctors and nurses will be glad to know that you are keeping an eye on the situation and will understand your concern for your child.

KNOW WHOM TO GO TO WITH A CONCERN

Never let a resident or nurse perform any procedure on your child without checking with the doctor in charge. Direct questions about your child's treatment to your child's doctor. If you have a concern that is not being addressed, most hospitals have a social worker who mediates between the hospital staff and patients. Some hospitals have Child Life specialists, offered through Child Life Council (see Resources), whose role is to prepare children for medical procedures and tend to their emotional needs.

DO NOT NEGLECT YOUR OTHER CHILDREN

Even though your focus needs to be on your ill child, recognize that your other children need you, too. Alternate stints at the hospital with your spouse, if possible, and try to get a grandparent or friend to stay with your other children to give them extra attention. If you are nursing another child, make sure your hospital will let your nursing baby room-in as well. Let older children help care for the sick child as much as they can, by making cards and visiting. Reassure your children that they have not caused the illness of their sibling, and that he is getting the best possible care.

After a Hospitalization

Once your child is home from the hospital, the healing process is just beginning. It can take lots of time and attention to help children heal emotionally from a hospitalization for a serious condition. Here are some things you can do to speed your child's emotional recovery, from mother and writer Anita Courtney, whose three-year-old daughter recovered fully from a brain tumor.

SPEND TIME PROCESSING THE EXPERIENCE

Encourage your child to talk about it as much as he is ready to, explaining again what happened and why. Your child may want to draw a picture of what happened, or act it out with dolls. Do not be surprised if this drawing or acting out is quite violent, as medical procedures can be physically brutal to children.

BE PREPARED FOR LITTLE HURTS TO BECOME A BIG DEAL

Some children may relive the trauma of their operation or hospitalization the first time they get hurt afterwards. Even something as insignificant as a splinter may become an occasion for panicked

tears. Allow your child to go through this catharsis with lots of love and gentle support from you.

When to Call a Doctor

As you become intimately familiar with your child's body signals and behavior when healthy, you will be more aware of your child's signs of illness. Linda White, MD, counsels parents to contact the doctor if your ill child:

- Has a fever over 104 degrees F., or a fever accompanied by chills or excessive sweating.
- Appears unusually limp, apathetic, or difficult to awaken.
- Complains of severe pain.
- Has a bulging fontanel (soft spot) with a very strong pulse (a sign of meningitis). A healthy fontanel should not sink in or protrude, and the pulse should be regular but not especially strong.
- Has had diarrhea or been vomiting for more than a day and appears dehydrated (signs of dehydration include loss of skin elasticity, going eight hours without urinating, dry lips, sunken eyes, or a sunken fontanel).
- Has problems with balance or coordination, or numbness in any area.
- Has difficulty breathing.
- Loses consciousness.
- Has not improved after three days of home treatment.
- Is under two months old.

RELISH—AND SHARE—SUPPORT

Knowing about the people who showed concern for your child can help her heal. Let her look through the cards that people wrote, and spend time talking about the people who prayed for her or brought food or presents. You may want to encourage your child to share that kind of support by going back to the hospital to visit and bring presents to other children who are having operations.

ENCOURAGE LAUGHTER—THE BEST MEDICINE

Laughter can be a powerful healing tool. Play silly games with your child—look at it as a chance to develop your creativity and acting skills.

CHAPTER 14

What Makes a Healthy Family?

It may seem as if the American family is facing greater challenges today than at any other time in its history. Legislation favors the worker over the parent, placing a tax burden on the middle class that makes it difficult for parents to stay home with young children. We read about the deterioration of society—the rising crime rate, increasing impersonalization due to technology, deadly diseases like cancer and AIDS—and we may begin to wonder if there is any way to raise an emotionally and physically healthy family in today's world.

In truth, the American family is alive and well. Recent statistics are telling: Ninety percent of adult Americans describe their relationship with their mother as "close"; almost 70 percent say they are close to their father, and 85 percent report feeling close to their siblings.[1] Over 90 percent of American children say they feel loved by their parents and think their parents are doing a good job of raising them.[2] Mothers say their top priorities are spending time with their children and communicating with them.[3] Families today are strong and diverse: They include children adopted from foreign countries, interracial families, and families with same-sex parents.

Concern over the future of the family is not new. Social critics pointed out a few centuries ago that children were little more than possessions or servants in the eyes of their families. Even in our own century, child labor laws had to be enacted to protect children. We have come a long way in upgrading the status of children, and though we still have a long way to go, society is beginning to recognize the value of the family, and to offer more support and information to families than ever before.

Healthy Families Start with Love

That love is the foundation of healthy families is no secret. Of course we love our children, but love is more than a feeling—it is a commitment, an action. The successful translation of love from feeling into action defines why some families work and others do not.

Ross Campbell, in his book, *How to Really Love Your Child*, reminds us that the only kind of love that is truly affirming is unconditional love. If we express our love to our children only when they please us, we are really only loving ourselves by reassuring ourselves of our own values. Our love for our children cannot be dependent on what they do. The secure parent will risk self-doubt by loving children even when their behavior is emotionally challenging.

Loving a child no matter how he behaves does not mean forsaking discipline—but there is a difference between disliking the deed and disliking the doer. The wise parent will recognize that a child who misbehaves is crying out for help.

One of the best ways to express love to your child is by touching. Hugging, kissing, and stroking your child, holding hands, putting an arm around your child's shoulder, and giving a back rub communicate love more concretely than any words. Look into your child's eyes. Don't just reserve eye contact for when your child has done something you don't like. Maintaining physical contact as your children get older may be more difficult, because of our cultural distrust of touching. If you did not come from a touching family, you may have to relearn to touch your older children, and consciously remember to convey your love to them physically.

Part of unconditional love is giving your children more than they ask for. So often, we are encouraged to give our children the bare minimum we can get away with. If a baby seems content in a crib or swing, people will advise us not to carry her around. When she does cry, we are told to give her a pacifier or distract her with toys before nursing her. Why pack school lunches for your child, people will ask, if he is old enough to do it himself?

But what about doing those extra things that convey love—picking up your baby for a cuddle just because you love to see that smile, or sending your child off to school with a lunch that is lovingly prepared? Responding only to your children's demands for attention may make them feel they need to step up the intensity of their demands, or, worse yet, may make them settle for less than they deserve. Consider how much more you appreciate the unsolicited attentions your spouse gives you than those you have to ask for, and consider giving your children more than they demand.

Love Yourself

We cannot truly love our children without first loving ourselves. If we have not been well-loved as children, we must work on our own concept of self-worth in adulthood. Our journey with our children is a unique opportunity to relive our own childhoods. If we are to grow healthy families, we must begin with ourselves, and welcome the challenges of parenting as a chance to reexamine the values that we inherited from our own families. Parenting is our chance to finally "get it right." The beauty of parenting is that it is never too late to grow and change; we can make a fresh start with our children every day.

Teresa

My youngest son was five when I divorced my husband, and suddenly Jeremy wanted to sleep in my bed. I tried lying beside him until he fell asleep, or letting him sleep with his siblings or on a mattress on the floor beside my bed. He rarely protested, but made it clear that he really wanted to sleep with me.

Finally, I suggested an alternate night routine. One night Jeremy could sleep with me; the next night he would sleep in his own bed. It worked... sort of. Jeremy would happily climb into bed with me and sleep soundly on the nights he was allowed to. On the alternate nights he would say (with a big sigh), "I guess I have to go to my own bed," and look at me sadly.

One night I glanced at his dejected face, pulled back my comforter and said, "Come on." He looked at me, stunned. "You really want me to sleep with you?" he asked. I nodded. He climbed into bed, snuggled up to me, and fell asleep with his face still glowing. I lay awake for a long time. I had heard the delight in his voice when I had invited him to sleep with me. Why had I spent so much energy trying to get him to sleep alone? It wasn't that I didn't want him to sleep with me—in fact, I probably slept better next to him—it was just that I thought he was too old to be sleeping with his mother.

Jeremy slept with me every night for more than a year. During that year he made remarkable progress. The divorce had been more difficult for him than for the older kids, but suddenly his schoolwork improved, he made new friends, and he started to participate in other activities.

Eventually, my son decided he didn't want to sleep with me anymore. But he still knows that he is welcome in my room any time. Love is a verb as well as a noun; and it's giving a little more than we have to that makes it love in action.

"Giving Children More," Teresa Pitman, *Mothering,* Fall 1997.

Raising a healthy family means trusting yourself to do the best job that you know how at parenting. All parents experience moments of panic—times when we wonder what we have gotten ourselves into. When this happens, the only way to learn to mother is to plunge in, trusting yourself to figure it out because you have done so before.

It all comes down to trust—trust in the fact that your child has a good reason for her behavior and trust in yourself to figure out what that is. There is a danger in over-intellectualizing the parenting experience. Each "expert" promises the secret to perfect parenting, attempting to encapsulate the human experience in a single book, tape, or video. Sorting through all of this information becomes overwhelming unless you come back time and time again to your child. Ideas are only ideas; opinions are culturally dictated. Your child, however, is new and unspoiled, without any of the learned trappings of modern civilization or the dichotomies of intellectual reasoning. Your child operates on an instinctive level, and if you stay quiet and listen to your own instincts, you will find that the answers to your parenting questions lie within you.

What Makes a Healthy Family

Beyond the important qualities of love and trust, healthy families share certain other characteristics. Here are some traits of healthy families, adapted from Dolores Curran's *Traits of a Healthy Family* and Harville Hendrix's *Getting the Love You Want*.

COMMUNICATION

Healthy families have good communication skills. They feel safe talking about anything and are comfortable expressing their emotions. Some families find it valuable to set aside a weekly meeting time during which grievances are aired, achievements are recognized, and special occasions are planned. The family meeting is not a substitute for open communication, but an additional forum for communication. If you dislike the formality of a family meeting, you can still make communication a priority by designating the dinner hour as family sharing time, for example.

For tips on effective communication, see Chapter 15.

RESPECT. HEALTHY FAMILIES RESPECT ONE ANOTHER

This pervasive attitude begins in a family with the parents' model of self-respect and respect for each other. Families who respect one another value all members equally and allow all members to share in decision making.

An atmosphere of mutual respect does not mean that everyone has equal say; parents in healthy families don't abdicate decision-making responsibility in the name of democracy. Because adults have valuable experience and knowledge, they must take the lead. By the same token, children have a unique perspective on the small details of life and the importance of the moment, and at times it is appropriate for them to lead. Healthy families neither exclude children from the decision making process, nor allow too much decision making to be directed by the children.

TIME

Healthy families make time for each other. One of the best gifts you can give your children is to simply spend time with them. By spending time together, you develop mutual trust, ensure time for touching and communicating, and get to know your children well enough to understand what type of discipline and guidance they need and to recognize the first signs of distress. Quality time cannot be scheduled into neat time slots—relationships need quantity time in order for quality moments to occur.

A great challenge to the family today is lack of time. Our culture defines people by what they do; thus we feel a compulsion to do things in order to have a sense of achievement as a person. You may feel that, besides being a parent, you must have a career, be involved in volunteer activities, stay in shape by working out, keep up on current events, and attend cultural activities. Perhaps we are trying too hard to fulfill societal dictates about what we should be, or are applying outmoded models of what we could do as a single person to what we can do as a parent. Isn't it enough to have intense, gratifying relationships with the members of our families day in and day out; to consciously try to be honest and loving in all of our interactions with them? Why must it always feel as if this sense of connection has to be slipped in between car pools and other commitments?

If we are to have healthy families, we must be in charge of our lives. We have to learn to value ourselves not in terms of our productivity, but in terms of our relationships. We have to set priorities and be selective in what we do outside of the home. In response to every new activity, ask yourself the questions, "Why do I want to do this?" "How will it affect our family life?" "Is it worth it?" Learn to say "No" as often as possible outside of the family and "Yes" as often as possible within the family.

Susan

I used to rush my children around the block, through the grocery store, and out the library door, hollering, "Come on, let's go!" One day, after trips to three different stores, Nicholas started crying in his car seat. When I asked what was wrong, he said, "Too much places!"

Today, on those days when I have not made any plans or we only have one place to go, I notice my kids' eyes meet mine. They smile more often. They seem to feel better about themselves, because their pace and preferences are taken into account. By scheduling less, I'm building my children's self-esteem more.

Susan W. Specht, "Zen and the Art of Mothering," *Mothering,* November/December 1998.

SPIRITUALITY

Healthy families have a sense of a greater good or power in life—a belief that gives them strength and purpose. For some families these beliefs have a traditional religious base; for others they do not. Regardless of spiritual beliefs, in healthy families, parents give their children a clear sense of right and wrong and hold them responsible for their own moral behavior.

Sometimes, in an attempt to be democratic and nonauthoritarian, parents do not share their belief systems with their children, wanting them to be free to make their own decisions. But as adults, we have an obligation to share our values and teach our morals to our children so that they have a basis on which to operate in the world. We can give them the freedom to question these values later in life, but in the early years we cast them adrift if we don't give them the moral foundation of our experience and beliefs.

RESILIENCE

Healthy families are not without problems. They are, however, able to view stress and crisis as an opportunity to grow. They are certainly not perfect. Imperfection is God's gift; it makes us compassionate as well as deserving of compassion. Imperfection allows us to take risks, to fail and succeed, to learn and grow, to ask questions.

Healthy families are a safe haven—home should be a place where families can fall apart, act out, and hold onto one another. Healthy families know that humor can be a tremendous stress release, and they remember to laugh. Healthy families are willing to ask for help.

Sharing Family Responsibilities

In a healthy family, responsibility is shared by all members. The secret to teaching children to be accountable is giving them responsibility. Allowing them to be responsible means giving them the freedom to make mistakes and to learn from them.

Even young children want to be responsible for their lives. When we relinquish control over them, they may choose mismatched socks, decide on chocolate pudding and green beans for breakfast, or clean their rooms up in ways that make no sense to us, but that look orderly in their eyes. When children are allowed to risk choosing for themselves, they learn to trust their feelings and intuitions.

Making the transition from fulfilling your children's needs in the early years to letting them take responsibility for themselves as they get older can be difficult. It is easier for you to pick up your children's messes, or to get them dressed in the morning because you are in a hurry—but it is not better for them. You may have to relax your standards of perfect cleanliness and order to give your children the freedom to grow into responsible adults.

The healthy family allows its members to learn the consequences of irresponsibility. We handicap our children if we teach them that they need other people in order to wash their hair, feed themselves, or dress themselves "right." To bail children out is tempting for parents, but if we hover over our children too much and do not allow them to learn from experience, they will miss valuable lessons that are better learned within the safety of the home.

In addition to taking responsibility for themselves, children can be given responsibilities within the family starting at a young age. The benefits of regular chores extend beyond the tasks themselves: A study by professor of psychology Joan Grusec at the University of Toronto found that children who are given family chores show increased concern for the family. "Children who perform routine tasks that benefit others come to think of themselves as caring, helpful people and behave accordingly," concludes Grusec.

Here are some tips for assigning family chores:

ARTICULATE YOUR REASONS
"Because I said to" is not the best motivator for doing chores. You can explain to your children that the task of keeping the household running smoothly needs to be shared by all members. Some children respond to the idea that the more they pitch in around the house, the more free time Mom has to spend with them. Your happiness is also valid justification: Children need to learn to get along with other people, and knowing how to keep Mom happy is a valuable lesson.

TAILOR THE CHORES TO THE CHILD
You can start giving your children chores even before they can read. Assign them a few age-appropriate responsibilities such as setting the table or emptying the trash, and draw pictures to remind them of their duties. As they get older, you can post a weekly list of duties, rotating tasks periodically. Resist gender stereotyping by assigning the same type of work to sons and daughters.

You will probably find that you have to keep gently reminding (try to refrain from nagging!) your children to do their chores. But eventually they will learn that chores are a part of family life, and you may be amazed to see your son whipping through his list of duties on Saturday morning before he heads out to play.

MAKE RULES ABOUT MAKE-WORK
"Make-work" is any mess someone creates that someone else has to clean up. Your children can learn that taking care of popcorn they spilled or wet towels they left on the floor is their responsibility. Make a deal with them: You won't create make-work for them if they don't create make-work for you.

MAKE ALLOWANCES FOR ALLOWANCE
Some families start giving children an allowance at a young age so they can begin learning fiscal responsibility. Others disagree with the idea of an allowance, preferring to give their children opportunities to earn money, through car washes and pet-sitting, for example. Either way, your children can learn a lot from investing their own money in a savings account, and making their own purchases.

ENLIST THE HELP OF YOUR PARTNER
Most women still assume the lion's share of responsibility in the home, directing the housework and cooking, scheduling activities, and taking care of social courtesies. For one person to have to take on the burden of that responsibility alone is unfair. You and your spouse can set a good example for the children by sharing traditional gender-oriented tasks such as cooking, grocery shopping, carpooling, taking out the garbage, mowing the lawn, and taking care of the cars.

Easing up on Housework

Housekeeping is no longer a top priority for mothers today. According to a nationwide Gallup survey of mothers with children eighteen or younger, moms today believe they spend more time with the family than their mothers did, but when it comes to keeping a spotless home, their mothers win hands-down. This change appears to be a healthy shift in values: For children, cleanliness and order run a very distant second to spending time with their parents.

But you don't need to sacrifice a clean house in order to spend time with your children. Try a compromise: Ease up on your standards a little, and involve your children in the work.

INVOLVE YOUR CHILDREN

Young children love working alongside you. A baby can be carried in a sling or backpack while you work, and a toddler can help you dust the furniture or match socks, or can simply play beside you while you clean. Be sure to use natural, nontoxic cleansers, and make it fun by singing and talking to each other while you work.

Household work can provide as many lessons as preschool: Your toddler can learn about the safe use of tools, the workings of everyday items, sorting and sequencing, liquid and dry measurements, and following directions. He can also learn the pleasure of a job well done.

Karen

Recently, the children and I spent most of an afternoon cleaning our garage. Three-year-old Zachary, who had been especially industrious, grabbed my hand when we were finished. Walking to the entrance, he said to me, "Let's step back here and look at what a good job we did, Mom!"

Karen Miles, "Housekeeping With Little Ones," *Mothering*, Winter 1989.

CREATE A CLEANING SCHEDULE THAT WORKS FOR YOUR FAMILY

Some people prefer to get all the household cleaning done on one day; others prefer to spread out the tasks throughout the week. Whatever approach works for you, create a schedule that is realistic, so that you are not constantly playing catch-up, and there is time left over for other activities.

DO A "CLEAN SWEEP" SEVERAL TIMES A DAY

Some people find the clutter of toys strewn about the house overwhelming; others see it as evidence of a creative household. Requiring children

to put each toy or project away before they move on to the next one may be too rigid. But you can call for a ten-minute clean-up several times a day, before an outing or dinner, for example. Put on lively music and make sure everyone pitches in to put things away.

RELAX YOUR STANDARDS

Our standards of cleanliness have increased in the last century far beyond sanitary requirements. If you don't mind a little dirt, you can lessen your load by doing less. Let a few toddler fingerprints smudge the windows, and let your child wear the same shirt a few times, even if it has stains on it.

Joyce

Some of the most creative people I know love messes—unfortunately, seven of them live in my house. Before I had children, I believed that every family was naturally blessed with an equal proportion of neatniks and slobs. Somewhere there must be a family with seven compulsive cleaners wondering what happened to bring them all under one roof.

I used to fight the creative clutter in my house. Now I enjoy my children's individuality and rejoice in the clutter. Maybe someday I will even finish the needlework saying, "May your house be dirty enough to be happy and clean enough to be healthy."

Joyce Good Reis, "Creative Clutter," *Mothering*, Spring 1985.

FORGET ABOUT SPRING CLEANING

Spring is the time to be outdoors with the children, planting a garden or exploring the woods. Open up the windows to let the fresh breezes through in spring, but save your major cleaning for fall, when the family will be spending longer hours indoors.

HIRE HELP

While the easiest approach, this strategy is financially out of reach for many families. One way to get help might be to trade cleaning chores with another family: If you hate housecleaning, but

love to cook, you might be able to make dinner one night a week for a friend in exchange for housecleaning services. If you work outside of the home, figuring out a way to pay someone to clean the house while you work may let you spend more of your free time with your children.

What Makes an Unhealthy Family?

In contrast to the model of shared responsibility, cooperation, and communication, is the family in which one or both parents dominate. Such an approach is an easy way to raise a family in some regards, since it requires very little consideration, negotiation, or change. It is practical, and settles some matters expediently—but it does very little for matters of the heart.

Families in which children are raised in a parent-centered way—in which decisions are based on arbitrary mandates of the parents rather than the needs of the child—do not often remain friends once the children grow up. Those who advocate the parent-centered family may be afraid that cooperative, compassionate family life means that the children dominate the family. For the children to dominate the family wouldn't be any healthier than for the parents to dominate.

If you want more from family life than peace and quiet, then you must learn to listen for and trust what goes on beneath the surface. If you want true intimacy with your children, you must use your experience with them—and not an arbitrary idea of what the rules should be—to guide you in your decision making.

A National Issue—Family- "Unfriendly" Policies

Raising a healthy family can be difficult in a country that lacks basic support structures for families. No other industrialized nation enacts less legislation for families or provides less money to offset the costs of parenthood than the United States does. Ours is the only industrialized democracy that has no universal prenatal and postnatal care, no paid parental leave policy, and no provisions to encourage at-home care in the early years of life. Along with Somalia, we are the only nation in the world that has not signed the United Nations Convention on the Rights of the Child, a pledge to end illegal child labor, sexual exploitation, and violent abuse of children.[7]

Although our national prosperity is growing, our child poverty rate has not fallen. One in five American children lives in poverty today, according to the Children's Defense Fund. Poor children have more health problems, are more likely to fall behind or drop out of school, and earn lower wages when they grow up.

Despite expressions of concern about families and children, we in fact value the worker above the parent. Legislation in this country effectively penalizes the at-home mother. If the federal government sincerely wanted to help families with children, legislation would support families through tax credits, reimbursements, or direct payments, rather than applying Band-Aid solutions such as increased government day care funding. In contrast, countries like Germany, Holland, Sweden, and Japan consider children a precious national resource—a source of continued national wealth, stability, and growth—and enact legislation that encourages and aids families.

We need legislation and social programs that attack poverty, give families choices, and support the family unit. We have a diverse society made up of people of many cultural and racial backgrounds. Some want children and some do not. Some families want one balance of work and family life, and other families want another. Each family should be supported in making its own choices.

Toward a More Family-Friendly Workplace

A nationwide survey of 1,000 men and women shows that eight out of ten parents would sacrifice rapid career advancement to spend more time with their families.[8] Parents are demanding

more flexible options from their employers, and employers are beginning to respond. Flexible scheduling—including part-time employment, job sharing, and flexible work hours—is now offered by over half of the nation's major companies.[9] Companies are pioneering innovative programs to make the work environment more family-friendly. Management and consulting firm Corporate Family Solutions, for example, helps employers create family support programs like "Kids in the House": When schools close due to bad weather, the company works with employers to convert conference rooms into snowy day playrooms and learning centers for children, thereby reducing parent absenteeism.

Employees who seek flexibility are no longer seen as less committed to their jobs. Women on flexible work schedules stay on them for an average of five years, and more than half get promotions while working part-time, job-sharing, or engaging in some other alternative to the forty-hour work week. Over half of women on flextime say they would quit if flexible arrangements were not possible.[10]

Parents are also finding ways to work from home. Over 50 million Americans are currently working from home, according to the National Association of Home-Based Businesses, and home-based businesses are the fastest-growing segment of the United States economy. Home-based workers are self-employed or are on salary or contract, doing everything from graphic design to computer programming to knitting and sewing. The Internet has made working from home easier than ever and has provided a whole new category of opportunity.

The Transformative Power of Parenting

Increased support for families from the federal government and corporate America would give parents a much-needed break, but ultimately, healthy families begin at home. Raising a healthy family is an endeavor worthy of our best efforts. Developing an ethic of parenting based on trust and unconditional love can create more than a strong family unit—it can cause personal transformation. Having a child can teach you more about the nature of the human being and the power of love than you could possibly ever suspect. By giving us a sense of connectedness to and compassion for other parents and children all over the world, parenting can truly civilize us.

PART 5

Family Matters

CHAPTER 15 # Discipline

Imagine being able to discipline your child without punishment. Not only without spanking, but without time-outs, grounding, or any other form of punishment. Imagine the freedom in realizing that you do not have to constantly control your children's behavior.

Parenting without punishment is not just possible—it is the *only* effective way to discipline your child. Consider the roots of the word discipline: from "disciple," or learner. The goal of discipline is to teach.

Effective discipline is based on loving guidance. It is based on the belief that children are born innately good and that our role as parents is to nurture their spirits as they learn about limits and boundaries, rather than to curb their tendencies toward wrongdoing. Effective discipline presumes that children have reasons for their behavior and that their cooperation can be engaged to solve shared problems.

Forgoing punishment does *not* mean loss of authority. On the contrary, when you rely on your authority as a parent and your relationship with your child as the basis for problem solving, you actually gain power. When you rely on punishment, you lose power, as punishment must be constantly escalated to work. Effective discipline means teaching your child self-discipline.

But conflicts are a normal part of life. All children have conflicts. They fight with their siblings. They grab things. They do things you don't like. How can you discipline if you don't have punishment to rely on?

Here's how: You communicate with your child— you examine the problem and work toward a solution together. You rely on your authority as the parent. You use positive reinforcement, natural consequences, or any of the other alternatives to punishment described below.

Parenting without punishment does not mean being permissive. You still need to be vigilant. But you can use a different language, relating to your children in a cooperative rather than an authoritarian way.

Developing new skills takes time. But discipline without punishment is really just a choice. During a conflict, you have a brief moment between your child's action and your reaction, in which you can choose. You can choose to control the situation by punishment. Or, you can choose to go deeper—to use the situation to teach your child, and in the process, to learn something yourself.

Punishment Does Not Work

The children are bickering; the toddler is having a tantrum; the teenager just broke the house rules. What do we do when these behaviors arise? We punish. We scold, threaten, deprive, and, when pushed far enough, we yell and even slap.

But do we ever stop to think about whether these techniques work? They may work to stop the behavior in the short term, but they do not work over the long term. Punishment is ineffective, because:

IT DOES NOT TEACH

Punishment teaches a child nothing about why his actions were wrong. Logical consequences—such as taking away a bike for a few days if a child was caught bike riding in the street—allow a child to make a connection between her actions and the result. But time-outs, spanking, and grounding have no connection to a child's behavior.

How often do we send a child to her room or a time-out chair, saying, "I want you to think about what you just did?" How often do you think that child truly reflects about what she just did? In reality, she seethes with indignation, frustration, or humiliation. These powerful feelings effectively block out any remorse; the child focuses on the punishment rather than the lesson to be learned. Haim Ginott, parent educator and author of *Between Parent and Child*, used to say, "The child who has just been spanked or sent to his room does not think, 'Thank God for my father or mother who just punished me. When I grow up I want to be just like them.' Instead, all he thinks is 'revenge.' "[1]

Punishment leaves little room for guilt or contrition. Feelings of guilt can be a wonderfully educational thing. Punishment refocuses the child's feelings on anger at the parent, so guilt gets canceled out.

Punishment may frighten a child—as in the case of a toddler getting spanked for coloring on the walls—but it is very unlikely that he will make the connection between the misdeed and the punishment, especially if the punishment is delayed until the parent discovers the crime. Even if the punishment is administered immediately, he may be so overwhelmed by it that any verbal messages about why he is being punished are lost.

And even if the child understands the punishment, it still does not teach him anything. A child who is grounded for a bad report card cannot go back and change his grades, and he learns nothing about how to get better grades in the future. The most the punisher can hope for is that the child will avoid that behavior in the future in order to avoid punishment. Such a change is a lot to ask, even of adults. If punishment worked, our jails would not be full of repeat offenders.

IT DOES NOT ENCOURAGE SELF-DISCIPLINE

Your goal should be to teach your child to discipline himself. Punishment does not teach a child to control his actions—it teaches him to avoid getting caught. Children who are put in time-out whenever they say a swear word quickly learn to swear only when their parents are not around.

IT ADDRESSES SYMPTOMS, NOT CAUSES

Children usually have good reasons for acting out. We can either take the quick way out and attempt to put a stop to the offending behavior, or we can take the time to figure out the underlying causes of it.

Children are, by nature, dependent—they cannot fulfill their own needs. When a child "misbehaves," it may be that she is simply frustrated by a legitimate need. She may be tired, hungry, or overwhelmed by a disruption of her routine; she may be feeling jealous, frustrated, confused, or afraid; or she may be simply too young to understand or to express her emotions. When we eliminate the symptoms of the problem by punishing, the problem does not go away.

IT REQUIRES CONSTANT ESCALATION

When we punish a child, and the next day she does the same thing again, do we think "this isn't working, let's try something else?" Or do we punish again, maybe even harder? Punishment quickly loses its effectiveness the more it is used, just as yelling to get your children's attention does not work if you yell all the time. The dangerous thing about the escalation of punishment is that it can eventually cross the line from reprimand to abuse.

IT IS NOT MOTIVATING

Do you find it more motivating when your boss says, "Thanks for all your hard work on the presentation; why don't you take tomorrow off?" or "You took an extra hour at lunch today; I'm going to dock your paycheck"? Positive reinforcement is so much more motivating than negative feedback. Punishment produces resentment, fear, and anger—definitely not mental states conducive to learning, or to good communication.

IT IS NOT FAIR

Punishment often requires that you play Supreme Court Justice: The children begin wailing from the other room, "He scratched me!" "No, she pinched me first!" You rush in and try to determine who really started it, or you simply throw up your hands in frustration and send both children to their rooms. You cannot possibly be all-seeing and all-knowing.

Punishment Harms

Not only does punishment not work long-term, it can cause longterm harm. It can damage the trusting relationship with your child that you have worked so hard to build. In extreme cases, it can cause physical damage. Punishment harms because:

IT SETS UP AN ADVERSARIAL RELATIONSHIP

Punishment is based on control, coercion, and an imbalance of power; effective discipline is founded on trust, cooperation, and communication. If you view discipline as loving guidance, and always keep your love and trust for your child in mind, you can work together at an effective solution. If you use punishment to maintain your position of authority, you set yourself up for battles that no one really wins.

You don't have to give up your authority when you give up punishment. As the parent, you are the one in charge, and you can demonstrate that to your child in lots of ways without having to rely on punishment.

IT TEACHES CHILDREN TO STIFLE THEIR FEELINGS

When a child is sent to her room or put in time-out because she is screaming or lashing out at another child, she gets the message that her parents do not want to be around her when she is angry or upset. Eventually, she will learn to keep her uncomfortable or difficult feelings to herself.

IT CAN PERPETUATE A CYCLE OF ANGER

How many parents vow never to do the things their parents did, then find themselves doing exactly that? The rage, frustration, and helplessness you may have felt when spanked or punished gets channeled into bottled-up feelings of anger, which may explode once you are grown up and dealing with your own children. Do you ever wonder why your children's misbehavior can engender such fury in you? Often, that anger has its roots in the way you were punished as a child. If you feel you were treated unfairly by your parents, you must make a commitment to treat your own children differently. It is up to you to stop the cycle of anger and abuse.

IT IS CONFUSING

What is a child to think when his parent spanks him, saying, "I'm only doing this because I love you"? Hurting a child in the name of love—whether physically or emotionally—sends a terribly mixed message.

Even a time-out is viewed by a child as a temporary withdrawal of his parents' love. Children want their parents' love and approval more than anything. A child who is sent to his room or a time-out chair feels rejected and unlovable—even if his parents tell him, "I love you, but you need to go to your room right now." His feelings of anxiety and abandonment are so strong that they override any reassurances from his parents.

Never Hit a Child

If we are to look truthfully and honestly at spanking, we must first of all call it what it really is: hitting. Even when done gently, using physical force to discipline a child is always wrong.

Although spanking is on the decline in the United States, over 90 percent of parents in national surveys report spanking toddlers at least occasionally[2], and over half of parents say they have spanked their children in the past year.[3] In a survey of 130 pediatricians in the United States, 70 percent said that spanking is acceptable when a child engages in dangerous behavior, and 38 percent concluded that spanking is an appropriate response to hitting, pushing, or scratching.[4]

In many European countries—including Austria, Italy, and all of Scandinavia—spanking a child is illegal. Corporal punishment in schools has been prohibited in some European countries for centuries, and in the last ten years was banned in England and South Africa. In the United States, corporal punishment in schools is not federally banned and is still permitted in about half of all states.

Hitting a child is always wrong because:

IT TEACHES THAT HITTING IS THE WAY TO SOLVE PROBLEMS

We cannot expect to teach our children the value of peaceful conflict resolution if we hit them. Spanking only teaches a child that it is okay to hit someone smaller or weaker than you. Children need to learn compassion, patience, and understanding from adults who teach by example.

IT HUMILIATES AND DEMEANS

Hitting a child—however gently—lowers his self-esteem. It makes him feel bad and unlovable. Eda LeShan, a family counselor and author of over thirty books, including *When Your Child Drives You Crazy*, says, "No matter how children may behave—even with bravado—being hit is demeaning. In my work in prisons, I have never met a person convicted of serious crimes who wasn't beaten as a child. Hitting can only lead to abject withdrawal or hurting oneself or others."[5]

IT CAN BE ABUSIVE

There is a fine line between spanking and abuse. Most parents who spank for disciplinary purposes recoil at the thought of child abuse—but it is easier to cross the line than you may think. Spanking is often motivated by anger and fear—anger at our inability to control our children and fear that they will grow up badly behaved. These strong emotions cause the release of adrenaline into the bloodstream, which can easily overpower us and cause us to hit harder than we intended.

When a husband slaps his wife in anger it is called wife-beating and could land him in jail. Why are children—whose size disadvantage makes them so vulnerable to harm—not entitled to the same protection?

IT IS NEVER JUSTIFIED

Hitting is never the best way to teach a child. Even in the case of real danger—as when a child runs out into the road—you can grab him, sit him down, look him in the eyes, and tell him why he must never do that again. The panic in your voice will communicate your message much more effectively than any spanking. You can be dramatic without being abusive.

Terry

I occasionally think that my life would be easier in some ways if I spanked Travis. It is difficult to realize that a project will have to be put away unfinished, a book left unread, or a phone call cut short. When he started crawling, things really got busy. He was old enough to be mobile but too young to reason with. It seemed I was constantly jumping up to divert, distract, or remove him from dangerous situations. Rather than preventing the negative from happening, I tried to allow the positive to occur.

Not spanking has a lot going for it, difficult though it may be at times. For one thing, it forces you to develop the maturity to deal with your anger rather than physically venting it upon your child. (And there is no guilt afterward.) I don't worry that my son had a "might makes right" attitude ingrained in him from infancy on. You don't waste time spanking, but instead devise disciplinary methods that are more effective.

Terry McElhiney Dunn, "Some Thoughts on Spanking," *Mothering*, Spring 1982.

The Problem with Time-Out

Many of us abhor the thought of spanking our children. Instead, we have decided to rely on the popular disciplinary tool known as time-out. Sending a child to a corner or to her room, we reason, gives her time to cool off and think about her misbehavior.

The problem with time-out is that it doesn't work. As explained earlier, time-out teaches a child little about her behavior, or how to act differently in the future. A time-out is supposed to give a child a chance to collect herself and reflect on her wrongdoings—but such reflection is a lot to expect of a child who is probably too overwhelmed by her own emotions to think clearly about her actions. Rather, the child is apt to focus on her feelings of frustration at not having her needs met, rejection at being sent away when she needed her parents' understanding, and anger at not being heard. And time-outs quickly become ineffective the older your child gets: Imagine telling a child who is almost as tall as you are to go sit in a chair in the corner.

Instead of being silenced and isolated in time-out, what a child needs most when she is out of control is a loving parent to hold her, listen to her, and allow her to release her pent-up emotions in a constructive way so that she may develop the ability to verbalize her feelings rather than to act out.

Buddhist monk Thich Nhat Hanh, author of *Being Peace,* suggests that each family have a small breathing room—a simple space with a cushion for each family member, and perhaps a vase of flowers.[6] When a child is agitated, rather than sending him to his room or time-out, you could take his hand and walk into the room to sit quietly together and just breathe. Parents could also use the breathing room when they need a time-out to calm themselves down.

Children Have Good Reasons for Their Behavior

Your children don't bicker and yell because they are trying to drive you crazy, although at times it may feel that way. They are testing their limits, developing their social skills, and defining their relationship to the world.

Young children are naturally impatient, forgetful, stubborn, loud, messy, and demanding. They are childish. It is unrealistic to expect them to act in socially acceptable ways until they have the maturity to do so. Most youngsters under five do not have the language and cognitive skills needed to share or work out disagreements, so they fight or cry instead.

You can prevent some undesirable behavior by simply by sticking to a routine. A child who is hungry and tired is much more likely to fall apart if she cannot have candy at the grocery store than a child who is well-fed and well-rested.

Your child's behavior can teach you something about his needs, if you take the time to listen.

Almost all acting out is a cry for help. Your child may be jealous, afraid, lonely, or in a situation that is out of his control. Often the child who is acting most unlovable is the most in need of love.

Mary

Michael and I were going through a rocky period when he was four, and I just couldn't figure it out. It seemed that he objected to everything I said or did, and picked on his baby sister, Emily, constantly. He wasn't verbal enough to tell me what was bothering him, so I had to guess by listening to his surly, belligerent actions.

One day I guessed correctly. I talked a bit about how he must get tired of sharing all the time and how it must seem like Emily was always grabbing his things. The relief on his face was indescribable. I told him that it wasn't necessary to share all the time and that he could play alone when he wanted to. I told him he could go into another room and close the door or he could ask me to distract Emily with a different activity. I told him it was OK to feel mad at Emily and me.

He was so overwhelmed that he cried in my arms. He hasn't been belligerent since then.

Mary Ehrmin, "Instead of Spanking," *Mothering,* Winter 1985.

Besides understanding your child's reasons for her behavior, understanding your own reasons for getting angry with your child is important. If you are annoyed because your daughter insists on wearing an old sweatsuit instead of a dress to a birthday party, you need to ask yourself whose problem it really is. You don't need to let your child have her way, but acknowledging that it is your issue may help you to deal with the situation.

By the same token, try to avoid misplacing your anger on your child. It is all too easy to get an annoying phone call from a friend and immediately lose your temper with your child for tugging at your sleeve, when it is really your friend you are upset with. When you feel yourself getting angry for reasons that have nothing to do with your child, take a parental time-out until you can regain your composure.

Alternatives to Punishment

Punishment is always a quick fix. If you view conflict as an opportunity for you and your child to learn and grow, you can choose from many creative alternatives to punishment. Teaching—not punishing—is the goal of effective discipline.

Effective discipline means approaching conflict with your child as you would any other conflict. Identify the problem, evaluate the possible solutions together, choose a solution that is mutually considered, act on the solution, and discuss the consequences. You can do this even with a very young child. However, for a young child, direct action and simple words work best.

Effective discipline means recognizing that your child does not "misbehave." Children act out of their needs. Your responsibility is to communicate to your child how his actions affect you for better or for worse. When they affect you for the worse, assume that your child, too, wants to work out a solution—one that will leave you both with

your self-respect intact. Effective discipline has more to do with being involved with and tuned into your child than with being permissive or strict.

Look over this list of alternatives to punishment. Not all of them will work for you—some may be more appropriate for certain ages or situations; some may even be contradictory. The point is to have a repertoire of approaches to draw from in any given situation.

And give yourself time to change. Changing our approach to discipline doesn't happen overnight just because we have changed our minds. (For a quick reference list to post someplace handy, see the one-page summary at the end of this chapter.)

USE POSITIVE REINFORCEMENT

Too often, we take good conduct for granted and pay attention to our children only when their behavior disrupts us. When your children put their shoes away, share nicely with each other, or do their chores without being asked, let them know that you appreciate it.

CREATE A POSITIVE ENVIRONMENT

"Provention" is a term used in conflict resolution, meaning being proactive in order to avoid conflict. Create an environment in which you do not constantly have to say 'no.' Childproof your house. Let your children keep toys they don't want to share in their rooms. If your child keeps getting into your makeup, move it to a higher shelf.

SAY YES AS MUCH AS POSSIBLE

Between the things you cannot be flexible on, and the dictates of society, your child will encounter plenty of no's. Try to say yes as much as possible at home. Saying yes does not mean being overly indulgent; it means allowing your child to be a child. Remind yourself to be more positive when your child wants to do something that you feel like saying no to just because it is messy or time-consuming. See if you can figure out a win-win solution. You don't have to be a martyr.

SAVE NO FOR THE IMPORTANT THINGS

There are some things you cannot be flexible on. "No" will have more impact if you use it less frequently.

USE NATURAL CONSEQUENCES

Within the boundaries of safety, let experience be your child's teacher. If she wants to go outside in winter without a coat, she will learn that she gets cold. If she does not put her dirty clothes in the laundry hamper, she will learn that her clothes are still dirty after wash day. Once your child has learned her lesson, avoid the temptation to say "I told you so."

USE LOGICAL CONSEQUENCES

If you must provide a consequence for an action, make it a logical one. Say your child goes to a friend's house after school without telling you—have her check in with you even more formally before going anywhere until you feel that she's back on track. Logical consequences must be fair, respectful of the child, and connected to the behavior. The cause-effect relationship makes this form of discipline more effective than a punishment that has no connection to the offense.

USE RESTITUTION

Show your child how to make amends for a wrongdoing. An older child could do extra chores to pay for a neighbor's smashed window; a younger child could offer to help tape torn pages back in a book or give up one of his toys to replace a broken one. If restitution is not possible, your child could write a note or make a drawing to express his apology.

LEAVE IT UP TO YOUR CHILD

So often we jump in to solve our children's problems, when they are really capable of figuring it out themselves. Whether the issue is that your son's friend will not share the toy truck with him, or that he wants to use the computer at the same time you need to work on it, ask him, "What do you think you should do?" An older child can run through some possible scenarios and propose a solution. Younger children may need suggestions of possible solutions: "You and Charlie could take turns with the truck. Or Charlie could play with that truck and you could play with this one." As Adele Faber and Elaine Mazlish, authors of *How to Talk So*

Kids Will Listen and Listen So Kids Will Talk, say, "See your children as problem solvers, and they will begin to see themselves this way." Realizing that you don't need to solve your child's every problem is liberating.

COMPROMISE

If the issue is something you can be flexible on, try to arrive at a solution together that works for both of you. Your five-year-old could go to her friend's house now if she agrees to help clean up the playroom when she gets home. You need to use the computer from 3 to 5 p.m., but your teenager could use it from 5 to 7 p.m. Elicit your child's agreement in the compromise up front, by asking questions like, "How does that sound to you? Can you do that?"

STATE YOUR EXPECTATIONS, AND GET OUT OF THE WAY

Hovering over our children does not teach them to take responsibility for themselves. State your expectations clearly—"You need to be dressed in five minutes if you want to come with me," or "There is only one cookie and three of you. You need to work it out"—and then leave.

GIVE SPECIFIC INSTRUCTIONS

Young children may need specific instructions as well as clear expectations. Instead of "Clean up the playroom," say, "Put the books on the shelf, the crayons in the box, and the coloring books in the drawer." A young child may also need you to show her how to do something: "This is how we pet the dog gently."

GIVE A REASON

Explain to your child why we don't wear muddy shoes in the house, or why we don't pull on the dog's ears.

OFFER HELP

Do not do tasks for your child, but do them with your child. Say, "Why don't you clean up the blocks and I'll put away the paints." Instead of asking, "Why are you taking so long?" say, "Can I help you with this so we can get to Sally's house on time?"

GIVE A CHOICE

Children need to have choices in order to feel they have some control over their world. Even a choice as simple as "Would you like to brush your teeth now, or after the story?" gives a child a sense that his opinion is valued. You can always come up with choices; just make sure they are real choices and that you can live with all the alternatives.

REDIRECT

Give your child another option to redirect his behavior: "You can't hit the baby, but you can hit a pillow." Or, "You can't ride your truck in the dining room because it scratches the floor, but you can ride it in the kitchen."

REMOVE

Take your child out of a situation that is deteriorating, but rather than isolate her in time-out, stay with her, hold her, and listen to her until she is ready to act appropriately. Don't, however, be nicer than you feel.

MAKE POSITIVE STATEMENTS

Consider the difference: "We can read a story as soon as you brush your teeth," rather than, "If you don't brush your teeth right now, we won't be able to read a story."

GIVE IN OCCASIONALLY

"We can skip brushing your teeth tonight because you're so tired." You don't want to become a pushover, but you don't want your child to think of you as a tyrant, either.

GIVE YOUR CHILD TIME TO AGREE

Issuing too many ultimatums teaches your child that his opinions do not matter. Backing your child into a corner may mean that he has to rebel in order to save his self-esteem. Try to find a compromise so that your child can save face.

SIMPLY INSIST

With things you feel strongly about—especially where your child's safety is concerned—compromise is not possible. In that case, insist. Do not make threats—"Do this, or I'll . . ."—simply insist.

Threats and punishment give your child a choice—he can either comply, or be punished. Sometimes a child is relieved when you take responsibility for a decision.

MAKE RULES

There are certain things your children need to know, like, "In this family, we don't hit each other." If a child breaks a rule, remind her of it firmly. Let the children be involved in devising the family rules. You may even want to write them down together and post them in a place where everyone can see them. Just make sure you abide by the rules along with everyone else, and that you forgive yourself and your children and start over when the inevitable backsliding occurs.

IGNORE SOME BEHAVIOR

Behavioral scientists tell us that whatever is noticed is reinforced. Ignore your son when he starts saying "dammit," and he will soon tire of it. Overlook little things that do not really matter. We do this all the time in our relationships with our spouses.

AVOID NAGGING AND THREATS

Your child may be acting out just because she is craving attention. Try to notice her in more positive ways than nagging.

DISTRACT

Often you can diffuse a tense situation with a diversion. The more you dig your heels in, the deeper your child will dig his in. Haim Ginott liked to say, "Don't change a mind; change a mood."

USE HUMOR

Humor is wonderful at dissolving tension. Suggest that you and your child get your aggressions out with a playful pillow fight. Be silly. One mother says, "My son loves it when I turn him upside down and shake all the grumpy stuff out of him. He thought it was hilarious when I moaned and sobbed in my most melodramatic style, 'I don't want to fix dinner. It's too hard, and it takes too long. Why do I always have to feed you?' His task—taking a bath—seemed fun after that."

MAKE IT A GAME

Pretend that you are the Cat in the Hat's helpers, and you have to get the playroom picked up before Mother gets home. Set a timer, and challenge your daughter to get dressed by herself before the buzzer rings.

BE WILLING TO ADMIT YOUR MISTAKES

If a consequence was too punitive, be willing to change your mind. Be willing to tell your child you are sorry for overreacting. He may learn more from your admission than from anything else; he will learn that even grown-ups make mistakes and are able to admit they are wrong. On some days, say to your children, "Let's start this day over again." And do.

STOP AND THINK BEFORE YOU ACT

How often have you said something to your child—or your spouse—that you wish you could take back as soon as you said it? How often have you lashed out in anger that was not really justified? We all do it. One of the most important things you can do when disciplining your children is to take a deep breath before you do anything. Sometimes you may need to admit, "I'm really upset right now. I'm going to go in the other room for a minute, then come back and talk to you." Disciplining children requires control—self-control for adults, that is.

DON'T MAKE A BIG FUSS OVER LITTLE THINGS

Getting upset at a child for spilling her milk humiliates her, and accomplishes nothing. Save your energy for the things she can control.

STICK TO ROUTINES

If you want to avoid melt-downs, make sure your children get enough sleep. Do not try to run errands just before nap time. Give your children a snack before you go to the grocery store or the post office.

DON'T HURRY YOUR CHILDREN TOO MUCH

Allow them enough time to get dressed in the morning so that you won't lose your temper over their inevitable dawdling. Give them an early warning when it is almost time to leave the

park. Make a deal: "Three more slides, and then we have to go."

GET TO THE ROOT OF THE PROBLEM

If your child hits his baby sister, encourage him to tell you why he is upset, and address his feelings of anger or jealousy. Accept your child's feelings, but teach better behavior. "You sound really angry. I can't let you hit your sister. Why don't you hammer your blocks instead, and then when she goes down for a nap, you and I will work on that puzzle together."

CORRECT ONE BEHAVIOR AT A TIME

Do not try to deal with your daughter's lousy table manners, messy room, and inability to get dressed in time for school, all in the same week. Tackle one issue at a time.

GIVE YOURSELVES TIME

Change takes time. Children are forgetful and may have to be told the same thing ten times—in the same day. Be patient with your children, and with yourself.

USE THE GOLDEN RULE

Think to yourself, "If I were the child, how would I want to be treated?" Treat your children at least as well as you would treat your friends—with tolerance, respect, and understanding.

MODEL APPROPRIATE BEHAVIOR

Children learn more from our actions than from our words. Do you expect your children to keep their rooms neat when the rest of the house is disorganized? Do you and your spouse spend a lot of time bickering and blaming each other? Do you spank your children to teach them that hitting is wrong? You can't expect your children to act any differently than you do.

THINK OF YOUR CHILD AS AN EQUAL

Think of your child as another person whom you care deeply about, but who exists independently of you. Enjoy knowing that you are not responsible for your child's every action.

ALWAYS KEEP YOUR LOVE FOR YOUR CHILD IN MIND

No matter how unlovable your child is acting, remember how much you love her. Take her by the hands and look into her eyes. If you keep your love for your child in mind, whatever you do will be right.

Claiming Your Authority

Disciplining in a cooperative, nonadversarial way does not have to mean a loss of authority. There are plenty of ways to remain in charge without relying on control or coercion.

One way to claim your authority as the parent is to avoid "parenting by permission." If you find yourself asking your children's permission for everything—"It's time to go home now, honey, okay?" "Your pirate pajamas are in the wash tonight, okay?"—you will find that it is hardly ever okay. Simply removing the question mark from the end of your commands can do wonders for your authority.

Claim your authority with dramatic action and strong language, but without threats or verbal abuse. Get loud and angry if you need to, without attacking or blaming. "Look at this! My closet is a mess! My new makeup is on the mirror, my shoes are everywhere, my dresses are on the floor!" As Adele Faber and Elaine Mazlish say, you do not need to be nice—you need to be real.

As the parent, you are always the one in charge. Even when you do not know what to do, you are still the one in charge. You can elicit your children's cooperation and work toward compromises, but ultimately, you have to make the final decisions. Be prepared, at times your children will not like you.

Peaceful parenting does not mean passive or permissive parenting: It is the combination of authority and mercy that helps children to grow up with self-respect and concern for others.

Mary

At some point in my growth as a mother, I made up my mind that I would not punish—physically or otherwise. It wasn't long, of course, until a child stood on her little flat feet and refused my request for cooperation. There were moments of pure panic, but miraculously a way was always given. I believe in grace, something that breaks through from the beyond, because this is how it has appeared in my own life—one little miracle after another.

I owe a lot of my education to my daughter, Miriam, a pint-sized diva of the temper tantrum. At the age of twenty months, she had been transplanted from Korea, and after resting for a few weeks, she spent most of her third year with a major chip on her shoulder. Intellectually, I knew she had a reason to be angry, and I also knew there was no point in adding fuel to the fire, but being shrieked at by this dainty virago made me want to start shrieking back. I had stayed calm and reasonable through the boys' two-year-old snits, but hers could reduce me to the emotional level of another tot.

By trial and error, I learned to plant my feet wide apart, neither advancing nor retreating, and absorb her anger without giving it back. After the storm, we got back to the business at hand. I was, after all, the grown-up.

Mary Liston Liepold, "Parenting Without Punishing," *Mothering*, May/June 1998.

Communication That Engages Cooperation

The key to effective discipline is effective communication. You won't be able to engage your children's cooperation if you can't communicate in a loving, nonjudgmental way.

Good communication skills must be worked at. Just as couples often turn to counseling to help them communicate effectively, parents need to learn to talk so that their children will listen. Here are some tips for improving your family communication:

USE "I" STATEMENTS

You can express strong disapproval without insulting your child. Instead of "You are such a slob!" or "Why do you always do that?" use statements like "I have a really hard time coming home to a sink full of dirty dishes," or "I'm afraid if you leave your toys all over the floor that I'm going to trip over them." Separate the deed from the doer. The message should be, "How can we solve this?" rather than "Look what you did!"

DESCRIBE

Faber and Mazlish counsel parents to point out what is bothering them, without attacking a child, by simply describing the situation. "This room is a mess. Wet clothes on the floor. And apple cores on the bed. And dirty underwear on the chair." Describe, and leave. If you are really angry, feel free to yell: "Hey Johnny, apple cores belong in the garbage!" Saying something like this is a much better alternative than the other damaging things you might say in anger.

REDUCE

Resist the temptation to always lecture, add Faber and Mazlish. Instead of saying, "Johnny, you just left your new jacket on the floor for the fifth time this week, and I don't want to have to remind you again to hang it up," just say, "Johnny—the jacket."

EMPATHIZE

Trying to minimize a child's feelings usually has the opposite effect. When a tearful child shows you a little scrape, and you say, "Oh, that's nothing," he will probably cry even harder. But if you say, "You got a scrape. That must hurt," he is likely to say, "It doesn't hurt that much," and run off to play.

ADMIT TO YOUR OWN FEELINGS

If you are feeling angry or frustrated, you can simply say, "I'm starting to fall apart!" Being honest about your emotions teaches your child to express his own feelings in conflicts with others.

MAINTAIN EYE CONTACT

When you listen to your child, get down on her level, look her right in the eyes, and give her your full attention. This one habit can do more to make your child feel heard than you can imagine.

It can be extremely annoying to have a child tugging at your sleeve while you are trying to finish an adult conversation. But if you simply take a moment to give your child your full attention and ask her what she needs, you are much more likely to be able to carry on your conversation without interruption.

When you are reprimanding your child, take her by the hands, look in her eyes, and explain why her actions were wrong. Your words will have more impact on her, and you will be reminded of the lovable person behind those eyes.

DON'T DO ANYTHING

When you jump in and attempt to solve your child's problems, you are not allowing her to think for herself. Instead, if you allow her to vent her emotions while you simply listen nonjudgmentally, she will most likely come to a solution on her own. We must resist the temptation to always do for our children. As Haim Ginott used to say, "Don't just do something; stand there."

LET YOUR CHILD SPEAK FOR HIMSELF

Attempting to interpret your child's feelings yourself can lead to inaccuracies and frustration. Allow your child to speak freely, without interruption. Afterward you can paraphrase what he just said to let him know that you heard him correctly, and he can correct you if you did not.

Eileen

I was not allowed to say no to my parents. Saying no was considered a sign of disrespect. Saying no was a prerogative reserved for grown-ups, and my parents used it liberally. In my childhood diary, I referred to my father as "Mr. No." Recording his answer to a rare challenge of "Why can't I?" I wrote: "Because you kids have got to learn the meaning of the word no." In retrospect, I see how ridiculous it was to try to fathom the meaning of a word I was not allowed to use.

When my daughter says no, it means "I am different from you, mother. I am my own person. I want something you don't want for me. I am making my own way. I am fighting back."

I am learning that motherhood is not about getting my daughter to behave in a certain way, or convincing her to do things for her own good, or filling her up with all she needs to know, as if she were an empty vessel. What she needs from me is attention, affection, and protection—but only from whatever she cannot protect herself from. Every time I allow my daughter the freedom she needs to grow, every time I let go of rigid expectations of her, every time I discover another respectful way to be with a child, I say yes to life.

Eileen Mullen, "The Meaning of No," *Mothering,* Fall 1993.

HELP YOUR CHILD EXPRESS HER FEELINGS

If you want to encourage your child to share her feelings, you must be prepared to listen. Eda LeShan says we can help children tell us how they feel by reading them stories and following up with conversation, by listening to accounts of their dreams, and by paying attention when they have something to tell us rather than saying "I'm busy now," or "Wait until I get off the phone."

DO NOT PRY TOO MUCH

In our attempts to elicit our children's feelings, we sometimes overanalyze or ask too much. One seven-year-old girl said, "I like talking to Dad better than Mom—he doesn't ask so many questions." Your child is more likely to tell you about the bully who frightened him on the school playground if you don't ask about it. And avoid making too much of a small thing. By tomorrow, when you ask him if the bully was still there and how he handled it, he is likely to have forgotten about the whole incident.

Ineffective Communication

Effective communication does not happen overnight. It takes time to change ingrained habits. As you work toward improving your communication skills, it is helpful to notice what kinds of messages alienate rather than foster understanding. Poor communication techniques include:

- blaming
- accusing
- name-calling
- threatening
- commanding
- lecturing
- warning ("If you don't . . . , you'll be grounded.")
- evoking martyrdom (as in, "I'm the one who always has to clean up after you.")
- comparing ("Why can't you be more like your sister?")
- prophesying ("You'll never amount to anything if you don't study.")
- using sarcasm

Parenting with Encouragement

Loving discipline is a matter of building your child's self-esteem. Children who have a good opinion of themselves are better able to control themselves and have more confidence in solving conflicts.

Children absorb messages about who they are from their parents, and later from their peers. If you communicate to your child through your words, your tone, and your touch that she is loved and important, she will grow up feeling lovable and confident. If you attack or demean your child—"You can't do anything right! You drive me crazy"—your words will define who she is and what she feels that she deserves in life.

Helping Your Children Combat Verbal Abuse

Even if you are careful not to demean or invalidate your children, they are likely to encounter verbal abuse at the hands of their peers. Louise Hart, author of *The Winning Family: Increasing Self-Esteem in Your Children and Yourself,* and Jay Carter, author of *Nasty People,* offer the following advice for children dealing with insults and verbal abuse:[10, 11]

- *Inquire.* Throw the responsibility back on the insult-giver by asking, "What do you mean by that?" or "Are you in a bad mood or something?"
- *Repeat.* Look directly at the insult-giver, and very enthusiastically ask him to repeat the comment. This approach often gets people thinking about what they said. They may back down or repeat the comment with less emphasis.
- *Confront.* If a comment hurts, acknowledge it, by saying, "I don't like that" or "Ouch!" A harmless way to retaliate is by acting like a snake—making a hissing sound and pointing two fingers at the person.
- *Withdraw.* There is no reason to stick around people who are mean. Try staying away from that person for a while.

To discipline your children without damaging their self-esteem, keep the following tips in mind:

EXAMINE YOUR EXPECTATIONS

Expectations that are too high set our children up for failure and set us up for disappointment, says Louise Hart, author of *The Winning Family: Increasing Self-Esteem in Your Children and Yourself.*[8] Expectations that are too low tell our children that we do not believe in them, and they learn not to believe in themselves. Maintain high, attainable expectations for yourself and your children, and then cheer each other on!

THINK BEFORE YOU SPEAK

When you say hurtful things to your children, their self-esteem suffers, and so does yours. Matthew Fox, in his book *Original Blessing,* writes, "Healthy families remind each other of their goodness; unhealthy families remind each other of their failings."[9]

FOCUS ON THE POSITIVE

Instead of always looking for shortcomings, focus on what is wonderful about your child. Some schools are now sending home "We caught your child being good" certificates instead of failure or discipline notices.

GIVE CONSTRUCTIVE CRITICISM

Parents may fear giving criticism because they do not want to damage their child's self-esteem. But constructive criticism is necessary to lifelong learning. When correcting a child, use phrases like, "I see why you may have thought that, but it's not quite right," or "That's not the answer. Let's see how you came to that." Children need to engage in the hard work of correcting their own mistakes in order to achieve competence and self-esteem.

The Problem with Praise

Although it may seem ironic, too much praise can be equally as damaging as invalidation. Praise that is too vague or too frequent may set a child up for failure. Blanket praise—"You're so smart" or "You're a good girl"—is meaningless. When praise is overdone, it loses its effectiveness as a motivator.

Here are some ways to praise your child effectively:

BE SPECIFIC

Instead of simply, "You're a good artist," you can say, "Wow. You drew a perfect circle." This comment gives the child a view of her abilities that she can then duplicate and feel good about.

DESCRIBE, RATHER THAN JUDGE

Instead of "That's a very nice painting," try saying, "Look at all the bright colors you used." Again, this type of praise gives the child something specific to feel good about.

BE HONEST

Children will quickly sense when you are being insincere. If you don't like a painting, you can say, "It looks like you enjoyed painting that." Beware of telling your child she is the greatest artist since Van Gogh, unless it is really true.

GIVE ENCOURAGEMENT

"You did that puzzle all by yourself!" is better than "Good boy!"

EXPRESS APPRECIATION

Tell your child, "I like it when you help me clean up the kitchen."

DON'T CRITICIZE WHILE YOU COMPLIMENT

The surest way to defeat the value of praise is to couple it with a reminder: "You did a great job putting away your toys today. I hope you won't forget again tomorrow." The negative reference to tomorrow's expectations takes the pleasure out of today's praise.

PRAISE EFFORT

Try to focus on your child's efforts rather than her talents. A series of six studies of fifth graders by Columbia University psychologists demonstrated that children commended for their intelligence instead of their effort became performance-oriented; handling failure was difficult for them. They tended to blame their failure on lack of intelligence, and therefore saw no way to improve their performance. When children who had been praised for hard work performed poorly, they tried harder next time.

Staying out of Danger with Anger

Even if you understand the importance of building your child's self-esteem, and try to consciously use effective communication techniques, it is still easy to say things you wish you had not said in the heat of the moment. Why? Because you get angry. Anger is a part of life.

Anyone with young children knows that for tempers to have flared several times before breakfast is even served is not unusual. Children express their anger often and loudly, and children's behavior can easily provoke their parents' wrath. Anger is a normal, healthy emotion, and its expression can be a tremendous release. Far more constructive than bottling up anger—only to express it indirectly through slammed doors or sarcastic remarks—is the ability to air strong emotions and hurt feelings in the open. When two people can listen to each other in anger and work through a conflict, their relationship is stretched and strengthened.

To avoid making hurtful remarks, however, you need to keep your temper from getting the best of you. Here are some steps to take next time you feel yourself about to blow up at your children (or your spouse), from Kathy Collard Miller, author of *When Love Becomes Anger:*[12]

RECOGNIZE THE EARLY WARNING SIGNS

Think back to what happened the last time you lost your temper. Did you feel tense and hurried inside? Were you gritting your teeth? Were you on the verge of tears? Had you just had a confrontation with your spouse? Learn to identify when you have reached the end of your rope, so that you can take steps to avoid lashing out.

RECOGNIZE THE CAUSE OF YOUR ANGER

Before you overreact to something your child just did, take a second to think about why you are really angry. Chances are, something else is bothering you, and your children do not deserve to bear the brunt of your wrath. You may need to step back from your emotions before you can think clearly enough to recognize what is really bothering you.

TAKE A TIME-OUT

When you feel yourself about to lose control with your children, you need to remove yourself temporarily from the situation. Try taking several deep breaths, counting to ten, or taking three steps backward. If you need more time to cool off, call a friend to watch the children while you take a walk or a shower.

VERBALIZE YOUR ANGER

Once you have figured out why you are angry, you can go about expressing your anger in an appropriate way. Confront the source of your anger—your spouse, your child, perhaps yourself—and explain how you feel. Be sure to use "I" messages—"I feel…" or "It bothers me when…"—to avoid putting the other person on the defensive. If you are too emotional to talk about it immediately, you can take time to calm down, or write your feelings in a note. You may find that you do not even need to send the note; the mere act of writing down your feelings can be cathartic enough.

Tempering Tantrums

A two-year-old's temper tantrum can be a frightening thing to witness. He may throw himself on the ground, kicking and thrashing; shriek and sob for something he cannot have; and wring his hands or rhythmically tug on a piece of clothing.

Not surprisingly, most temper tantrums occur in public places, where the pressure on your child to control his behavior is the most intense. Whether you are in the grocery store, at a restaurant, or at church when a tantrum strikes, you are likely to get disapproving stares from adults who think you should do something to control your child.

Recognize that temper tantrums are a normal, healthy, necessary release for toddlers and that you can do nothing to control them. Young children lack the verbal skills or cognitive awareness to interpret the powerful emotions they feel, and sometimes fear, anger, or frustration explode in a very physical way. A no-holds-barred tantrum can be very cleansing to a child, who will usually emerge calm and renewed.

A tantrum is as overwhelming to the child experiencing it as it is to the adults witnessing it. The best thing you can do for your child when he is in the midst of a full-blown tantrum is to stand by quietly and give him the time and space to work out his rage. If you are in a public place, you may have to remove him to a place where he won't disturb others. Instead of shutting him in a room by himself, stay with him until his fury subsides, so that he can climb onto your lap, be comforted, and then get on with the business of learning about the world in a trusting, open way.

Coping with Sibling Rivalry

Ask any parents of more than one child what they find themselves disciplining their children about most often, and the answer is likely to be squabbles between brothers and sisters—sibling rivalry.

In truth, tussles between siblings should be the least of your discipline problems. The last thing children need when they are having a confrontation is for their parents to step in and try to break it up or demand restitution. Letting siblings work out their differences—within the framework of some important ground rules—is a wonderful lesson in social skills for children, and a huge relief for parents.

Children are, by nature, uncivilized. Until they learn how to express themselves in other ways, they solve conflicts by grabbing, hitting, or yelling. These interactions can be upsetting for parents to watch, but they provide valuable learning experiences in acceptable and unacceptable behaviors for the children. When one child grabs a toy from another, he learns what reaction that produces, and he is on his way toward learning to take the feelings of others into account.

Siblings are good sounding boards for practicing social skills, says Eda LeShan. Not until adolescence do children usually feel secure enough to fight with their parents. But the sibling relationship is, from the start, a great place for expressing and acting out all kinds of feelings—negative as well as positive ones.

When your children begin to quarrel, don't try to play referee. Attempting to mediate your children's conflicts teaches them that they are unable to solve their own problems. Once you let them work it out, you may be surprised to find that they arrive at compromises you might not have thought of.

Your keeping out of your children's conflicts assumes, of course, that you are not really needed as a referee, that you have established family rules such as no hitting, biting, or hurtful insults. When you witness the rules being ignored, you should break up the fight.

Short of bodily harm or below-the-belt barbs, however, the best thing you can do is stay out of your children's way. When one of them comes running in to you, crying, "She's being mean to me!" you can simply listen and be sympathetic—and you can be sympathetic to both sides. Most likely, you will soon hear the sounds of two happy children playing together again. Eventually you may find that your children are having fewer fights. They will learn important lessons about limits and power, and giving in—and you will discover the value of staying out of their business.

Peaceful Parenting: The Roots of Nonviolence

Perhaps the most exciting thing about peaceful parenting is the possibility of nurturing future peacemakers who can create a better world. If we teach our children to use nonviolent ways to solve conflicts, perhaps they will help influence a future in which world peace is possible.

The building blocks for peace start within the family. A unique cross-cultural survey that put together anthropological studies from 400 different sources around the world found that cultures with the least occurrence of interpersonal violence and militarism were those that displayed childbearing characteristics such as late weaning, a high degree of touching and holding of infants, and a low incidence of punishment. [13]

Anthropologist Ashley Montagu, author of *The Nature of Human Aggression*, *The Elephant Man*, and dozens of other works, writes that "man is not born with innate drives toward violence and destruction...every living creature carries within itself the seeds for healthy growth and development." He concludes, "Violence toward children in any shape or form breeds and perpetuates violence. The only discipline children need is the firmness of love and the encouragement to grow and develop in their unique and authentic selves." [14] Psychoanalyst Alice Miller further explores connections between orthodox disciplining practices and the development of violent individuals and nations—particularly Nazi Germany—in her brilliant book, *For Your Own Good: Hidden Cruelty in Child-Rearing and the Roots of Violence.* [15]

If we want to raise children who will foster both inner peace and peace for future generations, we must go about it peacefully. "Peace is

not the absence of conflict. Conflict is an inevitable fact of daily life," write Kathleen and James McGinnis in *Parenting for Peace and Justice.* "Peace is the process of working to resolve conflicts in such a way that both sides win. This style of parenting is neither permissive nor authoritarian. It is mutual. Parents do not make all the decisions, but neither do they give in to the children when their own essential needs are at stake." [16]

The act of parenting civilizes us. Being a parent makes us want to create a better world for our children. One leader of an organization that assists thousands of children who are victims of war explains, "We do not believe in saving all children or one hundred children or ten children. We believe in saving one child. If one child is not

202

Alternatives to Punishment

Copy this list and post it where you can see it, as a constant reminder.

Use positive reinforcement.

Create a positive environment.

Say yes as much as possible.

Save no for the important things.

Use natural consequences.

Use logical consequences.

Use restitution.

Leave it up to your child.

Compromise.

State your expectations, and get out of the way.

Give specific instructions.

Give a reason.

Offer help.

Give a choice.

Redirect your child.

Remove your child.

Make positive statements.

Give in occasionally.

Give your child time to agree.

Simply insist.

Make rules.

Ignore some behavior.

Avoid nagging and threats.

Distract your child.

Use humor.

Make it a game.

Be willing to admit your mistakes.

Stop and think before you act.

Don't make a big fuss over little things.

Stick to routines.

Don't hurry your children too much.

Get to the root of the problem.

Correct one behavior at a time.

Give yourselves time.

Use the golden rule.

Model appropriate behavior.

Think of your child as an equal.

Always keep your love for your child in mind.

---

worth being saved, then two are not. The basis of everything is one child."

An equally simple devotion to our own children is the root of all peace work. The act of attending to our children's daily needs in a lov-ing, conscious way nurtures both parent and child into peacemakers. The more love you give to your own children, the more your heart and arms ache to give love and life to those beyond your own family. Peace truly begins at home.

CHAPTER 16 # Adolescence

Only the rare parent looks forward to a child's adolescence. As one father joked, "I'm not at all worried about living through my daughter's teenage years. From age thirteen to seventeen, she's going to move in with her grandparents." After all, few of us have fond memories of our own adolescence, and we are none too eager to relive those tumultuous times with our children.

Parenting a teen is, in some ways, like parenting a two-year-old. Like two-year-olds, teens have a healthy narcissism and rebelliousness. They know their preferences and sometimes cannot be reasoned with. They begin again to constantly question, "Why, Mom, why?" They are stubborn, intractable, rude, unaware of other's needs, and emotionally volatile. In short, they are in the process of discovering their limits.

At the same time, teens require a very different approach than two-year-olds. As psychiatrist Lynn Ponton, mother of two teenagers, says, "Teenagers are not little, they are not cute, and they talk back." Suddenly the rules change in adolescence, and many parents are caught off guard by the fact that what worked with a three-year-old or a ten-year-old no longer applies with a fourteen-year-old.

We can be tempted to be smug; to allow ourselves to believe that if we parent "right"—if we breastfeed, don't spank, and encourage healthy communication with our children—we will be spared the turmoil associated with the teen years. But the power struggle between teens and

adults is necessary for the child to grow into an adult. This parent *vs.* teen conflict is the stuff of the adolescent years, and it can't be avoided by better parenting. In fact, avoiding the struggle now may mean that your child will have difficulty with power and authority later in life.

The teen years are confusing, turbulent, and challenging for both child and parent, but they are also enlightening, touching, and at times, very funny. Wise parents will recognize when their child is ready to take the driver's seat and will act as a bumper rail on the bridge to maturity. Once your children are teens, you will learn that you can no longer protect them all of the time. You will realize you will have to live without them sooner than you thought. Hopefully, if you have laid the foundation for a loving, trusting relationship, you can both emerge the more resilient from these years, on your way to remaining lifelong good friends.

The Kids Are All Right

Adolescence has a terrible reputation. The media paint a picture of teens today as highly troubled by focusing on alarmist statistics such as rates of teen pregnancy, suicide, and drug use and abuse. Television sitcoms portray teenagers as dazed idiots fixated on fashion and vulgar music, possessing insatiable appetites, and capable of wild mood swings. Teenagers see the media images, too. One adolescent wrote in a letter to the editor of a teen magazine, "There is a popular belief that teenagers are antisocial creatures for whom responsibility is a dirty word."

Adolescence sometimes sounds like a terminal disease. We hear about pot-smokers who skip classes, high school students who gun down their classmates, or teenage mothers who abandon their babies in public restrooms. But what about the teens who make the honor roll, or who are active in their local church groups? That's different, we think; those good kids are the exception. As it turns out, they are the majority.

Contrary to popular opinion, about 80 percent of teens are not particularly troubled, apart from the normal adolescent anxieties, says Daniel Offer, a psychiatrist at Northwestern University who researches teenagers. The reason we hear more about the 20 percent of teens who are not well-adjusted is that they make up a sizeable number—about three to four million kids.

A different set of statistics counters the popular image of the apathetic, self-indulgent teen. The first Scholastic Poll of American Youth indicates that teens care about the world around them; they are concerned about the economy, AIDS, and drugs; and they believe that strong political leadership can make a difference.[1] They care deeply about the environment: In a survey of over 200,000 college students, 26 percent of freshmen said that getting involved in programs to clean up the environment is a "very important" life goal.[2] They contribute their time: In 1989, 58 percent of teens engaged in voluntary charity work—usually through their school, church, or synagogue—compared with 54 percent of adults.[3]

Teens: The Prophets and Scapegoats of Society

Teens are both the scapegoats and the prophets of society. We criticize them for what we see as their reckless, rebellious behavior, and yet they are often simply acting out the incongruities of society. The teen craze of wearing clothing that is several sizes too big, for example, might be a backlash to our obsession with clothes, size, and thinness. Teens' fascination with drugs and alcohol could be seen as a response to our own

hypocrisy: On the one hand, our society preaches a "Just say no" approach, while on the other hand, we abuse social drugs like cigarettes, alcohol, and caffeine, and prescription drugs like Valium and Prozac.

Teens are the agents of social change. Each new generation transforms society—it only makes sense that every generation would improve upon the last. With each new generation of teens, everything comes up for review again. It was largely student protests to the Vietnam War—challenging the unquestioning patriotism of their parents' generation, the World War II generation—that caused the United States to end its involvement there.

Teens are the most alive among us. They are brutally honest and straightforward, because they have nothing to lose. They are refreshingly and sometimes irritatingly idealistic, because they see the world with new eyes. They feel as if every new idea they have is incredibly unique and original.

The current generation of teenagers has the potential to alter society in a profound way. Many of them have been raised in a conscious, open way by parents who are idealists themselves. They have access to and a firm grasp of the transformative power of technology. Witnessing the contributions they make as they come of age will be exciting.

The Struggle Toward Adulthood

Renowned psychiatrist Erik Erikson says that the work of the adolescent is to establish a stable self-identity. Adolescents are not quite sure who they are, but they are becoming sure of who they are *not*. They are creating themselves.

A necessary step in the development of self-identity is rejection of the family. For the first time, adolescents see their families with some objectivity, and they realize that the way their family does things is not the same way everyone does them. They must reconcile this new knowledge with their love for their family and their growing attachment to their peers. The result is their critical scrutiny of everything about the family.

It helps to realize that this rejection is a part of growing up. In your child's infancy, you and he

are like the same person. In his early years, you are like God. Then, as your child grows, you are less divine, but still perfect. During your child's adolescence, you are not only imperfect—you are the problem.

Teen rebelliousness is often difficult for parents to deal with because it challenges them at a time when they may be in state of flux themselves. Adolescence runs parallel to the period of mid-life crisis, when parents may be reevaluating their own lives. The teens are thrusting outward; the parents are looking inward. Teens feel flush with immortality and potential; parents are bumping up against their own mortality and limits. This counterpoint is probably necessary: It keeps parents from getting too introspective and helps teens keep their feet on the ground.

The teen years are necessarily a time of upheaval. This turmoil is part of the transformation from childhood toward adulthood, from dependence to independence. Adults and teens are involved in an intimate transfer of power: Teens grab for power, then refuse it; adults are both eager to give it up and jealous of its loss. Consciousness is never won without a struggle.

The teen is neither child nor adult—she is somewhere in between. In this in between state, everything is experienced with a sense of heightened awareness. The protective veil of the family parts a bit, and the teen sees that there is a discrepancy between what people say and what they do. This necessary loss of innocence begins the process of unfolding awareness so vital to the emerging adult.

Teens are highly self-conscious. Often it is as if they have just awakened from a dream and realized that they are here. This sudden, confusing awareness may be why many teens go through a black phase—they dye their hair black, wear black lipstick and nail polish, and don black clothing, as a way of hiding. We wear black both in mourning and in adolescence, because during both times, we are lost.

Joseph Chilton Pearce, author of *Magical Child*, and Rudolph Steiner, father of Waldorf schooling, postulate that for the first seven years of a child's life, his mother is the matrix; that all learning takes place in relationship to his mother. Between age seven and fourteen, nature becomes the template for learning. By age fourteen, the child's focus has shifted to his peers. At age twenty-one, he begins seeking God, or a deeper meaning in life.[4]

During adolescence, then, the child is totally defined by his peers, while at the same time he is preparing to bond with God, to find a sense of purpose in life. This is why teens join gangs or cults, why they dress and look exactly the same—because they just want to feel connected, to belong.

The shift to adulthood does not happen automatically at age eighteen or twenty-one. Just as babies each have their own developmental timetable, adolescents each mature at a different rate. Just as you completely fulfilled your baby's dependency needs in the early years, so you must be prepared to encourage your child's growing independence in adolescence.

The Rules Have Changed

Perhaps you and your child have had an enviable relationship for thirteen years. You were the first one she turned to with important questions, and you could talk openly on any subject—in short, you were best friends. Then suddenly—overnight it seems—she became sullen, uncommunicative, and defiant. You have not changed, but she has. What happened to your relationship?

The reason that most parents are caught unawares by their children's adolescence, according to Michael Riera, author of *Uncommon Sense for Parents with Teenagers*, is that they fail to recognize one important fact: In adolescence, the rules change.[5]

In the early years, parents play an active role in their children's lives—arranging rides and activities, helping with homework, and being there to offer support, encouragement, and advice. But when children reach adolescence, they want to figure it out for themselves. They begin to question your attitudes and beliefs. They are confused and overwhelmed by the hormonal upheaval taking place in their bodies, and you become the scapegoat rather than the confidante.

Most parents do not know how to react to this shift in roles, says Riera, and they make one of two mistakes: They either over-parent, treating their adolescents like children and trying to take

an even more active role in their lives; or they under-parent, treating their teenagers like adults and relinquishing involvement in their lives in order to avoid conflict.

You must understand this fundamental shift in the relationship if you are to give your children what they need during the teen years. Riera likens it to the shift from a managerial to an advisory role: As an advisor, you offer input only when asked; you save your influence for the really important issues; and you learn not to take feedback personally. Instead of insuring that your child makes the "right" decisions, you focus on helping your teenager learn to make his own decisions. As Mark Twain said, "Good judgment comes from experience, and experience comes from bad judgment."

What Teens Need from Parents

The challenge during these years is to give your teen the independence he craves along with the support and guidance he needs. Teens need to learn from their mistakes, yet you don't want to set them adrift in an unsafe world. They want to feel that they are in charge of their own destiny, yet they don't want to feel abandoned. It is a continual give-and-take. Your teen needs to earn your trust by behaving responsibly; and he needs to be given independence and trust in order to learn responsibility. You cannot expect the process to go smoothly; try to view occasional lapses in responsibility as learning opportunities rather than failures.

Teens need to solve their own problems. Remember how you left your squabbling children alone to work out their own differences? Now you need to give your teens the freedom to resolve their own difficulties. Not giving them that freedom invites either dependency or rebellion.

Still, your teen needs to know that you are available to offer your opinion when asked. The trick is to wait until she asks for help, and even then, not to respond right away. A good rule of thumb, says Riera, is not to offer advice until the third time your teenager asks. Sometimes a teen will ask for advice because she has temporarily lost belief in herself. What she really needs is a listening ear—not someone to solve her problems for her. As one parent says, "The less advice I offer, the more he talks to me." You don't need to get involved unless your child's health or safety are at stake, and then, get involved!

Allowing teens to solve their own problems means letting them do some of the worrying, adds Riera. Doing all of the worrying for your teen lets him off the hook. Your goal is to let your teenager take responsibility for himself by worrying about his own problems—but not to let him worry so much that he becomes overwhelmed or immobilized.

At the same time, because the decisions your teens are making—about driving, sex, drugs, and their futures—could be life-and-death ones, they need your counsel more than ever. They don't need you to control them, but neither should you relinquish them to the world. Like toddlers, teens want to know their limits.

Teens need a wide leash from their parents, with a few non-negotiable boundaries. Your goal should be to say yes most of the time, but you must be totally uncompromising about anything illegal, immoral, or unsafe. Family chores are another area in which you should make a firm stand. As much as they may complain about them, doing chores helps teens learn responsibility and a sense of commitment. You may also want to anchor your teen to family life by making his presence at family gatherings—such as Sunday dinners, birthday parties, holidays, or church—non-negotiable.

Here are some other things your adolescent needs from you:

AVAILABILITY
Your teen needs to know that you are there for her when she needs you, that you will pick up the pieces when things fall apart. Teens may act as if they want you to stay out of their business, but they don't ever want to feel ignored or neglected.

EMPATHY
There will be many times when your teen will need your sympathy and compassion. Adolescents put themselves and their lives under a microscope, so the most minor problem—a pim-

ple, a missed phone call—can turn into a cause for major hysteria. Having been through it all yourself, you can assure your teen that she will survive. Offer empathy, but avoid getting too worked up yourself—that will only add fuel to the fire.

RESPECT
Your adolescent is trying very hard to act like an adult, and she wants to be treated like one. Show her respect, and she is likely to show you that she deserves it. Above all, avoid belittling her by holding her hand when she crosses the street or by second-guessing her in front of her friends. Teens are notorious for being easily embarrassed by their parents.

TRUST
Once you have laid out clear boundaries, your teen must make his own decisions. If you trust that your upbringing has given him the tools to know right from wrong and to know when to ask for help, you can trust that he will make the right choices.

FRIENDSHIP
You must always remain the parent, but that does not mean that you and your teen can't be good friends. Treat your teen as well as you would your friends. But know that you will have to make some decisions that will be unpopular. There will be times when your teen will dislike you—maybe even hate you. These strong feelings are all part of your teen's carving out a separate self-identity for himself.

INTEREST
Showing an interest in your teen's life and friends—without being nosy—communicates to him that you care. And believe it or not, your teen is interested in knowing about your life as well.

APPRECIATION
Your teen is becoming her own unique, grown-up person—someone you will hopefully want to be good friends with for life. Even though there may be periods when you cannot see eye to eye, be sure to let her know you are proud of the person

she is becoming. Just as she did when she was younger, your teen will respond better to positive reinforcement than to reprimands.

HIGH STANDARDS

Keep your expectations high, and your children will live up to them.

A GOOD EXAMPLE

Set high standards for yourself as well. Remember that your teen is scrutinizing everything that you do, and your actions speak much louder than your words. Be aware of how many drinks you have at night or how fast you drive on the freeway, and don't preach what you don't practice.

SUPPORT

Your teen needs to know that you will not give up on him—no matter what. For all their bravado, teens are much more fragile than people think. Keep in touch; keep talking; show no ambivalence about your devotion to your teen. He needs to know how much he is worth to you.

TIME AND SPACE ALONE

Teens need time to decompress from the stresses of their day just as adults do, in their own room, often to the accompaniment of loud music. Respect your teen's privacy, and try to resist yelling, "Turn that noise down!"

A THICK SKIN

There will be many times when you will bear the brunt of your teen's volatile emotions and emerging rejection of the family. Try not to take it personally—the rejection is more about her than about you.

Expect estrangement. You and your teen have to fight a little, or she will never want to leave home.

A CONNECTION TO THE ADULT WORLD

Teens are yearning to take their place in the adult world. If we do not provide them with a meaningful way to enter the society of adults, they may seek it through more harmful activities such as smoking or drinking. Encourage your child's friendship with interesting adults, get him involved in an activity that has strong adult leadership, or help him to secure a job or internship where he can work in the company of adults who truly enjoy what they do. Give him a glimpse of the possibilities open to him in adult society, and he will be more likely to grow into a mature adult.

How to Talk to a Teen

How many parents and teens find it easy to communicate with each other? "You never listen to me," or "You just don't understand," are common complaints—heard as much from teens as from their parents.

Much of the communication that goes on in a household with teens involves demands and complaints, says Don Dinkmeyer, PhD, author of *Systematic Training for Effective Parenting of Teens (STEP/TEEN)*.[6] Commands like "Stop that" and "You will follow my rules as long as you live here" serve to shut down, rather than open up communication. They offer little in the way of sharing feelings and beliefs.

True communication is a two-way street. It requires an open, honest relationship in which you can each express your feelings, listen without making judgments, and attempt to understand the other's point of view. The biggest obstacle to effective communication is our own egos. When we insist on being right, we lose the opportunity to engage in meaningful dialogue.

Dinkmeyer suggests asking yourself the following questions, to determine if you are communicating openly with your teen:

- Am I honest with my teenager? Do I really say what I feel, in a non-hurtful way?
- Can my teen be honest with me? If he shares his beliefs with me, and they are different than mine, am I still able to accept them?
- Do I listen before debating or retorting?
- Do I give positive feedback, without demanding a change?
- Am I open to receiving feedback from my teenager?
- If I were a teen, would I come to me to share a feeling or a goal?

Here are some tips for communicating more effectively with teenagers:

LISTEN OPENLY
Your teen needs to know that she can come to you with a problem, and that you will listen without making judgments or placing blame. You always learn more through listening than through talking.

LISTEN ACTIVELY
Active listening means following what the person is saying carefully, and repeating it back to make sure you got it right. You may feel as if you are restating the obvious, but there is plenty of room for miscommunication between parents and teens. Dinkmeyer suggests using phrases like, "Were you saying...," "You believe...," or "You feel...because..."

AVOID THREATS AND ACCUSATIONS
Your teenager won't respond to shouting any better than your three-year-old did. You can easily get whipped into a frenzy when dealing with a teenager—just as you can with a toddler—but it is precisely because teens are so volatile that they need you to remain calm. A quiet firmness will give your teen something to lean on (or push against); shouting will only turn him off. A change in tone can turn an accusation into a concerned question—and improve the chance that it will be answered.

AVOID NAGGING AND NITPICKING
Even more so with adolescents than with young children, you cannot expect to control everything they do. Forget commenting on hair and dress, and save your input for the things that matter. Then, as you did when your children were younger, state your expectations clearly and get out of the way.

GIVE CONSTRUCTIVE CRITICISM
At times, natural consequences will not be enough—when you feel strongly about something and need to let your child know how you feel. In this case, a loving tone, careful attention to word choice, and strict adherence to the subject are important if you want your adolescent to hear you. As you warm up to the subject, remember that bringing up different problems, with admon-ishments like "and another thing...," will only convince your teens that you think they can't do anything right. If other issues need attention, discuss them later.

USE HUMOR
Humor is your ally; use it to diffuse a tense situation and to let your teen know that you are both on the same side.

SNEAK IN MINI-LECTURES
One of the biggest turn-offs to effective communication is sitting down to have a "little talk" (although sometimes you must). Try to work in your words of wisdom in the car, at the dinner table, or around the house. Your teens need to know what you think, but they don't want to be lectured to.

FIND SPORTS OR ACTIVITIES TO SHARE
Communicating can be easier in the midst of a shared activity. Simply working on a project together is good nonverbal communication. Tossing a baseball, building a bookshelf, or cooking a meal all allow parents and children to develop skills together and to take joint pride in what they have accomplished. At the same time, the activity creates a nonthreatening atmosphere. Conversation can happen in fits and starts, and if it gets too close to a sore point, attention can be diverted for a while to the project at hand. Even though your teen is spending more time with her peers, try to find a common interest that will keep you communicating.

ESTABLISH RITUALS
Rituals can keep your family close. A ritual could be Sunday night supper, or a weekly family meeting, or a tradition of reading aloud together after dinner. For a ritual to last, establish it early on, and be sure every family member participates in and gets pleasure out of it.

WRITE IT DOWN
If you and your teen are at an impasse, you may need to put your thoughts on paper to allow her to digest them more openly and less defensively. If a letter seems too formal, try making a tape.

PUT IT IN YOUR OWN WORDS—OR SOMEONE ELSE'S

By sharing your own experiences, you can let your teen know where you stand on an issue, as well as show that you understand what he is going through. Sometimes you may need to let someone else do the talking. As Michael Riera says, what you tell your children may be ignored, but the same piece of advice from an admired teacher is brilliant.

COMMUNICATE THROUGH TOUCH

Don't forget, as your children grow, the importance of touch. Sometimes a hug or a backrub is the best way to tell your child that you are concerned and you care.

TRUST THAT YOU HAVE DONE A GOOD JOB OF COMMUNICATING YOUR VALUES

You have shared your moral standards with your child all along, through your words and your deeds. Now, when your child is poised on the brink of adulthood, you need to trust that your upbringing will "take." You can be ready to share your values when your adolescent needs to hear them again, but you cannot dictate his values for him. Even if his values ultimately end up being similar to yours, he needs to think them through and to open up the possibility of rejecting them before he can make them his own.

The Importance of Risk-Taking

Today, more than ever, parents worry about the dangers available to their teenagers. True, today's youth is exposed to more opportunities for dangerous risks than at any other time in American history—including readily available drugs, the threat of sexually transmitted diseases, the lure of violent gang activity, and the widespread prevalence of harmful eating disorders.

However, it is also true that risk-taking is normal adolescent behavior. Adolescents have always needed to take risks in order to find out who they are and to understand the consequences of their behavior. Try to recognize that risk-taking is not rebellion directed against parents, but actually a critical step in determining self-identity. The challenge to parents is to understand the difference between healthy and unhealthy risk-taking behavior, and to know when to step in.

Lynn Ponton, author of *The Romance of Risk: Why Teenagers Do the Things They Do,* points out that most teens are not at high risk for unhealthy behaviors. Assuming that all risk-taking is dangerous, argues Ponton, denies teens the tremendous benefits derived from healthy risk-taking. "It is because today's parents have many legitimate reasons to be frightened for their children that it is especially important that they work not to be frightened by their children," says Ponton. "In learning how to assess risks and make reasonable choices, young people begin to realize just how powerful they can be, how much control over they own lives they do have, and what promise their futures hold." [7]

The point is to make sure that adolescents have healthy risk-taking opportunities available to them so that they don't have to choose more harmful behaviors. Healthy adolescent risk-taking opportunities are activities that allow teens to stretch themselves and to move outside of their "comfort zone," within safe boundaries. They include:

- participation in team sports
- safe participation in "adrenaline" sports, such as snowboarding and rock-climbing
- outdoor activities, such as camping out with friends
- creative pursuits, such as drama and art
- travel, such as car or bus trips or time abroad
- work opportunities, internships, or volunteer commitments

Unlike your child's early years, when you could sign her up for a dance class and drive her there, you cannot expect to direct your teenager's choices. But you can make suggestions, expose her to a variety of opportunities, and support her involvement in healthy risk-taking behavior.

Much teenage rebellion is a simple attempt to assert individuality. Harmless rebellions that affect only the rebel include choices in clothing, hairstyles, and music. If your teenager gets a purple mohawk, consider it a safer alternative than some other risks she might take. Body piercing and tattoos are also fairly innocuous rebellions, although they can also cross the line to more dangerous body mutilations.

While you need to recognize what constitutes healthy or harmless risks, be on the lookout for signs of unhealthy behavior. You can be vigilant without being controlling. Warning signs for dangerous risk-taking behavior include:

- ongoing, debilitating emotional distress (beyond normal teenage mood swings)
- withdrawal or alienation
- frequent crying or violent outbursts
- lack of friends
- drop in school performance or attendance
- not checking in or abiding by curfew
- engaging in illegal activities
- lying

Harmful things that your teens should not experiment with include:

- fast cars (especially in combination with drugs or alcohol)
- unprotected or exploitive sex
- hard drugs

Teen Drug Use and Abuse

At some point in your child's adolescence, she will probably experiment with drugs. You may not agree with this statement. But remember that the term "drugs" includes legal substances such as caffeine, nicotine, alcohol, and over-the-counter prescriptions, as well as more illicit drugs. These legal substances are widely used and abused in our society, and they are as potentially harmful as illegal drugs. Nicotine, for example, is more addictive than heroin.

Our society's idea of drug education has been to counsel teens to "Just say no." This simplistic approach gives teens no information on which to base their decision making if drugs are offered to them or to differentiate between drugs if they do choose to experiment. It is hypocritical to assume that teenagers will turn a blind eye to drugs, when alcohol, tobacco, and prescription drugs are advertised relentlessly and consumed routinely in our culture, and when half of adults age eighteen to thirty-five have tried marijuana.[8]

A more reasonable approach would be to recognize that drug use doesn't equal abuse. Psychologists Meyer Glantz, PhD, and Roy Pickens, PhD, found that while over 90 percent of people in the United States experiment with legal and illegal drugs, only a few develop substance abuse problems. They point out that contrary to popular belief, experimentation with drugs does not inevitably lead to addiction. The number one protective factor against substance abuse that they identified was a strong mutual attachment between parent and child. Parental support, communication, and affection can prevent drug abuse because these qualities lead to an understanding of the consequences of one's actions, foster an inner sense of security, and enable children to feel more in control of their lives.[9]

Another study found that adolescents who experiment with drugs are better adjusted than both those who abstain from drugs and those who abuse them. Teens who used drugs frequently were described as "alienated, deficient in impulse control, and distressed," in comparison with experimenters, while those who abstained from drug use were described as "anxious, emotionally constricted, and lacking in social skills." These findings indicate not that experimentation with drugs is beneficial, say the pyschologists who conducted the study, but rather that such experimentation is not catastrophic.[10]

What teens need is plain facts about drugs. The Consumer Reports book *Licit and Illicit Drugs*, by Edward M. Erecher and the editors of *Consumer Reports*, for example, offers a detailed analysis of drug research. As mentioned before, teens need healthy outlets for their risk-taking behaviors, and parents with whom they can communicate and ask questions. Well-adjusted teenagers with high self-esteem won't abuse drugs or alcohol.

What teenagers don't need are black-and-white prohibitions. Any teenager who is old enough to drive a car or go to high school can find access to drugs or alcohol if he wants to. An authoritarian approach doesn't work with a child old enough and smart enough to think for himself. If you simply forbid your teenager from trying drugs, you are giving up whatever power and influence you have over him, and encouraging him to come up with ways to experiment behind your back.

Recognizing that you cannot control your child's behavior, you need to look for ways to educate your child about the dangers of drug abuse. Robert Schwebel, PhD, author of *Saying No is Not Enough: Raising Children Who Make Wise Decisions about Drugs and Alcohol*, suggests that you open up a dialogue with your teenager about drugs. For such a dialogue to be successful, you must be willing to forgo making judgments or giving lectures. Instead, offer suggestions or ask thought-provoking questions to help your chil-

dren to broaden their thinking about drugs and to consider the downside of drug use.[11]

Once you have had an honest discussion about drugs, says Schwebel, you can work on getting your child to agree to your terms. You may be opposed to all drug use, or you may be open to some experimentation. The key issue, says Schwebel, is assessing harm: If your teen has already tried drugs and exhibited danger signs such as driving after drinking or cutting classes, you should opt for immediate, strong intervention, with the hope of reopening a dialogue later.

Says Schwebel, "To some people, a dialogue approach sounds quite permissive. These people confuse discussion with surrender. Dialogue increases mutual understanding and respect in the family. Parents who talk with their children do not surrender their authority and can continue to set a high standard of behavior."

John Holt, founder of the contemporary home schooling movement, suggested that the appeal of smoking and drinking for teenagers is that those are some of the few adult activities available to teens. If adolescents had opportunities for a meaningful connection to the adult world, Holt theorized, they might not be as eager to mimic the superficial trappings of adulthood.

By making sure that your child has contact with interesting adults and safe outlets for recreation and excitement; by setting high standards; and by being a good role model, you will help your adolescent make the transition to adulthood in a healthy, safe way.

How to Cope with a Teen

The realization that you cannot control your teen's behavior—that you can no longer protect your child—can be a terrifying one. In light of this realization, what can you do to cope? Here are a few things you can do:

- Be the example you want your children to follow—someone they can respect and admire. Share your experiences with them, and let them know that they don't have to make the same mistakes you did. But don't be surprised when they do the things you did.
- Talk to them. Don't think because they act mad at you that they don't want to listen to you. Don't think because they act like they have all the answers that they aren't still full of questions.
- Make sure that they have a place where they can hang out. Teens really have no place to go in our society. Restaurants do not want them because they have no money to spend. Convenience stores forbid them from "loitering." Local governments ban skateboarding and rollerblading in public places, and do a poor job of providing teen centers where they can gather.
- Make your home a place where your teens and their friends want to hang out. Get a ping-pong table. Feed them. Teens are always hungry. Try listening to their music, even going to a rock concert. If nothing else, you will get an eye-opening glimpse into their world.
- Make your home a safe haven, where your teen can feel free to vent frustrations, release pent-up emotions, and brood. Many teens are afraid to act this way around their peers, so you should feel comforted by the fact that your teen is willing to let down his defenses at home.

Being a parent of a teen requires great reserves of confidence, self-esteem, and resiliency—if for no other reason than to be able to confront six tall young men in a messy kitchen and demand that they clean it up. Being a parent of a teen requires a willingness to claim your authority as the parent and to insist on your right to protect your teens even when they don't want protection. And being a parent of a teen requires a sense of humor. As humorist Dorothy Parker said, "The best way to keep children home is to make the home atmosphere pleasant—and to let the air out of the tires."

CHAPTER 17 Approaches to Sexuality

Sex doesn't have to be a scary topic for parents. Normal sexuality should not have to be taught: It can be communicated to your children through your own attitude and the example you set for them. Your goal with your children's sex education should be to help them become sexually healthy, happy adults.

One of the strongest foundations for healthy sexuality is a secure attachment in infancy. "The experience of being in love recapitulates the mother-child relationship in its intimate physical attachment, trust, and dependency. It has been shown even in the animal realm that adequate sexual functioning in adulthood depends on satisfactory relations with the mother in infancy," writes Maggie Scharf in *Unfinished Business*.[1]

A natural approach to family life means rejoicing in the human body and all its capabilities. Through natural childbirth and breastfeeding you may have realized a newfound respect for your body. Watching your child grow, you cannot help but be awed by the perfection of the human form. By communicating your respect for the body, its form, power, and function, you will help foster in your children healthy attitudes toward their own bodies.

Sexuality in Young Children

Even though children will not really discover their sexuality until puberty, they begin learning about and experimenting with their bodies in infancy. The messages you give your children during these formative years can have a lasting impact.

Children are naturally comfortable with their bodies. You can encourage this sense of ease by giving your child the message that all bodily functions are natural and not dirty. Touching your child—hugging, kissing, and massaging, as well as showing physical affection to your spouse or partner in front of your children—will help your child to be comfortable with intimacy. Here are some issues you may face with your young child:

NAMING BODY PARTS

As your child begins to learn names for different body parts, you can introduce the words "penis" and "vagina." There is no reason to invent euphemisms for the sexual organs: Being straightforward and making your child comfortable with the correct terms now will make it easier—for both of you—to talk about the function of the sexual organs later.

GENITAL EXPLORATION

Sometime in infancy, just as your baby discovers his fingers and toes, he will find his genitals. There is no need to treat this discovery any differently than your child's exploration of any of his other body parts. Later, as your child gets a little older, you can communicate the message that touching oneself should be done in private.

NUDITY

Young children are very happy being naked—in fact, many toddlers go through a phase where they would prefer never to wear clothes. In your own home, you need not worry about your child's nudity or your own in front of your child, until she starts to show modesty. This increased self-consciousness usually takes place sometime between when children start school and when their bodies begin changing—around the ages of seven to ten. Once this happens, you must respect your child's need for privacy. If your child is comfortable being naked past the age you think is appropriate, you may need to explain the concepts of modesty and privacy.

Children's Sexual Play

Between the ages of four and seven, children become more aware of their sexuality and begin to explore each other's bodies. Such sexual play is almost universal. If you do not remember engaging in it yourself, it may be that you were too young to remember, or you blocked it out because of your parents' frightening response.

The most harmful reaction to children's sexual exploration is judging and punishing the behavior. If you express anger, shock, or alarm, you can squelch a child's curiosity about her body and make her feel that what she did was abnormal. Reacting negatively may send your child the message that something is wrong with sexual curiosity.

Here are some tips for responding to your child's sexual play:

KEEP IN MIND THAT IT IS A NORMAL PHASE IN A YOUNG CHILD'S DEVELOPMENT

Children are curious about everything, including their bodies. This kind of play is a rehearsal for grown-up activities, but it does not have the same sexual meanings that it does for adults. Reassuring your children that their curiosity is normal gives them the message that their body is not something to be ashamed of.

DON'T IMPLICATE OR TRY TO EDUCATE THE OTHER CHILD

Immediately sending the other child home sends the message that you blame him. Instead, suggest another game they could play, and wait until the other child has gone home—since his parents may have different views about sex education—to talk to your child about the incident.

TURN THE INCIDENT INTO A LEARNING OPPORTUNITY

This situation provides the perfect occasion to satisfy the curiosity your child is expressing about body parts and functions. You can bring out some anatomical pictures, saying to your child, "It's interesting to find out how other people's bodies look, isn't it?" (See Resources at the end of this book.)

VIEW IT AS A CHANCE TO SET LIMITS

Sexual curiosity is natural, but children also need to learn about privacy and the limits of society. You can teach your children that sex and nudity are considered private matters. You can say, "I know you're interested in the fact that you and your friend are made differently: You have a vagina and he has a penis. But as you get older you don't take off your clothes around other people outside of the family."

DO MONITOR THE ACTIVITY

Occasional sexual experimentation is harmless, but if it becomes a frequent occurrence, you may need to take action. Overexposure to the media, with its emphasis on sex, can lead to a preoccupation with sexual games. Too much sexual play could be a sign of deeper emotional problems. If you feel your child's friends are more sophisticated about sex than you are comfortable with, you may want to limit your child's exposure to those friends. If sexual experimentation ever becomes aggressive or forced, it should be stopped immediately.

Talking with Your Children About Sex

Many parents fear sitting down with their children to have the "birds and the bees" talk. But the fact is, in today's world, children are exposed to sex from a young age. If you don't talk to your children about sexuality, their friends and the media will. Do you want your child to get the message from you, or from someone down the street?

Sex education needs to begin at home. Your children need to hear your point of view. Children want to talk about sex with their parents and to know what their values are.

The best way to approach sex education is not to wait until the day when you think your children are old enough for "the talk," but to answer their questions as they come up, and to look for opportunities to incorporate the subject into day-to-day conversations. Here are some tips on talking about sexuality with your children, from the Sex Information and Education Council of the United States (SIECUS) and Planned Parenthood:

DON'T OFFER MORE THAN YOUR CHILD IS READY FOR

Until adolescence, children ask simple questions about sex, and they are usually satisfied with simple answers. You may want to start out by asking "What do you want to know?" to help you understand the question, and then answer it directly. It isn't necessary to have a major conversation with your child each time he asks about sex.

If your child is interested in knowing the facts of life, keep it simple until he is old enough to understand more. For a three- to five-year-old, you could answer with, "You grew inside of Mommy. When an egg from Mommy and a sperm from Daddy came together, you started to grow."

LET YOUR CHILD KNOW THAT YOU WELCOME QUESTIONS

Reward questions by saying "Thank you for asking me that. I'm glad you came to me with that question." Never tell your children to wait until they are older before you will answer their questions; find a way to respond to what they are asking in terms they can understand now. Always answer questions honestly. If you don't know the answer, tell your child you will find out and get back to her later—and be sure to follow through.

DON'T WAIT UNTIL YOUR CHILD ASKS

While all children have questions about sex, many don't ask their parents. They may think they should already know the answers, or they may

believe that they know everything already. Young people often know more about sex than their parents think they do, but less than they themselves think they know. You have a responsibility to teach your children what you want them to know about such things as love, intimacy, birth control, and sexually transmitted infections, before they hear it from someone else or before a crisis occurs.

TEACH YOUR CHILD YOUR VALUES ABOUT SEXUALITY

In addition to the facts of life, your child needs to know where you stand, and the reasons you hold your values. Most of us have very good reasons behind our beliefs. Explaining those reasons to your child rather than simply trying to impose your values teaches your child to think.

DON'T WORRY IF YOU ARE UNCOMFORTABLE TALKING ABOUT SEX

Be honest—let your child know that sex is a difficult topic for you to discuss, but you are going to do it anyway because you want to help. The fact that you are willing to talk about sex may be more important than what you actually say, because your openness lets your child know that he can come to you with concerns or questions.

Sexuality and Adolescents

Once your child reaches puberty—anywhere between age nine and seventeen for girls, and usually a year or so later for boys—sex education becomes critical. Although most parents would prefer that their children wait until they are adults to have sexual relations, the reality is that the majority of all teens in the United States have had intercourse by the time they leave high school.[2] It is critical for adolescents to know how pregnancy occurs and how sexual diseases are transmitted—as well as what healthy, intimate relationships are all about—before they get into an environment where the majority of their peers are having sex.

Some of the sexual issues teens face today—sexually transmitted diseases, rampant sex in the media—are new, while others are timeless. You are best qualified to help your adolescent navigate these complicated issues. They are not going to learn what they need to know in school: Fewer than 10 percent of children in the United States receive comprehensive sexuality education in school, according to SIECUS, and often, what young people think they know about sexuality is incorrect. Talking about sex does not encourage teenagers to have sexual relations; actually, young people whose parents discuss sexuality with them tend to be less likely to have intercourse of any kind, including unprotected sex or multiple sex partners.[3,4]

The best time to raise these issues is during the preteen or early teen years when your child is beginning to experience the changes of puberty and is thinking about sexuality in a whole new way. Waiting too long to bring up these issues may mean that your child will enter high school ignorant or misinformed.

As you explain the facts to your child, you should also communicate your values, and establish limits. Do recognize, however, that you cannot control your child's sexual activity, and attempts

to be too rigid may backfire. By acknowledging that teens are surrounded by sex in our culture and that sexuality is a normal part of life, you can help guide your child to the right decisions.

Following are suggestions for topics you may want to cover with your child, adapted from Planned Parenthood. For a guide to talking about sex with your child, contact Planned Parenthood or SIECUS (see "Resources Section," page 339).

PUBERTY

This phase can be very confusing for adolescents, as they struggle to cope with the physical and emotional changes that accompany adulthood. Reassure your child that everyone changes at a different rate, and that although she may feel overwhelmed while her body is changing so rapidly, eventually she will begin to feel normal again. Relating some of your own experiences about going through puberty may help.

SEXUAL INTERCOURSE AND PREGNANCY

If you have not already, you need to explain to your son or daughter how pregnancy occurs. Some common misconceptions young people have about pregnancy are that it cannot happen if:

- it is the girl's first time having intercourse, or if she does not have intercourse often.
- she has not yet had her first period, or she has intercourse during her period.
- she does not have an orgasm.
- she urinates or douches immediately afterwards.
- the man "pulls out" before ejaculating.

After explaining the facts, you can discuss with your child when and under what circumstances you think people are ready for intercourse. You can acknowledge that desires for touching and loving are very strong once a person reaches puberty, and that sexual intercourse is one way to express these desires and share feelings for another person. You can also make it clear that sexual intercourse is usually not the best choice young, unmarried people can make, because, in addition to the risk of the woman getting pregnant, or of either partner getting a serious disease, they may not be emotionally ready. Let your child know that there are alternatives to intercourse—including kissing, hugging, touching, and masturbation—that can be healthy expressions of sexual feelings.

MASTURBATION
Most people masturbate—girls as well as boys—usually beginning during puberty. It is not harmful, and it is often the first way a person knows sexual pleasure. Sexual urges are very strong at this age, and masturbation is one safe way to satisfy them. Negative responses to masturbation from their parents can lead children to negative feelings about their sexuality as adults. It is important for your child to know that masturbation is normal.

BIRTH CONTROL
Whether or not you expect your child to be sexually active, he or she should know about birth control. You can tell your child that the only 100 percent effective method of preventing pregnancy and sexually transmitted infections is abstinence. However, most young people become sexually active when they feel they are ready. Your child needs to know how to protect himself or herself. Discuss pros and cons of the various birth control methods (contact Planned Parenthood or your church for more information, if you need it), stressing that condoms reduce the risk of sexually transmitted infections as well as pregnancy.

SEXUALLY TRANSMITTED DISEASES
One out of four Americans will contract a sexually transmitted infection (STD) such as herpes, gonorrhea, or chlamydia, throughout the course of a lifetime.[5] Some STDs can be cured; others stay in the body for life. Some can cause sterility or death. Proper diagnosis and treatment are essential—another reason your children need to know they can talk to you openly about their sexual health concerns.

SEXUAL ABUSE
In order to recognize when something is wrong, your children need to know that sexual abuse includes forced sexual intercourse as well as any invasion of someone's sexual privacy. Let them know that no one has the right to touch them, expose themselves to them, or make them do something sexually without their permission, and that they can come to you with any concerns in this area.

SEX AND LOVE
Children's feelings of sexual desire can be very strong at this age, and it can be easy for a child to confuse those feelings with love. You can help your child understand the difference by explaining that sexual desire is a strong physical excitement, while love is a deep caring for someone else; that sexual desire can exist without love, and vice versa, but that the most satisfying relationships are those in which love and sexual desire are shared by both partners.

THE JOY OF SEX
Finally, a critical component in any discussion of sexuality is the acknowledgment of desire. If we only warn our children of the dangers of sex without letting them know that sex is pleasurable and natural, we are not truly informing them. Our ultimate goal is to have our children experience

their sexuality in joyous and healthy ways. To accomplish this goal, we must give them an idea of what healthy sexual relationships are all about.

Sexual feelings are usually taken for granted in boys, but besides educating our daughters about pregnancy, rape, and exploitation, we need to acknowledge their sexual desires as well. They need to know that female sexual development is not about resisting male sexuality but about understanding and expressing their own desires.

When Your Daughter Begins Menstruation

For many girls, the start of menstruation can be a frightening and shameful experience, if they are not adequately prepared. If you have been open with your daughter about bodily functions all along, she is probably aware of what having your period is all about. If the subject has not come up, it is up to you to prepare her by the time puberty hits—anytime from about age nine on. You should also prepare your son for the fact that he will probably start experiencing erections and wet dreams around this time.

Necia

"Oh, yeah, Mom. I forgot to tell you. I started my period yesterday." Joie, the youngest of my three children, was on her way to the shower, her lips still heavy and red from sleep and her eyes barely open. The announcement startled me. Joie had just turned eleven, and was nearly a year younger than I had been at the onset of puberty.

"Already?" I exploded. "Do you need anything? Are you ok?" I hugged her close, feeling her solid warmth through our thin summer robes.

"No thanks, I've got it covered," she laughed, breaking away from me and heading toward the bathroom.

"Well, God. Don't you even need to *talk* to me about it?" I wailed.

"Give me a break, Mom," she said in her droll tone. "We've talked about it for years."

Unfortunately, menstruation is often viewed as a curse, rather than the joyful rite of passage that it should be. Through your example, your daughter can glimpse what it means to be a woman—to give birth, to nurse a baby—and can welcome her own passage into womanhood.

HELP HER KEEP TRACK OF HER CYCLES

Most anxiety that teen girls feel about their period comes from uncertainty about when they will get it. Help your daughter mark the days of her period on a calendar each month, and explain to her that she can expect to bleed with some degree of regularity every twenty-five to thirty-five days, lasting for three to seven days, but that her cycles may not become regular until after the first year or two.

LET HER REST AND "GO WITH THE FLOW"

There is no need to limit her activity during her period if she feels good. But this is a good time to be quiet and introspective, if she is so inclined. Some women find that their creativity peaks during their period. Encourage your daughter to listen to her body during this time, to meditate, write, think, or simply daydream.

GIVE HER A CHOICE OF DIFFERENT SANITARY PRODUCTS

Although tampons are less bulky and more convenient for swimming and other sports, sanitary napkins are generally considered safer. Tampons can irritate the vagina and increase the risk of vaginal infections. They can also lead to toxic shock syndrome, which can be fatal. The culprit appears to be superabsorbent tampons. Tampon users are cautioned to use tampons with the minimum absorbency needed to control their flow, and to change them frequently.

Give your daughter a variety of products to try, explaining the pros and cons of each, but let her make her own choice. Peer pressure is a powerful force at this age, and she will probably be most comfortable with what her friends are using.

EXPLAIN WHAT MENSTRUATION MEANS

You may want to explain that her body has cycles just as the moon and stars and seasons do, and help her to notice the phase of the moon—full, new, or in between—when her period starts, so she can sense the connection between her inner cycles and the rhythms of nature. You can also let her know that the onset of menstruation means she is becoming fertile, although she is probably far from emotionally ready to have a baby.

Safer Sanitary Products

For the same reasons that mothers choose cloth diapers for their babies—chemical-free, reusable products are better for baby's health and for the environment—some women choose cloth menstrual pads or organic cotton tampons or pads, available from natural food stores.

Cloth menstrual pads are worn on a belt around your waist or in a liner that snaps around your panty crotch. They can be washed by hand or in the washing machine. They are considerably cheaper than disposable pads in the long run (especially if you make your own), have minimal impact on the environment, and contain no harmful chemicals.

Some women prefer the convenience of disposable sanitary protection, but choose chemical-free products. Conventional sanitary pads and tampons may contain residues of dioxin—a byproduct of the paper-bleaching process—which has been shown to cause cancer and birth defects. Chemical-free or organically grown cotton tampons or pads do not contain dioxin or other chemicals or perfumes that might cause allergic reactions, and they cause less environmental impact in their production.

CREATE A RITUAL FOR HER RITE OF PASSAGE

You and your daughter might want to consider celebrating the onset of her menses with a ritual, such as preparing her a special bath with red and white rose petals floating in it, or lighting a white, red, and green candle to represent maidenhood, womanhood, and the wisdom of old age. You could give her a gift of a red piece of jewelry or clothing to wear each month during her period, to remind her of the new world of women she is entering. However, be cautious about embarrassing your daughter by making too much of her period.

Daughters and Body Image

Raising a daughter in today's society offers you, her mother, the challenge of helping her to develop a positive body image. The statistics are dismaying: 60 percent of girls under twelve in the United States develop a distorted body image and overestimate their body weight,[6] 81 percent of girls have already been on a diet by the time they turn 10,[7] and seven million girls are affected by an eating disorder.[8] The message that girls in our society begin to absorb at a very young age is that unrealistic thinness means beauty, which is necessary to success and happiness. Once this message sinks in, it can lead to a lifetime of poor self-image and weight battles, or, in its most extreme form, to potentially fatal eating disorders.

You cannot control the media, but you can help your daughter to learn that food is her friend, by following the guidelines in Chapter 11, "Healthy Eating for the Whole Family"—particularly teaching her to trust her own appetite. You can also help combat media stereotypes through your positive example. If your daughter sees that you are comfortable with your own body, it will give her a chance to accept herself. If she hears you complaining about the weight you have not lost since the last baby was born, or sees you cooking separate meals for yourself, it cannot help but affect her newly forming, fragile body image. It is up to you to model the message that beauty is not measured by a number on a scale; rather, it comes from finding inner peace, discovering a passion for living, eating wholesome foods, and rejoicing in your body through sports, dance, and exercise.

Babies are not born hating their bodies, but delight in the discovery of them. They are their own best judges of their appetites, crying when they are hungry and eating until they are full. The more you can encourage your daughter to listen to and love her own body, the better off she will be.

Broaching the Subject of Homosexuality

About 10 percent of the population is gay, meaning that in a group of twenty children, chances are that one, two, or three of them will be gay or lesbian.

Sexual orientation isn't something that children choose for themselves, or that parents can predict for their children. According to most experts, it seems to be established before birth, just like gender. Children are often in their teens when they first realize they are gay. For most people, it is a devastating realization. Surrounded by fears and myths about sexuality, gay teens in our culture often become suicidally depressed. Nearly one-third of all teen suicides are committed by gay youth, and gay youth are two to three times more likely to commit suicide than straight teens, according to Planned Parenthood.

Talking about homosexuality with your child in no way promotes it—but broaching the subject early on can help combat negative stereotypes. Just as with racism, if you do not take steps to counteract ignorance and misconceptions, your children may grow up fearful and intolerant.

You can begin when your child is six or younger by pointing out that some families have two mommies or two daddies, and that people of the same gender can care about each other and choose to spend the rest of their lives together. Help your child to understand that homophobic slurs—just like racial insults—are hurtful. It is also important to differentiate gender roles from sexual orientation, by explaining to your child that the job a person has or the way he or she dresses does not have anything to do with whether or not the person is gay.

As your child becomes a teenager, raising the subject of homosexuality once in a while lets your child know that you are open to conversation on the topic.

If Your Child Is Gay or Lesbian

Teenagers often feel pain, guilt, and terrible loneliness when they discover they are homosexual. Many are terrified to tell their parents, and choose instead to live a lie or to leave home. If you suspect or know that your child is homosexual, you can help your child come to terms with it by having an open, accepting attitude. Here are some tips for parents of a homosexual child, from Judith Dutton, a psychotherapist specializing in gay and lesbian issues, and Andrea Warren and Jay Wiedenkeller, authors of *Everybody's Doing It: How to Survive Your Teenagers' Sex Life (and Help Them Survive It, Too).*[9]

DON'T TRY TO CHANGE YOUR CHILD
Pre-teens can develop crushes on people of the same sex that they mistake for homosexuality. If your child seems confused, now is the time to have an honest discussion about why your child thinks he or she might be gay. You may want to seek guidance from a counselor trained in gay and lesbian issues.

However, most teens have grappled for some time with their homosexuality and are certain of their difference before they tell their parents. You know your child best, and can probably tell whether this is a passing confusion or whether your son or daughter really is gay. Trying to "talk your child out of it" at this point can do more harm than good.

DON'T BLAME YOUR CHILD
Your child did not choose his or her sexual orientation. Most gays and lesbians say that if they had a choice, they would choose to be straight.

DON'T BLAME YOURSELF
You may feel a sense of failure or loss. Remember, you did not cause your child's sexual orientation by anything you said or did.

DON'T REJECT YOUR CHILD
Your acceptance is critical to your child's happiness. Homosexuals who are well-adjusted are those whose parents love and accept them unconditionally.

DON'T GO INTO THE CLOSET WHEN YOUR CHILD COMES OUT
Your child's homosexuality may not be easy for you to accept. Give yourself time to work through any anger or grief you might feel. Educate your-

self on homosexuality, and seek the help of support groups. Most importantly, don't try to hide your child's homosexuality from your relatives, friends, or church. The message your child will get is that you are ashamed of him or her.

Setting a Positive Example

We all know that actions speak louder than words. The best sex education you can give your children is showing them what a loving relationship looks like.

Unfortunately, it is easy for parents of young children to be so consumed by day-to-day demands that they let the passion in their own relationship die out. Both for your sake and your children's, take time out to cherish each other and to keep alive the spark that brought you together in the first place. Set aside some time for yourselves once a week, to take a walk with just the two of you, go out to dinner, go to a cafe and read a magazine to each other, or take a dance class together. Seize opportunities for sex when you can, and keep your sense of humor about it (for hints on finding time for sex after children, see "Sex and Breastfeeding," page 56). Don't be afraid to hug and kiss and show affection for each other in front of your children. One of the best gifts you can give your children is happy parents who love each other.

Is a perfect marriage essential, then, for your child to develop a healthy attitude toward sexuality? No. Children of divorced parents often report feeling more comfortable with dating and sexuality, because they may have a parent who is going through the same experiences. The main thing is to remain honest, aware, and available to your children.

CHAPTER 18

High Technology— Uses and Abuses

Technology does have its place in a natural lifestyle. Television and, increasingly, the online medium are interwoven into the fabric of popular culture. To deny or ignore their influence would be unrealistic. But how do your protect your children's innocence from the aggressive marketing tactics and undesirable messages they are barraged with by the media?

You could, as some families do, choose *not* to own a television, VCR, or computer, and to engage in more old-fashioned forms of family entertainment. However, you cannot prevent your children from coming in contact with today's media culture. They will be exposed to it in school, at friends' houses—just about everywhere they go in society. More importantly, you would be doing them a disservice to deny them the tremendous educational benefits, as well as the immediacy and interactivity, of computers and quality media.

You can, however, advocate the wise use of technology in your home. Using technology wisely means carefully screening and limiting the material your children view by relying on the assessments of quality rating organizations, as well as your own judgment. It means setting clear guidelines about media viewing and not using the television or computer as an electronic babysitter. It means giving your children the tools of media literacy so they can understand the impact of what they are watching. In short, using technology wisely means controlling the media in your home, rather than letting the media control you.

Television: The Boob Tube?

Chances are, like most of us, you grew up with "Bullwinkle," "Beaver Cleaver," or any number of other lovable television characters. But television today is not as benign an influence as it was back then. The proliferation of cable channels has made it harder than ever to control what your children watch. The nature and amount of violence on television has moved far beyond what was acceptable in more innocent days. Even the news has become more frightening and graphic than anyone ever imagined, with television cameras taking us into the courtroom for murder and rape trials, and onto the streets during riots and bombings.

At the same time, the quality of educational programming continues to climb. The 1997 Children's Television Act—which requires network stations to broadcast a minimum of three hours of educational programming per week—has led to some innovative new kids' programming, as well as the reintroduction of old favorites like *Captain Kangaroo*. Studies have shown that preschool-age children who watch quality educational programs aimed at their age level, such as *Sesame Street*, have better pre-reading skills than children who don't watch television.[1]

Even educational programs, however, are no substitute for reading to and spending time with your children. Here are some issues to be aware of with children and television viewing:

TELEVISION CAN STIFLE THE IMAGINATION

Listening to stories and reading are wonderful exercises for a child's imagination. Television, however, supplies the images as well as the sound, leaving nothing to the imagination. Kids watching television often appear to be in a stupor—a state that is definitely not normal for young children, says Marie Winn, in *Unplugging the Plug-In Drug*.[2]

TELEVISION CAN HARM INTELLECTUAL DEVELOPMENT

The average American child spends twenty-eight hours per week watching television—more time than he spends learning in elementary school. Television viewing can cut into time spent developing verbal and reading skills. Studies have shown that children who watch cartoons or other pure entertainment shows during the preschool years have poorer pre-reading skills at age five than children who don't watch television.[3]

Television programs are usually "dumbed down" to reach the widest possible audience, encouraging an overly simplistic view of the world. Most television programs—other than educational ones—break material down into thirty-second chunks. Continued exposure to these sound bites keeps children from developing their attention spans, according to a Carnegie study.

TELEVISION CONTRIBUTES TO A VIOLENT VIEW OF THE WORLD

The average child will have witnessed 8,000 murders and over 100,000 other acts of violence on television by age 10.[4] Cartoons, though they may be considered harmless, are often more violent than live-action programs.

Numerous studies have demonstrated a relationship between television violence and aggressive behavior in children.[5,6,7] The National Association for the Education of Young Children warns that children who watch violent shows on television may become aggressive and desensitized to the suffering of others.

TELEVISION CAN FRIGHTEN CHILDREN

Joanne Cantor, PhD, professor of communication arts at the University of Wisconsin and author of *Mommy, I'm Scared: How TV and Movies Frighten Children and What We Can Do To Protect Them*, says that children under age seven are particularly frightened by media images of monsters and scary-looking animals, while older children are more alarmed by real events shown on the television news. Cantor has found that many children are so disturbed by something they saw on television that they have long-lasting nightmares as a result.[8]

TELEVISION PROMOTES CONSUMERISM

Children younger than about eight cannot distinguish between fantasy and reality on television, nor can they tell the difference between programming and commercials. Thus they are particularly susceptible to being manipulated by advertisements.[9]

Madeline Levine, PhD, author of *Viewing Violence: How Media Violence Affects Your Child's and Adolescent's Development*, sums up the problem when she says that children who are heavy viewers of television are "more aggressive, more pessimistic, less imaginative, less empathic, and less capable students than their lighter-viewing counterparts."[10]

Smart Family Television Habits

Short of giving away your television, what can you can do to keep television-viewing from having a negative impact on your children? Here are some suggestions:

LIMIT TELEVISION VIEWING

The American Academy of Pediatrics recommends limiting television viewing to developmentally-based programs, no more than one or two hours a day, and advocates no viewing at all for children under two. Select quality, age-appropriate programs or videos with your children. Don't use the television as background noise—turn it off during mealtimes, playtime, and study time. Set ground rules, such as no television or videos during daytime hours, or before homework is done. One good tip from David Walsh, PhD, author of *Selling Out America's Children*, is to not keep the television in a prominent location in the house, or in kids' rooms, where it is more likely to be watched.[11]

SUBSTITUTE OTHER ACTIVITIES

Reading, sports, crafts, or science projects...there are a million things your children can do besides watch television. Don't feel you have to always entertain them—children need time to be self-directed, to use their imaginations. For television-free entertainment and recreation ideas, see Chapter 20.

WATCH WITH THEM

Watching television alongside your children gives you an understanding of what they are seeing, and allows you to turn television viewing into an educational experience by discussing what you watch.

As mentioned before, avoid using the television as an electronic babysitter. If you find yourself plunking your children in front of the television so that you can get something done, consider hiring a babysitter for a few hours a week if you can afford it, trading with other mothers for babysitting time, or asking a friend or relative to help you out.

Becoming "Media-Literate"

If your children do watch television, you can keep them from becoming passive couch potatoes by teaching them some critical viewing skills. Media literacy means learning to question and challenge programming and advertisements, by understanding how and why media messages are constructed. Coursework in media literacy is now required in school curriculums in every industrialized country except the United States.

For example, media literacy teaches students to deconstruct advertisements so they can recognize how advertisements attempt to manipulate them. Understanding that commercials use techniques like repetition, flattery, hyperbole, and even lies makes children less susceptible to their messages.

The New Mexico Media Literacy Project offers a number of teaching tools for both parents and educators, including an excellent CD-ROM containing hundreds of examples of media, as well as a less expensive activity guide containing tools and activities for deconstructing media. The Center for Media Literacy publishes books, videos, and curriculum resources intended mainly for educators; some of these may also interest parents. The Lion & Lamb Project's free parent action kit gives parents tips for talking to young children about television violence. See Resources.

Choosing Quality Children's Videos and CD-ROMs

As foolish as allowing your children unrestricted television viewing would be, denying them the learning benefits of the many wonderful children's videos and CD-ROMs on the market would be equally shortsighted.

Videos have the advantage over television of being commercial-free, allowing parents control over what their children watch, and, in the case of adaptations from books, of being a conduit to literature. Quality children's videos are those that appeal to a child's sense of imagination and wonder—videos that cause a child to laugh, ask questions, and be amazed. A good test of a video's caliber is whether you enjoy watching it with your child.

Although most Disney films and videos are flawless productions with wonderful music, they have been criticized for being sexist (the heroine of the *Little Mermaid* is willing to give up her voice to get the prince to marry her), frightening (Simba in *The Lion King* witnesses his father being trampled to death), and containing cultural stereotypes (the portrayal of Arabs in *Aladdin*, or Turks in *Mulan*). Disney has also recently been criticized for selling goods produced in sweatshops. The National Labor Committee published a list of the nine worst corporate offenders in this regard and Disney topped the list.

Many of the most delightful children's videos are made by smaller producers, and they are not necessarily available from the corner video store, although they may be found in your local library. You can find quality titles through Kids First!: The Coalition for Quality Media—a not-for-profit organization that rates videos, using a volunteer jury of child development professionals, teachers, parents, and children of diverse socioeconomic and ethnic backgrounds. To qualify for endorsement, a title cannot include any gratuitous violence or sexuality; physical or verbal abuse; bias in terms of race, gender, culture, or religion; or

condescension toward children. Kids First! also reviews children's CD-ROMs, and is currently developing endorsements for quality children's television programs and Internet sites. For lists of endorsed titles, contact Kids First! See "Resources," page 339.

Here are a few tips from Kids First! on children's video viewing:

MAKE SURE VIDEOS ARE AGE-APPROPRIATE

Martha Dewing, publisher of the *Children's Video Report*, suggests the following guidelines:

- Children under four prefer uncomplicated stories with simple, rhythmic language and lots of music. Superheroes and bad guys teach the wrong message to children who are learning to communicate with words rather than fists.
- After age four, mildly frightening stories with a happy ending—like fairy tales—can be empowering.
- From five to eight, children relate to quests, fantasies, and inspirational stories.
- From eight to twelve, children need more challenging stories with well-developed characters and logical plots, especially stories about resolving conflicts or examining important life questions.

- Most experts agree that videos and television are not appropriate for children under age two, unless a program encourages—rather than acts as a substitute for—parent-child interaction, such as a "Mommy and Me" activity video.

CD-ROMs bring children's storybooks to life and teach subjects from astronomy to foreign languages, all in an interactive environment. While they captivate children's attention with animation, sound, and graphics, they give them a chance to develop their reading, math, or problem-solving skills. Most CD-ROMs keep children challenged on several different levels.

Here are a few tips from Kids First! on choosing CD-ROMs:

- Match the program to a child's age and interests. Children will not "grow into" new media—if the fit is not right, they will not use the program.
- Let your children test software ahead of time at computer stores with stations set up for this purpose.
- Help younger children to install and set up a new program. Older children, however, will probably be better at this than you are!

To get a list of Kids First!-endorsed CD-ROM titles, contact them or look up their website, listed in Resources.

The Brave New World of the Internet

If you have a computer in your home, the chances are that your child has figured out, or will soon figure out, how to "surf" the Internet or World Wide Web. The Internet is both an incredible resource for children and a source of potential exploitation. It has the potential to democratize our nation's education and health care systems, as well as to promote equal access to information in general. Some liken its impact to the invention of the printing press. The Internet is a powerful research tool and a way for children to connect with people all over the world. At the same time, it is a rapidly expanding field, where children can be subjected to overt marketing and sexual harassment. Be as cautious about overuse of computers as you are about overuse of television. Computers and the Internet, like any other electronic media, can be overused. If you feel that your children are using the computer inappropriately or too much, try suggesting other forms of entertainment (see Chapter 20 for ideas).

The Interactive Shopping Mall

Unlike television, which is regulated by the Federal Communication Commission (FCC), the Internet is still largely unregulated. As a result, online marketers engage in all manner of unethical practices to target children on the Web, including promising children gifts or prizes in exchange for personal information about themselves and their families. This information is then used to create personalized interactive ads designed to "microtarget" the individual child. "Never before has there been a medium with this kind of power to invade the privacy of children and families," says Kathryn Montgomery, PhD, President of the Center for Media Education (CME).

According to CME's 1996 report, "Web of Deception," advertisers have hired teams of cultural anthropologists and psychologists in order to study how children's developmental needs can be exploited online. Advertising and content are often seamlessly interwoven in new online "infomercials" for children. Children are enticed to play games with product "spokescharacters" like Kellogg's Tony the Tiger, and are immediately transported to advertising sites by clicking on game icons.

In response to CME's report, Congress in late 1998 passed the Children's Online Privacy Protection Act, authorizing the FCC to develop rules for regulating data collection on commercial Web sites targeted to children. Dr. Montgomery of CME called it "an important first step, one that balances the need for effective safeguards with the goal of providing children with the full benefits of interactivity on the Web."

Selling Alcohol and Tobacco to Minors Online

Alcohol and tobacco interests are a particularly alarming commercial force on the Internet. Beer and spirits companies routinely use cartoon characters, hip language, games, and contests in their Web sites to appeal to a youthful market. A 1997 report by CME, "Alcohol and Tobacco on the Web: New Threats to Youth," found that, with few exceptions, alcohol company Web sites offered no warnings about the dangers of substance abuse while offering easy access to minors, who could simply lie about their age. Minors can even purchase alcohol over the Internet, although ostensibly someone over twenty-one would have to sign for the delivery.

Although the report found that tobacco companies did not attempt to entice minors in their Web sites, many so-called "smoking lifestyles" sites, created by independent parties, glamorize the image of smoking, with photos of celebrities smoking and blatant slogans like "smoking is sexy," "smoking rules," and "smoking is good for you." Almost none of these sites refer to smoking age restrictions or substance abuse, and many offer online purchasing of cigarettes.

Clearly, more regulation regarding children and the Internet is needed. To find out more or to get involved, contact CME at *www.cme.org*.

Internet Rules for Kids

As easily as your child can find a pen pal in China or look up biographical facts on Marie Curie on the Internet, she can as easily "chat" and even arrange a meeting with a pedophile, or download instructions for making a bomb. That's why, just as you taught your child not to talk to strangers on the street, you will probably want to set up rules for her Internet use. Consider establishing these basic rules:

PROTECT YOUR IDENTITY

Don't ever give out your name, phone number, address, name of your school, or e-mail address to strangers on the Internet. Choose an e-mail name that is different from your real name. Don't ever exchange photographs with someone you don't know.

BE CAUTIOUS OF E-MAIL FROM STRANGERS

If you get a strange e-mail, show it to your parents.

NEVER AGREE TO MEET SOMEONE YOU CORRESPONDED WITH ONLINE

Immediately let your parents know if someone asks you to meet him or her in person.

Internet Guidelines for Parents

Several sites also offer guidelines on how parents can protect their children while they use the Internet.

- The National Center for Missing and Exploited Children Web site (*www.missingkids.com*) lists a ready-to-use agreement between parents and children.
- The Department of Education (*www.ed.gov*) is preparing a manual of guidelines for safe Internet usage, as well as educational children's sites.
- The Direct Marketing Association (*www.cyber savvy.org*) teaches parents how to talk to their children about privacy in the online world.

Blocking Access to Certain Sites

The Web is full of pornographic sites, which can easily turn up as someone does a search for information—for example, while searching for sites on breastfeeding. Although censorship is a tricky issue, you may want to look into ways to protect a young child's innocence as he surfs the Web. You can use Web filtering devices or parental control software to block your child's access to certain areas, just as you might not allow your twelve-year-old to watch an R-rated movie. Unfortunately, screening out the more insidious threat of marketing messages is more difficult, because they are so interwoven with Internet content.

Parental control software falls into three main categories:

ONLINE SERVICE PARENTAL CONTROLS

All of the major online services—AOL, Microsoft Network, and the like—include parental controls that give children limited access to the Internet.

WEB-FILTERING SOFTWARE

Filtering programs allow you to screen the material your child has access to—by blocking sites with the word "sex" in them, for example. They include programs such as CyberSitter, NetNanny, and SurfWatch.

CHILD-FRIENDLY SEARCH ENGINES

These services provide a controlled way for children to search the Web, by filtering out what are considered objectionable sites. In some cases the filtering is done by humans—the sites are hand-picked—while in other cases it is done via computer blocking out of sites containing certain words. To date, these search engines include:

- Yahooligans (*www.yahooligans.com*)
- Ask Jeeves for Kids (*www.ajkids.com*)
- Disney Internet Guide (*www.disney.com/dig/today*)
- Lycos Safetynet (*http://personal.lycos.com/safetynet/safetynet.asp*)
- AltaVista Family Filter (*www.altavista.com*)

An updated directory of kid-friendly search engines can be found at *www.searchenginewatch.com/facts/kids.html*.

The Best of the 'Net for Kids

Of course, the best way to monitor your child's Internet use is the same way you monitor her television use: By talking to her about what to be aware of and by spending time with her on the computer. Ultimately, as with anything else, it comes down to a question of trust.

You can also begin creating your own personal directory of quality Internet sites. Here are some highly recommended sites for children, many created by children:

- *www.kids-space.org*—"everyone's home page," featuring art and stories from kids around the world.
- *www.kidlink.org*—engages ten- to fifteen-year-olds in a global dialogue.
- *www.exploratorium.edu/learningstudio/sciences.html*—the site of the Exploratorium Museum in San Francisco, with links to many other science, art, and education sites.
- *www.globalearn.org*—takes children on expeditions to learn about other cultures.
- *www.coloringbook.com*—a virtual coloring book.
- *www.pluggedin.org*—the project of a low-income community center, giving low-income kids a chance to explore the Internet.
- *www.mtlake.com/cyberkids/*—stories written by kids.
- *www.kaleidoscapes.com/current.html*—an online gallery of animated artwork by children.
- *www.ala.org/yalsa/yasites/yasites.html*—The American Library Association's index of sites for young adults.

The Internet as a Parenting Tool

The Internet can be an invaluable resource for parents. Web sites—many created by individual moms or dads—offer parenting advice and support on subjects from home birth to homeschooling, and chat rooms give stay-at-home moms a chance to share thoughts and ideas with other mothers.

Although, like anything else on the Internet, the parenting sites represent every possible point of view, there are a number of excellent natural parenting sites. For a good starting point with links to new sites every month, check out The Natural Child Project at *www.naturalchild.com*. Also check out *Mothering* magazine's site at *www.mothering.com*.

CHAPTER 19 Toys and Family Values

Play is the work of the child—an expression of the imaginative world of early childhood. Play is more important than any early academic training in shaping your child's physical, mental, and emotional development in the early years.

Child's play has no goals outside of the activity itself. The rules are personally imposed and can be changed at will. It is self-initiated and self-rewarding. Imaginative play, especially, can result in a wellspring of creativity that continues into adulthood. Children who never lose their delight in imaginative play may grow up to be artists, inventors, or musicians.

For young children, play means doing, not watching. Children need to experience new objects with all five of their senses. Ever wonder why babies put everything in their mouths? That is their way of learning. Watching figures on a television or computer screen can never be as satisfying to a child as touching and moving the objects themselves.

You can encourage your children's creative play by providing them with toys that stimulate the imagination, such as dolls, puppets, playhouses, and dress-up costumes. Give them toys that are open-ended and allow lots of room for creativity, such as blocks, and make sure you include classic toys that have withstood the test of time.

The best toys are the simplest ones. Toys that merely suggest an object—a piece of knotted yarn with a cloth head, instead of an anatomically correct doll, for example—allow the child to complete the rest in her imagination. You don't need to go out and buy expensive toys once you have a child. Homemade toys and games, hand-me-downs, cleaned-up garage sale items, old pots and pans, objects from nature, and recycled materials lying around the house can all become jumping-off points for your child's creativity.

The Stages of Play

Babies are engaged in the process of learning about their bodies and their relationship to the world around them. They need no special toys other than their fingers and toes, your face to play peek-a-boo with, and perhaps a wooden spoon to grasp.

Toddlers delight in the joy of newfound mobility. Plenty of playtime spent running, climbing, and jumping will help them develop their large motor skills. The most important piece of equipment at this stage is the child's own body. You can help your child exercise his new skills by childproofing his environment so that you don't have to inhibit his movement with too many no's, and by roughhousing and playing miming games like standing on one foot or walking on a line—an imaginary tightrope—on the floor. As your child gets older and better able to follow directions, you can add a listening element to these games by playing Simon Says or Red Light, Green Light.

Toddlers are also developing small motor skills—an important precursor to reading and writing. Encourage your child to string beads, stack blocks, and move objects from one container to another. Help your toddler to sharpen his senses by playing "I spy" games, describing an object you see in the environment (later you can make it more challenging by adding letters: "I spy, with my little eye, something that begins with S"). Put an object in his hand and have him try to guess what it is with his eyes closed, or close your eyes together and describe the sounds you hear around you.

At about age three, children begin to engage in make-believe play. The bed is magically transformed into a pirate ship; a row of lined-up chairs becomes a train. The child's play at this stage will mimic the world around him, as he begins to assimilate and make sense of that world. Through fantasy play, the child can try on different roles and act out suppressed emotions (jealousy over a new baby, for example). Cardboard boxes for making playhouses and costumes for dressing up in are great tools for your child at this stage.

Though toddler play is usually solitary or parallel (two children playing side by side, without interacting), after about age three children enjoy social play. Spend time at the park or invite other children over to encourage this interaction. By age five, playmates are a must. Siblings are also wonderful for interaction, and siblings of all ages can play well together in the early years of life.

The Value of Leaving Your Children Alone

Children need time and space to play, to discover—to simply be. Our generation has fewer children and more resources than any previous generation, making us intensely focused on our children. From her observations of South America's Stone Age Indians, Jean Liedloff, author of *The Continuum Concept*, feels that parenting that is too "child-centered" deprives a child of his ability to learn about the world by observing the adults around him. Instead, she says, when the adults around him are focused on the child, he becomes confused and demanding.[1]

Children don't need adults to constantly plan play dates and activities for them. They need to be bored—to discover their own inner resources. They need to be left to their own devices to direct their games with siblings or neighborhood friends. When play is managed by adults, children become dependent on adults for direction and problem solving, but when children are left alone, they get to figure out a method of determining who goes first, and what to do if someone isn't following the rules. In neighborhood play, there are no agendas, and no one has special privileges, because no one is "the guest."

Margaret

"Mum, I'm bored," announces my six-year-old daughter. I remind her that I am writing. She stomps off to her room.

When my daughter's humming seeps into my consciousness, I knock on her door. It cracks open, and a small girl with a gappy grin peers up at me. She has created a post office, with envelopes made from folded and taped scraps of paper, adorned with handmade stamps.

Later I look up when I hear my son's exclamations of joy as he pulls a string tied to bells and a toilet paper roll—an amusement his big sister has fashioned for him. Beaming, he comes into my office and rests his head on my leg. I rub his back. After a few moments, he toddles away to discover other things that can be taken apart while I write and parent with benign neglect.

Benign neglect—the purposeful inclusion of solitude in my children's lives; the refusal to over-manage and over-schedule them. Benign neglect—giving my daughter and son the time alone that I believe they must have to grow up independent, thoughtful, observant, self-reliant, persistent, creative, joyful, and moral.

Margaret Dean Daiss, "Benign Neglect," *Mothering*, Winter 1994.

Classic Toys

Classic toys have proven themselves with generations of children. They are not advertised in multimillion dollar campaigns, so you may not hear much about them, but their appeal is timeless.

For a toy to become a classic, it must intrigue parents as well as children. It must have many uses—like a good pun, it can be appreciated on several levels. It must be hands-on and engage the imagination of the child rather than relying on gimmicks to entertain. Here are some ideas to start with:

- *Teddy bear.* Boys and girls alike love teddy bears. They are still the perfect bedtime companion. Choose one with an expressive face and moveable arms and legs who can sit up on its own.
- *Red wagon.* A shiny red wagon can be many things to a child—a stroller, baby carriage, fire truck, train. The old-fashioned kind with removable side railings is useful for other jobs, too, like bringing in firewood or vegetables from the garden.
- *Magnifying glass.* A wonderful tool for inspecting bugs, stamps, or Dad's whiskers. Try an optician's office for a quality glass.
- *Magnets.* Find a small, heavy-duty magnet at a hardware store, and pack it in a cookie tin with a supply of nuts, bolts, and paper clips.
- *Bug kit.* Assemble a butterfly net, bug-catching box, magnifying glass, and a field manual with which to identify bugs.
- *Tool kit.* A child as young as two can be taught to use real tools, with supervision. Get a metal toolbox and fill it with a small hammer, screwdrivers, saw, square, tape measure, and sandpaper.
- *Doctor kit.* Instead of a cheap imitation, put together the real thing. In a zippered shaving kit, put a real stethoscope (found through medical supply companies or medical school bookstores), "forceps" (scissored tongs from the grocery store), a box of bandages, tongue depressors from a drugstore, and a flashlight.
- *Miniature cars and trucks.* Buy small, quality vehicles with doors that open and shut at hobby or toy stores. Make your own raceway from a piece of green felt with a "road" glued on it. Add miniature stop signs and trees from a hobby store that carries train set accessories.

- *Easel.* A child-sized easel might have a blackboard on one side, and a magnetic or wipe-off board on the other, with a roll of paper for making paintings. Include colored chalk, an eraser or sponge, and magnetic letters.
- *Dollhouse.* If you are not lucky enough to have a dollhouse in the family, you can make your own from an unpainted wooden shelf. Younger children can make furniture from thread spools, small boxes, and scraps of fabric; older children could make more elaborate furniture from balsa wood. Buy small dolls, or make them out of clothespins.
- *Small toys and gifts.* Other ideas include: wind-up toys, tops, marbles, yo-yos, jacks, and wooden paddle and rubber ball sets.

"New" Classics

If a toy is still manufactured by the company that invented it, that means somebody still cares about producing it. Here are some brand-name classics and some newer toys, destined to become classics:

- *Slinky.* The company that makes this flexible toy recently celebrated its golden anniversary, releasing an $85 gold-plated Slinky to commemorate the occasion. The Slinky is an incredibly simple toy—nothing goes with it, and nothing can break it.
- *Koosh.* Only about ten years old, but destined to last as long as the Slinky, the Koosh is a simple rubber "ball" that throws well and is easy to catch. Another great toy from Koosh is the StickBall—nothing to do with a stick, but actually a Velcro-covered ball that sticks to target discs.
- *Klutz Books.* Children can learn how to play the harmonica, juggle, make a French braid, and more with the help of these colorful books. Each book contains clear instructions and comes with an attachment that is essential to the activity—the harmonica or juggling balls, for example, are included. The originators, who were Stanford students at the time, distributed their first juggling book on their bicycles to local merchants around the campus. Now it has sold millions of copies.

- *SS Adams magic tricks.* These magic tricks have been around since 1917—in fact, the little boy on the cover of one of their card magic books now runs the company. Each trick is sold separately, and some can be mastered by children as young as four. The company also sells practical jokes, like candy that makes your mouth turn blue.
- *Brio Trains.* These train sets are made in Sweden, out of high-quality maple. Their wooden tracks are interlocking, and the brightly colored trains stick together with magnets. Brio also makes indestructible child-sized garden tools and wooden baby toys.
- *Breyer Horses.* These plastic horse models are very true-to-life.

Blocks: Back to Basics

Blocks are a fundamental learning material, since they don't come with a prescribed recipe that children are supposed to follow. Similar to paint and clay, blocks become whatever children want them to become.

At the same time, blocks are not malleable like paint and clay—providing an additional challenge. If a child wants to make a tunnel out of blocks, she can't just draw it or shape it—she has to figure out how to use the blocks to create a three-dimensional reality.

Younger children will have fun seeing how high a tower they can build (and then knocking it down), or making a simple bed for a doll. Older children, when given the space and materials, will make elaborate structures designed to last for more than a few hours. Wooden blocks are the most durable and hold the most possibilities.

You may be tempted at first to sit next to your child and build with him, or to build your own structure. But by letting your child set his own standards and devise his own engineering solutions, you are giving him the best opportunity for learning. If two children are building side-by-side, make sure each has plenty of space to prevent catastrophes. If you have the space, allowing block structures to stay up for a while can be wonderful, so that your child can keep adding details.

Just be sure to shield the structures from accidentally destructive younger siblings.

And remember that all of these toys are appropriate for girls and boys. Expose your children of both sexes to a variety of toys.

Dolls: Free Rein for the Imagination

A doll is a child's first friend. A young child tries to feel a kinship with everything around him. The doll—the image of the human being—can help him experience a one-on-one relationship for the first time. Of course, boys enjoy dolls as a first playmate and a tool for nurturing just as much as girls do.

The less formed a doll is, the more possibilities it holds. Rudolf Steiner, father of the Waldorf School movement, says that just as muscles grow strong through use, the child's brain is exercised by toys that require the use of the imagination. A doll with only a suggestion of a mouth can be happy or sad, depending on the situation, while a doll with a fixed smile implies an artificial mood. The novelty of a plastic doll that drinks, wets, or speaks quickly wears off, but a simple soft doll can be a friend forever.

A doll made of natural materials will warm to the touch as the child holds it. Simple clothing is best, as it gives free reign to the child's imagination, while also making dressing and undressing the doll easier. Cloth wrappings, or pieces of fabric with a hole cut in the middle for the head, and a piece of yarn for belting around the waist, can instantly transform a doll into a sorceress, prince, or baby. The only other accessories your child might need would be a bunting bed or knotted hammock and a few little wooden bowls and spoons.

Soft dolls such as those used in Waldorf schools can be purchased through HearthSong Catalogue (see Resources). Or you can make your own from the patterns in books listed in Resources. Don't forget about the old-fashioned pleasure of paper dolls, either.

Puppets: World's Oldest Actors

Puppetry is the oldest form of performing arts, predating live theater and probably even mime.

Children take naturally to puppetry. Young children will enjoy putting on simple shows behind the couch with sock puppets, while older children can master more complicated puppets and perform intricate plays.

You can make simple sock puppets, or try this technique: Use a Styrofoam ball for a head and two eight- by ten-inch squares of fabric, sewn together except at the bottom, for the body. Make a hole in the Styrofoam ball deep enough for a child's finger. Place the fabric square over your hand, and stuff the top of the fabric into the hole with your index finger. You may want to cover the head with the toe of a nylon stocking. Decorate the head with yarn hair; draw on a face. Or make simple puppets from cut-out photographs of family members glued to a popsicle stick. An empty, cardboard refrigerator box makes a great stage.

Children can make up their own plays, or choose fairy tales or favorite scenes from a book—the Mad Tea Party from Alice in Wonderland, for example. If your puppeteers want to make their performances appear professional, give them a few tips:

- Play up and forward so that the audience can see the action.
- Puppets should enter and exit from the sides of the stage, rather than simply dropping out of sight.
- When more than one puppet is on stage, only the speaker should move, and the others should face the speaker.
- Make each movement count, instead of just jiggling the puppet aimlessly.

Encourage your children to practice their productions, then assemble an audience, add music and lights, and let them show you what they can do.

Educational Toys

Although there are some wonderful educational toys on the market today (see Resources), you don't have to buy expensive toys that are rendered useless once a few pieces get lost. Make your own toys that are built to last, or make instant, throwaway toys out of paper and other materials—when your child is ready to move on

Creating a Playful Environment

You can encourage your child's self-reliance and imagination by making her environment child-friendly, and by making play materials readily available to her. A child-friendly environment means that off-limit and breakable items are out of reach, and children's toys and activities are within reach.

A child's mind loves order. If toys each have their place, the child will know where to find them and can get in the habit of putting them away. Keep toys organized, using stackable boxes, recycled containers with lids, and drawstring bags. (You can make drawstring bags by cutting the legs off an old pair of pants, sewing across the bottom, and putting a drawstring through the belt loops.) Go through the toys periodically to mend or get rid of those that are broken or are missing pieces. Rotate toys periodically, too, putting some out of sight so that they will seem new again when you reintroduce them. You can also start a regular toy trade with friends. When certain toys have outgrown their purpose, have your child select a few to donate to a local children's charity.

Young children love to play near you. Rather than putting all toys in a playroom—especially if it is in an out-of-the-way part of the house, like a basement—consider designating "activity corners," such as an art or costume area, in rooms where you spend a lot of time. Baskets and plastic or wooden tubs with handles are great for young children to use to carry favorite toys from room to room.

to the next stage, you can simply make more, age-appropriate toys.

If you are handy with a drill, make your own toy to teach the "round peg in the round hole" concept, with a block of wood and an assortment of different size dowels. Otherwise, use an empty yogurt container; cut a round hole for bottle caps, a thin slit for small pieces of cardboard, and so on.

Teach matching concepts by pasting colored paper on index cards—two of each color—and have your child find the matches. (She can also try to match the color to objects around the house.) Using the same concept, cut out identical shapes from construction paper, make matching patterns with swatches of fabric, or write letters and numbers on index cards to match.

Instead of plastic stacking cups, use empty aluminum food cans in graduated sizes. They can be fitted into each other or stacked in towers. Make your own puzzles by pasting a color copy of a photograph of your child, or a picture she has drawn, to a piece of cardboard, and cutting it into pieces. If you lose a piece, simply make another puzzle.

Board Games: A Family Tradition

Board games can be played by all ages, depending on the intricacy of the game. Some, like chess, cannot be mastered in a lifetime. Board games provide a "sneaky" way to foster learning: They teach simple concepts such as how to take turns or read dice, as well as imparting facts about history, science, and geography.

Start a family tradition of playing board games, and you will have a lifelong shared activity. Playing board games around the fire at night is a wonderful alternative to evening television. Families who grew up playing Scrabble or backgammon together quickly reconnect over the game board after the children have moved away from home.

The best games are the classics: chess, checkers, backgammon, and others you may not have heard of, like Africa's mancala—a thinking game with hundreds of variations—or Asia's version of chess, called "go." Chess, the oldest and greatest board game ever invented, dates back to ancient China, India, and Persia, and draws upon metaphors of chivalry. Mancala is a game played in Africa for over 3,000 years, requiring planning, foresight, and psychology. It can be played by young children and adults alike. It is wonderful to touch, too, with its routed wooden playing board and smooth beads.

In addition to the tried-and-true favorites, here are some newer games to get your family traditions started:

- *Music Maestro* (Aristoplay, age four and up) introduces children to musical instruments past and present, with five levels to choose from. Conductor Says, for example, teaches the names and shapes of instruments in the orchestra, while in Sound-Off, players identify the sounds of instruments played on a beautifully clear cassette.

- *Enchanted Forest* (Ravensburger, age six and up) is a stunningly illustrated fairy tale game that involves strategy and imagination. Players are not limited to the classic fairy tale story lines, but can make up their own tales as they go along.

- *SomeBody* (Aristoplay, age six and up) comes complete with a diagram of the human body and stick-on organs. Physiological facts come to light at the higher levels of the game. This game is a fun one if you want to hear your kids shout, "I need a gallbladder," or "I've got a spleen."

- *The A-MAZE-ing Labyrinth* (HearthSong, age eight and up) requires perception, skill, planning, and intricate maneuvering to move your counter toward a treasure.

- *Where in the World* (Aristoplay, age eight and up) is actually two card games and three board games aimed at expanding a player's knowledge of geography and the cultural and economic details of specific regions. The sixth level demands extensive research beyond the game.

- *Save the Whales* (Animal Town, age eight and up) supplies a wealth of information about endangered whale species. Players work cooperatively to save eight whales by trying to avoid oil spills, radioactive waste, and the catcher ship. The game also contains a booklet offering possible solutions to the problems whales face.

- *True Science* (Aristoplay, age ten and up) is a kind of Trivial Pursuit for science buffs, based on the popular Nova television program. Kids will learn all sorts of amazing facts that are stranger than fiction, and the Genius level will challenge the most advanced budding scientist.

- *The Book of Classic Board Games* (Klutz Press, age five and up) includes boards and playing pieces for fifteen games, ranging from well-known favorites to less familiar classics—including Nine Men's Morris, an Egyptian game dating from 1400 B.C., and Fandango, a fast-action game from Madagascar. There is even a challenging three-D version of tic-tac-toe.

INVENT YOUR OWN GAMES

Older children will like the challenge of creating a game with a theme and rules of their own making. Younger children can help you make simple, educational games by drawing the illustrations.

Simple games call for following a path by rolling the dice and moving spaces, obeying instructions along the way. You can make your games more challenging by having your child name or match cards to shapes, colors, or letters on board spaces.

Use poster board or a piece of cardboard from the inside of a recycled cereal box for a playing board. Decorate your games with hand-drawn illustrations or pictures cut out of comics or magazines. Preserve your board with plastic laminate, or iron it between two sheets of wax paper (waxy side in). Game pieces can be buttons, coins, or little toy animals.

Neighborhood Games

When you think of games for your children, don't forget about neighborhood standards like jump rope, hopscotch, and tag. Some neighborhood games have a legacy of thousands of years. Hopscotch originated in ancient Greece, when youths would compete in tests of endurance to see who could stand motionless, balanced on one foot, for the longest time. An ancient hopscotch diagram was found scratched onto the floor of the Roman Forum. Jump rope was first played with hops vines stripped of leaves.

As well as passing on a rich historical tradition, neighborhood games teach children important democratic and socialization skills. You can help keep the legacy alive by reintroducing these games to your children.

Do Violent Toys Make Violent Kids?

Parents and educators have expressed growing concern about war and weapon toys promoting violence and aggression in children. Highly realistic toy guns, computer and video games of mass destruction, and action figures like Power Rangers and Small Soldiers—which often have their own violent television shows—are some of the most popular items in toy stores today.

These toys give children the message that pretending to kill is fun. Hasbro's Chip Hazard is an action figure that comes equipped with "blow-apart legs," their Small Soldiers toys "do not understand the meaning of the word quit—or mercy," and Brick Bazooka "shoots first and asks questions later." War toys help create an environment in which war, not peace, appears normal, and militarism, not nonviolence, is acceptable.

Cooperative Play

As a society, we value competition for its ability to bring out the best in people. But some parents and educators feel that cooperation is more motivating to children than competition, and that the skills learned through cooperative play are more relevant to real life than those learned through competitive games.

Young children can be made particularly anxious by competition. No child likes to feel like a loser, or be left out. Cooperative play, on the other hand, can provide a chance to learn and practice consensus-building skills.

You can engage your children in cooperative play in different ways. Imaginative and open-ended activities like make-believe and blocks are naturally cooperative, but you can modify many other games to eliminate the competitive element. A cooperative way to play musical chairs, for instance, would be to take away a chair after each round, but keep all the people, letting them pile on the remaining chairs. And, instead of seeing which player gets the highest individual score as you play Scrabble, you could keep a family score, trading letters with each other and helping each other to spell words.

Family Pastimes makes games designed for cooperative play. See Resources.

On the other hand, children have a natural impulse to brandish weapons as a way of expressing themselves. Many children—especially boys—go through a fascination with guns, swords, or knives, usually around age two or three, when they are beginning to develop a self-identity. The play weapons they construct out of sticks or blocks allow them to assert some power and control over a big world.

Censuring play weapons in the name of nonviolence may be worse than allowing them. Children's interest in weapons is usually much more innocent than what adults read into it. They are readily able to distinguish between make-believe play and real violence. Nancy Carlsson-Paige and Diane Levin, authors of *Who's Calling the Shots? How to Respond Effectively to Children's Fascination with War Play, War Toys, and Violent Television*, say that homemade weapons go back to

being sticks or blocks when children are finished play-fighting with them, while toys such as action figures or guns remain a constant invitation to violent play.[2]

Although you cannot prevent your children from making play weapons, you should lay down some ground rules regarding their use—such as not using them to hurt animals, each other, or any living thing. You could channel a persistent interest in weapons into a positive outlet, like fencing or archery. You could definitely restrict your child's exposure to graphic and commercial war toys by limiting his television viewing. For advice about violent toys, get the Lion & Lamb Project's Parent Action Kit (see Resources).

Marilyn

I hate violence, am terrified of guns, and see war as a childish, ineffectual, and largely male response to conflict. I'm an unconditional pacifist.

My son, however, is not. At nine months he crashed his trucks, and at fifteen months he added the staccato effects of a battlefield. At two, he "badoom!ed" with guns fashioned from Legos, Tinkertoys, and blocks. My stomach sank with each badoom, and I pontificated endlessly on the dangers of guns, to which he replied, "But Mama, it's only make-believe."

I have come to believe that it is okay to let my son, who is now four and is not at all violent or aggressive toward his playmates, enjoy weapons. And I felt much better about things when I overheard this backseat conversation between him and a seven-year-old friend:

"Maybe I'll get to fight in a war with rifles like yours!"

"But real wars are terrible," replied his friend. "You could get killed. If one side threw out their guns, and then the other side did, there wouldn't be any more wars."

Marilyn Kaggen, "Badoom!," *Mothering*, Fall 1990.

Bitten by Barbie

Just as parents of boys fear weapons in the home, some parents of girls despise the thought of sharing their home with that icon of womanhood, Barbie. They fear that her impossibly curvaceous figure will permanently color their daughters' body image and that her persona will fill their minds with flighty thoughts of weddings and fashion.

The fact is, just as some boys are fixated on guns, some girls—and boys—are drawn to weddings and fashions. Playing with Barbie dolls, however, does not preclude their becoming rocket scientists. Barbie has broadened her image in recent years and is now into sports like windsurfing and rollerblading, as well as careers like medicine. When a talking Barbie uttered such inanities as "Math is hard" a few years ago, consumer pressure convinced Mattel to change her dialogue.

Barbie is such a pervasive part of popular culture that even if you don't own a television, your daughter is likely to come in contact with her. You can provide a positive counterpoint to Barbie by helping your daughter to celebrate her own body image (for more on daughters and body image, see Chapter 17). You can also point out to your daughter how unreal Barbie is and how you feel about "her" at the same time that you respect your child's play choices.

Tony

I thought—no, I knew—that my daughter would never have a Barbie doll. That was before I had a daughter.

Now all my best efforts have been bushwhacked by some Madison Avenue huckster and a sister who remembered being Barbied herself. So she sent my daughter a Barbie.

Life goes on. I now raise a four-year-old in the company of a glitter-faced, big-haired, big-breasted babe. But my daughter—McKenzie, named after a wild and rambunctious Oregon river—gives me perspective.

"You know, Dad," she says, frustrated with my clumsy efforts at sabotaging her love for Barbie, "Barbie's not real. She's just a doll. So let me play."

Tony Kneidek, "Bitten by Barbie," *Mothering,* Fall 1995.

Plastic Toys: A Health Hazard

If your child owns a Barbie, a Teletubby, or just about any other plastic toy, chances are she has come in contact with polyvinyl chloride—or PVC—which can be hazardous both to a child and to the environment.

Greenpeace tested 131 PVC children's products from the large toy store chains and found that 21 percent of the products contained lead, which is released to the surface of the products as they age.[3] Lead poisoning causes irreversible nervous system damage—which is one reason why we don't let our children eat paint.[4] In addition, the Greenpeace study and further studies found that flexible PVC items like teethers contained large amounts of toxic chemicals called phthalates, which may leach out into the child's mouth when they are chewed on and have been shown to cause damage to the liver and kidney.[5]

Besides its health hazards, PVC is bad for the environment. Both its manufacture and its incin-

eration can produce dioxin, one of the most toxic substances known.[6] And PVC is currently not recyclable.[7]

In response to consumer pressure, most large toymakers began in 1998 to phase out the use of phthalates in teething toys and other toys that babies can put into their mouths. Some toy manufacturers, such as Lego, have pledged to stop using PVC entirely. Several European countries—including Denmark and Sweden—have initiated bans on phthalates in all PVC toys.

If you are concerned about PVC in your children's toys, buy toys made of other materials, like wood, metal, cloth, or even other plastics. If you do buy plastic toys, look for ones made of non-chlorinated plastics, marked with the triangle of "chasing arrows" with a 2, 4, or 5 in the middle. If a product is not labeled with a number, don't buy it. You can also put pressure on manufacturers to make non-PVC toys by writing or calling toy manufacturers and retailers. For more information, contact Greenpeace or the Children's Health Environmental Coalition Network (see Resources).

Old-Fashioned Birthday Fun

Birthday parties grew out of a tradition of holding a ceremony each year to protect a child from evil spirits. Even the ritual of blowing candles out on a birthday cake has its roots in the ancient tradition of lighting candles on altars.

Unfortunately, most parties today—with their reliance on commercial decorations and favors and store-bought gifts—have gotten away from the simple idea of honoring the child. Here are a few ideas for birthdays with presence:

KEEP IT SMALL

A good rule of thumb is to have the number of guests equal the birthday child's age. Your child may also want to have just the immediate family. The fewer the guests, the more meaningful and intimate the celebration can be.

KEEP DECORATIONS SIMPLE

Balloons are hard to beat for creating a festive atmosphere. Shea Darian, author of *Seven Times*

the Sun: Guiding Your Child Through the Rhythms of the Day, suggests making reusable decorations like a special tablecloth, dried flowers, or colorful flags. Your children's artwork can be turned into invitations or placemats. The birthday child's friends and family can all help to draw a giant birthday card in colorful chalk on the driveway or the basement or garage floor.

HONOR THE CHILD

The birthday child might enjoy wearing a crown and cape or necklace made especially for the occasion. Reminisce with your child about her babyhood by selecting a few photos from each year of her life to arrange on a posterboard or throughout the room.

GIVE GIFTS FROM THE HEART

Encourage friends and family to think of personal gifts, such as a poem, a picture, a special rock, an IOU for a day together, or a batch of cookies. Use handmade wrapping paper made out of stamped newsprint or brown paper bags (make stamps from potatoes or sponges cut into interesting shapes, and dip in paint), and tie the packages with string.

If you don't want a frenzy of gift-unwrapping, consider spreading out the present-opening over the course of the day, or even a week. Start a tradition of making something special for the birthday child yourself, like a set of felt finger puppets, a cassette of stories that you create and narrate, or a broomstick hobby horse.

OFFER SPECIAL PARTY FAVORS

The birthday child could also choose or make a small gift for each person at the party—a seashell, handmade candle, soap, bookmark, or friendship bracelet.

GIVE IT A THEME

Themes, such as a pirate treasure hunt or a tea party, can be fun for older children. Guests can come in costumes, and the food and decorations can reflect the theme.

MAKE IT FUN

Simple activities are the most successful. Play games like Ring Around the Rosy and Simon Says, do a craft like necklace-stringing or making robots out of cardboard boxes, or put on a puppet show together.

MAKE IT MEANINGFUL

You might also consider creating a ritual to celebrate the child, such as having her walk once around the "sun" (a candle) for each year of her age, passing a candle around for each person to hold as they say a blessing for the child, or sprinkling the child with "fairy dust" (glitter).

CHAPTER 20 Wholesome Family Entertainment

Making mud pies on a spring morning; stargazing on a summer evening; playing checkers by the fire on a winter night...there are so many old-fashioned, wonderful ways you can spend time together as a family, without relying on television or other outside forms of entertainment.

Start with the simple ideas here, and build on your repertoire of favorite family activities. Remember, too, at the same time you are opening up new worlds to your children, you will be rediscovering the delightful realm of child's play for yourself.

The Magic of Books

What better gift can you give your child than a love of literature? Once your child discovers the joy of reading, books will continue to strengthen, nourish, and delight her for the rest of her life.

Excellent contemporary children's books abound, but some of the best stories you can read to your children are still the classic fairy tales of Hans Christian Anderson, the Brothers Grimm, and the like. Fairy tales address universal themes that speak to us all. The heroes go on quests, face injustices and hardships, but always emerge triumphant. In his book, *The Uses of Enchantment: The Meaning and Importance of Fairy Tales*, noted child psychologist Bruno Bettelheim says, "Nothing can be as enriching and satisfying to child and adult alike as the folk fairy tale."[1]

Children are engaged in the complex process of making sense of the universe, and fairy tales can help them to do this in a simple, direct way. Not that fairy tales encourage a simplistic view of the world—yes, they have fairy tale happy endings, but they also teach the child that struggling is a means for growth. Perhaps most importantly, they give the child a notion of a life filled with magic and limitless possibilities.

You may find yourself recoiling as you read some of these tales, at their violence, sexism, and other signs of a less politically correct era. Peter Neumeyer, professor of literature and author of children's books, says, "Folktales, like museums, hold the history of the human race...What evils and inequities there have always been! A family atmosphere of love and trust provides strong magic against the real-life cruelties and outrages that are the subject of much of the world's art. In sharing folktales with our children, we enable them to rehearse symbolically powerful ways of exorcising the terrors of the world."[2]

Here are some classic children's stories and fairy tale collections, available in many different editions, to consider for your family library:

The Complete Fairy Tales and Stories,
  Hans Christian Anderson
The Complete Fairy Tales of the Brothers Grimm,
  Jakob and Wilhelm Grimm
In the Beginning: Creation Stories from Around the World, Virginia Hamilton

The Adventures of Brer Rabbit, Julius Lester
The Tale of Peter Rabbit, Beatrix Potter
Just So Stories, Rudyard Kipling
The Wind in the Willows, Kenneth Grahame
Alice's Adventures in Wonderland, Lewis Carroll
Charlotte's Web, E.B. White
The Lion, the Witch, and the Wardrobe, C.S. Lewis
Little House on the Prairie, Laura Ingalls Wilder
The Story of Babar, Jean de Brunhoff

When your children get older, don't abandon the habit of reading to them. Adolescents, like young children, are in a questioning period in their lives, and the themes in great literature can help them to fashion their view of themselves and the world. Once they are busy with their own schoolwork and activities, a family tradition of reading aloud can be the glue that holds your family together.

Try to carve a time out of your family's schedule for reading—maybe right after dinner, or on Sunday afternoons. Start with just ten to fifteen minutes, but don't be surprised to find your children begging for "one more chapter!" Take turns reading, or do the reading yourself—whichever your children prefer.

Older children often prefer stories about adventures or quests, as well as stories about young adults in different eras. Here are some favorites:

The Old Man and The Sea, Ernest Hemingway
The Hobbit and *The Lord of the Rings,* J.R.R. Tolkien
The Adventures of Huckleberry Finn, Mark Twain
Cheaper by the Dozen, Frank B. Gilbreth, Jr., and
    Ernestine Gilbreth Carey
A Wrinkle in Time, Madeleine L'Engle
Endurance, Ernest Shackleton
A Tree Grows in Brooklyn, Betty Smith
Little Women, Louisa May Alcott

The Lost Art of Storytelling

It is no coincidence that every culture uses stories to communicate its beliefs and creation myths to its youngsters. The oral tradition of storytelling is a rich cultural legacy that we can pass along to our own children.

Read the classic folk and fairy tales to refresh your memory, then retell them to your children.

When a story is told rather than read, you imbue it with your own personality, as you unconsciously edit certain parts.

Make-believe stories are another source of shared delight. Don't worry if you are not a storyteller—draw upon your own experience and your children's lives, and you will find that you have an eager audience. Tell stories as you tuck your children into bed at night, in the car on long trips, during waits at restaurants or doctors' offices, and around campfires on summer nights.

Here are a few tips to spark your storytelling talents:

CULL FROM YOUR OWN CHILDHOOD

Children love to hear stories about when their parents were little, especially if they concern an event or an issue that the child is currently facing himself. Recount special times that you remember—how your family celebrated holidays, for example. Recall how you felt at the time—that you were scared too, on your first day of school.

INVOLVE YOUR CHILDREN AS CHARACTERS

Children love to hear about themselves. "The day you were born" is always a favorite. Tell stories of what happened to them when they were little, or make up stories, using your child as the hero. After about age four, children appreciate the ambiguity of having a character "almost" named after them—"Lucinda" instead of Lucy, for example. They sense the identification, but are not sure if it is intended, adding a touch of wonder. You can also tell stories about their favorite stuffed animals or dolls, using your child as a supporting character.

USE CHARACTERS FROM YOUR CHILDHOOD

Recreate characters from stories your parents told you, preserving your family's oral history. One mother tells her children stories about the Friant Jog—a giant green frog character created by her father.

MODERNIZE FAMILIAR TALES

Tell Cinderella, using a pumpkin that turns into a stretch limousine. Give the story your own ending.

DON'T PREACH

Your stories can have a moral, but nothing is duller than a thinly veiled lesson.

TELL ONGOING STORIES

You can have a lot of fun with "The Continuing Adventures of...." Just remember to be consistent. Your children will probably amaze you with how well they recall the details from the last story.

TAKE TURNS DOING THE TELLING

Develop a character, then let your child take over. You might take turns, each picking up where the other left off.

Storytelling Springboards

If you need further inspiration, consider using the following list of words, from Alexandra Kennedy, editor of *Bridging the Worlds*, a newsletter on the imagination, as a springboard. Write each list on a stack of index cards—one word per card—and choose a card from each group. Then you or your child can create a story based on the words you have chosen.

- *Places:* mountain, bazaar, sea, valley, pool, lake, desert, castle, village, cave, tunnel, meadow, tree, garden, forest, fire, dungeon, church, temple, bridge, city, crossroads, fountain, hollow, island, palace, river, ship, tower, volcano, house.
- *Magical beings:* unicorn, dragon, troll, giant, fairy, goblin, mermaid, angel, sorceress, dwarf, monster, wizard, soothsayer, fairy godmother, phoenix, centaur, griffin, gnome.
- *Magical objects:* egg, gold, cauldron, ring, ivory, stone, crown, shell, cross, treasure, seed, chalice, drum, star, horn, anchor, pearl, bell, arrow, ladder, sword, rose, book, ax, bone, candle, cloak, crystal, diamond, feather, fire, flute, goblet, helmet, key, mirror, rope, moon, sun.
- *People:* hermit, knight, princess, prince, queen, king, mother, father, grandmother, grandfather, musician, old man, old woman, child, farmer, priest, nun, monk, tailor, carpenter, healer, pirate, gypsy, fool, boy, girl, brother, sister, orphan.
- *Creatures:* turtle, crow, worm, serpent, dove, whale, horse, fish, sparrow, camel, lamb, rat, owl, frog, swan, fox, crocodile, dog, cat, bear, lion, eagle, monkey, bee, pig, dolphin, peacock, ox, hare, cock, wolf, bull, butterfly, elephant, leopard, spider, stag, vulture, hawk.

Poetry: Fun with Words

Don't be afraid to try poetry. You already know so much about it—the body, the month, the universe all have their rhythms. And so do your children—after nine months with the steady backdrop of your heartbeat, no wonder they thrill to the thumpity-thump of good poetry.

You do not have to know an iamb from a haiku to introduce your children to poetry. You simply need to make the most of the richness of the human language. "A poet," said the great writer W.H. Auden, "is someone who has fun hanging around words." Start hanging around words with your children.

You no doubt have your personal favorites, but here are some poets and poetry collections you might try out on your family:

The Oxford Nursery Rhyme Book, Iona and Peter Opie, Oxford University Press, 1955.

Oxford Poetry Book series, John Foster, Oxford University Press, 1988.

The Tall Book of Mother Goose, Harper & Row, 1942.

A Rocket in My Pocket: The Rhymes and Changes of Young Americans, Carl Withers, Henry Holt, 1988.

Talking Like the Rain, X.J. and Dorothy Kennedy, Little, Brown, 1992.

Where the Sidewalk Ends, Shel Silverstein, HarperCollins, 1974.

When We Were Very Young, A.A. Milne, Puffin Books, 1992 (Reissue Edition).

All the Colors of the Race, Arnold Adoff, Beech Tree Books, 1992.

Neighborhood Odes, Gary Soto, Harcourt, 1992.

Creating Poetry

Children are natural poets—they have an unadulterated sense of wonder about the world, and they are instinctively drawn to repetition and rhyming sounds. Even before your children can write, they will often come up with wonderful images that you can record.

You and your children can have fun writing poetry together. Help spark your child's poetic talents by offering the following suggestions:

- *Start a line.* Offer a jumping-off point, like "I wish..." "If I could be...I would..." "With my magic...I...."
- *Pick a subject.* Suggest a subject to explore. Animals are always popular; so is the weather.
- *Pick a letter.* Try making up a poem full of words beginning with the same letter.
- *Describe an image.* Tell me what you see in that tree, cloud, or painting.

Anna

When Riley was less than two months old, I started getting a little bored singing the same old songs over and over again. Then I began to tire of the running monologue I would try to keep up so he wouldn't think I was ignoring him: "Now Mama's changing your diaper, now Mama's blowing her nose...."

During one long car ride, I began reciting bits of half-remembered poems. Sadly, I could not get much further than a couple of first lines. The next day, however, I pulled my trusty volume of Robert W. Service from the shelf and started in with "The Cremation of Sam McGee." What a response! Riley's face lit up in huge grin, his eyes crinkled in pleasure, and he swung along to the rhythm with his feet and arms.

Since that first success with Service, Riley and I have branched out to Poe, Kipling, Longfellow, Ogden Nash, T.S. Eliot, and A.A. Milne. Whenever I search for a new poem, I look for a gripping tale and rollicking rhythm—rip-snorting poems that roar along, as my father puts it. Sometimes when Riley seems to be cranking up a bit, all I have to do is lean over and whisper breathlessly, "There are strange things done in the midnight sun by the men who moil for gold!" and he starts to grin and boogie.

Anna Watson, "Poetry That Children Love," *Mothering,* Winter 1997.

Music: The Universal Language

Music belongs in every child's life. Besides providing a creative outlet for expressing thoughts and feelings, music is a preverbal realm of communication, as rich and resonating as any we engage in.

Don't be intimidated by music. Yes, studies have shown that listening to Mozart may raise a child's IQ and that children who play the piano have better abstract reasoning skills, necessary for math and science.[3,4] But you needn't rush your child into formal music lessons, or limit his musical diet to strictly classical works. Good music is whatever strikes a chord with you. It doesn't matter if you know "quality" music from bad, can read music or even carry a tune. What is important is that you share the joy of music with your child. Sing and dance together, tap to the beat, fill your house with music you love, and you will open up a marvelous doorway for your child.

Start with lullabies. If you can remember favorites that your mother sang to you, sing them as a way to strengthen family ties and preserve your family's oral history.

Encourage musical awareness by playing music often—in the car, during dinner, on weekend mornings. Each time your child hears the notes of a particular song, says early childhood educator and violinist Ellen Babinec Senisi, he is actually refining basic music skills such as pitch, rhythm, and dynamics.

The only way to identify a "good" piece of music is to really listen to it. If you find you still like it after ten or twenty hearings, chances are your child will too. Listen to all kinds of music. Go to concerts and music festivals together. Generate your family's own hit parade. Musicologist Hewitt Pantaleoni's family liked to listen to such diverse favorites as Verdi's "Requiem," the Beatles' "Sgt. Pepper's Lonely Hearts Club Band," "The Rain in Spain" from *My Fair Lady,* Scott Joplin's "Maple Leaf Rag," and Patsy Cline's "Tennessee Waltz."

Here are some suggestions for your listening enjoyment:

- *I Got Shoes,* Sweet Honey in the Rock (Music for Little People). Spirituals, traditional African songs, and African-American children's songs.

- *Peter, Paul, and Mommy*, Peter, Paul, and Mary (Warner Brothers). Old, contemporary, funny, and sad songs, including "Puff, The Magic Dragon."
- *Songs for Singing Children*, John Flagstaff (Revels Records). Classic folk songs, singing games, and story songs.
- *Beauty and the Beast* (Walt Disney Records). Like most Disney productions, this movie score features exquisite music, with clever lyrics, sung by well-known artists.
- *American Folksongs for Children*, Mike and Peggy Seeger (Rounder Records). A new collection from the heirs of the first family of folk music. Also consider the original, *Songs and Stories for Little Children* by Pete Seeger.
- *Platinum Too* (Sony Music). The Sesame Street gang's greatest hits.
- *Around the World and Back Again*, Tom Chapin (Sony Music).
- *Reggae for Kids* (Real Authentic Sound).
- *For Our Children* (Disney). Artists from Paula Abdul to Bruce Springsteen singing their favorite kids' songs; benefits children with AIDS.
- *Singable Songs for the Very Young: Great with a Peanut Butter Sandwich*, Raffi (Rounder Records). Raffi is the most popular children's recording artist. Also try *Rise and Shine; One Light, One Sun;* and *Baby Beluga*.
- *Free to Be, You and Me*, Marlo Thomas and friends (Arista). Encourages children to explore their hopes and dreams, free of sexist and other limiting notions.
- *American Children* (Alacazam!). A crazy-quilt of folk-blues songs by a variety of artists.
- *Star Dreamer: Night Songs and Lullabies*, Priscilla Herdman (Alacazam!). Contemporary and traditional lullabies.
- *Gula Gula*, Marie Boine Person (Virgin/Realworld). An extraordinary tape for quiet times, with singing and hand drums.
- *The Balafon Marimba Ensemble* (Shanachie). African percussion music; a great accompaniment for family chores.
- *Slugs at Sea*, The Banana Slug String Band (Music for Little People). A great car tape, including the irreverent "Butts Up" about a feeding habit specific to ducks.
- Classical favorites: Prokofiev's *Peter and the Wolf* and Saint-Saens' *Carnival of the Animals* were written just for children. Other classical works that children respond quickly to include Tchaikovsky's *Nutcracker Suite* and *1812 Overture*, Copeland's *Rodeo*, Haydn's *The Surprise Symphony*, Mozart's *Eine Kleine Nachtmusik* (and just about anything by Mozart), and Wagner and Rossini's overtures.

Making Music

Music is not just for the ears alone; it is a full-body experience. Here are some other ways to encourage your child's natural inclination to sing along and move to the sound of music:

DO FINGER-PLAY SONGS

Young children love finger-plays like "The Itsy Bitsy Spider" and "Chin Chopper," which have the added benefit of developing manual dexterity (see Resources for good finger-play books).

DANCE TOGETHER

Do impromptu waltzes in the kitchen, moonwalk across the bedroom floor, watch Hap Palmer videos together like Creative Movement and Rhythmic Expression (Hi Tops Video) that invite movement. Encourage your children to perform for you, complete with costumes. Take them to the ballet or contemporary dance performances.

TAKE MUSIC CLASSES TOGETHER

While you needn't rush your child into formal lessons on a musical instrument, you both might enjoy the many enriching age-appropriate programs designed to nurture children's innate musicality. Some popular ones include Kindermusik, Kodaly programs, Dalcroze programs, the Orff Schulwerk system, and the Suzuki method. For more information, see Resources.

FORM A FAMILY BAND

Rhythm instruments like triangles, tambourines, finger cymbals, castanets, maracas, and drums of all kinds are great fun. Consider getting your child a traditional folk instrument, such as an autoharp, ukelele, wooden flute or recorder, or kalimba (thumb piano). They are just as easy to play as toy store instruments, but much more melodic. Or you can make your own instruments from spoons, pot lids, a paper-wrapped comb, or a metal tin filled with pebbles.

SING, SING, SING

Great CD or cassette and songbook collections include:

Rise Up Singing: The Group Singing Songbook, Sing Out, 1992.

The Book of KidSongs (1 and 2), *KidsSongs Jubilee* and *KidSongs Sleepyheads,* Nancy Cassidy, Klutz Press, 1986-1992.

Woody's 20 Grow Big Songs, Woody and Marjorie Mazia Guthrie, HarperCollins, 1992.

Shake It to the One That You Love the Best: Play Songs and Lullabies from Black Musical Traditions, JTG, 1986.

Animal Folk Songs for Children, Ruth Lawrence, Shoe String Press, 1993.

Nurturing Your Budding Artist

Children love to make art. They will grab every opportunity to doodle, scribble, paint, and make clay sculptures. They love mastering new tools and trying new techniques. Art gives children a way to communicate their feelings and discover the beauty in the world.

Here are some suggestions for stocking your art cupboard, from Kim Solga, owner of KidsArt, a mail-order catalogue specializing in art supplies for children:

PAINTS

The best all-purpose paint for children is powdered tempera, a powder that when mixed with water makes a brilliant, durable paint that will not spoil or stain clothes. Invest in five basic pigments (the primary colors plus black and white), and your young artists can mix any color they want. Use the basic paint powder for many different kinds of paint:

- Shake it up in a plastic jar with a small amount of water for thick poster paint.

- Thin it with lots of water for opaque watercolors.
- Mix 3 tablespoons cornstarch with 3 tablespoons water, then stir into 1 cup of just boiled water. Cool, then divide into small jars and color with tempera for finger paints.
- Add salt, sand, or sawdust to poster paint for texture paints.
- Mix with white glue and water for shiny acrylic-type paints.

A good addition to your painting supplies might be water-soluble acrylic varnish. It can be mixed with paints to make glazes, used as a brush-on glue for collages, or brushed over any painting, clay, or papier-mâché project to give it a shiny, protective finish.

DRAWING AND COLORING

Crayola crayons are hard to beat for value and quality. Most children, even toddlers, prefer the regular size to the thicker "jumbo" crayons. Buy a box with lots of colors. When the crayons break, peel away the paper and hold the crayons on their sides for broad, sweeping impressions. Carve notches in the sides to produce striped marks. Rub crayon pieces on paper held over coins, tennis shoe soles, and other textures to make rubbings. When the pieces get tiny, put peeled crayon pieces in a muffin pan and place in a 350 degree F. oven for ten minutes. Once they cool and harden, pop out rainbow play "cookies."

Colored pencils allow for greater control and variety for artists age five and up. They can be dipped in water, used to draw on damp paper, or water can be brushed over a finished picture for different effects. Felt-tip markers are also fun to use.

Pastel chalks are a delightful medium. Use them on brown-paper grocery bags or any rough-textured paper. Try them on damp paper, or on pieces of cotton fabric dipped in buttermilk (the milk protein "sets" the chalk into the cloth as it dries). And what could be better than sidewalk chalk drawings on a summer morning? To save chalk drawings on paper, spray them lightly with hairspray.

PAPER

Different sizes and textures of paper will suggest different types of art. Try these possibilities:

- Student-grade white drawing paper can be purchased at art or school supply stores.
- Construction paper comes in pads of assorted colors.
- Newsprint can often be found for free at newspaper offices; ask for "roll ends."
- Thick, textured pieces of paper can be found at printing shops; ask for scraps and trim pieces.
- Adding machine rolls are a fun, different shape.

SCULPTURE

Traditional, muddy potter's clay is great fun. Buy it at pottery shops. If you want to preserve your child's pieces, you will need to take them to a pottery shop kiln to be fired.

There are several great modeling clays on the market:

- Sculpey creations can be baked in a kitchen oven.
- DAS Terracotta Clay dries hard in the air.
- Fimo or Sculpey III polymer clay transforms into sturdy plastic in the oven for making beads, jewelry, miniature toys, and lots more.

A final addition to your art cabinet should be a low-melt hot glue gun, which dries glue instantly, is safe enough for kids eight and older to use alone, and is indispensable for any kind of gluing project.

Art Appreciation

Trips to your local art museum can be an eye-opener for both of you, as you learn to appreciate art on your child's level. You may want to enrich the experience by getting some children's books on the world's great artists and art styles. Here are a few to start with:

- *What Makes a...*, Richard Muhlberger, Metropolitan Museum of Art and Viking Publishers, 1993, ages eight to fourteen. This series of six inexpensive paperbacks examines the paintings of some of history's greatest artists. Several stylistic traits of the artist are examined in detail, answering the question in the title.

- *A Child's Book of Art: Great Pictures, First Words,* Lucy Micklethwait, Dorling Kindersley, 1993, age five to ten. Teaches children the alphabet, using gorgeous, full-color illustrations from the world's great paintings to illustrate each letter.
- *Picture This: Perception and Composition,* Molly Bang, Little, Brown, 1991, age twelve and up. Explains why we feel what we do when we look at different designs, shapes, and colors. Striking black, white, and red examples illustrate basic visual principles.
- *Getting to Know the World's Greatest Artists,* Mike Venezia, Children's Press, 1988, ages five and up. From Picasso to Van Gogh, this series uses original cartoons and works, and simple, lighthearted text to explain the artists' lives and works in terms young children can understand.

Discovering the World of Science

Children are scientists by nature, eager to figure out how and why things work. Encourage your children's curiosity by doing your own science experiments together.

Even if you know nothing about science, you can learn alongside your child. One of the best ways to understand an unfamiliar subject is to read a book written for the fifth grade level. Start with your local library, or buy one of the many books on science projects for children (see Resources). Your initial experiments may be met with such enthusiasm that you will find yourself starting a local science club!

Here are a few simple experiments to get you started:

- Place an empty glass bottle in a saucepan of water with a balloon stretched over the top. Turn on the heat, and watch the balloon inflate as the air inside the bottle expands. Or pour about 1/2 cup of vinegar into a bottle and shake one spoonful of baking soda into a balloon. Put the balloon over the top of the bottle, and when the soda falls into the vinegar, it will produce CO_2, inflating the balloon.

- Sink your teeth into a large hunk of modeling clay, pushing the clay up to gum level and as far back in the mouth as comfortable (being careful, of course, not to push it too far). Remove the clay from your mouth and pour prepared plaster of Paris into the mold. When it is hardened and you peel the clay away, you have a model of your teeth!
- Draw a small (four- by two-inch) American flag on a piece of white paper. Make the stripes black and bright blue, the background for the stars bright yellow, and the stars black. Stare at the center of the flag for a minute or so. Then look at a blank wall, and a red, white, and blue flag will appear before your eyes.

If your child is the kind who likes to take apart old telephones or radios to see what is inside, encourage that inventive spirit. Children as young as twelve have patented inventions ranging from the OOPS! Proof No-Spill Feeding Bowl to the Double Decker wire baking rack, which holds three trays of cookies at a time in an oven.

Be a sounding board for your child's ideas, and provide the tools and space for experimentation and model-building. Create an "inventor's box" of junk from garage sales and recycling bins, such as tin cans, thread spools, rubber hose pieces, parts from broken appliances, an eggbeater, an old bicycle wheel. Then let your budding scientist go to work! For more information on invention books and contests, see Resources.

Getting Down and Dirty

Making mud pies is about the simplest and most satisfying thing you and your child can do. So is squishing mud between your toes. Here are some recipes for other squishy substances you and your child can sink your hands into—but don't forget about good old backyard mud.

PLAYDOUGH

Mix 2 cups flour, 1 cup salt, 4 teaspoons cream of tartar, 2 cups water, 2 teaspoons cooking oil, and food coloring of your choice. Stir in a saucepan over medium heat until the dough leaves the sides of the pan. Cool and knead. Store in an airtight container to keep soft and malleable.

UNCOOKED PLAYDOUGH

Mix 2 cups flour, 1 cup salt, and 1 cup water with food coloring added to it. This dough doesn't keep as long, but it is easier for children to make.

BAKER'S CLAY

Mix 1½ cups flour with 1½ cups salt; add ¾ to 1 cup of water and knead until stretchy. Creations from this dough can be baked in a 350 degree F. oven for twenty minutes and then painted with poster paints.

SAND DOUGH

Mix 2 cups corn starch, 4 cups fine sand, and 3 cups cold water in a pan. Cook over medium heat until thick. Let the dough cool, and use it to make a sandcastle or sculpture. Decorate with shells, beads, and other objects. Your creations will harden and last.

PEANUT BUTTER PLAYDOUGH

Mix 1 cup peanut butter, 1 cup honey, 1 cup powdered milk, and 1 cup oatmeal. Roll the dough and cut it out with cookie cutters, or make freeform sculptures. When you are finished with your creations, eat them!

SLIME

Mix a box of cornstarch with ½ cup of water. Add green food coloring. This dough isn't for making sculptures—it's just fun to ooze between your fingers! When it dries out, simply add more water.

SILLY PUTTY

Mix equal parts of Elmer's glue and liquid starch. Food coloring can be added. Store in airtight container.

Good Clean Fun

When you've gotten messy from your mud and clay creations, clean up with a little bubble fun. Here are a few bubble ideas that appeal to kids and parents alike:

BUBBLE SOAP

Mix 1 cup dishwashing liquid, 10 cups water, and ¼ cup glycerin (available at the drugstore; for longer-lasting bubbles). Make bubble wands from straws, cardboard toilet paper rolls, or thin wire bent in creative shapes.

BUBBLE PAINT

Add a few drops food coloring to bubble solution. Blow a bubble and let it pop on a sheet of white paper. Mix different colors and pop them on the same sheet. Soon you will have a colorful piece of artwork.

MONSTER BUBBLES

Roll a piece of poster board into a cylinder and paper clip the ends together. Dip into a bowl of bubble solution and wave it in the air. To make bubbles galore, dip the plastic rings from a six-pack container into the solution and wave them in the air.

Mary

I'd started the day consumed by the question of which preschool to choose for Anna for next year. By mid-morning, I had decided that the future of our family rested entirely on my choice. Just then, Anna asked if I wanted to join her on the front step for some bubble blowing.

I held the little plastic wand in front of me, puckered up, and blew, ever so sloo-o-owly, nice and steady. Aha! There they went: fat, glistening, perfect bubbles sailing up and away. Pretty soon my preschool worries just floated away with them.

Chances are some area in your house replicates almost exactly the arts and crafts closet in a psychiatric ward. Take advantage of it. When you feel crazed by toothbrushing battles, and the cost of college, and what your neighbors just sprayed on their lawn, call "Hey kids, want to do some finger painting?" Then take your place at the kitchen table and concentrate very hard on technique, swirling thick orange paint into yellow paint. After awhile, things don't seem so bad. And you've got a nice picture to hang on the refrigerator.

Mary Button Hopkins, "Bubble Therapy," *Mothering*, Fall 1995.

Sports and the Great Outdoors

Encouraging your children's love of the outdoors and physical activity will help to keep them healthy and in touch with the world around them. The Surgeon General recommends that children, as well as adults, participate in moderate physical activity at least thirty minutes a day. Although most children don't need to be encouraged to move, physical activity decreases with age, and physical education is emphasized less in school as children reach higher grades.

Executive director of the National Association for Sport and Physical Education (NASPE) Dr. Judith Young recommends that parents encourage physical activity at home and on weekends, and take as much interest in their child's physical education as in their academic coursework. NASPE and Shape Up America! offer a brochure called "99 Tips for Family Fitness Fun," including tips for activities like walking in charity fundraisers and organizing a family hopscotch or badminton tournament. To get a copy of the brochure, see Resources.

Some families establish a tradition of Sunday morning hikes or bike rides as their form of spiri-

tuality—a way of connecting with each other and with nature. If you love to hike and bike, incorporating your children into your active lifestyle is a natural. Using a sturdy child carrier backpack, you can transport your toddler on day hikes or overnight camping trips. Once your children are five or older, they can hike a few miles on a trail and even carry a little backpack. Be sure to pack lots of high-energy snacks, water, and field guides so the children can identify flowers and bugs.

Bicycling with children is made easier by all the gear options available today. For transporting toddlers, a trailer—which accommodates two children, plus snacks and toys, and is comfortable enough for them to nap in—is your best bet. A child seat that fits on the back of your bike is a simple, relatively inexpensive choice. Once your child is old enough to pedal herself, a trailer cycle—a half-bicycle appendage that turns an adult bike into a tandem—allows her to pedal with you, or just go along for the ride. Older children will enjoy riding their own bikes alongside you. Make sure your child always wears a helmet, and remember to wear yours as well. For more information on backpacking or bicycling with children, see Resources.

Exploring the Night

Night walks are a way for you and your child to see the world from a different perspective. A familiar trail takes on a magical quality by moonlight. Sitting very still, with your flashlights turned off, you might hear an owl hooting or see the flickering light of a firefly. Check your newspaper for listings of guided night walks, or set out on your own.

Sue

The moon is out tonight, full and luminous, nearly bright enough to read by. And to think that last Saturday at this time, I had no idea what phase it was in—half-moon or new or that thin sliver that always reminds me of a fingernail clipping. Neither did my husband or our two children. We were busy watching TV, Dorito dust on our lips, our faces illuminated by the glow of the screen.

Not this evening, however. Tonight, with flashlights and sweatshirts, we followed a volunteer Friend of the Canyon into the night. We hiked along a rocky path until the sound of a thousand lovesick frogs finally drowned out the white noise of a distant highway. The frogs' chorus stopped our usually unstoppable son in his tracks. Our daughter noticed the silhouettes of the trees, reaching like gnarled "fingers" into the night.

Our guide was informative enough. As it turned out, however, he was upstaged by another man: the one in the moon. Midway through our two-mile hike, the moon in all its fullness beamed out from behind the clouds. Seemingly summoned, we stopped, every one of us husbands, wives, children, friends, and strangers—and in silence turned our faces toward its light. At that moment, I knew that the moon needs no interpreter. It speaks for itself, its shimmering voice full of the mysteries of time and tides.

Sue Diaz, "Moon Walk," *Mothering*, Winter 1994.

Stargazing sparks children's sense of awe and wonder. It helps them to realize the vastness of the universe, while at the same time connecting them to people of all ages through the telling of the myths for which the constellations are named.

The only equipment you need for stargazing is a good star map or chart, perhaps a book about the stories of the constellations, and a pen flashlight to read by. Pick a warm, clear, summer night; spread a blanket in the backyard or on a knoll; and discover the mystery of the night skies together.

To enhance your nighttime expeditions, check out the following books:

Stargazers, Gail Gibbons, Holiday House, 1992.
The Young Astronomer, Harry Ford, DK Publishing, 1998.
Night Sky, an interactive action pack, DK Publishing, 1994.

Creepy Crawlies

You don't have to go to the zoo to observe the animal kingdom. All you have to do is poke around your own backyard.

Children have an instinctive fascination with insects. And why shouldn't they? Bugs are amazing creatures. Some species of ants "shepherd" aphids on plants, collecting their honeydew the way we milk cows. Monarch butterflies migrate 1,000 to 1,500 miles to lay their eggs. After they die, their offspring make the return trip—never having traveled that route before. If insects were not around to pollinate plants, most plants would die, animals would die—indeed, the human race would perish.

Girls, as well as boys, often delight in creepy, crawly things. If you want to encourage your daughter's interest in nature, try to quell any of your own squeamishness by really looking closely at the creatures she collects and by educating yourself about their fascinating behaviors.

Go on bug safaris with your children. Head out in the early morning, when cobwebs shimmer, and dew-soaked butterflies rest on tall grasses. Head out after a rain, when sidewalks are littered with worms and snails. Roll back stones or logs to find what creatures reside beneath them. (Just remember to roll them back.) Get an ant farm. Catch a caterpillar and house it in a jar with a lid that has holes, feeding it leaves from the plant you found it on. You may be rewarded by watching "your" caterpillar metamorphose over the next few weeks into a beautiful butterfly that you can set free.

Sally

Our daughter Sadie was five when she found our first praying mantis pet on the front porch. "Mantie" was nearly three inches long and light green. Her triangular, almost heart-shaped face was recognizably animal-like with its big, round eyes and pointed mouth. In her normal resting posture—with her "hands" held together as if in prayer—she was quite peaceful looking.

From the start, Mantie acted as though she wanted to be held. When we took the lid off the terrarium to drop a bug in for her to eat, she reached her "arms" up into the air as though she were asking to be picked up. Soon Sadie discovered that she could hand-feed her: Holding a cricket by the legs, she waved it back and forth in front of Mantie to get her attention. Within a few seconds, Mantie had snatched it—cleanly, daintily—without ever touching Sadie's fingers. Having a microcosm of nature in our house has taught us a good deal about life, death, and the ways of the animal kingdom.

Sally Kneidel, "Romancing the Bug," *Mothering*, Spring 1990.

Forts and Playhouses

Woodworking projects can be very satisfying with children. If you have a few tools and are handy with a saw, you can make anything from a simple doll bed to an elaborate playhouse. Let your children help design the project, and, with plenty of supervision and guidance, let them do as much of the work as possible.

Junkyards are a great source of materials: Collect plastic barrels, old tires, and sheets of metal to make boats, swings, and slides. Of course, sand all wood carefully for splinters, check for any sharp edges, and test each creation yourself before your children use it.

If you don't know a Phillips-head from a flat-head screwdriver, remember that large cardboard boxes—available from appliance stores—make great playhouses and castles. Or build a teepee in the backyard from sticks or bamboo poles and an old sheet. Have fun painting your creations together.

Remember, too, that the simplest structures—pillow forts, or a sheet draped over a card table—are often the favorites.

Sewing Projects

Children can quickly master a sewing machine to make simple costumes and gifts. Start young children out sitting on your lap, while you operate the foot pedal and place your hands over theirs. Once you feel they have mastered the basics, you can supervise them as they operate the machine themselves, always keeping it on low speed. Shop for patterns and fabrics together. A boy might want to make a magician's cape or a pillow for the cat; a girl might want to try a tote bag or princess headdress.

You can also handstitch dolls or stuffed animals. Knitting, needlepointing, or cross-stitch embroidery are just a few of the many needleworking projects for children to try. See Resources for books on needlework.

Children's Museums and Other Child-Friendly Places

Unlike many other countries, where children are welcomed and even revered in public, most American establishments are not particularly child-friendly. Taking your children out into society can be downright intimidating.

An organization working to change that attitude is the Child-Friendly Initiative. A panel of experts in child development has developed criteria for child-friendly businesses, from restaurants to post offices. Establishments that meet the criteria can display a "child-friendly" logo, and parents can find out about child-friendly places in their area through the organization's website. For more information, see Resources.

One kind of establishment that invites children to touch and explore is children's museums, which have grown from just a few in the mid-1980s to hundreds today. San Francisco's Exploratorium is the granddaddy of them all, with an enormous space devoted to the exploration of science. At Denver's Children's Museum, children can learn to ski on a 150-foot artificial ski slope. Most major cities and quite a few smaller towns now have children's museums offering hands-on art projects, working models of the human body, and pint-sized grocery stores and banks where children can experiment and learn about the world. If you don't have a children's museum nearby, your family might want to plan to visit one on your next vacation. For more information, contact The Association of Youth Museums (see Resources).

On the Road: Traveling with Children

Family vacations provide an opportunity to expand your horizons and strengthen family bonds. If the idea of car travel with children causes you to groan, you may not be looking at it from the right perspective.

The key to successful travel with children is learning the lesson that children, in their infinite wisdom, already know: The journey is more important than the destination. You may not get where you are going as quickly by taking the back roads and stopping every few hours, but you certainly will find more interesting stops along the way and arrive at your destination more refreshed.

Here are a few tips for successful family road trips:

INVOLVE YOUR CHILDREN IN THE PLANNING

Maybe an interest in dinosaurs has sparked an idea for a trip to Dinosaur National Monument in Colorado, or your family has always wanted to view the fall foliage in Vermont. Plan out a route together, marking it on a map that your children can follow along in the car. Get some books on the history and geology of the area you are visiting, and learn as much as you can before you go.

TAKE THE BACK ROADS

Children need lots of stops to rest or burn off energy. Smaller highways that go through small

towns offer more choices for good stops, as well as more colorful scenery. Good places for rest stops, in addition to points of interest along your route, include:

- Public libraries
- School playgrounds in the off hours
- Municipal parks or ball fields
- Public or commercial campgrounds
- College or university campuses
- Community recreation centers or YMCAs, where you can pay a drop-in fee and use the basketball courts, or go swimming.
- Hotel lobbies (in a city, if all else fails, a lobby can be a place to escape traffic noise and stretch your legs).

PACK DISTRACTIONS

Bring lots of things to do in the car, like bubbles, felt boards, and card games. Klutz Press makes the *Kids Travel: Backseat Survival Kit*, including board games, puzzles, quizzes, and activities. Pack plenty of children's tapes, both songs and stories. Sing your own songs and tell your own stories. Play guessing games like "20 Questions" and "I Spy."

PACK SNACKS

Pack a cooler with fruit, snacks, and drinks. Water is a very underrated liquid—kids drink it only if thirsty, leading to fewer potty stops. Consider feeding your children in the car—a peanut butter sandwich and an apple will not create too much mess, and will keep them busy for a little while.

PLAN TRAVEL TIMES AROUND YOUR CHILDREN'S RHYTHMS

Doing some driving while your children are sleeping makes sense if you want to eventually make it to your destination. When there are two drivers, some people prefer taking turns driving and sleeping at night. A safer option may be to leave before dawn, transferring your sleeping children from their beds to the car and letting them sleep in the car until the sun comes up. With a breakfast stop and several rest stops, you can still get in six hours on the road, pulling off before rush hour hits and motels begin to fill up.

TAKE SCHOOL WITH YOU

If the best time to travel does not coincide with your child's school vacations, you can collect lesson plans from his teacher and devote a portion of each day to studies. You can also develop your own lessons based on the places you visit.

KEEP LASTING MEMORIES OF YOUR TRIP

Encourage your child to keep a travel journal and to take photographs along the way. Even a very young child can draw pictures in a journal and take snapshots with an inexpensive disposable camera. And don't forget to send postcards to friends and family as you go from place to place.

More Ways to Have Fun with Your Family

- Make a detailed map of your house and yard, based on accurate measurements.
- Put on a treasure hunt for each other.
- Practice some magic tricks and put on a magic show.

- Invite the neighborhood over for a circus. Make costumes, dress the dog up as a lion, place a tightrope on the floor, practice juggling...use your imagination!
- On a windy day, make a kite and fly it.
- On a warm day, wash the car. Offer to wash the neighbor's car.
- Make boats from wood scraps and corks, with paper or fabric sails, and sail them down a creek.
- Play store with your children's toys and paper money.
- Play restaurant, writing up a menu of the day's lunch offerings.
- Learn a new language together, with tapes or CD-ROMs. Use index cards to label items around the house in the new language.
- Celebrate a holiday from another country, like Bastille Day or St. Brighid's Day. Research the holiday, make traditional foods, and listen to music from that country.
- Do crossword puzzles.
- Do origami.

- Trace around your child's body on a long sheet of newsprint, and let him color in his face and clothing.
- Decorate each other's faces with face paints.
- Paint on each other's tummies or arms with watercolors. Then take a bubble bath together!
- Using a parachute or sheet, have children hold the edges and bounce a ball on it, get under it, or ride on it as adults hold onto the edges and walk around.
- Enjoy the old pastime of visiting. Visit artists, craftspeople, musicians, or inventors.
- Make a trip to a home for elderly people in your community.
- Polish your silverware or pots. Use lemon juice and salt for copper; silver polish for silver.
- Bake bread. Children will love kneading it, letting it rise, punching it down, smelling it bake, and eating it!
- Finger paint with shaving cream.
- Cut paper dolls and clothing from catalogues.
- Make macaroni jewelry: Mix food coloring in rubbing alcohol, and stir in uncooked macaroni. Let it dry and string it on yarn for bracelets and necklaces.
- Make seed necklaces: Dye dried melon seeds in food coloring mixed with water. Let them dry, and string them together with a needle and thread.
- Make flower arrangements with pipe cleaner stems and colored tissue or construction paper flowers.
- Plant a vegetable or flower garden together.
- Force paperwhite or amaryllis bulbs indoors.

- Start some seeds indoors. Stick four toothpicks in a potato or avocado pit and suspend it halfway in a jar of water. Plant orange and lemon seeds in a little potting soil in eggshells. Put them in a sunny window, and watch them germinate.
- Grow a tray of bean or alfalfa sprouts, or wheatgrass—then eat them for good health!
- Make a felt board, covering a piece of cardboard with a felt background, and cutting animals, shapes, or letters out of felt to stick on it. (This felt board is a great game for the car.)
- Write letters to relatives, and take a trip to the post office to find out how the mail gets delivered.
- Start a stamp collection.
- Start a neighborhood food drive, and deliver canned goods to a local church or social service agency.
- Set out birdseed and a birdbath, and watch the birds gather.
- Fill walnut shell halves with candle wax and a tiny wick. Light them around the garden or on a pond at night for a magical scene.
- Research your family tree, gathering information from relatives, libraries, and the Internet.
- Have each family member write an autobiography, illustrated with photos and drawings of themselves.
- Take turns bringing a favorite passage from a book or poem to dinner. Copy them into a blank book to save.
- Write and illustrate a children's book to give to a friend or relative.

PART 6

Educational
Alternatives

CHAPTER 21 # Public Schooling

Universal education, begun in the mid-nineteenth century in the United States, started with a lofty democratic ideal: To educate all classes and ethnic groups, regardless of income or ability level. The birth of this idea signaled a new era of respect for every child's mind.

Today, however, public schools receive more negative publicity than praise. Schools are criticized for being overcrowded, impersonal institutions, mired in bureaucracy, relying on outmoded standardized curriculum and tests. They struggle with low student achievement scores, teacher apathy, and the increasing influence of drugs and sex on campus.

Parents who can afford to send their children to private school or to move to a district with better schools have always had options, and a growing number of parents are choosing to educate their children at home. But nine out of ten American school children still attend public school.

Today, however, parents are no longer content to send their children unquestioningly to the public school down the street, trusting that they will emerge educated thirteen years later. Parents are demanding accountability and innovation from the educational system, and as a result, public education is transforming itself. The progressive movement of the 1960s and '70s has had a lasting influence on mainstream education. As a result, many traditional public schools are offering a more experiential, child-centered, diverse curriculum, and are experimenting with different ways of learning. There are many options for an excellent education in public school today.

Where Do You Fit into Your Child's Education?

Free education has its price—helping your child to get the best public school education demands as much involvement as does home or private schooling.

You may wonder where you fit into your child's education. You cannot expect the school to give you instructions about your role. You may even get the feeling that your participation in the school is not needed or wanted.

However, your involvement is probably the most important element in making the public school system work for your child. Several studies have found that when parents become involved in schools, children's academic achievement goes up.[1]

You have always been an integral part of your child's learning, and there is no reason that should stop once he or she goes to school. By staying closely involved, you can better augment your child's learning and can find out quickly if anything is amiss. Here are some steps to take to help your child get ready for school and get the most out of school:

REQUEST A TEACHER

Before class assignments are made in March or April, find out about the teaching styles of the

teachers your child might be assigned to, by talking to other parents and observing classes. Then make a phone call or visit to the school principal, and request to have your child placed with the teacher who appealed most to you and your child. The principal may tell you the school has a no-request policy because it would be impossible to accommodate all requests. However, very few parents do actually request a teacher for their child. You can make it clear that your request is based on your belief that your child will function best with a particular teacher.

OBSERVE YOUR CHILD'S CLASSROOM

Early in the year, arrange a time with the teacher when you can sit in on your child's classes. Most teachers are very open to having parents observe, and doing so a few times throughout the year will give you a sense of the teacher's rapport with the students and how the material is being taught.

VOLUNTEER IN YOUR CHILD'S SCHOOL

Getting involved in your child's school gives you a chance to maintain contact with your child and to observe the dynamics of his school life. There are many ways to volunteer: You can be a room parent, tutor in the classroom, work in the library or playground, or help design teaching tools or materials. Some parents prefer to spend time in the classroom—where they have the most contact with their children—while others prefer to take a more background role.

If you have limited time or have a young child at home, you can still get involved by making phone calls to organize fund-raisers or academic events, working on school materials from home, or driving to an occasional field trip. Even indirect involvement with your child's classroom will give you more of a sense of ownership about the school, will help you get to know the teachers and administrators better, and will give your child a sense of pride that you are contributing. It also pays dividends to your child: Most teachers cannot help making an extra effort for a child whose parent is involved.

SHARE YOUR EXPERTISE
Another way to get involved is to offer your talents or areas of knowledge to augment the classroom curriculum. If you are a musician, you might offer to play for the classroom, or even help organize a music appreciation program. If you have contacts with local artists, you could put together an artist-in-residence program. You could share stories and slides of a country you know well, or act as the classroom computer consultant, or share details about your work. Your child's teacher will probably be very receptive to a parent presentation or consultation.

KEEP IN TOUCH WITH YOUR CHILD'S TEACHER
The conventional forums for parent-teacher contact—parent-teacher conferences, back-to-school night, and the like—discourage real interaction. Parents are put in the role of outsiders, visiting the school and discussing their child's progress for a very limited time, only when invited. Building a trusting and cooperative relationship with your child's teacher—the person who is directing and influencing your child six hours a day, five days a week—requires an ongoing effort on your part.

Start within the first month of school, by setting up a conference or writing a letter. Describe your child's temperament, interests, and habits. List your child's strong points and explain any concerns you might have. Define your goals and objectives for the school year. Ask what the teacher expects of you, both at home and in the classroom. Express your desire to communicate regularly, through notes, e-mail, phone calls, or brief after-school visits. Although it may sound like you are asking too much of a teacher's time, most teachers welcome communication with parents. Parents who are kept informed are better equipped to help their children succeed in the classroom, and are able to become partners in their children's education.

You may also want to organize a few social events where you can get to know your child's teacher better as a person. Most towns are too big for the lives of teachers and parents to overlap. You can invite your child's teacher out for an occasional cup of tea, or join with other parents to host potlucks, barbecues, breakfasts, or work groups for playground construction or other projects.

SUPPORT TEACHERS WHO ARE DOING A GOOD JOB
A note of praise to a teacher and school administrators carries a lot of weight, and can help support a teacher who is criticized for having the courage to be innovative.

Try to get involved in the hiring process. More schools are now looking for input from committees of parents, students, and other teachers when new teachers are hired.

LOOK INTO YOUR SCHOOL'S DISCIPLINE POLICY
Read school policies on disciplinary practices. Spanking, or "paddling," is still used legally in many school districts. If you do not spank in your home, you need to express your objection in writing. Take a letter to each of your children's teachers—to be filed later with the principal—stating that you withhold permission for your children to be spanked, but will back up teachers in reasonable alternatives should your children need to be disciplined.

GET INVOLVED AT A POLICY LEVEL
At one time, parents were an integral part of the nation's public school system. Parents built the schools, hired and housed the teachers, and financed each endeavor. Today, however, the real control of public education is in the hands of administrators and school boards, with a little input from the Parent-Teacher Association (PTA).

In many school districts, however, parents are demanding a larger decision-making role, and their input is being welcomed by administrators. Parents can serve on task forces and advisory groups to establish the curriculum, hire teachers, allocate the budget, and determine policies. Committees from several school districts acting together can effect statewide changes, and if need be, can take issues to the national level.

Never underestimate the power of a small group of committed parents and teachers to transform education.

Reinforce Learning at Home

We are all, in effect, homeschoolers. School is only a part of your child's education—we learn constantly from our environment and people around us.

You can augment your child's schoolwork at home by coming up with activities that reinforce what your child is learning. In addition to reading with your child as she is learning to read, and doing addition and multiplication flash cards, you can plan a theme dinner around a country your child is studying in school, and do neighborhood nature walks and kitchen chemistry experiments to keep alive an interest in science. Share your ideas with your child's teacher—he or she may want to use some of them in the classroom, or pass them along to other parents.

Many parents are frustrated that budget-cutting has limited music and art opportunities in public schools. While you can work with other parents to find ways to bring these important elements back into schools, you can also enrich your child's education with after-school music or art classes, or simply listen to different types of music at home, or visit museums. (For more ideas of activities to supplement your child's education, see Chapter 20.)

Helping your child with homework is one of the best things you can do to ensure his success in school. A national PTA-World Book survey found that the most important ways that parents can help children in elementary school are by regularly encouraging them with their homework, helping them to perceive themselves as problem solvers, instilling a strong work ethic, showing pride in their academic growth and achievements, and listening to and talking to them about school.

Asian families in the United States provide a strong example of homework success. A study of 536 Indochinese children who immigrated as "boat people" to the United States found that, although many of the children knew no English when they first arrived, within three and a half years, half of them ranked in the top 25th percentile of students nationwide, and one-quarter of them in the top 10th percentile. The key ingredient in their success was devotion to homework. Compared with their classmates, the Indochinese children spent about twice as much time on school assignments. The study found that after dinner, siblings in Indochinese families usually sit down to help each other with homework, while their parents stay nearby, doing household chores and providing watchfulness and motivation.[2]

Ways that you can help your child with homework include:
- Making homework a family priority.
- Establishing guidelines for your child's homework and incorporating homework time into the family's daily schedule.
- Providing a clean, well-lit, distraction-free space for studying.
- Keeping telephone numbers of teachers and other students handy.
- Discussing with your child how you can be of assistance with homework without being intrusive or controlling. Be aware of school policy regarding how much teachers expect parents to help with homework. Be sure that you and your child share a common set of expectations regarding your role in the homework process.

Talking to Your Child About School

Keeping up on your child's school life requires some effort on your part. Your child may not volunteer information about what goes on at school, and may respond to your questions with one-word answers, or that universal conversation-stopper, "I dunno."

You can learn a lot about your child's school life from being involved in his classroom and maintaining regular contact with his teacher. You can also work on drawing your child out to communicate about school. Nancy Wilson, author of *Children and Television* (PPI Publishing, 1988) and *Teenagers and Stress* (PPI Publishing, 1990), suggests the following techniques:

ASK OPEN-ENDED QUESTIONS

Instead of "How was your day at school today?" ask specific questions like "How did that spelling test go?" or questions that evoke feelings, like "You sure look happy. Did something good happen today?" To find out about learning experiences, ask your child about the specific topics he or she is studying. Ask if she agrees with the teacher or the other students on discussions involving current events or environmental issues.

Hovering over your child the minute she walks through the door can make her feel overwhelmed. Instead, give her time to decompress and open up when she is ready. Some parents find that comments about school life surface during relaxed conversation over dinner. Others find that they learn something by going over school papers and homework with their children.

OFFER ACKNOWLEDGMENT AND EMPATHY

Young children need to have their feelings recognized. When your child bursts in the house yelling "I hate my teacher!" she needs to first of all have her emotions validated. Give her an opportunity to vent her feelings without advice or criticism, before you start trying to get the facts. Then try to get to the root of her feelings.

If there is a problem at school that needs addressing, go to your child's teacher first, and if that fails, to the principal. Without attacking the teacher, explain that you want to hear both sides of the story. Most teachers care about their students and appreciate parental sensitivity to school problems. While it is important to realize that children's perceptions can often be exaggerated and influenced by their peers, it is equally important to recognize your child's feelings as valid.

ADDRESS HYPOTHETICAL SITUATIONS

Your child may be hesitant to tell you about a playground bully or a cheating incident for fear of retaliation from classmates. You can address these issues before they come up by asking hypothetical questions, like "What would you do if your friend asked to copy your test paper?" or "How would you

Being Your Child's Advocate

You know her. She is that woman over there with the disheveled hair, the strident voice. She is the one who is a little too involved with her child, a little too interfering. She is that crazy mother.

What is it about becoming a parent that turns a reasonably polite, discreet woman into a guerrilla warrior for her child? And why is it that no matter how righteous the cause, whenever we assert ourselves on behalf of our children we must be prepared to do battle with the crazy mother stereotype?

In school, a child has inevitable conflicts with friends and with teachers. It is challenging for a parent to be an advocate for a child in a classroom and not make things more difficult for the child. And yet, children must never doubt that we will defend them. Children at this age do not always know how to identify or deal with unkind or inappropriate behavior. They sometimes need their parents to appear crazy to their friends, to be the bad guy, to say no, in effect, for them. All of us run the risk of being labeled troublesome parents by just speaking up. Even so, it is always worth the risk to speak up for our children, even when our children are embarrassed by our behavior.

As Elaine Heffner writes in *Mothering* (Doubleday, 1980), "Those who believe they should be in charge often attach too little importance to a mother's point of view. The mother's differing perception becomes an obstacle to overcome, and if she persists, she is labeled a 'difficult' mother.

Over and over again, determinations are made on the basis of limited observations, which have a major effect on a child's future. It is simply taken for granted that such observations and decisions are valid because they have been made by an expert. But a mother's understanding of her child's behavior—her awareness of his functioning in a great variety of situations—makes it essential that her point of view be taken into consideration in drawing conclusions about him. It is the mother who must stay in charge of decisions that affect the course of her child's development. Staying in charge means that a mother will follow her own judgment on two fronts: She will interpret the advice and recommendations she is given in ways that seem to her most applicable to her own child; and she will insist that others who make decisions affecting her child will take her understanding and point of view into consideration.

It is good to be crazy about your child and to get crazy for him. Your child is supposed to have someone who thinks he is the greatest no matter what; who rushes to defend him without knowing the whole story; who sympathizes even after hearing it. You can tell crazy mothers by a certain gleam in their eye. They are the ones who are willing to get crazy for love.

handle it if someone were teasing you on the playground?" Help your child rehearse what to do and say without angering another child or hurting another child's feelings. (For tips on helping your child deal with bullies, see "Helping Your Children Combat Verbal Abuse," page 199.)

BRING FAMILY NEWS TO SCHOOL

Just as you need to know what issues your child is dealing with at school, your child's teacher needs to know what is going on at home. If your family is coping with a major event that may affect your child's behavior at school—such as a new baby, a death, or a separation—you should let your child's teacher know about it. Even an event that may seem minor to you—such as a child's pet dying—may affect your child's emotional state. By maintaining regular contact with your child's teacher, you can share this kind of information on an ongoing basis

When to Start Your Child in School

In today's achievement-oriented society, children are being pushed to start academics earlier and earlier. When did we decide that children are vessels, to be crammed full with knowledge, and how have we become so competitive that it matters to us if our child is the first on the block to learn to read?

Some of world's greatest achievements have been made by people who were considered to be "slow learners" as children—Einstein, Edison, and Faulkner, among them. When children are simply given encouragement and allowed to develop according to their own timetable, they can grow into their true potential.

Joseph Chilton Pearce, author of *The Magical Child* (Bantam, 1977), says that when children are forced into academics too early and deprived of the critical period of creative free play, they leave the magical world of early childhood before they would have outgrown it naturally. He considers the first seven years of life to be the absolute sacrosanct period for leaving the child alone and allowing her to be a child. Rudolf Steiner, father of Waldorf education, also felt strongly that for the first seven years of life, children express themselves through imaginative play and physical movement. Thus, Waldorf schools do not pressure children to learn to read or master other academic skills until they have lost their baby teeth, at the age of six or seven.

Raymond Moore, longtime educational researcher with the United States Department of Education and author of more than sixty books on human development, recommends that children refrain from formal study until they are eight, ten, or even twelve, depending on maturity level. Prior to this, he recommends allowing children to learn at home through playing, singing, being read to, and exploring their own interests. According to Moore, early home schooling can provide a sound basis for formal education. He cites numerous studies showing that too early formal schooling constraints can be detrimental. Particularly in the case of boys, he says, who mature a year or so later than girls, readiness for school should not be presumed too early.

However, Maria Montessori, founder of Montessori education, felt that children's minds are particularly "absorbent" between the ages of three and six, and that there are "sensitive periods" in their development at these ages when they are open to acquiring certain language abilities or mathematical skills. In a Montessori primary classroom, through the use of concrete, hands-on, self-correcting materials, children often learn to read and write, add and subtract and even work with fractions before they are six or seven. This kind of learning, however, would not be considered by most to be "forced" or "formal" learning—rather, children learn through self-discovery and self-motivation.

The best advice is to do what is best for your child. If you are home full-time with your child, he is probably getting all he needs from being around you and engaging in imaginative play. As a culture, we are asking our children to cope with lengthy parental separations at increasingly early ages. There is no reason to feel that your child needs to begin school before age five or six, or even later.

On the other hand, you may have a wonderful Montessori preschool in your neighborhood that you feel your child would benefit from, or you may want your child to attend preschool to get "ready" for kindergarten, or you may work outside of the home and need to find a good preschool environment to send your child to.

Just as you respect your child's timetable in learning to talk and in weaning, you need to look to your child for school readiness. When children are pushed too early into an academic experience that they are not ready for, they may fail to thrive and end up being at the bottom of the class, or labeled "learning disabled" as a result.

Some schools are now offering a "Pre-First Grade" year between kindergarten and first grade, for those students who are not developmentally ready for first grade. A good start upon entering first grade gives children a better chance in school. Elementary school counselor Dale Warren Hill cautions parents not to "overplace" their children in school. If you have questions about your child's school readiness before enrolling her in kindergarten, he counsels, ask your principal or counselor to evaluate your child's developmental readiness based on a variety of criteria. Don't send your child to school just because of chronological age, peer pressure, or work demands. "The best time to give your child a developmental 'gift of time' is before she goes to school," says Hill. "If you think that you might overplace your child by sending her to school, consider a gift of time at home."

Standardized Tests: Poor Measures of Success

Standardized, multiple-choice tests have become the yardstick by which we measure intellectual ability. Most school districts rely on exams for entry to school, placement in ability-grouped "tracking" programs, promotion from grade to grade, and graduation from high school. Student test scores are used in decisions regarding school funding and teacher promotion. Parents depend on test results to measure how their children stack up against their peers. Most educators and government leaders put ultimate faith in standardized tests as a way to strengthen academic achievement and improve our national educational standards. However, there is strong evidence that tests do more harm than good. Here are some of the arguments against standardized tests:

THEY ARE NOT A VALID MEASURE OF INTELLIGENCE

Monty Neill, associate director of FairTest, points out that tests measure only a narrow range of skills and abilities. On a standardized spelling test, for example, students must pick the correct spelling from a few choices, rather than spell a word correctly. This measures spelling recognition, not spelling ability. Knowledge is simply not a multiple-choice reality.

The worst offender is the IQ test, which measures not intelligence, but the ability to take IQ tests. IQ tests are notoriously inaccurate: Students retaking them over time have scored as many as twenty points above or below their original results.[3] Even so, they are still widely used to assign an arbitrary number to a child's intelligence and worth.

THEY ARE NOT OBJECTIVE

The only objective thing about standardized tests is the method by which they are scored, says Neill. Decisions about what areas to cover, what questions to include, what terminology to use, and how scores are interpreted are all subjectively determined.

THEY ARE BIASED

Most tests questions are based on the experiences of white, middle-class children. As Neill points out, every test assumes a language, a culture, and a set of experiences, and therefore cannot help but favor test takers who have had those particular life exposures. As a result, minority and lower-income children do poorly on standardized tests, compared to their white peers. Test makers insist that they examine tests to remove bias; however, biases are not always obvious.

Girls also do not score as well on the Scholastic Aptitude Test (SAT)—perhaps because girls tend to do better with essay tests than multiple choice questions—even though young women earn higher grades in both high school and college.[4]

THEY FAVOR THE WEALTHY

For those who can afford them, there are expensive courses, workshops, and computer programs that promise to increase student's scores on college entrance exams. Students have the option of taking these entrance exams over as many times as they like—only the highest score is considered. Children who cannot afford these aids are therefore put at a disadvantage.

THEY ARE USED TO PERPETUATE DAMAGING TRACKING SYSTEMS

Based on their test scores, "slower" children are placed in low-ability groups, where they are exposed to less challenging material than their higher-scoring classmates. This creates a vicious cycle which low-testing children cannot break out of, because they never receive the grade-level instruction or encouragement need to bring their scores up. Research shows that tracking damages lower-ranked students and does not help advanced students, who do just as well in mixed-ability groups.[5]

THEY ENCOURAGE TEACHERS TO "TEACH FOR THE TEST"

Pressured to have their students score well, teachers may design their curriculum around test content, diverting attention from meaningful instruction. For too many of today's students, says Neill, schooling has been reduced to test-coaching.

THEY INHIBIT DEVELOPMENT OF THE INTELLECT

Education and creativity consultant Alan Garten-haus points out that although many real-life problem-solving activities require divergent thinking—the ability to generate a range of possibilities in order to make a decision—most school activities and multiple-choice tests instead measure convergent thinking—the ability to select a correct response from a list of choices. As a result, creativity and inventiveness may be lost. It is difficult to engage in intellectual risk-taking under the looming presence of evaluations based on "right" or "wrong" responses. Tests emphasize speed over depth of thought, and short-term memorization over true understanding—the recall of the dates and battles of World War II, for example, rather than an inquiry into why the war occurred.

These arguments are beginning to have an effect on the use of tests. In response to the call for test reform, the Educational Testing Service undertook a major study of the SAT, and the American College Testing (ACT) program substantially revised its admission test. A growing "test optional" movement reflects increasing concerns about the ACT and SAT. At least 280 colleges and universities now disregard ACT or SAT results to make admissions decisions for many applicants.

FairTest conducted a state-by-state survey of educational testing in 1997 and found that most states now use writing samples in addition to multiple choice tests, and are making an effort to reduce biases in tests. However, the survey also found that the majority of states still rely on outmoded multiple choice tests and mandate testing as a requirement for high school graduation.

If you are concerned about the reliance on standardized tests or tracking systems at your child's school, educator Stephen Schmitz suggests you take the following steps:

- To ensure that your child is appropriately placed, ask to see the documentation used to determine class placement. Do not accept standardized test scores as the primary criteria. Instead, insist upon the inclusion of grades, classroom performance, motivation, and interest.

- Refuse IQ testing of any sort for your child. Even school districts that do not require parental permission before testing will allow parents the right of refusal.
- Formally request that your child be exempted from standardized aptitude and achievement tests. While most states require all educational facilities to administer testing for funding purposes, few require scores on individual students. If administrators are reluctant to exempt a child, keeping your child home on testing day will accomplish the same goal.
- On the other hand, if your child is struggling in school and you are seeking special placement for him, you might want to allow your child to be tested, but also be very active in getting proper interpretation of the results.
- Finally, do not judge the intellectual potential of your child on the basis of test results.

For more information, contact FairTest (see Resources).

Making the Grade

We all want our children to do well in school, and the most common measure of success in school is grades. In the same way that standardized tests are flawed, however, there are dangers in relying too much on a report card to reflect your child's abilities.

Grades encourage a narrow scholastic definition of success. If we are to broaden our thinking, we must recognize that intelligence can take many forms. Some children are linguistic or mathematical thinkers, who memorize well and tend to perform well on tests and get good grades. Other children, however, excel in leadership skills, wisdom, creativity, or persistence—talents which are not as easily measured or graded. Other kinds of intelligence—not reflected by standard grading systems at all, but which could be considered measures of success in later life—include artistic,

musical, and athletic aptitudes. (For more on the theory of multiple intelligences, see page 286.)

Grades may actually stifle motivation to learn, argues school psychologist Fred Luskin, by placing emphasis on academic status rather than natural curiosity and the satisfaction of learning as an end in itself. No one grades a child on learning to walk or talk, and yet her desire to learn these skills is limitless. But once a child enters school and recognizes the value placed on getting good grades, her innate curiosity gives way to a narrow focus on learning the prescribed curriculum.

In addition, grades foster competition and can damage self-esteem. Jack Canfield, author of *Chicken Soup for the Soul* cites studies showing that most children enter kindergarten feeling good about themselves and their ability to learn, but by fifth grade, less than half of all students feel good about themselves as learners, and by high school, only a small proportion do.

Luskin suggests the following tips for parents who want to protect their children from a school's overemphasis on grading:

NURTURE YOUR CHILD'S TALENTS AND MOTIVATION FOR LEARNING

Encourage your child to try many different activities. Acknowledge your child's full range of abilities, and she will be more likely to discover areas in which she excels.

LET YOUR CHILD KNOW THAT YOU CONSIDER GRADES SECONDARY TO LEARNING

Reward efforts rather than outcomes. Encourage curiosity and natural learning. Recognize the limitations inherent in school curricula, and support your child's attempts at self-expression, both in school and at home.

AT THE SAME TIME, LET YOUR CHILD KNOW THAT GRADES ARE THE WAY SUCCESS IS MEASURED IN SCHOOL

To some extent, your child needs to work within the system. While grades may not be the best measure of intelligence, students who want to do well need to do their work and pass their subjects. The challenge is to encourage your child to work for good grades while not letting the pursuit of good grades take precedence over the ability to learn and think for oneself

DISCUSS YOUR VIEWS WITH YOUR CHILD'S TEACHER

If your child is getting poor grades, meet with his teacher to see how you can collaborate in helping your child to learn. Explain that you consider grades to be only a partial measure of your child's achievement. Ask your teacher to pass on information about which subjects seem to inspire motivation in your child and which are a struggle, and explain how your child behaves at home.

SUPPLEMENT LEARNING AT HOME

If you feel your child's school does not fully support his strengths, you can compensate at home, by bringing movement, art, or music to homework assignments (for more on tapping into each child's way of learning, see "Multiple Intelligences," page 286). You may want to consider transferring your child to a school that emphasizes multiple ways of learning and uses nontraditional methods of assessment (for more on Alternative Education, see Chapter 22).

Above all, keep a clear perspective. School draws to a close, and grading comes to an end, but learning goes on for life

The Learning Disability Debate

More than one out of ten American schoolchildren is labeled learning disabled (LD). Children considered to have an LD are not mentally retarded, but they cannot function normally in a classroom. They may have trouble—ranging from mild to severe—with speaking, writing, reading, arithmetic, logic and reasoning, and motor skills. Of the twenty identified LDs, dyslexia—reading disability—is one of the best known.

For parents of a learning disabled child, it is a very real problem that touches every aspect of their lives. Patrice Fitch, mother of a daughter who is learning disabled, describes how, at age eight, her daughter had the motor skills and temperament of a five-year-old. She had to constantly be reminded to wipe and flush after going to the toilet. Her two-year-old brother could run faster than she could. Although she could read at her grade level, she could not write legibly or perform abstract reasoning because of a congenital right brain abnormality.

Students with learning disabilities are guaranteed special education in public schools by the Individuals with Disabilities Act. Generally, LD students are put in special education classes for reading, writing, and math, as well as physical and speech therapy. The rest of the day, including lunch, recess, art, and music, may be spent with their age-group classmates.

The Attention Deficit Epidemic

The most commonly diagnosed learning disability—Attention Deficit Disorder (ADD), with or without hyperactivity (ADHD)—is diagnosed in 3 to 10 percent of all American schoolchildren. Children with ADHD may constantly seek out new sources of stimulation, and are often too impatient to wait more than a few seconds for something. Many of them are very bright, but they have difficulty functioning in school because of behavioral difficulties. They may sincerely want to sit still and concentrate, but they cannot, no matter how hard they try.

No one knows what causes ADHD. Researchers are pursuing a possible genetic theory. Some attribute it to diet, or allergies. Others feel that it is fad diagnosis made by teachers who have trouble controlling spirited children in the classroom. Richard Vatz, PhD, and Lee Weinberg, PhD, associate psychology editors of *USA Today Magazine* and contributing authors to the book *Discovering the History of Psychiatry* (Oxford University Press), claim that "ADHD is not a bona fide disease. It is not even a clearly defined behavioral pattern. It is a debilitating label too frequently imposed on children." They point out that the *Diagnostic and Statistical Manual of Mental Disorders* (DSM-IV), published by the American Psychiatric Association, defines ADHD in strictly nonmedical terms, based largely on teachers' and parents' observations.

Most of the children diagnosed with ADHD are prescribed Ritalin (methylphenidate) and other amphetamines, which are purported to control their distractibility, impulsiveness, disruptive behavior, and difficulty in school. Prescriptions for Ritalin have risen 300 percent in just four years. While Ritalin may improve attention span and decrease hyperactivity for many children, it has also been shown to have a number of adverse side effects, including insomnia, headaches, appetite loss, stunted growth, and nervous tics—perhaps not surprising, considering that it is in the same drug family as diet pills.

Parents have reported that their children's personalities appear changed by the drug, and that their behavior is worse once the effects of the drug—which lasts about four hours—wear off. Perhaps most disturbing about these prescriptions is that they give children the message that they need to take drugs long-term to be "normal."

The Problem with Labeling

Although for many children, special education is a godsend, educational consultant and former special education teacher Thomas Armstrong disagrees with the notion of special education. He feels that putting children in special education classes does them more harm than good. Labeling children "learning disabled," he says, focuses on what is wrong with the child, when in fact, many children simply have unique learning styles that public schools are not prepared to deal with. Howard Gardner's theory of multiple intelligences—including artistic, physical, and social ways of learning—supports this notion (see "Multiple Intelligences," page 286).

Armstrong paints the following scenario of what happens to a child who is labeled learning disabled: A child who has difficulty sitting still or who is overwhelmed by the foreign and intimidating atmosphere of public school is sent by her teacher to a specialist for an evaluation. She is diagnosed with a learning disability. Being told that there is something wrong with her brain, she becomes even more confused and unable to concentrate. She is placed in a special class where she is subjected to a variety of esoteric exercises, including staring at a rubber ball on a string and completing dull worksheets, for which she is rewarded with prizes. Returning to her homeroom, she is teased about being in the "retard class."

Melvin Levine, of the Clinical Center for the Study of Development and Learning at the University of North Carolina, agrees that labeling can result in self-fulfilling prophecies. He cautions that emphasizing disabilities over strengths can easily harm a youngster with an "attention deficit" who may exhibit an extraordinary imagination, or a child with "language disabilities" who may have superb nonverbal reasoning and conceptual abilities. In the end, he notes, "Children may grow up feeling 'defective' if adults pay too much attention to their disabilities."[6]

Alternative Approaches to Learning Disabilities

Many parents who are dissatisfied with special education or wary of putting their children on prescription drugs have investigated other options in addressing LDs. Here are some of the more successful approaches:

PUBLIC SCHOOLING ALTERNATIVES

Instead of placing children in special education classes, Armstrong suggests working with your child's teacher to try to improve the environment in the regular classroom. You can do this by offering to aid in the classroom and provide special materials to help your child learn. Since schools are used to parents demanding more special education services for their children rather than less, your request may be met with positively.

ALTERNATIVE SCHOOLING

Often what specialists term a "learning disability" may simply be a poor relationship between teacher and child. In that case, suggests Armstrong, consider moving your child to another class or another public school. Better yet, he suggests moving your child to an alternative school that emphasizes individual styles of learning and a nonpressured, child-centered environment. Unfortunately, this is usually the opposite kind of environment found in most special education classes.

For the same reasons, Armstrong counsels parents to consider homeschooling. When children are allowed to learn at their own pace, they usually blossom. Even if the experts try to convince you that only an expert can teach a child with a so-called learning disability, the fact is that you are the expert where your child is concerned. (For more on alternative schools and home-schooling, see Chapters 22 and 23).

IMPROVING ATTENTION SPAN

Armstrong also suggests a number of things you can do to improve your child's attention span, including limiting television and video games, enrolling your child in a martial arts class, using background music to focus and calm, and removing common allergens from your child's diet. For more suggestions, read Armstrong's *The Myth of the ADD Child: 50 Ways to Improve Your Child's*

Sheri

My four children were born at home, breastfed for over a year, minimally immunized, treated with homeopathic medicine, and enrolled in a Waldorf school. Imagine, therefore, the struggle we have been through since my son was first diagnosed with ADHD. My son's teacher expressed strong negative opinions about the use of medication, and at her suggestion, we used various therapeutic approaches more aligned with the philosophy of Waldorf education. However, our son's behavior was an ongoing problem, his self-esteem decreased, and his teacher's frustration rose.

He entered third grade in public school virtually a nonreader. He was found to have a learning disability as well as ADHD. Again, we chose alternatives to medication, including a vision-training program, homeopathic remedies, and craniosacral adjustments. These approaches provided some relief. However, after he was detained at school three times because of impulsive behavior, we decided to try Ritalin.

In the six weeks since he began a course of Ritalin, he has not missed recess or been detained after school. He is very pleased with himself. He has gained an ability to focus, follow directions, participate constructively in school, and realize that he is a capable student!

Leslie

Our nonverbal three-year-old son was referred to our school district for an evaluation. Our only concern was his lack of speech. After a single two-hour evaluation, the Pupil Placement Team concluded that our son was severely delayed in many areas and recommended that he be placed in the special education class.

After our shock wore off, our skepticism grew. How can any team come to such a life-altering conclusion after a two-hour session? No retests, no second meetings, no other follow-up whatsoever! We felt the special ed class was completely inappropriate for a child who we felt needed only speech therapy.

We searched out a second, independent opinion and were told that our son scored at or above average for all areas except speech. Completely confused, we decided to listen to our hearts and wait a year. Six months later, our nonverbal three year old has become a completely verbal three and a half year old. He "cured" himself.

Behavior and Attention Span Without Drugs, Labels, or Coercion (see Resources).

HOMEOPATHIC TREATMENT OF ADD

Judyth Reichenberg-Ullman and Robert Ullman, cofounders of The Northwest Center for Homeopathic Medicine and authors of *Ritalin-Free Kids: Safe and Effective Homeopathic Treatment of ADD and Other Behavioral and Learning Problems* (Prima Publishing), have found homeopathy to be 70 percent effective in treating ADD and ADHD. Improvement is noticeable within a few days or weeks, and one dose of the right remedy may last six months to a year. To contact the Ullmans see Resources, "Health and Alternative Medicine," or read their book.

OTHER ALTERNATIVE THERAPIES FOR ADD

The Feingold diet—which eliminates food colorings, dyes, and other preservatives from a child's diet—has been found to be helpful with ADD in some cases, as have diets that eliminate sugar and common food allergens. (See Resources,

277

"Health and Alternative Medicine.") Parents have also reported success in treating ADD with craniosacral therapy and calming herbs. For more on these remedies, see *The Ritalin-Free Child: Managing Hyperactivity and Attention Deficits Without Drugs*, in Resources.

THE TOMATIS METHOD

The Tomatis Method stimulates the muscles of the middle ear to enhance the development of listening, language, and communication skills. It has been shown to treat learning disabilities, hyperactivity, autism, stuttering, and a variety of other disorders. Special equipment, including an "Electronic Ear," accentuates and diminishes different frequencies of sound, stimulating the muscles of the ear to improve their response to a wide variety of sound frequencies. There are Tomatis Centers throughout the United States. For more information, see Resources.

Education in the Twenty-first Century

Education in the United States has undergone greater transformation in the last thirty years than at any other time in its 150-year history, and it is poised for many additional changes in the twenty-first century. Here is a brief look at just a few of the issues currently influencing educational reform:

COMMERCIALISM IN SCHOOLS

Middle schools and high schools—with their captive audience of young consumers—have increasingly become an attractive market to advertisers. Commercialism in schools can take the form of billboards, corporate-sponsored educational materials (an Exxon-sponsored lesson plan about the wildlife in Prince William Sound, Alaska, for example), and company-sponsored contests or sampling programs.

The most blatant example of school commercialism is Channel One: a twelve-minute news program, containing two minutes of advertising, that is broadcast to 40 percent of United States middle and high schools each day. In exchange for lending schools a satellite dish, VCRs, and televi-sion sets, Channel One requires that students spend class time watching the commercial program. According to the Center for Commercial-Free Public Education, Channel One is shown disproportionately in schools located in low-income communities, where the least money is spent on textbooks and other academic materials. Schools that can afford to say no to Channel One do. The program is opposed by almost every national educational group. To find out more about Channel One, or to oppose its airing in your child's school, contact the Center for Commercial-Free Public Education (see Resources).

MULTICULTURALISM

As English-speaking Caucasians become less of a dominant minority in America, minority groups have begun to oppose the teaching of literature and history based on western European culture. At the same time, feminists challenged the focus on the accomplishments of men. As a result, "multiculturalism"—the inclusion of literature by minorities and women, and the study of the role of African-Americans and Hispanics in American history—has been introduced at some level in most schools around the country.

Multiculturalism is expected to become a more dominant force in American education, as proponents push for sweeping reforms in practices that put minorities at a disadvantage. These practices include subtle or unintended discrimination by teachers, tracking systems that place minorities in remedial programs based on standardized test scores, and a language that is not the native or home language of minorities.

ARTS EDUCATION

When budgets are cut at schools, the arts are usually the first thing to go. However, arts education has been making a comeback in recent years.

The Association for the Advancement of Arts Education reviewed nearly 400 studies in the four art disciplines of dance, music, theater, and visual arts, and found that the arts are necessary for many aspects of students' success in school and in life. The studies demonstrate that the arts give children self-discipline, creativity, and confidence; that they help students comprehend math, reading, and science; and that they remove boundaries and give children new ways of exploring the world.

In 1994, the Consortium of National Arts Education Associations developed National Standards for Arts Education, to provide schools in the United States with guidelines for quality education in the four art disciplines. That same year, the "Goals 2000: Educate America Act" was signed by President Clinton, marking the first time in history that the United States government recognized the essential role the arts play in education, and codified music and arts education as core subjects. Since then, almost every state has overhauled school curricula to include the arts. For more information on education in arts, see Resources.

TECHNOLOGY

The Internet is expected to have a major impact on education, just as it has on many other aspects of culture. Part of the "Goals 2000: Educate America" legislation directs states to develop plans describing how they will use technology to support education reform and help students achieve high standards. Authentic uses of technology in the classroom include the use of desktop publishing tools and the use of the Internet as an information resource. For example, at the Open Charter School in Los Angeles, where there is one computer for every two students, students relied on the computer as a design and research tool to devise a model city.

The Internet has the capacity to transform education by bringing the classroom to students all over the world, including rural or hard-to-reach areas. Already, several homeschooling programs have been developed to educate high schoolers over the Internet

SCHOOL LUNCH REFORM

The fifty-year-old National School Lunch Program—established to provide nourishing, low-cost or free meals in schools, and which currently feeds 60 percent of all school-aged children every day—got its first major update a few years ago. "Team Nutrition" was launched by the United States government in 1995 to give students healthier food choices. Other grassroots programs have sprung up as well. EarthSave Foundation's Healthy School Lunch Action Program is an effort begun in 1994 to educate students about the health and environmental benefits of plant-based foods. Chefs Collaborative 2000 is an program that teaches students about the diversity of food, through cooking foods from around the world in the classroom.

The result of these programs has been healthier options in school cafeterias, from fresh fruit and vegetable "food bars" to vegetarian main dishes. For more information about school lunch reform or to get a community action kit, contact Team Nutrition or EarthSave Healthy School Lunch Program (see Resources).

In some areas, students are learning about the entire food cycle, through growing their own food on school property. In the Edible Schoolyard program—launched a few years ago by Chez Panisse chef Alice Waters, at Martin Luther King Jr. Middle School in Berkeley—students cultivate organic vegetables that supply the school's lunch program. Food from the 'Hood takes the process a step further: Students at Crenshaw High School in South Central Los Angeles grow the ingredients to make all-natural salad dressings, which they sell to raise scholarship funds. A sister business in Ithaca produces applesauce. For information on these programs, see Resources.

College: It Isn't Over Yet

You have done your best to provide your child with a rich and diverse educational experience. Now your child is ready for college, and you have another whole set of decisions to guide her through. Academic counselor and college administrator Ron Hale suggests taking the following factors into consideration:

ENCOURAGE YOUR CHILD TO CONSIDER WHY SHE WANTS TO GO TO COLLEGE

Some young people decide not to go to college, or to take a few years off after high school; in fact, more than half of those attending college today are over the 18-to-22-year-old age bracket. Some people prefer approaching learning and personal development through a job, travel, community

Peggy

Last fall, my oldest daughter went to college. And she came back. I thought that maybe at eighteen, they grew up and left home. No. It ain't over yet. This has turned out to be one of my most profound mothering experiences.

The reality of life away from home turned out to be very different for my daughter than the widely accepted fantasy of college. We place our vulnerable young adults in a new situation that carries heavy personal, societal, and financial expectations. They leave their support network to live with someone they've never met, in a room so small that furniture must be stacked.

I was cautioned to hold a hard line when I received "the call" from my child asking to come home. Quite frankly, I could not. I have always trusted my daughter's perceptions. She knew when she wanted to walk, to talk, to wean, to go to school.

Like childbirth, sending a child to college requires us to prepare as well as we can, knowing that we must also be able to respond to the unexpected. There is a name for what my daughter is doing. It's called taking a year off. Many of her former classmates are choosing similar paths. They have recognized at a young age that life is not only about going after something, but also about getting there in the style to which they have become accustomed.

service, or artistic pursuits. A college education does not make a person "better" or "smarter."

Still, there are very good reasons for going to college: to experience the excitement of being part of a learning community, to gain exposure to new and exciting fields of knowledge, to prepare for a career offering fulfillment and economic security, to make lifelong friendships, and more.

CHOOSE A SCHOOL BASED ON THE QUALITY OF THE EDUCATION IT OFFERS

Try to help your child find a school that matches her style of learning. Read school catalogs carefully, and read through college directories and books that rate colleges, available at public libraries and high school guidance offices. Talk to people whom you and your child consider "educated" in the best sense of the word.

CONSIDER SIZE AND LOCATION

How far away from home does your child want to go? What sort of environment will she thrive in: a campus with access to the resources of a city; a quiet, rural setting; or a student-oriented university town?

A small liberal arts college can provide individualized attention and a chance to form relationships with faculty. A large university can offer a wide range of learning opportunities. A local community college can offer accessible and affordable options as well.

CONSIDER ALTERNATIVE SCHOOLS

"Alternative" colleges may offer individualized programs of study and experiential learning. For example, at St. John's College in Annapolis and Santa Fe, students learn by reading and discussing the great works of Western civilization. At Antioch University in Yellow Springs, Ohio, students alternate semesters of full-time study with semesters of employment, travel, or political or social work. Prescott College in Prescott, Arizona, has an environmental-wilderness focus. Friends World College in Huntington, New York, offers a multinational education infused with the traditional Quaker values of social awareness and pacifism. Investigate these and other options through a college directory.

DON'T LET COST BE A DETERRENT

There are many creative ways of financing a college education. Financial aid is available if you demonstrate need. Many merit-based scholarship opportunities are also available. Dee Garretson and Ann Braithwaite, founders of Scholarship Advantage, Inc., offer the following suggestions for pursuing scholarships:

- Encourage your children to become well-rounded, independent, and enthusiastic learners by simply cultivating their interests. This is the best way to ensure that they will appeal to scholarship organizations.

- Encourage them to take varied and challenging courses. The types of courses taken are more important to college admissions and financial aid counselors than grade-point averages.
- If your children are academically advanced, suggest that they take advanced placement (AP) courses. Students enrolled in independent study programs or schools that don't offer AP courses may still take the AP examinations. You can find out about these exams from high school guidance counselors.
- Encourage your children to participate in school clubs and extracurricular activities as a way to gain new friendships, new interests, and leadership opportunities.
- Suggest that your children get to know a few teachers and adults outside of school, who can provide invaluable insights into their careers, as well as being a source for letters of recommendation.
- Think twice about part-time jobs for your children. Although a job can provide lessons in responsibility as well as financial independence, your children's time may be better spent studying, or engaging in volunteer activities or an internship in a field of interest.

CHAPTER 22

Alternative Education

Albert Einstein—who didn't speak until he was four and who was labeled a "slow learner" in school—once said, "It is nothing short of a miracle that the modern methods of instruction have not yet entirely strangled the holy curiosity of inquiry."

Many parents would agree with Einstein. Children are all individuals, with their own patterns of development and unique styles of learning. Parents have different family values and educational goals for their children. The one-size-fits-all approach to schooling no longer works. Fortunately, there are many more options in education today than there were even ten years ago. School choice programs such as voucher systems, charter schools, and open enrollment have introduced competition and accountability into the public school system, driving all schools in a district to raise their standards in order to remain viable.

As a result, parents can choose from a wide range of alternative schools, both public and private. Your local school may offer a "school-within-a-school" program, with open classrooms and an emphasis on child-centered learning. Or, your city may boast a racially-integrated magnet middle or high school, which offers smaller classes and a special focus on the arts or science. Other schools in your area may include a progressive "free" school, a back-to-basics "Core Knowledge" school, or a Montessori or Waldorf school. Whatever your educational goals for your child, you are likely to find a school suited to his or her needs.

School Choice

In most states, school choice programs have become a reality only in the last few years. School choice means giving parents the opportunity to choose the school they send their child to, through the following programs:

CHARTER SCHOOLS

Charter schools are independently operated public schools started by educators, parents, and community leaders. Because they are free from traditional school bureaucracy and are schools of choice, they can offer innovative programs tailored to community needs.

Charter school laws are currently on the books in thirty-four states. In the twenty-six states that offer charter schools, they have been extremely popular, with 65 percent having a waiting list averaging 135 students.[1] Required by state law to be tuition free, nonsectarian, and nondiscriminatory, charter schools are judged on how well they meet the student achievement goals established by their charter. They must operate with the highest regard to equity and excellence; if they fail to deliver, they are closed.

City on a Hill—a charter high school in Chelsea, Massachusetts—requires its students to perform community service, do independent research, and attend weekly school "town meetings." At Michigan's Noah Webster Academy, over one thousand students from across the state learn at home, from state-certified teachers, via computers and toll-free telephone lines. Colorado's charter schools include academies for the arts or science and technology, schools for the gifted, and a preschool for at-risk children.

VOUCHER SYSTEM

Full school choice programs—or vouchers—give parents an education tax credit to use at the school of their choice. If parents decide not to send their child to the local public school, they are reimbursed all or a portion of the funding allotted for their child in public school, which they can use toward private school, parochial school, or in some cases, homeschooling. Offered statewide in Vermont and Maine since the 1800s, as well as in several isolated school districts around the country, voucher programs are being introduced in many more areas.

OPEN ENROLLMENT

Under open enrollment, you are not bound to send your child to your neighborhood public school, but can choose any school in the district, or cross boundaries among districts. Usually, neighborhood students have first priority, with outside students admitted by lottery. Currently, thirty states offer open enrollment in some or all parts of the state.

What Makes an "Alternative" School?

Spurred by school choice laws, the range of alternatives to mainstream education today is quite diverse, including religious and traditional, "back to basics" schools as well as child-centered progressive schools. In a more specific sense, however, the term "alternative" refers to progressive schools—those schools favored by parents who are uncomfortable with the teacher-centered, competitive, often impersonal approach of mainstream public schooling.

Although progressive alternative schools take many forms, they all share certain key characteristics. These include:

A CHILD-CENTERED APPROACH

In contrast to traditional schools—where the teacher stands in front of the class and does most of the talking—alternative schools give students an opportunity for self-directed learning. The teacher serves as a facilitator or guide, while the students work in small groups or individually. Schools and classes are small. Developmental, rather than chronological age is emphasized, with classrooms typically grouping children of multiple ages together. Often teachers remain with the same class for several years.

AN OPEN AND UNSTRUCTURED ENVIRONMENT

Rather than desks in rows, the classroom usually consists of open areas where students can work together, with "learning centers" of tools and materials grouped around the room. The curriculum is not predetermined, but is flexible, depending on student interests and ideas. Children are treated as individuals and are given a fair amount of freedom to pursue their own interests. One fundamental difference in progressive education is the belief in children's natural desire to learn, as opposed to the fear that, without structure, children will do just enough to get by.

INTERDISCIPLINARY LEARNING

Instead of dividing the day into periods devoted to the study of distinct subjects, many different subjects are integrated into comprehensive, in-depth projects. A class might devote several weeks or months to the study of early humans, incorporating reading skills in their research, mathematical and art skills in designing a timeline, and language skills in making a presentation to the rest of the school.

Alternative schools acknowledge that children have multiple ways of learning, and incorporate a variety of approaches to a topic. All aspects of a child's development—emotional, artistic, social, vocational, physical, spiritual, as well as intellectual—are honored.

A DEMOCRATIC APPROACH

Students are given a substantial voice in the running of the classroom or school. They can be involved in deciding curriculum, setting rules, even hiring staff and setting the budget.

MULTIPLE METHODS OF ASSESSMENT

Most alternative schools eschew grades and standardized testing in favor of other forms of assessment, including written reports, oral presentations, student work journals, and teacher conferences.

INDEPENDENT OPERATION

Because most alternative schools are independently operated, they are free from bureaucracy and can pursue innovative approaches to learning.

A COOPERATIVE APPROACH

Rather than individual, competitive learning, children learn from each other and from working in groups. The absence of grades or tracking systems also fosters cooperation.

A MULTICULTURAL CURRICULUM

Often multiculturalism—the study of achievements and literature by cultures other than western European—is emphasized. In communities with a large minority population, alternative schools may be bilingual.

INTEGRATION INTO THE COMMUNITY

Rather than being windowless institutions that are isolated from the community, alternative schools take advantage of the resources in the community through field trips and apprenticeships, and involve parents and community leaders in the school. Children learn from real-life activities—research and hands-on projects—in addition to textbooks.

The Influence of Progressive Education

The progressive movement has had a major influence on mainstream education. Ideas that were once thought of as radical have now found their way into many public and traditional schools. You should be aware of these progressive approaches when evaluating different schools. You can also incorporate these ideas into your child's learning at home. Here are some ways in which the progressive movement has influenced the "Three Rs":

READING: WHOLE LANGUAGE

Inspired by progressivism, schools began teaching a "whole language" rather than phonetic approach to reading in the 1980s. In the phonetic approach, students must learn the sounds of letters and the many rules and exceptions that govern the English language before they can begin sounding out words and reading. They start out with elementary "readers" and gradually progress to more challenging material.

The whole language approach lets students start with the whole and later break it down into parts. Teachers read to the class from large-print books while students follow along and begin to learn to recognize whole words by sight. Rhymes, repeated phrases, contrasting colors, and drawings form cues that help children identify words. They may learn to memorize short stories or poems and "read" them back to the teacher or each other. Although whole language used to be taught as an entirely separate approach from phonics, most schools now combine the two approaches, introducing phonics rules once children are already reading.

A new approach to reading—which is supplanting whole language in some schools—is based on teaching children to hear and manipulate the individual sounds in words, called phonemes. This approach is taught in programs like "Read Right" and "Reading Fundamentals." For more information, see Resources section for Diane McGuiness's book, *Why Our Children Can't Read and What to Do About It: A Scientific Revolution in Reading.*[2]

WRITING: INVENTED SPELLING

In the same way that the whole language approach allows children the pleasure of reading before they have mastered all the rules of the language, the "invented spelling" approach to writing encourages children to write before they learn to spell.

When our children are learning how to talk, we delight in their growing vocabulary, and we certainly don't correct every pronunciation or grammatical error they make. However, the traditional attitude in schools has been that children should not write until they know how to spell.

Children learn their letters by copying sentences from the blackboard or workbooks, practicing until their handwriting is neat and legible. They do not begin writing compositions until the upper grades, and when they do, the teacher corrects all spelling and grammatical errors before handing their work back to them.

With the invented spelling approach, a child's natural inclination to write is encouraged. Mimicking what they see their parents doing, children "write" stories, letters, poems, and shopping lists, learning through the process of writing. Thus, their writing may start out as unrecognizable letter combinations, proceeding to invented spellings, and finally to standard spelling. Their handwriting and spelling are not corrected at first, but are allowed to naturally evolve as they gain more practice with writing. They learn spelling rules later on through lessons, or often, pick them up naturally from their reading and from observing each other's work. Letting children write before they know how to spell gives them confidence in their writing ability and allows them a way to record their emotions and the important events in their lives at a young age.

MATH: A REAL-LIFE APPROACH

One criticism of traditional schooling is that it takes concepts out of the context of reality, and teaches them as abstractions. Children learn math from reading textbooks and solving problems. Fractions, geometry, and algebra, in this context, have no connection to real life.

Progressive education, on the other hand, always seeks to apply concepts to everyday life. Thus, children might learn fractions from working with recipes, or laws of averages and probability from estimating the number of jelly beans in a jar. One teacher in East Harlem takes her eighth-graders into the neighborhood to take photographs, draw maps, and notice the math inherent in everything from the geometric shapes in buildings to the number of times a day the bus stops at the corner. One very concrete way to teach math is through handling school or family finances. By preparing a budget and balancing a checkbook, children not only learn math concepts, but gain important life skills.

One of the biggest advantages of this approach is that it helps counteract the stigma that some students often feel about "not being good at" math. Children learn that anyone who finds pleasure in completing a jigsaw or crossword puzzle, cooking, taking photographs, building a bookcase, or drawing in perspective has a bent toward mathematics.

Multiple Intelligences: New Ways of Learning

The theory of multiple intelligences, outlined in Harvard School of Education professor Howard Gardner's 1983 book *Frames of the Mind*, has had a major impact on education. For the first time, using current neuropsychological and child development research, Gardner verified the idea that our concept of intelligence—as measured by IQ testing and developed in traditional schooling—is much too limited. His book outlined seven different forms of intelligence: linguistic, logical-mathematical, spatial, bodily-kinesthetic, musical, interpersonal, and intrapersonal. Of these, only the first two—linguistic and logical-mathematical—are reinforced and assessed in schools. Children who instead excel in other forms of expression, such as art, dance, music, leadership, and contemplation, are often labeled "learning disabled."[2]

Linguistic thinkers learn primarily through words; logical-mathematical thinkers learn through numbers and abstract concepts; spatial thinkers learn (as artists and engineers do) through perceptions of objects in space; bodily-kinesthetic thinkers through movement and bodily sensations; musical thinkers through sounds and rhythm; interpersonal thinkers through social interactions; and intrapersonal thinkers through introspection.

Gardner's theory was radical in that it called for more than just offering specialty classes in art, music, and physical education in schools. He recommended that schools balance their curriculum by integrating all of the intelligences, accommodating different learning styles, and basing assessments upon multiple intelligences.

Thomas Armstrong, PhD, an educator who has been instrumental in implementing the theory of multiple intelligences, proposes creating lessons so that all of the intelligences are developed. Lessons could be conducted using the spoken or written word; numbers and logic; visual aids, color, or art; singing and rhythm; hands-on experiences; group activities; and self-directed learning. Armstrong also suggests creating specific areas in the classroom to nurture each of the intelligences. For example, the classroom might include a book nook, a math/science lab, an art area, a carpeted open space for movement, a corner with musical instruments and tape recordings, a group discussion area, and a quiet loft.

While the theory of multiple intelligences has had a major influence on educational reform—inspiring numerous conferences and workshops, and influencing the curriculum at a number of public and independent schools—it actually incorporates ideas that have been used in progressive education for a long time, such as integrating subjects in in-depth projects and using multiple assessment methods. Thus, whether they label it as such or not, most alternative schools incorporate a multiple intelligences approach.

The Educational Reform Movement

Dissatisfaction with mainstream schooling began as long ago as the early 1800s, influenced by French philosopher Jean-Jacques Rousseau, who believed that human beings are innately good and that children are naturally motivated to learn. In the late nineteenth century, reformer Francis Parker began to attack the use of grades and corporal punishment as motivators and argued for creating challenging, self-directed learning environments.

In 1894, John Dewey became the director of a laboratory school launched by the University of Chicago to experiment with new approaches to learning. His ideas about meaningful learning—as opposed to rote memorization and reciting—formed the core of American progressive education in the twentieth century.

In Europe, around the same time, progressive thinkers Maria Montessori, Rudolf Steiner, and Alexander Sutherland Neill were forming schools that are still the dominant forces in alternative education in the United States today. Italian doctor Maria Montessori founded the child-centered schools that bear her name in the early 1900s. Waldorf education grew out of Austrian philosopher Rudolf Steiner's spiritual-scientific research known as anthroposophy. In the 1920s, A.S. Neill founded a democratic school called Summerhill in Suffolk, England, that inspired a number of democratic or "free" schools in America.

The social unrest of the 1960s and early '70s spawned an explosion of alternative public schools in the United States, many of which began on a shoestring budget and failed within a few years. The conservatism of the '80s produced a backlash against progressive schools and a resurgence of a back-to-basics curriculum. However, progressive ideas are still being incorporated into many mainstream public schools, and quite a few avowedly progressive schools continue. In addition to charter schools and alternative schools founded on progressive ideals, there are three distinct types of schools within the progressive movement: Montessori schools, Waldorf schools, and democratic schools.

Montessori Schools

At the core of the Montessori philosophy is founder Maria Montessori's respect for the child. Through her work with retarded and disadvantaged children, she found that children have a natural curiosity to learn and much greater powers of concentration than they are given credit for. When children are offered an opportunity for self-directed learning, she discovered, they naturally flourish.

Montessori called the years from birth to age six the peak receptivity period for a child's "absorbent mind," when children are constantly absorbing information through all of their senses. She was one of the first to recognize that children develop in stages, which she called "sensitive periods," when they are particularly capable of learning a concept. Children are in the sensitive period for learning to walk, for example, when they are willing to pick themselves up over and over again and put one foot in front of the other.

INSIDE A MONTESSORI CLASSROOM

Within a Montessori classroom, children's activities are referred to as "work." Because she felt that a child's task during childhood is to develop toward his full human potential through practicing new skills and establishing social roles and values, Montessori refused to trivialize those endeavors as "play."

The tools for Montessori's method of self-directed learning are her beautifully designed, self-correcting materials. Wooden graduated cylinders, for example, fit correctly into only one particular hole, teaching the child the concept of discriminating between sizes, without intervention from the teacher. Because Montessori understood that learning progresses from the concrete to the abstract, all of her materials are hands-on. Children learn the abstract mathematical concept of the decimal system, for example, by working with chains of beads that are marked off every tenth bead. The materials are designed to challenge children at many different levels and to build on concepts they have already mastered. Lessons are introduced simply and concretely in the early years and are reintroduced several times over the following years with increasing degrees of abstraction and complexity.

In the carefully designed environment of a Montessori classroom, all equipment is child-sized, with the materials invitingly arranged on low, open shelves. The room is divided into four distinct areas: practical life, sensorial, mathematics, and language. The practical life skills area gives young children a chance to develop everyday skills like pouring and sweeping. By mastering these activities, they are also laying the foundation for academic learning. The sequencing of steps in table-washing, for example, is left to right, preparing children for the left-to-right eye motion of reading.

Sensorial materials teach children to recognize differences and relationships in shape, size, color, temperature, weight, tone, value, texture, taste, and scent. Each sensory concept is isolated. These exercises are designed to prepare the child for reading, writing, math, geometry, art, music, and more.

Math skills are learned through counting rods, spindles, cards, and beads, progressing from manipulating objects to mental calculations. Children learn to understand the concept of "how many" because they actually hold the amount in their hands.

In the language skills area, children learn to write before they can read, building words and sentences phonetically with a wooden moveable alphabet. They learn the kinesthetic feel of the alphabet by tracing over sandpaper letters with their fingers, which teaches them the motions that they will need for writing.

Children in a Montessori classroom take responsibility for their environment. They learn to put materials away when they are finished with them and to care for the plants and animals in the classroom. They learn not to interrupt or disturb each other's work.

Grouping together children within a three-year age span allows the children to learn from each other. Each child gets to experience being the youngest in the class and to learn from observing the older children, as well as eventually taking the leadership role as the oldest in the class. Montessori teachers often witness an "explosion in learning" during the child's third year, both from the repetition of materials and the child's increasing confidence in the nurturing community of the classroom.

Teachers prepare and maintain the environment with calm and order, warmth, care, awareness, and joy. The Montessori teacher's role is that of facilitator and observer. The teacher never unnecessarily interferes or corrects. She or he presents material to the children—usually one-on-one or in small groups—and gives the children an opportunity to repeat the lesson. If the child is not yet ready for the material, it is simply put away for another time.

Children are free to choose their own materials and to work with them as long as they need to. The most striking thing about observing a Montessori classroom is the quiet and concentration evident when children as young as three are totally absorbed in what they are doing. Because each individual child sets her own learning pace, a Montessori classroom invites learning without overstimulating the child. Six-year-olds who have completed the Montessori primary program usually have been reading and writing for a few years, and have experience working with addition, subtraction, multiplication, and division. More importantly, by experiencing the pleasures of mastering skills on their own, the children establish a lifelong love of learning.

MONTESSORI METHODS WITH OLDER CHILDREN

Although Montessori's ideas are most often applied to early childhood education, she did design a curriculum and philosophy for older children. In the elementary classrooms—for children age six to ten and those ten to fourteen—children get a chance to explore increasingly abstract concepts through in-depth projects. Throughout the day, small groups of students meet with the teacher for lessons, which require follow-up such as reading more about the subject, arranging an interview with an expert, building a model, or organizing a field trip. Each child keeps a journal of the day's work, which the teacher reviews periodically.

Throughout the Montessori experience, the child develops independence, self-motivation, responsibility, and a sense of community. Older children help the younger ones academically and socially, even serving when asked as mediators in conflicts.

TYPES OF MONTESSORI SCHOOLS

Because Maria Montessori never patented her methods, Montessori schools may vary quite a bit. Sometimes her method and materials are used without incorporating her essential underlying philosophy of respect for the individual child and freedom to grow in a stimulating learning environment, leading to a criticism of some Montessori schools for being too rigid.

Another criticism of the Montessori approach is that it does not include a creative arts program or opportunity for fantasy play. There are actually two distinct factions within the Montessori philosophy. American Montessori Association (AMA) accredited schools attempt to adapt Montessori's methods to the American way of life, by incorporating toys and opportunities for creative play into the classroom. Association Montessori Inter-

nationale (AMI) certified schools adhere more strictly to Montessori's methods, which they feel have been proven to give excellent results. These schools believe that group activities and playtime interrupt the blocks of concentrated time children need to master their work.

The success of the Montessori method—evidenced in the academic achievements and self-discipline of the students—has made it extremely popular. In fact, Montessori preschools have become so accepted in the United States today that they are not even considered alternative.

Waldorf Schools

Waldorf education reflects founder Rudolf Steiner's philosophy of anthroposophy, best described as the knowledge of man. It is a diverse discipline that seeks a fuller understanding of the inner nature of the human soul and spirit and its enormously expansive potential for further development. Steiner, an astonishingly versatile scholar who edited the works of Goethe and founded the fields of bio-dynamic gardening and anthroposophical medicine, was asked by his followers in 1919 to design an educational system based upon his unique vision.

At the heart of Waldorf education is Steiner's understanding of the three major stages of development in the life of the child, occurring in seven-year cycles. During the period from birth to about age seven, the child learns through imitation and movement, which Steiner called the development of will. Around the time that the child loses his baby teeth—about age seven—he enters a stage of feeling, in which he learns through the imagination and artistic expression. Once he reaches puberty—at about age fourteen—he reaches the thinking stage, when abstract concepts and intellectual thought become his main ways of learning.

WALDORF KINDERGARTENS

Waldorf kindergartens create an environment rich in opportunities for imitation and imaginative play. Simple toys made of natural materials—such as dolls, puppets, blocks, and lengths of cloths for costumes—engage the child's imagination. Finger plays and circle games that incorporate elements of rhythm, repetition, and movement are used to inspire imitation and movement. Classic fairy tales nourish the child's inner, imaginative life. Stories are told—rather than read—to evoke their aliveness, and are often repeated for two or three weeks at a time to allow the children to enter deeply into the story's images.

Children generally do not start Waldorf kindergarten before age five or six, as Steiner felt that children are best served by being home with their mothers up to this age. He considered the period of childhood up to age seven to be sacred. Thus, play, movement, and fantasy are the most important activities in a Waldorf kindergarten. Reading, writing, and arithmetic are not introduced until the next stage, at around age seven, so as not to deprive children of the last year or two of the magical, dream-like state of childhood. This period of fantasy play is not considered frivolous; rather, a wide, rich imaginative life is considered the foundation for language skills in the next stage of development.

WALDORF ELEMENTARY SCHOOLS

In a Waldorf elementary school, imitation and movement are replaced by activities that awaken feelings. Subjects are taught through the use of images and stories, always emphasizing the subject's relationship to the human being.

Intellectual work is still not pushed on the child. Academic subjects are approached through in-depth study "blocks." Fifth-graders who study ancient Greece might learn history interwoven with legends and myths, then paint scenes from the myths, and finally make papier-mâché masks and enact a Greek play.

Arts, crafts, and music are viewed as integral elements of learning. Children make models with colored beeswax and paint with watercolors. There is a definite sequence of activities, based on the curriculum developed for the first Waldorf school: Children learn to knit in first grade, crochet in second grade, do woodcarving and metalwork in fifth grade. All children learn to sing and play an instrument, beginning with the recorder in first grade and progressing to string instruments in third grade.

Waldorf education differs from progressive education in that it is teacher-centered and structured. Steiner believed that children up to age fourteen need a symbol of authority to obey and love. Thus, Waldorf elementary teachers stay with the same class and teacher for all eight years. Teachers give a daily main lesson, following a prescribed curriculum. No textbooks are used except those the students write and draw themselves from the daily lesson.

Days have a definite pattern. The daily lesson is given in the morning, when student's intellectual capacities are the freshest. In the middle of the day the emphasis is on the rhythmical element through classes in music; foreign languages, taught through recitation of poems and stories; and Eurythmy—movement based on speech or music, developed by Steiner. The afternoon usually involves physical activity, such as noncompetitive sports or handicrafts.

WALDORF HIGH SCHOOLS

In a Waldorf high school, class teachers are replaced by specialists in each subject. At this stage, thinking and the intellect are given free rein. Although intellectual development proceeds slowly at the elementary level, by high school, Waldorf students have caught up with their peers and delve more deeply than most public school students into the humanities and sciences. Arts and crafts and music are still an important part of the curriculum. Students all play in the orchestra and sing in the choir. They learn how to weave a shawl and make a copper candlestick.

A Waldorf high school has a strong nondenominational spiritual element. The adolescents' idealism and search for meaning in life are developed through the philosophy of anthroposophy. Waldorf education demonstrates that when the soul is nurtured, academic learning occurs naturally and spontaneously.

Free Schools

In the 1920s, Alexander Sutherland Neill founded Summerhill, the first "free" school, in Suffolk, England, where it is still going strong as a primary and secondary boarding school. Summerhill

was based on Neill's vision of a school as a place where children could learn purely through interest—a place where they could have the freedom to do whatever they liked, as long as it did not endanger them or interfere with others.

Neill felt that if the emotions are free, the intellect will follow. "I'm not against learning. I'm against making learning the only thing in schools," he said.[3] He held steadfastly to Jean-Jacques Rousseau's notion that children are innately good and will pursue self-fulfillment if surrounded by an atmosphere of freedom and love.

THE SUMMERHILL EXPERIENCE

Summerhill's radical approach allows total freedom for its students. Lessons are optional—children may attend, or they may stay away. Usually, most children go to classes in the first few weeks of the school year, but only the really interested children continue. The younger ones often prefer to play.

291

Neither homework nor tests are given. Observers have noted that students at Summerhill absorb material at a much faster rate than do students at most schools—and without studying outside of the classroom. Neill maintained that the Summerhill children learn more quickly because they are emotionally free and can better concentrate on what they are doing.

Democracy is another guiding principle at Summerhill. Each adult and student at the school—down to the six- and seven-year-olds—has an equal voice. Decisions are made at a weekly meeting, in which expenditures are voted on, staff is hired, and grievances are aired.

Neill's experiment at Summerhill stimulated radical criticism of the American educational system. Neill—along with John Holt, founder of the "unschooling," or homeschooling, movement—argued that traditional schooling actually interferes with learning; that learning goes on all the time in daily life. Canadian author Frank Smith expressed this idea in a 1988 speech to educators: "...man is by nature a learning animal. Birds fly, fish swim, man thinks and learns. Therefore, we do not need to 'motivate' children into learning, by wheedling, bribing, or bullying...all we need to do is bring as much of the world as we can into the school and the classroom; give children as much help and guidance as they need and ask for; and then get out of the way. We can trust them to do the rest."

FREE SCHOOLS IN THE UNITED STATES

With the publication of Neill's book, *Summerhill: A Radical Approach to Child Rearing*, schools modeled on Summerhill began springing up in the United States.[4] By the late 1970s there were more than a thousand free schools throughout the country, most of which failed for lack of funds and a backlash against idealism in the following decades. About 350 free schools are still in operation in the United States today. They differ in specifics, but they are all guided by the principles of freedom and democracy, and they all accept any child who wants to attend, often charging very low or sliding-scale tuition. The largest of these is the Sudbury Valley School for kindgarteners through high schoolers in Framingham, Massachusetts.

At Sudbury Valley, explains one of its founders, Daniel Greenberg, children learn not because they are pushed to do so, but because they are inwardly driven to conquer the unknown, to understand. There are no textbooks, and no formal lessons are given.

Students are not "taught" to read; rather, they pick it up on their own by being read to, or by teaching themselves letter sounds. "To be honest, we do not know how they do it, and rarely can they tell us," says Greenberg. "Left to their own devices, children see for themselves that the written word is a magic key to knowledge. And they find that, compared with the task of learning how to speak, reading is a breeze." Students may not learn to read until they are age eight or ten or even twelve, but when they are ready to learn, they easily master it.

Math is grasped with the same ease, once students develop an interest in it. Greenberg describes a group of a dozen nine- to twelve-year-olds who approached him wanting passionately to learn all of the basics of arithmetic—addition, subtraction, multiplication, division, fractions, decimals, percentages, and square roots. Up to that point, they had had no formal lessons in these math fundamentals. They met twice a week, for a half-hour. At the end of twenty weeks, every student had completely mastered material that usually takes six years to learn. Elementary math specialist Alan White, hearing of this phenomenon, was not surprised. "Everyone knows that the subject matter itself isn't that hard," he commented. "What's hard is beating it into the heads of youngsters who hate every step. Give me

a kid who wants to learn the stuff—well, twenty hours or so makes sense."[5]

Graduates of Sudbury Valley who go on to college usually get into the college of their first choice, says Greenberg. Those who don't opt for college go on to careers in the arts, various trades, and business. A study of Sudbury Valley's graduates in the *American Journal of Education* concluded that they show a degree of self-confidence and self-knowledge rare in this day and age.[6] "No one who meets our older students would be able to guess the age at which they first learned to read, write, and compute," says Greenberg. "And even if someone could, why should it matter?"

Choosing a School

Each child is unique, and no one school is right for everyone. You may find that the school your neighbors love for their child is not one you would even consider for yours. The important thing is to think about what learning environment is best suited to your child's personality and to make sure that the school you send your child to will serve her needs.

How does your child learn? Does she need structure, or does she thrive in a more open environment? Does she do well with competition, or is she more motivated by a cooperative approach? Also take into account your own values. Do you believe in a back-to-basics educational curriculum, or do you believe the arts are an integral part of education? Do you want your child to be exposed to the great works of Western civilization, or do you favor a more multicultural approach?

Once you have thought about what kind of school is best suited to your child, you are ready to begin the process of looking into all the options. In his excellent book, *The Parents' Guide to Alternatives in Education*, Ronald E. Koetzch, PhD, gives a comprehensive overview of all types of alternative schools. To locate all of the schools in your area, look in the phone book under Education and Schools,[7] and get a copy of *The Almanac of Educational Choice*, which lists schools around the country (see Resources). Once you have pinpointed a few schools, you can take the following steps with each one:

VISIT THE SCHOOL

Go when school is in session, so you can observe both the physical environment and the students. Visit the playground, library, gym, and cafeteria. Do they feel cheerful and inviting? Are the facilities up-to-date and well-maintained? Is students' work displayed? What are interactions between students like? Do children generally seem happy and well-adjusted, or restless and anxious?

OBSERVE CLASSES

Sit in on all the classes at the grade level your child will attend. How do the teacher and students interact? How large are the classes? What kinds of work is going on? Do the students seem involved and stimulated? Notice how the classroom operates: Do students work independently or in groups? Is there time for discussion, or does the teacher do most of the talking? Are children free to move about, or do they stay at their desks most of the time?

TALK TO THE PRINCIPAL

The principal sets the tone for the school. Set up an interview with the principal to get a feel for the school's philosophy. These are some questions you might want to ask:

- Do you follow a standard curriculum?
- Are subjects integrated, or is the day broken up into separate subjects?
- How are teachers chosen?
- When do children start getting homework? How much?
- How are children tested, graded, or assessed? How does the school compare to other schools in the state in terms of student test scores?
- How and when are reading and writing taught?
- How much time is spent on art? music? physical education?
- What method of discipline is used?
- How much interaction is there between the school and the community?
- How are parents involved in the school?

TALK TO THE TEACHERS

Arrange a time to talk to your child's prospective teachers. A confident, knowledgeable teacher should welcome questions from parents. Remember, you are actually interviewing teachers for a job—that of teaching your child. Here are some ideas of questions to start with:

- What do you like about teaching at this school?
- What don't you like?
- How do you believe children learn best?
- How do you handle discipline problems?
- What reading, math, language, science, etc., program do you use?
- How do you deal with children who fall behind? Children who are ahead of their classmates?
- Do you keep in touch with any former students?
- What are your outside interests? A challenging, stimulating teacher will probably have a variety of interests.

TALK TO PARENTS

Talk to other parents about the perceived strengths and weaknesses of a school, but keep in mind that a school that may be right for one child may not be right for yours. You may also want to get the names of parents who took their children out of the school, to find out why they left.

Well-known educator Herbert Kohl, author of Growing Minds, says that at minimum, a decent learning situation should:[8]

- Respect the arts as essential to life, treat science and mathematics as arts, and nurture all of these areas in classical and experimental ways.
- Help young people learn to analyze events in the world (both near home and far away) and to speak intelligently about their opinions.
- Introduce the magic of literature, focus on a work's content, and be sensitive to the author's intent.
- Help children learn to accept criticism offered in the spirit of love and to offer criticism in the same way.
- Help young people feel solidarity with all of the people, animals, and plants on earth and

be willing to act on this feeling.
- Make it possible for young people to know adults who live the beliefs they teach, no matter how imperfectly.
- Create a writing environment in which the writer is not afraid to express his or her ideas, opinions, and feelings.
- Eliminate all grading and testing procedures that do not help children know how to learn what they want to learn.
- Respect classical learning and children's creativity, bouncing them off each other.
- Abandon the notion that some students are "better" than others.

CHAPTER 23 # Homeschooling

More than a place of schooling, homeschooling is a philosophy of learning. Education reformer John Holt—founder of the contemporary homeschooling movement—outlined this philosophy in his landmark book, *How Children Learn*: "Children learn out of interest and curiosity, not to please the adults in power....They should be in control of their own learning, deciding for themselves what they want to learn and how they want to learn it."[1]

This belief in natural learning guides many progressive alternative schools; however, homeschoolers take the idea of freedom in education one step further. Homeschoolers who are followers of Holt's philosophy don't see themselves as their children's teachers—instead, they give their children the freedom to teach themselves. Rather than viewing education as a particular body of knowledge that a child must acquire, they think of learning as a lifelong, ongoing process whose emphasis should be determined by a person's interests. Children learn without schooling until they are age five, and again after they are eighteen or twenty-two, homeschoolers reason, so why do they need schooling to learn in between those years?

Whether you choose homeschooling or formalized schooling, your involvement in your children's education is essential. Even if you have no interest in homeschooling, you can use the ideas and resources in this chapter at home to supplement your child's learning.

The Growth of Homeschooling

Although the number of children who are homeschooled in the United States has tripled in the last few years, homeschooling is not a new movement. In the early days of America—as in all cultures throughout history—the only kind of schooling was homeschooling.

With the creation of universal schooling in the mid-1800s, however, the responsibility for education shifted to the state. Public schools had the final decision in what and how children learned. Children who were kept home from school were considered truants.

Criticism of public schools—spurred by the idealism of the 1960s—led to an explosion of alternative schools. By the 1970s, many of these schools were mired in internal politics and power struggles, and most failed.

Disillusioned with the failure of the alternative school movement, Holt put forth the idea of "unschooling" in the late-1960s, with the publication of his book, *How Children Learn*, and a newsletter, *Growing Without Schooling*. He argued that education was simpler than schools made it seem, that children learn all the time from the world around them. Holt felt that schools, by their nature, discourage real learning. True education, he argued, occurs only when individuals are motivated to learn for themselves.

Today, between 1 million and 1.6 million children are homeschooled in the United States,

according to the National Home Education Research Institute. The majority of those are fundamentalist Christians, who initiated a homeschooling movement in the 1980s because they did not want their children to be exposed to morals and teachings that they disagreed with by attending public school. About 200,000 to 350,000 homeschoolers, however, are inheritors of Holt's philosophy that education occurs naturally, and that home is the best base for learning. These alternative homeschoolers are not so much against public schools as they are in favor of learning at home. As interest resurges in birthing babies at home and in working from home, it makes sense that parents also consider schooling at home.

Reasons for Homeschooling

Some homeschooling families live in rural areas where good schools are not available close by.

Others are not satisfied with either their public or alternative school options, or they cannot afford private school. Others simply feel that their children will learn best at home. Here are some of the common reasons that families choose the Holt style of homeschooling:

IT EMPHASIZES "NATURAL" LEARNING

According to "unschoolers," the traditional school system makes it seem as if learning can take place only within the confines of a school, Monday through Friday, nine months of the year. Homeschoolers believe that learning is a dynamic process that cannot be contained in a room or a book. When children are taught to think of home as their base for learning and the world as their classroom, they are motivated to learn year round, from a rich variety of sources.

Instead of artificially separating subjects into different periods throughout the day, homeschooling allows children to get a truly interdisciplinary education, from real-life experiences. At the same time, it permits parents to continue their own lifelong pursuit of knowledge, as they learn alongside their children.

IT ALLOWS CHILDREN TO LEARN AT THEIR OWN PACE

For parents who have trusted their children to wean themselves and to sleep through the night when they were ready, allowing their children to learn to read, write, and compute at their own pace makes sense. A homeschooled child has no grade-level expectations to keep up with, and no remedial classes to take if he "falls behind"; similarly, he is not held back from forging ahead in subjects he is interested in. His pace of learning is determined only by his desire and readiness.

IT OFFERS INDIVIDUALIZED ATTENTION

To give each student much individualized attention is almost impossible for a teacher with a class of twenty or thirty children. Most education experts agree that there is no substitute for one-on-one teaching, which is exactly what homeschooled children get all the time.

Parents sometimes wonder how they will have time to teach their children six hours a day. John

Holt's response to this concern was, "Who is teaching your kids six hours a day? I was a good student in supposedly the best schools, and it was a rare day that I got five minutes of teaching ... of somebody's serious attention to my personal needs, interests, or concerns."[2]

IT OFFERS FLEXIBILITY

Parents who homeschool can respond to their children's needs in a way that schoolteachers cannot. If a child is feeling introspective, she can do some quiet work; if she is full of energy, she can tackle a big project. The parent-teacher can tailor the material, the approach, and the pace to the child's needs. For a schoolteacher to be that flexible or sensitive to each of her students is difficult.

Families who homeschool can also travel whenever they want to, simply continuing their learning wherever they are.

IT STRENGTHENS THE FAMILY BOND

Homeschooling families get to experience being together much of the time, much like families in traditional cultures, or in the days before public schooling. Children are exposed to their parents' values, rather than their peers' values. Homeschooling parents recognize that children will leave the security of their home for the outside world at some point, but many of them would rather not have that passage happen at a young, impressionable age.

Many homeschooling parents are also concerned about their children being separated from them at a young age. Some parents homeschool in the early years for this reason, and send their children to school later.

Homeschooling Concerns

In the early 1970s, parents had to fight an uphill battle to homeschool. Neighbors reported them to the authorities, relatives were aghast, and school officials took them to court for negligence and child abuse.

Today, homeschooling is much more widely accepted. Approximately six percent of parents homeschool, according to a March, 1997, *Wall Street Journal*/NBC News poll. Homeschooling is legal in all fifty states. Hundreds of packaged curriculum programs are available to homeschooling parents, and many accredited independent study schools offer high school diplomas. The Internet has begun to blur the line between school-based and home-based education, by bringing school into the home.

Here are answers to some common concerns parents have about homeschooling, from Patrick Farenga, president of Holt Associates, Inc., which publishes *Growing Without Schooling* magazine and offers homeschooling materials and support:

IS IT LEGAL?

The right of parents to homeschool their children was first established in 1974 in a New Mexico Supreme Court case. By the late 1980s, homeschooling was legal in all fifty states. Each state has its own regulations regarding homeschooling. Some states require parents to submit a plan to the local school district; some states require filing with the State Department of Education. In other states, parents can register their home as a private school.

The best source for current information about laws and regulations is the homeschooling support group in your state. For a state-by-state listing of homeschooling organizations, contact Holt Associates; for legal concerns, contact the Home School Legal Defense Association (see Resources).

WILL MY CHILDREN GET ENOUGH SOCIALIZATION?

Many parents worry that their children will not have a normal social life if they are homeschooled. The issue hinges on how you define "normal." Homeschooling advocates argue that a family unit is a much more normal social group than thirty children of the same age in a classroom with one adult. As Holt pointed out, human beings tend to behave worse in large groups. As a result, children in school learn to be cliquish, conformist, bullying, and teasing. Human virtues like kindness, patience, and generosity are best learned in intimate relationships, such as those within the family.

Studies have shown that homeschooled children are as well socialized as their public school peers, and have a more positive self-image.[3,4] According to family psychologist Urie Bronfenbrenner of Cornell University, children up to age ten or twelve are better socialized at home, by their parents, rather than by other children. The more children in a group, says Bronfenbrenner, the fewer meaningful contacts each one has. Educational researcher Raymond Moore adds that children who interact more with parents than peers are more often thinkers rather than mere parrots of other children's thoughts. Independent and self-directed in their acquisition of values and skills, they largely avoid peer dependency.

Children can have a full social life without school. They can join local scouting groups, take after-school drama, music, or sports classes, play on community sports teams, join clubs, meet with friends in the neighborhood, and get together with other homeschoolers. Some public schools let homeschoolers play on school teams or participate in other school activities. Homeschoolers also have a chance to form meaningful relationships with adults in the community, through volunteering and internships.

Some might argue that attending public school gives children a chance to mix with children of other races and socioeconomic classes. Homeschooling proponents counter that, in reality, little mingling between children of different backgrounds takes place in schools. As Farenga says, "Compulsory schooling's regimen of competition among students for status and standing, pitting child against child...actually creates social inequality. Let's minimize our thinking of schools as engines of racial harmony, and instead think of supporting families and building local communities that are racially tolerant."

WHAT IF I DON'T HAVE TEACHING EXPERIENCE?
You are not required to be a certified teacher to homeschool your children. Most private schools don't require their teachers to be state certified—instead, they hire teachers who are knowledgeable in their subject areas. John Holt argued that an education background is actually a disadvantage in homeschooling, because he felt that the teaching approaches taught in education classes are wrong.

As for teaching experience, you have been teaching your child her whole life. No one knows how your child learns best or what motivates her better than you do. You don't need to be an expert in every subject in order to teach your child. You can learn alongside her, and help direct her research efforts. When she develops an interest in a subject you know nothing about, you can steer her toward the Internet and the public library, take her on field trips, and help arrange meetings and even internships or apprenticeships with people who are experts in that area.

HOW CAN I AFFORD THE TIME TO TEACH MY CHILDREN?
You needn't teach your children for six hours a day. Because they are getting individual attention, they will probably learn more in much less time than children in public school.

One of the best things about homeschooling is that it can be a very self-motivated, self-directed process. Many homeschooling parents start out spending a lot of time with their children each day, but find as their children get older that they don't need as much structured attention. Sometimes parents want to spend a lot of time with their children just because they enjoy it. But most parents find that their children can work very well independently, occasionally checking in for guidance or suggestions.

Some parents worry about giving up a career to homeschool. Homeschooling usually does require that one parent—often the mother—stay home to teach the children. But staying home doesn't necessarily mean giving up a second income; it is possible to work part-time from home while homeschooling, especially as children get older and more self-reliant.. Two-income families who work outside of the home have found ways to homeschool by working split shifts. Single parents also have homeschooled successfully, by working from home. Families who run a home-based business, such as a farm, can involve their children in helping out and in learning to run the family business as part of their homeschooling education.

HOW DO HOMESCHOOLERS COMPARE IN TERMS OF ACADEMIC ACHIEVEMENT?

A study published in 1997 by the National Home Education Research Institute (NHERI) found that homeschoolers score in the 80th to 87th percentile on national achievement exams—thirty points higher, on average, than children in public school.

Because their learning is directed by their interests and is based on real life experiences more than lectures and textbooks, homeschoolers can usually absorb material quickly and retain it better than students in public school. Even though homeschoolers who learn at their own pace may learn to read and do math later than students in public school, they usually catch up quickly, and soon surpass their public school peers.

Homeschooling Day by Day

The only typical thing about homeschooling is that there is no typical day. Flexibility is one of the main advantages of homeschooling. Rather than running their home like a school, most homeschoolers prefer to let their child's interests dictate the schedule.

Some families like to spend at least a little time each day on structured academic work. Others find that this becomes unnecessary as children get older and more self-directed in their work habits. Generally, a large part of the day is devoted to independent work, such as reading, writing, completing assignments, doing an art project, building something, or practicing music. Most homeschoolers also take full advantage of community resources, going on field trips each

Louise

After examining my children's home-study program, the local school superintendent said, "These are all things any interested parent would do with their children in addition to school."

There's the catch. How many of those enriching activities can actually be offered to children when they are in school all day? There simply is not enough time. When I first began homeschooling Heidi and Michael after a few years in the local public school, they hounded me with a long list of activities they wanted to do at home that we had never had time for previously because so much of their lives was taken up with school and extracurricular activities. The first thing they insisted I teach them was how to use the sewing machine, a skill which they have developed steadily from that point. Yet when they were going to school there simply was not time for it.

Louise Andrieshyn, "A Homeschooling Solution," *Mothering,* Summer 1980.

Candace

I keep a teacher's plan book (bought from the stationery store) for each child, with categories labeled "Reading/Language Arts," "Math/Logical Thinking," "Physical/Natural Science," "Social Studies (History/Sociology/Anthropology/Geography)," "Music/Art/Drama," "Physical Education/Health/Social Activities," and "Consumer/Practical Education." At the end of each day, I record whatever we've done—field trips, reading, discussions, cooking, etc.—under the appropriate category. At the end of each semester, I fill out an evaluation. Not only is all this nice and official; it is an interesting record of our activities to have. When I read old record books of our homeschooling, they always inspire me—a real boost on down days.

Candace Syman-Degler, "Our Home School," *Mothering,* Spring 1984.

week to museums, the library, parks, or aquariums, or visiting local artists or craftspeople. Homeschoolers also usually spend some time each week on outside activities such as 4-H clubs; music, art, or sports classes; book discussion groups; and volunteer or paid jobs.

One unique advantage of homeschooling is that it provides an opportunity to learn from real life. Children can learn to write from writing letters, poems, or articles for the local newspaper. They can learn to read from being read to and being exposed to great books. They can learn math from measuring ingredients for cooking and handling money; history, from talking to older people.

Homeschooling Tools

You don't need to buy a lot of expensive materials for homeschooling—in fact, you should not have to spend any more money than you would normally on your child's interests. Homeschoolers can take advantage of the library and used book

stores. Local homeschooling support groups may also barter or lend materials. Here are some of the tools that homeschoolers find valuable.

CURRICULA

Some homeschooling families feel more comfortable starting out with a packaged curriculum from a correspondence school. For curriculum sources, contact Holt Associates (see Resources).

Other homeschoolers prefer to stay away from the "school at home" approach. Just as in alternative schools, which often don't use a set curriculum, they let their children's interests guide their learning.

Parents who want to have an idea of what students are expected to learn in each grade may be able to get a copy of their public school's curriculum, or they can consult the Typical Course of Study, K-12 pamphlet (see Resources).

Textbooks and workbooks are available through textbook supply companies as well as school supply stores and local public school book depositories—ask your public school administration office or local homeschooling group where to find these. Sometimes schools give away old books. In addition, universities often have resource libraries for teachers, where individual books and teaching aids can be checked out.

However, don't feel that you must work from textbooks or educational materials. One of the biggest advantages of homeschooling is being able to learn from the world around you.

BOOKS

The public library is probably the most important resource for homeschoolers. Once your child has developed a love of books and an interest in a subject, his capacity for knowledge is limitless. Introduce your child to the world's great writers, and let them be his teachers.

David Colfax, whose homeschooled sons went on to Harvard, suggests that homeschooling parents set up a reference library consisting of a good encyclopedia set, a dictionary, world atlas, current almanac, book of world records, Bartlett's Familiar Quotations, thesaurus, and reference volumes on sports, art, or music, depending on your child's interests.

COMPUTERS

A computer can greatly enhance a homeschooling education. Children can learn from educational CD-ROMs, do research on the Internet, and connect to other students and classrooms around the country and the world. According to the National Home Education Research Institute, homeschoolers own computers at a higher rate than other American families; at least 86 percent of homeschoolers own a computer, which they use to teach their children.

Nancy

Ishmael learned to write neatly by copying his favorite poems into his handwriting notebook, and we taught him spelling by playing Scrabble. We thought that science and social studies textbooks were useless for the most part—since they were so arid and boring—so we relied mostly on books from the library and magazines like National Geographic. But language and math textbooks came in handy.

Nancy Wallace, "Homeschooling's Unique Structure," *Mothering,* Summer 1985.

ART SUPPLIES

Quality art supplies will give your child an outlet for creativity and self-expression. For suggestions on materials to buy, see Chapter 20. If your child develops a strong interest in art, you can enroll her in community art classes, or arrange lessons with a local artist.

APPRENTICESHIPS

Apprenticeships can broaden a homeschooler's horizons and give her an opportunity to pursue an interest and investigate future career options. Penny Barker arranged for her homeschooled daughter Britt to travel across Canada at age sixteen for eight weeks with a Canadian nature writer and her field biologist husband, as they gathered material for a book they were writing. Britt also worked in the layout department and wrote a weekly puzzle column for the local newspaper, sold articles to *The Mother Earth News*, and waitressed and played piano in a local inn.

Homeschoolers have pursued apprenticeships with architects and auto technicians, artists and musicians, sheep farmers and restaurant chefs. Barker suggests that you make a point of keeping track of people you meet who are dedicated to their work or a hobby, and who might share their interest or skill with a homeschooled child.

The First Day of School at Fourteen

Some families homeschool in the early years, but send their children to junior high or high school to enable them to engage in social life with their peers and to prepare them for college. At first, these homeschoolers may experience culture shock as they adjust to being in a classroom with many other students, following the class curriculum rather than their own interests, and not having the freedom to come and go as they please. Most, however, adjust readily after the first few months and find that their homeschooling background serves them well in school.

Homeschooling for Teens

For the same reasons that they chose it in the first place when their children reached school age,

Peggy

My eldest daughter began high school after eight years of home schooling. She had learned easily at home and had been presented with a diversity of material. She passed a test to enter a private school and was advised to take math in summer school to prepare for the first year.

Those initial few months required intense adjustment. She was adjusting not only to the challenging new subject matter, but also to the realities of test taking, the sometimes puzzling school procedures, and a newly school-centered social life. However, after this adjustment period, school became manageable. By the end of the year, she had received high honors, doing particularly well in math.

My eldest son entered a public junior high school at the beginning of eighth grade, after attending a Waldorf school for a few months at the end of seventh grade. Even more than his sister, he was eager for the social life that school represented to him. He had more catching up to do in his subjects, but he, too, surprised me by how quickly he did this. The adjustment to the frenetic school social scene was as difficult as the adjustment to the academics. But then, for both children, the "first day of school" came a lot later than for most.

some families choose to continue homeschooling throughout the teenage years. Homeschooling families with teens may continue to follow a laissez-faire, "unschooling" approach, letting their teenager work independently and pursue his own interests. Many homeschooled teens who followed this approach have been able to get into the college of their choice. Other homeschooled teens for whom college is not important have gone on to careers in the arts or other trades.

Some families, on the other hand, prefer a more structured approach in the high school years, to ensure that their child is covering all of the required subject areas, and to create a "paper trail" to use on college applications. Some homeschoolers are eager in their teenage years to work with teachers other than their parents, and to

find out how they measure up with other students in terms of grades.

For homeschoolers wanting more structure and objectivity, independent study programs are available nationwide, allowing students to work within a prescribed curriculum, be in contact with teachers, receive an official high school transcript, and earn a high school diploma from an accredited school. Clonlara Home Based Education Program and the American School are two of the better known of these programs. Some local public schools will also allow a homeschooled student to follow the school curriculum, participate in extracurricular activities, and receive grades and a diploma.

For a complete list of homestudy schools nationwide, contact Cafi Cohen, author of *And What About College: How Homeschooling Leads to Admissions to the Best Colleges and Universities* (see Resources).[5]

Getting into College

Although most colleges and universities ask for high school transcripts or a diploma in their applications, homeschoolers have been successful at getting into college without either. Most colleges require homeschoolers to take the Scholastic Aptitude Test (SAT) or American College Test (ACT) for admission.

If a student does reasonably well on standardized tests and can demonstrate a well-rounded course of study and self-directed learning, he is a good candidate for college. Often, the larger, more prestigious universities have more liberal admissions requirements than smaller schools. Stanford University, for example, accepts several homeschoolers each year, and admissions officers say they are more interested in "intellectual vitality" than in grades or a prescribed curriculum.

Judy Gelner, author of *College Admissions: A Guide for Homeschoolers,* helped her son Kendall work his way through the college admissions process without a high school diploma, transcript, or other objective measurements. The Gelners' homeschooling approach was very unstructured, so they had no grades or standard coursework to show on college applications. Instead, they provided simple, direct descriptions of their home-schooling experience. They created a transcript, describing Kendall's learning so it would fit into the framework of typical admissions requirements. Kendall's mother wrote his counselor recommendation, and the coach of a sports team he played on wrote the required teacher recommendation. Kendall was admitted to all the colleges he applied to, and attended Rice University. He also applied for and received a considerable amount of financial aid.

Cafi Cohen suggests that homeschoolers create a portfolio of documentation for college applications, including such things as:

- award certificates
- letters of recommendation
- correspondence school transcripts
- programs from arts or musical performances or sports competitions
- sports team practice schedules
- church youth group activity calendars
- standardized test scores.

An Emphasis on Learning

Instead of the question "What school do you go to?" homeschooling puts the focus on "What did you learn today?" The success of homeschooling reminds us that every experience carries its lesson and that the world is our teacher.

PART 7

When
Bad Things
Happen

CHAPTER 24 Handling Divorce

Divorce is always a tragedy when there are children involved. But it is not necessarily a failure. We may think of divorce as an act of running away, of taking the easy way out. However, divorce may actually be an act of great courage when it has as its motivation the continued growth and health of the family.

The act of divorce changes many lives irrevocably. Divorce is painful, embarrassing, depressing, exhausting, and expensive. It is difficult to believe that anyone would choose divorce unless she or he were severely oppressed emotionally, psychologically, physically, or spiritually.

Now that women have access to birth control and economic independence, we do not have to marry for money, property, status, or to legitimize children. For the first time, we are taking a hard look at what makes a good marriage, and what honest communication between men and women is all about. For the first time, we are realizing that a marriage vow does not simply take care of itself, and that a relationship with others is not possible without a relationship with oneself. Rather than being aghast that so many marriages are ending, we might look in awe at how many are surviving or beginning anew.

Both people in a marriage are equally responsible for what happens in that marriage, even though one may look like the "bad guy," or be the first to call the alarm. Making a divorce someone's fault implies that it could have been avoided. In most cases of divorce, the break is sadly unavoidable.

The good communication essential to a healthy marriage takes effort. We can try to learn new ways to express negative emotions, or to respond to criticism. Sometimes learning new communication skills can save a marriage. Sometimes, however, two people are simply incompatible. We can be compatible with someone at one time in our lives, and not at others. Some of us divorce because, ironically, marriage has given us the comfort to discover our true selves and to realize that our new self is no longer happy in the marriage.

Becoming a parent may change a marriage. We may immerse ourselves in mothering and forget ourselves as women. In the joy of parenting, we must remind ourselves that all of our intimate relationships deserve our attention, and that having parents who love each other and are committed to their marriage is one of the best gifts we can give our children.

At some point, however, we may find ourselves questioning whether commitment to marriage precludes all other commitments; we may wonder how we can balance commitment to ourselves and our children with our obligation to our marriage. These questions never have easy answers.

The real tragedy in divorce happens when parents cannot get past their anger and hostility to salvage the *family* for the children, even if the marriage cannot survive. After the marriage ends, the couple can either continue their suffering into a bitter postdivorce relationship, or they can choose to relate in a new way. For the sake of the children, they can transcend the loss of the marriage and let it go.

Families who are able to recover from the pain and disappointment of divorce can indeed be healthy and happy families again—in fact, can even be healthier families. Acknowledging this possibility isn't an endorsement of divorce. But children may be less harmed by a "good" divorce than by a bad marriage. For, when love dies in a marriage and cannot be revived, staying together without love does not teach joy—it teaches hardship, disappointment, and withdrawal. This pretense of love does not give children a true model of a loving relationship to aspire to—and that may be a greater tragedy than divorce.

More and more divorced parents today are learning to tolerate each other's personal limitations and to develop a coparenting relationship that is cooperative, though no longer intimate. They consult with each other on child-related matters and attend the same school functions. Their children don't feel that they are from a "broken home"—they may live in two homes, but neither of them is broken. Children can recover from a divorce if they are kept informed, have free access to both parents, and do not feel abandoned.

Here are some things you can do to reassure your children as you are going through a separation or divorce:

- Make sure your children know that both parents love them. Children want and need both their parents.
- Reassure them that they will continue to have a relationship with both parents. They need to know that you are divorcing each other—not them.
- Make sure they understand that they are not the cause of the divorce. Young children may feel guilty about a divorce and blame themselves, while adolescents tend to blame their parents.
- Make it clear that the divorce is final.
- Don't make light of the situation—while divorce may not compare with the death of a parent, it is the death of the family that the children have known.
- Help them talk about painful feelings.

Liz

After trying to weave together two disparate parenting styles, my husband and I finally got divorced. Professional counseling only highlighted our differences and left me wondering how we had managed to stay together for twelve years. My five-year-old stopped wetting his bed the week his dad moved out; and my nine-year-old is now getting A's and B's on her report card. Empirical evidence shows that divorce has not been bad for these children.

They see their father on Sundays. He lavishes more attention on them than he ever did while feeling trapped here. I believe our divorce has saved not only his relationship with them, but theirs with him and mine with myself.

Liz Lo Cicero, "Letters," *Mothering,* Spring 1992.

Children and Divorce

Divorce may not be as harmful to children as we once thought. Ironically, the generation that coined the terms "dysfunctional family" and "inner child" is the generation whose parents "stayed together for the children." A troubled marriage may have as much impact on children as a marriage breakup.

Recent studies support this conclusion. In analyzing data from large-scale longitudinal studies of children of divorce, Johns Hopkins University sociologist Andrew J. Cherlin, PhD, found that problems stem as much from family conflict *before* a divorce as from the divorce itself. He concluded, "At least as much attention needs to be paid to the processes that occur in troubled, intact families as to the trauma that children suffer after their parents separate.[1]

"In general," adds Cherlin, "kids are hurt by family conflict whether parents are married or not. In the most troubled families, some children may [even] benefit from a divorce, but this only applies to the most extreme cases."[2]

There is also no reason to believe that children of divorce are destined for unhappy marriages themselves. Pamela S. Webster and colleagues at the University of Michigan's Institute for Social Research found that 43 percent of married children of divorce termed their marriages "very happy" and "were no more likely to think they will get divorced in the future than equally happily married children of two-parent families."[3]

Keeping Children Out of the Middle

Although divorce may not be as damaging to children as once thought, we're not saying that chil-

dren emerge from a divorce unscarred. No one wins in a troubled marriage or a bitter divorce—least of all the children.

Despite any hurt or anger you feel, remember that your ex-spouse is still your child's parent—the other most important person in your child's life. When you slander each other in front of your children, they are left reeling, wondering which one of you is the good guy and which is the bad guy; who is telling the truth and who is lying.

The challenge is to talk about the other parent in ways that are compassionate, healing, and also

truthful, says Shoshana Alexander, author of *In Praise of Single Parents: Mothers and Fathers Embracing the Challenge.* We must learn ways to honor our children's other parent while honoring and healing our own pain.

The general rule, says Alexander, is to remain positive. Say nice things about your ex-spouse, and don't let your own emotions get in the way of your child's relationship with her other parent.

The "talk nice" rule becomes difficult, however, when an ex-spouse is truly destructive or dangerous. In this case, you are put in an ethical bind: How do you acknowledge the other parent's harmful behavior in a way that does not cause your children to feel torn or somehow tainted?

The only thing you can do in this case, offers Alexander, is to tell the truth compassionately. Giving your children a deceptively one-dimensional portrait of their other parent tends only to heighten their confusion. If you speak only about your ex's good points—especially if you were the one who left the marriage—your child may question why you left in the first place, and even wonder whether you could do the same thing to her. By acknowledging some of your resentment about your ex-spouse, you may give your child a chance to discuss her feelings; perhaps she may admit how her other parent hurt her as well. Telling the truth allows your children to move on with their lives.

Here are some suggestions for keeping your children out of the middle of your disputes with your ex.

DON'T USE THE CHILDREN AS A PAWN
What went wrong in your marriage is between you and your ex-spouse. No child is ever responsible for an adult's problems.

DON'T SPEAK BADLY OF THE OTHER PARENT IN FRONT OF THE CHILDREN
Never denigrate your ex-spouse to your children unless you feel you must to protect their safety or to give them a clear picture of what went wrong in the marriage. If you do decide to speak to your children critically and honestly about

your ex-spouse, wait until they are old enough to handle it—at least seven or eight—and pick a time when you are calm enough to discuss it rationally.

DON'T USE THE CHILD AS A MESSENGER
Find ways to communicate parent-to-parent. Don't ask the child for information about the other parent; if you want to know something, ask the parent directly.

DON'T PROJECT YOUR EX-SPOUSE ONTO YOUR CHILD
If your child reminds you of your ex, be cautious of critical comments like, "You're just like your father," which may cause your child to fear that you will someday reject him. Instead, try to recognize the positive qualities in your child that remind you of why you might have fallen in love with his parent in the first place.

DON'T TRY TO PREVENT YOUR CHILD FROM SEEING HER OTHER PARENT
There is no reason to keep your child apart from her other parent unless you genuinely fear for her safety. If your child is never given an opportunity to know her parent, she may imagine that parent to be much worse—or better—than he or she really is. Children are more securely attached when they have a relationship with both their parents. Promoting your child's bond with her other parent—even if doing so is difficult for you—is in your child's best interests.

The Custody Battle

Judges hate custody cases. "Of all the grim things we deal with, nothing is sadder than two adults tearing apart the child who loves them best in the world," says The Honorable Sara P. Schechter, a family court judge for the state of New York and author of a book on family law.[4]

Fortunately, most custody and visitation cases are settled before trial by parents who would rather decide their child's future together than leave the decision to a stranger in a black robe. Settling custody and visitation issues is not easy—but it is vastly preferable to the alternative. "You would run into a burning building to save your child," offers Schechter, "and avoiding custody litigation will prevent at least as many scars."

Consider using a mediator—a professionally trained, neutral third party who can help you negotiate a fair settlement. Mediation is much less costly than going to court, and, more importantly, does not drag your children into the battle.

Divorce mediation exists in nearly all fifty states as a voluntary process. Several states require mediation before courts will hear a custody or visitation case. To find a qualified mediator, get a referral from a good family law attorney, therapist, or friend, or use the national referral service at the Academy of Family Mediators (see Resources).

There are, however, some things you should never sacrifice while negotiating. "Never bargain away adequate child support, which every child has as much a right to as he does to two loving parents," cautions Schechter. "And never compromise your child's safety or your own."

Unfortunately, no matter how hard you try, some cases cannot be settled. If the case does go to trial, no matter how much you try to shield your children from the proceedings, they will be in the thick of it. Schechter offers the following suggestions for helping your children get through a custody battle:

DON'T BURDEN YOUR CHILDREN WITH SECRETS
Young children will be incapable of keeping a secret, and older children will have difficulty balancing their loyalties between battling parents. Usually, children will give in to whichever adult is questioning them at the moment, then feel frightened and guilty afterward.

DON'T TRY TO COACH YOUR CHILDREN FOR ANY OF THE INTERVIEWS THEY WILL UNDERGO
Judges are experts at detecting signs of coaching. Young children will reveal promises or bribes you made to them; with older children, it will be obvious if they have been given a script to recite.

DON'T CRITICIZE YOUR SPOUSE IN FRONT OF YOUR CHILD
Not only is this harmful for all the reasons mentioned above, it can also be counterproductive. The child may become defensive about his other parent, and hide his own fears or negative feelings about the parent during an interview.

NEVER ASK YOUR CHILDREN TO CHOOSE WHICH PARENT THEY WANT TO LIVE WITH
Which of your children would you give up? That is a question you cannot answer, and neither can your children decide which parent to sacrifice. Reassure them that, no matter what happens, both parents will continue to love them and be part of their lives.

In the Best Interests of the Child

Theoretically, parents stand on equal footing in a custody case. In the past, this was not always true. Mothers used to be considered more fit to care for young children. Today, however, the courts are recognizing that children need both parents, and, in some cases, that the father is the better guardian.

When both parents remain actively involved in their children's lives, children end up much better adjusted. Although 90 percent of children of divorce end up living with their mothers, the trend toward joint legal custody is growing.

Joint physical custody is another thing, however. True joint custody implies that a child will spend 50 percent of the time with each parent, alternating days or weeks or months. This kind of arrangement is difficult on a child, at best.

Attempting to split a child down the middle this way raises moral questions, says Nancy Black, PhD, a clinical psychologist specializing in family therapy, and marriage and divorce counseling. Is this kind of arrangement in the best interests of the child, or is it based on the parents' desires? Do we own our children? Can we treat them as possessions to be divided fairly in a divorce—or have they simply been given over into our custody during the temporary period of their childhood for us to nurture and guide?

WHEN BAD THINGS HAPPEN

A more flexible, child-centered joint custody arrangement would give the child easy access to both parents, allowing the child the freedom to go to whichever parent she needs at the time. This kind of arrangement requires that the parents continue to live near enough to each other that the child can easily go back and forth between houses and get to school from either house. It means doubling up on bedrooms and belongings for the child. It also requires extremely good communication between parents, as well as compatible values and lifestyles.

In the long run, it usually makes more sense for a child to live with one parent and to visit the other frequently, or for long vacations. When setting up a custody and visitation arrangement, putting the needs of the child first—and being flexible enough to allow the arrangement to change as the child's needs change—is essential.

Breastfeeding, Attachment, and Visitation

One critical thing to take into account in determining a custody and visitation arrangement for a young child is the child's attachment history. If a child is used to nursing on demand, with little separation from his mother, being apart from her for longer than he is accustomed to might be tramautic.

Although a mother may need to spend more time with her child during the infant and toddler years, the father's role becomes more important as the child gets older. The challenge is to protect the breastfeeding relationship in the early years, while still preserving the father's bond with his child.

Judges, lawyers, and the baby's father may need to be convinced about the importance of breastfeeding, counsels attorney Elizabeth Baldwin, legal advisor to La Leche League, International. To help you make this argument, get "Breastfeeding Rights Packet" and "Custody/Visitation Arrangements for the Breastfeeding Child" from La Leche League (see Resources).

At the same time, breastfeeding should not be used as a tactic to limit a father's visitation. A judge in this case may decide that the mother could pump her milk during separations, or that the child should be weaned immediately.

What is really at stake in a custody case involving a nursing child is the mother-child bond that develops from a close breastfeeding relationship. Children who are securely attached to their mothers can be traumatized by even brief separations. But in most cases, for the child to have a relationship with Dad is important as well. For a nursing child, visitation may simply need to be introduced a little more gradually until the child is older or weaned.

Here are some visitation guidelines for young children, from Baldwin and her husband, attorney Kenneth Friedman:

- For a child under age three, it is best that the child remain with the parent to whom she has been most securely attached—usually the mother. Visits with the father should not exceed the amount of time that the child is used to being away from her mother.
- The younger the baby, the more important it is to have frequent, rather than lengthy, contacts with the father. Babies do not have long memories. Seeing their fathers every day, rather than every other weekend, will deepen their bond. Consider the time that the father is used to spending with his child: If they are accustomed to going to the playground for an hour every evening, try to incorporate that time into the visitation plan.
- With children age three to five, visitation could gradually increase to full-day visits on weekends and possibly overnights. At this age, securely attached children are still probably best off with their mothers.
- By age six, a child should be able to handle a standard visitation schedule, defined in most states as alternating weekends, and one or two weeks in the summer. A child might also be ready at this age to live with his father full-time.

These guidelines are obviously generalizations, and any individual custody case should be decided based on the needs of the child. The point is to start thinking about what works best for the child in her situation, over and above the parents' desires.

The Reality of Coparenting

Parenting, of course, does not end with divorce. Divorce is between husband and wife, not parents and children.

A paradox is inherent in true shared parenting, however, says psychologist Black. To be able to coparent effectively takes a tremendous amount of flexibility, cooperation, emotional maturity, and willingness to put the needs of your children ahead of your own. It takes all of those admirable traits in both parents. The challenge is for parents to do all this together when they were unable to work out the problems of their marriage in the first place. The same kinds of incompatibilities that spoiled the marriage can easily spoil the day-to-day workings of any coparenting agreement.

Even if parents are able to work out a coparenting agreement, adds Black, additional factors complicating the arrangement can intensify over time. One is financial. The economics of divorce are such that there is rarely enough money to go around. The custodial parent may be seen as stingy for not being able to buy something for the child, and the support-paying parent may feel resentful of requests for more money.

Subsequent marriages can be another force that drives a coparenting agreement apart. New husbands or wives—particularly if they have children of their own—may feel protective of their own children and to be less than supportive of their spouse's involvement with her or his first family.

Even the best-intentioned coparenting arrangements are subject to changes brought about by time. Parents may move away, lose a job, or alter their views toward child-rearing substantially. The situation also changes as the children get older.

These complications don't make coparenting impossible—but it is helpful to be aware of the stresses that you will have to cope with, so that you are better prepared to deal with problems as they come up. Perhaps the best thing you could do would be to enter into an agreement at the time the divorce and custody arrangements are made that you will seek out counseling and arbitration when difficult issues do arise.

Above all, work as a team for your child. Your child does not need to be burdened with your anger and hostility; now, more than ever, he needs your love and attention.

In the best of all worlds, try to think of coparenting as the beginning of a new relationship with your former spouse. You will be coparents for the rest of your child's life, hopefully sharing graduations, weddings, and the birth of your grandchildren. In spite of your differences, you have given each other the gift of parenthood, and given your child the gift of life. Make the most of it.

Child Support That Really Is

Black says she has yet to see a recipient of child support who feels that it is enough money, or a provider of child support who believes that it is being spent properly. Divorce causes tremendous financial stress, giving rise to a new poverty class composed of divorced women and their children. Less than half of absentee fathers continue to pay child support four months after the split, according to the United States Census Bureau's Survey of Income and Program Participation. While most divorced mothers join the work force, they are unable to approach their former standard of living. Studies indicate that after divorce, a woman's income drops dramatically, while a man's usually increases.

That is the bad news. The good news is that there are fathers out there who sincerely want to do all in their power to support their children—even paying more than the court-ordered amount of child support.

Bruce Low, who got divorced when his son was eighteen-months-old, is one of these fathers. His main concern when he and his wife split up was for his son's welfare. He felt strongly about providing enough child support so that his ex-wife could stay home full-time with their son until the boy started school and could work flexible hours after that. He wanted to be sure that his son could live in a safe neighborhood, near good schools, and that his ex-wife could afford a reliable car. After taking all of this into consideration, he and his ex-wife came up with a child support amount that totaled 65 percent of his monthly take-home pay—approximately seven times as much as the average court-ordered amount.

"It makes no difference to me whether or not my ex-wife is grateful for the large support," says Low. "I am only supporting her indirectly. I am really supporting my son. I am trading my current comfort, as parents have throughout history, for his future. None of us has ever wanted a medal; we love our kids."[5]

Low urges fathers involved in a divorce not to let their anger and frustration toward their ex-wife affect their children's needs. To ensure that their children are well taken care of, Low suggests that fathers can increase their child support any time by paying more than the court has required and can even offer to have the divorce decree rewritten to legally increase the amount of child support.

The Divorced Dad

We tend to hear stories about deadbeat fathers, the ones who dodge their child support payments and drop out of their children's lives after a divorce. But what about the committed fathers, for whom being separated from their children is the worst thing about the divorce? As one father says, "I see my daughter only on alternating weekends. When I drop her off at her mother's house, I feel horrible. Sometimes I get so depressed that I think it would be better if I didn't see her at all. It hurts so much, I can't stand it."

Jack Maslow, a clinical social worker who offers workshops on divorced parenting, says that when the family breaks up, fathers are bombarded with intense feelings of guilt, hurt, and anger. They are lonely and miss their children.

They are suddenly single, yet still have the responsibilities of fatherhood. They are still part of a family, yet they must live apart from their family.

Society does little to help the divorced father figure out his new role. Conventional wisdom is that fathers should see their children every other weekend, pay child support, and be content with that. Divorced fathers are led to believe that spending fifty-two days and a few overnights a year with their children is enough to maintain a healthy parenting relationship.

Just because society expects little from a divorced father, however, fathers needn't resign themselves to that role. For the dedicated father who is willing to confront his feelings of pain and loss, divorce can actually provide an opportunity to develop a new relationship with his children— one that is not linked to the pain of a difficult past or to some preconceived notion of what divorced parenting is supposed to be.

Maslow offers the following suggestions for fathers who want to be more than a "weekend dad" (as well as for noncustodial mothers):

- Stay in touch. If you are unable to be with your children, phone them regularly.
- Stick to your word. Be there when you say you will. The more you maintain a solid foundation of trust, the more your children will know that they can count on you.
- Make your home their home, too, regardless of how little time they spend there. Create a home atmosphere that is warm and inviting. If possible, have a room for them, complete with clothes, toys, books, and art supplies. When they come, treat them like family, not like visitors.
- Don't be afraid to discipline your child or to say no—your relationship will be stronger for it.
- Do the things families do. Shop together, cook together, do chores together. Kiss them goodnight and tuck them into bed. All of these activities create the togetherness of a family unit, even a single-parent family unit.
- Plan activities that are meaningful to both of you. Consider an ongoing project, such as

setting up an aquarium or building a tree-house. Your children can look forward to the project, and knowing that it is there will give them a sense that your home is their home, too.

- Get to know their friends. Let them have overnight guests. Be willing to take them places and do things with them.
- Attend school functions, and get to know their teachers. Help them with their homework and school projects.
- Go to their games, performances, and other special events.
- Make them part of your social world, and include them in on your significant relationships.
- On birthdays, holidays, and other meaningful occasions, have your own celebrations with your children.

- Don't be fooled into thinking that every moment together has to be perfect. It is the cumulative experiences that count. Remember that you are a parent—not Santa Claus. You don't need to buy your child toys every visit.
- Above all, think about the kind of father (or mother) you would like to have if you were a child. Then think about the kind of parent you would like to be. And finally, do whatever you can to be that kind of parent.

Living in a Stepfamily

In the past decade—now that one in three children in the United States is living in a stepfamily—sociologists and psychologists have begun to take a serious look at what makes stepfamilies different from "unbroken" families. As a result, the postdivorce family is now becoming recognized as a "real" family with its own unique characteristics, not as something less than a traditional family.

Jane Mickelson, who grew up in a stepfamily and is now raising one of her own, says the challenge for parents in stepfamilies is to openly acknowledge the ways in which they are different from the "unbroken" family, and to attempt to blend themselves and their children into a new family. Only then can the family begin to establish a new kind of kinship.

The most obvious difference in a stepfamily is that one of the adults in the household is not the children's natural parent. A stepfamily has little time to develop the closeness that exists in a parent-child relationship. A child's loyalty to the other parent can form a barrier between child and stepparent. Children who have lived with a single parent for an extended period of time are often closely bonded with that parent, in ways that can challenge the development of new family ties.

Siblings complicate matters further. In a stepfamily, instead of the gradual introduction of a new baby into a home, siblings are thrown together suddenly. Conflicts over room sharing, chores, and other normal areas of sibling rivalry can be heightened and bitter.

A child in a new stepfamily is struggling with loss—not only the loss of a parent, but the loss of a family unit, or, in the case of a bitter divorce, an entire family branch, including grandparents, aunts, uncles, and cousins. Some children are also separated from their siblings. Family patterns, customs, and ways of doing things—all the comforting habits that contribute to a child's sense of security—may be altered or eliminated. These losses, combined with a possible change in home, neighborhood, school system, and friends, can be very traumatic.

Stepfamilies can, however, weather the initial adjustment period and emerge healthy and strong. Mickelson offers the following suggestions for members of a new stepfamily:

SPEND PLENTY OF ONE-ON-ONE TIME WITH YOUR CHILD
Children in a new stepfamily need lots of reassurance that the love shared with a parent before remarriage still exists. Spending special time alone with your child will help ease his shock at being plunged into an entirely new lifestyle. At the same time, you need to devote time to your new marriage, to ensure the survival of the new family, and to show your children what a healthy relationship looks like.

TAKE A BACKGROUND ROLE AT FIRST WITH STEPCHILDREN
A new spouse must be understanding of his or her new stepchildren's needs, and recognize that when children remain secure in their parent's love, they feel less threatened by the stepfamily.

Many new stepmothers—anxious to meet society's expectations of them in their new role—jump right into trying to be a nurturing mother. This eagerness can not only put children on the defensive, but it may have the unintended result of usurping the father's role in his children's lives. The best advice is for stepmothers to hold off as much as possible on major alterations in the daily routines.

For the same reasons, the natural parent is also the best disciplinary guide. The wise stepparent will hold off on behavioral measures until a solid friendship and trust have been established.

PLAN ACTIVITIES WITH YOUR STEPCHILDREN AND THEIR FRIENDS
Simply including a friend in a shopping excursion or a movie is a pleasant way to see another side of your new stepchild. And buffered by the familiar presence of a friend, your stepchild will have a perfect opportunity to get used to you.

PLAN ACTIVITIES THAT INVOLVE THE WHOLE FAMILY
Shared activities lead to a common storehouse of memories. At the same time, creating new traditions helps to establish the new family as a unit.

KEEP THE LINES OF COMMUNICATION OPEN
Honest discussions about what is and isn't working are vital. It can be helpful to hold a weekly family meeting to air grievances and share ideas.

Even if a problem is not immediately resolved, sometimes simply being heard is enough. Other times, when communication becomes blocked, you may need to consult an outside advisor such as a clergyperson or family therapist.

Review "What Makes a Healthy Family?" (page 175). Stay committed to creating a unique new family, and give your children and stepchildren time to adjust to the new family dynamics. As Jeannine Parvati Baker, stepmother and teacher of midwifery, says, "This process [of creating a blended family], painful as it can be at times, is a paradigm for the larger family of humanity. If we can resolve conflicts in stepfamilies, then we can heal conflicts between nations."

A NEED FOR COMPASSION

As a society, we could do better at recognizing that divorce is sometimes the least damaging option. We could learn to be kind to ourselves and others about divorce. Perhaps if we increase our compassion for those who divorce and begin to reduce the stigma that goes along with it, we will create an environment in which healthy marriages can really thrive, and new, healthier families can be born after divorce.

CHAPTER 25 Handling Death

As much as we would like to protect them from it, death will touch our children at some time in their lives, bringing with it the grief that accompanies loss. Death—of pets, grandparents, and for some children, of parents or siblings—is inevitable. Grief is not a pathological illness, but a natural response to death. We all grieve. We all die.

Yet, educating our children about death and guiding them through grief are neglected in our society. Because we are uncomfortable with the subject, we "protect" our children from what can be one of the most important learning experiences of their lives. In shielding them, we deny them not just the richness and openness that is unique to the occasion but the opportunity to express honest feelings, too. We fail to recognize that by teaching our children about death and grief, we also teach them about life and joy.

When death occurs in the family or close by, children draw on their earlier coping skills. Loss and sadness are familiar childhood experiences. Separation fear—one of the dominant feelings expressed when someone in the family dies—is something nearly all infants know by a few months of age; by age two, children are very familiar with feelings of sadness and measures of comfort. These responses to past separations are the cues children draw on when faced with death. Our choice as parents is to stand by silently or to participate in the process. By participating, we can create a new learning experience. We can reinforce the healthy coping skills, introduce new

ones, and help our children externalize and deal with the deep feelings that accompany loss.

Talking to Children About Death

Joy Johnson is author and editor of more than one hundred books on grief. With her husband, Dr. Marvin Johnson, she is also founder of the Centering Corporation, the oldest bereavement resource center in the country (see Resources). She offers the following suggestions for talking to children about death:

BE HONEST

Children do not naturally fear death. We instill fear in them, put a black shroud around death, and worry it into power. Once, when a little girl was crying over the death of her cat, her mother tried to comfort her. "Don't worry, honey," she explained. "Your cat is with God in heaven." The little girl looked at her mother, her eyes widening. "What does God want with a dead cat?" she asked.

When talking about death with your child, saying the word "death" is best—not "passing away," "asleep," "gone" or "lost." When flowers wilt, we do not say that flowers have passed away; we say that they have died. Flowers, people, and the family pet all die. Once we get used to saying the word, it becomes less frightening.

If a child who attends her grandfather's funeral is told that Grandpa is "asleep" in the casket, she may be afraid to go to sleep at night, fearing that she, too, might end up in a casket. You can tell your child simply and honestly, "Grandpa is dead. He was very old and very sick, and his body just stopped working. He won't ever come back. But we'll always remember him, and we'll always love him, and we'll remember that he loved us too."

TELL YOUR CHILD YOURSELF

When someone your child cares about dies, make sure you are the one to tell your child. Let your child know early on that nothing is too frightening or too sad to talk about together.

One grandmother whose daughter had committed suicide refused to tell her six-year-old grandson how his mother had died. Joy Johnson asked her, "Would you rather he hear it from you, knowing that you love him and will be there to answer questions—or do you want him to hear it from a classmate during a moment of childhood cruelty, or to overhear it during a family get-together?" If the child discovered the truth either of those ways, she explained, he would most likely feel betrayed, left out, not-to-be-trusted, and deeply hurt.

"But how can I talk about such a terrible thing to a little boy?" the grandmother asked. She ended up taking the boy on her lap, and saying, "Tony, there's something I want you to know, and I want you to hear it from me because I love you, and I'm here to answer your questions. Your mommy's mind was very, very, sick. She wanted to die and couldn't think clearly. She killed herself and thought that would solve her problems. She didn't know it wouldn't solve anything, and she didn't know how sad it would make us." Grandma began to cry. Tony began to cry. They held each other. Now Tony could ask the questions he needed to ask, and Grandma didn't have to waste the horrendous amount of energy it takes to keep a skeleton in the closet.

SAY IT IN TERMS YOUR CHILD CAN UNDERSTAND

In Joy Johnson's book *Tell Me, Papa*, a kindly grandfather explains death in a way that can be easily grasped: "When someone dies, everything inside of that person stops. The heart stops. The breathing stops. The thinking and the feelings stop. When a person is dead, that person cannot think about things. They cannot feel any hurt. They cannot feel hot or cold. When we are dead, we do not have any life in our bodies anymore. What is left is just the body...like a peanut shell without the peanut. Like an apple peel with no apple. Like a school with no children."[1]

SHARE YOUR BELIEFS

If you are a religious family, sharing your faith with your children during a time of grieving is important. Let them know, however, that God does not pull strings to keep us safe or deprive us of life, but rather provides loving support through all we face. Some people find the idea of "God's will" to be a comfort, but to children, the idea that "God came and took Daddy" is about as frightening as you can get. Share your beliefs, but at the same time be careful that no one makes God into a people-snatcher. You may want to say, "After your brother Timmy died, God came and took his soul to heaven—the part of Timmy that loved and laughed. That part is gone now."

BE REAL

Let your children know that families who love each other laugh together and cry together. Tell your children how you feel. Even though children are people-readers and know how we feel, articulating our feelings sets an example and forges a bond. Children need to know that it is all right for adults to cry too. Sharing tears can bring you closer together.

One two-year-old girl, Heather, refused to talk about her nine-month-old sister who had died. She would not even say Jessica's name. A sensitive friend pointed out that Heather talked about Jess and asked questions when she was with the friend, but every time she mentioned her sister at home, both parents began to cry.

Heather's father took her into Jess's room and sat with her in the rocking chair. He told her it was okay to talk about Jess any time she wanted to, and that it was all right if he and Mommy cried—they would be sad for a long, long time, but they were still a family.

"You don't have to be afraid of our tears," her father said. "It helps to cry, and it helps to talk about Jess."

"Jessica!" Heather squealed. "Jessica! Jessica! Jessica!" She ran into the living room and started looking at Jessica's pictures and talking about her. It was a powerful release for a small child.

HELP YOUR CHILD DEAL WITH FEELINGS OF GUILT

Children often fear that they did something to cause a death. When Kisha's sister died, the seven-year-old suddenly stopped speaking. At last she told a very patient bereavement counselor that before her sister was hit by a car, Kisha had yelled, "You should be dead! I hate you. Go away." It took some convincing before Kisha really believed that her words and thoughts couldn't make anyone die.

If your child is older, you might want to talk about the difference between guilt and regret. Guilt is what we feel when we deliberately, consciously, intentionally hurt or do harm. Regret is what we feel when we wish we could have done something to prevent hurt or harm. Every child, no matter what age, needs to know that she did not make a death happen.

REASSURE YOUR CHILD THAT DEATH DOES NOT MEAN ABANDONMENT

When the movie Bambi recently reappeared in video form, some parents groups opposed its release because they felt that children would be frightened by the scene in which Bambi's mother dies. "A mother's death is what a child fears most," one group announced, "and this movie encourages that fear."

Johnson counters: "What a child fears most is abandonment, and Bambi's father moves in immediately, letting Bambi know that he will care for him. Bambi is allowed to be sad, and his love for his mother is expressed."

Children grieving the death of a loved one need to know that they will not be left alone to fend for themselves. Your children may need you to tell them that if you were to die, Daddy would take care of them, and if you were both to die, Grandma and Grandpa would look after them.

Respect the Age of Your Child

Children have varying reactions to death, depending on their age. Johnson offers the following guidelines for what to expect from different age groups:

INFANT TO AGE THREE

Even a newborn will pick up on your body language and your emotions. If you are tight from stress and grief, your baby will feel it through your arms and hear it in your voice. Parents have reported increased crying in very young infants during times of grief—it is as if they are insisting you notice that they are part of the family, too.

Children this age cannot understand the finality of death. While they can comprehend that the dead person cannot feel anything and does not breathe anymore, they may not seem very sad because they think the person is coming back.

"When are we going to pick up Jess?" two-year-old Heather asked months after her sister died. Each time her mother explained that Jess was not coming back. When Heather wanted to draw pictures to send to Jess, her parents let her mail them. Gradually, Heather began to accept the notion of permanence.

Three-year-olds may not grasp the full concept of death, but they do understand sadness. Tell them why you are sad, let them know that sadness is a normal feeling when someone dies, and that even though you are sad, at times you will still laugh. You may want to tell your child that when you are sad, you need a hug. Fulfilling this request will give the child something helpful to do.

AGE THREE TO SIX

Death still does not seem permanent at this age. But now you can begin to explain to the child the difference between sick, very sick, and very, very sick.

Children this age may surprise you with their reactions to death. Six-year-old Cathy had leukemia. Her best friend Julie was also six and also had leukemia. The two girls met regularly at the cancer clinic and spent overnights together. When Julie died unexpectedly, Cathy's mother was extremely concerned about Cathy's reaction. She took Cathy on her lap and said, "Cath, I have some really bad news. Julie got very sick yesterday. Her mom took her to the hospital, and the doctors and nurses tried to help her, but they couldn't make her better. Honey, Julie died last night."

Cathy looked at her mother for a minute. "Geez," she said. "What did they do with her toys?"

With children this age, be sure to give them permission to play and laugh as well as to grieve and cry. Children don't think in a linear manner. They will play, then grieve; grieve, then play. Frankly, we could probably learn a lot from their style of sorrow.

AGE SIX TO NINE

At this stage, kids are interested in details. "How did he die?" "Who killed him?" they want to know. Children this age see death as someone or something that comes and gets you. They think they can catch it. They become scared. If the death is violent, they are traumatized. Even a death after a long illness can make children fear that someone else close to them may die unexpectedly.

With children this age, sharing details of the death can help them understand the difference

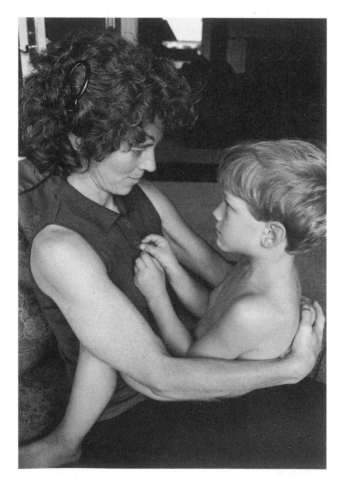

between an earache and cancer. The older the child, the more details they need. Nine-year-olds may be satisfied with, "Aunt Liz's heart was very weak. It finally stopped. It's not at all like your healthy young heart." Older children would want to know if Aunt Liz had a heart attack or heart disease.

AGE TEN THROUGH TEENS

Children in this age group have feelings that are similar to those of adults. They want details, and often they will use black humor or attempt to "gross you out" with death jokes or overly vivid descriptions. You are likely to see more anger and acting out from this age group. Teens may withdraw or take risks to prove they are invincible, throwing parents into panic and despair. Sharon Turnbull, who wrote *Who Lives Happily Ever After?* about violent death, says you must approach a teen as you would a deer: quietly, softly, slowly.[2]

Do not assume teenagers can handle grief alone. They cannot. Even if they are distant and don't want to listen, talk about how you feel— your fears, needs, and expectations. Provide a journal or a blank notebook so your teenagers can write down feelings, song lyrics, or poems. An excellent resource is the Centering Corporation's journal for teens, *Fire in My Heart: Ice in My Veins.* Also, tell teachers and school counselors that your teen may need extra attention.

> ### Rob
>
> At 2:00 in the morning, my youngest daughter, five-year-old Elisa, woke me up. She stood in front of me in the half-light of the bedroom. Her hair was mussed, and her pajamas were ruffled. She had been crying. In a voice that barely trembled, she said, "I can't remember what Mommy looked like."
>
> At that moment, her grief was inconsolable. At that moment, the world had snatched another thing from her: Her mother's face no longer existed as a ready and reliable memory. For Elisa, the time to cry and say goodbye to her mother was not at the official funeral, but in her pajamas on a warm August night thirteen months later.
>
> Rob Loughran, "Talking to Children About Death," *Mothering,* Summer 1994.

Let Your Child Say Goodbye

Attending a funeral can provide needed closure for a child. Although a child should never be forced to attend, he needs to know what will happen and how the family will be gathering to say good-bye. Children need to be part of important family events.

Viewing the body can be a tender learning experience, and need not be frightening. You should prepare your child ahead of time for how the body will look and feel. You can explain that though Grandma may look like she is sleeping, you can see that her body is not working. What is left is like a shell, a body that Grandma had used and enjoyed.

A child may want to touch the body. There is nothing frightening or creepy about a body. If you have never felt one, rub the cover of this book.

That is what a body feels like. Explain to your child that the body will feel cool and solid, and let him rub his grandmother's hand or touch her face.

Saying goodbye makes death less frightening and grief more acceptable. Children can say good-bye to someone they love in any number of ways. Perhaps your child would like to draw a picture to be placed in the casket. Or maybe he would like to make a tape recording of personal memories. A child can easily accept the idea that "Grandma cannot hear us like she used to, but talking about her will help us, and it is one way we can keep her memory alive."

A balloon goodbye can be appropriate for a child. One eight-year-old girl stood on her father's grave a few weeks after he died and dictated a message to her mother, who wrote it with a magic marker onto a red balloon. It said: "Dear Daddy, I

Helena

My dear husband Tom died at age thirty-two of a heart attack. There were no flowers surfacing to my lips when I told our six-year-old daughter, Mignon. I knelt before her on the floor, took her hands in mine, and said, "Dolly, Daddy is dead."

She was instantaneously horrified. She screamed and sobbed and said, "I won't let him be dead! I can't live without my daddy!" Within moments she calmed down and said very adamantly, "I have to see his body." I was stunned, and explained to her that bodies get cold and stiff when we die.

"I don't care," she responded. Just as I had needed to see Tom's body to say goodbye, she did too. I promised her we would see him on Monday at the funeral.

On the day of the funeral, she ran as fast as she could to the coffin and stretched up on her toes to look in at Tom. When I caught up to her, there were tears streaming down her face and she reached in and grabbed his hand, which, of course, didn't move very far.

"He's stiff!" she shrieked and looked at me with questioning eyes.

"We discussed that, darling," I said softly. She started to climb up in with him; I helped her.

"He's hard and cold, Mom. He's freezing." She was crying so hard, my heart bled for her.

"We discussed that too, darling. Here, touch his hair, that's warm." She was pleased by the warmth of his hair, and her tears fell on his face.

At the grave site, Mignon had been prancing and playing about the graveyard while I watched as Tom's casket was lowered into the grave. But when the lowering device began to creak, she too came over to watch. "Why are they putting him down in that hole, Mom?" she demanded. She started pacing nervously all around the hole, scrutinizing each of the workers. Finally, she came and sat on my lap and together we cried as the dirt forever sealed our contact with the physical body of her beloved Daddy.

We now visit the grave frequently. She frolics through the graveyard very light and free. She assures those who begin to shower her with sympathy that Mommy's the only one who is sad now. For those who think children are too young to understand death, I discovered that they can teach us, if only we listen to them.

Helena Kosmides, "The Death of a Father," *Mothering*, Summer 1983.

love you very much. You were the best daddy in the whole world, and I know you are the best daddy in the whole cemetery. I will always love you." The little girl read the message aloud—to her father and the world—then released the balloon into the sky.

Older children might like to keep a journal, write poems, or talk privately into a tape recorder. Any artwork, poetry, or tapes can be put into the casket or taken to the cemetery later and buried under the grass.

Ask for Help

Know that you don't have to go through a death alone. Ask for help. Find a bereavement counselor. Talk to teachers, school counselors, your funeral director, and minister or rabbi. Read everything you can find on grief. Ask about support groups and centers for grieving children.

Grief is love's sorrow. As soon as children know love, they prepare to know grief. Only in the last ten years have we come to truly recognize the needs of grieving children and the need of all children to know about death.

Sharing information about death with your children allows them to know that you are there for questions and are not afraid of honest answers. Sharing feelings honestly with your children removes the tremendous burden that you may feel of taking care of everyone else. When given love, support, and simple answers to their questions, your children may surprise you with how well they understand grief and grow through the experience. It is up to us to take the black shroud off the image of death and let the light in.

Trusting and Taking Care of Yourself as a Parent

I hope that this book gives you hope; a bigger sense of who you are, of who your child is, and of your family. If there is any advice I would give after twenty-five years of parenting, it is to be yourself. Go your own way. Use this book as a guide, not a bible. The most natural kind of family living is what is natural to you.

The greatest lesson I have learned from my children is that I am okay the way I am. It's the message I raised them with, and now one that they give back to me.

As much as we have a responsibility to follow our own way—which is sometimes the hardest way—so, too, must we examine our lives and our beliefs anew once birth, babies, children, and family come along. It is much easier to be more than who we are than to be simply who we are.

Often we feel the need for a script, a philosophy, a book, a guru. Certainly, we fear the unknown world of life with our child without some rules. We fear we can't just go our own way.

But we must. All of evolution depends on us going our own way. Genius only happens by happy accident. It can't be predicted, controlled, or manipulated. It just happens. It must be, therefore, that what seem like happy accidents are, in fact, grand schemes. There must be, after all, a script of which our own intuition is the only author.

Dance legend Martha Graham says, "There is a vitality, a life-force, an energy, a quickening, that is translated through you into action and because there is only one of you in all of time, this expression is unique. And if you block it, it will never exist through any other medium and be lost. The world will not have it. It is not your business to determine how good it is nor how valuable nor how it compares to other expressions. It is your business to keep it yours clearly and directly, to keep the channel open. You have to keep open and aware directly to the urges that motivate you. Keep the channel open."

Keeping the channel open in this era of rapid change is no easy task. Not only in the realm of microchips is our world changing. Our culture, our customs, and our world views are also changing. Some liken this time of cultural transformation and its metaphor, the Internet, to the printing press and the changes that followed that invention. More information than ever is available to parents; therefore, more critical thinking than ever is necessary.

What this availability does is not only to democratize information, but also to demystify it. With so much information coming to us from so many sources, we have to figure out how to discriminate among the sources, how to filter it, and how to recognize the sources of information that are the most reliable for us. Grounding the channel in our own personal beliefs and values rather than in some prescription or current fashion keeps us honest. Following our own way without examining our beliefs, however, is foolishness. Examining our own beliefs and deciding to follow them is enlightened.

Being open to change is an essential prerequisite for our time and for our lives as parents. At the same time that parenting opens us up to personal transformation, so too does it remind us that some things never change.

The basic integrity, perfectibility, and goodness of the child never change. All decisions and actions should flow from this faith in the innate goodness of the child.

When we see that the child is basically good, trustworthy, and authentic, we will follow the child's lead as parents rather than molding the child to our own wishes. It only makes sense that the next generation is smarter than the last. They communicate the biological imperative, the way humans have survived for centuries in close contact with one another. It is no longer an era of domination, but of cooperation. History favors responsive, sympathetic parenting. History favors intimacy.

Following the lead of the child only works, however, when we claim our authority as a parent. It will not work if we abdicate our responsibility and give up our authority to our children. Following the lead of the child acknowledges that the child is equal to us in terms of emotional experience and personal integrity. Claiming our authority as a parent ensures that we are the ones in charge. Being in charge does not require coercion—it requires persuasion.

If being a natural parent has to do with finding our own way; with believing in our children and their biological imperative; with claiming our authority as a parent and using that authority with discretion, then we have a lot cut out for us. What kind of support and information do we need to become the kind of parents we want to be? How do we take care of ourselves as we take care of others?

I used to think that taking care of myself meant doing aerobics or something that got me away from the kids. Since I prefer walking to aerobics and like being around my kids, I thought I had it figured out. But, now I realize that taking care of myself has more to do with my inner experience of myself than with what I do. And, when I think better of myself, I do things for myself.

Because society expects so much of us as parents—and we expect so much of ourselves—we can easily be overly critical of ourselves. After all, parenting is something we can learn only by expe-

rience, and it takes many years to feel confident as a parent. It makes it easier if we can be nice to ourselves.

Sometimes being nice to ourselves means replacing a limiting and critical inner dialogue with a gentle and encouraging one. When things are tough with our children, we shouldn't be tough on ourselves. Really knowing ourselves means not underestimating ourselves. It is the circumstances of life with family that expand that capacity, that develop in us reserves of character we never thought possible. We learn how to handle difficult circumstances by handling them; we learn how to love by loving.

It helps to get to know yourself; to become a fair witness. Self-knowledge builds a foundation for self-trust, which in turn generates self-love. Begin by getting to know yourself through self-observation. Observe your inner experience of life. Notice your body language, facial expressions, posture, and mental attitudes.

It's also important to know some facts and opinions that will help you in parenting. It's important to know something about human development, perhaps from different points of view. How do medicine, science, religion, philosophy, and culture view human development?

What makes a healthy family? Sometimes as parents we know what we don't want to do, but we're not sure what our other options are. One way to nurture the health of your family is to develop new communication skills. Communication is the key to strong relationships within the family. Also work on developing coping mechanisms for tough times. Look at how athletes, performers, political leaders, and others who put themselves on the line every day handle pressure. Realize that your own unique life as a parent is your teaching ground.

As you learn new communication skills and coping mechanisms, and work on growing a healthy family, go easy on yourself. Change takes time. The best coping mechanism of all is the ability to start over again and again. That is what we do every day with our children. That is what it means to be gentle on ourselves.

It sounds simple to advocate that we be gentle on ourselves while we change and grow as a parent, but what does that mean, and how important can it really be? It is essential. If the authority for making intuitive, authentic decisions about our child's well-being rests in us, then we must support and strengthen ourselves with great attentiveness. The kinder we are to ourselves, the more we will believe in ourselves.

It is easy to feel that you have no free time as a parent, but you can always find fifteen minutes. Here are some things you can do in fifteen minutes that will allow you to catch your breath and settle your mind:

- Take a walk.
- Go to a park.
- Take a bath.
- Call a friend.
- Read a poem.
- Have a cup of tea.
- Lie in the hammock.
- Look at the clouds.
- Sit by the fire.
- Sit by the window.
- Lie in the grass.
- Lie on the floor.
- Water the plants.
- Give yourself a facial.
- Read the headlines.
- Sing a song.
- Dance around the living room.

Being gentle on yourself means appreciating signs of overload in yourself not as signs of weakness, but as cries for help. When we are tired all the time, or easily angry, on the verge of tears, or afraid of everything, we need to rest. We cannot expect ourselves to make important decisions regarding our children when we are not at our best. Sometimes we don't realize that the simple solutions of getting enough sleep, eating good food, and creating some unstructured time for relaxation can make most problems disappear.

Being gentle on yourself also means having the good sense to allow yourself to catch your breath and think something over. Trusting yourself means that you appreciate that you sometimes need more information. Making decisions on your own timing, even if it takes longer than you and others think it "should," and having enough time for your mind to wander gives you much needed processing time for deep decision making.

Deep decision making requires a dialogue with the heart. If going your own way as a parent is the truly natural way, then the language of your heart is the language you will be listening to. We listen to our heart, our intuition, our gut, all the time. I once heard that the most frequently used word in the Bible is "listen." The language of the heart is everywhere.

But how does it speak to us? How do we know what we feel? We know what we feel by observing ourselves and developing an inner-truth sense, a sense within us that allows ready recognition.

The heart speaks to us when we are alone or when we let our minds wander. Although finding time alone when you have children is almost impossible, setting aside ten minutes to meditate is a worthwhile goal. A walk in the woods with a baby in a backpack provides a way to find mental room. Using breastfeeding as an opportunity for contemplation is a possibility.

Getting out into nature often puts things in perspective. Remembering and writing down dreams can give you insights into your deeper experience of things. The heart often speaks through emotions, either our own or others. Pay attention to what evokes emotion in you and what in life is most meaningful to you.

Intuition works many times through what appear to be coincidences. It speaks through first impressions, your own body language, and even through what you find humorous. Pay attention to the nonverbal side of life. Begin to understand how you respond to the world around you and notice what your intuitive sense of things is.

Emotion and intuition have the disadvantage of having their own timetable. The biggest challenge in parenting from the heart is having the patience to get to know yourself.

> Do you have the patience to wait
> till your mud settles and
> the water is clear?
> Can you remain unmoving
> till the right action
> arises by itself?
> —*Tao Te Ching*

Emotion and intuition are the strong suits of the feminine, both the feminine in women, and also the feminine as it applies to the receptivity in all of us. The feminine ideal is often portrayed in classic art with one hand outstretched and one hand toward the heart, as if to say, "As I give to you, so do I give to myself."

We can easily feel used up by parenting; tired and overwhelmed much of the time. Taking care of ourselves when we can barely take care of others can seem impossible, but we need to continuously keep trying to figure out how to balance giving to others with taking care of ourselves.

In order not to overuse ourselves, we have to set priorities. Frequently, we believe one thing, but don't know how to live it. Try this experiment with the following words: "Friends, Self, Work, Family, God, Relatives." Put them in the order of what you value most. Give it some time.

Now reflect on how well the priorities you set in life reflect these values. With so much competing for your time, living your personal values may not be easy, but it is worth the effort.

One of the biggest challenges to living our personal values is the simple overload of daily life. Many days with children are simply out of control. When inconvenient, challenging, or downright bad things happen, that is where the gentle inner dialogue comes in. We can compound the bad situation by harshly judging ourselves or our loved ones as well, or we can "Roll with the punches" as my aunt used to say, "Flow with it" as the hippies used to say, or "Chill" as the new generation says. Just surrendering to things as they are does much to improve any day.

Besides accepting things, other strategies can help in tough times. Let go of the past. Release old sorrows. If it never worked out before, it just might now. Every moment is another chance.

Schedule only a manageable number of activities. And don't forget to leave room for the unexpected. It always happens. If you schedule yourself so tightly that you have no room for the unexpected, you will be the only one who will pay when it does occur.

Allow plenty of unstructured time for relaxation. This is always a challenge. Never give up trying to figure out how to do it. Remember that unstructured time is unstructured. Do nothing. Don't orchestrate it.

Look at things from an objective point of view. Be a fair witness. It's self-indulgent and inaccurate to look only at what's wrong with things or what's wrong with you.

Do not stay in extreme positions or states of mind. Be flexible. Sometimes it's better to be kind than to be right.

Allow fun and pleasure in your life regardless of what you face emotionally.

Build relationships within the family and without that are special and equal.

Communicate directly. Move always at first glance. Trust your first impressions and act on intuitive information.

Trust your inner experience, your gut feelings.

Give immediate attention to what has you most worried or anxious, to the priorities and commitments of the present moment. Take care of the things on your "list" that you are the most anxious about, no matter what others think you "should" do. When setting priorities, be kind to yourself. Do things in such a way in the present that you don't set yourself up for overload in the future. Don't overcommit yourself or your family. Don't expect yourself to continually clean up your past excesses. Give yourself a break.

Do things step by step. If something seems overwhelming, break it down into small steps that you can accomplish comfortably day by day over a certain period of time.

Have faith. Look back and see how everything worked out in the past as if by some grand scheme. Trust that it will work out again even though you can't always figure it out.

Often when we look back, however, we have regrets. We would have done things differently if we knew then what we know now. But, the fact is, we didn't. Trusting ourselves means that we have to trust our mistakes as well. We never intentionally make a mistake. If we turn them into learning experiences, mistakes are opportunities.

Regrets about the past are what we want to avoid by parenting from the heart. The more we trust ourselves, the more we can forgive ourselves.

If we trust our child's innate integrity, then we must trust our own. We must believe that in some existential or mystical sense, our child picked us. There is an inherent rightness about each parent and child couple, and thus some blessing on the process they go through together.

We heal and develop our capacity for self-trust as we allow our children to grow in an atmosphere of trust. The reasons we distrust ourselves are usually negative mental habits we learned from our own childhood or simply the lack of the right mental attitudes for tough times. Or just the inevitable overload.

Often our cloudy days have a silver lining. It is always darker before the dawn of our understanding. Just as we are at our wit's ends with our children, the cloud lifts and we are transformed. We see the light. In many myths of creation, chaos precedes creation. Life with children is ever chaotic, ever creative. Life with children is inherently out of control. It's supposed to be.

Children are agents of change; their freshness and newness invigorate the culture. As parents, we have the opportunity to make the world a better place by modeling an authentic life for our children. We don't have to perfect, however. We just have to be ourselves. This integrity is our greatest security.

Whether or not you are smart, pretty, witty, or have any idea what you're doing, you are the one in charge. And you have all the right qualifications. You are the expert witness.

Would you volunteer for this job?

Wanted: *Men and women for a job in which no experience is required, no predictability or control is possible. This job demands long hours and offers no pay, no training, and little praise. Society will hold incredibly high standards for this job, but will give little support for it. Everyone else in society will think they know how to do the job better than you do, yet you will be the only one blamed if something goes wrong.*

This job offers the potential to develop the thinking and emotional capacity of another unique individual. The potential to inexorably affect the quality of life on the planet. The potential to improve the environment, ensure world peace, and eliminate nuclear war.

This job is totally unlike any other, and yet will prepare you for anything. It has been known to be a religious experience.

The job is priceless, so payment is made in self-esteem, intimacy, epiphanies, and personal transformation.

This is a totally improvisational position. Individuals are handpicked for the position."

Chapter 1 Preconception

1. Schwartz, L., *Bonding Before Birth*. (Boston: Sigo Press, 1991).
2. Verny, T., and Kelly, J., *The Secret Life of the Unborn Child*. (Loveland, OH: Summit Books, 1981).
3. Verny, T., and Kelly, J., ibid.
4. Mehl, L., "Preventing Prematurity." *Mothering*, Fall 1988.

Chapter 2 A Healthy, Wide-Awake Pregnancy

1. Brennan, Patrick, et al, *New Scientist*, Issue 1476, June 10, 1999.
2. Flessig, Anne, and Cartwright, Ann, "Women's preference for place of birth." *British Medical Journal*, Volume 305, August 22, 1992, letters to the editor.
3. Tew, M., "Place of Birth and Perinatal Mortality" *JR Coll Gen Pract* 35, 1985.

Chapter 3 Natural (Drug-Free) Childbirth

1. Jacobson, B., et al. (1990), "Opiate addiction in adult offspring through possible imprinting after obstetric treatment." *British Medical Journal*, 301: 1067–1070.
2. Morton, Sally, PhD et al., "The effect of epidural analgesia for labor on the Cesarean delivery rate." *Obstetrics and Gynecology*, Volume 83, no. 6, June 1994.
3. "The Bad News about Epidurals." *Time* magazine, March 24, 1997.
4. Hughey, M. J. et al, "Maternal and Fetal Outcome of Lamaze Prepared Patients." Obstetrics and Gynecology, *Journal of the American College of Obstetricians and Gynecologists* 51, no. 6 (June 1978).

5. Klaus, M.H., and Kennell, J.H., *Maternal-Infant Bonding*. (Hanover, MO: C.V. Mosby Co., 1976).
6. Klaus, M.H., and Klaus, P., *Your Amazing Newborn*. (Reading, MA: Perseus Books, 1988).
7. Golding, J., et al., "Childhood Cancer, Intramuscular Vitamin K, and Pethidine Given during Labour." *British Medical Journal* 305, 1992.
8. LeBoyer, F., *Birth Without Violence*. (New York: Knopf, 1975).

Chapter 4 Breastfeeding

1. N.M. Layde et al., "The Independent Association of Parity, Age at First Full-Term Pregnancy and Duration of Breastfeeding with the Risk of Breast Cancer." *Journal of Clinical Epidemiology* 42, 1989.
2. R. Morely et al., "Mothers' choice to provide breastmilk and developmental outcome." *Archives of the Diseases of Childhood* 63, 1988.
3. Roger V. Short, "Contraceptive Effects of Extended Lactational Amenorrhea." *Lancet*, March 23, 1991.
4. "Commonwealth v. Carol A. Michaud, Normand R. Michaud." 389 Mass. 491, 451 NI 2nd 396, 1983.
5. Jelliffe, D., and Jelliffe, E., *Human Milk in the Modern World*. (New York: Oxford University Press, 1978).
6. Lawrence, Ruth, A., *A Review of the Medical Benefits and Contraindications to Breastfeeding in the United States*. (Arlington VA: National Center for Education in Maternal and Child Health, 1997).

Chapter 5 Circumcision

1. Johnson, A.A.W., "On an Injurious Habit Occasionally Met with in Infancy and Early Childhood." *Lancet*, 1860.

2. Campbell, M.F., *Campbell's Urology*, Vol. 2. (Philadelphia, PA: W.B. Saunders Company, 1970).

3. Diamond, M., and Sigmundson, H.K., "Sex Reassignment at Birth: Long-Term Review and Clinical Implications." *Archives of Pediatrics and Adolescent Medicine* 151, 1997.

4. Williams, N.,"Complications of Circumcision." *British Journal of Surgery*, October, 1993.

5. Taddio, A., et al,"Effect of Neonatal Circumcision on Pain Responses during Vaccination in Boys." *Lancet* 345, 1995.

6. Stang, H.J., et al., "Local Anesthesia for Neonatal Circumcision: Effect on Distress and Cortisol Response." *Journal of the American Medical Association*, 1988.

7. Davenport, M., "Problems with the Penis and Prepuce: Natural History of the Foreskin." *British Medical Journal* 312, 1996.

8. Altschul, M., "Cultural Bias and the UTI Circumcision Controversy." *Truth Seeker*, July 1989.

9. Frisch, N., et al, "Falling Incidence of Penis Cancer in an Uncircumcised Population: Denmark 1943–90." *British Medical Journal* 311, 1995.

10. McCance, D.J., et al, "Human Papillomavirus Types 16 and 18 in Carcinomas of the Penis from Brazil." *International Journal of Cancer*, 1996.

11. Lawler, F., "Circumcision: Decision Analysis of its Medical Value." *Family Medicine*, 1991.

12. Bazett, H.C., et al, "Depth, Distribution and Probable Identification in the Prepuce of Sensory End-Organs Concerned in Sensations of Temperature and Touch; Thermometric Conductivity." *Archives of Neurology and Psychiatry* 27, 1932.

13. Hammond, T., "Awakenings: Preliminary Poll of Circumcised Men." NOHARMM, 1992.

14. *British Journal of Urology* 83, 1999.

Chapter 6 Vaccinations

1. Odent, M.R., Culpin, E.E.; Kimmel, T., "Pertussis Vaccination and Asthma: Is There a Link?" *Journal of the American Medical Association*, 272, 1994.

2. Newacheck, P., and Taylor, W.R., "Childhood Chronic Illness: Prevalence, Severity and Impact." *American Journal of Public Health* 82, 1992.

3. Newacheck, P., McManus, M., and Fox, H., "Prevalence and Impact of Chronic Illness among Adolescents." *American Journal of Diseases of Children* 145, 1991.

4. Newacheck, P., and Strickland, B., et al, "An Epidemiologic Profile of Children with Special Health Care Needs," *Pediatrics* 102, 1998.

5. Adams, P.F., and Marano, M.A., Current Estimates from the National Health Survey, 1994. Vital Health Statistics. 10 (193). Hyattsville, MD: National Center for Health Statistics. Department of Health and Human Services, Publ. No.(PHS) 96–1521.

6. Classen, J. Barthelow, MD, *New Zealand Medical Journal*, May 24, 1996 and "Public Should be Told that Vaccines May Have Long Term Adverse Effects." *British Medical Journal*, 318(7177):193.

7. Wakefield, A.J., MD et al, "Heal-lymphoid-nodular Hyperplasia, Non-specific Colitis and Pervasive Developmental Disorder in Children." *The Lancet* 9103, February 28, 1998.

8. "Measles Vaccine Link with Autism Studies." *London Times*, February 27, 1998.

9. "Hepatitis B Vaccine Reaction Reports Outnumber Reported Disease Cases in Children According to Vaccine Safety Group." Press Release, National Vaccine Information Center, Vienna, Virginia, January 27, 1999.

10. *Center for Medical Consumers: HealthFacts*, Volume 24, Issue 2, February 1999.

11. Smith, Jane S., *Patenting the Sun: Polio and the Salk Vaccine.* (New York; William Morrow, 1982).

12. "The Vaccine Business Gets a Shot in the Arm." *The Wall Street Journal*, February 25, 1998.

Chapter 7 Crying

1. Frey, W., *Crying: The Mystery of Tears.* (New York: Harper & Row, 1985).

2. Frey, W., ibid.

3. Pierce, R. A, Nichols, M.P., and Dubrin, J.R., *Emotional Expression in Psychotherapy.* (Gardner Press, 1983).

4. Sagi, A., and Hoffman, M., "Empathic Distress in the Newborn." *Developmental Psychology*, 1976.

5. Bell, S., and Ainsworth, M., "Infant Crying and Maternal Responsiveness." *Child Development*, 1972.

6. Devore, I., and Konner, M., "Infancy in a Hunter-Gatherer Life: An Ethological Perspective." *Ethology and Psychiatry*, 1974.

7. Harlow, H.F., and Harlow, M.K., *Behavior of Nonhuman Primates.* (San Diego, CA: Academic Press, 1965).

8. Clinical studies presented at plenary session of American Academy of Pediatrics annual meeting, November 1997.

9. Hunziker, U.A., and Barr, R.G., "Increased Carrying Reduces Infant Crying: A Randomized Controlled Trial." *Pediatrics*, 1986.

10. Jones, S., *Crying Babies, Sleepless Nights*. (Boston: Harvard Common Press, 1992).
11. Chapman-Smith, D., "Infantile Colic—A New Study from Denmark." *The Chiropractic Report*, 1989.

Chapter 8 Night Waking

1. Konner, M., *Childhood*. (Boston: Little, Brown, & Company, 1991).
2. Verny, T., and Kelly, J., *The Secret Life of the Unborn Child*. (Loveland, OH: Summit Books, 1981).

Chapter 9 Attachment Parenting

1. Restak, R., *The Brain*. (New York: Doubleday, 1979).
2. Ainsworth, M.D.S., "Attachments Across the Life Span." *Bulletin of the New York Academy of Medicine* 61, 1985.
3. Magid, K., and McKelvey, C., *High Risk*. (New York: Bantam Books, 1988).
4. Bell, S., "Long-Term Effects of Responsive Parenting." unpublished study, 1998.
5. Klein, P.F., "The Needs of Children." *Mothering*, Spring 1995.
6. Barker, E., "The Critical Importance of Mothering." *Mothering*, Spring 1988.
7. Klein, P.F., ibid.
8. Liedloff, J., *The Continuum Concept*. (Reading, MA: Addison-Wesley, 1975).
9. Hallet, J-P, *Pygmy Kitabu*. (New York: Random House, 1973).
10. Konner, M., *The Tangled Wing: Biological Constraints on the Human Spirit*. (San Diego, CA: Holt, Rinehart and Winston, 1982).
11. Small, M., *Our Babies, Ourselves: How Biology and Culture Shape the Way We Parent*. (New York: Anchor Books, 1998).
12. Liedloff, J., ibid.
13. Bowlby, J., *Attachment and Loss*, Vols. I, II, III. (New York: Basic Books, 1969).
14. Bowlby, J., ibid.
15. Salk, L., *What Every Child Would Like His Parents to Know*. (New York: Warner Books, 1973).
16. Fish, M., and Belsky, J., *American Journal of Orthopsychiatry*. July 1991.
17. Fish, M., and Belsky, J., ibid.
18. Brazelton, T.B., *Touchpoints*. (Reading, MA: Addison-Wesley, 1992).
19. Crosby, F.J., *Juggling*. (New York: The Free Press, 1991).
20. Liedloff, J., ibid.
21. Siegel, C., "The Brave New World of Childcare." *New Perspectives Quarterly*, Winter 1990.

Chapter 10 First Food

1. L. Businco, et al., "Is Prevention of Food Allergy Worthwhile?" *Journal of Investigative Allergies and Clinical Immunology*, 3, 1993.
2. Lawrence, R., *Breastfeeding: A Guide for the Medical Profession*. (Hanover, MO: Mosby, 1989).
3. Wiles, R., Davies, K., and Campbell, C., "Overexposed: Organophosphate Insecticides in Children's Food." Environmental Working Group/The Tides Center, January 1998.

Chapter 11 Healthy Eating

1. Zemel, M.B., "Calcium Utilization: Effect of Varying Level and Source of Dietary Protein." *American Journal of Clinical Nutrition* 48, September 1988.

Chapter 13 Common Ailments

1. Diamant, M.B., "Abuse and Timing of Use of Antibiotics in Acute Otitis Media." *Archives of Otolaryngology* 100, 1974.
2. *Science News*, November 19, 1994, pp.332–333.
3. Nsouli, T.M., et al, "Role of Food Allergy in Serous Otitis Media." *Annals of Allergy* 73, 1994.
4. Jung, T.T.K., "Prostaglandins, Leukotrienes, and Other Arachidonic Acid Metabolites in the Pathogenesis of Otitis Media." *Laryngoscope* 98, September 1988.
5. Kleinman, L.C., et al, "The Medical Appropriateness of Tympanostomy Tubes Proposed for Children Younger Than 16 Years in the United States." *JAMA* 271, 1994.
6. It requires 2.5 milligrams of sodium fluoride per pound of a person's weight to kill. There are 260 milligrams in a family-sized tube of toothpaste.
7. *Review of Fluoride: Benefits and Risks*. U.S. Public Health Service, pp. F1–F7, 1991.
8. The Brown University Child and Adolescent Behavior Letter, January 1997.
9. Fung, K.P., et al, "Attenuation of Exercise-Induced Asthma by Acupuncture." *Lancet*, 20–27 December 1986.
10. Nagarathna, R., and Nagendra, H.R., "Yoga for Bronchial Asthma: A Controlled Study." *British Medical Journal* 291, 1985.

Chapter 14 Healthy Families

1. Gallup poll, reported in *American Demographics*, 1990.

2. Roper Organization survey, reported in *Pediatrics for Parents,* October, 1987.

3. Gallup poll, reported in December, 1991.

4. Campbell, R., *How to Really Love Your Child.* (Colorado Springs, CO: Victor Books, 1980).

5. Curran, D., *Traits of a Healthy Family.* (Akron, OH: Winston Press, 1983).

6. Hendrix, H., *Getting the Love You Want.* (New York: Harpers Perennial Library, 1992).

7. "The State of America's Children Yearbook 1998." Children's Defense Fund.

8. Survey by Robert Half International, 1989.

9. "Work and Family Benefits Provided by Major US Employers," Hewitt Associates Study, 1991.

10. *The Wall Street Journal,* August 10, 1993.

Chapter 15 Discipline

1. Ginott, H., *Between Parent and Child.* (New York: Macmillan, 1965).

2. Murray Straus, *EPOCH-USA.*

3. National Committee for the Prevention of Child Abuse Alert, March 1993.

4. Pediatric Management, cited in *Your Child's Wellness Newsletter,* April 1994.

5. LeShan, E., *When Your Child Drives You Crazy.* (New York: St. Martin's Press, 1985).

6. Hanh, T.N., *Being Peace.* (Albany, CA: Parallax Press, 1987).

7. Faber, A., and Mazlish, E., *How to Talk So Kids Will Listen and Listen So Kids Will Talk.* (New York: Avon, 1980).

8. Hart, L., *The Winning Family: Increasing Self-Esteem in Your Children and Yourself.* (New York: Dodd, Mead, and Co., 1988).

9. Fox, M., *Original Blessing.* (Santa Fe, NM: Bear and Co., 1983).

10. Hart, L., op. cit.

11. Jay Carter, *Nasty People.* (Chicago: Contemporary Books, 1993).

12. Miller, K.C., *When Counting to 10 Isn't Enough: Defusing Anger.* (Port Charlotte FL: Shaw Publishing, 1996).

13. "Body Pleasure and the Origins of Violence." reported by James W. Prescott, *Bulletin of the Atomic Scientists,* February, 1988.

14. Montagu, A., *The Nature of Human Aggression.* (Lafayette, CA: Acadian House, 1995).

15. Miller, A., *For Your Own Good: Hidden Cruelty in Child-Rearing and the Roots of Violence.* (New York: Noonday Press, 1990).

16. McGinnis, J. and K., *Parenting for Peace and Justice.* The Institute for Peace and Justice, Maryknoll, NY: Obis, 1981.

Chapter 16 Adolescence

1. Scholastic Poll of American Youth. *Scholastic Inc.,* March 3, 1992.

2. *In Business,* March/April, 1990.

3. *The Christian Science Monitor,* December 6, 1990.

4. Pearce, J.C., *Magical Child.* (New York: Bantam, 1977).

5. Riera, M., *Uncommon Sense for Parents with Teenagers.* (Berkeley, CA: Celestial Arts, 1995).

6. Dinkmeyer, D., PhD, *Systematic Training for Effective Parenting of Teens (STEP/TEEN).* (Circle Pines, MN: American Guidance Service, 1983).

7. Ponton, L., *The Romance of Risk: Why Teenagers Do the Things They Do.* (New York: Basic Books, 1997).

8. Zimmer, L., and Morgan, J.P., *Marijuana Myths, Marijuana Facts.* (New York: Open Society Institute, 1997).

9. Glantz, M., PhD, and Pickens, R., PhD, *Vulnerability to Drug Abuse.* (Washington, DC: American Psychological Association, 1992).

10. *American Psychologists,* May, 1990.

11. Schwebel, R., *Saying No Is Not Enough: Raising Children Who Make Wise Decisions about Drugs and Alcohol.* (New York: Newmarket Press, 1989).

Chapter 17 Sexuality

1. Scharf, M., *Unfinished Business.* (New York: Ballantine Books, 1981).

2. The Alan Guttmacher Institute: Sex and America's Teenagers, New York and Washington, 1994.

3. Newcomer, S.F., and Udry, J.R., "Parent-Child Communication and Adolescent Sexual Behavior." *Family Planning Perspectives,* 17, July/August, 1985.

4. Holtzman, D., and Robinson, R., "Parent and Peer Communication Effects on AIDS-Related Behavior Among U.S. High School Students." *Family Planning Perspectives* 27, November/December, 1995.

5. The Alan Guttmacher Institute, op. cit.

6. St. Jeor, S., "The Role of Weight Management in the Health of Women." *Journal of the American Dietetic Association,* September, 1993.

7. Rodin, J., *Body Traps.* (New York: Quill William Morrow Press, 1992).

8. Virginia Meehan, MD, President, Anorexia Nervosa and Associated Disorders.

9. Warren, A., and Wiedenkeller, J., *Everybody's Doing It: How to Survive Your Teenagers' Sex Life (and Help Them Survive It, Too).* (New York: Viking Penguin, 1993).

Chapter 18 High Technology

1. MacBeth, T., *Tuning Into Young Viewers.* (Thousand Oaks, CA: SAGE Publications, 1996).
2. Winn, M., *Unplugging The Plug-In Drug.* (New York: Viking Penguin, 1985).
3. MacBeth, T., op. cit.
4. Huston, A.C., et al., *Big World, Small Screen: The Role of Television in American Society.* (Lincoln, NE: University of Nebraska Press, 1992).
5. National Institute of Mental Health, "Television and Behavior: Ten Years of Scientific Progress and Implications for the Eighties," Summary Report (Vol. 1), 1982.
6. Surgeon General's Scientific Advisory Committee on Television and Social Behavior, "Television and Growing Up: The Impact of Televised Violence." 1972.
7. Report of the American Psychological Association Commission on Violence and Youth, 1992.
8. Cantor, J., *Mommy, I'm Scared: How TV and Movies Frighten Children and What We Can Do to Protect Them.* (San Diego, CA: Harcourt Brace, 1998).
9. Liebert, R.M., et al., *The Early Window: Effects of Television on Children and Youth.* (Tarrytown, NY: Pergamon Press, 1982).
10. Levine, M., *Viewing Violence: How Media Violence Affects Your Child's and Adolescent's Development.* (New York: Doubleday, 1996).
11. Walsh, D., *Selling Out America's Children.* (Minneapolis, MN: Fairview Press, 1994).

Chapter 19 Toys

1. Liedloff, J., *The Continuum Concept.* (Reading, MA: Addison-Wesley, 1986).
2. Carlsson-Paige, N., and Levin, D., *Who's Calling the Shots? How to Respond Effectively to Children's Fascination with War Play, War Toys, and Violent Television.* (Branford, CT: New Society Publishers, 1996).
3. Di Gangi, J., "Lead and Cadmium in Vinyl Children's Products." Greenpeace USA, September 1997.
4. Moller, S., et al., "Environmental Aspects of PVC." Danish Environmental Protection Agency, 1995.
5. Vinkelsoe, K., et al., "Migration of Phthalates from Teething Rings." Danish Department for Environmental Chemistry, April 15, 1997.
6. Gibbs, L., and Citizens Clearinghouse for Hazardous Waste, *Dying from Dioxin.* (Cambridge, MA: South End Press, 1995).
7. Washington Citizens for Recycling: *Plagued by Plastic Packaging,* Seattle, Washington, 1995.

Chapter 20 Wholesome Family Entertainment

1. Bettelheim, B., *The Uses of Enchantment: The Meaning and Importance of Fairy Tales.* (New York: Vintage Books, 1989).
2. Neumeyer, P., "Classic Books for Children." *Mothering,* Fall 1992.
3. Rauscher, F., Shaw, G., and Ky, K., "Listening to Mozart Enhances Spatial-Temporal Reasoning: Towards a Neurophysiological Basis." *Neuroscience Letters* 185, 1995.
4. Rauscher, F., Shaw, G., et al., "Music Training Causes Long-Term Enhancement of Preschool Children's Spatial-Temporal Reasoning." *Neurological Research* 19, February 1997.

Chapter 21 Public Schooling

1. Kathleen Cotten and Karen Reed Wikelund, *Parent Involvement in Education.* (Eugene, OR: Northwest Regional Education Laboratory, 1989).
2. *Scientific American,* February, 1992.
3. Arthur R. Jensen, *Straight Talk About Mental Tests.* (New York: Macmillan, 1981).
4. "Civil Rights, Feminist Leaders Challenge National Merit Formula." *FairTest Examiner,* Summer 1988.
5. Jeannie Oakes, *Keeping Track: How Schools Structure Inequality.* (Princeton, NJ: Yale University Press, 1985).
6. *The Brown University Child and Adolescent Behavior Letter,* February 1992.

Chapter 22 Alternative Education

1. Center for Education Reform, "Charter School Survey," 1996–1997.
2. McGuinnis, D., *Why Our Children Can't Read and What to Do About It: A Scientific Revolution in Reading.* (New York: Free Press, 1997).
3. Gardner, H., *Frames of the Mind.* (New York: Basic Books, 1983).
4. Herb Snitzer, *Summerhill: A Loving World.* (New York: Macmillan, 1964).
5. Neill, A.S., *Summerhill: A Radical Approach to Child Rearing.* (New York: Hart Publishing Company, 1960).
6. Alan White, in an article by Daniel Greenberg, "Learning Without Coercion: Sudbury Valley School." *Mothering,* Winter 1991.
7. *American Journal of Education,* Chicago University Press, February, 1986.

8. Koetzch, R.E., *The Parents' Guide to Alternatives in Education.* (Boston, MA: Shambala Publications, 1997).

9. Kohl, H., and Featherstone, J., *Growing Minds: On Becoming a Teacher.* (New York: Harper Collins, 19850.

Chapter 23 Homeschooling

1. Holt, J., *How Children Learn.* (New York: Bantam, 1967, rev. 1983).

2. Interview with John Holt in *Mothering,* Spring 1981.

3. Van Galen, J., and Pittman, M.A., *Homeschooling: Political, Historical, and Pedagogical Perspectives.* (Stanford, CT: Ablex, 1991).

4. Mayberry, Knowles, Ray, and Marlow, *Home Schooling: Parents as Educators.* (Thousand Oaks, CA: Corwin Press, 1995).

5. Cohen, C., *And What About College: How Homeschooling Leads to Admissions to the Best Colleges and Universities.* (Cambridge, MA: Holt Associates, 1997).

6. Gelner, J., *College Admissions: A Guide for Homeschoolers.* (out of print).

Chapter 24 Divorce

1. NICHS "News Notes." November 18, 1993.

2. *Science,* June 7, 1991.

3. *The Psychotherapy Letter,* September, 1993.

4. The Honorable Sara P. Schechter, in "Tell Them to Stop Fighting: A Judge's View of Custody Battles." *Mothering,* Fall 1997.

5. Bruce Low, in "Child Support That Really Is." *Mothering,* Winter 1987.

Chapter 25 Death

1. Johnson, J., *Tell Me, Papa.* (Omaha, NE: Centering Corporation, 1980).

2. Turnbull, S., *Who Lives Happily Ever After?* (Omaha, NE: Centering Corporation, 1990).

Note: Please be aware that the phone numbers and Web site addresses included in this book are up-to-date as of publication, but they may be subject to change.

Chapter 1 Preconception

Baker, Jeannine Parvati, Frederick Baker, and Tamara Slaytor. *Conscious Conception: Elemental Journey Through the Labyrinth of Sexuality.* Monroe, Utah: Freestone Publishing Co., 1986.

Balaskas, Janet. *Preparing for Birth with Yoga.* Boston, MA: Element, Inc., 1994.

Chamberlain, David B., Ph.D. *Babies Remember Birth.* Los Angeles, California: Jeremy P. Tarcher, 1988.

Montagu, Ashley. *Life Before Birth.* New York: New American Library, 1964. *(not in print)*

Nilsson, Lennart. *A Child Is Born.* New York: Delacorte Press, 1990.

Noble, Elizabeth. *Essential Exercises for the Childbearing Year* (4th edition). Harwich, Massachusetts: New Life Images, 1995.

Schwartz, Leni. *Bonding Before Birth: A Guide to Becoming a Family.* Boston: Sigo Press, 1991.

Verny, Thomas R., M.D., with John Kelly. *The Secret Life of the Unborn Child.* New York: A Delta Book, Dell Publishing, 1986.

Association of Prenatal and Perinatal Psychology and Health (APPPAH)
40 Colony Road
Box 994
Geyserville, CA 95441
Phone: 707-857-4041
Fax: 707-857-4042
E-mail: *apppah@aol.com*
www.birthpsychology.com

Chapter 2 Pregnancy

Balaskas, Janet and Gayle Peterson. *Natural Pregnancy: A Practical, Holistic Guide to Wellbeing from Conception to Birth.* Brooklyn, NY: Interlink Publishing Group, 1991.

Bing, Elisabeth and Libby Colman. *Making Love During Pregnancy.* New York: Bantam, 1989.

Gardner, Joy. *Healing Yourself During Pregnancy.* Freedom, California: The Crossing Press, 1987.

Haire, Doris and members of ICEA. *The Pregnant Patient's Bill of Rights/The Pregnant Patient's Responsibilities.* Minneapolis, MN: International Childbirth Education Association, 1975.

Heinowitz, Jack. *Pregnant Fathers: Challenges and Discoveries on the Road to Being a Father.* Kansas City, MO: Andrews and McMeel, 1997.

Jordon, Sandra. *Yoga for Pregnancy: Safe and Gentle Stretches.* New York: St. Martin's Press, 1988.

Kippley, John and Sheila Kippley. *The Art of Natural Family Planning* (4th edition). Cincinnati, OH: The Couple to Couple League, 1996.

Kitzinger, Sheila. *The Complete Book of Pregnancy and Childbirth.* New York: Alfred A. Knopf, 1996.

———. *Sex During Pregnancy.* Minneapolis, MN: International Childbirth Education Association (ICEA) 1979.
www.sheilakitzinger.com

Marti, James with Heather Burton. *Holistic Pregnancy and Childbirth: A Month-by-Month Guide.* New York: John Wiley & Sons, 1999.

Moskowitz, Richard, M.D, *Homeopathic Medicines for Pregnancy & Childbirth.* Berkeley, California: North Atlantic Books, 1992.

Noble, Elizabeth. *Having Twins: A Parent's Guide to Pregnancy, Birth & Early Childhood (2nd edition).* Boston: Houghton Mifflin, 1991.

Olkin, Sylvia Klein. *Positive Pregnancy Fitness: A Guide to a More Comfortable Pregnancy & Easier Childbirth Through Exercise & Relaxation.* Garden City, New York: Avery Publishing Group, 1987.

Sears, William, M.D. and Martha Sears, R.N. *The Pregnancy Book: A Month-by-Month Guide.* Boston: Little, Brown and Company, 1997.

Verny, Thomas R. *Nurturing the Unborn Child: A Nine-Month Program for Soothing, Stimulating, and Communicating with Your Baby.* New York: Dell, 1992.

Yntema, Sharon. *Vegetarian Pregnancy: The Definitive Nutritional Guide to Having a Healthy Baby.* Ithaca, NY: McBooks Press, 1994.

American College of Home Obstetrics
2821 Rose Street
Franklin Park, IL 60131
Phone: 847-455-2030

American College of Nurse Midwives
818 Connecticut Avenue, Suite 900
Washington, DC 20006
Phone: 202-728-9806
E-mail: *info@acnm.org*
www.midwife.org

American College of Obstetricians and Gynecologists
409 12th Street SW
P.O. Box 96920
Washington, D.C. 20090-6920
Phone: 202-638-5577
www.acog.org

ASPO/Lamaze International
1200 19th Street, NW, Suite 300
Washington, DC 20036-2422
Phone: 800-368-4404 or 202-857-1128
Fax: 202-223-4579
E-mail: *lamaze@dc.sba.com*
www.lamaze-childbirth.com

Association of Labor Assistants and Childbirth Educators (ALACE)
P.O. Box 382724
Cambridge, MA 02238

888-22-ALACE
E-mail: *alacehq@aol.com*
www.alace.org

Association of Women's Health, Obstetric and Neonatal Nurses (AWHONN)
2000 L Street, NW, Suite 740
Washington, DC 20036
Phone: 800-673-8499 (US)
800-245-0231 (Canada)
Fax: 202-728-0575
www.awhonn.org

Chapter 3 Natural Childbirth

Arms, Suzanne. *Immaculate Deception II: A Fresh Look at Childbirth.* Berkeley, CA: Celestial Arts, 1994.

Balaskas, Janet. *Active Birth (revised edition).* Boston: Harvard Common Press, 1992.

Baldwin, Rahima. *Special Delivery.* Berkeley, CA: Celestial Arts, 1995.

Bradley, Robert A. *Husband-Coached Childbirth (4th edition).* New York: Bantam, 1996.

Castro, Miranda. *Homeopathy for Pregnancy, Birth, and Your Baby's First Year.* New York: St. Martin's Press, 1993.

Cheatham, King and Bartz. *Childbirth Education for Women With Disabilities and Their Partners.* Minneapolis, MN: International Childbirth Education Association, 1994.

Cohen, Nancy Wainer, and Lois J. Estner. *Silent Knife.* South Hadley, MA: Bergin & Garvey Publishers, 1983.

Cohen, Nancy Wainer. *Open Season: A Survival Guide for Natural Childbirth and VBAC in the '90s.* Westport, CT: Bergin & Garvey, 1991.

Crawford, Karis, Charles S. Mahan, M.D. and Johanne Walters. *Natural Childbirth After Cesarean.* Malden, MA: Blackwell Science Inc., 1996.

Davis-Floyd, Robbie. *Birth as an American Rite of Passage.* Berkeley, CA: University of California Press, 1992.

Dick-Read, Grantly. *Childbirth Without Fear.* New York: Harper & Row, 1984.

Dunnewold, Ann, Ph.D., and Diane G. Sanford, Ph.D. *Postpartum Survival Guide.* Oakland, CA: New Harbinger Publications, 1994.

England, Pam and Rob Horowitz. *Birthing From Within: An Extra-ordinary Guide to Childbirth Preparation.* Albuquerque, NM: Partera Press. 1998.

Flamm, Bruce. *Birth After Cesarean: The Medical Facts*. New York: Fireside Paperbacks, 1990. *(out of print)*

Gaskin, Ina May. *Spiritual Midwifery (3rd edition)*. Summertown, TN: The Book Publishing Company, 1990.

Gillmor, Mickey. *Squatting for Labor and Birth*. Minneapolis, MN: International Childbirth Education Association, 1989.

Goer, Henci. *Obstetric Myths Versus Research Realities: A Guide to the Medical Literature*. Westport, CT: Bergin & Garvey, 1995.

Haire, Doris. *Cultural Warping of Childbirth*. Minneapolis, MN: International Childbirth Education Association (ICEA), 1972.

Jordon, Brigitte. *Birth in Four Cultures: A Cross Cultural Investigation of Childbirth in Yucatan, Holland, Sweden, and the United States. (4th edition)*. Prospect Heights, IL: Waveland Press, 1993.

Jones, Carl, with Jan Jones. *The Birth Partner's Handbook*. New York: Meadowbrook Press, 1989.

Jones, Carl, Henci Goer, and Penny Simkin. *The Labor Support Guide: For Fathers, Family and Friends*. Minneapolis, MN: International Childbirth Education Association (ICEA), 1984.

Klaus, Marshall, Phyllis Klaus and John Kennell. *Mothering the Mother*. Reading, MA: Addison-Wesley, 1993.

Kitzinger, Sheila. *Your Baby Your Way: Making Pregnancy Decisions and Birth Plans*. New York: Pantheon Books, 1987.

———. *The Experience of Childbirth*. London: Penguin Books, 1987.

———. *Being Born*. Rutherford, New Jersey: Berkeley Publishing Group, 1992.

———. *A Celebration of Birth*. Minneapolis, MN: International Childbirth Education Association (ICEA), 1986.

———. *Giving Birth: How It Really Feels*. New York: Farrar, Straus, Giroux, 1989.

Kitzinger, Sheila and Penny Simkin. *Episiotomy and the Second Stage of Labor*. Minneapolis, MN: International Childbirth Education Association (ICEA), 1986.

Korte, Diana. *The VBAC Companion: The Expectant Mother's Guide to Vaginal Birth After Cesarean*. Boston: The Harvard Common Press, 1997.

Korte, Diana and Roberta Scaer. *A Good Birth, A Safe Birth (3rd edition)*. Boston: The Harvard Common Press, 1992.

Leboyer, Frederick. *Birth without Violence: The Book that Revolutionized the Way We Bring Our Children into the World*. Rochester, VT: Inner Traditions, 1995.

Machover, Ivana, and Angels and Jonathan Drake. *The Alexander Technique Birth Book: A Guide to Better Pregnancy, Natural Birth and Parenthood*. New York: Sterling Publications, 1993.

Maternity Center Association. *Journey to Parenthood*. New York: Maternity Center Association, 1997.

McCutcheon, Susan and Peter Rosegg. *Natural Childbirth the Bradley Way*. New York: Penguin Putnam, 1999.

Noble, Elizabeth. *Having Twins: A Parent's Guide to Pregnancy, Birth & Early Parenthood (2nd edition)*. New York: Houghton Mifflin, 1991.

Odent, Michel. *Birth Reborn*. New York: Birth Works, 1994.

Peterson, Gayle. *Birthing Normally: A Personal Growth Approach to Childbirth (2nd edition)*. Berkeley, California: Shadow & Light, 1991.

———. *An Easier Childbirth: A Mother's Guide for Birthing Normally (2nd edition)*. Berkeley, California: Shadow & Light, 1993.

Placksin, Sally. *Mothering the New Mother: Your Postpartum Resource Companion*. New York: Newmarket Press, 1994.

Rooks, Judith Pence. *Midwifery & Childbirth in America*. Philadelphia: Temple University Press, 1997.

Rothman, Barbara Katz. *The Encyclopedia of Childbearing*. New York: Henry Holt, 1994.

Sears, William, M.D. and Martha Sears, R.N. *The Birth Book: Everything You Need to Know to Have a Safe and Satisfying Birth*. Boston: Little, Brown & Co., 1994.

Simkin, Penny. *The Birth Partner: Everything You Need to Know to Help a Woman Through Childbirth*. Boston: The Harvard Common Press, 1989.

———. *Turning a Breech Baby to Vertex*. Minneapolis, MN: International Childbirth Education Association (ICEA), 1983.

Simkin, Penny, Janet Whalley, R.N., B.S.N., and Ann Keppler, R.N., M.N. *Pregnancy, Childbirth, and the NewBorn: The Complete Guide*. New York: Meadowbrook Press, 1991.

Tew, Marjorie. *Safer Childbirth? A Critical History of Maternity Care*. New York: Chapman and Hall, 1990.

Wagner, Marsden. *Pursuing the Birth Machine: The Search for Appropriate Technology*. Australia: ACE Graphics, 1994.

Weed, Susun S. *Wise Woman Herbal for the Childbearing Years*. Woodstock, New York: Ash Tree Publishing, 1986.

Young, Diony and Charles Mahan. *Unnecessary Cesareans: Ways to Avoid Them (2nd edition)*. Minneapolis, MN: International Childbirth Education Association, 1989.

BIRTH, published quarterly
Blackwell Science, Inc.
Commerce Place
350 Main Street
Malden, MA 02148
Phone: 617-388-8250 or 888-661-5800
Fax: 617-388-8255
www.blacksci.co.uk/usa

The Bradley Method
(American Academy of Husband Coached
    Childbirth)
P. O. Box 5224
Sherman Oaks, CA 91413-5224
Phone: 800-4-A-BIRTH or 800-423-2397
or 818-788-6662
Fax: 818-788-1580
www.bradleybirth.com

Cesareans/Support, Education and Concern, Inc.
    (CSEC)
22 Forest Road
Framingham, MA 01701
Phone: 508-877-8266
Include SASE if contacting by mail.

Citizens for Midwifery (CFM)
P.O. Box 82227
Athens, GA 30608-2227
Phone: 888-CFM-4880
E-mail: *shodesmwy@peachnet.campus.mci.net*
www.cfmidwifery.org

Coalition to Improve Maternity Services (CIMS)
2120 L Street
Suite 1202
Washington, DC 20037
Phone: 202-478-6138
Fax: 202-223-9579

Depression After Delivery (DAD)
P.O. Box 1282
Morrisville, PA 19067
Phone: 800-944-4PPD

Doulas of North America (DONA)
1100 23rd Avenue East

Seattle, WA 98112
Phone: 206-324-5440
E-mail: *AskDONA@aol.com*
www.DONA.com

The Farm
Birth Gazette
42 The Farm
Summertown, TN 38483
Phone: 931-964-3798

Informed Homebirth and Informed Parenting
P.O. Box 1733
Fair Oaks, CA 95628
Phone: 916-961-6923

International Cesarean Awareness Network (ICAN)
1304 Kingsdale Avenue
Redondo Beach, CA 90278
Phone: 310-542-6400
Fax: 310-542-5368
E-mail: *ICANinfo@aol.com*
www.childbirth.org/ICAN

International Childbirth Education Association (ICEA)
P. O. Box 20048
Minneapolis, MN 55420
Phone: 612-854-8660 or 800-624-4934
Fax: 612-854-8772
E-mail: *info@icea.org*
www.icea.org

Midwifery Education and Accreditation Council
    (MEAC)
220 West Birch
Flagstaff, AZ 86001
Phone: 520-214-0997
Fax: 520-773-9694

Midwifery Today, Inc.
P.O. Box 2672-350
Eugene, OR 97402
Phone: 541-344-7438 or 800-743-0974
Fax: 541-344-1422
E-mail: *Midwifery@aol.com*
www.midwiferytoday.com

Midwives Alliance of North America (MANA)
P.O. Box 175
Newton, KS 67114
Phone: 888-923-6262
www.mana.org

National Association of Childbearing Centers (NACC)
3123 Gottschall Road
Perkiomenville, PA 18074
Phone: 215-234-8068
Fax: 215-234-8829
E-mail: *reachnacc@birthcenters.org*
www.birthcenters.org

National Association of Parents and Professionals
for Safe Alternatives in Childbirth, International
(NAPSAC)
Route 4, Box 646
Marble Hill, MO 63764
Phone: 573-238-2010
Fax: 573-238-2010
E-mail: *napsac@clas.net*

National Association of Postpartum Care Services
P. O. Box 1012
Edmonds, WA 98020
Phone: 800-453-6852
E-mail: *mthrcre@gte.net*

North American Registry of Midwives (NARM)
5257 Rosestone Drive
Lilburn, GA 30047
Phone: 888-842-4784
E-mail: *cpminfo@aol.com*

Postpartum Support International (PSI)
927 North Kellogg Ave.
Santa Barbara, CA 93111
Phone: 805-967-7636
E-mail: *THonikman@compuserve.com*

Read Natural Childbirth Foundation
P.O. Box 150956
San Rafael, CA 94915-0956
Phone: 415-456-3143

Stork Smart
Robin Elise Weiss
173-D Sears Ave.
Louisville, KY 40207
E-mail: *pregnancy.guide@about.com*
www.pregnancy.about.com
www.childbirth.org

Chapter 4 Breastfeeding

Auerbach, Kathleen G., Jan Riordan. *Study Guide for Breastfeeding and Human Lactation (2nd edition)*. Boston: Jones & Bartlett, 1999.

Baumgarner, Norma Jane. *Mothering Your Nursing Toddler (revised edition)*. Schaumberg, IL: La Leche League, 1999.

Hale, Thomas, Ph.D. *Medications and Mothers' Milk: 1998-1999*. Amarillo, TX: Pharmasoft Medical Publishing, 1998.

Herzog-Isler, Christa and Klaus Honigmann. *Give Us a Little Time: How Babies with a Cleft Lip or Cleft Palate Can Be Breastfed*. Switzerland: Medela AG, 1996.

Huggins, Kathleen. *The Nursing Mother's Companion (3rd edition)*. Boston: Harvard Common Press, 1995.

Huggins, Kathleen and Linda Ziedrich. *The Nursing Mother's Guide to Weaning*. Boston: Harvard Common Press, 1994.

Jelliffe, D., and Jelliffe, E. *Human Milk in the Modern World*. New York: Oxford University Press, 1978.

Kippley, Sheila. *Breastfeeding and Natural Child Spacing*. Cincinnati, OH: Couple to Couple League International, 1989.

Kitzinger, Sheila. *Breastfeeding Your Baby (revised edition)*. New York: Knopf, 1998.

La Leche League International. *The Womanly Art of Breastfeeding*. New York: Plume, New American Library, 1997.

Lawrence, Ruth A., M.D. *A Review of the Medical Benefits and Contraindications to Breastfeeding in the United States. Maternal & Child Health Technical Information Bulletin*. Arlington, VA: National Center for Education in Maternal and Child Health, 1997.

Lee, Nikki and Margot Edwards. *An Employed Mother Can Breastfeed When*. Minneapolis, MN: International Childbirth Education Association, 1991.

Mohrbacher, Nancy, I.B.C.L.C. and Julie Stock, B.A., I.B.C.L.C. *The Breastfeeding Answer Book (revised edition)*. Franklin Park, IL: La Leche League International, 1997.

Odent, Michel. *The Nature of Birth and Breastfeeding*. Westport, CT: Bergin & Garvey, 1992.

Pryor, Karen and Gale Pryor. *Nursing Your Baby*. New York: Pocket Books, 1991.

The Association for Breastfeeding Fashions
(National clearinghouse for information about nursing wear.)
Send SASE for free brochure of companies designing nursing wear.
Box 4378
Sunland, CA 91041

International Lactation Consultants Association
  (ILCA)
4101 Lake Boone Trail, Suite 201
Raleigh, NC 27607
Phone: 919-787-5181
Fax: 919-787-4916
E-mail: *ilca@erols.com*
www.ilca.org

La Leche League International
1400 N. Meacham Road
Schaumburg, IL 60173-4048
Phone: 847-519-7730
Breastfeeding Helpline: 800-525-3243
Taped Message: 900-448-7475, ext. 26
Fax: 847-519-0035
www.lalecheleague.org

The Parent Center for Breastfeeding and Parenting
  Services
6145 N. Beulah
Ferndale, WA 98248
Phone: 360-384-1755
Fax: 360-384-2694
E-mail: *kga@telcomplus.net*

Chapter 5 Circumcision

Bigelow, Jim, Ph.D. *The Joy of Uncircumcising!*
  Exploring Circumcision: History, Myths, Psychol-
  ogy, Restoration, Sexual Pleasure and Human
  Rights. (2nd edition). Aptos, CA: Hourglass, 1995.
Goldman, Ronald, Ph.D. *Circumcision: The Hidden*
  Trauma: How an American Cultural Practice
  Affects Infants and Ultimately Us All. Boston: Van-
  guard Publications, 1997.
———. *Questioning Circumcision: A Jewish Perspec-*
  tive (2nd edition). Boston: Vanguard Publications,
  1997.
O'Mara, Peggy, ed. *Circumcision: The Rest of the*
  Story—A Selection of Articles, Letters, and
  Resources 1979-1993. Santa Fe, NM: Mothering,
  1993.
Ritter, Thomas J., M.D., and George C. Denniston,
  M.D. *Say No to Circumcision! 40 Compelling Rea-*
  sons Why You Should Respect His Birthright and
  Keep Your Son Whole (2nd edition). Aptos, CA:
  Hourglass, 1996.
Wallerstein, Edward. *The Circumcision Decision.*
  Minneapolis, MN: International Childbirth Edu-
  cation Association (ICEA), 1990.
Whose Body, Whose Rights? Examining the Ethics
  and the Human Rights Issue of Infant Male Cir-

cumcision. Award-winning documentary. 56 min.
  VHS. Personal use: VideoFinders, 800-343-4727

Doctors Opposing Circumcision (DOC)
2442 NW Market Street, Suite 42
Seattle, WA 98107
Phone: 206-368-8358
www.faculty.Washington.edu/gcd

National Organization of Circumcision Information
  Resource Center (NOCIRC)
P.O. Box 2512
San Anselmo, CA 94979-2512
Phone: 415-488-9883
E-mail: *nocirc@concentric.net*
www.nocirc.org

National Organization to Halt the Abuse and Rou-
  tine Mutilation of Males (NOHARMM)
P.O. Box 460795
San Francisco, CA 94146-0795
Phone: 415-826-9351
Fax: 415-642-3700
www.noharmm.org

Nurses for the Rights of the Child
369 Montezuma, Suite 354
Santa Fe, NM 87501
Phone: 505-989-7377
www.cirp.org/nrc/

Chapter 6 Vaccinations

Coulter, Harris L. and Barbara Loe Fisher. *DPT: A*
  Shot in the Dark: Why the P in the DPT Vaccina-
  tion May Be Hazardous to Your Child's Health.
  Garden City Park, NY: Avery Publishing Group,
  1991.
James, Walene. *Immunization: The Reality Behind*
  the Myth (revised 2nd edition). Westport, CT:
  Bergin & Garvey, 1995.
Lange, Robert W., M.D., M.P.H. *The Doctor's Guide to*
  Protecting Your Health Before, During and After
  International Travel. Greenport, New York: Pilot
  Books, 1997.
Moskowitz, Richard, *The Case Against Immunizations.*
  173 Mt. Auburn Street
  Watertown, MA 02172
  Reprints of lectures on vaccinations given by Dr.
  Moskowitz available for $3.00.
Neustaedter, Randall. *The Vaccine Guide: Making an*
  Informed Choice. Berkeley, CA: North Atlantic
  Books, 1996.

O'Mara, Peggy (ed.) *Vaccination: The Issue of Our Times.* Santa Fe, NM: Mothering Magazine, Inc., 1997.

Offit, Paul A., M.D. and Louis M. Bell, M.D. *What Every Parent Should Know About Vaccines.* New York: Macmillian, 1998.

Plotkin, Stanley A., M.D. and Edward A. Mortimer, Jr., M.D. *Vaccines (2nd edition)* Philadelphia, PA: W. B. Saunders Co., 1994.

Rozario, Diane. *The Immunization Resource Guide (3rd edition).* Burlington, IA: Patter Publications, 1998.
Patter Publications
P.O. Box 204
Burlington, IA 52601-0204
Phone: 319-752-0039

Stratton, Kathleen R., Cynthia J. Howe, and Richard B. Johnston, Jr. (eds.) *Adverse Events Associated with Childhood Vaccines: Evidence Bearing on Causality.* Washington, DC: National Academy Press, 1994.

Autism Research Institute
4182 Adams Avenue
San Diego, CA 92116
Fax: 619-563-6840

The Bell of Atri, Inc.
J. Anthony Morris
23-E Ridge Road
Greenbelt, MD 20770
Phone: 301-474-5031

Determined Parents to Stop Hurting Our Tots (DPT-SHOT)
Marge Grant
915 S. University Avenue
Beaverdam, WI 53916
Phone: 920-887-1133

Philip Incao, M.D.
Anthroposophic and Homeopathic Medicine
Steiner Medical Associates
Gilpin Street Holistic Center
1624 Gilpin Street
Denver, CO 80218
Phone: 303-321-2100
Fax: 303-321-3737

Michigan Opposing Mandatory Vaccines
P.O. Box 1121
Troy, MI 48099-1121
Phone: 810-447-2418

Missouri Citizens' Coalition for Freedom in Health Care
P.O. Box 190318
St. Louis, MO 63119-0318
Phone: 314-968-8755

National Vaccine Information Center (NVIC)
512 West Maple Avenue, Suite 206
Vienna, VA 22180
Phone: 800-909-SHOT or 703-938-0342
Fax: 703-938-5768
www.909shot.com
NVIC publishes the book *The Consumer's Guide to Childhood Vaccines*
($9.00 plus $2.00 shipping)

National Vaccine Injury Compensation Program (NVICP)
Health Resources and Services Administration
Parklawn Building, Room 8A-35
5600 Fishers Lane
Rockville, M.D. 20857
Phone: 800-338-2382
www.hrsa.dhhs.gov/bhpr/vicp

Ohio Parents for Vaccine Safety
Kristine Severyn, RPh, PhD
251 W. Ridgeway Drive
Dayton, OH 45459
Phone: 937-435-4750

Amy Rothenberg, ND
Paul Herscu, ND
115 Elm Street
Enfield, CT 06083
Phone: 860-763-1225

Vaccine Adverse Events Reporting System (VAERS)
Department of Health and Human Services
P.O. Box 1100
Rockville, M.D. 20849-1100
Phone: 800-882-7267
www.fda.gov/cber/vaers.htm

Vaccine Information and Awareness (VIA)
Karin Schumacher
12799 La Tortola
San Diego, CA 92129
Phone: 619-484-3197
Fax: 619-484-1187
E-mail: *via@access1.net*
www.access1.net/via

Chapter 7 Crying
Chapter 8 Night Waking

Frey, William H. III. *Crying: The Mystery of Tears*. New York: Harper & Row, 1985.

Jones, Sandy. *Crying Baby, Sleepless Nights*. Boston: Harvard Common Press, 1992.

McClure, Vimala Schneider. *Infant Massage: A Handbook for Loving Parents (revised edition)*. New York: Bantam, 1989.

Sears, William, M.D. *The Fussy Baby: How to Bring Out the Best in Your High-Need Child*. La Leche League International, 1982.

_____. *Nighttime Parenting: How to Get Your Baby and Child to Sleep*. Schaumberg, IL: La Leche League International, 1996.

Small, Meredith F. *Our Babies, Our Selves: How Biology and Culture Shape the Way We Parent*. New York: Anchor Books, 1998.

Thevenin, Tine. *The Family Bed: An Age-Old Concept in Child Rearing*. Garden City Park, New York: Avery, 1987.

Chapter 9 Attachment Parenting

Berends, Polly Berrien. *Whole Child/Whole Parent (4th edition)*. New York: Perennial Library, 1997.

Bernhard, Emery and Durga Bernhard (illustrator). *A Ride on Mother's Back*. San Diego, CA: Harcourt Brace, 1996.

Bowlby, John. *Attachment (Attachment and Loss Series, Volume 1)*. New York: Basic Books, 1983.

_____. *Separation Anxiety and Anger (Attachment and Loss Series, Volume 2)*. New York: Basic Books, 1986.

_____. *Loss, Sadness and Depression (Attachment and Loss Series, Volume 3)*. New York: Basic Books, 1986.

Campbell, Ross. *How to Really Love Your Child*. Wheaton, IL: Victor Books, 1980.

Cardozo, Arlene Rossen. *Sequencing: A New Solution for Women Who Want Marriage, Career, and Family*. New York: Collier Books, 1986.

Curran, Dolores. *Traits of a Healthy Family: Fifteen Traits Commonly Found in Healthy Families by Those Who Work With Them*. New York: Ballantine Books, 1990.

Dawson, Connie and Jean Illseley Clarke. *Growing Up Again: Parenting Ourselves, Parenting Our Children*. Center City, MN: Hazelden, 1989.

Eyre, Linda. *I Didn't Plan to Be a Witch: And Other Surprises of a Joyful Mother*. New York: Fireside Books, 1988.

Fraiberg, Selma H. *The Magic Years: Understanding and Handling the Problems of Early Childhood*. New York: Charles Scribner's Sons, 1959.

Gosline, Andrea and Lisa Burnett Bossi with Ame Mahler Beanland. *Mother's Nature: Timeless Wisdom for the Journey into Motherhood*. Berkeley, CA: Conari Press, 1999.

Granju, Katie with Betsy Kennedy, B.S.N., M.S.N. *Attachment Parenting: Instinctive Care for Your Baby and Young Child*. New York: Pocket Books, 1999.

Hallet, J.P. *Pygmy Kitabu*. New York: Random House, 1973.

Hendrix, H. *Getting the Love You Want*. New York: Harpers Perennial Library, 1992.

Hymes, James L., Jr. *The Child Under Six*. Englewood Cliffs, NJ: Prentice-Hall, 1963.

Jones, Sandy. *To Love a Baby*. Boston: Houghton Mifflin, 1981.

Karen, Robert. *Becoming Attached: Unfolding the Mystery of the Infant-Mother Bond*. New York: Warner, 1994.

Kitzinger, Sheila. *The Year after Childbirth*. New York: Fireside Books, 1994.

_____. *Sex After the Baby Comes*. Minneapolis, MN: International Childbirth Education Association, 1980.

Klaus, Marshall, John Kennell, and Phyllis H. Klaus, C.S.W., M.F.C.C. *Bonding: Building the Foundations of Secure Attachment and Independence*. Reading, MA: Addison-Wesley Publishing Company, Inc., 1996.

Klaus, Marshall H., M.D. and Phyllis H. Klaus, C.S.W., M.F.C.C. *Your Amazing Newborn*. Reading, MA: Perseus Books, 1998.

Kline, Christina Baker, (ed). *Child of Mine: Writers Talk about the First Year of Motherhood*. New York: Hyperion, 1997.

Konner, M. *The Tangled Wing: Biological Constraints on the Human Spirit*. Austin, TX: Holt, Rhinehart and Winston, 1982.

LeShan, Eda. *Natural Parenthood*. New York: Signet, 1970.

_____. *The Conspiracy Against Childhood*. New York: Atheneum, 1967.

Liedloff, Jean. *The Continuum Concept*. Reading, MA: Addison-Wesley, 1985.

Lim, Robin. *After the Baby's Birth...A Woman's Way to Wellness: A Complete Guide for Postpartum Women*. Berkeley, CA: Celestial Arts, 1991.

McClure, Vimala. *The Path of Parenting: 12 Principles to Guide Your Journey*. Novato, CA: New World Library, 1999.

Montagu, Ashley. *Touching: The Human Significance of Skin*. New York: HarperCollins, 1986.

Moorman, Chick. *Where the Heart Is: Stories of Home and Family*. Merrill, MI: Personal Power Press, 1996.

Peck, M. Scott. *The Road Less Traveled*. New York: Simon & Schuster, 1978.

Restak, R. *The Brain*. New York: Doubleday, 1979.

Salk, L. *What Every Child Would Like His Parents to Know*. New York: Warner Books, 1973.

Small, Meredith F. *Our Babies, Our Selves: How Biology and Culture Shape the Way We Parent*. New York: Anchor Books, 1998.

Spangler, David. *Parent as Mystic, Mystic as Parent*. New York: Putnam, 1999.

Sweet, Win and Bill. *Living Joyfully with Children*. Lakewood, CO: Acropolis Books, 1997.

Attachment Parenting International
1508 Clairmont Place
Nashville, TN 37215
Phone/Fax: 615-298-4334
www.attachmentparenting.org

Children's Defense Fund
25 East Street, NW
Washington, DC 20001
Phone: 202-628-8787
www.childrendefense.org

Empathic Parenting
Journal of the Canadian Society for the Prevention of Cruelty to Children
Annual Subscription (four issues) $12.00
Phone: 705-526-5647
E-mail: *cspcc@bconnex.net*
356 First Street
Box 700
Midland, Ontario
L4R 4P4
Canada

National Association of Home-Based Business
Phone: 410-363-3698
www.usahomebusiness.com

Natural Jewish Parenting
173 Speedwell Avenue, Suite 127
Morristown, NJ 07960
Phone: 973-538-5454
E-mail: *njpmail@mindspring.com*

Chapter 10 First Food
Chapter 11 Healthy Eating for the Whole Family

Colbin, Annemarie. *The Book of Whole Meals: A Seasonal Guide to Assembling Balanced Vegetarian Breakfasts, Lunches & Dinners*. New York: Ballantine, 1985.

———. *The Natural Gourmet: Delicious Recipes for Healthy Balanced Eating*. New York: Ballantine, 1991.

Crook, William G., M.D. *Tracking Down Hidden Food Allergy*. Jackson, TN: Professional Books, 1978.

Katzen, Mollie and Ann Henderson. *Pretend Soup and Other Real Recipes: A Cookbook for Preschoolers & Up*. Berkeley, CA: Tricycle Press, 1994.

Katzen, Mollie. *The Moosewood Cookbook (revised edition)*. Berkeley, CA: Ten Speed Press, 1992.

———. *Still Life with Menu Cookbook (revised edition)*. Berkeley, CA: Ten Speed Press, 1994.

———. *Enchanted Broccoli Forest (revised edition)*. Berkeley, CA: Ten Speed Press, 1995.

Kenda, Margaret and Phyllis Williams. *The Natural Baby Food Cookbook*. New York: Avon Books, 1988.

Hirschmann, Jane R. and Lela Zaphiropoulos. *Preventing Childhood Eating Problems: A Practical, Positive Approach to Raising Children Free of Food & Weight Conflicts*. Carlsbad, CA: Gurze Books, 1993.

Johnson, Roberts (ed). *Whole Foods for the Whole Family (2nd edition)*. Schaumberg, IL: La Leche League International, 1993.

Lair, Cynthia. *Feeding the Whole Family: Whole Foods Recipes for Babies, Young Children and Their Parents (2nd edition)*. Seattle, WA: Moon Smile Press, 1998.

Lappe, Frances M. *Diet for a Small Planet (20th editon)*. New York: Ballantine, 1991.

Lawrence, R. *Breastfeeding: A Guide for the Medical Profession*. Hanover, MD: Mosby, 1989.

Madison, Deborah and Edward Espe Brown. *The Green's Cookbook: Extraordinary Vegetarian Cuisine from the Celebrated Restaurant (5th edition)*. New York: Bantam, 1988.

Robertson, Laurel, Carol Flinders and Brian Ruppenthal. *The New Laurel's Kitchen*. Berkeley, CA: Ten Speed Press, 1986.

Rockwell, Sally, Ph.D. *Calcium Rich and Dairy-Free: How to Get Your Calcium Without the Cow*. Seattle, WA: Diet Design, 1997.

Rombauer, Irma S., and Marion Rombauer Becker. *The Joy of Cooking*. Indianapolis, IN: Bobbs Merrill Co., 1972.

Shandler, Michael and Nina. *The Complete Guide and Cookbook to Raising Your Child as a Vegetarian*. New York: Schoecken, 1987.

Watson, Susan. *Sugar-Free Toddlers: Over 100 Recipes Plus Sugar Ratings for Store-Bought Foods*. Charlotte, VT: Williamson Publishing, 1991.

Warner, Penny. *Healthy Snacks for Kids (Nitty Gritty Cookbooks)*. San Leandro, CA: Bristrol Publishing Enterprises, Inc., 1996.

Yntema, Sharon. *Vegetarian Baby* (1991), *Vegetarian Children* (1994), and *Vegetarian Pregnancy* (1994). Ithaca, New York: McBooks.

Feingold Association for the United States
P.O. Box 6550
Alexandria, VA 22306
Phone: 800-321-3287
www.feingold.org

Chapter 12 Alternative Medicine and Family Health
Chapter 13 The Natural Approach to Common Infant and Childhood Ailments

American Pharmaceutical Association. *American Pharmaceutical Association Practical Guide to Natural Medicines*. New York: William Morrow, 1999.

Annas, George. *The Rights of Patients: The Basic ACLU Guide to Patient Rights*. (An American Civil Liberties Union Handbook). Totowa, NJ: Humana Press, 1992.

Bach, Edward and F. J. Wheeler. *The Bach Flower Remedies*. New Canaan, CT: Keats, 1979.

Castro, Miranda, R. S. Hom. *The Complete Homeopathy Handbook*. New York: St. Martin's, 1990.

Cumming, Stephen, M.D., and Dana Ullman, M.P.H. *Everybody's Guide to Homeopathic Medicines (expanded and revised)*. New York: Tarcher/Putnam, 1984.

Fuentes, Robert, M.D., and Carl Lowe. *The Family First Aid Guide*. New York: Berkley Books, 1994.

Gerson, Scott, M.D. *Ayurveda: The Ancient Indian Healing Art*. Boston: Element Books, 1997.

Grist, Liz. *A Woman's Guide to Alternative Medicine*. Chicago: Contemporary Books, 1988.

Handle, Kathleen. *The American Red Cross First Aid & Safety Handbook*. Boston: Little Brown, 1992.

Hodgkinson, Neville. *Will To Be Well: The Real Alternative Medicine*. York Beach, ME: Samuel Weiser, 1986.

Inlander, C. B. and J. L. Dodson. *Take This Book to the Pediatrician With You*. Allentown, PA: People's Medical Society, 1992.

Keville, K., and M. Green. *Aromatherapy: A Complete Guide to the Healing Art*. Freedom, CA: The Crossing Press, 1995.

Korte, Diana. *Every Woman's Body: Everything You Need to Know to Make Informed Choices About Your Health*. New York: Ballantine Books, 1994.

Kuttner, L.A. *Child in Pain: How to Help, What to Do*. Point Roberts, WA: Hartley & Marks, 1996.

Lad, Vasant. *Ayurveda: The Science of Self-Healing*. Santa Fe, NM: Lotus, 1984.

Lockie, Andrew Dr. *The Family Guide to Homeopathy: Symptoms and Natural Solutions*. New York: Fireside, 1989.

Lust, John. *The Herb Book*. New York: Bantam, 1974.

Morton, Mary and Michael. *Five Steps to Selecting the Best Alternative Medicine: A Guide to Complementary & Integrative Health Care*. Novato, CA: New World Library, 1996.

Murray, Michael ND. *Natural Alternatives to Over-the-Counter and Prescription Drugs*. New York: Quill, 1999.

Norman, L. *Feet First: A Guide to Foot Reflexology*. New York: Simon & Schuster, 1988.

Ohashi, W., with M. Hoover. *Touch for Love: Shiatsu for Your Baby*. New York: Ballantine Books, 1985.

Panos, Maesimund B. M.D., Jane Heimlich. *Homeopathic Medicine At Home*. New York: Jeremy P. Tarcher/Putnam Book, 1980.

Pantell, Robert H., M.D., James F. Fries, M.D. and Donald M. Vickery, M.D. *Taking Care of Your Child: A Parent's Guide to Complete Medical Care (4th edition)*. Reading, MA: Addison-Wesley Publishing Company, 1993.

Parsa-Stay, Flora D.D.S. *The Complete Book of Dental Remedies: A Guide to Safe & Effective Relief to the Most Common Dental Problems. Using Homeopathy, Nutritional Supplements, Herbs, & Conventional Dental Care*. Garden Park, New York: Avery Publishing Group, 1996.

Schmidt, Michael A. *Healing Childhood Ear Infections (2nd edition)*. Berkeley, CA: North Atlantic Books, 1996.

Schmidt, Michael A., Lendon H. Smith and Keith W. Sehnert. *Beyond Antibiotics: 50 (or so) Ways to Boost Immunity and Avoid Antibiotics*. Berkeley, CA: North Atlantic Books, 1994.

Ullman, Dana. *Homeopathic Medicine for Children and Infants*. Los Angeles: Jeremey P. Tarcher, 1992.

———. *The Consumer's Guide to Homeopathy: The Definitive Resource for Understanding Homeopathic Medicine and Making It Work for You*. New York: G. P. Putnam's Sons, 1995.

Ullman, Robert and Judyth Reichenberg-Ullman. *Homeopathic Self-Care: The Quick & Easy Guide for the Whole Family.* Rocklin, CA: Prima Publishing, 1997.

White, Linda B., M.D. and Sunny Mavor, A.H.G. *Herbs, Kids, Health: Practical Solutions for Your Child's Health, from Birth to Puberty.* Loveland, CO: Interweave Press, 1999.

Wootan, George and Sarah Verney. *Take Charge of Your Child's Health: A Guide to Recognizing Symptoms and Treating Minor Illnesses at Home.* New York: Crown, 1992.

Yiamouyiannis, John, M.D., *Fluoride: The Aging Factor.* Delaware, OH: Health Action Press, 1993.

Zand, Janet, L.A.C., O.M.D., Rachel Walton, R.N. and Bob Rountree, M.D. *Smart Medicine for a Healthier Child: A Practical A-to-Z Reference to Natural and Conventional Treatments for Infants & Children.* Garden City Park, New York: Avery Publishing Group, 1994.

Alive and Well
Eucapnic Breathing
100 Shaw Drive
San Anselmo, CA 94960
Phone: 415-258-0402

Allergy and Asthma Network
Mothers for Asthmatics, Inc.
2751 Prosperity Avenue, Suite 150
Fairfax, VA 22031
Phone: 800-878-4403 or 703-641-9595
Fax: 703-573-7794
www.aanma.org/

American Association of Naturopathic Physicians
601 Valley Street, Suite 105
Seattle, WA 98109
Phone: 206-298-0126
Fax: 206-298-0129
Referral number: 206-298-0125
www.naturopathic.org

American Chiropractic Association
1701 Clarendon Boulevard
Arlington, VA 22209
Phone: 703-276-8800
Fax: 703-243-2593
E-mail: *memberinfo@amerchiro.org*

American Holistic Health Association
P.O. Box 17400

Anaheim, CA 92817-7400
Phone: 714-779-6152
E-mail: *ahha@healthy.net*
www.ahha.org

American Holistic Medical Association
Phone: 703-556-9728
www.holisticmedicine.org

Associated Bodywork and Massage Professionals
28677 Buffalo Park Road
Evergreen, CO 80439-7347
Phone: 800-458-2267
Fax: 303-674-0859
www.abmp.com

Association for the Care of Children's Health (ACCH)
19 Mantua Road
Mt. Royal, NJ 08061
Phone: 800-808-2224
Fax: 609-423-3420
www.acch.org/

Nelson Bach USA
Source for Bach Flower Essences
Phone: 800-334-0843

BodyBio Corporation
Patricia Kane, Ph.D.
5 Osprey Drive
PO Box 809
Millville, NJ 08332
Phone: 609-825-8338

Council for Homeopathic Certification
1199 Sanchez Street
San Francisco, CA 94114
Phone: 415-789-7677

Flower Essences Services
Box 1769
Nevada City, CA 95959
Phone: 530-265-0258

Healthy Child newsletter
Future Generations
1275 Fourth Street, Suite 118
Santa Rosa, CA 95404
Phone: 707-575-5065
E-mail: *info@healthychild.com*
www.healthychild.com

HealthWorld
A comprehensive holistic health care site with over 40,000 pages of information.
www.healthworld.com

International Chiropractic Pediatric Association
5295 Highway 78, Suite #D362
Stone Mountain, GA 30087-3414
Phone: 770-982-9037
Fax: 770-736-1651
E-mail: *info@4icpa.org*
www.4icpa.org

National Acupuncture and Oriental Medicine Alliance
14637 Starr Road Southeast
Olalla, WA 98359
Phone: 253-851-6896
www.acuall.org

National Center for Homeopathy
801 North Fairfax Street
Suite 306
Alexandria, Virginia 22314
Phone: 703-548-7790
www.homeopathic.org

National Certification Commission for Acupuncture and Oriental Medicine
11 Canal Center Plaza Suite 300
Alexandria, VA 22314
Phone: 703-548-9004
Fax: 703-548-9079

The National Institute of Ayurvedic Medicine
584 Milltown Road
Brewster, NY 10509
Phone/Fax: 914-278-8700
Phone: 888-246-NIAM
www.niam.com

North American Society of Homeopaths (NASH)
1122 East Pike Street, Suite 1122
Seattle, WA 98122
Phone: 206-720-7000
www.homeopathy.org

The Northwest Center for Homeopathic Medicine
131 3rd Avenue N
Edmonds, WA 98020
Phone: 425-774-5599
Fax: 425-670-0319
www.healthy.net/jrru

The Office of Alternative Medicine (OAM)
National Institutes of Health
9000 Rockville Pike
Building 31
Rooms 5B-38
Bethesda, M.D. 20892
Phone: 888-644-6226
Fax: 301-402-4741
www.altmed.od.nih.gov

Physician's Association for Anthroposophical Medicine
1923 Geddes Avenue
Ann Arbor, MI 48104-1797
Phone: 734-930-9462
Fax: 734-662-1727

Chapter 14 What Makes a Healthy Family

Berends, Polly Berrien. *Whole Child/Whole Parent (4th edition)*. New York: Perennial Library, 1997.

Bernhard, Emery and Durga Bernhard (illustrator). *A Ride on Mother's Back*. San Diego, CA: Harcourt Brace, 1996.

Bowlby, John. *Attachment* (Attachment and Loss Series, Volume 1). New York: Basic Books, 1983.

———. *Separation Anxiety and Anger* (Attachment and Loss Series, Volume 2). New York: Basic Books, 1986.

———. *Loss, Sadness and Depression* (Attachment and Loss Series, Volume 3). New York: Basic Books, 1986.

Campbell, Ross. *How to Really Love Your Child*. Wheaton, IL: Victor Books, 1980.

Cardozo, Arlene Rossen. *Sequencing: A New Solution for Women Who Want Marriage, Career, and Family*. New York: Collier Books, 1986.

Curran, Dolores. *Traits of a Healthy Family: Fifteen Traits Commonly Found in Healthy Families by Those Who Work With Them*. New York: Ballantine Books, 1990.

Dawson, Connie and Jean Illseley Clarke. *Growing Up Again: Parenting Ourselves, Parenting Our Children*. Center City, MN: Hazelden, 1989.

Eyre, Linda. *I Didn't Plan to Be a Witch: And Other Surprises of a Joyful Mother*. New York: Fireside Books, 1988.

Fraiberg, Selma H. *The Magic Years: Understanding and Handling the Problems of Early Childhood*. New York: Charles Scribner's Sons, 1959.

Gosline, Andrea and Lisa Burnett Bossi with Ame Mahler Beanland. *Mother's Nature: Timeless*

Wisdom for the Journey into Motherhood. Berkeley, CA: Conari Press, 1999.

Granju, Katie with Betsy Kennedy, B.S.N., M.S.N. *Attachment Parenting: Instinctive Care for Your Baby and Young Child.* New York: Pocket Books, 1999.

Hymes, James L., Jr. *The Child Under Six.* Englewood Cliffs, NJ: Prentice-Hall, 1963.

Jones, Sandy. *To Love a Baby.* Boston: Houghton Mifflin, 1981.

Karen, Robert. *Becoming Attached: Unfolding the Mystery of the Infant-Mother Bond.* New York: Warner, 1994.

Kitzinger, Sheila. *The Year after Childbirth.* New York: Fireside Books, 1994.

_____. *Sex After the Baby Comes.* Minneapolis, MN: International Childbirth Education Association, 1980.

Klaus, Marshall, John Kennell, and Phyllis H. Klaus, C.S.W., M.F.C.C. *Bonding: Building the Foundations of Secure Attachment and Independence.* Reading, MA: Addison-Wesley Publishing Company, Inc., 1996.

Klaus, Marshall H., M.D. and Phyllis H. Klaus, C.S.W., M.F.C.C. *Your Amazing Newborn.* Reading, MA: Perseus Books, 1998.

Kline, Christina Baker, (ed). *Child of Mine: Writers Talk about the First Year of Motherhood.* New York: Hyperion, 1997.

LeShan, Eda. *Natural Parenthood.* New York: Signet, 1970.

_____. *The Conspiracy Against Childhood.* New York: Atheneum, 1967.

Liedloff, Jean. *The Continuum Concept.* Reading, MA: Addison-Wesley, 1985.

Lim, Robin. *After the Baby's Birth...A Woman's Way to Wellness: A Complete Guide for Postpartum Women.* Berkeley, CA: Celestial Arts, 1991.

McClure, Vimala. *The Path of Parenting: 12 Principles to Guide Your Journey.* Novato, CA: New World Library, 1999.

Montagu, Ashley. *Touching: The Human Significance of Skin.* New York: HarperCollins, 1986.

Moorman, Chick. *Where the Heart Is: Stories of Home and Family.* Merrill, MI: Personal Power Press, 1996.

Peck, M. Scott. *The Road Less Traveled.* New York: Simon & Schuster, 1978.

Small, Meredith F. *Our Babies, Our Selves: How Biology and Culture Shape the Way We Parent.* New York: Anchor Books, 1998.

Spangler, David. *Parent as Mystic, Mystic as Parent.* New York: Putnam, 1999.

Children's Defense Fund
25 East Street, NW
Washington, DC 20001
Phone: 202-628-8787
www.childrendefense.org

National Association of Home-Based Business
Phone: 410-363-3698
www.usahomebusiness.com

Natural Jewish Parenting
173 Speedwell Avenue, Suite 127
Morristown, NJ 07960
Phone: 973-538-5454
E-mail: *njpmail@mindspring.com*

Chapter 15 Discipline

Carter, Jay. *Nasty People.* Chicago. IL: Contemporary Publishing Group, 1989.

Faber, Adele and Elaine Mazlish. *How to Talk So Kids Will Listen & Listen So Kids Will Talk.* New York: Avon, 1980

_____. *Siblings Without Rivalry: How to Help Your Children Live Together So You Can Live Too.* New York: W.W. Norton & Co, 1987.

_____. *Liberated Parents, Liberated Children.* New York: Avon, 1974.

Fox, Matthew. *Original Blessing* (revised). Santa Fe, NM: Bear & Co., 1996.

Ginott, Haim. *Between Parent and Child: New Solutions to Old Problems* (17th edition). New York: Macmillan, 1965.

Hanh, T. N. *Being Peace.* Berkeley, CA: Parallax Press, 1987.

Hart, Louise. *The Winning Family: Increasing Self-Esteem in Your Children and Yourself.* Berkeley, CA: Celestial Arts, 1993.

Hyman, Irwin. *The Case Against Spanking: How to Discipline Your Child Without Hitting.* San Francisco: Jossey-Bass Publishers, 1997.

Kohn, Alfie. *Punished by Rewards: The Trouble with Gold Stars, Incentive Plans, A's, Praise, and Other Bribes.* Boston: Houghton Mifflin Company, 1995.

LeShan, Eda. *When Your Child Drives You Crazy.* New York: St. Martin's Press, 1985.

McGinnis, J. and K. *Parenting for Peace and Justice.* Maryknoll, NY: Obis, 1981.

Miller, Alice. *For Your Own Good: Hidden Cruelty in Child-Rearing and the Roots of Violence* (3rd edition). New York: Noonday Press, 1990.

Montagu, Ashley. *The Elephant Man.* Lafayette, LA. Acadian House, 1995.

Sears, William. *The Discipline Book: Everything You Need to Know to Have a Better-Behaved Child from Birth to Age 10.* New York: Little, Brown & Co., 1995.

Thich Nhat Hanh. *Being Peace.* Berkeley, CA: Parallax Press, 1988.

End Physical Punishment of Children Now (EPOCH-USA)
Center for Effective Discipline
155 W. Main Street
Suite 100-B
Columbus, OH 43215
Phone: 614-221-8829
Fax: 614-228-5058
E-mail: *nblock@infinet.com*

University of New Hampshire
Family Research Laboratory
www.unh.edu/frl
(see "papers online")

Chapter 16 Adolescence

Baum, Dan. *Smoke and Mirrors: The War on Drugs and the Politics of Failure.* Boston: Little Brown, 1996.

Brecher, Edward M., and the Editors of *Consumer Reports. Licit and Illicit Drugs.* Boston: Little Brown, 1972.

Dinkmeyer, D., PhD. *Systematic Training for Effective Parenting of Teens.* Circle Pines, NM: American Guidance Service, 1983.

Elkind, David. *Parenting Your Teenager.* New York: Ballantine Books, 1993.

Erlbach, Arlene. *Worth the Risk: True Stories about Risktakers Plus How You Can Be One, Too. Minneapolis,* MN: Free Spirit Publishing, 1998.

Glantz, M. PhD, and Pickens, R. PhD. *Vulnerability to Drug Abuse.* Washington, DC: American Psychological Association, 1992.

Henkart, Andrea Frank and Journey. *Cool Communication.* New York: Perigree, 1998.

Hersch, Patricia. *A Tribe Apart: A Journey into the Heart of American Adolescence.* New York: Fawcett Columbine, 1998.

Kalergis, Mary Motley. *Seen and Heard: Teenagers Talk About Their Lives.* New York: Stewart, Tabori & Chang, 1998.

Kaster, Laura and Jennifer Wyatt. *The Seven Year Stretch: How Families Work Together to Grow Through Adolescence.* Boston: Houghton Mifflin, 1997.

Landsman, Julie (ed). *From Darkness to Light: Teens Write about How They Triumphed Over Trouble.* Minneapolis, MN: Deaconess Press, 1994.

Llewellyn, Grace. *The Teenage Liberation Handbook: How to Quit School and Get a Real Life and Education (revised edition).* Eugene, OR: Lowry House, 1998.

Pearce, Jospeh Chilton. *Magical Child.* New York: Dutton, 1976.

Pedersen, Anne and Peggy O'Mara (ed). *Teens: A Fresh Look.* Santa Fe, NM: John Muir Publications, 1991.

Ponton, Lynn E., M.D. *The Romance of Risk: Why Teenagers Do the Things They Do.* New York: Basic Books, 1997.

Riera, Michael. *Uncommon Sense for Parents of Teenagers.* Berkeley, CA: Celestial Arts, 1995.

_____. *Surviving High School.* Berkeley, CA: Celestial Arts, 1997.

Schwebel, R. *Saying No Is Not Enough: Raising Children Who Make Wise Decisions about Drugs and Alcohol.* New York: Newmarket Press, 1989.

Steinberg, Lawrence and Anne Levine. *You and Your Adolescent: A Parents Guide for Ages 10–20.* New York: Harper Perennial, 1997.

Zimmer, L. and Morgan, J. P. *Marijuana Myths, Marijuana Facts.* New York: Open Society, 1997.

The American Academy of Child and Adolescent Psychiatry
Phone: 800-333-7636
They have fact sheets on many topics relevant to adolescents and their parents.

New Moon Network
Box 3587
Duluth, MN 55803-3587
Phone: 800-381-4743
Fax: 218-728-0314
E-mail: *subscriptions@newmoon.org*
www.newmoon.org
Newsletter and other publications for "adults who care about girls," with frequent pieces about sexuality and related topics.

Chapter 17 Approaches to Sexuality

Alyson, Sasha, ed. *Young, Gay and Proud!* Boston: Alyson Publications, 1985.

Bell, Ruth. *Changing Bodies, Changing Lives.* New York: Random House, 1988.

Borhek, Mary V. *Coming Out to Your Parents.* New York: The Pilgrim Press, 1983.

_____. *My Son Eric: A Mother Struggles to Accept Her Gay Son and Discovers Herself.* New York: The Pilgrim Press, 1979.

Calderone, Mary and James Ramey. *Talking with Your Child About Sex: Questions and Answers for Children From Birth to Puberty.* New York: Random House, 1983.

Calderone, Mary and Eric Johnson. *The Family Book About Sexuality.* New York: Harper & Row, 1981.

Gravelle, Karen and Jennifer Gravelle. *The Period Book: Everything You Don't Want to Ask But Need to Know.* New York: Walker and Co., 1996.

Griffin, Carolyn Welch, and Arthur G. Wirth. *Beyond Acceptance: Parents of Lesbians and Gays Talk about Their Experiences.* Englewood Cliffs, NJ: Prentice-Hall, 1986.

Kindlon, Dan, PhD., and Michael Thompson, PhD. *Raising Cain: Protecting the Emotional Life of Boys.* New York: Ballantine, 1999.

Madaras, Lynda and Diane Saavedra. *The What's Happening to My Body? Book for Boys: A Growing Up Guide for Parents and Sons* (2nd revised edition) New York: Newmarket Press, 1991.

Madaras, Lynda and Area Madaras. *The What's Happening to My Body? Book for Girls: A Growing Up Guide for Parents & Daughters* (revised). New York: Newmarket Press, 1991.

Rodin, J. *Body Traps.* New York: Quill William Morrow, 1992.

Scharf, M. *Unfinished Business.* New York: Ballantine, 1981.

Warren, A., and Wiedenkeller, J. *Everybody's Doing It: How to Survive Your Teenagers' Sex Life (and Help Them Survive It, Too).* New York: Viking Penguin, 1993.

Federation of Parents and Friends of
Lesbians and Gays (P FLAG)
Family and Chapter Support Office
1101 14th Street, NW, Suite 1030
Washington, D.C. 20005
Phone: 202-638-0243
E-mail: *info@pflag.org*
www.pflag.org

Good Vibrations
938 Howard Street, Suite 101
San Francisco, CA 94103
Phone: 800-289-8423
www.goodvibs.com

Melpomene Institute of Women's Health Research
1010 University Avenue
St. Paul, MN 55104
Phone: 651-642-1951

National Gay and Lesbian Task Force
1734 14th Street NW
Washington, DC 20009-4309
Phone: 202-332-6483

Planned Parenthood
"Talking About Sex: A Guide for Children"
Phone: 800-230-PLAN
www.ppfa.org/ppfa

Sexuality Information and Education Council of the
US (SIECUS)
130 W. 42nd Street, Suite 350
New York, NY 10036
Phone: 212-819-9770
Publishes *Growing Up: A SIECUS Annotated Bibliography of Books about Sexuality for Children and Adolescents*

Chapter 18 High Technology—Uses and Abuses

Cantor, Joanne, Ph.D. *Mommy, I'm Scared: How TV and Movies Frighten Children and What We Can Do To Protect Them.* San Diego, CA: Harcourt Brace, 1998.

Chen, Milton, Ph.D. *The Smart Parent's Guide to Kids' TV.* San Francisco: KQED Books, 1994.

Children's Partnership. *Parent's Guide to the Information Superhighway: Rules and Tools for Families Online.* National PTA and National Urban League, 1998.

Huston, A. C., et al. *Big World, Small Screen: The Role of Television in American Society.* Lincoln, NE: University of Nebraska Press, 1992.

Ivey, Mark and Ralph Bond. *The PC Dad's Guide to Becoming a Computer-Smart Parent.* New York: Dell, 1999.

Levine, M. *Viewing Violence: How Media Affects Your Child's and Adolescent's Development.* New York: Doubleday, 1996.

Liebert, R. M., et al. *The Early Window: Effects of Television on Children and Youth.* Tarrytown, NY: Pergamon Press, 1982.

Palmer, Edward L. *Television and America's Children.* New York: Oxford University Press, 1988.

Walsh, David. *Selling Out America's Children.* Minneapolis, MN: Fairview Press, 1995.

Winn, M. *Unplugging the Plug-In Drug.* New York: Viking Penguin, 1985.

Center for Media Education
2120 L Street, NW, Suite 200
Washington, DC 20037
Phone: 202-331-7833
www.cme.org

Center for Media Literacy
4727 Wilshire Blvd., Suite 403
Los Angeles, CA 90010
Phone: 323-931-4177
www.medialit.org

KidsFirst!
Coalition for Quality Children's Media
112 West San Francisco St., Suite 305A
Santa Fe, NM 87501
Phone: 505-989-8076
www.cqcm.org

The Lion & Lamb Project
4300 Montgomery Ave., Suite 104
Betheseda, MD 20814
www.lionlamb.org

New Mexico Media Literacy Project
6400 Wyoming NE
Albuquerque, NM 87109
Phone: 505-828-3129
www.nmmlp.org

Chapter 19 Toys and Family Values

Carlsson-Paige, Nancy and Diane Levin. *Who's Calling the Shots? How to Respond Effectively to Children's Fascination with War Play, War Toys, and Violent Television*. Philadelphia, PA: New Society Publishers, 1996.

Flugelman, Andrew, ed. *The New Games Book and The Second New Games Book*. New York: Doubleday, 1977.

Orlick, Terry. *The Cooperative Sports and Games Book and The Second Cooperative Sports and Games Book*. New York: Pantheon, 1978.

Children's Health Environmental Coalition Network
P.O. Box 846
Malibu, CA 90265
Phone: 310-589-2233

Greenpeace International Toxics Campaign
Box 416
564 Mission Street

San Francisco, CA 94105
Phone: 800-326-0959
www.greenpeaceusa.org

Companies that make quality, imaginative toys and games:

Animal Town
P.O. Box 757
Greenland, NH 03840
Phone: 800-445-8642

Aristoplay
450 South Wagner Road
Ann Arbor, MI 48103
Phone: 800-634-778

Back to Basic Toys
1 Memory Lane
Ridgely, MD 21685
Phone: 800-356-5360

Family Pastimes
RR 4
Perth, Ontario
Canada K7H 3C6
Phone: 888-267-4414

Hearth Song
1950 Waldorf NW
Grand Rapids, MI 49550-7100
Phone: 800-432-6314

Klutz Press
455 Portage Avenue
Palo Alto, CA 94306
Phone: 800-558-8944

Magic Cabin Dolls
1220 North Main Street
Viroqua, WI 54665
Phone: 707-585-9711

MindWare
2720 Patton Road
Roseville, MN 55113
Phone: 800-999-0398

Mother Child
P.O. Box 4406
Mountain View, CA 94040
Phone: 800-864-0131

North Star Toys
HC 81 Box 617
Questa, NM 87556
Phone: 800-737-0112

Rosie Hippo
P.O. Box 2068
Port Townsend, WA 98368
Phone: 800-385-2620

t. c. timber
P.O. Box 42
Skaneatelef, NY 13152
Phone: 315-685-6660

Toys to Grow On
P.O. Box 17
Long Beach, CA 90801
Phone: 800-542-8338

Tree Blocks
2022 Cliff Drive, Suite 292
Santa Barbara, CA 93109
Phone: 800-873-4960

Chapter 20: Wholesome Family Entertainment

Adams, P., and J. Marzollo. *The Helping Hands Handbook.* New York: Random House. 1992.

Ardley, Neil. *101 Great Science Experiments.* New York: D/K, 1993.

Bettelheim, Bruno. *The Uses of Enchantment: The Meaning and Importance of Fairy Tales.* New York: Vintage, 1989.

Blakey, Nancy. *The Mudpies Activity Book: Recipes for Invention.* Berkeley, CA: Tricycle Press, 1994.

———. *More Mudpies: 101 Alternatives to Television.* Berkeley, CA: Tricycle Press, 1994.

Caney, Steve. *Invention Book.* New York: Workman Publishing, 1985.

Carlson, Laurie. *Kids Create!* Charlotte, VT: Williamson Publishing, 1991.

Cromwell, Liz, Dixie Hibner and John Faitel, *Finger Frolics: Finger Plays for Young Children.* Mount Rainer, MD: Gryphon House, 1983.

Dean, M. The Sierra Club *Family Outdoors Guide.* San Francisco: Sierra Club. 1994.

Diehn, Gwen and Terry Krautwurst. *Science Crafts for Kids.* New York: Sterling Publishing, 1994.

Krueger, Garyl Waller. *1001 Things To Do With Your Kids.* Nashville, TN: Abingson Press, 1988.

Milford, Susan. *Adventures in Art.* Charlotte, VT: Williamson Publishing, 1993.

Orlick, Terry. *The Cooperative Sports and Games Book* and *The Second Cooperative Sports and Games Book.* New York: Pantheon, 1978. .

Press, Judy. *The Little Hands Big Fun Craft Book.* Charlotte, VT: Williamson Publishing, 1996.

Solga, Kim. *Paint! Make Sculptures! and Make Prints!* Portland, OR: North Light Publishing, 1991.

Steward, Mary and Katy Phillips. *Yoga for Children.* New York: Simon & Schuster, 1992.

Wilkes, Angela. *The Fantastic Rainy Day Book.* New York: D/K, 1995.

———. *The Amazing Outdoor Activity Book.* New York: D/K, 1996.

Song Books:

Fox, Dan (ed). *Go In and Out the Window: An Illustrated Songbook for Young People.* New York: Henry Holt, 1987.

Guthrie, Woody and Marjorie Mazia Guthrie. *Woody's 20 Grow Big Songs.* New York: HarperCollins, 1992.

Krull, Kathleen, composer. *Gonna Sing My Head Off! American Folk Songs for Children.* New York: Alfred A. Knopf, 1992.

Ladybug Magazine. *Music, Movement and Me,* songbook and activity set. P.O. Box 388, Ashland, OR 44805. 800-967-2085.

Swinger, Marlys. *Sing Through the Day,* songbook and CD ROM. Farmington, PA: The Plough Publishing House, 1999.

Wessels, Katherine Tyler. *The Golden Song Book.* Chicago: Golden Press, 1981. (out of print)

The Association of Youth Museums
1300 L. Street NW, Suite 975
Washington, DC 20005
Phone: 202-898-1080

Child Friendly Initiative
184 Bocana Street
San Francisco, CA 94110
Phone: 800-500-5CFI
www.childfriendly.org

US Patent Model Foundation
Invent America! Contest
1505 Powhatan Street
Alexandria, VA 22314
Phone: 703-684-1836
www.inventamerica.org

Art Supply Catalogues:
  Daniel Smith
P.O. Box 84268
Seattle, Wa 98124-5567
Phone: 800-426-6740

KidsArt
P.O. Box 274
Mt. Shasta, CA 96067
Phone: 530-926-5076
www.kidsart.com

Sax Arts & Crafts
P.O. Box 510710
New Berlin, WI 53151-0710
Phone: 414-784-6880

Music Education Programs:
  American Orff Schulwerk Association
P.O. Box 391089
Cleveland, OH 4419-8089
Phone: 440-543-5366

Kindermusik International
P.O. Box 26575
Greensboro, NC 27415
Phone: 800-628-5687

Organization of American Kodoloy Educators
P.O. Box 9804
Fargo, ND 58106
701-235-0366

Suzuki Association of The Americas
P.O. Box 17310
Boulder, CO 80308
Phone: 303-444-0948
E-mail: *suzuki@rmi.net*
www.suzukiassociation.org

Chapter 21 Public Schooling

Armstrong, Thomas E. *In Their Own Way: Discovering and Encouraging Your Child's Personal Learning Style.* New York: Putnam Publishing Group, 1988.

———. *The Myth of the ADD Child: 50 Ways to Improve Your Child's Behavior and Attention Span Without Drugs, Labels, or Coercion.* New York: Dutton Signot, 1995.

Faber, Adele and Elaine Mazlish. *How to Talk So Kids Can Learn at Home and in School.* New York: Simon & Schuster, 1995.

Fiske, Edward B. *Smart Schools, Smart Kids: Why Do Some Schools Work?* New York: Simon & Schuster, 1992.

Freed, Jeffrey and Laurie Parsons. *Right-Brained Children in a Left-Brained World: Unlocking the Potential of Your ADD Child.* New York: Simon & Schuster, 1998.

Heffener, Elaine. *Mothering.* New York: Doubleday, 1980.

Hunter, Diana. *The Ritalin-Free Child: Managing Hyperactivity and Attention Deficits Without Drugs.* Chicago, IL: Consumer Press, 1995.

Jensen, Arthur R. *Straight Talk About Mental Tests.* Old Tappan, NJ: Macmillan, 1981.

Kohl, Herbert. *The Question Is College.* Portsmouth, NH: Boyton Cook Publishers, 1998.

———. *The Discipline of Hope: Lessons from a Lifetime of Teaching.* New York: Simon and Schuster, 1998.

Lavin, Paul. *Parenting the Overactive Child: Alternatives to Drug Therapy.* Lanham, MD: Madison Books, 1989.

Levine, David, et al (ed.). *Rethinking Schools: An Agenda for Change.* New York: The New Press, 1995.

Oakes, Jeannie. *Keeping Track: How Schools Structure Inequality.* New Haven, CT: Yale University Press, 1985.

Pearce, Joseph Chilton. *Magical Child.* New York: Dutton, 1976.

Reichenberg-Ullman Judyth and Robert Ullman. *Ritalin-Free: Kid's Safe and Effective Homeopathic Treatment of ADD and Other Behavioral and Learning Problems.* New York: Prima Publishing, 1996.

Riera, Michael. *Surviving High School.* Berkeley, CA: Celestial Arts, 1997

Stein, David B., PhD. Ritalin Is Not the Answer: A Drug-Free, Practical Program for Children Diagnosed with ADD or ADHD. San Francisco: Jossey-Bass, 1999.

Vatz, Richard, PhD, and Lee Weinberg, PhD. Discovering the History of Psychiatry. New York: Oxford University Press, 1994.

Wilson, Nancy. *Children and Television.* Kettering, OH: PPI, 1988.

———. *Teenagers and Stress.* Kettering, OH: PPI, 1990.

Center for Commercial-Free Public Education
1714 Franklin Street, #100-306
Oakland, CA 94612
Phone: 510-268-1100
Fax: 510-268-1277
E-mail: *unplug@igc.org*
www.commercialfree.org

The Davis Dyslexia Association
  International
1601 Old Bayshore Highway, Suite 245
Burlingame, CA 94010
Phone: 650-692-8995 or 888-999-3324
Fax: 650-692-7075
E-mail: *ddai@dyslexia.com*
www.dyslexia.com

EarthSave International
600 Distillery Commons, Suite 200
Louisville, KY 40206-1922
Phone: 800-362-3648
E-mail: *earthsave@aol.com*
www.earthsave.org

The Edible Schoolyard
178 Rose Street
Berkeley, CA 94703
Phone: 510-558-1335
Fax: 510-558-1334
E-mail: *edible@lanminds.com*

Food from the 'Hood
Phone: 888-601-FOOD or 800-4U-YOUTH

FairTest
342 Broadway
Cambridge, MA 02139
Phone: 617-864-4810
Fax: 617-497-2224
E-mail: *fairtest@aol.com*
www.fairtest.org

National Coalition of Education Activists
P.O. Box 679
Rhinebeck, NY 12572
Phone: 914-876-4580
E-mail: *rfbs@aol.com*

Rethinking Schools
"The Real Ebonics Debate"
1001 East Keefe Ave.
Milwaukee, WI 53212
Phone: 800-669-4192
Fax: 414-964-7220
E-mail: *rethink@execpc.com*
www.rethinkingschools.org

Tomatis Center
2701 E. Camelback Road, Suite 205
Phoenix, AZ 85016

Phone: 602-381-0086
www.soundlistening.com

USDA Team Nutrition
3101 Park Center Drive, Room 802
Alexandria, VA 22302
Phone: 703-305-1624
E-mail: *teamnutrition@reeusda.gov*

Chapter 22 Alternative Education

Baldwin, Rahima. *You Are Your Child's First Teacher.* Berkeley, CA: Celestial Arts, 1995.

Gardner, Howard. *Frames of Mind: The Theory of Multiple Intelligences.* New York: Basic Books, 1993.

Holt, John. *What Do I Do Monday? Innovations in Education Series.* Portsmouth, NH: Boyton Cook Publishers, 1995.

_____. *Teach Your Own: A Hopeful Path for Education.* New York: Dell, 1982.

_____. *Learning All the Time.* Reading, MA: Addison-Wesley, 1990.

Illich, Ivan. *Deschooling Society.* New York: Pennenial Library, 1972.

Koetzsch, Ronald E., Ph.D. *The Parents' Guide to Alternatives in Education.* Boston: Shambhala Publications, Inc., 1997.

Kohl, Herb, and Featherstone, J. *Growing Minds: On Becoming a Teacher.* New York: Harper Collins, 1985.

Llewellyn, Grace. *The Teenage Liberation Handbook: How to Quit School and Get a Real Life and Education* (revised edition). Eugene, Oregon: Lowry House, 1998.

Markova, Dawna, PhD. *The Open Mind: Exploring the 6 Patterns of Natural Intelligence.* Berkeley, CA: Conari, 1996.

McGuinness, Diane. *Why Our Children Can't Read and What to Do About It: A Scientific Revolution in Reading.* New York: Free Press, 1997.

Mintz, Jerry (ed). *The Almanac of Education Choices: Private and Public Learning Alternatives and Homeschooling.* New York: Macmillian Publishing, 1995.

Montessori, Maria. *The Secret of Childhood.* New York: Ballantine, 1966.

_____ *The Absorbent Mind.* New York: Henry Holt, 1967, rev. 1995.

Neill, A.S. Summerhill: *A Radical Approach to Child Rearing.* New York: Hart Publishing, 1960.

Snitzer, Herb. *Summerhill: A Loving World.* Old Tappan, NJ: Macmillan, 1964.

Steiner, Rudolf. *The Spirit of the Waldorf School.* Hudson, NY: Anthroposophic Press, 1995.

Center for Education Reform
1001 Connecticut Ave., Suite 204
Washington, DC 20036
Phone: 800-521-2118
Fax: 202-822-5077
www.edreform.com

Montessori Institute of America
5901 NW Waukomis
Kansas City, MO 19401

National Association of Charter Schools
2722 E. Michigan Avenue
Suite 201
Lansing, MI 48912
Phone: 517-772-9115

National Association for Legal Support of Alternative Schools
P.O. Box 2833
Santa Fe, NM 87504-2823
Phone: 505-471-6928

National Center for Montessori Education
PO Box 1543
Roswell, GA 30077
Phone: 404-434-1128

National Coalition of Alternative Community Schools
1266 Rosewood, Unit 1
Ann Arbor, MI 48104-6205
Phone: 734-668-9171

Sudbury Valley School
2 Winch Street
Framingham, MA 01701
Phone: 508-877-3030
Fax: 508-788-0674
www.sudval.org

Waldorf Early Childhood Association
1359 Alderton Lane
Silver Spring, MD 20906
Phone: 301-460-6287
Fax: 301-460-6145
E-mail: *jalmon@erols.com*

Chapter 23 Homeschooling

Cohen, C. *And What About College: How Homeschooling Leads to Admissions to the Best Colleges and Universities.* Cambridge, MA: Holt Associates, 1997.

Colfax, David and Micki. *Homeschool for Everyone.* New York: Warner, 1988.

Dobson, Linda. *The Homeschooling Book of Answers.* Rocklin, CA: Prima, 1998.

Farenga, Patrick. *The Beginner's Guide to Homeschooling* (2nd revised edition). Cambridge, MA: Holt Associates, 1998.

Griffith, Mary. *The Homeschooling Handbook.* Rocklin, CA: Prima, 1997.

———. *The Unschooling Handbook.* Rocklin, CA: Prima, 1998.

Hegener, Mark and Helen. *The Homeschool Reader.* Tonasket, WA: Home Education Press, 1995.

Holt, John. *How Children Learn.* Aulander, NC: Pittman, 1964, rev. 1983.

Pedersen, Anne and Peggy O'Mara (ed). *Schooling at Home: Parents, Kids, and Learning.* Santa Fe, NM: John Muir Publications, 1990.

Pride, Mary. *The Big Book of Home Learning.* Volume I, Volume II. and Volume III. Westchester, Illinois: Crossway Books, 1986.

Reed, Donn. *The Home School Source Book. Bridgewater,* ME: Brook Farm Books, 1994.

Van Galen, J. and Pittman, M. A. *Homeschooling: Parents as Educators.* Thousand Oaks, CA: Corwin, 1995.

American School of Correspondence
2200 East 170th Street
Landsing, IL 60438
Phone: 708-418-2800 or 800-531-9268

Cafi Cohen
160 Cornerstone Lane
Arroyo Grande, CA 93420
www.concentric.net/~ctcohen

Clonlara: Full Service to Home Educators
1289 Jewett
Ann Arbor, MI 48104
Phone: 734-769-4511
Fax: 74-769-9629
E-mail: *clonclara@delphi.com*
www.clonclara.org

Holt Associates
John Holt's Bookstore and Growing Without Schooling magazine

2269 Massachusetts Avenue
Cambridge, MA 02140
Phone: 617-864-3100
Fax: 617-864-8235
www.holtgws.com

Home Education Magazine
P.O. Box 1587
Palmer, AK 99645
Phone: 907-746-1336
Fax: 907-746-1335
E-mail: *HomeEdMag@aol.com*
www.home_ed_press.com

Home School Legal Defense Association
P.O. Box 3000
Purcellville, VA 20134
Phine: 540-338-5600
Fax: 540-338-2733
E-mail: *mailroom@hslda.org*
www.hslda,org

National Home Education Research Institute
P.O. Box 13939
Salem, OR 97309
Phone: 503-364-1490
www.nheri.org

Oak Meadow, Inc.
PO Box 740
Putney, VT 05346
Phone: 802-387-2021
Fax: 802-387-5108
www.oakmeadow.com

Worldbook International
Educational Services Dept.
Typical Course of Study: K-12
101 Northwest Point Blvd.
Elk Grove Village, IL 60007
Phone: 312-876-2200

Sycamore Tree
2179 Meyer Place
Costa Mesa, CA 92627
Phone: 949-650-4466

Chapter 24 Handling Divorce

Fisher, Bruce. Rebuilding: *When Your Relationship Ends*. San Luis Obispo, CA: Impact Publishers, 1981.

Friedman, Gary J., J.D. *A Guide to Divorce Mediation*. New York: Workman Publishing, 1993.

Lyster, Mimi E. *Child Custody: Building Parenting Agreements That Work*. Berkeley, CA: Nolo Press, 1996.

Riccie, Isolina. *Mom's House, Dad's House: Making Shared Custody Work*. New York: Collier Books, 1980.

Shoshana, Alexander. *In Praise of Single Parents: mothers and Fathers Embracing the Challenge*. New York: Houghton Mifflin, 1994.

Trafford, Abigail. *Crazy Time: Surviving Divorce*. New York: Bantam Books, 1984.

Viorst, Judith. *Necessary Losses: The Loves, Illusions, Dependencies and Impossible Expectations That All of Us Have to Give Up in Order to Grow*. New York: Simon & Schuster, 1988.

Wallerstein, Judith, and Sandra Blakeslee. *Second Chances: Men, Women, and Children a Decade after Divorce*. New York: Ticknor and Fields, 1989.

Wallerstein, Judith, and Joan Berlin Kelly. *Surviving the Breakup: How Children and Parents Cope with Divorce*. New York: Basic Books, 1980.

The Academy of Family Mediators
5 Militia Drive
Lexington, MA 02421
Phone: 781-674-2663
Fax: 781-674-2690
E-mail: *afmoffice@mediators.org*

Chapter 25 Handling Death

Davis, Deborah L., Ph.D. *Empty Cradle, Broken Heart: Surviving the Death of Your Baby*. Golden, Colorado: Fulcrum Publishing, 1996.

Doka, Kenneth (ed). *Children Mourning, Mourning Children*. Washington, DC: Hospice Foundation of America, 1995.

Fitzgerald, Helen. *The Grieving Child: A Parent's Guide*. New York: Simon & Schuster, 1992.

Huntley, Theresa. *Helping Children Grieve: When Someone They Love Dies*. Minneapolis, MN: Augsburg, 1991.

Ilse, Sherokee. *Empty Arms: Coping After Miscarriage, Stillbirth, and Infant Death* (revised). Maple Plain, MN: Wintergreen Press, 1990.

Jarratt, Claudia Jewett. *Helping Children Cope With Separation and Loss*. Boston: Harvard Common Press, 1994.

Johnson, Joy, and Marvin, MD. *Tell Me, Papa: A Funeral Book for Children* (revised) . Omaha, NE: Centering Corporation, 1996.

———. *Grief: What It Is and What You Can Do*. Omaha, NE: Centering Corporation, 1995.

———. *Children Grieve Too: A Book for Families Who Have Experienced a Death.* Omaha, NE: Centering Corporation, 1998.

Krementz, Jill. *How It Feels When A Parent Dies.* New York: Alfred Knopf, 1999.

Kubler-Ross, Elisabeth. *Questions and Answers on Death and Dying.* New York: Macmillan, 1974.

McCue, Kathleen. *How to Help Children Through a Parent's Serious Illness.* New York: St. Martin's Press, 1996.

Mellonie, Bryan, and Robert Ingpen. *Lifetimes: The Beautiful Way to Explain Death to Children.* New York: Bantam Books, 1983.

Roberts, Janice and Joy Johnson. *Thank You for Coming to Say Goodbye: A Funeral Home Orientation for Children.* Omaha, NE: Centering Corporation, 1994.

Schaefer, Dan, and Christine Lyons. *How Do We Tell the Children? A Step-by-Step Guide for Helping Children Two to Teen Cope When Someone Dies.* New York: Newmarket Press, 1993.

Traisman, Enid. *Fire in My Heart, Ice in My Veins: A Journal for Teens Experiencing a Loss.* Omaha, NE: Centering Corporation, 1992.

Turnbull, Sharon. *Who Lives Happpily Ever After? For Families Whose Child Has Died Violently.* Omaha, NE: Centering Corporation, 1990.

Wheeler, Sara Rich and Margaret M. Pike. *Goodbye My Child: A Gentle Guide for Parents Whose Child Has Died.* Omaha, NE: Centering Corporation, 1992.

Loving Arms
Quarterly Newsletter for the Pregnancy and Infant Loss Center, Inc.
1421 East Wayzata Blvd., #30
Wayzata, MN 55391-1939
Phone: 612-473-9372

Centering Corporation
1531 North Saddle Creek
Omaha, NE 68104
Phone: 402-553-1200
A nonprofit organization that supports and provides resources for bereaved children and their families.

Children's Hospice International
2202 Mt. Vernon Ave., Suite 3C
Alexandria, VA 22301
Phone: 800-24-CHILD (242-4453)
Fax: 703-684-0226

E-mail: *chiorg@aol.com*
www.chionline.org
Information on children's hospice care for the general public, referrals to local hospice programs or other health professionals, and printed materials.

The Compassionate Friends
P. O. Box 3696
Oak Brook, IL 60522-3696
Phone: 630-990-0010
Fax: 630-990-0246
E-mail: *tcf_national@prodigy.com*
www.compassionatefriends.org
A national self-help organization for families that have lost a child.

Hospice Education Institute
190 Westbrook Road
Essex, CT 06426
Phone: 860-767-1620
Fax: 860-767-2746
E-mail: *hospiceall@aol.com*
"Hospice Link" toll-free hotline: 800-331-1620
Referrals to a regularly updated directory of hospice and palliative care programs nationwide, plus general information on hospice care and bereavement services.

National Hospice Organization
1901 North Moore Street, Suite 901
Arlington, VA 22209
Phone: 703-243-5900
For referrals to hospices in your area, call: 800-658-8898
www.nho.org

Afterword: Trusting and Taking Care of Yourself as a Parent

Bing, Elizabeth and Libby Coleman. *Emotional Life of New Mothers.* New York: Henry Holt, 1997.

Boyer, Ernest L. *A Way in the World: Family Life as Spiritual Discipline.* New York: Harper & Row, 1985.

Campbell, Leslie Kirk. *Journey Into Motherhood.* New York: Riverhead Books, 1996.

Choquette, Sonia, Ph.D. *The Wise Child: A Spiritual Guide to Nurturing Your Child's Intuition.* New York: Three Rivers Press, 1999.

Erlich, Louise. *The Bluejay's Dance: A Birth Year.* New York: HarperCollins, 1995.

Frymer-Kensky, Tiva. *Motherprayer.* New York: Riverhead Books, 1995.

Fuchs-Kreimer, Rabbi Nancy. *Parenting as a Spiritual Journey: Deepening Ordinary & Extraordinary*

Events into Sacred Occasions. Woodstock, VT: Jewish Lights Publishing, 1996.

Kabat-Zinn, Myla and Jon Kabat-Zinn. *Everyday Blessings: The Inner Work of Mindful Parenting.* New York: Hyperion, 1997.

Kitzinger, Sheila. *The Year After Childbirth.* New York: Fireside Books, 1994.

Lamott, Anne. *Operating Instructions: A Journal of My Son's First Year.* New York: Fawcett Books, 1994.

Lewis, Cynthia Copeland. *Mother's First Year: How to Cope with the Exhausting, Exasperating, Exhilarating Experience Called Motherhood.* New York: Berkeley Publishing Group, 1992.

Lim, Robin. *After the Baby's Birth. . A Woman's Way to Wellness: A Complete Guide for Postpartum Women.* Berkeley, CA: Celestial Arts, 1991.

Martin, William. *The Parent's Tao Te Ching: Ancient Advice for Modern Parents.* New York: Marlowe & Co., 1999.

McClure, Vimala. *The Tao of Mothering.* Novato, CA: New World Library, 1997.

McGinnus, Kathleen and James. *Parenting for Peace and Justice.* Maryknoll, NY: Orbis, 1981.

Saavedra, Beth Wilson. *Restoring Balance to a Mother's Busy Life.* Chicago: Contemporary Books, 1996.

Fathering

Cosby, Bill. *Fatherhood.* New York: Simon & Schuster, 1986.

Ehrensaft, Diane. *Parenting Together: Men and Women Sharing the Care of Their Children.* Champaign, IL: University of Illinois Press, 1990.

Glennon, Will. *Fathering: Strengthening Connection With Your Children No Matter Where You Are.* Emeryville, CA: Conari Press, 1995.

Greenberg, Martin. *The Birth of a Father.* New York: Continuum, 1985.

Hall, Nor and William R. Dawson. *Broodmales.* Dallas: Spring Publications, 1989.

Levine, James A. *Who Will Raise the Children? New Options for Fathers (and Mothers).* Philadelphia, PA: Lippincott 1976. (out of print)

Louv, Richard. *FatherLove: What We Need, What We Seek, What We Must Create.* New York: Simon & Schuster, 1993.

Osherson, Samuel. *Finding Our Fathers.* New York: Ballantine/Fawcett, 1987.

Pittman, Frank, M.D. *Man Enough: Fathers, Sons and the Search for Masculinity.* New York: G. P. Putnam, 1993.

Pruett, Kyle. *The Nurturing Father: Journey Toward the Complete Man.* New York: Warner, 1987.

Spacek, Tim. *Fathers: There at the Birth.* Chicago: Chicago Review Press, 1985.

Thevenin, Tine. *Mothering and Fathering: The Gender Differences in Parenting.* Garden City Park, NY: Avery Publishing Group, 1993.

Thorndike, John. *Another Way Home: A Single Father's Story.* New York: Crown Publishers, 1996.

Vanwert, William F. *Tales for Expectant Fathers.* New York: Dial, 1982.

Parenting: Special Needs

Campion, M.J. *The Baby Challenge: A Handbook on Pregnancy for Women with a Physical Disability.* New York: Routledge, 1990.

Cowen-Fletcher, J. *Mama Zooms.* New York: Scholastic, 1993.

Preston, P. *Mother Father Deaf: Living Between Sound and Silence.* Cambridge, MA: Harvard University Press, 1994.

Rogers, J. and M. Matsumara. *Mother to Be: A Guide to Pregnancy and Birth for Women with Disabilities.* New York: Demos Publications, 1991.

Brimstone Bulletin (newsletter)

Mothers From Hell: Advocating for disability rights
P.O. Box 21304
Eugene, OR 97402

Disabled Parenting Today (newsletter)
Sullivan Publishing
Box 3827
Courtney, BC V9W 7P2 Canada
Fax: 250-337-0041
E-mail: *sullsb@mars.ark.com*

Disability, Pregnancy and Parenthood International (newsletter)
Auburn Press
9954 South Walnut Terrace, #201
Palos Hills, IL 60465

It's Okay! Adults Write about Living and Loving with a Disability (newsletter)
Phoenix Counsel
1 Springbank Drive
St. Catharines
Ontario, Canada L2S 2K1
Phone: 905-685-0486

Parenting with a Disability Newsletter
Through the Looking Glass
2198 6th Street, Suite 100
Berkeley, CA 94707
Phone: 800-644-2666 (voice and TDD)
www.lookingglass.org

Diana Michelle's Home Page
The Internet's One-Stop Resource for Parents with
    Disabilities
*www.ourworld.compuserve.com/homepages/Trish_
    andJohn/disabilitycool*

Parenting with Disabilities Project
6301 Northumberland Street
Pittsburg, PA 15217
Phone: 412-244-3081
www.trfn.clpgh.org/star/

Through the Looking Glass
Research and Training Center for Families with
    Adults with Disabilities

2198 6th Street, Suite 100
Berkeley, CA 94707
Phone: 800-644-2666 (voice and TDD)
E-mail: *TLG@lookingglass.org*
www.lookingglass.org

The Reflexology Association of America
4012 S. Rainbow Boulevard
Box K585
Las Vegas, NV 89103-2059

The Upledger Institute
(craniosacral therapy)
11211 Prosperity Farms Road
Palm Beach Gardens, Florida 33410
Phone: 561-622-4706
Fax: 561-627-9231
E-mail: *upledger@upledger.com*
www.upledger.com

math, 286, 288, 293
Mathison, Linda, 5
Mattel, 243
Mazlish, Elaine, 193, 196, 197
McClure, Vimala, 91
McGinnis, James, 202
McGinnis, Kathleen, 202
McGuiness, Diane, 285
McKenna, James, 100
measles, 75, 76, 77, 83
meat, 127
media literacy, 229
mediation, divorce, 313
Medical Research Council, 76
Medical Research Institute of Infectious Diseases, US, 81
medications
    during breastfeeding, 54–56, 59
    during labor, 20, 28–30
    during pregnancy, 9
    See also Herbs
medicine, alternative, 147–57
meditation, 22, 31, 106
meningitis, 47, 77, 78, 83, 165, 173
menstruation, 222–23
Merck Institute, 83
mercury, 75, 77, 170
messages, mixed, 189
methylphenidate (Ritalin), 275
Mica, John, 80
Mickelson, Jane, 318
Micklethwait, Lucy, 254
microwave ovens, 8
midwives, 16–18
Midwives Alliance of North America (MANA), 17
Miles, Karen, 180
milk, 127, 128, 138, 139–40
    See also Breastmilk
Miller, Alice, 202
Miller, Kathy Collard, 200
minerals, 6–7, 160–61
miscarriage, 7, 15, 25, 79, 170
MMR vaccine, 76, 77, 78, 79
Mommy, I'm Scared (Cantor), 228
Montagu, Ashley, 171, 202
Montessori, Maria, 271, 287–89
Montgomery, Kathryn, 231
Moore, Raymond, 271, 300
Morgan, Nancy, 93
morning sickness, 23–24
Mother Earth News, The, 303
motor skills, 110
moxibustion, 149
MSG (monosodium glutamate), 128, 171
Muhlberger, Richard, 253
Mulan, 229
Mullen, Eileen, 198
multiculturalism, 278, 285
multiple intelligences, 286–87
mumps, 77–78, 83
muscle aches, 24, 138
museums, children's, 258–59
music, 250–52, 268
Myth of the ADD Child, The (Armstrong), 277

nagging, 194, 211
naps, 39, 106–7
Nasty People (Carter), 199
National Academy of Sciences, 74
National Association for Sport and Physical Education (NASPE), 256

National Association for the Education of Young Children, 228
National Association of Home-Based Businesses, 183
National Center for Health Statistics, 65
National Center for Infants, Toddlers, and Families, 118
National Center for Missing and Exploited Children, 232
National Child Care Staffing Study, 118
National Childhood Vaccine Injury Act, 74
National College of Naturopathic Medicine, 157
National Foundation for Infantile Paralysis, 83
National Home Education Research Institute (NHERI), 298, 301, 303
National Institute of Ayurvedic Medicine, 156
National Institute of Neurological Disorders and Stroke, 163
National Institutes of Health (NIH), 76, 83, 148, 149
National Labor Committee, 229
National School Lunch Program, 279
National Vaccine Information Center (NVIC), 80
National Vaccine Injury Compensation Program (NVICP), 74
Natural Child Project, The, 233
Nature of Human Aggression, The (Montagu), 202
naturopathy, 152–53, 157
nausea, 149, 170
NBC News, 299
neglect, benign, 236
Neill, Alexander Sutherland, 287, 290–92
Neill, Monty, 272
Neonatal Behavioral Assessment Scale, 29
Neumeyer, Peter, 247
newborns. See Babies
New England Journal of Medicine, 163
New Mexico Media Literacy Project, 229
New York Times, 80
nicotine, 7, 55, 172, 213, 231
night, exploration of, 257
nightmares, 103, 228
Night Sky, 257
Night waking, 97–107, 154
nipples, 33, 49, 54
nitpicking, 211
Noah Webster Academy, 283–84
North American Registry of Midwives (NARM), 17
Northwest Center for Homeopathic Medicine, The, 277
Northwestern University, 206
nose drops, 168
Nova Southeastern University, 154
nudity, 39, 218
nursing. See Breastfeeding
Nutrition, team, 279
nuts, 23, 127, 138, 165, 259

obstetricians, 16, 17, 18
Odent, Michel, 76
Offer, Daniel, 206
Office of Alternative Medicine (OAM), 2, 148, 149
On Becoming Baby Wise (Bucknam), 52
Open Charter School, 279
open enrollment, 284
Orient, Jane M., 80
Original Blessing (Fox), 199
osteoporosis, 48
Our Babies, Ourselves (Small), 100
outdoors, 256
overfeeding, 89
overstimulation, 89, 102
oxytocin, 28, 30, 33, 48, 56, 88, 109

pacifiers, 51, 113
Pain
    of worms, 103